COMPARATIVE SOCIETIES : SOCIAL

HM 51 R8648

P9-DWP-694

DATE DUE

DE 2 '91		
AG 27 '92		
MR 18 '94		
MY 20 '94		
OC 20 '95		
DE 10 '96		
FE 10 '99		
MR 10 '99		
DE 20 00		
MR 25 08		

DEMCO 38-296

COMPARATIVE SOCIETIES
Social Types and Their Interrelations

Daniel W. Rossides
BOWDOIN COLLEGE

Prentice Hall, Englewood Cliffs, New Jersey 07632

Riverside Community College
Library
4800 Magnolia Avenue
Riverside, CA 92506

Library of Congress Cataloging-in-Publication Data

Rossides, Daniel W., 1925-
    Comparative societies : social types and their interrelations /
Daniel W. Rossides.
        p.   cm.
    ISBN 0-13-155318-6
    1. Sociology--Comparative method. 2. Policy sciences.
3. Political science. 4. Political anthropology.   I. Title.
HM51.R8648   1990
301--dc20   89-22790
                                                         CIP

For Marilyn, as always

Editorial/production supervision: Susan Alkana
Cover design: Miriam Recio
Manufacturing buyer: Carol Bystrom

© 1990 by Prentice-Hall, Inc.
A Division of Simon & Schuster
Englewood Cliffs, New Jersey 07632

All rights reserved. No part of this book may be
reproduced, in any form or by any means,
without permission in writing from the publisher.

Printed in the United States of America
10 9 8 7 6 5 4 3 2 1

ISBN 0-13-155318-6

Prentice-Hall International (UK) Limited, *London*
Prentice-Hall of Australia Pty. Limited, *Sydney*
Prentice-Hall Canada Inc., *Toronto*
Prentice-Hall Hispanoamericana, S.A., *Mexico*
Prentice-Hall of India Private Limited, *New Delhi*
Prentice-Hall of Japan, Inc., *Tokyo*
Simon & Schuster Asia Pte. Ltd., *Singapore*
Editora Prentice-Hall do Brasil, Ltda., *Rio de Janeiro*

CONTENTS

PREFACE

Comparative Societies has been designed as a text for courses in comparative societies, modernization, social system change, comparative social stratification, comparative public policy, and the sociology of peace and war. It should also prove useful as collateral reading in courses on international politics, comparative government and economics, and comparative rural or Third-World sociology. Its main purpose is to provide readers with a comprehensive grasp of the various types of human society and their interrelations, both in the past and especially in the contemporary world. I hope it will contribute to the broader base of foreign studies that the United States needs if it is to overcome its "shortfall in international competence."[1]

---

[1]*What We Don't Know Can Hurt Us: The Shortfall in International Competence* (Washington, D.C.: The Commission on International Education, American Council on Education, 1984). Starting in 1984, a large number of other national education reports appeared stressing the need to internationalize the undergraduate curriculum.

Part I, The Spectrum of Social System Types, provides the indispensable historical dimension for understanding the present world. Societies do not emerge full blown from natural processes, human nature, or constitutional conventions—they are the product of historical variables, that is, they emerge from unique mixtures of changing, half-understood sociocultural causes. Of special importance in understanding how a society modernizes is whether it emerged from feudal absolutism or from a more decentralized agrarian-horticultural background (those emerging from feudal absolutism have been more successful in becoming industrial societies). In addition, Part I establishes that no society beyond simple hunting-gathering societies can be understood without understanding the relation between its domestic power structure and the outer world of other power structures.

The United States has been chosen to represent the developed capitalist societies. For a number of reasons, it receives by far the fullest treatment. It is the most powerful country in the world and the leader of the developed capitalist societies (and capitalism is the dominant force in today's world). It was also chosen because those who compare must have a clear idea of what it is they are comparing. Our picture of the United States will certainly not receive universal assent but it should provide a standard reference point on which to base comparisons and discussions.

The Soviet Union is also treated at length, though not as fully as the United States: it too is a superpower and it represents the other major type of developed society, socialism. In addition to the treatment of the two superpowers there are case studies of various lengths (Canada's is the longest) of 12 other countries, each chosen because it represents either a typical society, typical relations with more powerful societies, or typical problems. The complexity of the contemporary universe of societies is indicated in Chapter 17, which discusses a variety of societies that have exceptional features and in Chapter 18, which discusses the changing power structure of the world system.

One of the main purposes of this study is to analyze and evaluate the *adaptive capacity* of various kinds of society. Pure and applied science are not opposing activities and there are signs that this is being recognized in social science. In recent years government, business, and a wide variety of voluntary groups have all stressed the need for a more explicit translation of knowledge into policy.

Progress in policy studies requires a more intimate association between researchers and decision makers. In addition, therefore, to providing a theoretical analysis of social types and their interrelations, I have also tried to provide a framework for raising and discussing a wide range of questions. The United States' adaptive capacity is based on a market economy, political democracy, professionalism, and voluntarism. The Soviet Union's adaptive capacity is based on a centrally controlled economy and polity, and professionalism. How effective are these institutions? Has the United States entered a mature stage of capitalist development

marked by slow growth, declining living standards, stalemated politics, and formalism. Has a similar fate befallen the Soviet Union?

Broad theoretical concerns of this sort are focused wherever possible on concrete policy problems. What are the issues in the confrontation between the First and Third worlds? Do similar issues arise in the relation between the Second and Third worlds? What are the facts of and problems with the world's military buildup? What are the issues and national interests involved in the attempt to rewrite the law of the sea, effect technology transfers, or reduce barriers to the flow of labor, capital, commodities, and services between societies? Case studies are provided in these areas and an effort is made to identify incipient problems that have not yet reached the state of public awareness. For example, it is known that the world's minerals and fossil fuels are being depleted and once gone cannot be replaced—it is not so well known that an absolute decline in the production of renewable commodities may have started.

Throughout the study I have emphasized the link between a society's past and its present structure and dynamics. The deeply ingrained rationalism of the West has led many to believe that social problems can be solved through scholarship and research. In contrast to seeing social problems as a problem in knowledge, I focus on the deep tangle of power groups that causes problems and clogs the process of social adaptation. Indeed one of the disheartening prospects that this study broaches is the possibility that all complex societies (developed and developing, capitalist and socialist alike) are incapable of easing the burden of social and world problems because it would threaten elite power. Nonetheless, I have tried throughout to extract policy leads and lessons from the record of comparative behavior, especially for American citizens and policy makers.

The policy theme of the text, along with the two appendices on studying and working abroad, and on career opportunities for students in comparative studies, should help students see the relevance of a comparative societies course and perhaps entice them to do further comparative work either in sociology or some other discipline.

Chapter 1 outlines the text's general perspective and its basic organizing ideas. To minimize bias I have alternated the main theoretical orientations in sociology, the functional, the conflict, and the interactionist perspectives. However, these perspectives are not enough—to develop them fully and to relate them to policy analysis, I have also contrasted *liberalism* (the thought forms and values of capitalism) with *socialism* (of various kinds, but especially Marxism). Both supply perspectives that are needed to understand the present world and both have consensus, conflict, and interactionist perspectives in them.

This study also uses multiple perspectives by showing how various societies view themselves and each other. Concepts derived from the consensus-conflict perspectives and from liberal and socialist thought are used to understand how, for example, the U.S.S.R. and the United States see themselves, and how typical Third-World countries view the superpowers. However, many societies frame their outlook on the world in religious terms or do not use Western modes of thought. Where appropriate, therefore, the text develops perspectives that fall outside Western rationalism.

Chapter 1 also provides a refresher in sociological analysis for sociology students and should prove useful to students from other disciplines. It also has a fairly complete description of the topics and themes that will be covered in the remaining chapters, something that should prove useful in developing topics for student research papers (the appendix on researching the undergraduate paper in comparative studies should also help in this regard).

The text is anchored in sociology but there is also a heavy reliance on history, political science, economics, and anthropology. The existing division of labor among the various disciplines is an anachronism from the nineteenth century. A sociology that does not take into account other disciplines makes little sense. However, the text provides no formal introduction to these other disciplines. Learning is easier and retained better if ideas are introduced as needed in the context of issues and subject matter. For example, the basic elements of the full-scale political analysis that informs this study unfold chapter by chapter: Chapter 1 discusses political science, modernization theory, and comparative public policy; Chapter 2 discusses the sociopolitical structures of the preindustrial world; Chapter 3 discusses the political and legal ideals of the West developed by ancient Greece and Rome; Chapter 4 discusses the origins and nature of the modern state; Chapter 5 discusses intersocietal stratification and the international political economy, and Chapters 7 and 10 develop the basic ideas of political science through a comparative analysis of American politics, government, and law. Thus the basic elements of political science emerge gradually between Chapters 1 and 10. The same is true of concepts from other disciplines. By the end of Chapter 10, which also ends the analysis of American society, students should have a good grounding in comparative analysis (both temporal and spatial) and a good picture of the United States. After that point, other societies can be analyzed and comparisons drawn with greater economy and, hopefully, with increased understanding.

In developing the text's themes I have paid considerable attention to how students learn. The heart of effective learning is to build on what learners already know. Accordingly, I have chosen topics and examples known to readers and built on them chapter by chapter. Concepts are explained as they are introduced and then used and reused to give students a sense of mastery over both concepts and subject matter. Wherever possible I have illustrated concepts with examples familiar to students and have focused them on topics that interest and concern them. A Glossary at the end of the text reinforces learning.

The text contains Boxes to provide a change of pace, amplify topics, and to develop themes. In addition, I have included extensive bibliographic notes and instructors should find it relatively easy to assign collateral reading. A number of public and private agencies provide data about the United States and other countries on a continuous basis and I have used as many of these sources as possible so that instructors and students can easily update their understanding of social trends and problems.

It should be noted that the framework of concepts, issues, and social types established in Chapters 1–10 easily lends itself to an expansion of topics and themes and makes it possible to substitute other societies for some of the ones that I've chosen. This should make it possible to adapt this text to existing comparative societies courses as well as to use it to develop new courses. Part VI is especially designed to facilitate adoption by instructors with different interests by providing synopses of and bibliographic notes about a wide variety of countries.

The sociological perspective behind this work is derived largely from Max Weber. Weber saw behavior as a function of economic and social institutions rather than biology or psychology. Throughout he focused on norms, values, and technologies (culture) and thought of human behavior as meaningful interaction. His image of society saw stability and integration as well as conflict, tension, and change. In short, Weber's work contained all the elements of what today are known as the functional, conflict, and interactionist perspectives on society.

Weber's general perspective included a deep skepticism about capitalism's prospects. This text captures this perspective in its insistence that we must think of modern society as a problem and not merely as a society with problems. This tends to give the text the flavor of the conflict perspective. However, I try throughout to present all the perspectives in sociology faithfully and fully.

The educational philosophy behind this work is also derived from Max Weber, and outlined in his "Science as a Vocation." A text, no less than education in general, should provide students with clear contrasts and choices in tackling scientific and social problems. Accordingly, I have done my best to frame scientific problems from a variety of perspectives. I have also stressed the political dimension in scientific and other problems and have made every effort to provide readers with clear, meaningful choices about basic issues confronting them. My hope is that this text will broaden and inform the choices of its readers and increase their commitment to problem solving through political and social action even as it portrays the narrowness and rigidity of much in their social worlds.

The history of the modern West has no counterpart elsewhere and provides little guidance for understanding the non-Western world. Actually, it provides little guidance for Westerners as they grope their way into their own future. For all their science and free institutions, Westerners are badly handicapped by their assumption that Western society is somehow rooted in the essential nature of things. *Comparative Societies* will succeed in its purposes to the extent that students and prospective policy makers become aware that the entire spectrum of social system types may be problematic and that maybe none by itself provides a way for humanity to survive, much less to enjoy the earth.

CHAPTER

1

THE STUDY OF HUMAN SOCIETIES AND THEIR INTERRELATIONS

MODERNIZATION: DOUBTS AND CONTROVERSIES

The contemporary world of approximately 165 nation states has been in the making for over 600 years. The rise of capitalism, which produced the distinctive capitalist nation state, also released a worldwide process of exploration, imperialism, and cultural diffusion. Today the world is filled with a wide variety of dissimilar societies: developed capitalist and socialist societies, developing right- and left-wing dictatorships, multicommunal societies, struggling political democracies in the developing world, wealthy and poor developing countries, and secular and religious societies. Making sense of societies as diverse as these is not easy. Understanding the modern world poses special problems for the elites of each of the above societies. Characteristically, human beings take much of their world for granted, and if what they assume is wrong or out of focus, even the obvious will escape

them. In the United States, liberalism (the thoughtways of capitalism) established itself so fully during the course of American history that the basic structure of capitalist society became part of the taken-for-granted world (that is, it merged with American conceptions about human nature, nature, religion, history, and human destiny).[1] As a result of this near monopoly, Americans rarely raised questions about the core values

---

[1] Liberalism is discussed more fully in the sections below, The Liberal Perspective on (Domestic) Society and The Liberal Perspective on Intersocietal Relations. Essentially, it refers to the acceptance of private property, private economic motives and actions, and political and legal equality as central social institutions. Thus, both Democrats and Republicans in the United States are liberals; that is, both accept the validity and superiority of capitalist (liberal) society while disagreeing on how to run it. For a fuller discussion of historical and European developments in liberal social thought, see George H. Sabine's unsurpassed commentary, *A History of Political Theory*, 4th ed. (New York: Dryden, 1973).

and beliefs of capitalism (e.g., private property, individualism, economic growth) or of the international system (e.g., the nation state, private property, free trade, and the convergence of all societies toward Western ideals).

Until recently, even sociologists (and social scientists in general for that matter) took it for granted that progress was a law of history and that the West was simply leading humanity out of its dark past. More concretely, sociologists, perhaps the majority in the United States, saw the basic trend of the past 600 years as a growth in the adaptive capacity of society. Mainstream sociologists (and social scientists) argued that modern society (by which they usually meant the liberal or capitalist democracies of the West) has or represents

1. increased social differentiation toward functional specialization and concretely defined achievement statuses (leaving behind the static, diffused ascriptive world of feudalism).
2. the emergence of abstract, disposable facilities (money, technology, rational law, abstract labor force, abstract electorate, abstract nature)—in short, a rational market economy, polity, and society.
3. the emergence of a hierarchy of statuses known and accepted by most in which economic, political, family, religious, and educational rights and duties are spelled out and arranged in an order of priority, thus providing predictability, stability, and direction.
4. a growth of knowledge (provided by natural and social science).
5. the application and transmission of knowledge through the professions and education to yield higher living standards and social adaptation.
6. the rise of rational organizations (bureaucracies) to ensure efficiency in the economy, professions, voluntary sector, and government.

In recent years sociologists have become less certain about where the overall trend of modern development is leading. Despite a revival of the evolutionary perspective, sociology (along with the other social sciences) is no longer so positive that economic and technological growth is automatically good for society. And it is not as optimistic as it once was about the ability of the professions, electorates, or markets to direct society and solve its problems. Accordingly, there is now a fairly wide difference of opinion about modernization in general. The liberal (capitalist) faith in the adaptive capacity of economic and political markets, aided and directed by professionalism, is being modified. In addition, there is wide criticism of the liberal perspective on modernization among radicals. Western society, argue some radicals, has been industrialized for only a short time. A mature urban-industrial society has occurred only in the past 50 years. The question—is an industrial society sustainable? (that is, really possible)—has yet to be answered. To complicate matters, the countries of the world are modernizing in very different ways and the prospects for many preindustrial societies are grim—too many people and not enough work to do or food to eat. In addition, the countries of the world appear to be so deeply interconnected that making sense of one requires making sense of the others.

IS THE UNITED STATES EXCEPTIONAL?

Americans characteristically think of their society as an exception to the run-of-the-mill humanity. They believe that the United States has been specially favored by God, history, and geography and that it stands as a model for the world to copy. Two things make one hesitate about America's belief in its exceptionalism. One, almost all other societies believe the same thing. And two, many distinctive things about American society are not flattering, indeed, they are a cause for concern. The United States, for example, leads the world in divorce, rape, teenage pregnancy, and crime, tends to have more unemployment than other developed countries, has the lowest rate of political participation among the liberal democracies, pays far more than other countries for the same health care results, and is one of only three industrial countries (along with the Soviet Union and the Union of South Africa), and the only liberal democracy, to execute people for crime.

Americans are aware that they live in a society that has problems. By and large, they believe that they live in a sound (just) society with problems, not a problem society. Their usual response to a problem is to search for a way to solve it, taking it for granted that the United States has the will and resources to reform itself. But if American society causes such a wide variety of world-class problems, might they stem from a society that is fundamentally unsound? What if poverty, segregated minorities, recession, unemployment, crime, and an ineffectual foreign policy stem from the core nature of American society? What if the United States is losing ground against its problems? As later chapters will show, there is evidence that the United States has had little success in curbing unemployment and poverty, that it appears to have a permanent underclass composed largely of minorities, and that old and new problems appear to be piling up with no solutions in sight. Is the United States, after all, simply another fallible human society whose string has run out?

Societies rarely encourage much thought about their fundamental nature. Questions about the constituent principles of society are usually answered by myth and emotion, lodged deeply in the unconscious layers of the personality (the *mores*). We Americans are no exception—like other peoples we take our society for granted. Even sociologists, who are far more interested in such questions than other social scientists, do not as a rule raise questions about the fundamentals of our society. By and large, sociologists take it for granted that the United States is a reformable society with problems, not a problem society.

The social sciences, including those in the United States, were profoundly affected by the national societies in which they emerged and developed. American social science, including sociology, developed social theories largely in keeping with the values, norms, and practices of American capitalism. In recent decades sociologists and other social sci-

entists have begun to paint a more realistic picture of the United States and its outer world of other societies. Of special importance in all this is the comparative method.

SCIENCE AND THE COMPARATIVE METHOD

To compare is to examine something in relation to something else in order to point out similarities and differences. In its most fundamental meaning, to compare is to think. The comparative method in social science is the attempt to think systematically about human behavior and to pit ideas against facts to see if the ideas are true. The comparative method, therefore, is not really a separate method—it is synonymous with science itself.

When people in social science speak of the comparative method, however, they usually mean a distinctive branch of study both in terms of approach and subject matter. Most often they mean macro-sociology (or concern with large-scale analysis), cross-cultural analysis, or comparing something found in one society with a similar thing in another society. Less often, they mean the comparison of total societies, either of the same type or of different types. The comparative method can also mean a comparison of the past with the present (either a comparison of forms of behavior in past and present societies or a search for patterns in social change). In this sense the comparative method is also historical.

In probing the unknown, social scientists start with a basic and perhaps unprovable axiom—that human behavior is lawful (patterned, ordered, structured). According to mainstream social scientists, finding that order and making generalizations about it constitute the first order of business. As a consequence, the main thrust of social science has been to uncover universals, sometimes inside one society, sometimes across societies, sometimes as a linear pattern of social evolution. Facts and regularities that can be generalized have been preferred to facts and regularities that are situation-specific. The latter tend to be seen as half-knowledge, as a secondary world of diversity that has to be overcome.

The search for universals, however, can be a bias rather than a safeguard against error and half-knowledge. Searching for universals often means taking things out of context, thus distorting their meaning. It can mean a bias in favor of the static and away from the dynamic and unstable. Often the search for universals becomes psychological rather than sociological—that is, a search for the underlying manifestations of a psychologized human nature rather than a focus on institutions and groups. Often the search for universals results in equating attitudes with behavior. The search for universals may make us assume that beneath the world's diversity lurks consensus, unity, and convergence.

The comparative-historical method must guard against these and other distortions. Scholars are not immune to economic and political biases, including *ethnocentrism* (taking one's own society as the center of the universe and judging other societies by one's own standards). Even the great comparative thinkers of the past such as Herodotus, Aristotle, Vico, Montesquieu, Comte, Herbert Spencer, Karl Marx, Tocqueville, Emile Durkheim, and Max Weber could not escape the pull of their own time and place. Fortunately, theorists in recent decades have developed an increasingly reliable set of tools for conducting comparative studies.[2] However, much remains to be done and the development of a vocabulary and syntax (or

method) to enable scholars, policy makers, and citizens to talk fruitfully about societies and their relations is still a pressing priority in social science.

There are other difficulties to overcome in conducting comparative research. William Form has related his problems with respondent distrust and the difficulty of getting the parties in a power relation to respond openly and fully.[3] Linguistic diversity presents a special problem in cross-cultural research. The languages of the world are not interchangeable and thus conclusions derived from cross-cultural surveys are far from valid, if taken at face value.[4] Linguistic diversity raises the problem of cultural diversity. Regardless of underlying linguistic similarities, the people of different societies give the world and all the things in it different meanings. For better or worse, the people of the world, including social scientists, live in historically specific cultures. The problem of language, therefore, raises a more profound problem than the need for accuracy in translating one language into another on a questionnaire. Cultures provide their members with very different world views, and given forms of behavior can have very different meanings depending on culture.

In its simplest meaning, science provides a picture of causation and thus the ability to predict. But science is also conducted by humans who see (and must see) the world in terms of ideas and meanings. Lay people and scientists alike are immersed in national cul-

[2]A good library on comparative methodology would have to include Ivan Vallier, ed., *Comparative Methods in Sociology* (Berkeley: University of California Press, 1971); Donald P. Warwich and Samuel Osherson, eds., *Comparative Research Methods* (Englewood Cliffs, N.J.: Prentice-Hall, 1973); Michael Armer and Allen D. Grimshaw, eds., *Comparative Social Research: Methodological Problems and Strategies* (New York: Wiley, 1973); Neil J. Smelser, *Comparative Methods in Social Science* (Englewood Cliffs, N.J.: Prentice-Hall, 1976); Arthur L. Stinchcombe, *Theoretical Methods in Social History* (New York: Academic Press, 1978); J. Berting, F. Geyer, and R. Jurkovich, eds., *Problems in International Comparative Research in the Social Sciences* (New York: Oxford University Press, 1979); and

M. Niessen and J. Peschar, eds., *International Comparative Research: Problems of Theory, Methodology, and Organization in Eastern and Western Europe* (New York: Pergamon Press, 1982).

[3]William H. Form, "Field Problems in Comparative Research: The Politics of Distrust" in Michael Arner and Allen D. Grimshaw, eds., *Comparative Social Research: Methodological Problems and Strategies* (New York: Wiley, 1973), Chapter 3.

[4]Irwin Deutscher, "Asking Questions Cross Culturally: Some Problems of Linguistic Comparability" in Donald P. Warwich and Samuel Osherson, eds., *Comparative Research Methods* (Englewood Cliffs, N.J.: Prentice-Hall, 1973), Chapter 8.

tures and there is no easy way to overcome the blind spots, the biases, and the fads of inherited traditions, including those in science. Given all this, sociologists are probably best safeguarded from error and ethnocentric bias by consciously employing a variety of basic perspectives. The comparative sociologist, therefore, must draw on a wide variety of perspectives and concepts.

THEORIES OF SOCIETY, DEVELOPMENT, AND INTERSOCIETAL RELATIONS

Perspectives on society, social development, and intersocietal relations vary across a broad spectrum. For purposes of general orientation, the best start is to arrange them into two rough-and-ready groupings: the liberal and the socialist perspectives. These two groupings will also make it easier to translate academic orientations into their political counterparts and thus help us understand how scholarly studies are related to policy orientations.

The Liberal Perspective on (Domestic) Society

The term *liberalism* refers to the thought forms and values of the historic middle class in the modern West. From the seventeenth century to the present, Western liberals have stressed the reality of the individual, the sanctity of private property, the respectability and social value of work, the possibility and necessity of economic growth, especially through science and technology, and political and legal equality. Liberals in the Anglo-American world have also stressed the validity of market mechanisms, the efficacy of voluntarism, the irrationality of politics, and the incompetence of government.

This use of the term liberal, while standard in Europe, is not familiar to Americans. For Americans, liberals as opposed to "conservatives" are those who stress political and governmental solutions to problems. It is clear, however, that conservatives (Republicans) and liberals (Democrats) in the United States represent two versions of liberalism—Republicans tend to stress classic (or early liberal) ideas such as individualism, private initiative, and market mechanisms while Democrats believe that government action is necessary to make sure that all have a chance to become individuals and that markets work properly (late liberalism).

Early liberals (1650–1850) tended to assume that humans shared certain elemental needs and that all right-thinking people would agree on such things as liberty, equality, justice, and fraternity. These assumptions were plausible in a simpler age and certainly useful in fighting against parasitic and tyrannical monarchies. Later liberals (1850–present) began to diversify human needs and to stress human inequality and the emotional (and alleged darker) regions of human nature. Consensus and stability remained dominant concerns but new sources for them were found. Some liberals argued that consensus and stability came from mobility and achievement, while others argued that they came from education, the welfare state, or a publicly regulated market. Liberals continued to assume that society could be based on self-evident values: life, liberty, happiness, and the pursuit of material goods. But while these assumptions were revolutionary in the seventeenth and eighteenth centuries, they are the mark of conservatism in the twentieth, especially when combined with concepts of self-interest and market mechanisms.

Liberal thought is not limited to consensus models. Liberalism has many conflict themes—in Saint Simon, in classical economics (for example, David Ricardo), social Darwinism (for example, Herbert Spencer and William Graham Sumner) and in various ways in the thought of Emile Durkheim, Charles Horton Cooley, and contemporary theorists. But liberals have a tendency to explain conflict as a temporary problem caused by social change and vestiges from the past. The liberal interpretation of the conflicts brought about by increased social differentiation is a case in point. Liberals from Durkheim to Talcott Parsons looked on increased social *differentiation* as the mark of modernity. The growing complexity of the division of labor was seen as a natural process leading to enhanced adaptive capacity. Any problems associated with social differentiation were defined as transitional. Obviously an entirely different tradition from Rousseau to Marx to contemporary socialist thinkers defines social differentiation (or the division of social labor) as a problem in and of itself.

The Liberal Perspective on Intersocietal Relations

The liberal perspective on domestic society was extended toward all other subject matter (the past, other societies, and intersocietal relations). In American sociology the key figures in this extension are Marion J. Levy,[5] Seymour Martin Lipset,[6] Gerhard Lenski,[7] Talcott Parsons,[8] Wilbert Moore,[9] and Robert M. Marsh.[10] Liberal sociologists who pioneered empirical cross-cultural research—for example, the analyses of "modern man" (attitudes, values, behavioral dispositions) by Daniel Lerner, Alex Inkeles, and David H. Smith[11]—deserve special mention.

The basic perspective in mainstream sociology (represented by these thinkers) is known as *modernization theory.* This theory, which coincided with the emergence of the United States to unrivaled world leadership, dominated American social science in the 1950s and 1960s. During these decades, mainstream sociology thought of world modernization in terms similar to modernization in the West. Economic growth was taken as a given and it was assumed that the rationalization of life requires noneconomic institutions to change. Early modernization theorists simply assumed that the world was changing to become modern, something the West had already become.

Liberal sociologists openly acknowledge the importance of economic and technological factors. Some, for example, Gerhard Lenski and Inkeles-Smith, even give them primacy. But liberals do not think of the economy as a scientific problem—by and large, they assume that the economy reflects natural forces and that, on the whole, it has benign and progressive consequences. Liberals are aware of international conflict and imperialism but they define them as somehow separate from the nature of private power groups and do not link world troubles easily to economic development itself or to the inherent nature of capitalist society. Some, like Talcott Parsons and Gerhard Lenski, explicitly argue that a symbolic culture (knowledge, rules for living) has evolved naturally to yield *modern society* (the end of development for the foreseeable future). Wilbert E. Moore thinks of modernization as the growth of efficiency (rationalization) and rejects concepts derived from social stratification and imperi-

---

[5]*The Structure of Society* (Princeton, N.J.: Princeton University Press, 1952); *Modernization and the Structure of Societies,* 2 vols. (Princeton, N.J.: Princeton University Press, 1966); and *Modernization: Latecomers and Survivors* (New York: Basic Books, 1972).

[6]*The First New Nation: The United States in Historical and Comparative Perspective* (New York: Basic Books, 1963).

[7]*Power and Privilege: A Theory of Social Stratification* (New York: McGraw-Hill, 1966) and (with Jean Lenski) *Human Societies: An Introduction to Macrosociology,* 5th ed. (New York: McGraw-Hill, 1987).

[8]*Societies: Evolutionary and Comparative Perspectives* (Englewood Cliffs, N.J.: Prentice-Hall, 1966); *The System of Modern Societies* (Englewood Cliffs, N.J.: Prentice-Hall, 1971); and Victor Lidz and Talcott Parsons, eds., *Readings on Premodern Societies* (Englewood Cliffs, N.J.: Prentice-Hall, 1972).

[9]*Order and Change: Essays in Comparative Sociology* (New York: Wiley, 1967); *World Modernization: The Limits of Convergence* (New York: Elsevier, 1979).

[10]*Comparative Sociology* (New York: Harcourt, Brace, and World, 1967).

[11]Daniel Lerner, *The Passing of Traditional Society: Modernizing the Middle East* (New York: Free Press, 1958); Alex Inkeles and David H. Smith, *Becoming Modern* (Cambridge, Mass.: Harvard University Press, 1974).

alist theory as aids in understanding the process.[12]

Modernization theory in sociology has had parallels in economics and political science. A theory of international economics emerged during the post-World War II period as an extension of laissez-faire domestic economics. Liberal economists simply looked at the world economy in the same way that they looked on the domestic economy: economic drives and interests are given; economic behavior is a natural process that can and must be severed from nonrational politics and national customs; trade and investment must be free (private); and nations must pursue what they are best suited for in a grand global division of labor. If all this takes place, argue liberal economists, a mutually beneficial world economy will emerge and with it prosperity, stability, and peace. Socialism and communism, they argue, are wrongful limits on natural domestic and international economies, which, ultimately are part of a one-world economy.[13]

The same pull of time and place can be seen in American political science. In the period after World War II, while their country was prosperous and exercised world leadership, American political scientists optimistically promoted democracy at home and abroad. As troubles developed at home during the sixties and as American power went into relative decline in the seventies, American thinkers began to stress elitism, stability, and value consensus.[14]

During the 1960s and 1970s, the United States suffered foreign policy reverses. The debacle in Vietnam stands out but there were others. One way to state all this is to say that it became increasingly clear that the United States did not know how to read other societies or to interpret the world it lived in. Misled by domestic interest groups, by its tradition of a bipartisan foreign policy, and by modernization theory in its social science, the United States found itself increasingly at odds with its European allies and isolated from much of the Third World. These trends were accentuated by the Reagan administration in the 1980s, which brought America's ineptitude in foreign affairs and its excessive reliance on military strength to new heights.

A main purpose of this book, therefore, is to contribute a clearer picture of the outside world than the one now used by American policy makers. This book also provides an extended case study of the United States (Part II) because one of the reasons we do not understand the outside world is that we do not understand ourselves.

The Socialist Critique

The essential difference between liberal and socialist thought is that the latter rejects the equation of private property (ostensibly productive property used in business or farming to yield profits) with economic progress, justice, social stability, and peace. Socialists feel that ultimately even science and economic growth are hampered and distorted by a private property, market economy and that, therefore, capitalism is also bad for the economy (as well as the natural environment).

The socialist perspective is quite varied, ranging from materialist Marxism to Christian socialism, and from Fabian gradualism to theories that advocate immediate action to overthrow the existing social order. Some socialists in the West tend to take the nation state and representative government for granted while others see them as barriers to social change and transformation. Outside

---

[12]Wilbert E. Moore, *World Modernization: The Limits of Convergence* (New York: Elsevier, 1979), pp. 52–6, 154–55.

[13]For a well-written and balanced presentation and defense of the liberal position, (which is also the major textbook on international economics used in American business schools), see Franklin R. Root, *International Trade and Investment*, 5th ed. (Cincinnati: South-West Publishing Co., 1984), Chapters 1, 2, 18–20.

[14]For an analysis of American political science from this perspective, see Donal Cruise O'Brien, "Modernization, Order, and the Erosion of the Democratic Ideal" in David Lehmann, ed., *Development Theory* (Totawa, N.J.: Frank Cass, 1979).

the West, socialism is associated with liberation movements and with nation building. Despite their differences, however, socialists have a number of views that separate them from liberals.

For socialists, known forms of society are all marked by violence, conflict, coercion, and exploitation. Socialists are critical of liberal social scientists who depict social development as a gradual process sparked by creative individuals and animated by ideas and morality. They discount the liberal emphasis on individual rights, seeing it as a smokescreen for economic exploitation. They are also critical of the liberal assumption that there are autonomous societies and that the creative ones develop on their own and help to foster development in the others. And socialists are also skeptical of the liberal assumption (not as prevalent today as it was in the immediate past) that societies are converging on a common type (a capitalist society on the order of the United States).

Socialists feel that liberals have not understood the role of the state in the development of capitalism. From its origins capitalism has required massive state aid to build roads and ports, enforce laws protecting property, adjudicate disputes, suppress labor, subsidize business and farmers, supply the navy, merchant ships, and army that made imperialist plunder possible, and regulate the economy either by manipulating interest and tax rates or through its own spending. By minimizing the role of the state, say socialists, capitalist theorists not only falsify the nature of capitalism but they make it difficult for people to think of using the state to construct a socialist society.

As outsiders (despite the fact that socialist leaders and intellectuals are invariably drawn from the middle or upper classes), socialists render capitalist society problematic, that is, as not necessarily natural or fixed. Socialists (like liberals) are marked by a scientific respect for facts, but they combine science with values with the same spontaneity (and confusion) as liberals. Socialists see social science as a way to change society fundamentally, not merely as a way to know it, reform it, or administer it.

The key figures in rendering capitalist society as inherently problematic are Karl Marx (1818–83) and Vladimir Lenin (1870–1924). While appreciating capitalism as a progressive phase in the evolution of humanity, Marx defined its basic forms of social experience and its basic beliefs and values as relative to time and place. Far from being the terminal of history, capitalism is subject to inner contradictions that will lead to its demise and transcendence. All capital investment, argued Marx, must come from underpaid labor. Invariably, the ability of a concentrated capitalist economy to extract value from labor will diminish, eventually reaching a point where it will be obvious that capitalism must be replaced with socialism.

Marx predicted that property groups would become ever more concentrated and this has occurred. But he also predicted that the general populace would become ever more miserable (through mass unemployment) and politically revolutionary, and this has not happened—Western capitalist societies raised their standard of living significantly during the latter half of the nineteenth century and developed stabilizing political institutions that muted class conflict. In an extension of Marxian theory, Lenin argued that the capitalist countries were prolonging their lives through imperial expansion. In waves of exploration and conquest, the emerging capitalist and then the maturing capitalist societies of the nineteenth century grabbed huge chunks of the planet as colonies. The European empires made huge profits from their colonies by trading in raw materials and labor (slaves). One result was to upgrade the occupations and incomes of the Western working class. Another was to make it possible for Western governments to pacify their populations with welfare programs. However, capitalist imperialism would eventually cease to pay, he argued, and Marx's original theory would be validated.

More recently, socialists, following Lenin, argue that imperialism is an outcome of capitalism's inherent nature, that without the unearned profit from colonies the capitalist class could not appease its own working class. However, some contemporary Marxists and others on the radical left disagree with Lenin's belief that colonies would eventually industrialize, become independent, and thereby create a crisis in the older industrial countries. On the contrary, argue these theorists (known collectively as *dependency* theorists), imperialism has led to *lasting* inequality. The institutions of countries affected by imperialism have been shaped to serve the needs of the industrial world. The developing world is marked by two general types of dependency: dependent development and underdevelopment. Dependent development is when a society has undergone significant industrialization but does not have control over its own destiny (for variations of this form of dependency, see the analyses of South Korea, Canada, Yugoslavia, and Brazil). Underdevelopment refers to a society that has been developed away from industrialization to become a supplier of raw materials and cheap labor (much of Latin America, Africa, and Southeast Asia fit this pattern). Here again, argue dependency theorists, liberals have falsified their picture of the world by downplaying the role of the state. Dependency in the developing world requires a coercive state that collaborates with outside capitalists and imperial powers.

Dependency theorists distinguish sharply, therefore, on the one hand, between old fashioned conquest and colonialism and, on the other hand, the imperialism of the world market economy in which powerful industrial nations exploit weaker nations and render them dependent, primarily through market mechanisms. But whether emanating from Lenin or from dependency theorists, the socialist theory of imperialism is deeply critical of the basic liberal perspective on world modernization, which emphasizes human nature and immanent domestic processes, and on intersocietal relations, which emphasizes abstract and benign economic and cultural factors.[15]

The world economy, argue socialists, is not necessarily good nor does it proceed out of natural processes. The world economy is a *capitalist* economy and favors the developed countries over the developing ones. Even developing socialist countries are forced to participate in it, often to their disadvantage. For socialists, the actors in the world economy are social classes, corporations, schools, foundations, professions, churches, labor unions, and governments. They argue that over the past few centuries international power relations have produced a highly diversified set of nation states stratified among themselves and stratified internally to suit the world capitalist economy. Socialist thinkers vary widely in how they frame their analyses but, by and large, they see nation states as part of a worldwide process of exploitation in which industrial elites exploit their own people and, in cooperation with native elites, exploit the masses of the developing nations. Even something like food and agricultural aid is suspect (see Box 1-1, The Green Revolution: Progress or Disaster?).

BASIC PERSPECTIVES IN SOCIOLOGY

The broad contrast between liberal and socialist perspectives was presented first for purposes of general orientation. To study the world's societies, however, requires a more technical inventory of concepts. To minimize bias we will follow a settled convention in sociology and present three contrasting views of human behavior: the functional, the conflict, and the interactionist perspectives.

---

[15]For a valuable summary of the various kinds of imperialist thought, see Karl W. Deutsch, "Theories of Imperialism and Neocolonialism" in Steven J. Rosen and James R. Kurth, eds., *Testing Theories of Economic Imperialism* (Lexington, Mass.: D.C. Heath, 1974), Chapter 2. Imperialism is discussed again later in this chapter (Types of Intersocietal Relations) and more fully in Chapter 5.

BOX 1-1.   The Green Revolution: progress or disaster?

The Green Revolution refers to the many-sided effort by the United States (and other industrial countries) to increase the agricultural output of Third World countries through technology (new seeds, fertilizer, irrigation systems, tractors, harvesters). The same technology has made the United States incredibly productive in food and staples. When Third World countries needed more food, the United States simply assumed that what worked here would work there. But even the American Green Revolution has not been an unmixed blessing. Millions of Americans (of all skin colors and ethnic backgrounds) were dispossessed by the surge of agricultural technology and were forced to enter cities that were only partially ready for them.

The Green Revolution in the Third World has not had the industrial revolution to cushion its consequences, to soak up the labor it dispossessed from the countryside. Though it raised agricultural production, the Green Revolution seems to have had the ironic outcome of increasing food dependency, making people poorer and hungrier than they were. The Green Revolution has promoted cash-crop agriculture, which means production to stock the pantries and dining tables of America and Europe: coffee, sugar, pineapples, bananas, cocoa, nuts, artichokes, and so on.

The Green Revolution also means economic concentration in land and the dis-possession of former tenants. Third-World landlords import seed, fertilizer, and farm machinery and pay for them by exporting food and staples. The World Bank, other international agencies, the United States government, and a landlord-dominated home government provide ports, energy, and roads. The police become a national guard to provide protection. The value of the exports can never match the value of what is being imported (farm technology, Coca Cola, television sets, arms for the national guard) and a dependent right-wing society has been helped into being by the Green Revolution.

When food aid is sent either by the United States government or private charities to feed the dispossessed masses, the basic power structure is reinforced. The free or subsidized food is used to keep the national guard, the civil service, and urban workers fed and quiet. Some of the food is used to put rural labor to work—building roads, for example. But roads benefit landlords who can now get their crops out to be sold abroad. Food aid simply postpones the day of reckoning—the day the masses question a society in which economic growth produces poverty for most of the people. (For an actual example of a dependent right-wing society, including what happens when the questions begin, see the analysis of El Salvador in Chapter 5.)

The Functional Perspective

Sociologists in the functional school focus on society as an orderly system that survives and adapts through a series of subsystems. The questions they ask are: How does it work? What role does a given practice, element, or subsystem play in making the overall system function? To help them answer these questions, functionalists have drawn on natural science for ideas. Biology has provided the image of a biological system in which various bodily organs perform specific functions to keep the total enterprise healthy (the organic model). It has also supplied a more dynamic image in which biological forms evolve to adapt better to changing circumstances (social Darwinism). Physics has supplied the image of a system of forces in balance or in equilibrium (social Newtonianism, laissez-faire economics, constitutional checks and balances). For these and other forms of naturalistic thinking, see Box 1-2, Can Thought About Society Model Itself on Anything in Nature?

Functional theorists vary in their emphases and concerns. On the whole, however,

---

BOX 1-2. Can thought about society model itself on anything in nature?

Humans have probably always thought about themselves and their society in terms borrowed from nature. Eskimos whose existence depends on the deer focus their norms and values around the deer. Water plays a large role in early explanations of life and society. Animal and human fertility and the miracle of the seed and the annual birth, decay, death, and renewal of nature had a profound impact on how pre-industrial peoples thought about themselves and their society.

Scientific social theorists from the ancient Greeks to the present day have also sought inspiration in nature. Greek social philosophers thought of individuals and society in terms analogous to plant and animal life (teleological thinking). In the early modern period, capitalist thinkers such as Thomas Hobbes and John Locke thought of human nature and society along the same lines (mathematical mechanistic) that Isaac Newton was using to think about nature. Their social Newtonianism was elaborated by the thinkers of the French Enlightenment and had a profound influence on Thomas Jefferson and James Madison.

As a result, the American political system was consciously modelled on the static mechanistic image of the solar system that had emerged in natural science (separation of functions, checks and balances). In the late eighteenth century, Adam Smith popularized an economic theory (laissez-faire or market theory) in which economic forces were alleged to equilibrate themselves through markets just as the universe stayed in equilibrium because of gravity. Other members of the Scottish Enlightenment argued that human behavior was analogous to the behavior of bees who, though governed by instinct, created mathematically structured honeycombs and viable communities. Human appetites are blind and unintentional but, like the instincts of bees, are still rational. Biological processes, for example, blood circulation, work efficiently but do not require intention or will. We are lucky, argued the Scottish moralists, that reproduction does not come from conscious intent. Self-love is valuable to society and desire for gain leads to a rational division of labor.

In the nineteenth century, capitalist thinkers (such as the sociologist William Graham Summer) thought about society in terms analogous to how Charles Darwin thought about nature—an organism that evolves into new forms based on the survival of the fittest. Since then social thinkers have also argued that nature is a system of partnerships, mutual dependency, and cooperation, and that therefore society should also be thought of in these terms. And a wide assortment of thinkers have sought the explanation of human behavior in alleged causes in human nature itself (the brain, IQ, sex, race, hunger, aggression, pecuniary instinct, instinct for craftsmanship, and so on). A revival of this perspective in recent years is known as sociobiology.

they share the following assumptions about the nature of society:

Norms (or rules for behavior) and values are the basic elements of social life and thus the central subject matter of sociology. The success of society comes from consensus about basic norms and values.

Society is marked by solidarity, stability, cohesiveness, and integration. By and large, its parts are best understood as contributing to the success of the overall system.

The essential image of society consists of structure and order, a tendency toward equilibrium, a tendency to persist.

Society is a division of labor marked by cooperation, reciprocity, and authority—thus society is really a voluntary adherence to norms and values because they are deemed legitimate.

Tension and conflict are ever present but society is best seen as a system organized to overcome or manage disturbances.

Change does take place but occurs through consensus and should be thought of as a moving equilibrium.

It is apparent that functionalism shares the basic outlook of science. However, like any social theory, particular formulations of functionalism can succumb to political bias. Functionalism (in and out of sociology) is closely associated with the various stages of capitalism. Using images from Newtonian physics, functionalist theorists helped to develop and establish laissez-faire economic theory and the American concept of constitutional checks and balances during the eighteenth and nineteenth centuries. Using images from Darwin's theory of natural selection, they helped steel populations for the miseries and dislocations of industrialization during the nineteenth century. And using biological and physical concepts of order, system, and equilibrium, they produced a theory to help Americans through the Great Depression, World War II, and the Cold War. Functionalist theorists characteristically ask, what role does this practice or norm play in making society work? Judged by its history, we can also ask, what role does *functionalism* (or any social theory) play in preventing

elites from understanding their society and its problems?

The Conflict Perspective

Conflict theorists avoid identifying human behavior with the behavior of natural phenomena such as animals, plants, or molecules. Human behavior, they insist, is historical, social, and a function of social power. Accordingly, conflict theorists focus on the disagreements and rivalries among groups. The owners of a corporation, for example, have fundamental differences with their employees over the price of labor. Farmers have differences with urban workers and factory owners over the price of food. Quakers, pacifists, and advocates of social service programs oppose heavy spending on military programs. Black Americans, women's rights groups, and other minorities want strict enforcement of civil rights laws, while many traditionalists and many employers are opposed. Older citizens tend to vote against school budgets while parents with young children support them. In short, conflict is everywhere. Even in peaceful classrooms marked by common purposes, instructors have interests that run counter to those of their students. Higher wages for instructors, for example, mean higher tuition for students (or less money for student sports or clubs).

Conflict theory is also squarely in the scientific tradition and shares much with functionalism. What distinguishes conflict theorists are the questions they ask: Who rules? Who benefits from a given practice, norm, or value? What processes cause tension and lead to rivalry and change?

The basis assumptions underlying the conflict perspective (remember that individual theorists differ) are

1. society is essentially a loosely integrated collection of contradictory interests.
2. society's norms are often empty abstractions, its values merely ideals, not practice. The symbols of society often mislead and misinform people, often to the advantage of some groups over others—thus symbols are elements in the system of power. Society is made up of pow-

erful groups who achieve order by coercing people both psychologically and physically.

3. society spawns hostility and a questioning of authority.
4. society is always a system of uneasy power groups struggling to rule through a mixture of legitimate and illegitimate methods.
5. society is always on the brink of upheaval and change. However, conflict can sometimes promote solidarity leading to integration and adaptation.

Conflict theorists are of two types—capitalist and socialist.[16] Capitalist theorists sometimes use images from nature, for example, they adopted the concept survival of the fittest from Darwin's explanation of evolution to yield a distinctive theory called social Darwinism. Though no longer fashionable in sociology this perspective is quite common in American politics, especially among neoconservatives. Conflict theorists in the capitalist tradition are more likely today to think in terms of the conflict among institutions and the fragility of human interactions.

Socialist thinkers believe that private (productive) property and an economy oriented toward private gain are not compatible with justice and equality. Some socialists stress peaceful resistance to capitalism (for example, social democrats and Christian socialists) while others stress that life in capitalist society is a life-and-death struggle (not necessarily violent) between the nonpropertied and the propertied (Marxian socialists). Socialists assume that human behavior and society, while natural, are not patterned according to structures in nature. The key to understanding society is group structure, and groups develop for many reasons: some accidental, some deliberate. To know that society is not bound by the laws of physics or biology means that it can become the product of thought and conscious design. It means

that humans are free to change and direct their behavior. It means that thought about society is an aspect of politics and power relations.

The Interactionist Perspective

Functionalist and conflict theorists tend to see society from a macro-sociological perspective and to think of it as an objective structure and process. In contrast, interactionists tend to be micro-sociologists who focus on individuals and the relations among them. Interactionists place heavy emphasis on human subjectivity and tend to stress the individual actor as the source of human action. Theorists in this mode are especially interested in how humans create symbols and how they use them to create and cope with their world (hence the other term for this school, *symbolic interactionism*).

A major source of this tradition is Max Weber who stressed the meaningful nature of human interaction. Its American founders were the sociologist Charles Horton Cooley (1864–1929) and the philosopher and social psychologist George Herbert Mead (1863–1931). Variations on this general approach are known as exchange, dramaturgical, ethnomethodological, and phenomenological theories.

Again remembering that individual theorists differ, the basic assumptions of interactionism are

1. social reality consists of behaving individuals.
2. individuals create society, primarily by creating symbols.
3. interaction among individuals helps to create the self, which to a considerable extent is made up of acquired or internalized norms and values.
4. social relations consist of agreements and disagreements among individuals who incessantly define and redefine the world around them.
5. symbolic interactionists tend to assume that individuals can grow cognitively and that society can enlarge the area of consensus.
6. exchange theorists assume that individuals act to maximize benefits and avoid losses. Once excessively psychological and too nar-

---

[16]Robert E. Wood, "Conflict Theory as Pedagogy: A Critique From the Left", *Teaching Sociology* 10 (July, 1983): 463–86. Marxist sociology has had a revival in the United States in recent years and has become an important segment of the conflict perspective.

rowly modelled on economic theory (individuals consciously calculating advantages and disadvantages), exchange theory has broadened to include social influences and restrictions on individual choice and decision making.

7. dramaturgical theorists (Erving Goffman) and ethnomethodologists tend to assume that individuals live in a situation-specific world, which is often narrow, arbitrary, and precarious. Individuals, in these versions of interactionism, rely on their own inner resources. They negotiate, cope, improvise, and delude themselves and others in an effort to build a world they can live in.

8. phenomenological or social reality construction theorists (Peter Berger) also stress individual subjectivity but they are more likely to see it as leading to the construction of normative codes, institutions, and whole societies.

Science as the Interplay of Contrasting Perspectives

The three major perspectives in contemporary sociology do not exclude each other. Sociologists adapt particular modes of analysis by emphasizing certain assumptions and relegating others to a secondary position. But all three of the above perspectives are found in all creative sociology. Karl Marx, for example, was primarily a conflict theorist, but he paid a great deal of attention to how society integrated itself (for example, through the law and state) and he was also very interested in how people interacted (for example, workers in factories) and in their subjective worlds (class consciousness, religion, ideology). Emile Durkheim was primarily a functionalist, but conflict (anomie), interaction (association or moral density), and the collective conscience (norms and values) figured prominently in his thought. Max Weber was primarily a conflict theorist but he was also vitally interested in processes that integrated society (world views, the state, bureaucracy) and he made the meaningfulness of human interaction a central part of his sociology. And finally, Charles Horton Cooley and George Herbert Mead were symbolic interactionists, but they were not unmindful of the larger forces of economy and history and the role of inherited norms and values even as they probed into the intimate, small-scale processes of family, neighborhood, and play.

Basic Concepts in Sociology

Sociologists vary in the perspectives they use and have political orientations ranging from liberal to socialist. But, by and large, they share a core of basic concepts. These have been put into definitional form as Table 1-1.

COMPARATIVE SOCIOLOGY: BLENDING SCIENCE AND POLICY

Sociology as an Applied Science

The great classic tradition in sociology (as C. Wright Mills reminded us in his *The Sociological Imagination*) was composed of activist intellectuals: sociologists who did not hesitate to see practical benefits in their work for humanity-at-large. The great sociologists had many different orientations but they had at least one thing in common: a deep interest in using science to develop ways to direct society. Condorcet, Saint Simon, Fourier, Comte, Karl Marx, Herbert Spencer, Max Weber, William Graham Summer, and Lester Ward represent a wide range of sociological creativity across a number of countries—but all agreed that scientific knowledge should be incorporated into the life of society. In this century, American sociology pioneered the understanding of urban problems during the 1920s, played a significant role in changing American racist beliefs and practices, and was in the thick of the War on Poverty and the Civil Rights Movement of the 1960s. Today, sociologists are busy trying to develop practical solutions in many problem areas, for example, crime and punishment, mental illness, family pathology, and school integration.

Sociology, therefore, is both a pure and an applied science. Under its pure hat, it searches for generalizations about human behavior that are free of the distortions of time and place. Under its applied hat, it searches for knowledge that will help solve problems.

TABLE 1-1. Basic Concepts in Sociology

VALUES: The things, behaviors, states of personality, and states of existence in general that social actors (individuals and groups) deem good-bad, right-wrong, acceptable-unacceptable, desirable-undesirable. Values are usually stated in broad abstract terms, placed in a hierarchy of importance, and are effective in a general way in coordinating behavior. In complex societies values are both compatible (for example, individualism, civil rights, privacy) and contradictory (for example, competition vs. brotherhood, individualism vs. equality).

NORMS: The rules that ideally govern the behavior of an occupant of a status, especially in relation to someone in a related status. Whereas values provide general orientations, specific situations require specific directives, hence norms, or the rules of conduct appropriate to concrete situations. For example, the United States values human life but specific norms in law and medicine govern the way citizens and doctors must behave in order to realize the general value placed on human life. Murder is legally prohibited, killing someone in self-defense is legally permissible. Doctors must do all they can to keep people alive, they are not legally allowed to put patients with incurable diseases to death, and so on.

STATUS: A social position that directs behavior, especially toward the occupant of related statuses, according to rights and duties that are generally known and accepted.

GROUP: A social group forms when there is recurring interaction between the occupants of statuses who have expectations of each other.

INSTITUTIONS: A cluster of values, norms, statuses, and groups that emerges to provide one or more basic social needs (functions), i.e., obtaining food and shelter, having and raising children, defending one's territory, and settling disputes. Institutions tend to specialize: thus the family is a cluster of statuses organized around reproduction and socialization, the economy specializes in producing goods and services, religion in elaborating goals and arranging them in an order of priority, and the state in achieving social integration and defending against outside enemies. But institutions do more than one thing and are found in many combinations.

CULTURE: The complete set of values and norms that order (and disorder) the lives of society's members. The values and norms of a people considered as a complete range of symbols include definitions of people, statuses, groups, history, nature, artifacts (technology and the like), space, time, the hereafter, and so on.

Morris Janowitz has characterized these two traditions as "enlightenment" sociology (the stress on pure research and the belief that science can and should exert its influence but only on the general intellectual climate of the times, especially through teaching) and "engineering" sociology (the direct applications of science to problem solving).[17]

Eager to establish itself on the same basis as natural science, sociology (from roughly the 1920s to the 1950s) emphasized ahistorical, quantitative (pure) research and tended not to think of itself as an applied science. Today, all this has changed. For various reasons, sociology now openly avows that it is both a scientific and a humanistic discipline, interested in both pure (not immediately relevant) research and applied research (i.e., what is the best way to help children succeed in school, what will be the effects of an urban renewal project, what is the best way to introduce technological innovations, and so on). A call for more emphasis on social policy research has been heard lately in the addresses of presidents of the American Sociological Association. The programs of sociology conventions at both national and regional levels have also reflected a renewed interest in applied sociology. Perhaps, most important, the period from the 1960s on has seen a veritable explosion of applied sociology courses, programs, and degrees at both the undergraduate and graduate levels.[18]

---

[17]For this distinction and a brief history of sociology's attempt to develop an applied sociology, see Morris Janowitz, "Professionalization of Sociology", *American Journal of Sociology* 78 (July, 1972): 105–35.

[18]For a valuable summary of some important landmarks in social policy social science, see Louis G. Tornatsky, Trudy Solomon *et al.*, "Contributions of Social Science to Innovation and Productivity," *American Psychologist* 37 (July, 1982): 737–46.

Comparative Public Policy

The field of comparative public policy has burgeoned in recent years as social scientists have sought answers to both academic and policy issues by looking beyond their own societies. Political science has long had a comparative politics speciality that includes a policy dimension.[19] And more recently it has tackled public policy issues on a comparative basis more directly.[20] Sociologists have also begun to show interest in comparative public policy.[21] However, neither of these two otherwise admirable studies has any material on the impact of the international political economy on domestic policy. Interestingly, mainstream economics has shown little interest in comparative public policy, though it is by far the most influential adviser to government and politicians.

Nonetheless, the social sciences are far from being either comparative or applied and even the movements in this direction have their shortcoming. While we will draw on a wide variety of creative scholars, especially in sociology, economics, and political science, to fashion our analysis, we will also encounter resistance to a genuine policy science. This resistance is perhaps best seen in mainstream political science. Our reason for focusing on political science should be clear. The main avenue for the better management of society is political action. As we will see (in Chapter 7), the political institutions of the United States have serious deficiencies.

One way to summarize these deficiencies is to say that American politics has been deeply depoliticized. Mainstream political science also works to depoliticize politics largely by claiming to be empirical and value neutral.

Gabriel Almond, one of the most creative scholars in the field of comparative politics, epitomizes all that is good and bad about mainstream political (and social) science. The superb text he helped assemble is undoubtedly a leader in the field and has had a positive influence on generations of political science students.[22] Nonetheless, the text does not include the United States as one of the countries studied (references to the United States are used to develop the analytical tools with which to analyze the rest of the world, in effect, assuming that the United States and its political scientists are the benchmark for analyzing and understanding polities around the world), is still Eurocentric, is excessively focused on details about political institutions (if priority must be given to variables, economic and historical factors must come ahead of all others), and has almost nothing to say about the enormous impact of the international political economy on domestic social and political structures.

Almond has also written the summary statement for a recent collection of mainstream essays on Third World political development. His essay congratulates mainstream modernization theory in political science, affirms the empirical, value-neutral approach, and dismisses dependency theory altogether.[23]

The Sociology of Eternal Youth

One view of science is that it will accumulate knowledge and eventually ripen into a wise old age. An alternate view, expressed by

---

[19]Gabriel A. Almond and G. Bingham Powell, Jr., eds., *Comparative Politics Today: A World View*, 4th ed. (Boston: Little, Brown, 1988).

[20]Arnold J. Heidenheimer, Hugh Heclo, and Carolyn Teich Adams, *Comparative Public Policy: The Politics of Public Choice in Europe and America*, 2nd ed. (New York: St. Martin's Press, 1983).

[21]They have contributed important essays in an excellent multidisciplinary effort edited by Meinolf Dierkes, Hans N. Weiler, and Ariane Berthoin Antal, *Comparative Policy Research: Learning From Experience* (New York: St. Martin's Press, 1987). Sociologists have also done some important comparative work in the areas of family, education, and health care policy.

[22]Gabriel A. Almond and G. Bingham Powell, eds., *Comparative Politics Today: A World View*, 4th ed. (Boston: Little, Brown, 1988).

[23]Gabriel A. Almond, "The Development of Political Development [Sic]" in Myron Weiner and Samuel P. Huntington, eds., *Understanding Political Development* (Boston: Little, Brown, 1987), pp. 437–78.

the great German sociologist Max Weber, is that science (sociology) should aspire to "eternal youth." For Weber, the empirical world of human behavior is too diverse and ephemeral to ever be captured completely. Concepts and facts emerge and change according to historical conditions. As such, concepts and facts cannot lead to and cannot validate values. Ultimately, sociology is the analysis of social causation to enable humans to construct and manage their social environments on the basis of explicit value judgments. Weber's instrumental view of science put it in the service of policy—simply put, science is a means for helping human beings pass judgment on how society is being run. For Weber, the comparative sociologist does not create knowledge in the abstract (enlightenment sociology) but seeks to incorporate it directly into the life of society (engineering sociology).

For Weber, the sociologist is not merely a detached observer perceiving an outer objective reality. The sociologist must use *empathy* (understanding) as well as *perception* (empirical observation). The sociologist must be able to see and feel issues and phenomena as they are experienced by groups outside the United States, say the Peruvian military, the Iraqi government, or the Tanzanian peasant. American sociologists cannot remain within the confines of American culture when they pursue scientific work. And American sociologists cannot rely merely on balancing the ideas of rival Americans (all of whom may be trapped within American culture). The same is true of sociologists in any country—those who would see the world must leave their own worlds behind.

The genuine comparative sociologist, therefore, is careful to keep concepts, facts, and values separate but in fruitful interplay. A comparative study originating in the United States must go beyond mainstream American sociology and even beyond consensus versus conflict theories (since both can be liberal) to include the socialist tradition and since the socialist tradition is often vague and contradictory, it too must be clarified and balanced by opposing ideas and general perspectives. Above all, the comparative method must focus on the power groups and the power configura-

tions that comprise the causal reality of human behavior. The actors on the social stage are not values, attitudes, issues, or abstract processes of rationalization, modernization, or differentiation. The main actors are *groups:* corporations, churches, governments, armies, labor unions, lobbies, liberation or counterinsurgency groups, families, and international organizations like the United Nations, the World Bank, the Vatican, and the Arab League.

A special safeguard for sociologists in the developed world is to use versions of reality as seen by the sociologists, thinkers, and leaders of the developing world.[24] And thinkers in the developing world must do the same. "We balance one man with his opposite," said Emerson, "and the health of the state depends on the seesaw." Perhaps the same is true of the health of the comparative method, especially when it tackles the question, what types of society are there?

WHAT TYPES OF SOCIETY ARE THERE?

Society: A Working Definition

For a good working definition of a society, think of it as a population living in a given territory according to a comprehensive culture (that is, not a subgroup of any other group) and supplying itself with new members by reproduction. George Murdock has esti-

---

[24]No genuine comparative method is possible unless much more is done along the lines of Joseph A. Kahl's *Modernization, Exploitation, and Dependency in Latin America* (New Brunswick, N.J.: Transaction Books, 1976) which provides indispensable in-depth analyses of how the world is viewed by three prominent Latin American sociologists: Gino Germani, Pablo Gonzalez Casanova Jr., and Fernando Henrique Cardoso. Paul Sigmund, Jr., editor and author of the introduction, *The Ideologies of Developing Countries* (New York: Praeger, 1963) is a valuable compilation of excerpts from the writings and speeches of a wide variety of Third World leaders in the early post-World War II period. For more contemporary voices from the Third World, see Guy F. Erb and Valeriana Kallab, eds., *Beyond Dependency: The Developing World Speaks Out* (Washington, D.C.: Overseas Development Council, 1975).

mated that 5,000 such societies have existed in history though only about 2,000 have been studied and documented.[25] Many of these once autonomous societies have disappeared or are now part of the 165 or so contemporary nation states.

The above is only a working definition. Some societies are nomadic and do not live in a distinct territory. Many recruit substantial portions of their labor force from other societies. Some have no sense of being politically distinct. To complicate matters further, societies of any complexity are not as autonomous as we tend to think—all appear to be part of larger systems, regional blocs, military alliances, and especially the world-market economy.

The fact of the matter is that all societies beyond the subsistence level are heavily dependent on other societies. Even the advanced industrial societies are far from self-sufficient as witness, for example, the growth of the European Community, international trade and currency agreements, and military cooperation. The Western industrial countries are heavily dependent on other countries for oil and raw materials. Even the socialist societies, for all their talk of self-sufficiency, are now thoroughly involved in world trade and could not withdraw from it even if they wanted to. Beyond the developed and relatively stable nation states lie scores of countries racked by internal conflict and weakened by corruption, disease, overpopulation, and deteriorating natural environments. Without outside aid many of the nation states of the world could not exist.

The Classification of Societies

The transformation of feudal Europe into an expanding set of capitalist societies created a unique social and historical awareness among European intellectuals. By the eighteenth century, Western thinkers, anxious to understand the new society emerging around them, developed a genuine comparative sociology. From then to the present day, thinkers classified societies by core characteristics and tried to understand them as parts of an orderly, meaningful sequence of development. By and large, most theorists saw the terminal of historical development as an idealized capitalism. Another characteristic theme in these typologies is a distinction between customary-sacred-religious-static-agrarian-ascriptive-undifferentiated societies, on the one hand, and rational-secular-dynamic-urban-industrial-achievement-differentiated societies on the other (see Table 1-2).

TABLE 1-2. Types of Society in the Classic Literature of Sociology

Vico: Age of Gods, Age of Heroes, Age of Men

Montesquieu: Monarchy, Republicanism, Despotism

Saint Simon: Slavery-Militarism, Feudalism-Militarism, Industrialism

Comte: Theological, Metaphysical, Positive

Spencer: Military, Industrial (possibly, a future Ethical)

Marx: Ancient, Feudal, Capitalist, Socialist

Maine: Status, Contract

Durkheim: Mechanical, Organic

Toennies: *Gemeinschaft* (Communal), *Gesellschaft* (Society)

Weber: Traditional, Charismatic, Rational-Legal

MacIver: Unigroup (Unimyth), Multigroup (Multimyth)

Redfield: Folk, Urban

Sorokin: Ideational, Idealistic, Sensate

Becker: Sacred, Secular

Lenski: Hunting and Gathering, Simple and Advanced Horticultural, Agrarian, Industrial

Parsons: (Early typology) Universalistic-Achievement, Universalistic-Ascriptive, Particularistic-Achievement, Particularistic-Ascriptive
(Final evolutionary typology) Primitive, Archaic, Historic, Seedbed, Modern

---

[25]For a discussion of Murdock's estimate of the number of societies, see Robert M. Marsh, *Comparative Sociology* (New York: Harcourt, Brace and World, 1967), pp. 11–15.

The tasks that sustain human life and co-existence have been assigned in strikingly different ways during the course of history. The relative lack of behavioral instincts in human nature has led to enormous variability in human behavior, and thus types of social systems. However, the criteria and variables for classifying and explaining the many and varied forms of society are so numerous that despite many efforts at synthesis there is still neither an accepted typology nor a unified explanation among social scientists of the many ways that human beings have lived together. In exploring the universe of societies, ideas from the classic typologies of society can certainly be used. But these typologies overlooked a great deal so that we will also have to discover our own. We have already seen that theorists differ greatly in how they view society and its development. Earlier we also saw how they disagree about the relation of societies to each other. One aspect of the relations among societies, that they are not autonomous but interrelated, is a new and unsettling idea that we must consider again.

Types of Intersocietal Relations

Intersocietal relations have assumed many patterns: *diffused, bipolar, multipolar*. The most familiar of these took place among societies that had enough in common to develop norms to govern their relationships: the Greek city states, China (during the period of the Warring States), Renaissance Italy, and the European nation-state system over the past five centuries. Today there is a unique global system characterized by interaction among very *dissimilar* societies. To understand this multipolar world we will focus on the links between a society's domestic structures and processes and its behavior externally.

The essential link between the internal structure of Western societies and intersocietal relations over the past five centuries is that they both reflect the power of a novel market economy. Developing slowly from the eleventh and twelfth centuries on, the new market economy is fully evident in fifteenth-century Europe. By the sixteenth century a number of fully defined capitalist economies and societies have taken center stage. Understanding these societies, including their external relations (rivalry among monarchies up to the French Revolution and then among the various countries of Europe and their overseas offshoots) has long preoccupied Western social science. Perhaps the best (not the only) perspective on contemporary intersocietal relations is to see the entire European nation-state system as the outcome of an exchange economy that eventually organizes society in its service, pits societies against each other, and leads to a worldwide process of exploration, imperialism, and war.[26] The main causal chain stretches from an unleashed market economy that, having shaped society in its image, spills out beyond national boundaries for support and sustenance and eventually shapes the relations among societies themselves.

Intersocietal relations also reflect expansionist tendencies. Here there are two main patterns, the imperialism of empire and the imperialism of the world-market economy (taking advantage of others through economic means). The most prominent and important form of imperialism for most of the past five centuries has been that of conquest and colonialization. But rather abruptly (though reflecting long-term trends) the basic pattern shifted after World War II to an imperialism based on economic strength. Accordingly, our main focus in later chapters will be on links between domestic economic and class systems, on the one side, and international economic and stratification systems on the other.[27]

[26]Two key sources are Martin Wight, *Systems of States*, ed. and intro. Hedley Bull (Atlantic Highlands, NJ: Humanities Press, 1977) and Immanuel Wallerstein, *The Modern World-System: Capitalist Agriculture and the Origins of the European World Economy in the Sixteenth Century* Vol. I (New York: Academic Press, 1974); Vol. II, *The Modern World-System: Mercantilism and the Consolidation of the European World-Economy, 1600–1750* (New York: Academic Press, 1980), and Vol. III, *The Modern World System: The Second Era of Great Expansion of the Capitalist World Economy, 1730–1840s* (New York: Academic Press, 1988).

[27]For a fuller discussion, see Chapter 5.

THE TEXT'S BASIC PURPOSES AND ASSUMPTIONS

My analysis of the contemporary world of nation states will rest on a number of assumptions and beliefs:

My first assumption is that the modern world (1500–present) does not represent a clean break with the past either in the developed or developing world.

Second, the modern world was entered by different routes by those who are now in it, and those who are trying to get into it are pioneering still other routes.[28]

Third, there appears to be no uniform process of social development, which also means that there is no "modern" society if by that one means a society at the terminal of history that has figured out how to solve problems well enough to stave off failure as a society.

Fourth, societies beyond the simple subsistence systems are neither autonomous nor self-sufficient. Whether to contain internal pressures or to satisfy economic and other needs, societies develop relations among themselves. Given their different internal structures, interests, world views, and power, societies have conflicting aims and take conflicting directions. The fact that societies are not self-sufficient but must form *systems of societies* is an important theme of this study. Domestic and international phenomena are interconnected and cannot be separated into mere nation states, or types of individual societies, just as they cannot be captured in abstractions such as modernization, evolution, or rationalization. Thus while many chapters are devoted to the analysis of the various types of society, *the basic thrust of this text is to develop a conceptual framework to understand the interconnectedness of domestic and intersocietal relations.*

Fifth, my analysis relies on two basic images of society, the functionalist and the conflict models. I also employ interactionist assumptions to make sure that I am always talking about acting, evaluating, symbol-using human beings. However, my focus is always on social actors as personalities with acquired ways of perceiving, feeling, and behaving rather than as entities driven by biological or psychological forces. And while I stress the importance of symbols in human behavior, I try to avoid exaggerating their causal importance.

Sixth, my analysis contrasts capitalist and socialist systems and practices, being careful always neither to confuse ideals with reality nor to overlook the many versions of each.

My aim throughout is to find similarities among the diversity of social types. The comparative-historical approach must assume causation and must assume that societies subject to similar causes, for example, agriculture or industrialization, will have important similarities. But the comparative-historical approach also assumes that causes do not operate uniformly nor are they permanent. Social phenomena often have different meanings and different consequences, depending on time and place. Population growth and decline, for example, take place for various reasons and though studied defy unitary explanation.[29] Similar population phenomena have very different meanings for different societies—low population growth among the Russian and Israeli segments of the U.S.S.R. and Israel is a problem for these countries, whereas low population growth would be a boon for many other countries. Legal systems in various societies are quite similar in important ways because societies face similar social problems. But the law varies in relation to other forces of social control and the legal profession also develops in relation to national traditions.[30] To cite another example of the need

---

[28]For a full discussion, see the section, The Many Routes to the "Modern" World in Chapter 5. The comparative analyst must be alert to functional alternatives, the fact that similar ends can be achieved by different means; for a discussion and appreciation of the concept, see Robert E. Cole, "Functional Alternatives and Economic Development: An Empirical Example of Permanent Employment in Japan," *American Sociological Review* 38 (August, 1973): 424–38.

[29]Nathan Keyfitz, "Causes and Consequences of Population Change," in Amos H. Hawley, ed. *Societal Growth: Processes and Implications* (New York: Free Press, 1979), pp. 76–95.

[30]For an excellent introduction to the sociology of the legal profession (as well as comparative law), see Dietrich Rueschemeyer, "The Legal Profession in Comparative Perspective," *Sociological Inquiry* 47, nos. 3–4 (1977): 97–127.

to be wary of generalizations, civilian-military tensions seem not to be a characteristic of all contemporary societies. Societies differentiate civilian-military roles along a continuum ranging from none to a great deal and relations between them also form a continuum ranging from cooperation to conflict.[31]

The basic theme of this study is that modern society, capitalism or socialist, and the modern world (the world since 1500) need to be thought about at the deepest comparative level. Suspicions and doubts about modernization and about the health and prospects of industrial systems have appeared even in that most optimistic of societies, the United States. In the following chapters we will raise a variety of issues ranging from war and peace to environmental degradation, from women's rights to lagging productivity. But the overall context for discussing issues will always be the question: is modern society a society with problems or a problem society?

THE STUDY OF HUMAN SOCIETIES: A SUMMARY

Modernization and thus modern society (industrial capitalism) have become problematic. Social scientists are no longer sure of what modernization and modern society mean or where they are taking us.

Doubts about modernization have appeared among liberals as well as socialists.

The comparative method is synonymous with science: it means to compare things in different societies, things in one time period with another, and whole societies to each other.

The comparative method must be careful not to emphasize static, abstract generalizations and overlook change, instability, and historical diversity.

Liberal (that is, capitalist) thinkers in sociology, political science, and economics have seen the world in terms of private property, individ-

ualism, competition, and progress. Until recently, liberals have thought in terms of autonomous societies converging on one type.

Socialist thinkers see the existing world as characterized by conflict and instability and by the exploitation of the nonpropertied by the propertied. These thinkers emphasize the interdependence of societies and the exploitation of weaker societies by the stronger ones. Society, according to socialists, cannot achieve peace, stability, and the satisfaction of material needs until an organized public controls the basic economy.

Sociology has a long history of using models derived from nature to understand society. Most sociologists have adopted a consensus, functionalist image of society, while a minority have thought in terms of a conflict model. The interactionist perspective focuses on human individuals as willful, decision-making, symbol-creating actors. These perspectives are not mutually exclusive but are found in mixed forms in all creative sociology.

Sociology cannot be merely a naturalistic science but must also think of itself as a policy science. The comparative study of society and intersocietal relations is a valuable way to raise policy issues and provides insights into such issues that are not otherwise available.

Most social types developed by sociology have taken capitalist society for granted. This is no longer possible and comparative-historical analysis helps us render all societies as problematic.

A society is a population living in a given territory according to a comprehensive culture (that is, not a subgroup of any other group) and supplying itself with new members sexually. But this is only a working definition since societies can be nomadic or in need of foreign labor or part of a larger system of societies.

The relations a society has with other societies is an important part of its definition. Intersocietal relations can be diffused, polar, and multipolar. Inequality among societies can be the imperialism of empire or the imperialism of the world-market economy.

---

[31]For an incisive analysis, including a comprehensive bibliography, see David E. Albright, "A Comparative Conceptualization of Civil-Military Relations", *World Politics* 32 (July, 1980): 553–76.

Analyzing societies and world data requires a balance between generalizations and interpreting data in terms of unique cultural-historical contexts. Comparative analysis raises a host of policy issues, including what scheme of priority should they be put in, and provides insights about them not available to those who stay only inside their specialty and native society.

The basic purpose of this study is to gain knowledge and insights into modern society, the process of modernization, and the contemporary world of nation states, all as a preliminary toward social action. The question, is modern society a society with problems or a problem society? is especially important in deciding how society is to be better managed.

2

THE PREMODERN WORLD
Simple, Advanced Horticultural, and Agrarian Societies

A TIME PERSPECTIVE ON HUMAN SOCIETY

No understanding of human society is possible without first acquiring a time perspective on human and cultural development. Perhaps the most imaginative way in which the time frame of human life has been presented is James C. Rettie's. If someone, says Rettie, had taken one picture each year going back 757 million years and ran the pictures as a continuous film day and night for a year, humans would appear only at noon on December 31st. One hour to midnight humans would be chipping stone tools and then a few minutes later they would cultivate the soil. Christianity would appear 1 minute and 17 seconds before the end of the film. The Declaration of Independence would be signed 7 seconds before its end.[1]

THE BIOPSYCHOLOGICAL EVOLUTION OF HUMANS

Though there are gaps in the record, the fact of humans evolving out of the family of great apes is established beyond doubt. But while it is no longer necessary to argue the fact of human evolution, care must be taken to avoid the notion that the human animal emerged first and then as a superior being went on to exhibit human behavior and create culture. Our prehuman ancestors were using tools for at least 3 to 4 million years before they evolved into full humans, at least as early as 100,000 years ago. And the use of tools and other cultural behavior played a large part in furthering human evolution. Thus sociocultural behavior grew concurrently with human biopsychological evolution and both processes must be viewed as a single process of reciprocal cause and effect.[2]

---

[1]Cited by S. L. Washburn and Ruth Moore, *Ape Into Man* (Boston, Mass.: Little Brown, 1974), p. 28.

[2]For a compact account of how the human organism developed concurrently with tools, fire, and socioeconomic

The time span of evolution is difficult to grasp. The primates go back approximately 70 million years. Biopsychological evolution took place as random mutations in genes (the agent in cells that directs their development). Under selective pressure over millions of years, branches of the great apes developed an inventory of genes that enabled them to survive and increase their adaptability. The selective pressures that produced upright posture took millions of years and the achievement of bipedalism is a preeminently important stage of evolution. Further developments also took millions of years, but the tempo of development, though still slow, was speeded—bipedalism freed the front legs from the function of locomotion and thus the human hand could develop. The extensive use of the hands meant tool making and their use in a hunting environment thereby accelerating the pressure on brain development. In stressing the role of hunting in human evolution, care must be taken not to focus exclusively on males. Females played a central role in evolution both as innovative economic agents and as protectors and socializers of the young. The traditional image of "man the hunter" and "man the protector of the weak (women and children)" must be corrected.[3]

The increased tempo of biopsychological evolution probably began 15 million years ago, when the world grew drier and the earth's forests shrank. In consequence some apes moved onto the dry savannahs and bush country of South and East Africa. The new environment increased the pressure to stand upright (to see over the grass, for example) and to fashion tools (to become more efficient hunters in a harsher environment). The steady and more complex use of hands and eyes exercised the brain, which grew and specialized. Tool-making apelike-humanlike creatures with the brain size of contemporary apes have been discovered dating back 3 to 4 million years. Five hundred thousand years ago humanlike creatures with much larger brains and more complex tools were living in Asia. Fifty thousand years ago, human beings with brains the size of contemporary humans lived in many parts of the world. Between 50,000 years ago and the Neolithic Revolution of approximately 10,000 years ago human beings, biopsychologically the same as contemporary human beings, lived and flourished as highly skilled hunters and collectors in the first type of human society.

SIMPLE SOCIETY: THE SUBSISTENCE-ECONOMY PEOPLES

Simple societies can be composed of hunter-gatherers, simple horticulturalists or combinations of these. Regardless of their specific economy all are subsistence peoples, that is, they work for the direct satisfaction of their material needs. Hunter-gatherers satisfy their needs by hunting (and often fishing) and gathering wild vegetables and fruits.[4] Other simple societies hunt and gather, but may also

---

life, see S. L. Washburn, "Tools and Human Evolution," *Scientific American* (September, 1960) (now *Scientific American* reprint 601); also reprinted in a valuable, wide-ranging collection of readings in the areas of human and animal biology, biological evolution, prehistory, and ecology: *Biology and Culture in Modern Perspective: Readings From Scientific American* with introductions by Joseph G. Jorgensen (San Francisco: W. H. Freeman, 1972), pp. 143–55.

[3]As it has by Nancy Tanner and Adrienne Zihlman, "Women in Evolution. Part I: Innovation and Selection in Human Origins", *Signs* 1 (Spring, 1976): 585–608.

[4]Examples of simple hunting and gathering (including fishing) societies are Norman A. Chance, *The Eskimo of North Alaska* (New York: Holt, Rinehart and Winston, 1966), Keith H. Basso, *The Cibecue Apache* (New York: Holt, Rinehart, and Winston, 1979), C. W. M. Hart and Arnold R. Pilling, *The Tiwi of North Australia* (New York: Holt, Rinehart, and Winston, 1961), Emiko Ohnuki-Tierney, *The Ainu of the Northwest Coast of Southern Sakhalin* (New York: Holt, Rinehart and Winston, 1974), and Richard B. Lee, *The ! Kung San: Men, Women, and Work in a Foraging Society* (New York: Cambridge University Press, 1979). For an analysis of 11 hunting-gathering societies on five continents that have survived into the twentieth century, see M. G. Bicchieri, ed., *Hunters and Gatherers Today* (New York: Holt, Rinehart and Winston, 1972).

fish, herd, plunder, trade, or garden.[5] (For a list of the attributes of simple society as an abstract type, see the section below, Simple Society as an Abstract Type: The Folk Society.)

Prehistoric, Historic, and Contemporary Foraging Societies

The simplest society is one composed of a small group of families who live from hunting and gathering. At one time there were thousands of such societies throughout the world, but most have disappeared. Our knowledge of them derives from works of anthropology, especially from the nineteenth century on and from contemporary contact with the small number of surviving tribes that live in isolated areas like the Arctic, the Kalahari Desert, or in tropical rain forests.

European people began to collect information about other peoples largely in the eighteenth century. In the nineteenth century anthropology began to study simple societies in a systematic manner. Our knowledge of simple society and of what life must have been like before the advent of agriculture is based largely on the study of cultures that survived until and after that time, although archeological evidence is also important. Some simple societies disappeared because their ecological base collapsed; some were shattered when they came into contact with other cultures; many were destroyed by imperialism both ancient and modern. Those that survive are on the margins of the world economy. Unfortunately the world's economy is still expanding and native peoples are still being destroyed either by the very act of discovery or by exploitation (for example, the native peoples of Alaska and Canada and the Indians of the Amazon). Many members of these once proud and resourceful peoples now live on the skid rows of Anchorage, Vancouver, or Winnipeg.

For many thousands of years (at least from 30,000 to 10,000 years ago) all humans lived off the natural environment as foragers: mostly they collected wild vegetables, nuts, and fruits though they also hunted and fished. A hunting-gathering-fishing economy has no need to produce a surplus or to make capital investments and the members of a foraging society are relatively equal. Their division of labor is fairly simple and is based largely on ascriptive statuses (cultural definitions of kinship, sex, and age). The family is the basic focus of behavior and the basis of social organization. Nonetheless these small, often nomadic, societies became highly adapted to their environment and to their problems in general. Women and men both worked hard at economic tasks though men seem to monopolize the occupation of big-game hunter (something that led to a monopoly of military status in later societies and contributed to their superiority to women in other social statuses). Those who are especially skillful at the hunt are accorded a measure of extra prestige but it is not possible for any family to accumulate enough property to make them superior to other families. Though there are positions of leadership, they cannot be turned into hereditary statuses and passed on to children. Hunting and gathering societies are also polytheistic rather than monotheistic and peaceful rather than warlike. Also notable is the absence of slavery.

Mixed Subsistence Economies

At one time simple societies could be found throughout the world: in steaming jungles, the frozen north, well-watered valleys, deserts, mountains, forests, and by the sea.

---

[5]Simple horticulturalists gain some of their food by gardening with simple tools. For example, see Bruce G. Grigger, *The Huron: Farmers of the North* (New York: Holt, Rinehart and Winston, 1969), Napoleon A. Chagnon, *Yanomamo: The Fierce People* (New York: Holt, Rinehart and Winston, 1968), Jan Hogvin, *A Guadalcanal Society: The Kaoka Speakers* (New York: Holt, Rinehart and Winston, 1964), T. O. Beidelman, *The Kaguru: A Matrilineal People of East Africa* (New York: Holt, Rinehart and Winston, 1971), Robert Knox Dentan, *The Semai: A Nonviolent People of Malaya* (New York: Holt, Rinehart and Winston, 1968), and Lowell D. Holmes, *Samoan Village* (New York: Holt, Rinehart and Winston, 1974). Perhaps the best known of the simple subsistence societies that also live off plunder are the Vikings; in this regard see Michael H. Kirkby, *The Vikings* (New York: E. P. Dutton, 1977).

Based on a variety of natural habitats, early simple society took a variety of shapes. Some simple societies lived in more hospitable terrain, others were defeated by a harsh or changing natural environment and still others became specialized because of their special environments.

The mixed subsistence economies are somewhat different from foraging economies in that they have added simple farming (gardening or simple horticulture), herding, trading, or plundering to their economic behavior. Many mixed (or specialized) subsistence economies are marked by elementary political institutions. The preindustrial world was highly dependent on fragile and changing ecological conditions.[6] A successful hunt requires organization. A change of season may require movement from one locale to another. Provision must be made for lean years or for war. Nomadic peoples may trespass on lands used by others because rivers change their course, water holes dry up, or grasslands wither, and it is not uncommon for disputes to arise. As these domestic and intersocietal problems arise, political statuses emerge to provide direction, coordination, and protection. Contact with other peoples often leads to greater political, including military, organization. The ability to pool food and weapons and to act in concert greatly enhances a simple society's adaptation to both its ecological environment and to its neighbors.[7]

The ebb and flow of national development in the West, Western imperialism, and the growth of nation states throughout the world have left a large number of "simple" societies in the rural hinterland of countries all over the world. A number of anthropological (and sociological) classics have explored this world and have helped to bring simple society into relief. These studies were also often able to describe the beginning of the end for these communities as they came under the influence of industrial, urban, and governmental forces.[8] Later, when we focus on the contemporary nations of the world, we will encounter other peoples who have been bypassed by "modernization" inside such countries as the United States, Brazil, Vietnam, Nigeria, and others.

Simple Society as an Abstract Type: The Folk Society

The term *folk society*, coined by the anthropologist Robert Redfield,[9] presents the common features of a wide variety of simple societies:

1. Folk societies are small and isolated. Their members know each other, have predictable personal relations, and are not subject to ideas or values from the outside that challenge their own.

2. Folk societies have an elementary economic and social division of labor. Assignments to social labor are by sex, family status, and age. Folk societies have extensive empirical knowledge about the workings of nature but lack complex tools and elaborate techniques for dealing with nature (for example, irrigation systems), and do not employ high levels of inanimate energy. Production is for use and there is a relative equality of condition (not from choice but because of a shared scarcity).

3. Members of folk society view nature in personal terms. While there is a body of empirical

---

[6]Industrial societies are also subject to ecological conditions but, as we will see later, in a different sense.

[7]Elman R. Service uses political complexity to distinguish bands, tribes, and chiefdoms within the world of simple-subsistence peoples. For a valuable collection of essays on 14 variations on simple society, see his *Profiles in Ethnology*, 3rd ed. (New York: Harper and Row, 1978), Chapters 2–15).

[8]For a peasant village in Mexico studied by two anthropologists over a thirty year period, see Robert Redfield, *Tepoztlán: A Mexican Village* (Chicago: University of Chicago Press, 1930), Oscar Lewis, *Life in a Mexican Village: Tepoztlán Restudied* (Urbana, Ill.: University of Illinois Press, 1951), and Oscar Lewis, *Tepoztlán: Village in Mexico* (New York: Holt, Rinehart and Winston, 1960). For an Irish village, see Conrad Arensberg, *The Irish Countryman* (New York: Macmillan, 1937) and Conrad Arensberg and Solon T. Kimball, *Family and Community in Ireland*, 2nd ed. (Cambridge: Harvard University Press, 1968), originally published in 1965. For French Canada, see Everett C. Hughes, *French Canada in Transition* (Chicago: University of Chicago Press, 1943) and Horace Miner, *St. Denis: A French-Canadian Parish* (Chicago: University of Chicago Press, 1943). For a useful description of four "modern folk" societies in Mexico, Ireland, India, and China, see Elman R. Service, *Profiles in Ethnography* (New York: Harper & Row, 1978), Chapters 20–23.

[9]*American Journal of Sociology*, 52 (January, 1947): 293–308; widely reprinted.

knowledge derived from experience, there is no organized, scientific search for knowledge. Folk societies, like some advanced horticultural societies, do not have writing, and its absence makes the accumulation of knowledge and a sense of history difficult.

4. Social positions in folk societies are governed by specific norms that are accepted because they have always existed. Positions in all departments of life are not only constant but consistent with each other. Individuals view each other in personal terms.

5. Folk society personalities are relatively homogeneous, especially by sex. Identities are acquired and maintained easily. Social intercourse is relatively easy because individuals are either similar to each other or behave according to tightly prescribed and thus predictable norms.

6. Social control takes place through commonly accepted and cherished norms, and there are no specialized control agencies such as police, courts, government, and prisons. A folk society is basically an organization of families. Social control is maintained mostly through careful socialization and scrutiny by the multifunctional family. Shame rather than guilt is the main personality dynamic and keeps behavior in socially prescribed channels.

7. Social unity and stability are achieved through homogeneity and avoidance of novelty rather than through adaptation to new conditions and problems. Day-to-day problems are routinely addressed by a network of customary norms. The assumed causation of magic exists side-by-side with knowledge based on the validity of experience. The culture of folk society is not centered in a world governed by universal laws but in a polytheistic, multicausal world experienced as meaningful and noncontradictory. Folk peoples live an unambiguous, nonanomic way of life, in short, in a community.

The high-level abstraction folk society covers many different cultures, for example, the passive Zuni, the treacherous Dobu, the competitive Kwakiutl.[10] It includes hunting and gathering as well as simple horticultural societies that grow food in family or tribal gardens and also hunt, gather, fish, herd, or plunder.

The Transition to Complex Society

Nothing in the annals of human history surpasses the cultural (adaptive) achievements of *homo sapiens* between 30,000 and 10,000 years ago. The fact remains, however, that early society was heavily dependent on the natural environment, for example, the supply of large animals. Had the supply of large animals (caribou, deer) continued, homo sapiens would in all likelihood still be living as a hunter and collector of food.[11] The gradual decrease in the supply of large animals was a crisis of the first order. Early peoples adapted to this profound ecological change by intensifying the hunt and improving their hunting skills but this led only to a further depletion of the source of their basic sustenance. Like societies to come they *reacted to problems in terms of what had worked in the past* only to find that solutions eluded them. After considerable time and with apparently little forethought some hunters and collectors began to farm, thus introducing a revolution in the social environment. The eventual switch to an agricultural economy was one of the most profound transformations in human history. As with so many events in human affairs it took place without anyone noticing—a nonevent because there was no one to define or understand its meaning.[12]

COMPLEX HORTICULTURAL SOCIETY

The Neolithic Revolution

Many simple societies produce some of their food by cultivating plants and domesticating animals. Even some early hunting and

[10]For a classic discussion, see Ruth Benedict's *Patterns of Culture* (Boston: Houghton Mifflin, 1959); originally published in 1934.

[11]For an informative discussion see Marvin Harris, *Cannibals and Kings: The Origins of Cultures* (New York: Random House, 1977), especially the Introduction and Chapters 2 and 3; available in paperback.

[12]For an analysis that places food production much earlier than has been suspected (approximately 17–18,000 years ago) and that emphasizes that these momentous steps went unnoticed, see Fred Wendorf *et al.*, "Use of Barley in the Egyptian Late Paleolithic," *Science* 205:4413 (September 28, 1979): 1341–47.

gathering peoples were familiar with plant cultivation but remained uninterested in food production until the supply of big game began to run out. Food production economies introduced a profound revolution in human affairs, but the mere fact of food production does not automatically change simple society—some of them have had mixed subsistence economies for thousands of years. But the advent of plant cultivation about 10,000 years ago was revolutionary in that it led, in relatively short order, to advanced horticulture in a few places. And once developed the distinctive type of society known as advanced horticulture spread throughout the world. Such societies also appeared independently of each other.

Advanced methods of plant cultivation emerged in the Middle East between 9,000 and 6,000 years ago. A key technological element in crossing the threshold to complex society was the development of metallurgy.[13] Economic variables that affect the relations of humans to nature are quite varied and include the natural environment (soil, flora, fauna, topography, water, climate), tools, productive skills and knowledge, definitions of the natural environment, and definitions of humans. Societies that rely on the simple digging stick do not compare in productivity with those that have metal hoes. Productivity is significantly increased if:

water control is practiced either through irrigation or terracing;
crop rotation is practiced;
fertilizer is used;
a variety of plants are available;
and animal power is available.

For most of their millions of years on earth, prehumans and homo sapiens alike lived in a world of severe material scarcity. Leslie White has referred to the early pre-

agrarian period as "human-energy" culture or the "wild-food" stage of history. Humans had to rely on their own muscle power to get work done. The domestication of plants gave human beings a revolutionary new source of power—an efficient and readily available mechanism for harnessing solar energy. The cultivation of plants provided more than a dependable (other things considered) supply of food—it was also the basis for other advances in utilizing and controlling nature. And it had large implications for how humans would organize themselves as societies. As we see again and again, technological developments exert a profound influence on social organization. (See Box 2-1, Technology and Human Association for an introduction to this theme.)

Social Differentiation and Stratification

The new horticultural societies of Mesopotamia, Egypt, India, China, Mesoamerica, and Peru were marked by permanent settlements, a population increase, a marked growth in specialized occupations, technological and normative creativity, and the emergence of separate political institutions. In all six societies there appeared a full-fledged, autonomous state generated from internal sources alone. Four of these, the societies of the Tigris-Euphrates, the Nile, the Indus, and the Yellow rivers eventually went beyond advanced horticulture to become agrarian societies (which we will discuss shortly). The societies of Mesoamerica (Maya) and Peru (Inca), after an extraordinary advance in technical development and complexity of social organization, remained at the level of advanced horticultural society. Other advanced horticultural societies in sub-Sahara Africa (Ashanti, Zulu), North America (Cherokee), Southeast Asia (Siam), and in Polynesia also developed as state societies but through contact with other societies.

One of the striking features of the more advanced horticultural societies is the large increase in nonproductive activities: warfare, religious ritual and ceremonies, prestige practices and consumption, and administra-

---

[13]I am indebted to Gerhard and Jean Lenski, *Human Societies: An Introduction to Macrosociology*, 5th ed. (McGraw-Hill, 1987), Chapters 6 and 7 for their concise and informative analysis of horticultural and agrarian societies.

BOX 2-1. Technology and human association

Human interaction patterns are profoundly affected by technology. The first cities with their dense and rich social relations were made possible by agricultural technology (hoe, plow, draft animals, water control systems). The technology of writing split populations into literate and illiterate segments, made possible a bureaucratic form of power, and allowed people to interact with the dead. The mighty temple or palace reinforced hierarchical relations. The British House of Commons was deliberately rebuilt with too few seats for all its members so as to preserve a sense of intimacy and personal dialogue during political debate. The elevator has made possible high-rise buildings and new forms of urban density. The minutely specialized factory has separated workers from both their products and their fellow workers. The great public arenas of the past such as the Coliseum and the sports palaces of today, such as the Yankee Stadium and the Superdome, have always demanded a mass, spectator form of participation. The assorted technologies of birth control have had a profound impact on the relations between the sexes. New communications technology has facilitated totalitarian power, allowed diverse peoples to interact, and has put earth in contact with the remote planets, galaxies, and even the birth of the universe. The technology of nuclear energy may require so much monitoring and professionalism that it may promote an elitism bordering on authoritarianism.

tion. Also striking is the growth of specialized occupations: political heads, priests, warriors, tax collectors, merchants, artisans, servants, tenant-workers, serfs, slaves, entertainers, prostitutes, and bandits.

Perhaps the most striking feature of advanced horticultural society is the growth and formalization of special economic and political statuses. These statuses, which revolve around property rights, the organization of the labor force, and political authority, represent a significant change in power relations. Of special significance is the fact that these statuses become the attributes and transferable possessions of private individuals. Society is not only reconstituted, but its operation and maintenance over time are achieved through hereditary rights and processes. Another striking feature of advanced horticultural (and advanced herding societies) is the development of monotheism. In some advanced horticultural societies there is also the momentous development of writing and mathematics, both outcomes of the need to record and direct complex economic and social transactions.

Complex horticultural societies are marked by considerable internal rivalry among elites, by population pressures, both internal and external, and by economic problems (water shortages, pests, plant disease). The basic flow of resources is toward the top though there are some downward redistribution processes, most of them token and symbolic. The essential power structure derives from ownership of or control over land which in turn leads to occupations dependent on land ownership or control either directly or indirectly: king, nobility, priests, artisans, servants, serfs, slaves. The essential problem of power in this type of society (not necessarily seen clearly or fully) is how to maintain the heavy overhead of nonproductive activities in the face of population growth, diseases, crop failures, water shortages, and so on.

The power groups of advanced horticultural societies establish granaries to provide for lean years, institute welfare programs, undertake public works, some with direct economic significance such as irrigation and road-building projects, and expand their economic base by conquest and plunder. The association of advanced horticultural society (out of which grew some of the great agrarian civilizations) with irrigation and flood control is striking. Also striking is the independent emergence of an autonomous state in societies that geared their economies to water control. Though many societies copy or develop states as the result of pressure from other societies only six pristine state societies have emerged, all of them associated with drainage, flood control, and irrigation: the societies of the Tigris-Euphrates (Sumer), the lower Nile (Egypt), the country drained by the Indus River (India), the middle course of the Yellow River (China), Peru-Bolivia (Inca), and Mesoamerica (Maya).[14] Two of these failed to become agrarian societies and can be cited as the epitome of advanced horticultural society: the Maya (and Aztecs) and the Inca.[15]

Advanced horticultural societies develop primitive states. Their economic base can vary considerably since many primitive states result from outside influences or pressures, especially military pressures (for example, the Zulu, Ashanti, Siam, Cherokee). The crucial ingredient in the formation of states is that a particular group acquires a monopoly over the use of force. Given opportunities for coordinating production and trade in a diverse and productive natural environment (Inca), or the need to maintain independence from powerful neighbors

(Siam), or to fight against imperialist powers (Cherokee, Ashanti, Zulu), a unified production and redistribution system emerges, enforced by civil servants and soldiers. All this is often supported by hereditary political statuses (a nobility, often unified under a monarch), rudimentary legal orders, and a unified, normative-religious system (monotheism).

Advanced horticultural systems lack a number of vital sociocultural elements and thus are different from agrarian systems. A lack of large tracts of open land suitable for plant cultivation may force them to remain horticultural—accordingly their labor force must be composed of independent family units rather than serf families or slaves.[16] Many lack the wheel, the plow, domesticated animals, and writing (for example, the Inca lacked all of these). Such societies reach a certain level of socioeconomic development and go no further.

Evolution or History?

The Western world, perhaps especially Americans, see the world as a natural process of evolution representing progress. Before we analyze agrarian society, confusion about evolution-progress must be cleared up. Nature and society both exhibit change but of very different kinds—for one thing the time scales for each are very different. The movement from hunting-gathering society to advanced horticulture society and then to agrarian and industrial society is not evolution as that term is used in relation to animals, plants, geological formations, or the universe of galaxies. Social evolution should also not be interpreted as progress. The concept of progress is so deeply engrained in both social

---

[14]Morton H. Fried, "On the Evolution of Social Stratification and the State" in Robert A. Manners and David Kaplan, eds., *Theory in Anthropology* (Chicago: Aldine, 1968), pp. 251–60. For more general discussions, see Morton H. Fried, *The Evolution of Political Society* (New York: Random House, 1967), and Elman R. Service, *Origins of the State and Civilization: The Processes of Cultural Evolution* (New York: Norton, 1975).

[15]Sylvanus G. Morley, revised by George W. Brainerd, *The Ancient Maya*, 3rd. ed. (Stanford: Stanford University Press, 1956), J. Eric and S. Thompson, *The Rise and Fall of Maya Civilization* (Norman, Ok.: University of Oklahoma Press, 1954), Michael D. Coe, *the Maya* (New York: Praeger, 1966), George C. Vaillant, revised by Suzannah B. Vaillant, *Aztecs of Mexico: Origin, Rise, and Fall of the Aztec Nation* (Garden City, N.Y.: Doubleday, 1962), and Nigel Daires, *The Aztecs* (New York: Macmillan, 1973). For the Inca, see J. Alden Mason, *The Ancient Civilizations of Peru*, rev. ed. (Baltimore: Penguin, 1968).

[16]The type of crop is also important for social organization, for example, wet rice, coffee, rubber, bananas, sugar, and so on each have their own special economic requirements and opportunities. Further constraints or different opportunities develop depending on types of animals and other resources. For the variety of natural environments and the variety of rural economies in relation to efforts at modernization in the contemporary Third World, see below, especially Chapters 13 and 14.

science and popular culture that a special effort is needed to ward it off. Both liberal (Condorcet, Comte, Spencer) and socialist (Marx and Engels) thinkers interpreted history as progress. Evolutionary doctrines of progress suffered a decline during the early twentieth century but neoevolutionary theorists have worked hard to reestablish the idea (one version of this is modernization theory). My own view is that the evolutionary-progress model obscures more than it reveals and should be replaced with a historical model.

The evolutionary model contains a value judgment disguised as fact: that history reveals progress: progress in morals, knowledge, and general adaptive ability. Both liberals and socialists use the evolutionary model for political purposes (not always intentionally). The evolutionary (progress) model is so deeply planted in the West that many automatically interpret technological advance, writing, monotheism, ethical codes, law, philosophy, mathematics, modern natural and social science, liberal democracy, and state socialism with progress while overlooking negative outcomes.

As we move through each type and subtype of society, a number of features in each will be identified that run counter to the notion of progress. Of special importance is the need to be wary of claims that a particular society has developed an effective (and unique) problem solving capacity. Advanced horticultural societies resulted from a more effective division of labor and technology that yielded greater food supplies and new knowledge. But they are also marked by slavery, human sacrifice, head-hunting, warfare, imperial expansion, luxury amid deprivation, and exploitation. The leisure provided by horticultural society led to technical innovation and creativity in devising social forms. But the elites of horticultural society did not focus on existential problem-solving. Social problems were invariably defined and solutions proposed that enhanced and maintained the power of elites. *What is important about this is that the same is true of agrarian and industrial elites!* (The term *elite* will refer in later pages to historically and institutionally

created leaders and power groups. Some use the term differently to refer to human beings who allegedly have innate qualities that propel them to leadership.) Despite today's enormous emphasis on problem solving, one should be careful about assuming that contemporary societies (capitalist or socialist) have an improved or unique capacity for solving social problems. The relevant comparison is always between the problems of a society and its problem-solving capacity, not between the problem-solving skills and knowledge of different kinds of society. Far from having an improved ability to solve problems, contemporary societies (whether capitalist or socialist) may be unable to keep up with their problems. The high science, the technological achievements, the political and legal institutions, and the socioeconomic mechanisms of contemporary urban-industrial systems, including their education, look very different if they are evaluated in relation to their ability to solve *contemporary* problems rather than compared with the problem-solving capacity of past societies.

Advanced Horticultural Societies and the Modern World

Advanced horticultural societies are the basis of many "modern" countries. Western people tend to think in terms of an evolution (often revolution) from a centralized (advanced) feudal system to a liberal capitalist society (England), to an authoritarian capitalist society (Germany), or to a state socialist society (the Soviet Union). However, many of the regions of the world are struggling to "modernize" from an advanced horticultural (or simple feudal) base. By and large, such societies have failed to cross the threshold of sustained growth. When we assess the trials and assorted problems of the developing countries of the contemporary world in later chapters, it will be important to remember that many (for example, Tanzania) are modernizing from an advanced horticultural rather than an advanced agrarian base. (For an explicit contrast, see the last section in this chapter.)

COMPLEX AGRARIAN SOCIETY

Technological and Normative Developments

The first agrarian societies emerged out of advanced horticultural societies in the Middle East approximately 5,000 years ago. An advanced agrarian society is unique because it can produce food, tools, and other things, including belief and value systems, on a scale far exceeding even an advanced horticultural society. New technology, especially iron metallurgy and the plow, along with other productive techniques, such as irrigation and harnessing animal energy, combined with such economically central sociocultural inventions as slave and serf labor, family-tenant labor, administrative structures, standing armies, forms of taxation (including forced labor), money, writing, mathematics, religion, and legal codes, result in a unique type and level of social existence.

The revolution implicit in the domestication of plants and animals soon expressed itself in the "domestication" of human beings. A sedentary farm or village life became the characteristic form of human behavior in a number of places in the world. A few thousand years later, an even more important transformation in the quality and quantity of social interaction emerged, the city. The unique advantages of an urban division of labor augmented technological advances.[17] Once established, cities became the basis for a continuous growth of the productive arts (despite setbacks) until a series of technological-economic plateaus were reached in the

high civilizations of India, China, and medieval Europe.

The advanced horticultural societies all lacked one or more of the basic technological and normative elements that characterized agrarian society. The Aztecs, Mayas, and Sub-Sahara Africa, for example, lacked the wheel and draft animals. The Incas and Sub-Sahara Africa lacked writing. China had no plow or iron until relatively late. The emergence of iron is especially important because, unlike bronze, the ingredients from which it is made are both plentiful and durable. While bronze was restricted by cost to weapons and the decorative arts, iron found wide application in economic pursuits. The plow's importance can hardly be exaggerated—by digging deep it buries weeds and releases far more nutrients than the hoe. But no one item of technology should be singled out as the cause of quantitative and qualitative jumps in the level of social existence. A plow is really effective if made from iron and pulled by animals. The wheel is useful for carts and chariots and thus important for transportation and warfare. But the wheel is basically a lever and once in use it can lead to other applications such as wind-and-water mills and the use of gears. Ultimately the wide use of the wheel can lead to knowledge of mechanics. The wheel is also a circle and is related to the development of mathematics and astronomy—it is no accident, for example, that the New World societies that lacked the wheel also had no conception of the earth as a globe (circle) and that they developed no science of navigation based on the assumption that the world was round and the heavens circular.

The complex agrarian society develops a considerable economic surplus, thanks to an advanced technology and division of labor. Literacy, restricted to the elite in power, leads to the accumulation of technical knowledge and of a corpus of sacred writings, all easily transmitted under the custody of a privileged profession of priests or scholars. Agrarian society is characterized by mighty public works such as aqueducts,

---

[17]Two essays, Robert J. Braidwood, "The Agricultural Revolution" and Robert M. Adams, "The Origins of Cities," both in *Scientific American* (September, 1960), reprints 605 and 606, give quick introductions to this period. For fuller treatments see the highly readable accounts by V. Gordon Childe, *Man Makes Himself*, rev. ed. (New York: Mentor, 1951) and *What Happened in History*, rev. ed. (Baltimore: Penguin, 1954); William Howells, *Back of History* (New York: Doubleday, 1954); and Leslie A. White, *The Evolution of Culture* (New York: McGraw-Hill, 1959).

temples, roads, and fortresses, but little accumulation of productive capital; most production is for consumption. Any surplus over subsistence is expended on luxury, on "public" buildings glorifying the upper estates and the beliefs and values that benefit them, and on warfare. The surplus produced by the masses, in other words, is used to reinforce and perpetuate the system that dominates and exploits them.

A *simple* agrarian society is not much different from a horticultural society—in some ways it is less differentiated and less developed culturally. A simple agrarian or feudal system is centered on the economically self-sufficient latifundia, manor, or hacienda. It has a natural economy—little is produced for exchange. Simple feudal society is also marked by political self-sufficiency: the local lord (or patron or gentry) enforces laws and settles disputes. Decentralized feudalism generates simple market relations, mostly of a local character. Its outstanding characteristic is that land and labor are not commercialized. Work and nature are given fixed definitions and the economy is embedded in political, religious, and family institutions.[18]

Advanced feudal societies and folk, advanced horticultural, and simple feudal societies are similar in some important ways (all are static, sacred-value oriented rather than secular-scientific). But advanced feudal or agrarian societies possess important distinguishing features. Advanced agrarian societies (as found for example, in the river valley civilizations of the Middle East, India, and China) are typically large both in population and territory and exhibit a marked degree of institutional specialization. Above all, they everywhere exhibit a sharp cleavage between a small governing elite and a large unarmed peasant mass. Other features are a significant increase in food production and

an increase in craft specialization. The most important development, however, is the increased specialization of the dominant landlord stratum, an important mechanism for effective control of the many by the few.

Advanced agrarian societies derive their productive economies from a number of sources. Irrigation is a pervasive feature of agrarian civilizations. Feudal-absolutism (or state feudalism) was given considerable impetus by the development of centralized irrigation and water control systems. The so-called hydraulic societies[19] everywhere set up a leader and a state machine that legitimated itself in terms of an alleged derivation from both the supernatural and the people and an alleged devotion to their service. According to Wittfogel, large-scale irrigation in China, India, and pre-Spanish Mexico, led to state absolutism, whereas Europe, which relied on rainfall agriculture, was spared a centralized feudalism.

In addition to its advances in technology, agrarian society develops a variety of labor forms: the tenant family is the most productive unit when crops require intensive labor and a militarized slave force is productive in some forms of agriculture and transportation (slave galley), in mining, road building, and other public works. Productivity is also enhanced by the emergence of specialized crafts. The outstanding characteristic of advanced agrarian society is a concentration of land worked in a variety of ways by human and animal muscle. The essential economic power relation is between the owners/controllers of land and the landless. As a result, the goods and services produced by the economy are neither distributed equally nor are they distributed widely enough to raise per capita living standards (actually living standards decline). The essential flow of goods and services is upward into the coffers and service of the landlord (in the form of rent, interest, labor, or goods).

---

[18]For a useful distinction between types of economies and their societies, see C. B. Macpherson, "Status, Simple Market, and Possessive Market Societies" in his *The Political Theory of Possessive Individualism: Hobbes to Locke* (London: Oxford University Press, 1962), pp. 46–68.

[19]Karl Wittfogel, *Oriental Despotism: A Comparative Study of Total Power* (New Haven: Yale University Press, 1957).

Advanced agrarian societies are marked by pronounced expansionist tendencies.[20] Once productive levels reach their limits, the only way to increase an elite's holdings, to make up for reverses caused by drought or disease, to replenish a labor force, or to gain psychic benefits is physical expansion, invariably through conquest. A key perspective on complex agrarian societies is that they have the technological and organizational capacity to utilize their own as well as captured labor forces.[21]

The high agrarian civilizations are also marked by fully developed universalist, monotheistic religions. Monotheism and monarchy support and reinforce each other and religious and political institutions are formally intertwined; indeed religious values and norms permeate all institutional areas. In addition complex agrarian society develops practices and symbols in the realms of law, education, and art that reinforce and maintain elite domination. A marked feature of these latter developments is the explicit division of a population into two static categories, a tiny elite and a huge mass with an explicit parallel between religion, law, education, and art and the sharp inequality in economic and political power. Ultimately the basic symbolic system portrays the interests of the monarch and elite as synonymous with the interests of the masses.[22]

---

[20]Complex societies in general tend to be expansionist—see Chapter 5 for a discussion of the imperialism of empire (found among advanced horticultural, agrarian, and early capitalist societies) and the imperialism of the world-market economy (found among contemporary industrial systems).

[21]Industrial societies also know how to utilize foreign labor at home (immigrants, brain drain, guest labor, illegal aliens). In addition, industrial capitalism uses foreign labor abroad by exporting capital to compliant countries with large pools of cheap labor, for example, American capital goes abroad to manufacture television sets in Taiwan, textiles in the Republic of Korea, and automobile engines in Mexico.

[22]The historic middle class of the modern West did much the same—it proclaimed a universal humanity and gave itself as the definition of the human.

State Feudalism

In complex agrarian society the "owners" of land become immensely wealthy but do not remain an undifferentiated group of manorial lords. The wealth of advanced agricultural society leads to a significant and in many ways ominous development, the full-fledged state. The central problem in building an agrarian state is the decentralizing thrust of the local, self-sufficient economy. The central authority must subdue not the masses but the local landlords who in turn are intent on subduing the masses on their self-sufficient estates. Since the power that accrues to those who control land is enormous, the agrarian state never succeeds in fully freeing itself from its social base—its essential characteristic is a tension-filled collaboration between hereditary landlords and a central power (the monarch who is also an hereditary landlord).

The power of the decentralized feudal landlord is undermined in a number of ways. The warrior has already emerged as a specialized occupation. Under simple feudalism he (invariably male) is embedded in the local estate. The king must remove him from his local allegiance and make him part of a standing army. The standing army is the core of the agrarian state. A standing army is a bureaucracy: its members are employees who obey rules and orders and use equipment belonging to the owners of the bureaucracy. Supporting an army requires a considerable amount of money so the king must develop sources of revenue. The principle of bureaucratic administration is also used for civilian purposes. In its classic development the officialdom of Imperial China was chosen by civil service examinations. Not only does a bureaucracy lead to a more rational (efficient, responsible) administration than patrimonial administration (when officials administer hereditary offices and estates) but it supplies the central authority with officials who are unrelated by blood either to each other or to the "chief executive."

The king can also obtain loyal servants by using eunuchs, again forestalling the power of kin ties.[23] Foreign ethnic groups are also useful in performing political and economic functions since they are not easily drawn into power struggles. The assignments of administrative officials are often deliberately rotated and every effort is made to avoid assigning them to their place of origin. The king also undermines the power of concentrated local property by scattering the holdings of his aristocracy and by changing the laws of inheritance to require an equal division of family estates. The state also prevents the build-up of private commercial or manufacturing wealth by establishing state monopolies in lucrative economic sectors.

The agrarian state also develops a specialized priesthood bound to the service of the state. Specialization and professionalization emerge in other areas as well, for example, astronomers and astrologers, theologians, physicians, mathematicians, scholars, philosophers, and artists. Though king and nobility are at odds in some ways, their interests are reconciled somewhat by the fact that the upper reaches of the various professions are recruited either by law or de facto from the hereditary stratum of landlords. *The essential definition of complex agrarian society is domination by a landed propertied group that has specialized to control all functional areas—or, expressed differently, the propertied elite monopolizes the means of production, administration, warfare, and meaning.*[24]

Agrarian societies are stable, and yet comparative standards of stability are difficult to establish either in contrast to simpler societies or to industrial systems (whose time span has so far been very small). Advanced agrarian systems, however, experience unique types of instability. Advanced horticultural

societies are racked by rivalry and intrigue among the elite; in addition to palace rivalries, advanced agrarian societies face a new problem—challenges from below. A marked feature of advanced agrarian feudalism is peasant and slave revolt (and crime). Stated more broadly, class polarization and struggle are widespread in advanced agrarian society.

Advanced agrarian society is also more politicized than earlier societies. The government takes an active role in managing the economy, providing public works and storing food and other provisions for time of need.

Agrarian society has instability built into its power relations—the masses work hard, do not receive much in return, and can identify their oppressors.[25] Many reforms are "revolutions from above"—segments of the dominant oligarchy seeking to oust other segments, institute "reforms." A characteristic feature of Greece and Rome, for example, is caesarism—a reform movement initiated at the top in populist language but which leaves class relations substantively intact and distracts the masses by providing bread, circuses, and moral exhortation as substitutes for equality and justice.[26]

Estate and Caste Stratification

Both advanced horticultural and agrarian societies are rigidly stratified by hereditary estates and castes. The estate structure of stratification can vary considerably depending on geography, economic variables, patterns of conquest and migration, type of religion, and other factors. Thus, societies as dissimilar as ancient Egypt, the Inca and Maya, medieval Europe, Imperial Russia, China, and Japan all belong in the general category of estate stratification. But regard-

[23]Lewis Coser, "The Political Functions of Eunuchism" in *Greedy Institutions: Patterns of Undivided Commitment* (New York: Free Press, 1974), Chapter 2.

[24]Some important continuities and similarities between state feudalism and liberal democracy will be explored later.

[25]These are also the conditions that lead to economic and technological stagnation and that propel elites toward war as a way of maintaining revenues.

[26]The similarity with reform in liberal and socialist societies will be noted in due course. Revolution from above as a distinctive feature of contemporary modernizing societies is discussed in Chapter 5 and elsewhere.

less of variations, even some important ones, one overriding pattern characterizes pre-industrial estate society: a small group of families has succeeded in institutionalizing its domination of the vast majority of people through legitimated economic, political, military, religious, and intellectual power. Regardless of origin or specific history, a complex agrarian society tends to become "feudalistic"—that is, to develop as a hierarchy of explicitly articulated hereditary estates.

As economic surplus increases, so does social inequality. An increase in inequality begins with advanced horticultural society (characterized by a more productive and centralized gardening economy) and accelerates under agrarian society (characterized by an even more productive large-scale farming or agricultural economy). Agrarian society represents a significant advance in technology over horticultural society but the heart of its economy is still the production of food. Accordingly, the basis of social organization lies in the *control of land*. Under a feudal system of inequality, control over land is lodged in a small number of powerful families who supervise the labor and social existence of servants, serfs, tenants, and slaves. All positions in feudal society derive from this economic relation although religious and other ideologies obscure it. Land control determines superior and inferior, and this power relation is frozen by making statuses hereditary. The children of the feudal elite inherit their parents' position while the offspring of serfs and slaves automatically become serfs and slaves.

Economic hierarchy soon leads to hierarchies of prestige (what people are worth as determined by birth, breeding, consumption) and by political-legal-military hierarchies (property law, taxation, civil servants, the military). Social processes develop to insure the transmission of status from one generation to the next: hereditary wealth and occupations, socialization processes (apprenticeship, education), and legal norms (privilege). In addition, elaborate philosophies emerge to validate the status quo. The praises of the elite are sung and the masses are told that the hierarchy comes from God and that status obligations must be performed as a duty to the supernatural.

Advanced horticultural and agrarian societies develop an enormous range of transferable assets: not only land, weapons, and jewels, but amulets, songs, clothing, and masks. They also create transferable social statuses (children inherit their parents' position through the mechanism of birth). Most important, they create transferable personality traits and skills (children are socialized to be serfs or nobles and thus to live in different worlds).

Social stratification in advanced horticultural and agrarian societies takes two forms: *caste* and *estate*. In the caste system, economic inequality is legitimated by religion (and racist ideology). In the estate system, economic inequality is legitimated by family. Though it has a number of variations, the purest example of a caste system is India (see Box 2-2: The Indian Caste System).[27] Here one's identity is conferred by birth in a religious caste. In contrast, identity in estate stratification is conferred by birth in either a noble or ignoble family (classic cases are ancient Egypt, Imperial China, and medieval Europe). Neither system has much social mobility (movement from one caste or estate to another).

Feudal systems are very durable despite considerable internal conflict and struggle. Feudal nobles struggle among themselves and at the same time have to contend with peasant uprisings and slave revolts. But feudal societies are tough: when they decline, they usually revert to earlier forms or disappear. With the one exception of feudal Europe, they do not change to industrial systems.

Like the caste system, the estate system is focused formally on prestige rather than economic status. However, institutionalized inequality in estate society relies much more explicitly and heavily than caste society on political power (monarch, magistrate, state religion, tax collector, the military) to support economic inequality. Though economic vari-

---

[27]For the use of caste in a modern society, see below Box 4-3, South Africa: A Class-Caste Hybrid.

BOX 2-2. The Indian caste system

Agrarian societies are deeply and rigidly stratified. But agrarian caste systems go even further than estate systems in rendering their populations unequal. The feudal system of medieval Europe had at least a minimal sense of equality because of the Christian tradition (all souls are equal before God, all must obey God's norms). India's Hindu religion is unique—it declares people unequal *before God.* Its only universal rule is respect for the cow—otherwise Hinduism proclaims a different duty and a different existence for India's five broad castes and its thousands of subcastes. The caste system regulates everything: occupations, marriage, who can handle whose food, who drinks from what fountain, who enters into what gate, and so on. The radical inequality of the Hindu religion coincided with radical economic inequality to form history's most rigid and thoroughgoing system of social stratification.[1]

[1]For a more detailed picture of the Indian caste system (and modern India), see the section on India in Chapter 18.

ables are important in the origin of such societies, they eventually succumb to such power and prestige variables as military force, law and administration, a "rational" religion, styles of consumption, traditions of family honor, intellectual-educational forces, and the like. The fundamental similarity between caste and estate systems must not be overlooked. Both are based on an economic system characterized by a high concentration of landholding and a surplus of labor. Both develop normative systems that stress the hereditary rights of bloodlines. Both develop elaborate prestige systems (consumption, education, etiquette) to separate the elite from the mass. And in both force is ever-ready to enforce the rights of the elite.[28]

The Cycle of Advance, Decline, and Revival

The economic revolution signaled by the advent of agriculture did not come about through foresight or genius. As is true in almost all of human history events were in control and human beings were largely unaware of what was happening. The agricultural revolution that led to the high civilizations of the Middle East, India, and China was not progress in any but a limited sense. Despite the huge increase in productivity that came from harnessing solar energy, living standards fell as populations multiplied, diseases grew,[29] and material values were consumed by luxury, warfare, and state agencies of administration and control. Typical members of feudal and even early capitalist society were probably worse off than their paleolithic counterparts until approximately 1850 A.D. (in the West).[30] The advanced feudal system everywhere exhibits a pattern of centralized control, corruption, neglect, and decay of vital irrigation systems (as well as the environment), popular unrest, revival through feudal forms, and so on, in dreary repetition. Eventually the agrarian economy embedded itself in religious, political, and prestige forms that prescribed and legitimated the economic division of labor.

[28]For two informative articles on estate and caste systems see Hsiao-Tung Fei, "Peasantry and Gentry: An Interpretation of Chinese Social Structure and Its Changes, "*American Journal of Sociology* 52 (July, 1946): 1–17 and Gerald D. Berreman, "Caste in India and the United States," *American Journal of Sociology* 66 (September, 1960): 120–127.

[29]For an important study that points to the large and relatively neglected role played by disease in human history, see William H. McNeill, *Plagues and Peoples* (Garden City, N. Y.: Doubleday, 1976).

[30]For a fascinating discussion, see Marvin Harris, *Cannibals and Kings: The Origins of Cultures* (New York: Random House, 1977), especially the Introduction and Chapters 2 and 3.

Its essential weakness was that its major resource, cheap labor, destroyed all incentive to develop new technology or to transform economic surpluses into productive capital. Some capital formation took place but it occured largely to maintain existing levels of tools and facilities. Irrigation systems, aqueducts, roads, ports, and market places were built to establish agrarian society in the first place. And even much of this infrastructure was not productive—Roman roads, for example, served military and administrative needs but carried little commerce. Instead, the "gross national product" of agrarian society was consumed (and even mortgaged) by warfare, coercive military/police action, wasteful administration, luxurious living, and nonproductive public projects and buildings such as royal palaces and tombs, churches, sports arenas, and theaters. Only in Western Europe did the advent of centralized government lead to qualitative social-system change—and only because absolute monarchy in the West came after, and as a result of, economic change and growth and not before.

SIMPLE, ADVANCED HORTICULTURAL, AND AGRARIAN SOCIETIES: THEIR DIFFERING IMPACT ON DEVELOPMENT

Our look at the premodern world (which continues in Chapter 3) is no indulgence in historical curiosities. The modern world is a direct derivative of the past and we cannot understand it without knowing the various forms of society in the premodern world. Put simply, the types of social structure in the past are important for understanding the successes as well as failures in achieving modernity. Societies that start with horticulture (simple and advanced, for example, Black Africa) or simple feudalism (the latter's prime example is the type brought to Latin America and the Philippines by a backward monarchy, Spain) have, by and large, failed to modernize (build an industrial economy and a viable national state). Those with an agrarian background that took the form of

caste (India) have also had great difficulty in modernizing fast enough to overcome growing levels of poverty. Only the centralized estate (or feudal-authoritarian) systems have modernized successfully (the West, Russia, and the Sino-based societies of Japan, South Korea, Taiwan, Hong Kong, Singapore, and the People's Republic of China). For a summary of the characteristics of simple society (hunting-gathering, simple horticulture, simple feudalism), advanced horticultural society, and agrarian (feudal-authoritarian society), and for a glance at the characteristics of industrial society, see Table 2-1.

To know this is not to settle all issues in understanding modernization. On a lower level of abstraction societies must be known by the kinds of plants they cultivate and by their resource base. As we will see, it makes a considerable difference in the formation of a society's elite, its labor force, and its social power relations in general, if a country's economy is based on coffee, sugar, tin, or phosphate (often a question of whether it is capital or labor intensive). As we will see shortly, it is also vital to know if a society's economy is oriented toward subsistence or the market. We will also look at who controls the market: the farmer, government, creditors, mill owners, or private or public distributors. Often this latter question is best framed in terms of an economy's relation to the world-market economy and the society's relation to other societies.[31]

It is important, perhaps above all, to know the particular types of property relations, especially landholding, in societies that are attempting to modernize.[32] Historically, the

---

[31] For an important analysis (that we will discuss again) that emphasizes the importance of the specific type of agricultural economy for understanding the Third World, see Jeffrey M. Paige, *Agrarian Revolutions: Social Movements and Export Agriculture in the Underdeveloped World* (New York: Free Press, 1975).

[32] For a rich, pioneering analysis, contrasting rural property forms in both the premodern and modern worlds (the manorial, family-size tenancy, family freeholding, the plantation, and the ranch types of property), see Arthur L. Stinchcombe, "Agricultural Enterprise and Rural Class Relations", *American Journal of Sociology* 67 (1961–62): 165–76.

TABLE 2-1. Basic Characteristics of Premodern Societies and a Glance Ahead at Industrial Society

	Simple/Folk (Hunting-Gathering, Herding, Simple Horticulture)	Advanced Horticulture (including Simple Feudal)	Agrarian (Feudal-Authoritarian)	Industrial (Capitalist and Socialist)
Statuses and Roles	Roles are simple, congruent, and the same as statuses. Behavior takes place largely through ascribed statuses (age, sex, family).	Specialized statuses emerge, many nonfunctional. Inequality grows as economic and political hierarchies emerge.	Specialized statuses are pronounced. Roles deviate from statuses (ideal world). Statuses acquired through ascription birth into high or low families).	Statuses are deeply specialized and not always congruent. Roles often deviate from statuses. Capitalist (U.S.) and socialist (U.S.S.R.) elites think of their respective societies as based on a functional division of labor.
Groups	Family is central and the basis of social organization.	Family is important but nobles and ignoble families distinguished. Central government and permanent settlements emerge.	Family important but there is a hierarchy of noble and ignoble families. Courts, guilds, churches, and manor arise as special groups along with the state and cities.	Formal organizations predominate. Large private or state run corporations dominate the economy. The state and voluntary organizations also emerge as important groups.
Characteristic forms of Interaction	Differentiation is by age and sex. Interaction is local and personal and egalitarian by age and sex.	People interact by sex, age, kinship, and in a hierarchy based on noble versus ignoble birth.	Interaction local and primary but some impersonal because of royal bureaucracy. Interaction equal among peers, highly unequal between lords and serfs.	Impersonal interaction becomes dominant as large-scale bureaucracies direct economy, state, education, religion, and voluntary groups.
Institution	Family is primary. Other institutions embedded in family. Economic and political power egalitarian.	Family is important but economic and political institutions emerge along with religion. New institutions characterized by inequality.	Family is important but economy, state and religion emerge as specialized structures. Economic and political power is concentrated, unequal, and hereditary.	Economic institutions acknowledged as the mainspring of society but government, especially in socialist society, plays an important economic and social role. Economic concentration is pronounced. International economic and other activities increase.
Technology	Effective hunting tools and techniques. Muscle power primary; little use of animal or inanimate energy. Digging stick for gardening. Standard of living higher with less work than in agrarian society.	Emergence of metallurgy, and use of one or more of terracing, fertilizer, crop rotation, animal power make for large increase in food production.	Advanced use of water, wind, animal power, and metallurgy. Technology includes writing and organizational skills. Cultivation of large areas emerges (agriculture) but standard of living declines.	Spectacular technological growth, especially new machinery powered by inanimate energy.
Values and Norms	Empirical knowledge, custom, and magic blend into smooth mixture. No rival world views. People are not problem oriented—they live in a world of answers.	Empirical knowledge increases along with greater use of abstractions but magic increases most.	Empirical knowledge expands, magic challenged by religion (more abstract way to formulate causal process in world). Values and norms emerge to support hierarchical but still traditional, ascriptive world.	A pervasive rationalization of all aspects of life occurs or is attempted. Elites place great value on science and the creation of knowledge and technology. Heavy emphasis on economic achievement by all.
Social Control	Individuals are subjected to integrated statuses (community). There is little deviance.	Social control still primarily through family socialization but supplemented by public rituals and movements. State also enforces discipline.	Social control occurs largely through socialization and daily interaction but there is also need to weed out heretics, control conquered people, and to force labor—thus execution, imprisonment, slave galleys, etc.	Elaborate control structures: public education, standing armies, police, courts, prisons, bureaucracies. Mass and elite media also act to socialize within existing culture.
Social Change	Society still static and there is no inner dynamic for change except outward expansion.	None to speak of unless other cultures appear to disrupt it.	Except for outward expansion little social change—mostly cyclical—(decay, decline, revival, decay, etc.) Only West developed into a new society (rise of capitalism because of unique sociocultural factors).	Changes occur within capitalist and socialist societies but not social system change. There is no postindustrial society. All industrial societies are guided by active states but so far none has had much success in solving social problems.

power and behavior of large land holders are crucial for understanding the economic and political development of England, France, Prussia, Eastern Europe, and Russia. A large agricultural sector comprised of large land owners helps explain the failure of Argentina to modernize and may also be instrumental in retarding Australia's industrial development. It is not accidental that Japan, South Korea, Taiwan, and the People's Republic of China eliminated the power of large landlords before their spectacular economic growth.

Patterns of land holding are important to the history of all countries; the state socialist societies have eliminated private property in land, though some are now permitting private property to spur food production. The tension between landed elites and the growth of a national state (divorced from control by landlords) is found everywhere. It is not clear that landed elites have lost much in places where they have adapted (for example, Egypt, Mexico, Brazil, and much of the rest of Latin America).

And land ownership, in combination with the relative power of a commercial or industrial "middle" class, provides much of the explanation for the varied fortunes of most countries. A more complete explanation would point to the action of the state in either retarding or promoting development.

Agrarian societies are exceedingly durable. Despite large-scale problem-solving failures, they successfully resist revolt from below and changes from above. In only one place, the West, did agrarian society succumb to a new form of society and even here it imparted many of its characteristics to its successor. With their monopolistic control of symbol formation, technical intelligence, and administrative-military-legal-political skills, along with their highly developed forms of etiquette and taste, it is not surprising that agrarian feudal elites were highly influential in shaping the modern West. In England the feudal aristocracy had a profound impact on liberal society. In addition, one must think in terms of the blending of

interests and values between the feudal elite and the developing middle class rather than an abrupt break and reversal.[33] The feudal nobility was a powerful force in France well after the French Revolution while feudal elites remained dominant in industrial Germany[34] and Japan.

It is worth recalling that some landed elites did not adapt well to the modern world—the Junkers in Germany adapted well only in terms of militarism and the Russian aristocracy was defeated by ineptitude (and the German Army). And of course the landed classes in conquered territories stretching from all of Latin America to Southeast Asia (for example, Vietnam), India, and Africa (for example, Algeria and Rhodesia) have not adapted well to change at all.

The multiethnic systems developed by agrarian imperial expansion have also bequeathed a rich legacy of headaches for the modern world: Northern Ireland, Cyprus, Yugoslavia, Malaysia, and Nigeria are examples of segmented societies troubled by ethnic cleavage.[35]

Failure to understand the power of history goes a long way in explaining domestic and foreign policy mistakes, especially among America's ahistorical elites. We will return to the question of how and why modern society emerged in Chapter 4. Before that, though, we need to understand some of the premodern hybrid societies that were influential in shaping the rise of capitalism in the West.

---

[33]Walter L. Arnstein, "The Survival of the Victorian Aristocracy" in F. C. Jaher, ed., *The Rich, the Well-Born, and the Powerful* (Urbana, Ill.: University of Illinois Press, 1973), pp. 203–57.

[34]For an interesting analysis of how feudal and bourgeois values of inequality blended in Germany, which has implications for all modern societies, see Walter Struve, *Elites Against Democracy: Leadership Ideals in Bourgeois Political Thought in Germany, 1890–1933* (Princeton, N.J.: Princeton University Press, 1973).

[35]For a fuller discussion of segmented societies, see below, Chapter 4. For an analysis of representative examples, see Chapters 15 and 16.

SIMPLE, ADVANCED HORTICULTURAL, AND AGRARIAN SOCIETIES: A SUMMARY

Human beings emerged from a process of evolution lasting millions of years. Their biological evolution was greatly influenced by social and cultural factors. Social evolution is distinctly different from biological evolution. Human beings have not evolved bio-psychologically in any significant way in the past 10 thousand years but many different social types have emerged during that time.

Hunting-gathering societies (along with simple horticultural and simple feudal societies) have little social differentiation, rely on human muscle power, and have a coherent, homogeneous, and particularistic symbolic world. Complex horticultural societies are distinctly differentiated into nobles and nonnobles, have a more advanced technology (yielding more food from family gardens), a more complex symbolic culture, a central state, and are often warlike and expansionist.

Agrarian society is even more differentiated and has a more advanced technology, yielding larger amounts of food from the cultivation of large tracts of land. This society too tends to be warlike and expansionist. Another distinctive feature of agrarian society is the emergence of universalistic religions and normative codes, often to help manage its multicommunal empires.

The movement from simple to complex society saw an increase in inequality through the elaboration of transferable (hereditary) social statuses. It saw a movement from a particularistic, polytheistic world to a universalistic, monotheistic world.

Horticultural and simple feudal societies have had great difficulty in entering the modern world. Centralized agrarian societies with their well-developed symbolic world, including literacy, their well-disciplined, hierarchically organized populations, and their universal normative codes have found it much easier to modernize.

All complex societies have greatly influenced the nature of the contemporary societies that have emerged from them. The liberal democracies are no exception since they have been greatly shaped by the centralized feudal systems from which they emerged.

CHAPTER
3

THE PREMODERN WORLD
Hybrid Societies

The premodern world had societies that deviated from its three main types: the hunting-gathering, horticultural, and agrarian societies. As the Lenskis point out, there were a variety of specialized preindustrial societies, for example, fishing and herding societies and the maritime trading societies such as the Minoans, Phoenicians, and Venetians.[1] The Lenskis called mixed forms of society *hybrids*, a term they use mostly to describe industrializing agrarian and industrializing horticultural societies.[2] Unfortunately, the Lenskis do not single out the most important of the preindustrial systems (from the standpoint of understanding the modern world) that cannot be captured by the terms hunting-gathering, horticultural, or agrarian. The societies of ancient Greece and Rome, and in some ways ancient Israel, are mixed forms of society that lie outside the more typical preindustrial systems. In addition, Arab society (excluding Egypt) is also different from the conventional preindustrial societies. All these societies are important for understanding the modern world. To categorize them, I have borrowed the term *hybrid* from the Lenskis though I use it somewhat differently (they tend to use it as a catchall term for societies undergoing change).

Israel, Greece, and Rome were uniquely creative and must be distinguished from other hybrids. Talcott Parsons has referred to Israel and Greece as *seedbed* societies[3] and that term is an appropriate part of their definition (I include Rome). However, in discussing the nature of these complex preindustrial seedbed societies, and their indispensible

---

[1]Gerhard and Jean Lenski, *Human Societies: An Introduction To Macrosociology*, 5th ed. (New York: McGraw-Hill, 1987), Chapter 8.

[2]*Ibid*, pp. 360 ff.

[3]Talcott Parsons, *Societies: Evolutionary and Comparative Perspectives* (Englewood Cliffs, N.J.: Prentice-Hall, 1966), Chapter 6.

contribution to the modern world, I will not use Lenski's evolutionary scheme, and I will stress group structure, especially economic processes, rather than normative processes as Parsons does.

PREINDUSTRIAL HYBRIDS: THE SEEDBED SOCIETIES OF ISRAEL, GREECE, AND ROME

Social changes in the first millennium B.C. produced qualitative changes in the world views of a number of widely separated peoples. The basic movement was away from tribal particularism toward universalism. Between roughly 750 and 400 B.C. in Palestine, China, India, Persia, and Greece, a remarkable transformation took place in how humans viewed themselves and their world. The Jewish Prophets, Confucius, Buddha, Zoroaster, and the Greek philosophic tradition from Thales to Socrates all emerged in this relatively brief period. The basic normative thrust in China and India produced no tension with agrarian particularism; in point of fact it reinforced traditionalism. Judaism, and eventually Christianity and Greek philosophy, however, contained elements that were profoundly antitraditional and impossible to reconcile with tribalism or particularism. Israel and Greece ceased living in a congruent, customary world close to nature's rhythms and became more differentiated and questioning, at once intense and ingrown and outreaching and universalistic. Along with Rome (which they influenced), they became seedbed societies destined to have a considerable impact on the rise of capitalism, in the formation of the nation states of the West, and, through the latter, on the fortunes of the entire globe.

Israel, Greece, and Rome were creative for a number of reasons. All had natural environments and distinctive economies that in one way or another prevented them from becoming isolated or self-sufficient. At first a nomadic, pastoral people, the Jews then experienced the problems of settling and defending a more settled urban-horticultural economy at a major crossroads of the world. The element of contrast and the stimulus to thought and creation in Greece and Rome also stemmed primarily from economic causes. The basic creative thrust in Greece and Rome came from the relatively open, "free" market nature of their respective economies.

In discussing Israel, Greece, and Rome, I will not focus on these societies directly though I will describe their essential features briefly. My interest in them is twofold: as unique social forms and as contributors to the emergence of the modern West. In the first instance my focus is on ancient Israel, both as an interesting and creative herding and horticultural society in its own right and on Judaic-Christian culture, more specifically the Judaic-Christian cultural practices and symbols that have a bearing on the rise of capitalism.

THE JUDAIC-CHRISTIAN WORLD VIEW

The Separation of God, Human Nature, and Nature

A pronounced identification, even merger, between humans and nature is characteristic of simple societies, including simple horticultural societies. Simple societies make wide use of magic and taboos within a highly particularized world. Complex horticultural societies, especially complex herding societies, effect an important separation between human nature and nature and transcend particularism in important ways, especially by shifting from polytheism to monotheism. Herding societies often have a clear and straightforward relation to nature—a single person directs a herd of animals. Understandably, herding societies have a pronounced tendency to envision a single God who actively monitors the world and intervenes when he thinks it necessary. In short God is seen as a shepherd. The nomadic peoples of the Middle East (Jews and Arabs) conceived of God in these terms. Herding people also have another unique relation to nature. While their herds need pasture land and water they are not tied to a particular territory. This too helps to free them from nature worship. And it often brings them into contact (sometimes friendly, sometimes not) with other peoples and cultures.

The achievements of the ancient Jews must be placed against this background although other elements must be added. The Jews had a hybrid economy—at first a nomadic herding people they eventually became an "urban," horticultural society. And it was not their nomadic herding alone that brought them into contact with other peoples but the fact that they settled in the major crossroads of the world. In any case the distinctive achievement of the Jews (which took place roughly from 1500 B.C. to 500 B.C.) was to sharply separate God, humans, and nature and to make the relationship among them an intellectual and moral problem. The Jews strenuously fought nature worship and magic, eventually putting in their place a transcendent God, a universe governed by God's law, and an ethical orientation for both individuals and the corporate entity, the Jewish people. Personal identity was no easy thing for Jews because they had to struggle to fulfill a stern moral code and a demanding ethical tradition. One of their distinctive contributions to the eventual rise of capitalism was their severence of personality, society, and nature from each other. In short, they rendered human identity and society a problem for which there were no easy answers in nature (or in custom for that matter). In addition, by declaring that God had made nature subordinate to human needs, they gave religious sanction to the exploitation of nature that is such a marked feature of the modern world.

The Judaic-Christian Sense of History

Another distinctive creation of the Jewish people was a sense of history, a linear time perspective. Unlike other peoples who live close to nature in an eternal present, the Jews developed a sense of time, a distinction among past, present, and future: a way to note change and unique events. The main reason for this cultural innovation was undoubtedly the Jewish escape from Egyptian bondage, an event celebrated as unique and unrepeatable, that is, as a historical rather than a natural, seasonal, or cyclical phenomenon. Significantly, the celebration of Passover was substituted for an earlier nature festival marking a recurring stage in nature's unchanging cycle of seasons.

The advent of Christianity deepened the historical awareness available to later generations. In the Jewish panorama of time, God speaks to the Jews through Moses and then the prophets. In Christianity, God speaks to all humans by entering history directly and provides a permanent link and a permanent tension between the worlds of human society and the kingdom of God. The birth of Christ is a unique (historical) event and gives religious sanction to the idea that change in this world is both possible and good. And in both the Judaic and the Christian orientations, the glorification of God also leads to the dignity of humans and the celebration of earthly life (unlike the pronounced otherworldliness of, say, Hinduism).

Life as Moral Struggle

An important contribution of the Judaic-Christian tradition to the emergence of capitalism was its belief in a universal moral law existing independently of any individual, family, tribe, or nation. It was impossible for Jews and Christians to think of the moral realm as originating either from the person of a king or from sociohistorical variables. Their cultural achievement, which had such great significance later, was to create cultural components that were profoundly antitraditional. Both Jews and Christians were enjoined to obey ethical and moral laws that were not embodied in existing institutions. Though Judaism and Christianity often made their peace with the existing powers, they contained elements that were profoundly dangerous to the status quo. Foremost was the supreme importance of the individual personality and its relation to God.

Responding to the pressures of economic expansion and political nationalism, elements of the Judaic-Christian tradition emerged as the Protestant Reformation. The major cause of both Protestantism and capitalism was surely economic expansion but the economy could not have burgeoned to take command of Western society without help from Christianity, especially Protestantism, and from Greek and Roman cultural elements. Protestantism supplied a number of vital ingredients that helped capitalism succeed. Unable to obtain religious values through either the sacraments or Thomistic philosophy, Protestants dealt with their anxiety about salvation by working actively in the world. Prevented by their stern antipleasure religion from enjoying the full fruits of their labor, Protestants were net savers, thus furthering capital formation. By stressing individual responsibility for behavior, Protestantism also furthered economic and social individualism. To the extent that Protestants lived up to their demanding personal standards, they fostered the trust needed by the emerging capitalist world in which strangers found it necessary to interact. In a larger sense, the Christian idea that qualitative breaks in human life are both possible and good (the birth of Christ) gave religious sanction to the middle class's revolution against agrarian feudalism. And the Christian idea of Providence, the divine agency that works beyond human understanding, also gave Westerners the courage to face the uncertainty of economic and social change. With the secularization of Christian norms and values, the idea of Providence became the liberal idea of progress through laissez-faire and the magical market. (For a full discussion of the rise of capitalism, see Chapter 4.)

THE GREEK CITY-STATE

Olive Oil, Foreign Trade, and the Market Mentality

The natural environment of Greece is unsuited to large-scale agriculture and helped to prevent the emergence of large feudal landlords and large centralized kingdoms on the Greek peninsula. Greece's austere natural environment also promoted specialized agri-

culture, for example, olive orchards, rather than economic self-sufficiency. The surplus of olive oil in turn spurred pottery manufacture (as containers for oil), trade in oil, and thus a simple market economy. A common language and a common literature (Homer through Hesoid) as well as the contrasts and challenges afforded by trade and foreign enemies provided a loose, common pan-Hellenic culture that facilitated interaction among the diverse city-states (for example, the rise of "international" games and "international" religious centers such as Delphi).

The insufficiency of the Greek economy made it necessary for Greeks to buy and sell, and they eventually became deeply involved in market relations. The small-scale Greek economy based on a tradition of small, freeholding farmers produced a relative equality among Greek families (especially males), something that profoundly affected their political relations. The general insufficiency and specialization of the Greek economy also produced a unique market mentality (the ability to calculate the worth of one thing in terms of another). Greeks also experienced novelty, conflict, and insecurity as they engaged in domestic and international trade. By the fifth century B.C., Athens had broken with its customary feudal past and Athenians faced a unique social world— a society in which no power group was strong enough to subordinate the rest. For the first time in history, a human group had to reconcile the divergent interests of the many without the aid of magic, custom, or the supernatural. The result was the "invention" of politics and reason.

The Greeks invented both the practice and theoretical science of politics. The stem of the term *politics* simply means "the many"— Athens (and other city-states) was the first to promote the idea and practice that the many (all male citizens) should participate in all aspects of social life, including political and legal institutions. The Greeks invented the science of politics as part of their invention of a rational universe. Greek thinkers (starting in the new commercial centers of the Ionian Islands from 600 B.C. on) were the first to say that the human mind had a structure that corresponded to the outside world—thus they invented (discovered?) logic, including both teleological reasoning and mathematics, and natural and moral philosophy, which in their modern form are known as natural and social science.

Greek achievements were not due to blood or any special biopsychological endowments. Greek society created conditions that demanded adaptation and spurred creativity. The problematic, inquiring mentality developed by the Greeks stemmed from the fact that the social world they experienced was contradictory and problematic. The Greek stress on autonomy and equality (like the American emphasis on self-reliance) was in good part a reflection of their natural and social environment. The Greeks conceived of life as a struggle and like the Jews (but in a different way) they separated themselves from nature. To further self-reliance the Greeks insisted on equal inheritance of land. But this practice eventually divided the land into parcels that were too small to support a family. One result was land concentration, as the wealthy bought up bankrupt small farmers. Another was social tension because Greek society was generating a continuous supply of landless people with expectations of autonomy and equality. Out of this and other features of Greek society grew their unique political and rational tradition.[4]

The Preparatory Period

The period before the golden age of Periclean democracy holds special interest for understanding historical as well as contemporary societies. In 600 B.C. Attica (the general area in which Athens was located) was still a land of custom and supernatural explanations. The social structure was filled with tension and contradiction: small farmers were losing their land, debtors slipped

into slavery, and large landowners appeared. None of this was unusual—what was different about Attica was the tradition of self-sufficiency and individual autonomy.

The period before Athenian democracy was one of class struggle and radical reform. The Greeks invented the concept and practice of tyranny—concentrating power in one person to bring about the conditions of peace and justice. Two names stand out, Solon and Pisistratus, and the essential reforms they instituted were land redistribution and the abolition of debt slavery.

A preparatory period seems essential to the establishment of a new society. Society is not found in our genes. Society is not the release of human nature or human freedom or the reflection of divine will or cosmic forces. Society is a human creation, and new societies are wrought painfully out of conditions of social conflict and scarce resources. Preparatory periods are often wracked by civil and class struggle, by bitter arguments and considerable bloodletting. They often violate the norms and values of the society struggling to emerge. They often take considerable time and they often fail.

Think of the English Civil Wars as a preparation for parliamentary government and a dynamic English capitalism. It took from 1789 to 1870 to forge republican institutions in France, and even at that they were not fully established until 1945. The first election after the American Revolution had to wait eight years and that had a property qualification (the first white male suffrage took place in 1850). The twentieth century is filled with new societies in a preparatory stage toward somewhere. What most have in common, from the Soviet Union to Vietnam or from South Korea to Mexico, is dictatorship, a dictatorship that claims it is building the conditions for realizing a people's destiny.

The Greek preparatory period culminated in two achievements that profoundly affected future history. The Greeks invented a rational universe and they invented the ideal of human fulfillment in a rational society.

---

[4]For a discussion of the enduring impact of the natural environment on Greek society and for an analysis of modern Greece, see Chapter 13.

The Invention of a Rational Universe

In the two centuries from Thales in 600 B.C. to Socrates in about 400 B.C., the Greeks created a rational world view. In essence, the Greeks claimed that the world at large was lawful and that its lawfulness corresponded to the lawfulness of the human mind when it is doing logic. Socrates completed the idea of a rational nature by taking the revolutionary step of saying that human nature itself was rational and was governed by the same logic, teleology, that characterized the natural world. To know that logic is also to know how to act; human beings, argued Socrates, could schedule their lives according to the hierarchy of values established in logical discourse.

The invention of reason was a response to the diversity and temporality of the Greek experience. Existing side by side with religion, magic, and custom, reason eventually emerged as an autonomous force. Faced by the need to come to terms with the diversity and change spawned by a relatively complex division of labor, by foreign trade, and by warfare, the Greeks sought transcendence and certainty in the realm of abstraction. Though the Greeks preferred the logic of teleology, they also invented mathematics. The latter was to play an important part in the rise of modern natural science.

The Polis and Human Fulfillment

The Greeks thought of humans as entities who existed outside of nature but not outside of society. The Greeks would never have understood the modern, liberal idea that individuals have rights against society (government, corporations, any group) and an existence apart from it. In short, the Greeks understood the social nature of the human personality and human behavior. Accordingly, they developed the unique traditions of human fulfillment (for male citizens) through participation in public affairs.

The concept of participation went much deeper than the modern idea of voting or being civic minded. The human being reflects society—therefore, humans could develop fully only in a humane and rational social world. Social participation was essential to establish such a society and preserve it against internal and external enemies. Society was a human creation, not part of nature. Or rather, social existence was a continuous problem and solving this problem was as important as eating or breathing. How this tradition developed is also the story of ancient Greece.

Greece's thin rocky soil yielded a modest standard of living—not meager enough to defeat its inhabitants or affluent enough to enervate them. Even kings and the wealthy in Greece had nothing that compared to the luxurious lifestyle of Mesopotamia or Egypt. Above all, the specialization and interdependence of the Greek economy made the Greeks aware that society needed political direction. Given their adverse experiences during the long period of social change and conflict, the Greeks were well aware that people reflected diverse economic interests. Athenian democracy was set up to overcome the conflicts and cleavages of class, tribe, and family. Over time the Greeks of Periclean Athens developed extensive experience dealing with the diverse claims that came out of the division of labor. Ultimately they developed the idea that no (male) citizen could be truly human unless he involved himself in the life of society. Only in the vigorous give and take of political life could citizens transcend their parochial origins. Other societies suppressed diversity and suffocated life in a blanket of force, custom, and magic. The ideal of political participation (and the institutions needed to give it reality) as a solution to the diversity and instabilities of social life was an enduring legacy of the Greek city-state.

The Periclean ideal of resolving social problems by having citizens participate in policy making was not a formal doctrine. When Athens faltered, theorists began to ask why. One influential response was Plato's image of a rational society, one derived from reason and in the keeping of those with the most reason. But even more influential was Aristotle's image of society, an image much closer to actual Athenian practice. Like Plato, Aristotle assumed that the structure of the true and valid society was accessible to human reason. But Aristotle saw that society as a self-sufficient economic, political, and moral order that had authority over its members because they alone had fashioned it. And he knew that politics was essentially the unhappy story of rich versus poor—the only way to achieve a happy society was to neutralize these extremes with a large middle class.

ROME

Stoicism and the Universal State

Until well into the fourth century B.C., the Greek concept of society was limited to the city-state. For the Greeks, only a small society could be a true community. Plato and Aristotle, along with Athenian practice, assumed that all must participate directly in the life of society. Aristotle and Athens went further than Plato and stressed the need for and the equal right of those with property and leisure to attend to the business of society. For all their emphasis on reason, therefore, the Greeks developed a narrow view of social life. The city-state had a club-like exclusiveness that posed serious dangers for its life: women, resident aliens, and slaves, making up a large majority of the population, were excluded from citizenship. For all their emphasis on reason, practical and speculative, the Greeks failed to see that the problems of the city-state could not be solved within the confines of the city-state. The city-states were economically interdependent with each other and with the Mediterranean world, a fact belied by the Greek stress on the self-sufficiency and autonomy of each city-state. And the Greek achievement in philosophy and the other arts also led to a narrow ethnocentrism. Greeks considered themselves so superior to other people that it was impossible for them to even consider let alone confront the problem of how diverse people could live under common institutions. In point of fact the Greeks never even bridged the gap among themselves, especially the rival concept of life held by oligarch and democrat.

After the death of Aristotle (322 B.C.) social practice and theory underwent a startling transformation. Greek philosophy shook itself free of its focus on the city-state and its preoccupations with Greek practice and took on a universalist hue. Epicureanism, Cynicism, and especially Stoicism spoke of a private world of individual self-sufficiency in a rational and self-sufficient world. All humans, they claimed, had an identity which by and large made them equal. The earlier Greek distinctions between male and female, between free men and slaves, between Greeks and foreigners, broke down in the name of a common humanity. Admittedly, what individuals had in common was small and Stoic universalism tended to overlook the huge disparities among human beings derived from force, property, and custom. But the beginnings of a genuine universalism in which humans of diverse backgrounds could live together and interact were firmly implied in the spread of a Hellenistic rationalism.[5]

Roman Law

Stoicism was a reaction to the breakdown of the city-state and undoubtedly provided comfort during unsettled times. But its future was assured because it appealed to influential Romans; as such it was embodied in Roman social philosophy, especially Roman law. Its essential elements emerged later in Thomas Aquinas's philosophy as a full-blown theory of natural law. Still later, in John Locke and in the social theory of the French Enlightenment, the spirit of Stoic rationalism appeared as natural rights and helped shape the legitimating ideology of the middle class as it fought to overcome feudalism and agrarian absolutism.

Rome's economy was based on the labor of male slaves. A labor force composed of male slaves cannot replenish itself and the prime problem of the Roman economy was a chronic shortage of labor. The Romans "solved" the

---

[5]The spread of otherworldly religion, including Christianity, also supported the idea of an individual identity in a common humanity.

The Premodern World 49

problem of a slave economy by expanding outward as an empire. In essence, Roman greatness rested on military booty, especially captured slaves.[6] To legitimate its expansion, the Romans used Stoic and other Greek ideas. Responsible rule was distinguished from force; citizenship was open to diverse groups; lawful rule was distinguished from personal, arbitrary rule; and law was actively developed to facilitate interaction across ethnic, racial, and class lines.

The Roman economy was also characterized by market relations. A market economy in turn needs supportive political institutions. The Roman Empire was not a static feudal kingdom—its structure was designed to make a specialized slave economy work. The Roman state serviced large property owners who ran estates that were oriented toward urban and overseas markets. Thus the military conquered and maintained foreign markets and replenished the slave labor force while Roman law and state policy lubricated the complex relations among its various property owners, between citizens and noncitizens, and between property owners and nonproperty owners. *In short, the Roman contribution to the development of the modern West was its success in developing institutions that made it possible for a wide diversity of interests and peoples to think and act as effective members of the same society.*

Two aspects of the Roman achievement that have a bearing on the rise of the modern West should be emphasized (ignoring Rome's acceptance of Christianity). Rome continued the Greek ideal of a self-governing community, an ideal that was opposed to arbitrary, personal rule as well as to localism: the feudal tendency to dissolve society into private, particular in-

terests. Second, Rome developed a body of codified law that had a significant influence on the economic expansion of Europe almost a thousand years later. Rome derived its law from the practices of its diverse peoples. Under the Stoic assumption of a right reason pervading the universe, the Romans selected legal norms and practices that seemed fair and sensible, that protected dependents, and that stressed intent rather than empty formalities. Above all, Roman law facilitated economic transactions and legitimated political power based on economic power. No analysis of the rise of capitalism can fail to cite Roman law as a supporting cause.

THE LEGACY OF ISRAEL, GREECE, AND ROME

My survey of three hybrid, seedbed societies was intended to demonstrate the extraordinary variety of social forms in human history and at the same time to identify some of the causes of the rise of the unique industrial system that originated in the West and has now spread to influence, indeed, to shape the entire world. The societies of ancient Israel, Greece, and Rome, each in its own way, developed norms and values that made it difficult for traditionalism to ever again hold full sway. A belief in a world beyond experience is common to many cultures. All peoples create meanings to fortify themselves against the deficits of experience such as hunger, disease, death, and violence. Like other peoples, the ancient Jews (and ultimately Christians) and the ancient Greeks also developed meanings that pointed to a world beyond experience (Jehovah, salvation, truth). The uniqueness of both the Judaic-Christian and the Greek normative traditions is not so much that they universalized their meanings, though it is important to their achievement that they stressed ethics rather than the taboo, universal rather than particularistic norms, and methodical routine and reason rather than magic. The basic innovation in the Judaic-Christian-Greek achievement was to render the world problematic by developing a normative world in which truth was beyond this

---

[6]For a compact analysis stressing the relation between the deficiencies and contradictions of Rome's economy and its expansionist policies, see Max Weber, *The Agrarian Sociology of Ancient Civilizations*, R. I. Frank, tr., (London: NLB, 1976), Chapter 1. Here is a classic case of how complex society by its very organization generates outward expansion and war. The same tendency will be found in contemporary industrial and developing societies regardless of ideology. (For a discussion of the problem of war, see Chapter 19.)

world *but at the same time relevant and accessible for life in this world.*

The ancient Greeks (and Romans), and even Jews and Christians, did not subordinate the everyday world to otherwordly values, as is characteristic of other cultures ranging from simple hunting and gathering societies to complex civilizations such as India. Nor did they succumb to traditionalism, the tendency of societies everywhere to settle into mind-numbing routine. Both the ancient Jews (and Christians) and the ancient Greeks (and even the Romans) insisted that the unseen world had immediate and direct relevance for conduct in this world! In consequence the Judaic-Christian and the Greek normative systems stressed the problematic nature of experience and created tension in their respective customary practices and codes.

For its part Rome did more than simply transmit the Greek and Judaic-Christian traditions. Rome used selected elements from those traditions to develop the idea and the practices of the universal community. Rome was an expansionist oligarchy of slave owners. But internally and externally, it was too differentiated to become a centralized feudal state. It needed abstractions that could transcend its many internal diversities and conflicts, abstractions to legitimate its conquest of other peoples. The result was the idea of a republic and empire ruled by impersonal law and reflecting the fitness and morality of universal reason.

The Judaic-Christian, Greek, and Roman achievements can be epitomized as universalism, but this requires a word of caution. Universalism per se does not have effects, good or bad. Universalistic norms and values (abstract science, ethics, rule of law, logic, equal citizenship, equal opportunity) must first of all be institutionalized (as opposed to being empty ideals). Second, universalistic norms and values can have diverse consequences, often quite different from those intended by actors. Norms and values have consequences only in terms of historic contexts and in terms of power relations and functions. Judaic-Christian, Greek, and Roman universalism also functioned as a smokescreen

for oligarchy. Judaic norms and values all focus on sustaining a herding people in its struggle to secure land. Greek democracy was based on the subordination of women, slaves, and alien residents. Rome was a slave society that exploited its own free citizens and expended much of its energy on conquest.

These societies never solved the economic problem that was the cause of their malfunctioning. The best documented pictures of the instability caused by economic troubles and inequality are of ancient Greece and Rome. Strictly speaking, these were hybrid societies (that is, they had complex economies consisting not only of subsistence horticulture and agriculture, but extraction, construction, moneylending, manufacturing, and export agriculture and manufacturing), and complex political-legal institutions (that stemmed largely from the need to manage their complex economies). Nonetheless, their essential system of inequality was based on land and unfree labor (slaves and a variety of semifree serfs, tenants, and laborers). Without the consensus that marked this relation in the more straightforward agrarian systems, such as Egypt or China, this system was regarded as illegitimate (exploitative) by many and resulted in a chronic condition of class struggle.

The cleavage between rich and poor led not only to internal dissension but spilled out to cause instability among the Greek city-states and between Rome and its neighbors. Under pressure to pay higher taxes, the wealthier elements were always ready to lead and unite with the poor to seek booty in war.[7] This relation between inner and outer

---

[7]Alvin W. Gouldner, *Enter Plato: Classical Greece and the Origins of Social Theory* (New York: Basic Books, 1965), Part One; Robert Antonio, "The Contradiction of Domination and Production in Bureaucracy: The Contribution of Organizational Efficiency To the Decline of the Roman Empire," *American Sociological Review* 44 (December, 1979):895–912; Andrew Lintott, *Violence, Civil Strife and Revolution in The Classical City* (Baltimore: Johns Hopkins University Press, 1981); G. E. M. de Ste. Croix, *The Class Struggle in the Ancient Greek World: From the Archaic Age to the Arab Conquests* (Ithaca, N.Y.: Cornell University Press, 1981); and Alexander Fuks, *Social Conflict in Ancient Greece* (Jerusalem: Hebrew University Press, 1984).

power relations is a characteristic feature of all complex societies down to the present day.

Today universalism hides industrial society as much as it reveals it. (For example, equal rights and equal opportunity are meaningless abstractions for great numbers of Americans.) In short, like any sociocultural element, universalism can be ideological and dysfunctional. Nonetheless, its creation and elaboration remain the supreme achievement of the three seedbed societies of Israel, Greece, and Rome. Capitalism and liberal democracy are inconceivable without their fundamental assumption: that there are universal standards by which human beings can energize and judge historical institutions.

PREINDUSTRIAL HYBRIDS: THE UNIQUE ARAB WORLD

The Arab world encompasses a large and diverse territory. It is the site of a large number of contemporary countries: Iraq, Jordan, Syria, Egypt, Sudan, Saudi Arabia, Kuwait, the United Arab Emirates, Bahrain, Oman, Qatar, the People's Democratic Republic of Yemen, the Yemen Arab Republic, Libya, Tunisia, Algeria, and Morocco. It includes some of the peoples and regions of Lebanon and the stateless Palestinians. It includes Arabs who are citizens of Israel and Arabs who are residents of Israeli—occupied territories, the West Bank and Gaza. All these countries and peoples have their distinctive histories.[8] But the Arab world has a number of novel features that make it difficult to understand if one relies only on Western ideas and values.

The Warrior-Merchant Society

With the exception of Egypt, the premodern Arab world was not anchored in agriculture and cannot properly be called a feudal or agrarian society.[9] The Tigris-Euphrates River (fertile crescent) led to advanced agrarian societies such as Sumer and Babylonia but it did not yield a continuous agricultural society. Except for a few centuries (roughly the eighth to the tenth) its agricultural base lay in ruins. Only Egypt has had a continuous peasant-based civilization. The essential basis of Arab civilization was trade. The Arab world was centered in cities both in terms of population and economic activity. It was trade that supplied the surplus that allowed Arab-Islamic culture to shine so brilliantly from roughly the seventh to the twelfth centuries. It was even trade that supplied the surplus for the occasional reinvigoration of agriculture. The ebb and flow of Arab civilization follows the fortunes of the great long-distance trading routes that connect tropical Asia to the Mediterranean, Europe, and sub-Sahara Africa. In the agrarian societies, agricultural surplus led to markets and trade—in Arab society, trade led to surplus and urban life and even occasionally served as a stimulus to agriculture.

Though there are variations, Arab society never developed as an articulated social system with a well-established nobility and a well-established serf labor force. It was more a loose, fluid coalition of elites, ill-defined intermediate groups, and a diverse bottom. Neither inner boundaries nor external relations were crystallized. The reality of Arab society (that stretched from Persia to Morocco and from Syria down the coast of Africa) was anchored in the merchant-warriors who forged loose alliances with urban, military, and administrative elites, with nomadic tribal chiefs, and with landlords. With the decline of trade through the Middle East after Western Europeans developed maritime routes to the New World, Africa, and Asia, and with its absorption by the Ottoman Empire, Arab society stagnated.

---

[8]For general background, see Peter Mansfield, *The Arabs*, rev. ed., (New York: Penguin, 1985).

[9]Yves Lacoste, "General Characteristics and Fundamental Structures of Medieval North African Society," *Economy and Society* 3 (February, 1974): 1–17; Samir Amin, *The Arab Nation*, Michael Pallis, tr. (London: Zed Press, 1978); originally published in 1976, Chapter 1.

The Islamic Religion

The Islamic religion and the Arab world are deeply intertwined.[10] Islam has its sources in the Middle East and shares many elements with Judaism and Christianity. But it is also different, especially from modern Christianity, and the differences tell us much about present day Arab societies (and about many Islamic countries such as Iran, Pakistan, Indonesia, and Malaysia, which are not Arabic).

Islam believes itself to be the one true divine religion revealed to humanity by the prophets and most fully by Muhammad. There is one God, the source of all creation. It is the duty of the faithful to submit to His will. Those who disobey the will of God as revealed by the prophets will be punished both in this life and the next.

In all this Islam is identical to Christianity. What is distinctive about Islam is that religion and society are considered to be one and the same. Islam, both in the Koran and in developed "law," claims jurisdiction over the complete life of society. It provides norms governing marriage, family, and property, which the state and society are expected to enforce. It lays down rules governing personal and economic life (for example, it prohibits alcoholic consumption and taking interest). And it expects the state not only to enforce the specific norms of Islam but to promote Islamic ideals.

Islam has had wide popular appeal because it is a simple religion which envisions a society without nobility and commoner, without privileged ranks, a society in which all can exhibit spiritual virtue. In that sense Islamic religion is a revolutionary force. Those who are unhappy with given injustices or with alleged forms of economic and political backwardness can formulate their grievances in religious, i.e., spiritual, terms. Thus the history of Islam is filled with religious civil wars in which religious controversy and efforts at religious purification often mask socioeconomic struggles.

Islam is also a conservative force. It once accepted slavery and still believes in female inequality. Its ban on usury signifies a wider problem, the inability to separate morality from the workaday world. By blurring, often obliterating the distinction between society and religion, between the practical and the moral, and between the relative and the absolute, Islam interlocks all behavior into one and makes it difficult to solve any problem or pursue any goal without immediately involving it with other problems and other goals.

Judaism and early Christianity were similar to Islam, not only in religious-moral content, but in their attempt to absorb society in religion. The rise of capitalism transformed Christianity by restricting it to a narrow spiritual function and by turning it to an auxillary of economic and social development. No such development has taken place in the Arab world.

The Contemporary Arab World

The structure of Arab society was altered by the impact of Western imperialism, which by and large forced an amalgam of the various elites and directed them toward export agriculture. With the advent of World War II and the weakening of the European imperial powers, as well as with growing oil prosperity, the Arab world was again transformed. Led by vigorous independence movements at once Arab, nationalist, Islamic, and often socialist, the Arab world has changed from a collection of European colonies to a diverse group of sovereign nation states.[11] The ease with which the power of landlords was broken everywhere in the Arabian world (in contrast to that power in modern Europe, China, India, and Latin America) testifies to the shallow roots of agrarianism in Arab society.

---

[10]For a general background, see Bernard Lewis, *Islam and the Arab World* (New York: Knopf, 1976).

[11]For an analysis of contemporary Iraq against this background, see Chapter 14. For a vignette of Saudi Arabia, see Chapter 17.

The Arab world includes Algeria, which waged a long and bloody war of independence against France. It includes Libya, which seeks a domestic society based on the subordination of material values to the spiritual ideals of Islam but which also has a working relation with the Soviet Union to help it promote the downfall of other countries including Israel. It includes the Sudan, which is very poor. And it includes Saudia Arabia, an absolute monarchy sitting on huge reserves of oil.

The Arab world is volatile and unstable not because of any inherent defect in Arabs or in the Islamic religion but because of history. Always subject to the ebb and flow of history, the Arab has been subjected to unprecedented shocks in the post-World War II era. The complexity of Arab society cannot be reduced to any one problem. Most Arab societies lack the authority structures of settled agrarian absolutism. All were adversely affected by colonialism. All had modernity thrust on them in a rush. All have to cope with a world market dominated by industrial powers with well-developed and diversified economies.

THE PREMODERN WORLD—
HYBRID SOCIETIES: A SUMMARY

Chapter 3 rounds out the discussion of the premodern world by discussing four hybrid societies: Israel, Greece, Rome, and Arab society. These, along with the societies discussed in Chapter 2, provide indispensable background for understanding the rise and development of the modern world.

The Judaic-Christian world view is unique in its separation of God, human nature, and nature, in its sense of history, and in its depiction of life as a continuous struggle to fulfill moral and ethical ideals in this world.

Ancient Greece is important because it "invented" human reason, the idea that the human mind has a structure that corresponds to the universe at large. Human reason, applied to social behavior, supplied the West with the basic ingredients of social-type analysis. Greece's social practices and social theory assumed that humans are social animals and that the fullest development of human potential could take place only in a society designed for that purpose.

Despite its focus on a rational universe, early Greek thought (down through Plato and Aristotle) always assumed that rational society would be small and homogeneous (the city-state). With the breakdown of the Greek city-state system Greek philosophy became universalistic (Stoicism). Rome's contributions to the modern world were to embrace Stoicism and to develop a comprehensive legal code, all in an effort to organize a multiethnic empire.

Arab society is unique because it never developed (except in the case of Egypt) as an agricultural (feudal) system but was a unique hybrid of traders, warriors, and herders.

CHAPTER
4

THE MODERN WORLD
Capitalist and Socialist Nation States

The concept *modern world* refers to the developed world of capitalist and socialist nation states (it could also refer to all 165 countries in the contemporary world). The socialist nation state is fairly recent, in many ways an offshoot of capitalism, and the developed socialist societies represent only a small portion of the industrial world. Clearly, the modern world is primarily the story of capitalist society. The struggle to explain capitalism has also been the main task of social science since the seventeenth century. We came across one aspect of the effort to understand capitalism, the growing doubt (and controversy) about modernization in Chapter 1. In recent years serious questions have also been raised about the validity of capitalist values and beliefs and about the entire process of modernization outside the West. Our first step in understanding the modern world, therefore, is to gain a clear picture of the nature of capitalism. (Mature capitalism is also known as *industrial society*; for a quick summary of the

basic characteristics of industrial society, see Table 2–1.)

THE NATURE OF CAPITALISM

The essence of capitalism is the private ownership of nature, technology, including knowledge, and labor power (including professional skills), and their employment for gain (profit, rent, salaries, wages) through exchange relationships. Understood differently, capitalism means the transformation of nature and human nature into private productive forces for private gain. Under a capitalist (market or exchange) economy, the bulk of productive property (land, animals, factories, offices, and so on) is in private hands and its owners strive to profit from the use of their property. Under capitalism, work is performed by legally free individuals who sell their labor time. In the classic capitalist tradition, it is assumed that economic units are small and competitive, and that the free exchange of goods, services, and labor is the most rational way to allocate resources. The reality of capitalism is otherwise—the vast bulk of economic activity is conducted by giant, oligarchic corporations, and there are numerous distortions and barriers to the free exchange of goods, services, and labor, distortions and barriers that are both legal and illegal and that often represent other respectable social values.

Another distinctive feature of capitalism is its many-sided process of capital formation. Unlike even the highly productive agrarian society, which always remained a *use* or consumption society, capitalism reserved significant portions of its yearly output to invest in machinery, support facilities, research and development, and education. While a part of its surplus goes toward a rising standard of living and part for social overhead, part also goes for capital investment. Paying labor less than it produces, thrift, safeguarding property rights, tax policies that favor investments, norms of efficiency, research laboratories, the substitution of technology for labor, schools, the subsidization of necessary but unprofitable capital investments (such as canals, railroads, highways, airports, water supply, sanitation, fire and military protection) by public revenues are all part of the process of capital formation.

Historic capitalism based itself on a number of key beliefs: that its institutions expressed fundamental forces in human nature, that science and knowledge embedded in capitalist institutions are an unmixed good, and that the encouragement of self-interest is compatible, indeed a requisite, for social health. These beliefs were based on the master assumption that a hidden logic synthesizes the selfish, short-term initiatives of profit-oriented egoes. The magical belief in the hidden logic of social institutions, especially economic markets (laissez-faire market economy), political markets (representative government), and intellectual markets (competitive education, professionalism, research, creativity) has tended to protect capitalist society from scrutiny and evaluation.

THE RISE OF CAPITALISM

The transformation of feudal to industrial society is the most momentous event ever directly experienced and reflected upon by human beings (if we are right in assuming that the advent of agriculture was too gradual and too absorbed in mythology to stimulate much reflection). Many social scientists in the eighteenth and nineteenth centuries interpreted the rise of modern (capitalist or liberal) society as the outcome of "individualism." They assumed that human nature, suppressed for millennia by the forces of ignorance and superstition, had at last freed itself. Human beings, they felt, were now manifesting their natural biopsychological structures (or drives, instincts, needs, rights). Today a sociological perspective would insist that the order of causality be reversed, that capitalism emerged first and then developed individualism (including the full-range of vices and virtues called the modern Protestant-bourgeois personality) as its necessary personality type. If there's no human nature, then where did capitalism come from?

German thinkers in the nineteenth century were the first to ask this question. The nature and origin of capitalism was a problem for German intellectuals in a way that was not true in other Western countries, especially England and the United States. Given the gradual development of capitalism in England, its beginnings in small-scale enterprise, and its association with economic individualism and political-legal rights, English theorists gradually came to believe that the sources of economic and social development were in the individual. In Germany, however, capitalism emerged abruptly and was associated with large-scale economic units and authoritarian political and military policy. For German intellectuals, therefore, the origins and even the very nature and survival of capitalism were problematic.[1]

---

[1] Norman Birnbaum, "Conflicting Interpretations of the Rise of Capitalism: Marx and Weber," *British Journal of Sociology* 4 (June, 1953): 125–41.

Marx's Unified Theory of Economic Determinism

Karl Marx is a key figure in the development of this new outlook on capitalism. Marx rejected any notion of a fixed human nature with fixed differences, especially the idea that an individual's place in society rests on his or her innate talents. The key cause of human behavior for Marx stems from the relationship of humans to nature. Marx referred to this relation as the *forces of production,* or the material conditions of life (land, resources, technology, and technical skills). A given level of productive forces, he argues, leads to a distinctive set of social relations or *mode of production:* economic relations, the legal order, especially property forms, forms of the state, and the ideological order, including religion, philosophy, and art. In Marx's shorthand illustration, "the hand mill will give you a society with the feudal lord, the steam mill a society with the industrial capitalist" (for a concrete example of how technology and the rise of capitalism are related, see Box 4–1, Technology and the Rise of Capitalism).

Marx's economic determinism was not a simple mechanical explanation (as the above quotation might imply) in which one-to-one relations could be seen between economic causes and other phenomena. Marx was quite aware that political, religious, and family variables were also causes. Nonetheless, as a type of economy unfolded, economic variables would gradually prevail over and shape other social institutions.

Marx's economic determinism can also be seen in his metaphysical or unified theory. For Marx, human history is the story of the mastery of nature by humans, a mastery which then provides the basis for the human mastery of society and human development itself. For Marx, economic determinism meant that humans are dominated by material forces and it also meant that these forces would one day allow humans to escape from material bondage and construct societies devoted to the development and fulfillment of human capabilities, societies as "associations

in which the free development of each is the condition for the free development of all" (*Communist Manifesto*).

History, for Marx, therefore, is essentially the story of the changing relations of humans to nature. As the forces of production change, they upset and eventually contradict the society organized around the old economic forces. This leads to conflict between the groups and classes linked to the old and the new division of economic labor, and eventually to revolution, or social system change. As the new forces of production crystallize into a new modal form, they develop a new set of social relations to correspond to their new needs. The new society also develops a new personality type and a new conception of human nature in keeping with its needs. For Marx, therefore, society takes its essential structure from the prevailing level of technology, and it is the individual's relation to the means of production that determines his or her personality, consciousness, and social level. Rather than seeing economic and social structures as the result of innate human talents, drives, or needs, Marx always focused on economic and social variables, especially technology and the economic system in which it was embedded. Strictly speaking, the crucial factor in the creation of society's basic form is not technology as such but the *ownership* of technology—the means of production. The ability or inability of the owners of the means of production to wrest profits from the labor of their workers is the key to understanding the structure and process of all human societies. The simple dichotomy of owner and nonowner, therefore, is the key to understanding the fundamentals of social structure and change. All other factors, income, occupation, education, or political power, are for Marx derivative and secondary.[2]

---

[2]The easiest access to the substance of Marx's social theory may be found in the *Communist Manifesto* and on a more sophisticated level in *The German Ideology,* especially Part I.

BOX 4–1. Technology and the rise of capitalism

Looking at the rise of capitalism in terms of technology is instructive, even sobering. The technological perspective spotlights powerful causes in the everyday world that are often overlooked or misdefined. The rise of capitalism took place largely unnoticed, a nonevent much on the order of the agricultural revolution. The invention of the horse harness in the eleventh century is a good example of how easy it is to miss the significance of ordinary events. The harness seems simple by today's standards but is far from simple when put in historical context. Horses had been in use for a long time before the eleventh century but had been used mostly for hunting, warfare, transportation, and ceremony. Without an adequate harness, a horse's windpipe became choked if given a heavy load. By arranging leather straps to put the weight on the horse's shoulders, the new horse harness of the eleventh century released energy at a rate and in significance comparable to the better known steam engine of the eighteenth century (the historical context must be kept clearly in mind). Harnessing the full power of horses unleashed an important chain of causation. The horse could now pull a plow which digs deeper into the soil releasing more nutrients. The net result was greater food productivity. The food surplus of the countryside could now support urban dwellers (who worked in factories making leather harnesses and metal plows). But the chain of causation went much further. A harnessed horse would slip under heavy burdens—horses were therefore fitted with shoes to increase traction and protect their feet. Variations on the harness allowed teams of horses to be put in tandem. Harnessed animals could pull a heavier load which meant stronger wagons were needed. The mining and metal-working industries were stimulated by the new demand for metal to make plows, horseshoes, axles, and wheels.

The horse harness did not by itself cause capitalism. But in it one can see not merely a powerful cause but a new society. The horse harness meant that the society need no longer rely exclusively on human muscle power (serfdom), the economic basis of feudalism. By undermining serf labor, it undermined noblesse oblige, the feudal idea that all must adhere to status obligations and be responsible personally for the discharge of social functions. The new technology of the harness meant the growth of specialized businesses and occupations. The buyers and sellers of diverse products were forced to reduce their value to a common denominator, money, and an exchange or market economy grew. The new technology caused individualism and the growth of private property—for example, individuals, aided by the power of animals, could now run farms on their own. The harness also meant that society needed a more efficient and flexible form of labor than serfdom—hence "possessive individualism," the idea that individuals owned themselves and were free to use or sell their labor.[1] The new technology meant the self-propelled, self-controlled Protestant-bourgeois personality. If some humans could develop a self distinct from birth and human nature, it meant that eventually capitalism would declare that all should have a self.

[1] C. B. Macpherson, *The Political Theory of Possessive Individualism: Hobbes to Locke* (London: Oxford University Press, 1962).

Weber's Multicausal Historical Explanation

Oddly enough, Marx never directly answered the question, where did capitalism come from? He never asked, why did a new technology emerge in the West and not in the East, why from the eleventh century on and not before or later? Someone who did ask these questions and who provided perhaps our best answer to them was another German, Max Weber. As a German, Weber also experienced German's abrupt capitalist development and he too rejected human nature arguments (reason, pecuniary or profit instinct, hunger, sex and population growth, and so on) as the reason for the rise of capitalism.

According to Weber, capitalism was an outcome of the following sociocultural elements that came together by chance during the late middle ages:

1. Greek philosophy with its emphasis on abstraction, its assumptions about the lawfulness of human nature and nature, and its well-developed structures of logic (teleology and mathematics).

2. Greek and Roman political and legal theories with their distinctions between law and other types of norms, between the responsible and irresponsible exercise of power, and between public and private offices and norms.

3. The Judaic-Christian religious-moral orientation with its abstract theology (rational monotheism), its this worldly counterbalance to excessive other-worldliness, and its sharp separation between the realms of God, human nature, and nature.

4. An advanced material culture (plows, carts, the harness, animals, hearths, bellows, wind and watermills, ships).

5. A favorable natural environment (good soil, adequate rainfall, a temperate climate; good energy and other resources such as timber and ores; cheap water transportation).

6. Military factors.

7. Luxury trade.

8. But "in the last resort the factor which produced capitalism is the rational permanent enterprise, rational accounting, rational technology and rational law, but again not these alone. Necessary complementary factors were the rational spirit, the rationalization of the conduct of life in general, and a rationalistic economic ethic."[3]

Protestantism, argued Weber, was indispensable to the capitalist spirit. Protestant Christians, especially Calvinists, were called on, one and all, to do God's work in this world and to accept the world's problems as a challenge to their character. As Protestants they could neither withdraw from the world into mysticism nor accommodate themselves to it under the guidance of others (the medieval church). Given the need to avoid creatural temptations, Calvinism soon came to see work as a calling in which one administers what God has given. Eventually, argued Weber, there emerged a methodical, impersonal, individualist type of conduct, especially in economic affairs, which combined with a religious brake on consumption, stimulated both capital formation and the spirit of capitalism. Out of the Reformation came a merger of religious and economic behavior in which economic success signified religious worth and religious status provided economic motives and credentials.

Weber did not think of religion either as the only or even as the major cause of capitalism. If anything, his major emphasis was on economic factors, followed by political and then religious factors. But while his approach was multicausal, he put no emphasis on establishing priorities or on finding the unifying thread of human history as Marx had done. If anything, argued Weber, capitalism occurred because a large number of causes came together by chance. Thus he emphasized economic factors such as the emergence of technology, especially in the textile industry; the preeminent importance of coal and iron, which freed industry from inorganic and organic limitations; and the rise of new forms of economic organization such as the joint-stock company. But he also cited political factors such as the rising urban centers free of feudal political control, law, bureau-

---

[3]Weber's only summary of his position is in his *General Economic History*, trans. F. H. Knight, 1927 (New York: Collier paperback, 1961), Part 4. The quotation is on p. 260.

cratic state administration, warfare, and national states that competed for mobile capital as important causes. All these, along with Protestantism, said Weber, caused capitalism.

As they appeared, the above factors had the initial effect of diversifying the feudal society of the West. Combined with the decentralizing power of geography (it is important that Europe relied on rainfall agriculture and never developed the centralized agrarian monarchy characteristic of the hydraulic civilizations of China, India, and elsewhere), Europe became a cluster of "small" societies. Given centuries of economic growth these societies, especially England, became so diversified that they outgrew feudal definitions and social relations. By the sixteenth century the needs of commerce and manufacturing had resulted in a strong central state: a common currency, a law common to all, public roads, and a navy to protect shipping. It is important to note that the rise of the absolute monarchy came after the growth of a capitalist economy and was largely a support system for it. But by the sixteenth century the enormous diversification of English society had generated serious conflict among various economic groups, a conflict that also expressed itself in religious conflict. The protracted conflict among contending groups, including the violence of civil war, could not be resolved by a return to feudal particularism under a landed oligarchy. Instead, the stalemate led to a search for abstractions that could transcend particular points of view. The stalemate resulted in a new kind of oligarchy in which the English upper classes remained in an uneasy alliance astride the English people (Tory versus Whig from 1688 to 1832). Unable to coalesce, the stalemated power groups produced new norms and values: rule of law (as opposed to privilege), toleration, the right of free speech, petition, and assembly, the protection of the conscience of all individuals as individuals, the separation of law and morals, and a gradual growth of parliamentary government.

The real winner in all this was the emerging English capitalist "class." When Thomas Hobbes (1650) and John Locke (1690) developed an image of a society composed of individuals bounded by law and the state, the losers were the landed nobility. When parliament emerged victorious over the king, there was no reduction in the power of the state. Indeed the crown remained strong and now, in the hands of politicized aristocrats and other propertied interests, continued to grow in order to service the burgeoning capitalist economy.

Contemporary Debates About the Rise of Capitalism

Marx and Weber, especially the latter, were aware of the international aspects of the rise of capitalism, for example, it is obvious that war meant that countries had to organize in a certain way and to expend resources in a certain way. And international trade and banking were also commonplaces that Marx and Weber took for granted. However, international variables have begun to emerge as key factors in the thought of social theorists concerned with understanding modern society. Early in the twentieth century analysts focused on imperialism in an effort to understand the nature of developing capitalism. But it was not until after mid-century, perhaps first with Wallerstein, that the origins of capitalism itself were sought in international factors. Today the systematic exploration of such factors is known as *world system theory*, with theorists in this vein arguing that no understanding of the rise or the nature of contemporary capitalism is possible without emphasizing international factors (for a full discussion of world system theory, see Chapter 5).

Recent theorists have tended to emphasize noneconomic variables; such as geography, population, law, and politics. "Featuring Weber and a little bit of Marx," Daniel Chirot has provided one of the best of these new looks at the rise of the West. Chirot, who is one of the few American social scientists to understand Weber's "relativism," stresses Weber's emphasis on the accidental nature of the West's development. Within this framework, Chirot cites the role of rational law, religion, and the powerful influence of geography in decentralizing Europe. Chirot also cites the important role played by feudal political bodies (early "legislative" councils representing various contending social groups). However, Chirot overlooks the important role played by the absolute monarchy in modernizing Europe. And while rightly countering the excessive claims of world system theory, he goes too far in calling it "useless" in explaining the rise of the West. That rise depended greatly on international trade, overseas expansion, and international cooperation, alliances, and rivalry.[4]

Theorists have also argued that the basic reason that feudalism broke down and capitalism arose is population growth (with some arguing that population decline forced the landed nobility to adopt capitalist ways to make up for labor shortages). Population growth (or decline) allegedly outstripped resources (a neo-Malthusian argument) causing an agrarian crisis due to rising prices and food shortages. Others argue that elites also multiplied and were politicized when their children could not find places appropriate to their status in the restricted world of feudal society.

Population as *the* factor, especially if framed as a biological process, goes too far as an explanation. Population as a sociocultural variable is, of course, useful in understanding why many things happen from crime to the rise of capitalism.

Marxists have also entered the debate and have shown that they can supplement their focus on economic variables with a skillful use of other variables, including political-military factors, religion, population, and factors from antiquity. In the continuing debate (which also focuses on the causes of revolution)[5], it is probably wise to remember the major emphasis given to economic variables by both Marx and Weber.[6]

The Middle Class as a Historical Phenomenon

The middle class (the capitalist class that was in the middle between lord and serf in feudal society but which makes up the top classes in capitalist society) that created modern society also created the fiction that it was the bearer and creator of truth, somehow a thing apart from history. The great French historian Henri Pirenne raised suspicions about this early in the twentieth century.[7] Like Weber, he too, gives a different picture of the middle class, though his analysis is more descriptive than causal.

Until the eleventh century, says Pirenne, there were only "merchants of occasion." The first capitalists appeared in the eleventh and twelfth centuries but soon retired from commerce to become landed proprietors. A new batch of entrepreneurs emerged with the burst of capitalist activity that occurred in the thirteenth and fourteenth centuries. But here too the initial momentum of enterprise was soon exhausted, and the trading towns succumbed to rigid guild regulations, business monopoly, and moral and religious pressure. Capitalists sought security, and far from challenging the nobility, sought only to enter its ranks. Thus few of the same families were found among the new capitalistic elements of the fifteenth and sixteenth centuries. During these centuries the capitalist economy at last came into its own, but again the dynamism of economic expansion was stifled by conser-

---

[4]Daniel Chirot, "The Rise of the West," *American Sociological Review* 50 (April, 1985): 181–95.

[5]For a discussion, see The Many Routes To The "Modern" World in Chapter 5.

[6]For a good review of the various contemporary debates, see R. J. Holton, *The Transition From Feudalism to Capitalism* (New York: St. Martin's Press, 1985) and T. H. Aston and C. H. E. Philpin, eds., *The Brenner Debate: Agrarian Class Structure and Economic Development In Pre-Industrial Europe* (New York: Cambridge University Press, 1985).

[7]The following section is based on the classic analysis by Henri Pirenne, "The Stages in the Social History of Capitalism," *American Historical Review* 19: 3 (April, 1914): 494–515.

vatism (mercantilism). In the latter part of the eighteenth century, capitalistic behavior was vastly enhanced by industrialization; this new phase of capitalism, says Pirenne, saw a tenfold economic increase over the previous period. Again the prominent capitalist families of the previous period of economic expansion were unengaged by this new burst of economic energy (except in mining, because of its connection with ownership of land). And once again, during the nineteenth century, the spirit of economic conservatism and security reappeared in the guise of monopoly and high tariffs.

It is noteworthy in this sequence of events that the notion of a creative and revolutionary middle class is a fiction composed of convenient abstraction and ideology. Actually, there were numerous middle classes, each of which tended to stagnate well short of economic revolution, let alone social reconstruction. To a large extent, each of these capitalistic groups accepted feudal values, the most daring wanting change only to make their own lives easier or more profitable. Even on the eve of the French Revolution, the French middle class cannot be said to have had anything more than reform in mind.

The historic middle class has been creative since the latter part of the nineteenth century especially in Great Britain, France, and the United States. But the important point is that there is no guarantee that the middle class will remain creative and adaptive: the middle (or capitalist) class has been vastly transformed by the advent of corporate capitalism and its creative energies may be flagging.

If capitalism is not rooted in human nature and does not represent the unfolding of a rational process rooted in the cosmos, then capitalism becomes simply another type of society that must be analyzed and judged like any other type. Placed in a more contemporary light, the historical uniqueness of capitalism means that economic growth is not necessarily inherent in the destiny of humanity. Far from being in the nature of things for humans to exploit nature and ride the crest of endless economic growth, it is now recognized (at least by some) that the planet is finite and that it may not be able to sustain economic growth at current levels much longer. Perhaps more important is the fact that neither capitalist nor socialist societies can look for answers in alleged natural laws of economics, society, or history.

To understand capitalism and the modern nation state in the West, one must also raise questions about its overall system of inequality and, especially, its system of social stratification.

SOCIAL STRATIFICATION IN INDUSTRIAL SOCIETY

Modern industrial systems have many forms of inequality: by age, sex, ethnicity, race, and socioeconomic status. Social stratification refers to the inequality that emerges from economic power relations. The control of land is crucial to stratification in horticultural and agrarian systems (see Chapter 2). The control of property *in general* is crucial to stratification in industrial society, and is known as *class* rather than estate or caste stratification.

In general, therefore, social stratification refers to the structured way in which complex societies distribute material and psychic values. Essentially, complex societies make access to valued things a matter of birth into families that have different amounts of economic power. Thereafter individuals acquire values depending on the roles they are assigned and their passage from one group to another during their life cycle. Since we are talking of birth, we are also talking of the transmission of values through the family over time. Needless to say, when rewards are distributed by birth, they are often inequitable and nonfunctional. The concepts *legitimate* and *illegitimate inequality* will help us sort out such things.

The explanations offered by elites vary from the above perspective. Feudal elites claim that God wants a particular form of inequality or that birth is a valid mechanism for distributing values. Modern capitalist elites argue that equality before the law and equal opportunity neutralize the accident of birth and therefore individuals end up where nature intended them to be (the liberal explanation of inequality). As we will see, Soviet elites use an identical argument to explain inequality in their society.

For much of its history, American sociology tended to accept the liberal explanation of inequality (the functionalist and status attainment perspectives). In recent decades, conflict theorists have come to the fore. Since social class is central to understanding modern developed societies (as well as developing societies), it is important to understand the difference between functionalist and conflict explanations of social stratification.

Functionalist Theories

Functionalists believe that phenomena found universally must be making a functional contribution to the life of society and must somehow represent a necessary feature of social organization. In a classic analysis, Kingsley Davis and Wilbert E. Moore[8] argued that "the main functional necessity explaining the universal presence of stratification is precisely the requirement faced by society of placing and motivating individuals in the social structure." Assuming that different positions in society require different incentives and rewards, Davis and Moore conclude that "social inequality is thus an unconsciously evolved device by which societies insure that the most important positions are conscientiously filled by the most qualified persons."

Davis and Moore contend that, despite historical variations, inequality is inherent to society. Societies must define some positions as more important than others (in general, the leadership of major institutional areas) and must structure the distribution of social benefits to ensure an adequate supply of personnel for these positions, positions that re-

quire different talents, arduous training, and heavy responsibility.

In a celebrated rejection of the Davis-Moore position, Tumin argued

1. sacrifices in education are made more by parents than by students.
2. governments pay for education and direct the development of higher occupations.
3. society supports the higher occupations more than the lower ones.
4. social pressures and privileges waste a great deal of human talent.
5. social inequality results not in a functional heaven but generates resentment, hostile acts, and inefficiency.

Davis and Moore have simply stated popular prejudices as knowledge about society. Our perspective on inequality is quite different if we think in terms of powerful groups who define their jobs as important, keep them artificially scarce, give themselves high rewards in money, prestige, and job satisfaction, resist attempts to evaluate these jobs in terms of their consequences, and eventually persuade others that all this comes from human nature and the universal nature of society.

The Davis-Moore or functionalist position is really a discussion of social differentiation not social stratification. But, even as differentiation, this position is essentially empty. While it is worth knowing that individuals must be motivated and trained to occupy social positions, the important things to ask are, how is this done, by whom, for what functional purposes, and for whose benefit? The process of socialization has many arbitrary elements and suffers from gaps and ambiguities. Contrary to much belief, education has no positive relation to either work or citizenship (for details, see Chapter 8). In the final analysis, Davis and Moore are expressing the same elite complacency found in all complex societies—the existing system is just, natural, and functional.

In recent years, the functionalist perspective on social stratification has come to be known as *status attainment* theory. Despite

---

[8]"Some Principles of Social Stratification", *American Sociological Review* 18 (August, 1945): 242–49.

their new name, status attainment theorists still do not address the basic issues of social stratification. Instead, they take the United States at face value and assume that it is based on an open, competitive opportunity structure and its inequality is based on individual merit. As Horan has noted: "Status attainment rests on a functional conception of social structure in which social positions are conceived of as levels of performance, which are differently evaluated and rewarded within a competitive market situation."[9] As we will now see, sociologists in the conflict tradition reject his perspective.

Conflict Theories: Marx and Weber

The most creative currents in social stratification have come from conflict theorists who by and large agree on two things: one, known forms of social inequality have no direct basis in human beings and, two, no known form of society has figured out how to make people unequal in ways that are fair and socially useful. This does not mean that human beings may not be unequal, only that the effects of social conditioning are so powerful and so pervasive that natural inequalities (if any) are not easily identified. This also does not mean that inequality *per se* is unjust or unnecessary—conflict theorists openly discuss the merits and demerits of inequality in terms of social need. Conflict theorists (who politically are either left liberals or radicals), however, stress the illegitimacy of known forms of social inequality, while conservative thinkers (center and right liberals, Davis and Moore, status attainment theorists) tend to stress or to accept the legitimacy and functionality of existing forms and levels of inequality.

The two most creative thinkers in the field of social inequality were Karl Marx and Max Weber. As we said earlier, the key cause of human behavior and human consciousness for Marx is found in the relationship of human beings to nature. This relationship

expresses itself as an economy: forms of labor, states of technology, and sets of economic relations and meanings. In turn, the economy develops supportive institutions (the family, political system, law, art, religion, philosophy, natural and social science). The economy also divides a population into a hierarchy of families grouped into economic classes, fundamentally, the propertied (those who own the means of production) and the propertyless (those who must sell their labor to the owners of capital). Once economic classes emerge, they also become social classes since behavior (consumption, associational life, marriage, the education of children, religion, politics) outside of work tends to take on the characteristics of economic behavior, beliefs, and values.

The conflict between the propertied and unpropertied, argued Marx, is the great engine of historical development. Conflict, or in Marx's term, class struggle, is both a destructive and creative force. Those with property can pay labor less than the value of their work, oftentimes much less, and exploitation is thus "normal" to historical societies. In turn, exploitation leads to revolts and crime countered by coercion and repression by the propertied. But the conflict between classes is also creative—the propertied must continually rationalize production and by doing so both increase human mastery over nature and reduce the amount of labor needed in the economy. Progress then occurs because labor becomes conscious of exploitation and fights to construct a more humane economy. This spurs the propertied to rationalize production and so on. Thus the formation of classes and their conflict ensures the victory of progressive elements and the ultimate triumph of humanity.

An important aspect of Marx's explanation of class formation and his theory of the dynamics of class struggle and social change is his assumption that one can distinguish between progressive and reactionary technological forces (see box 4–2, Is It Possible to Distinguish Between Progressive and Reactionary Technology?). Progressive technology reduces material scarcity and enhances

[9]Patrick M. Horan, "Is Status Attainment Research Ahistorical?" *American Sociological Review* 43 (August, 1978): 538.

BOX 4–2. Is it possible to distinguish between progressive and reactionary technology?

Thinkers have disputed the value of technology for most of the modern period. Technology has been depicted as Frankenstein's monster and as Satan's handiwork. Both functionalist and conflict theorists have also hailed it as the liberator of humanity. By and large, the main currents of both capitalist and socialist thought endorse it.

Karl Marx saw technology as a progressive force because it promised relief from dehumanizing work. He saw the goal of history as liberating humanity from material scarcity: only then could humans develop their full potential and become conscious, choice-making beings. The conquest of nature, therefore, was seen as crucial to human liberation and anything that contributed to it was good, including technology. Actually, according to Marx, the way to tell if technology was good or bad was by its ownership. During the early period of

capitalism, the private ownership of technology was good because it liberated people from hunger and other hardships. This was no longer true, argued Marx, and public control of technology must complete the job.

Others have argued that only the private ownership of the means of production will ensure continuing creativity and fruitful production. Still others have ignored the issue of ownership, arguing that technology per se has gotten out of hand. Poisons from our factories and automobiles are ruining our soil, water, and air. These poisons are also forming an awning over the planet that is trapping heat and threatening our very existence. High technology must be lowered, say radical environmentalists, if we are to survive and remain human (for a fuller discussion of the environmental issue, see the section, Environmental Pressures in Chapter 19).

individual fulfillment—it becomes reactionary when it ceases to fulfill these liberating functions.[10]

Max Weber acknowledged the primacy of economic variables in the formation of social strata, but insisted that sociocultural variables outside of the economy were also influential in controlling the distribution of material and symbolic benefits. Religious beliefs and values, for example, were widely influential in determining the relationship of human beings to nature, the definition of work, and the worth of material values. According to Weber, such things as family beliefs and values, canons of taste or consumption, considerations of race or ethnicity, and political, legal, and military beliefs and values, once put into practice, were extremely

influential in determining the allocation of economic resources.

Even though these variables have their origin in the economy, argued Weber, they invariably take on a life of their own. He insisted, therefore, that in any analysis of social inequality three major clusters of variables must be included: *economic* variables (technology, wealth, income, occupation), *status or prestige* variables (status groups based on cultural evaluations involving matters of family, breeding, association, race, consumption), and *power* variables (political and legal forces).[11] (For Weber's multicausal theory and for the characteristics of households at the top and bottom of the stratification ladder in summary form, see Table 4–1).

---

[10]The substance of Marx's theory of social stratification may be found in *The Communist Manifesto* and in *The German Ideology*.

[11]"Class, Status, Party" in H. H. Gerth and C. Wright Mills, tr. and ed., *From Max Weber: Essays in Sociology* (New York: Oxford University Press, 1946), Chapter 7; widely reprinted.

TABLE 4-1. Weber's Multidimensional View of Social Stratification

	(Economic) *Class Variables*	*Prestige* *Variables*	*(Political-Legal)* *Power Variables*
	Income Wealth Occupation Education Family stability Education of children	Occupational prestige Subjective development Consumption Participation in group life Evaluations of Race, Religion, and Ethnicity	Political participation Political attitudes Legislation and governmental benefits Distribution of justice
Households in the Upper Social Class	Affluence: economic security and power	More integrated personalities, more consistent attitudes, and greater psychic fulfill- ment due to deference, valued associations, and consumption	Power to determine public policy and its implementation by the state thus giving control over the nature and distribution of social values
Households in the Lower Social Class	Destitution: worthless- ness on economic markets	Unintegrated personalities, inconsistent attitudes, sense of isolation and despair, sleezy social interaction	Political powerlessness, lack of legal recourse or rights, socially induced apathy

Status groups represent severe interferences with free markets, argued Weber. Open and explicit under feudalism, status groups are also profoundly important in capitalist society. As modern versions of medieval guilds, the professions and trade unions set up artificial nonfunctional barriers to entry, thereby ensuring themselves undeserved income. Education is largely a status phenomena (disguised by functional ideology) based on nonfunctional criteria whose main consequence is to cut the flow of labor into prized occupations. Status groups like prestigious clubs and associations also serve to restrict access to business and professional life. And political-legal variables (the state) also is used to support status groups and, further, to regulate or tax the economy, favoring some over others for no necessary functional outcomes.

The formation of social classes, therefore, results from variables in all three dimensions, says Weber. Most individuals and families have fairly consistent positions in the various dimensions and subdimensions. But people also have positions that are not consistent. A minister, the new rich, a call girl, a junk dealer, and a rock star all have inconsistencies among their class-prestige-power positions. But given systems of stratification, says Weber, tend to iron out inconsistencies over time (though some remain). Caste, estate, and class systems all respond to the nature of the economy and develop noneconomic statuses that are consistent with and supportive of those who have economic power.

Stratification in the Modern World

It is clear that capitalism has produced a new system of inequality. Capitalism's specialized and ever-changing division of labor cannot base itself formally or openly on ascription alone (the use of birth to assign social positions)—in its place there emerges the principle of individual achievement. By now readers will be wary of familiar phenomena. Individualism is a social phenomena, not the release of human nature. It is best understood as *possessive individualism,* the social doctrine that individuals own themselves. Individualism was enunciated clearly and loudly in the seventeenth century to provide symbolic justification for England's newly emerged capitalist society. Possessive individualism declares that since individuals own their labor, they also own the fruits of their labor. Through this idea capitalist theorists (for example, John Locke who had such great influence on the founders of the American republic) were legitimating the transformation of human nature and nature into private property. The theorists of possessive individualism also said that individuals were free to sell their labor. Here again theorists were providing for the needs of a capitalist economy: a labor force of legally free individuals whose labor could be bought to suit the needs of property owners.[12]

Seen from this perspective modern individualism is different than the usual meaning we give it. The same is true of modern egalitarianism. Individuals cannot achieve according to their natural talents unless they are free and can start the contest of life from the same starting gate. The tradition of equal opportunity, mass education, equal vote, and equality before the law are thought to ensure a fair contest. But this outlook, which is central to how Americans look on their society, is a partial truth. Children born to parents of wealth or with high income and important occupations have a far greater chance of becoming individualistic and successful than children born to middle level or poor parents. Industrial society's main characteristic, therefore, is not so much equality *as a changed way of producing inequality*. Industrial society is more open to individual achievement and movement up or down the hierarchies of inequality than feudal society. But inherited wealth and advantage and disadvantage by birth are still pronounced. The traditions of equal opportunity and political-legal equality should be seen as ways to produce an industrial form of inequality, not as forces that release or record the natural talents of human beings. *Modern industrial society is still very unequal and there is no long-term trend* *toward economic and social equality either in basic conditions or in economic, political, or educational opportunities.*

Social stratification in the contemporary world is quite varied if one focuses on all societies.[13] Capitalist and socialist developed societies, though largely similar in their stratification systems, have some differences. In addition, there are some important stratification differences among capitalist developing nations (for example, Brazil is more unequal than South Korea or Taiwan; the black African capitalist countries have unique mixtures that reflect their horticultural and colonial past). And there are differences between capitalist and socialist developing nations (the latter tend to be more successful in combating absolute poverty and have equalized the condition of women more than the capitalist societies). And there is the unique stratification system of South Africa, which combines class inequality with a racially-based caste system (see Box 4–3).

THE NATION STATE: ITS NATURE AND VARIETIES

The nation state emerged slowly in the West after the Middle Ages and reached its mature development during the nineteenth century. After 1945 the nation state spread rapidly outside the West. Today, all societies have assumed (or are struggling to assume) the shape of a nation state. What is a nation state? Despite variations (and the fact that many societies are only partially developed nation states), today's societies are all marked by centralized states (or by attempts to develop them). A centralized state comprises political mechanisms for reconciling power conflicts and producing a legitimate government, a legal code that expresses the results of the reconciliation process and that is sovereign

---

[12]C. B. MacPherson, *The Political Theory of Possessive Individualism: Hobbes To Locke* (London: Oxford University Press, 1962).

[13]For details on class inequality in the United States, with comparisons with other developed societies, emphasizing that class inequality is both pronounced and long lasting, see Chapter 9.

BOX 4–3. South Africa: a class-caste hybrid

South Africa was settled by the Dutch in the seventeenth century and taken over by the English at the end of the eighteenth century. The English lost control of the country to the Dutch Calvinist Boers after World War II who instituted a rigid system of racial segregation called *apartheid*. Today the 83 percent of the population who are black are kept in a subordinate position by the white population. What makes this a peculiar case is that the dominant whites are committed to economic development.

South Africa has representative government for certain segments of the population but blacks cannot vote. Blacks live in impoverished areas, use segregated facilities, and until recently had to carry passports. Interracial marriage and sex are illegal. Tension in South Africa is high because the white elite needs black labor to run their advanced economy. Even though whites monopolize the good jobs, blacks must be brought into cities, factories, and mines to work. Advanced societies develop "free" labor, that is, a labor force composed of individuals who are free to sell their labor and move to where there is work. South Africa's attempt to combine "slave" labor and a specialized, interdependent economy in which the majority must work hard for few rewards (and who are conscious of this, is contradictory and tension filled.[1]

[1]For background, including a valuable comparison with the United States, see G. M. Frederickson, *White Supremacy: A Comparative Study in American and South African History* (new York: Oxford, 1981). For a vignette of South African society, see Chapter 17.

---

vis a vis all other types of norms, and a bureaucratic form of administration (civil and military) to interpret, administer, and enforce the complex criminal, civil, and legislative elements in that code. Despite differences, all nation states identify themselves with a given piece of geography and all display nationalistic or patriotic emotions and beliefs, that is, deep, common, emotional-cognitive commitments to their constitutive values and norms and to the piece of geography on which they are located.

Despite these common elements, nation states differ in some important respects. Ideologically, some are liberal and others are socialist, some have representative government and some are dictatorships (often with functional equivalents of representative government). Organizationally, some are integrated (or associational) societies (both capitalist and socialist) and others are segmented (or multicommunal) societies (both capitalist and socialist).

The Liberal Nation State

It should be repeated that the term *liberalism* refers to the philosophic world view of the middle class and not to the political program or platform of political parties or organizations. In broad terms, the basic assumption behind the liberal world view is that human beings can achieve a mastery of themselves and of nature through the proper exercise of human reason (science) and the proper set of values (Protestant-bourgeois ethic). This value-idea system must be sharply separated from systems that seek world mastery through a mixture of tradition, religion, and philosophy (ancient and medieval societies in the West) as well as those that are based on a mastery of the world through magic, resignation, tradition, religion and/or philosophy (both folk societies and feudal societies such as India or China).

The outstanding feature of liberal society is its equation of social health with private property, individualism, a market economy (with or without explicit public direction), and private scientific-intellectual life. Ideally speaking, liberal society is secular, scientific, and dynamic. Geared to effect a mastery over nature and over human nature, liberal society institutionalizes individual achievement, futurism, and a highly specialized division of economic and social functions. Its general symbolic and status structure contains distinct public and private spheres of action and does not assume an identity of interest between individuals and groups. Its unity is based on universal (often excessively abstract and vague) values and beliefs as well as on specific mechanisms for ensuring social control and reconciliation (police, schools, courts, political parties, legislatures, government). Its social constitution is made up of hundreds of thousands (millions, counting families and economic units) of groups that cooperate, jostle, and disagree about this or that issue. Both competitive and managed economic markets settle many of the issues between groups and classes. The political system serves as a further arena of negotiation among groups and the results of the political process become law. There is an explicit generation and use of law (as distinct from agrarian societies that discover law), and legal norms as distinct from other norms are publicly enforced by coercive, allegedly referee structures and constitute the ultimate control system of liberal society. Private groups also play an important part in the process of social control since they develop fairly explicit norms to control their members. As Durkheim pointed out, much of the stability of a differentiated society comes from the social control exerted by occupational groups over their members.

Liberal society exhibits a considerable cleavage between its operational processes and outcomes, and its legitimating ideology. While there is much talk of equality of opportunity in all spheres and a strong normative tradition stressing equality of competition, in reality most competition takes place *within* classes and there is considerable concentration of economic, social, and political power.

While a powerful ideology stresses individual achievement, in reality, much of the ownership of the economy is ascriptive, and control of the economy and occupational placement is also hereditary either directly or through class-based socialization processes, including the private and public educational systems.

The inequality of liberal society is deep and much of it is at variance with its ideals. The evidence of the past decades suggests that it has made little progress in living up to its ideals and, further, that it may not be capable of bringing itself more in line with its normative value system. Personality structure, while homogeneous in some respects, is also quite diversified as between different classes. Members of liberal society behave according to a status structure that is highly specialized and impersonal—as we shall see, this status structure, while manageable for many, creates an enormous catalog of behavior problems for large portions of modern populations.[14]

The emergence of the liberal nation state was no easy matter. All Western nation states had their origins in royal centralization, that is, the process whereby a central power emerged, with the authority to integrate and manage the affairs of a given populace. While this process destroyed simple feudalism it did not always lead to liberal democracy. In the eighteenth century the tiny state of Prussia transformed itself into a bureaucratic (feudal) monarchy. Before the advent of industrialization Prussia (largely in response to outside military pressures) had a rational civil and military administrative structure wedded to a landed aristocracy. Even after industrialization (after 1840), the German middle class was too weak to wrest control of the state from the Junkers (the Prussian landed aristocracy). In addition, German industrialization took place abruptly in terms of a relatively large-scale factory system (aided by a centralized banking system eager to seek profits in large-scale industry), which

_____
[14]For an extended case study of the chief liberal society, the United States, see Chapters 6 to 10.

brought into being overnight a working class hostile to both landed aristocrat and capitalist. By 1900 the German middle class had made its fateful choice: it formed an open alliance with the Prussian aristocracy (as a de facto junior partner) to counter the threat of socialism. In Germany, therefore, the centralization of power and authority merely provided a new form through which feudal values and norms could remain dominant well into the industrial age. More precisely, the Prussian feudal aristocracy adapted itself to the modern world of science and industry by allying itself with the German middle class against the remainder of the German population. Thus Germany is the classic case of industrialization under capitalism without political democracy. Japan is an interesting variation on the same theme. South Korea is yet another variation on this theme.

Enough has been said to see that there is no one road to the modern world (see the section, The Many Routes To The Modern World in Chapter 5). This also means that there are neither set prerequisites for economic growth nor a set sequence for either economic or political development.[15]

In many ways the development of the liberal nation state in England and the United States is the exception. France was a great power on the eve of the industrial revolution but its rich agriculture and its extensive network of small family businesses made it difficult for it to industrialize at the same pace as first England and then Germany. And, given the political cleavages engendered by the French Revolution, it had difficulty establishing representative government before 1945 and could not get sustained state action to aid its economic development. Other countries such as Italy, Spain, Portugal, and Greece had little success with representative government. For most of their modern history these countries represent historic cases

of weak capitalist expansion with neither a transition to industrialization nor political democracy. While Germany and Japan are the classic cases of capitalist industrialization without political democracy, Italy, Spain, Portugal, and Greece are countries that spent most of their formative modern years as authoritarian capitalist societies with neither industrialization nor political democracy. The combination of capitalist institutions with authoritarianism is often accompanied by ideologies that stress innate human inequality and the need to think of society as an organic corporate whole in which all perform fixed functions—in short these were fascist societies until recently.

Liberal democracy (capitalism plus representative government) is now embodied in a relatively large number of developed and developing nation states (the United States, France, Canada, the United Kingdom, Denmark, Austria, Luxembourg, Sweden, Norway, Belgium, the Netherlands, Switzerland, Australia, New Zealand, Iceland, Ireland, and, since 1945, Germany, Italy, Japan, Israel, Venezuela, India, Sri Lanka, Malaysia, Jamaica, Cyprus, Greece, Portugal, and (until recently) Turkey.[16] Beyond these lie scores of developing societies that are somewhat akin to the authoritarian capitalist societies of the pre-1945 West, for example, the Republic of (South) Korea, Taiwan, the Philippines, Indonesia, Mexico and most of Central and South America, Nigeria and other African countries (some of these are now taking some steps toward representative government). This does not mean that the developing countries are easy to classify. It is only to suggest that all are becoming nation states and that one batch is capitalist, some with and some without representative government. But making sense of nation states is complicated because a large number claim to be unique—the socialist nation states.

---

[15]For an early discussion from this perspective, which focuses on Germany, Italy, and Russia, see Alexander Gerschenkron, *Economic Backwardness In Historical Perspective* (Cambridge, Mass.: Harvard University Press, 1962).

[16]Some of these countries have begun to experiment, of course, with socialist policies and governments. Some of these countries are also divided internally by ethnic diversity and consequently lack strong centralized states; for a discussion of segmented societies, see below.

The Socialist Nation State

Imperial Russia was undergoing a transformation toward industrialization and parliamentary democracy when it suffered a smashing military defeat in World War I. As a result the tiny communist party headed by Lenin came to power and began the task of establishing a Marxian society. Between 1917 and the 1960s, the U.S.S.R. developed as a one-party totalitarian state in relative isolation from the world (save for the brief NEP period when it invited outside help). Since the 1960s the Soviet Union has become authoritarian rather than totalitarian.[17] In general perspective, the Soviet Union is a case where industrialization succeeded with neither capitalism nor political democracy. Thus modern industrial nation states have emerged under the authoritarianism of both the right and the left as well as emerging as liberal democracies.

Between 1917 and 1939 the U.S.S.R. was the world's only society committed to socialism. After 1945 a number of Eastern European nations occupied by the Soviet Army became similar one-party Marxist societies. In addition a number of societies committed to socialism emerged in various parts of the world: China, Yugoslavia, Albania, Cuba, Tanzania, Vietnam, and assorted Arab socialisms.[18] Socialist societies are quite diverse. Marxist Yugoslavia has a one-party state that emphasizes a market economy, decentralized decision making, and mass citizen participation. There are also variations inside Soviet-dominated East Europe. Marxist Hungary has instituted many of the features of a market economy. In Poland the Communist Party, government, and military face strong opposition from the Roman Catholic Church and a politicized trade union movement. More recently China has adopted some "capitalist" practices to help it modernize.

Socialist societies are based on public property, public control of investment priorities, and comprehensive public planning and direction. Socialist society hopes to achieve many of the values of capitalism by removing what it believes is the chief obstacle to those values, private property. For socialists private property fragments populations into selfish, warring, wasteful units (individuals, groups, classes) and makes it impossible for society to achieve unity and self-direction, eliminate poverty and unemployment, or fully realize the ideals of individual fulfillment. Some socialist movements (for example, in Great Britain, France, and Germany) hope to combine liberal democracy with substantial social ownership of the economy. Socialist government in Sweden has ignored public ownership of economic units and has focused instead on reducing inequality through taxation and social services. And socialism elsewhere is associated with centralized political and economic forms without civil and political freedoms or rights. Variations on this latter pattern exist in the U.S.S.R., East Germany, the People's Republic of China, Syria, Algeria, and Cuba. A more "liberal" socialist system exists in Tanzania, Yugoslavia, and Hungary.

Segmented Nation States

Not all societies were successful in developing homogeneous populations or in producing free association among its diverse groups. An important distinction among contemporary societies, therefore, is between *integrated* (or associational) and *segmented* (or multicommunal) nation states.[19]

---

[17]In the past few years, the U.S.S.R. has taken some significant steps toward representative government.

[18]For a discussion of the variety of socialisms in the world, see the introduction to Chapter 14.

[19]Two pioneers in the field of cultural pluralism are J. S. Furnivall, *Netherlands India* (London: Cambridge University Press, 1939) *Colonial Policy and Practice: A Comparative Study of Burma and Netherlands India* (London: Cambridge University Press, 1948), and M. G. Smith, *The Plural Society in the British West Indies* (Berkeley, Calif.: University of California Press, 1965). The field branches out to include historians interested in the rise of nationalism, political scientists interested in nation-building, and sociologists interested in assimilation. And, of course, it includes all those interested in tribes, castes, religion, and race as diversifying forces.

Multicommunal societies are those that have a variety of tribal, ethnic, religious, or linguistic groups and are quite common in today's world. What is also quite common is that such societies suffer from intercommunal strife and political instability.

Multicommunal societies in the agrarian past seem to have been more peaceful, largely because each ethnic-religious-linguistic group could live by itself as almost a miniature society. Agrarian empires often allowed their conquered peoples to live as they had always lived, subject of course to imperial taxation and whatever laws and other norms were thought necessary to facilitate trade and political control.

The modern world has witnessed a new phenomenon—changing, economically growing or dynamic societies find it difficult to accommodate diverse ethnic, religious, or linguistic groups. Societies have often sought to avoid the threat (real or imagined) of having a plurality of ethnic minorities by expelling or killing them: the expulsion of the Jews from Spain and the Huguenots from France and Nova Scotia; the persecution of Jews and other minorities in Czarist Russia; the massacre of one and a half million Armenians by Turkey in 1915 and its expulsion of over one million Greeks in 1922 (in retaliation for Greece's invasion of Turkey); the Holocaust visited on six million Jews (and other minorities) by Nazi Germany; the violent expulsion of Asians by Uganda in the early 1970s; and the expulsion of Chinese from Vietnam after 1975. In some of the above cases it was the struggle to develop a nation state that led modernizing power groups to eliminate economically powerful groups in their midst (Turkey, Uganda). In other cases imperialist powers destroyed or undermined the cultures of weaker peoples (Spain in Latin America, the United States versus the native peoples of the continental United States, Hawaii, and some other Pacific islands).

Sometimes societies succeed in assimilating their various ethnic groups and becoming associational, with free movement and interaction among individuals under a central government. Modern Britain is an example of a successful amalgam of minorities (integrated society) by a dominant ethnic group (the English over the Scots and Welsh) and an unsuccessful attempt to dominate the Irish.[20] The United States is another example of a successful associational system. By and large, the United States has successfully absorbed a variety of ethnic groups, largely by imposing one language (except for Spanish-speaking groups) and one cultural system on all and by providing opportunities for many to succeed in its economy and polity. The U.S.S.R. is also an associational nation state but has important multiethnic, multilinguistic features. It is integrated under one ethnic group, the Russians, who promote multiethnic pluralism, but who also, whether under Czars or Commissars, have not hesitated to crush dissident ethnic groups (what the future holds for the U.S.S.R. in regard to its diverse nationalities will be discussed in Chapters 11 and 12).

However there are a number of contemporary societies where there is either a working accommodation or (more often) a nonworking stalemate among ethnic and racial groups. I have chosen the term segmented societies (successful[21] and unsuccessful) to refer to these societies but they are also called *plural, vertical, pluralist, segmented pluralist, consociationalist, consociational democracy, consensual democracy, pillarized, contractarian democracy, proportional democracy*, or as characterized by the *politics of accommodation*. Successful segmented societies are Switzerland, the Netherlands, Belgium (at least until the 1970s), Canada, Austria, Luxembourg, Lebanon (before the influx of armed Palestinian refugees in the 1970s), Nigeria (after the end of Biafra's uprising of 1968–70), Northern Ireland (before 1970), Jamaica and other Caribbean and Oceania Islands, Yugoslavia (less

---

[20]Scottish and Welsh nationalism remain strong but so far have been unable to overcome inertia and the visible benefits of being part of a dynamic larger society.

[21]The term successful simply means peaceful; peace in some cases results from a sharing of power, in others because of a more thorough domination.

successful in the late 1980s), Guyana, Malaysia, and Sri Lanka (less successful since 1983).[22]

Many societies have struggled with the problems of multicommunalism. Postcolonial India was segmented by religious cleavage (Hindu, Muslim) and India was divided first into India and Pakistan, and later Pakistan was divided into Pakistan and Bangladesh. But India has not been able to rid itself of communal strife. Other contemporary examples of communal strife are Cyprus, contemporary Northern Ireland, Lebanon, and Sri Lanka. Many nations, for example, Iraq, Iran, the Philippines, the Congo, Chad, Sudan, and Ethiopia, are marked by successionist or rebellious movements by dissident ethnic or tribal groups. In the 1970s the white-settler, racially segmented society of Rhodesia had its white minority overthrown and became Zimbabwe. Tension in racially segmented South Africa has produced considerable turmoil but so far no change.[23] One last example will suffice to illustrate the enormous diversity of segmented societies, Israel. Israel's population is divided by ethnic differences (Westernized and non-Westernized Jews, Arab citizens) and by religion (secular versus religious Jews), and at the same time Israel has occupied territory (which it deems vital to its security) composed of Arabs (Palestinians) deeply antagonistic to the occupation and often to the state of Israel itself (for further details, see Chapter 17).

Almost all complex societies originated through force. Those that became integrated nation states, by definition, managed to legitimate their act of social creation and to assimilate or at least render powerless their various minorities. Some new nations, however, were unable to destroy, expel, or assimilate their ethnic and racial minorities and thus became segmented societies. Most segmented societies also had their origins in conquest (the imperialism of empire). After independence many new nations found themselves with deeply divided populations (and often with artificial boundaries). These segmented societies also had their problems aggravated by outside interference, especially when dissident groups are helped by neighboring states and peoples. In any case, minority ethnic groups will continue to struggle for either political power or states of their own. Their struggle has been made necessary by the fact that a dynamic world market economy reaches everywhere and groups without power cannot hope to survive.

Stateless Peoples

There are numerous ethnic and racial groups with a distinct sense of identity or peoplehood but who do not have an autonomous existence, especially if judged by whether or not they are sovereign over a distinct territory. Some of today's stateless people were put in societies created artificially in the aftermath of wars. Some are conquered peoples and some are refugees. We will have more to say about all types of stateless peoples in subsequent chapters.

---

[22]Cultural pluralism in the developing world has been analyzed by Leo Kuper and M. G. Smith, eds., *Pluralism in Africa* (Berkeley: University of California Press, 1969); Leonard Plotnicov and Arthur Tuden, eds., *Essays in Comparative Social Stratification* (Pittsburgh: University of Pittsburgh Press, 1970), Part I; and Crawford Young, *The Politics of Cultural Pluralism* (Madison, Wisc.: University of Wisconsin Press, 1976).

Cultural pluralism in the developed world is the main focus of Arend Lijphart, *The Politics of Accommodation: Pluralism and Democracy in the Netherlands* (Berkeley: University of California Press, 1968), "Consociational Democracy," *World Politics* 21: 2 (January, 1969): 207–25, *Democracy in Plural Societies* (New Haven, Conn.: Yale University Press, 1977); and *Democracies: Patterns of Majoritarian and Consensus Government in Twenty-One Countries* (New Haven, Conn.: Yale University Press, 1984); and Kenneth McRae, ed. & intro, *Consociational Democracy: Political Accommodation in Segmented Societies* [Austria, Belgium, the Netherlands, Luxembourg, Canada] (Toronto: McClelland and Steward, 1974).

[23]For more details about Zimbabwe and South Africa, see Chapter 17. For case studies of developed capitalist (Canada) and socialist (Yugoslavia) segmented societies, see Chapter 15. For case studies of developing segmented societies, Nigeria, Malaysia, and Sri Lanka, see Chapter 16.

THE MODERN WORLD: CAPITALIST AND SOCIALIST NATION STATES— A SUMMARY

Chapter 4 focused on the modern world made up of developed capitalist and socialist nation states. The modern world did not come from a freed human nature but from historical causes that produced capitalism. Readers will have been prepared by the discussion of Israel, Greece, and Rome in Chapter 3 for this chapter's discussion of the rise of capitalism.

The discussion of the rise of capitalism featured the rival explanations of Karl Marx and Max Weber. Marx cited economic variables to explain political, legal, religious, and artistic developments. His theory was also unitary—that is, it purported to be a total explanation of human history (unified theory of economic determinism).

Max Weber cited economic variables in his explanation of capitalism but also identified political, legal, and religious variables as causes important in their own right. Weber denied that history has a unitary pattern (multicausal historical explanation).

In Chapter 2 we saw that socioeconomic inequality or social stratification varies by type of society. Hunting and gathering society cannot develop a full system of social stratification because it is too poor to generate the assets and statuses that enable superior individuals to pass their socioeconomic position on to their children. Advanced horticultural and agrarian societies develop full-bodied systems of social stratification (the transmission of superior economic, prestige, and political-legal statuses from parents to children via the principle of birth). Industrial society (capitalist and socialist) represents a new way (individual achievement through inherited economic and educational advantages) to transmit socioeconomic position from parents to children.

Functional theorists deny the reality of social stratification. The apologists for feudal and industrial systems (capitalist and socialist alike) argue that inequality comes from functional processes and that society is based on cooperating groups who agree on the values that lead to inequality. Conflict theorists such as Karl Marx and Max Weber deny this image and point to many illegitimate aspects of inequality (Marx would more than likely reject the Soviet image and explanation of Soviet inequality).

The heart of social stratification, they argue, is the difference between those who control or own property and those who do not. Actually, economic classes derive from gradations in economic assets: the ownership of physical assets and the ownership of personal traits and labor power deemed economically valuable—both can be fruitfully understood as property.

Property means the ownership or control of valued things, rights, or skills. In an agrarian society, the most important property is agriculturally productive land, followed by political-military-economic skills, tools, and human and animal muscle power. In industrial society, property means industrially productive technology, facilities, patents, legal rights, money, land, water, raw materials, air space, professional skills, and skilled and unskilled labor.

Marx focused on property as the source and basic dynamic of social stratification. Weber, while agreeing on the primacy of economic status also stressed the importance of prestige and political-legal variables (the multidimensional approach). Together with the contradictory nature of economic markets, these other variables also lead to inconsistency in overall class position for some.

The *nation state* is the characteristic form of contemporary societies. Developed (industrial) nations, whether capitalist or socialist, share many characteristics. These include centralized states, concentrated economies, investment decisions made at the top, and a commitment to mastery of nature through science and technology.

Nation states can be *integrated* (or *associational*) or *segmented* (*multicommunal*). In the former, individuals and groups are free to mix under institutions common to all. Segmented societies are those with two or more blocs of opposing ethnic, racial, religious, or linguistic groups who do not want to jeopardize their ethnic identity by associating freely with others (or where one group will not allow the others to associate freely). Segmented societies are common, and while some have succeeded in working out an accommodation among their diverse groups, most have not and suffer from strife and instability.

Stateless people are those who have a strong sense of peoplehood but who have no country of their own.

CHAPTER

5

THE WORLD SYSTEM
Stratification Among Societies

INTRODUCTION

Societies are characterized by "political" relations—they discuss, argue, and moralize among themselves, negotiate trade and military agreements, and agree or disagree on matters as varied as air rights, mail, customs, the rights of citizens, cultural and scientific exchange, and so on. Societies spy on each other and finance (even arm) political movements in other countries that favor their interests. Political relations can lead to mutual respect, a concern for the rights of the weak and minorities, including political opponents, and a willingness to compromise. But political relations also reflect differences in power and conflicting values. As is true of internal "political" relations, therefore, the relations among societies are also characterized by domination, conquest, exploitation, and dependence, in short, by stratification and imperialism.

INTERSOCIETAL STRATIFICATION: EMPIRE AND WORLD-MARKET SYSTEMS

The fact that societies interpenetrate as parts of larger systems, culminating in imperialism, has received various explanations. Karl Deutsch has classified these explanations as:

1. folk theories (biologic-instinctive, demographic-Malthusian, geographic-strategic, cultural organicism, or the people as a psychological entity), theories that today command little respect;

2. conservative theories (Jules Ferry, Disraeli, Rhodes, Kipling) that advocated imperial expansion to provide economic stability at home;

3. liberal theories (John Hobson and Norman Angell) that argued that imperialism was unnecessary and stood in the way of competition;

4. a sociological/psychological theory (associated with Joseph Schumpeter) that argued that imperialism was learned behavior and thus not inevitable;

5. Marxian theories of imperialism (especially those of Vladimir Lenin, Jon Galtung, and Samir Amin) that argue that capitalist economies necessarily reach outward to acquire colonies to support themselves (with Leninists arguing that imperialist nations weaken themselves by investing abroad and other Marxists arguing that they strengthen themselves by creating dependent, complementary colonial economies and societies).[1]

Perhaps the first systematic analysis of imperialism to influence mainstream sociology is Immanuel Wallerstein's *The Modern World System: Capitalist Agriculture and the Origins of the European World Economy in the Sixteenth Century.*[2] Wallerstein argues that a society's internal development is greatly affected by its relations with other societies. The uniqueness of capitalism is its commitment to economic growth through economic activity. The empires acquired by the capitalist societies were not ordinary empires. They were part of a new international division of labor roughly divided into technically advanced countries and countries that specialized in food, staples, ores, fuel, and labor. Gradually, modern imperialism shifted to a new kind of imperialism, one in which advanced societies could dominate others through new imperialist mechanisms such as free markets, trade agreements, loans, and investments (as well as through conquest and colonies). Historically, the imperialism of the new world-market economy emerged as a mercantile-financial operation (*portfolio investment*, or loans to foreign companies and governments—characteristic of British imperialism) and then shifted to *direct investment* in productive, especially industrial, enterprises (characteristic of American imperialism).

The key idea by which to escape the fallacy that societies are autonomous is to note that the division of labor within a (complex) society goes beyond the limits of the society itself.[3] Given societies may have too much of one thing and not enough of another, and economic intercourse develops between societies whose needs and surpluses are complementary. Sometimes a society will simply engage in conquest to obtain the things it needs. But whether the interdependence of societies is expressed in war or in peaceful trade, their relations are rarely those of equals. These two forms of international intercourse, conquest and trade, are also forms of international stratification.

AGRARIAN EXPANSIONISM: THE IMPERIALISM OF EMPIRE

It is useful to distinguish between the imperialism of an empire, in which a society expands by absorbing other societies (often becoming a larger society composed of different ethnic, religious, or linguistic groups), and the imperialism of the capitalist era in which a society expands by developing an economic superiority to other societies (as well as by territorial expansion) within an international division of labor.

Empires in some form or another have existed for 5,000 years and were made possible by the advent of agriculture. Their beginnings are the great river valley civilizations in the Middle East and their endings are in the dissolution of the Hapsburg Empire in 1918, the collapse of Imperial China between 1900 and 1945, the containment and contraction of the Ottoman Empire between 1450 and the 1920s, the dissolution of the British Empire and the overthrow of the French Empire after World War II, and the end of Portugal's empire in 1975. The essence of an

---

[1]For an extremely valuable analysis of these theories, including the fine shades of meaning that my summary has obscured, see Karl W. Deutsch, "Theories of Imperialism and Neocolonialism," in Steven J. Rosen and James R. Kurth, eds., *Testing Theories of Economic Imperialism* (Lexington, Mass.: D. C. Heath, 1974), Chapter 2.

[2]New York: Academic Press, 1974. For previous references to Wallerstein's work, see *Types of Intersocietal Relations* in Chapter 1.

[3]The implications for social science of the need to think in terms of systems of society have been succinctly stated by Wallerstein in his essay, "A World-System Perspective on the Social Sciences," *British Journal of Sociology* 27 (September, 1976): 343–52.

empire is expansion through military or political conquest and an attempt to control and profit from the economy of a conquered territory through military and political means. Empires are not able to integrate themselves through homogenization (because of feudal particularism and because they invariably contain a variety of racial and ethnic groups), though they are often accompanied by religious, missionary zeal (world religion).

Empires often last for considerable periods but they exhibit chronic internal turmoil, and all have decayed and disintegrated. Empires are marked by considerable economic surplus since they are based on a well-developed agriculture and a relatively advanced technology (irrigation, aqueducts, metallurgy, power from animals, water, wind, and sail, and from human muscle, especially serfdom and slavery). Characteristically, economic surplus is consumed in nonproductive activities: war, luxurious life styles, inefficient administration, public spectacles, art, and the construction of monuments, arenas, palaces, temples, churches, and tombs. Indeed, the cost of these activities, especially the military and administrative costs of maintaining empires, invariably become so great that they stagnate the economy. A stagnant or declining economy creates political and social unrest, which requires more coercion, more unproductive activities, and so on.

Empires may expand in terms of geographical size, population, and production but they are not dynamic systems. Unlike modern industrial systems they do not result in increased *per capita* living standards and do not provide incentives for productivity, technological advance, or capital investment. Actually, they institutionalize *disincentives* for production and efficiency. Their servile serf and slave labor, nonbureaucratic (nonrational) administration, punitive systems of tribute and taxation, otherwordly values, and institutionalized "waste" (prestige and military-political expenditures) militate against productivity, efficiency, and capital formation.

The elites of feudal systems see the acquisition of territory as the main way to enlarge the economic pie (which means that enemies are created because someone else'e pie shrinks). The orientation of industrial power groups is quite different. Modern Western elites strive to enlarge the pie through production and are even "wise" enough to give back territory (Philippine independence, the return of the Panama Canal) or "give away" economic values (Marshall Plan, foreign aid) in order to make sure that long-range economic and other values are preserved.

The mounting and conflicting claims that converge on the central state of empires lead to more inefficient centralization, political intrigue and conflict, ethnic and class rivalries, labor repression, and the suppression of political dissent through force. Ultimately, the military and political costs of running such a system outstrip the economy's ability to sustain them. It is argued that the same may be true of contemporary capitalist societies as they struggle to meet the expectations of their internal populations, protect their foreign interests against each other, contain the expansion of the socialist world, and ward off the demands of the developing countries.[4] This issue will concern us greatly later when we analyze the adaptive capacity of contemporary societies. However, we will apply the concept of a society living beyond its means to socialist and developing countries as well as capitalist society.

THE NEW IMPERIALISM: THE CAPITALIST WORLD-MARKET SYSTEM

New insight into the rise and nature of capitalism, modern class formation, the nation state, imperialism, and international stratification is provided by Wallerstein's concept

---

[4]The argument (from a Marxist perspective) that capitalist society is inherently prone toward living beyond its means is the main theme of James O'Connor's *The Fiscal Crisis of the State* (New York: St. Martin's Press, 1973). The problem of social overload has also been raised by conservative liberals such as Daniel Bell ("excessive entitlements"), Robert Nisbet ("too much equality"), and Samuel Huntington ("too much democracy").

of a capitalist world economy or, as we will refer to it, the world-market system. Using neo-Marxian ideas concerning imperialism, Wallerstein argues that solitary societies (except for simple subsistence societies) are not ultimate entities. On the contrary, all contemporary societies must be conceived of as part of a uniquely modern international division of labor. Unlike the inner structure of a single (precapitalist) society in which economic and political institutions are explicitly related, capitalist society separates economics and politics both in its domestic life and in the relations among societies. The essence of the international system is that an expansive world economy comes into being in which all benefit—but because unequal units are transacting business, the more powerful benefit disproportionately. And because there is no government common to the unequal and often exploitive economic relations of the world-market economy, there is no way to focus conflicts, effect compromises, assign blame and responsibility, and the dominant societies do not (at least at first) have to pay the full costs of maintaining order or institutionalizing exploitation.

Core, Semi-Periphery, and Periphery

According to Wallerstein three different types of units interact in the capitalist world-market system that emerged in the sixteenth century: *core states, peripheral areas,* and *semi-peripheral areas.* The core state develops an expanding economy based on capitalist agriculture (gentry, yeoman farmers), trade (for example, the East India and Hudson's Bay companies), manufacture (textiles, china, and ironware), and services (banking and insurance). A large component of this expanding economy is made up of foreign trade. Essentially, a core state specializes its economy (and its internal system of social stratification) to complement the specialization of its international trading partners. Over time it acquires many trading partners while peripheral and semi-peripheral types acquire few. Gradually, its labor force is up-

graded in skills and responsibilities, and a strong state emerges to create the conditions of internal economic expansion (roads, laws, currency) and external economic expansion (army, navy, foreign ministry).

Peripheral areas are marked by a distinctive form of development known as *underdevelopment*.[5] Development for them means the creation of unskilled, coerced, slave, or serf labor organized in extraction (for example, silver, gold, tin, oil, bauxite, copper) or in the production and export of labor and agricultural staples (slaves, cheap "immigrant," "migrant," or "guest" labor, sugar, cotton, coffee, rubber, tea, bananas, or cash crop specialty fruits and vegetables). Such areas are also politically underdeveloped: at first they are colonies but even after independence they are governed by a native upper and middle class that benefit from and thus have a stake in the new international division of labor.

The term *semi-peripheral* denotes societies that for one reason or another were able to avoid being subordinated by the capitalist core long enough to develop as core states themselves (such as Russia and Japan) or societies that are large enough, developed enough or have enough special assets to

---

[5]In this respect Wallerstein's work builds on the revisionist wing of Marxist imperial theory; for two pioneering essays, see Paul A. Baran, "On the Political Economy of Backwardness," *Manchester School of Economics and Social Studies* (January, 1952), reprinted in Robert I. Rhodes, ed., *Imperialism and Underdevelopment: A Reader* (New York: Monthly Review Press, 1970), pp. 285–301, and Andre Gunder Frank, "The Development of Underdevelopment," *Monthly Review* (September, 1966), reprinted in Andre Gunder Frank, *Latin America: Underdevelopment or Revolution: Essays on the Development of Underdevelopment and the Immediate Enemy* (New York: Monthly Review Press, 1969), pp. 3–17. Orthodox Marxism, stemming from Lenin, rejects the argument that imperialism creates chronic dependence. Rather, it believes that imperialism will either create competitors and weaken the advanced capitalist countries or lead to capitalist development and class conflict in the developing world. Bill Warren's *Imperialism: Pioneer of Capitalism* (London: New Left/Verso, 1980) has inspired a number of Marxist theorists (that we will come across in later chapters) along these lines.

have some of the features of core societies (such as India, the People's Republic of China, Brazil, Spain, Greece, Turkey, the Republic of Korea, and others). While not underdeveloped, many of these societies are also dependent on forces beyond their control and are thus forms of dependent development.

The concept of semi-periphery also serves as a caution against a mechanical one-way conception of the imperialist causal process. Every state, no matter how weak, has its unique traditions and has sources of strength and resilience. Thus dependent societies all have some power vis a vis dominant countries even if it only means the ability to participate in settling the terms of their dependence.

The basic elements of the capitalist world-market system can be summarized:

1. New geographical areas were added to the interaction zone of the European continent from 1450 onward. The geographic expansion of Europe was made possible by the new maritime technology that enabled Europe to do more than merely expand its contiguous frontiers as it had done between 1100 to 1250 (the Iberian peninsula, the basic Mediterranean Islands, parts of Palestine and Syria, Wales, Scotland, Ireland, and the Christianization of the Balts and Slavs in Eastern Europe).

2. New forms of labor emerged from 1450 on to correspond to various production zones.

3. Strong state machines emerged in the core states (bureaucracy, crown, national budgets, standing armies and navies, and concern over balance of payments, total production, and the state's share). The technology of the period made the modern state possible (compared to feudal decentralization) but significant capital formation was possible only in relatively small states (compared to an empire).

4. A combination of empire and market imperialism brought the entire world either within the capitalist orbit or into a one-world economy.

5. The contemporary countries of the world (both socialist and capitalist) participate in a single world-market system judged by the flow of four basic unfinished and finished commodities (crude materials, such as rubber, wood, and ores; mineral fuels; chemicals; and machinery and transport equipment) constituting a majority of world commodity trade, and there are distinct levels of exploitation with the core exploiting the semiperiphery and periphery, and the semiperiphery exploiting the periphery.[6]

Nationalism and Middle-Class Dominance

Caste and estate systems of social stratification explicitly promote strata consciousness and identification. A class system of stratification is markedly different. A society with an expanding economy cannot allow fixed values to develop. The historic middle class needed consciousness and symbolic legitimacy to rise against a feudal aristocracy but, at the same time, it did not want the masses to rise. It needed a strong state but had to prevent both feudal elites and the masses from using it for their own purposes. The basic solution adopted by the middle class was to define itself as the universal class, as human nature, as rational, normal, the spearhead of an emerging humanity, and the agent of progress. The net result of liberal social theory was to make aristocrats and workers look peculiar, warped, privileged, parasitic, dysfunctional, backward. Once in power, the middle class's basic orientation was to homogenize its population (one language, law, education, government, value-belief system, mode of labor, nation, and standardized consumption). Nationalism is a fundamental bourgeois emotion because it helps to promote all of the above. And while ensuring middle-class dominance internally, nationalism also provides motives and justifications for dominance over foreign countries.[7]

---

[6]For an empirical analysis of the points in #5, see Steven R. Steiber, "The World System and World Trade: An Empirical Exploration of Conceptual Conflicts," *Sociological Quarterly* 20 (Winter, 1979): 23–6.

[7]Here we are referring to the original nationalisms of developing capitalist Europe. Nationalism has also arisen in former colonies and has served to rally a variety of subjugated peoples against foreign domination.

The Disruption of Preindustrial Economies

The impact of the advanced nations of the West on preindustrial societies has been varied. British imperialism stressed elite control through British administration in cooperation either with a native elite or a white settler elite. British colonial government tended to be relatively efficient and honest. In addition, roads and ports were built and hygienic measures were taken. The French, on the other hand, thought of their colonies as extensions of French civilization and tended to avoid the overt racism and ethnocentrism of Britain. Variations on the British and French models can be found in the imperial policies of Portugal, Spain, Germany, the Netherlands, Belgium, and Italy. Russian and then later Soviet imperialism is somewhat different in that Czarist and Soviet Russia simply incorporated conquered lands into Russian society. English imperialism also consisted of incorporating contiguous areas, succeeding with Scotland and Wales, failing with Ireland. The United States has also expanded by incorporating new territory into itself, some through conquest, some through purchase.

Despite variations, Western imperialism has had one outstanding feature: everywhere traditional subsistence economies were transformed into export-oriented economies. From relative self-sufficiency, traditional societies became dependent on world markets (and, internally, rural and urban areas became dependent on each other). Colonial powers everywhere introduced and promoted cash-crop agriculture and (where resources permitted) the extraction and export of raw materials. The colonial power developed an infrastructure of roads, water and power supply, sanitation and medicine, currency, ports, railroads, land-use patterns, law, tax and other money incentives, and education, all of which furthered economic development in keeping with their needs. Even the white settler colonies of British North America (the American colonies, Canada), Australia, and New Zealand were shaped to suit the needs of England.

The dissolution of the European empires after World War II changed little in the economic relations between developed and developing nations. The former colonies were now independent nations but their economies were still geared to the world economy. Most former colonial powers adopted foreign aid programs, especially for their former colonies, and development loans were now made through international (Western-dominated) bodies such as the World Bank. The developing countries were still subject to private groups: multinational corporations, churches, universities, foundations, professional groups, and so on. The basic thrust of developmental aid, whether in the form of loans, grants, education, technical aid, or capital investment has been the same—to develop the human and natural resources of the developing world in keeping with the needs of the developed world.

The impact of imperialism on the non-West is extremely complex, and its interpretation has understandably become a source of considerable controversy. Probably the best strategy in assessing the impact of imperialism is to keep the issues close to concrete cases. Our next section is a case study of a particular type of dependency, the underdevelopment that occurs when developed countries promote the development of either horticultural or simple feudal societies.

El Salvador: A Classic Case of Development to Underdevelopment

An inflow of technology, money, and know-how into a simple feudal society results in economic concentration, especially in land. A road, a new supply of water, tractors, or a dependable customer for a product, each in its own way makes land more valuable. Before the arrival of imperial powers, the landlord had to develop labor-intensive methods of utilizing the land. Landlords and serf-tenants needed each other. The introduction of Western technology and supporting institutions made the land more valuable and labor cheaper. Everywhere in such societies landlords began to abrogate traditional relations with tenants, serfs, and other forms of labor. Unneeded labor was dispossessed, and a gradual concentration of land took place in keeping with economic power and the economies of scale. Today, most such societies are in a peculiar position: food production, even where it has risen dramatically, can no longer keep up with population, which has also grown spectacularly because of Western sanitation and medicine. Neither the Green Revolution nor food from abroad—whether bought or given free—seems to help.

Like much of Central and South America, El Salvador was greatly influenced by feudal traditions imposed by Spanish colonialization. And, like the other countries of Central and South America, El Salvador has outgrown its social form: the simple feudal society. Simple feudalism is a customary society centered on subsistence farming. The society is decentralized and revolves around a series of haciendas or large, self-sufficient estates. The patron is head of the hacienda, similar to the lord of the manor of yesteryear. He (invariably male) supervises an estate that is labor intensive, and provides for its own needs—furniture, clothing, leather goods, repairs, sickness, old age, and so on. A rudimentary polity, owned and operated by large landowners, provides a few services. There is no government in the sense of national education, health, transportation, postal or energy services (some of these are provided, especially in the few urban centers).

From the nineteenth century on, but especially in the past 50 years or so, El Salvador gradually developed a more specialized division of labor and its simple feudal system eventually broke at the seams. In clear view of the United States's government (actually with its help), American and other foreign companies brought new technology to El Salvador and introduced new products and services. The El Salvador government grew to provide more services to handle the increased economic activity, but ominously there was no extension of political participation. Essentially, political power remained in the hands of a few landowners and the tiny urban business and professional elite. Economic development resulted in a changeover from subsistence, labor-intensive farming. As in the rest of the Third World, the patron asserted absolute legal ownership of the estate and renounced all customary rights based on the previous feudal, patron-tenant relations. This was a preliminary, of course, to dispossessing the peasants and turning the estate into a business.

Gradually a new economy emerged under the euphemism, the Green Revolution. The Green Revolution refers to the many-sided effort by the United States (and other industrial countries) to increase the agricultural output of Third World countries through technology (new seeds, fertilizer, irrigation systems, tractors, harvesters). The same technology has made the United States incredibly productive in food and staples. When Third World countries needed more food, the United States simply assumed that what worked here would work there. But even in the United States the Green Revolution has not been an unmixed blessing. Millions of Americans, for example, (of all skin colors and ethnic backgrounds) were dispossessed by the surge of agricultural technology and forced to enter cities that were only partially ready for them.

The Green Revolution in El Salvador (and the Third World) did not have an industrial revolution to soak up the labor it dispossessed from the countryside. Though it raised agricultural production, the Green Revolution seems to have had the ironic outcome of increasing food dependency, making people poorer than they were and hungrier as well. The Green Revolution has promoted cash-crop agriculture, which means production to stock the pantries and dining tables of America and Europe: coffee, sugar, cotton, bananas, cocoa, nuts, artichokes, and so on. The Green Revolution means economic concentration in land and the dispossession of former tenants. Third World landlords import seed, fertilizer, and farm machinery and pay for them by exporting food and staples. The World Bank, other international agencies, the United States government, and a landlord-dominated home government provide ports, energy, and roads. The police become a national guard to protect the economy. The value of the exports can never match the value of what is being imported (farm technology, Coca Cola, television sets, arms for the national guard) and a classic example of a dependent right-wing society has been helped into being by the Green Revolution.

When food aid is sent either by the United States government or private charities to feed the dispossessed masses, the basic power structure is reinforced. The free or subsidized food is used to keep the national guard, the civil service, and urban workers fed and quiet. Some of the food is used to put rural labor to work—building roads, for example. But roads benefit landlords who can now get their crops out to be sold abroad. Food aid simply postpones the day of reckoning—the day when the masses question a society in which economic growth produces poverty for most of the people.

Despite some growth of industry and urban services, El Salvador's new economy could not absorb the dispossessed labor. People crowded into the cities, most of them as squatters without jobs. Government and other workers are insecure since their jobs are precarious—a slight change in the price of coffee or energy and many are out of work. The government is under the influence of landlords, banks, import companies, and manufacturing firms, many of them branches of multinational (mostly American) corporations. But all efforts by civil servants, workers, and peasants to obtain a voice in setting government policy are rebuffed. Gradually, a revolutionary situation develops in plain sight of all who could see, including the United States Embassy and American executives and professionals.

The major trend is clear: the fruits of economic growth are being hogged by a small set of oligarchic elites. The masses, who were always poor, are now poor in a new way: their poverty lacks meaning—they are idle while things around them are humming. Workers and civil servants are insecure, surrounded by consumer goods they cannot afford. Both the poor and the insecure employed can see the flow of profits to both native and foreign elites. Eventually, after repeated demands for reform are rebuffed, increasingly by violent means, the situation becomes polarized. Armed insurrection breaks out (using weapons supplied from abroad, especially the Soviet Union and Cuba, but also purchased from private dealers in the United States or stolen from the inept El Salvador military). There is also support from social democratic governments and forces in Europe as well as from the one-party conservative government of Mexico. The El Salvador government quickly schedules elections, which nobody takes seriously. It also beefs up its antiquated national guard (with emergency aid from the United States) in an effort to suppress the rebellion.

Official United States policy is that El Salvador is trying to develop representative government and that Soviet and Cuban forces are causing all the trouble. But the American government is not believed by even its own people let alone the rest of the world. Everyone knows that the main problem lies in the outmoded, unworkable institutions of El Salvador itself and the institutional disarray that the United States has helped to produce. Everyone knows that it is too late for meaningful elections. Tens of thousands have been murdered (by all accounts most of the blame is laid on the El Salvador military) and hatred consumes all parties. The United States, the world's oldest (liberal) democracy, finds itself on the side of an incompetent, greedy, feudal elite. The feudal elite gasps for breath as the American government funnels in the supplies it needs to stay alive. On February 25, 1982, President

Reagan makes a bold proposal to invigorate the economies of the Caribbean countries, especially El Salvador, so as to bring prosperity and stability to the region. As he throws gasoline on the fire, there is not even a hint of understanding that prosperity without democratization is the main cause of the problem and that the civilian government is in deep trouble because it has been unable to change the oligarchic economy and find a place in it for the large majority of the El Salvadoran people.[8]

New Developments in the World Economy

The penetration of the Third World by the advanced industrial powers has gone through a series of stages. The use by economically advanced countries of colonies (and independent countries) as exporters of food, staples, and raw materials is an early, and continuing, stage. In the post-World War II period, the developed countries began to establish manufacturing plants in less developed countries to take advantage of their cheap labor. And, gradually, the world economy has begun to internationalize capital flows and corporations. Huge geocentric (multinational) corporations now operate

routinely in as many as 60 countries and use the entire capitalist globe as a single market. These huge corporations are increasingly intertwined across national borders through joint ventures and mutual ownership.

Though international banking and finance have long histories, the 1980s saw a fully developed global system of financial institutions: large international banks, interconnected stock exchanges, global quasipublic banks (World Bank, regional development banks), and open coordination of exchange rates by the major capitalist countries. The power of the world market is nowhere clearer than in the fact that the Soviet Union and the People's Republic of China have abandoned their policies of national self-sufficiency and have fully committed themselves to participating in this market.

The World System

No understanding of the nature of society is possible, therefore, without placing it in an intersocietal context (or world system or system of societies). World system theory helps explain the behavior (and downfall) of ancient Greece and Rome. It is part of the explanation for war, for the rise of capitalism and modern science,[9] for revolution and social system transformation,[10] and, in general, why some societies develop and others do not.

World system theory also helps us understand many developments inside society. The economic growth attributable to profits from abroad has helped create welfare states and political peace in the developed countries. From the nineteenth century on labor skills and income in the developed world rose, at

---

[8]For a brief but meaty background on El Salvador, see Roland H. Ebel, "Political Instability In Central America", *Current History* 81 (February, 1982): 56ff. For more extensive data on the extreme and growing inequality in El Salvador, the brutality with which the tiny elite rules, and the complicity of the United States in perpetuating an unworkable system, see Enrique A. Baloyra, *El Salvador In Transition* (Chapel Hill, N.C.: The University of North Carolina Press, 1982); Tommie Sue Montgomery, *Revolution in El Salvador: Origins and Evolution* (Boulder, Colo.: Westview Press, 1982); Robert Armstrong and Janet Shenk, *El Salvador: The Face of Revolution* (Boston, Mass.: South End Press, 1982); and Raymond Bonner, *Weakness and Deceit: U.S. Policy and El Salvador* (New York: Times Books, 1984). For an eyewitness account by a priest of the role of local Christian communities in supporting insurrection in El Salvador, Guatemala, and Nicaragua (influential in the latter's success), see Philip Berryman, *The Religious Roots of Rebellion: Christians in Central American Revolutions* (Maryknoll, N.Y.: Orbis Books, 1984).

[9]Robert Wuthnow has cited the role of an international network of stimulation and support in the rise of science; see his "The Emergence of Modern Science and World System Theory," *Theory and Society* 8 (September, 1979): 215–43.

[10]For an example of the importance of international factors in these latter respects, see The Rise of Capitalism in Chapter 4 and the section, Current Debates About the Nature of Revolution, later in this chapter.

least in part because of the international economy. In recent decades, however, that same world market has caused labor skills and income in many developed countries to drop.[11] The world market has also increased economic inequality and poverty in much of the developing world.[12]

Countries that pursue development policies that fail to provide for an equitable sharing of economic growth appear to be prone to comparatively high rates of mass political violence.[13] Foreign penetration of a society has also been found to impede fertility decline.[14] World-system theory has also yielded a relation between dependency and the provision of basic needs: dependency produces a strong and negative effect on the satisfaction of human needs (complied in various ways to encompass all definitions).[15]

Political witch trials have helped nations assert their identities by conjuring up real and imaginary foreign devils and conspirators. A world-system analysis has found a rise in utopian literature in Great Britain and the United States (two core societies that were hegemonic or dominant global powers in their day) during periods of crisis (economic crisis or decline of hegemonic power).[16] The revival of religious concerns and religious extremism, in both the developed world (for example, the American South) and in the developing world (for example, Iran) are also partly traceable to the impact of foreign ideas, values, and gods. Urbanization patterns have also been deeply affected by international exploration, settlement, investment, and geopolitical concerns.[17] Foreign penetration has also been found to produce "urban bias" (government policies favoring urban areas relative to rural) in developing countries contributing to dependence and economic stagnation.[18]

The international economy has led to increased (or at least more visible) cooperation and linkage among capitalist elites. The United States cooperated with European elites after World War II to put capitalist Europe on its feet and to further the interests of American banks and manufacturers.[19] Useem has shown the extensive cooperation between American and British elites and their success in maintaining profit margins against the demands of their respective populations for greater public spending (the Reagan and Thatcher governments of the 1980s).[20] Annual economic summits among the lead-

---

[11]For a pioneering study of downward mobility by labor in terms of world-system theory, see Alejandro Portes and John Walton, *Labor, Class and the International System* (New York: Academic Press, 1981). For details on the biopolarization and downward slide of much of the American labor force, see Chapter 9. The adverse affects of the international economy on American communities, the general standard of living, politics, and world power position are analyzed in a number of places.

[12]For data from 103 countries and a review of the empirical literature, which concludes that multinational corporations have had an adverse effect on much of the Third World, see Volker Bornschier and Christopher Chase-Dunn, *Transnational Corporations and Underdevelopment* (New York: Praeger, 1985).

[13]Edward N. Muller, "Income Inequality, Regime Repressiveness, and Political Violence", *American Sociological Review* 50 (February, 1985): 47–61. The findings in this study are listed here under the assumption that development strategy is affected by a nation's location in the international political economy.

[14]Bruce London, "Dependence, Distorted Development, and Fertility Trends in Noncore Nations: A Structural Analysis of Cross-National Data", *American Sociological Review* 53 (August, 1988): 606–18.

[15]Bruce London and Bruce A. Williams, "Multinational Corporate Penetration, Protest, and Basic Needs Provision in Non-Core Nations: A Cross-National Analysis", *Social Forces* 66 (March, 1988): 747–73.

[16]Edgar Kisser and Kriss A. Drass, "Changes in the Core of the World System and the Production of Utopian Literature in Great Britain and the United States, 1883–1975", *American Sociological Review* 52 (April, 1987): 286–93.

[17]Many cities in the colonial or developing world prospered, especially if they served multiple purposes. For an interesting American example of urban development for a single purpose, exporting cotton, that led to stagnation, see David A. Smith, "Dependent Urbanization In Colonial America: The Case of Charleston, South Carolina," *Social Forces* 66 (September, 1987): 1–28.

[18]Bruce London and David A. Smith, "Urban Bias, Dependence, and Economic Stagnation In Noncore Nations," *American Sociological Review* 53 (June, 1988): 454–63.

[19]Kees Van der Pijl, *The Making of an Atlantic Ruling Class* (London: Verso, 1984).

[20]Michael Useem, *The Inner Circle: Large Corporations and the Rise of Business Political Activity In The U.S. and U. K.* (New York: Oxford University Press, 1984).

ing capitalist societies are further evidence of elite cooperation. And the changing world economy has brought about extensive new relations between the United States and Japan (and other dynamic capitalist societies in Asia). In effect, the shift of the world economy toward the Pacific Rim and the relative decline of the American economy have created a close system of geopolitical and economic cooperation between the United States and Japan (although only the coming decades will reveal its full contours, there is little doubt that Japan is subsidizing American indebtedness, penetrating its economy, and that there are many joint ventures between American and Japanese multinationals that are not necessarily good for their respective populations).

Social theory reflects social experience and world-system theory is no exception. The antecedents of world-system theory (Thucydides, nineteenth century imperialist theory) reflected the experience of the ancient Greeks with intersocietal relations and the experience of Europeans with the conquest of colonies. Contemporary world-system theory reflects experience with the emergence of 165 nation states interacting on a worldwide basis. It has seized on an important process that needs explaining and that promises to provide insights into a wide variety of subject matter.[21] However, despite the importance of world-system theory, it sometimes gets disconnected from its core insight, that domestic power structures are the mainspring of human behavior, including the world system. Understanding, the power relations within a society (and of course the various kinds of power in various kinds of societies) remains the central goal of sociology and social science. Despite the importance of the world system, therefore, it should not be for-

gotten that it derives largely from the outward thrust of domestic power structures.

The Contemporary International System

The modern international system has two phases:[22]

1. The main phase between 1450 and 1950 (roughly the end of World War II) was marked by acute rivalries among the various societies of the West. Part of the struggle represented a realignment between dynamic capitalist societies and the stagnant agrarian systems (for example, England versus Spain). Most of the rivalry, however, took place among the dynamic capitalist societies as they vied for the leadership of Europe and elsewhere in the world. The struggle between England and France lasted for centuries and was terminated only when both joined ranks to stop German expansionism. World War II, which marked the end of this phase, represented a vast struggle between the liberal capitalist societies and the authoritarian capitalist societies (this is not to minimize the major role played by the Soviet Union in World War II).

2. The end of World War II until the end of the Vietnam war marks a distinct phase in the nature of the modern international system. Between 1945 and the early 1970s the United States, having replaced Great Britain as the leading capitalist imperial power, exercised world leadership. The distinctive feature of this phase was not so much the rise of the United States to world leadership as the fact that the various capitalist societies closed ranks to confront a series of new threats. The foremost threat was the Soviet Union, which emerged from World War II as the second most powerful country in the world. The Soviet Union, like all nations, has national interests that run counter to the interests of other countries. In addition, it is a socialist society formally opposed to the

[21]For a fascinating collection that analyzes diverse phenomena ranging from American art, women, legitimating myths and hegemony to intersocietal conflicts, crises, ironies, and long-term cycles in relation to and as part of the world system, see Terry Boswell and Albert Bergesen, eds., *America's Changing Role in the World System* (New York: Praeger, 1987).

[22]For general background, see Daniel Chirot, *Social Change in the Twentieth Century* (New York: Harcourt, Brace, Jovanovich, 1977). For much of the same material but with more emphasis on the internal dynamics of capitalism, see Daniel Chirot, *Social Change in the Modern Era* (San Diego: Harcourt Brace Jovanovich, 1986).

spread of capitalism. Challenged by the growing power of the Soviet Union and its allies, and also by a diverse and volatile array of semi-peripheral nations, many marked by national liberation movements and almost all conscious of their exploitation by more advanced societies, the capitalist societies settled their rivalries and organized themselves under American leadership in relatively short order.

Since World War II the United States has scored some notable foreign policy victories (for example, the Marshall Plan, which restored the capitalist social systems of Western Europe and, through its occupation of Japan, which led to a demilitarized capitalist Japan). The United States also replaced Great Britain as the imperial power in the South Pacific, the Middle East, and in Greece and Turkey, though with mixed results in all cases.

The United States also scored a notable success (largely because it served China's interest) when it established relations with the People's Republic of China in the 1970s (thereby putting it in a position to benefit from China's estrangement from the U.S.S.R.). In Latin America the United States has scored successes in Chile (where it played a major role in undermining an elected Marxist regime) and in Panama (by returning the Panama Canal to Panama, an act symbolic of the entire shift from empire to world-market imperialism). Persistence also paid off when the United States helped mediate a pullout of South Africa from Nambibia and Cuba from Angola in 1988–89. Its aid to the Afghan resistance movement also helped ensure the Soviet Union's defeat and withdrawal in 1988–89.

The United States has also been adversely affected by the tide of national liberation. It suffered a major defeat in Vietnam when it foolishly allied itself with the jerry-built regime that emerged on the remnants of the former French colony. The emergence of a Marxist Cuba represents a significant failure of U. S. policy in its own backyard. It appears to have suffered another defeat in Nicaragua with the collapse in 1979 of the Nicaragua dictatorship that it established and supported for 40 years and the subsequent emergence of what appears to be a Marxist regime. In El Salvador and Guatemala, it is also reaping the harvest of policies that promoted economic development without mass participation.

In the Middle East, the United States has inherited the accumulated problems created by European imperialism, especially the actions of Great Britain and France. At present, it is handcuffed by its inability to solve the deadly deadlock between Israel and the Arabs (though it gained a considerable edge when, through little effort on its part, Egypt switched from the socialist to the capitalist camp) or to reconcile the rift between Greece and Turkey. The United States also suffered a defeat when the dictatorship in Iran collapsed in 1979 (a dictatorship it helped to establish and which it also helped to bring down by emphasizing a narrow policy of military strength instead of broad-based social development). In Africa, the United States has struggled to shore up and reform colonial regimes (often racist) against the onslaught of revolutionary movements supported by the U.S.S.R. and its allies.

The United States and all developed societies have also been confronted with a growing scarcity of resources compounded by environmental problems. Some cooperation on environmental matters among the developed countries has emerged in recent years to perhaps augur a better future. Third World debt and growing poverty, however, continued to burden the international system. However, the Cold War abated considerably in the late 1980s as the United States and the Soviet Union, experiencing growing domestic problems, muted their rivalry and even instituted some programs of positive cooperation.

Nonetheless, the basic unit of the international system, the nation state remains a problem. As we will see later, there is little evidence that the American people or its leaders in either the private or public sectors are aware of the limitations and liabilities of the nation state.[23] A genuine global sociol-

---

[23]American foreign policy is discussed in more detail in Chapter 10 and as seen from inside other countries in various other chapters.

ogy, therefore, undermines the fiction of the nation state as a self-sufficient entity by pointing to the permeability of national boundaries and to the indispensable roles of domestic and international processes in creating and maintaining each other. A global sociology may well include an awareness that liberalism and the world-market system are unique outcomes of a nonrepeatable capitalist development and that their contemporary relevance for humanity is problematic. Indeed, given the failure of liberal society to realize its own ideals of equal opportunity, equal justice, and the elimination of poverty, and its voracious appetite for the world's scarce resources, the relevance of liberalism for liberal society itself may well have become problematic. In any case, the ideology of nationalism continues strong in all countries despite the mutual dependence of nations on each other. One of the reasons for the world's ethnocentrism is that to explore the meaning and the implications of world interdependence threatens the power of all national elites, including many of its social scientists.

FIRST, SECOND, AND THIRD WORLDS

In recent decades three terms have gained currency as a shorthand for the world's countries. These terms, *First, Second,* and *Third World,* do not have a uniform meaning but are serviceable, if used with caution. In one usage, the term First World refers to the industrialized capitalist nations led by the United States (see Table 5–1). All are liberal democracies, and with the exception of Japan, all are white (by coincidence) and derive from the European Judaic-Christian, Greco-Roman tradition. In another sense, the term First World refers to both the developed countries and the developing capitalist countries aligned with them in varying degrees of dependency (see Table 5–4).

TABLE 5–1. The First World (Industrial Capitalist Countries) Ranked by GDP (With Per Capita Income and Population),[1] 1985.

	GDP (1985) (billions)	Per Capita Income	Population (rounded) in millions
1. The United States	$3,947	$14,565	239
2. Japan	1,325	9,452	121
3. The Federal Republic of Germany	625	8,950	61
4. France	512	8,126	55
5. United Kingdom	456	7,156	57
6. Italy	359	5,592	57
7. Canada	349	11,788	25
8. Australia	156	9,196	16
9. The Netherlands	125	7,710	14
10. Sweden	100	10,315	8
11. Switzerland	93	13,720	6
12. Belgium	81	7,408	10
13. Austria	66	7,631	8
14. Norway	57.9	11,784	4
15. Denmark	57.8	9,709	5
16. New Zealand	22	6,100	3
17. Luxembourg	4	11,960	.36

Source: The World In Figures, editorial information compiled by *The Economist* (Boston: G. K. Hall, 1988), pp. 8, 9, 13.

[1]Gross Domestic Product (GDP) differs from Gross National Product (GNP) in that it excludes property income from other countries. All such figures are dependent on exchange rates (modified by purchasing power indices) and should be used to obtain gross ratios among nation state economies.

The basic economic interests of the developed capitalist countries are three-fold: economic growth through private capital and an exchange economy, trade and investment abroad, and the importation of raw materials. The small group of capitalist countries outproduce by far the rest of the world, conduct most of the world's trade among themselves, and consume far more of the earth's resources than the rest of the world combined. The United States alone, for example, with only 6 percent of the world's population consumes 33 percent of its energy.

The classification of countries is rather arbitrary and it is best to keep the meaning intended by any particular grouping clearly in mind. The World Bank and the United Nations use a variety of standards to differentiate groups of countries: per capita income, capital surplus, oil exporting, and so on. The World Bank and the United Nations both have a larger list of developed capitalist societies than the list in Table 5–1 (for example, they include such countries as Argentina, Brazil, Israel, Mexico, and Spain). However, the countries in Table 5–1 not only have clearly crossed the threshold to affluence and economic viability (through various mixtures of industry, services, and extraction), but they have working political relations among themselves and most share

similar religious and moral-political traditions. For these reasons, the Union of South Africa, a developed capitalist country, is not included since its large black majority is dominated on racial grounds by minority whites and is more or less an outcast country.

The Second World is made up of the more developed socialist countries and is led by the U.S.S.R. (see Table 5–2). All are one-party authoritarian regimes. All are white (by coincidence) and derive from the European Judaic-Christian tradition, though their version of this tradition is distinctly less liberal and humanistic than its counterpart in Western Europe. The basic economic problem of these countries is to sustain economic growth in the face of popular restiveness over low living standards. Economically, the state socialist societies of Eastern Europe have developed extensive trade with the First World because of their decision (derived from need) to import Western capital, technological expertise, and food. As a result the Second World is an exporter of raw materials (to help pay for its imports) and has incurred sizeable debts to First World banks.

The term Second World also refers to both the developed Marxist societies and to the developing socialist societies (of various forms besides Marxism) aligned with them. A number of Soviet-led countries are

TABLE 5–2. The Second World (The More Developed Socialist Countries)[1] Ranked By GDP[2] (With Per Capita Income and Population), 1985.

	GDP (1985) (billions)	Per Capita Income	Population (rounded) in millions
1. The Union of Soviet Socialist Republics	$1,200	$4,200	279
2. The Democratic Republic of (East) Germany	100	5,400	17
2. Czechoslovakia	100	6,000	16
3. Poland	78	1,900	37
4. Romania	69	2,687	23
5. Bulgaria	31	3,200	9
6. Hungary	21	1,722	11

Source: The World in Figures, editorial information compiled by *The Economist* (Boston: G. K. Hall, 1988), pp. 8, 9, 13.

[1]Yugoslavia is a developed socialist society but does not follow the lead of the U.S.S.R.

[2]GDP figures are estimates and are even less reliable than usual because the Soviet bloc uses different accounting methods.

linked economically, but it cannot be said that there is a smoothly functioning communist world system whether considered economically, politically, or militarily (see Table 5-4).

The term *Third World* originated during the Cold War period soon after World War II and took on political reality in 1955 at the Bandung Conference led by Tito of Yugoslavia, Nehru of India, and Sukarno of Indonesia. Calling themselves unaligned, a number of developing countries proclaimed their right to act independently of the two superpowers. Since 1955 the unaligned nations (sometimes referred to as the Group of 77 but now numbering approximately 100) has met formally to coordinate their efforts.

The term Third World also has two meanings: (1) it is a catchall term for all nonindustrialized countries, and (2) it is used often to refer to nonindustrialized countries not aligned with either the First or Second Worlds. Table 5-3 separates the "nonaligned" developing nations into capitalist and socialist groupings while Table 5-4 presents the countries aligned with the First and Second Worlds. These are rough groupings—most of the developing countries call themselves nonaligned but are economically and militarily dependent on the First World. (Some exceptions are India, Yugoslavia, China, and the Arab socialist countries.) Dependent aligned countries tend to embody special economic, political, or military interests for the dominant countries. However, relations between dominant and dependent are not always smooth since "modernization" is politically unsettling and because of resentment over past and present forms of dependency and exploitation.

The outstanding characteristics of most Third World countries are their low technological levels, low energy consumption, an unskilled and surplus labor force, specialized economies geared toward exporting food and raw materials, and their inability to create capital fast enough to yield self-sufficiency and self-direction. A few key indicators such as per capita income and life expectancy tell us a great deal about the nature of a society (examples

TABLE 5-3. Nonaligned Developing Capitalist and Socialist Countries.

Capitalist	Socialist
Most developing capitalist societies cultivate an image of nonalignment mostly as a weapon against their de facto dependence on the First World. Some developing capitalist countries are openly aligned with the First World, for example, Greece, Turkey, Taiwan, Republic of (South) Korea, Spain, the Philippines.	1. Albania 2. Algeria 3. Angola 4. Cuba[1] 5. Democratic Kampuchea (Cambodia)[2] 6. Guyana 7. India[3] 8. Iraq 9. Libya 10. Mozambique 11. North Korea 12. People's Republic of China 13. The Socialist Republic of Vietnam[4] 14. Syria 15. Tanzania 16. Yugoslavia

[1]Cuba is a member of the Organization of Nonaligned Nations and is also an explicit ally of the Second World.

[2]Vietnam has agreed to withdraw from Democratic Kampuchea and its future is uncertain.

[3]India is formally socialist but operationally capitalist.

[4]Vietnam is allied with the U.S.S.R. and has a long history of enmity with both Imperial and Communist China.

TABLE 5–4.   Developing Countries Openly Aligned with or Dependent on Either the First or Second Worlds

First World	Second World[1]
The 125 or so capitalist countries of the Third World (including some of the less developed European countries) are either openly aligned with or dependent on the First World.	1. Afghanistan[2] 2. Angola 3. Congo 4. Cuba[3] 5. Ethiopia 6. Guinea-Bissau 7. Guyana 8. Iraq 9. Laos 10. Libya 11. Mozambique 12. People's Republic of Mongolia 13. Seychelles 14. South Yemen 15. Syria 16. Vietnam

[1]This is a loose grouping of countries that look to the U.S.S.R. for support in various degrees on various issues. A more formal Second World grouping, the Council for Mutual Economic Assistance, the Soviet bloc's economic and trade group, has 10 members (the U.S.S.R., East Germany, Poland, Hungary, Czechoslovakia, Rumania, Bulgaria and, from the developing world, Cuba, Mongolia, and Vietnam). Yugoslavia is an associate member while Ethiopia, Angola, and Laos have sent observers to its meetings. It cannot be said, however, that there is a socialist world political economy.

[2]The Soviet attempt to occupy Afghanistan ended in military defeat and withdrawal in 1988–89.

[3]Cuba, a close ideological and military ally of the Soviet Union, is also a member of the Organization of Unaligned Nations.

of other key indicators are infant mortality, energy consumption, debt, and the size of the manufacturing sector in relation to other economic sectors). Table 5-5 shows the diversity among Third World countries and at the same time the sharp contrast between most developing countries and the First and even the Second World (when comparisons are made with per capita incomes in those worlds as found in Tables 5-1 and 5-2). Another key indicator in assessing a society's internal structure and well-being as well as its place in the international system of stratification is degree and type of urbanization. The running sores called cities in the Third World are potent indicators of all that is awry in developing countries (for details see the section, Urbanization Outside the West in Chapter 6).

The polities of most Third World countries exhibit various shades of authoritarianism (though a number have evolved or are evolving into representative government) and exhibit various degrees of dependency on the core powers of the First and Second Worlds. Nonetheless, each country has its unique strengths and weaknesses, and analysts should be wary of using mechanical notions of causality or excessively abstract categories of classification when referring to the Third World or its relations to the developed worlds.

THE MANY ROUTES TO THE "MODERN" WORLD

There is no one route to modernity if by that one means becoming a nation state. If the definition of modernity means making a successful transition to industrialization, then here again societies have industrialized differently (and there is a possibility that many will never be successful). If the standard for mo-

TABLE 5-5. The Diversity of the Third World (By per capita income and average life expectancy, 1986. Examples include all the developing countries selected for this text—identified by italics).

Low-Income Countries (Total[1] 39; av. inc. $270; income range $120–420; average life expectancy 52, excluding China and India)
Ethiopia, Burma, *Tanzania*, Niger, *India*, Kenya, *China*,[2] *Sri Lanka, Vietnam*, Senegal

Lower-Middle-Income Countries (Total: 35; average income: $750; income range: $460–1570; average life expectancy: 59)
Indonesia, Philippines, *Zimbabwe, Nigeria*, Nicaragua, *El Salvador, Peru*, Turkey, *Cuba*, Chile, Syria

Upper-Middle-Income Countries (Total: 20; average income: $1890; income range: $1810–7410; average life expectancy: 67)
Brazil, Malaysia, South Africa,[3] *Yugoslavia*,[4] *Republic of Korea, Greece, Israel, Iraq*, Mexico, Algeria, Singapore

High-Income Oil Exporters (Total: 4; average income: $6740; income range: $6950–14,680; average life expectancy: 64)
Saudia Arabia, Libya, Kuwait, United Arab Emirates

Source: World Bank, *The World Bank Development Report, 1988* (New York: Oxford University Press, 1988), Table 1.

[1]Totals include only countries with a population of 1 million or more.

[2]China is not a typical low-income country—it not only has a life expectancy of 69 years and can feed itself but it is presently making a transition to industrialization.

[3]South Africa is a developed country but its general per capita income puts it in the Third World. It is peculiar also because its income distribution is skewed in favor of its white minority by South Africa's explicit racial policies.

[4]While Yugoslavia's per capita income puts it in the developing world, it is classified as a developed country in chapter 15 because it has a very high ratio of manufacturing to other economic activities and its savings/capital investment is high. The CIA places its per capita income considerably higher than the World Bank. Readers are reminded that per capita income is computed in terms of the U.S. dollar and prevailing exchange rates (modified somewhat by purchasing power indices) and that it should be used to obtain gross ratios.

dernity is representative government, here again the paths taken to it have varied (and most societies still have a long way to go). And if one's standard for modernity is socialism that too is being approached from many paths (and has little hope of success in numerous countries).

The Unique Bourgeois Revolutions

Social development in the West, long assumed to be the normal method of modernizing, is itself varied and can actually be considered as an abnormal departure from the rule. The rise of capitalism was a unique deviation from the sway of traditionalism. Agrarian societies do not yield easily to social-system change. Economic growth in Europe was no law of nature or history—it took place in a unique unrepeatable manner (see Chapter 4 for an earlier discussion of the rise of capitalism).

England's social development is instructive for it led to the first modern revolution. Responding to general economic conditions, both domestic and international, an English middle class emerged based on trade and fabrication. The lively commerce and manufacturing in the towns helped produce a profound and unusual transformation of the English countryside. Locked in rivalry with the monarch, the English landed class looked to their estates for their well-being. In a manner unique among the feudal nobilities of the world, the English landed class struggled to improve (modernize) their estates. Careful cultivation meant agricultural surplus and in turn that meant a commercial or capitalist agriculture. It also meant the abrogation of traditional rights among the rural lower classes and the removal of some excess labor from the countryside (the Enclosure Movement). The long-term development of "capitalist agriculture" in England transformed much of the landed class into a political interest group. Thus England on the eve of the English Civil War did not have a leisured consumption-oriented, economically backward landed class ready to support monarchy against parliament. England's growing agricultural economy also absorbed tenants either as owners or workers and, all in all, England was spared the peasant problem that was to plague other countries. The economic and thus political strength of the English nobility was a key element in England's break with tradition and in the eventual failure of royal absolutism. However, a commercial agriculture in England would not have been possible without a growing town economy and growing international trade.

The contest among landed, commercial, manufacturing, and crown interests plus religious fragmentation led to a uniquely "pluralistic" society. As the stalemated elites struggled for dominance they reached out for mass support and the result was an irreversible start on representative government. Barrington Moore has identified bourgeois revolution as one route to the modern world.[24] Thought of on an abstract level, the middle class effected the transformation of society in England, France, and the United States (American liberalism, argues Moore, triumphed not in 1776 but in 1865 when it smashed the power of the Southern plantation economy).[25]

The unique strength of the historic English and American middle class is not found elsewhere and failure to recognize

this is one of the reasons why Anglo-American social scientists have not been able to provide a well-grounded picture of how societies modernize.[26] Bourgeois revolution, however, was not a popular upswelling. The essential pattern is struggle among incompatible property groups, a struggle broad-based enough to prevent a reversion to feudal authoritarianism. The uniqueness of the Anglo-American path to the modern world not only means that it cannot be the model for other societies but that there are other paths to modernity.

Revolution From Above

Revolution from above culminating in fascism is another route to the modern world, argues Barrington Moore. The main countries here are Germany (1650 to 1848) and Japan (1868–1945) in which a monarchy used its landed class to forge a state machine strong enough to co-opt its middle class and build an industrial society subservient to its own values (militarism for the most part). The category of revolution from above can be broadened to include any and all attempts to modernize led by a property-oriented elite, often a military elite. The pattern is widespread: Mexico from 1910 on, Turkey from the 1920s on, Brazil from the 1930s on, Iran, Egypt, South Korea, Taiwan, Singapore, Hong Kong, Nigeria, Indonesia from the 1950s on, Peru from the 1960s on, Saudi Arabia, especially from the 1970s on, and so on.

The term *revolution* in the concept *revolution from above*, is misleading when applied to developing countries in the twentieth century. Unlike Germany and Japan, few of these countries have industrialized successfully (the exceptions are South Korea, Tai-

---

[24]Barrington Moore, Jr., *Social Origins of Dictatorship and Democracy: Lord and Peasant in the Making of the Modern World* (Boston: Beacon Press, 1966), especially Part III.

[25]Moore's analysis of the emergence of the modern world is a pioneering break with the dominant liberal theory that tends to idealize the middle class by emphasizing political norms and values, creative leaders, science, the role of education, benign economic growth, and continuity through reform. Moore, in contrast, stresses the neglected role of conflict and violence, the mixed and ironic effects of economic expansion, and the creative role of aristocrats and peasants.

[26]Another reason is that they have failed to place social development in an international context (Barrington Moore also neglects international factors). Not only did outside factors help England and France to modernize but both countries had an enormous impact on the rest of Europe and ultimately the world. Certainly revolution in Russia, China, and the ferment throughout the contemporary world must rely heavily on factors external to the society in question for their explanation.

The World System 93

wan, Hong Kong, Singapore). Unlike Germany and Japan, these societies do not enjoy substantial autonomy nor are they integrated nation states but rather are marked by significant degrees of dependency and instability (even large countries such as Brazil and Mexico). *The essential pattern here is an attempt by elites to bring their country up to date without interfering with property rights and without empowering the masses.* The developing nation states that are being revolutionized from above genuinely aspire to nationhood and want to control their destiny; they have some enclaves of modern industry and commerce, often an advanced military, and some state machinery, but, by and large, they lack economic self-sufficiency, a viable state machine, and other elements of a modern society.

Revolution from Below

The third route to the modern world, argues Moore, is the peasant-based revolution exemplified by Russia and China. In its simplest form, Russia and China were badly disorganized by war, giving a radical (urban) elite an opportunity to mobilize a discontented peasantry and seize power. Revolution in these countries meant a vast interference with previous property rights and a massive effort to mobilize the masses for state-led economic growth. Moore's category can be broadened to include mass-based revolutionary movements in Algeria, Cuba, and Vietnam.

Current Research and Debates About the Nature of Revolution

The main approach to revolution among both liberal and socialist theorists has been some version of conflict theory. Under this broad perspective theorists assume that members of society experience society's conflicts and act to resolve felt tensions and deprivations. The foremost example of the radical conflict theory of revolution is by Karl Marx. For Marx, society is essentially a struggle between the propertied and non-propertied. Under certain conditions (see

Chapter 4 for details), the struggle is heightened, class consciousness rises, and a revolution occurs. Marx did not say much about how people actually organize to promote revolution. Somehow, in some way, discontented workers would spontaneously organize and overthrow capitalism. To overcome this weakness in Marx's thought, Vladimir Lenin argued that the revolutionary class of capitalist society, the proletariat, must be led by a small, dedicated elite.

The conflict approach has also appealed to liberal theorists. Neil Smelser, for example, has argued that social movements emerge from conditions of social strain. When a society's norms and values are out of kilter, a general sense that something is wrong develops. Under these conditions it is easy to think and act in ways that will presumably reduce the tension and anxiety.[27]

A variation of conflict theory that became popular during the late 1960s and early 1970s as an explanation of social movements is relative deprivation theory. Liberal theorists in this vein also think of society in terms of discontented individuals who somehow act in concert to rid themselves of painful experiences. The best known attempt to use *relative deprivation theory* to explain revolution is James E. Davies's. Like other theorists, Davies avoids the equation of poverty, even extreme poverty, with discontent, social movements, and rebellion. Severe poverty tends to defeat people. If poverty is the normal condition of life, people do not rebel against it. Discontent rises only when there is movement away from the normal, when there is a rise in expectations and a sense of *relative deprivation*. Revolution, argues Davies, occurs only after a period of prolonged improvement in satisfactions and expectations. During this period people will tolerate a gap between a rising curve of expectations and a rising curve of satisfactions. Rebellion occurs if there is a sharp reversal in satisfactions (to yield a curve shaped like an up-side-down J)

---

[27]Neil J. Smelser, *The Theory of Collective Behavior* (New York: Free Press, 1963).

since expectations do not take a corresponding dip.[28]

Analysts have also benefitted by resource-mobilization theory to help them understand revolution. In their study of social movements, theorists such as McCarthy, Zald, Oberschall, and Gamson have rejected the notion that change movements arise from abstract individuals experiencing abstract conflicts. The things to look for, they argue, are resources and how well they can be mobilized, especially by elites.[29]

Against the background of conflict theory, research has gradually produced a better understanding of revolution. However no consensus exists and it is best to assume that it may not be possible to make generalizations covering the wide variety of revolution and all efforts to modernize.[30]

In surveying some of the recent creative work on revolution it is best to start by defining revolution. The concept *revolution* means the destruction of one system of society and its replacement by a new social order: the Anglo-American world had a bourgeois revolution between 1640 and 1865; France had a bourgeois revolution in 1789 (precariously established only during the Third Republic, 1870–1940 and fully in place only after World War II). Prussia's entry into the modern world was a revolution from above. The highly bureaucratized (efficient) Prussian state emerged under Frederick the Great (1740–86). Beaten by Napoleon, Prussia reformed itself and not only helped bring down Napoleon but was ready to beat back its own middle class (the failure of bourgeois revolution in 1848). By the end of the nineteenth century Germany had both feet in the modern world having co-opted its capitalist class to become a major industrial power under authoritarian auspices.

Russia was groping its way into the modern world through state-led economic development (essentially headed toward a capitalist economy) and had taken a few hesitant steps toward representative government when it suffered a smashing defeat by Germany in 1917. With its state shattered, a small communist party seized and held power. Russia's full entry into the modern world, therefore, took place under the direction of first a totalitarian and then an authoritarian socialist state (for details see Chapters 11 and 12). For its part, China (until 1945) was largely an agrarian society handicapped by a backward landlord class and unable to defend itself against foreign predators. Any hope of establishing a Chinese state and society was shattered by Japan's invasion in the 1930s. By the end of World War II Chinese society was in a state of utter disrepair. The only disciplined effective force was the Chinese Communist party and army. China's entry into the modern world began in 1949 with the victory of the Communists over the Nationalists. In the succeeding decades the Communist party established an effective central government and created a state-led economy able both to feed the Chinese people (for the first in China's history) and to industrialize (for details see Chapter 18).

Japan's revolution took place slowly over centuries but fell into place in 1868 (for details, see the section, Peaceful Social System Change: Japan, an Exception, in Chapter 18). Despite the fact that Japan's path to industrialization was constricted by the existing world economy prior to World War II, it did

---

[28]James C. Davies, "The J-curve Of Rising and Declining Satisfactions As A Cause Of Some Great Revolutions And A Contained Rebellion" in Hugh D. Graham and Ted Robert Gurr, eds., *Violence In America: A Report To The National Commission On The Causes And Prevention Of Violence*, Vol II (Washington, D.C.: U.S. Government Printing Office, 1969), chap. 19.

[29]John D. McCarthy and Mayer N. Zald, *The Trend of Social Movements In America: Professionalization And Resource Mobilization* (Morristown, N.J.: General Learning Press, 1973): reprinted as an appendix, along with other essays, in Mayer N. Zald and John D. McCarthy, eds., *Social Movements In An Organizational Society* (New Brunswick, N.J.: Transaction Books, 1987); Anthony Oberschall, *Social Conflict And Social Movements* (Englewood Cliffs, N.J.: Prentice-Hall, 1973); and William A. Gamson, *The Strategy of Social Protest* (Homewood, Ill.: Dorsey Press, 1975).

[30]For a superb collection of readings on almost every major and minor revolution in the modern period, which draws this conclusion, see Jack A. Goldstone, ed., *Revolution: Theoretical, Comparative, and Historical Studies* (San Diego: Harcourt Brace Jovanovich, 1986).

institute a new social order, became an autonomous world actor, and prepared itself to become an economic superpower in the post-World War II period.

The concept *revolution*, therefore, can mean a movement to either a capitalist or socialist industrial society and it can mean the use of old values, beliefs, and practices in new bottles. In studying revolutions one comes across the same variables that figure in the debates about the rise of capitalism: economy, polity, religion, population, international factors. Much of the recent creative work on revolutions has focused on political processes. In a creative analysis Trimberger identifies a political pattern that she labels *revolution from above* (Trimberger does not discuss Barrington Moore's three routes to modernity and her definition of revolution from above turns out not to be a revolution after all).[31] Trimberger calls attention to the role of the state in generating revolution from above (provided it is autonomous from the dominant class, and there are challenges from outside powers and forces). But her definition of revolution is vague, ultimately contradictory. On the one hand, she stresses that revolution does not mean a coup d'etat (mere change of personnel)—rather a revolution from above destroys the economic and power of the dominant social group of the old regime. On the other hand, however, she also stresses that her four examples of revolution from above all failed (even pre-World War II Japan). The revolutionary states in Japan and Turkey had to make compromises with its precapitalist landed class, while in Egypt and Peru the state coalesced with a rising capitalist class (Trimberger fails to note the continuing power of landed interests in Egypt and Peru). And Trimberger (taking a note from dependency theory) concludes that revolution from above has little chance to succeed in today's world since developing countries that fail to mobilize the masses will develop elites tied to the capitalist world economy. (Here Trimberger, writing in the mid-70s, was unable to see the successful industrialization from above of South Korea, Taiwan, Hong Kong, Singapore, and perhaps Saudi Arabia).

In another creative analysis, again featuring a state at once autonomous but inadequate, Skocpol has argued that revolution in France, Russia, and China were more similar than different.[32] She criticizes both liberal and Marxian theories for attributing purposfulness to revolutionary movements, ignoring international factors, and not taking the state into account as an autonomous actor. Skocpol argues that revolutions in the above countries occurred when autonomous but backward states (in relatively backward economies), under challenge from abroad, came into conflict with their dominant elites as they sought to raise more revenues. While noting similarities between these three revolutions and other revolutions, for example, in Mexico, Algeria, Vietnam, and Cuba, Skocpol wisely separates the latter from revolution in France, Russia, and China by emphasizing that revolutions vary depending on historical and international circumstances and by the structure and bases of state power (see her valuable conclusion).

The same stricture, however, applies to revolutions in France, Russia, and China. Skocpol rightly calls attention to the state and to international factors as causes. And she is right to emphasize that the class relations of landlord and peasant can be more important to historic revolutions than capitalist-worker relations. But her work is more successful arguing these commonplaces against the naive theories of revolution in American social science (see her valuable Chapter 1) than it is in establishing the similarity among revolution in France, Russia, and China. Her analysis also rightly criticizes the naive Marxist interpretation of revolution (a self-conscious middle class or proletariat will lead the way). But the alleged strong similarities that Skocpol sees in revolution in France,

---

[31] Ellen Kay Trimberger, *Revolution From Above: Military Bureaucrats and Development in Japan, Turkey, Egypt, and Peru* (New Brunswick, NJ: Transaction Books, 1978).

[32] Theda Skocpol, *States and Social Revolutions: A Comparative Analysis of France, Russia, and China* (New York: Cambridge University Press, 1979).

Russia, and China come only by focusing narrowly on revolution as distinct from broad social structural change, by exaggerating the role of the state, and by blurring distinctions among different kinds of international pressure.

Revolution in France came about because of centuries of capitalist growth that produced a large and unassimilated French middle class. The French state, torn between its allegiance to landed interests and its own interests, had helped create that middle class. Weakened because it could not raise taxes without losing power, especially to the middle class, cut off from illegitimate revenues (through the sale of titles for example) by the aristocratic reaction decades before the revolution, the French state found itself in a quandary because there were internal power groups beyond its control. In addition, the French Enlightenment was spearheading a liberal reinterpretation of the world. Whatever its proximate causes, the French Revolution came from the growth of French capitalism and its outcome could be nothing other than a bourgeois or capitalist France. (For a further discussion see the section, Violent Social System Change: France, the Typical Pattern, in Chapter 18.) As for Russia, the more likely prediction in the decades before World War I was that Russia would evolve into a bourgeois system of representative government given another decade or two of industrial growth. Russia's smashing defeat in World War I destroyed the Russian state and gave an obscure but ready political party a unique opportunity to take Russia in a direction that its historic development was not a preparation for. China is still a distinct third case of revolution. Woefully backward economically, politically backward and weak, China was preyed upon by outsiders. It was the unique combination of outside factors (a defeated Japan, a Marxist Russia as neighbor and ally, exhausted European colonial powers) in combination with an inept and corrupt "legitimate" government that allowed the Chinese Communist party to take over in 1949.

The need to see revolution in terms of a broad shift from one type of society to another, a shift that may take centuries, is also apparent in Goldstone's explanation of the English Civil War (1640), which he attributes to population growth and rising prices from 1520 on.[33] Goldstone rightly rejects the Marxian explanation that the enclosure movement led to conflict between gentry and peasants and between crown and gentry, and that parliamentary forces were capitalists and the royalists were feudal. However one need not resort to an unexplained growth of population and rising prices as the cause of the English revolution. One hundred years before the revolution England had a full-blown capitalist economy in which crown, gentry, merchants, manufacturers, small farmers, and skilled artisans were all deeply implicated. (The crown was deeply capitalistic in its activities as were the gentry). To confuse things further, there were strong feudal elements and strong and diverse religious feelings. In this deeply divided society there were no adequate mechanisms to resolve disputes or to put the stamp of legitimacy on losses and gains. In short, economic growth in unprecedented amounts and types had produced an anomic society[34] in need of a political system that could resolve disputes and provide legitimacy.

In recent years scholars have also focused on revolution in former colonial countries. By and large, theorists have found that revolution stems from the actions of the colonial powers, especially the destruction of the old order through the development of an economy geared to exporting food or raw materials (see the above discussion of El Salvador). Here too the role of the state in revolution has been highlighted by studies in a wide variety of developing countries. For one thing, the state often collaborates with the imperial

---

[33]Jack A. Goldstone, "Capitalist Origins of the English Revolution: Chasing a Chimera", *Theory and Society* 12 (March, 1983): 143–80; adapted as "The English Revolution: A Structural-Demographic Approach" in Jack A. Goldstone, ed., *Revolutions: Theoretical, Comparative, and Historical Studies* (San Diego: Harcourt Brace Jovanovich, 1986), pp. 88–104.

[34]See the Glossary for the definition of this important concept and for leads to related ideas.

power(s). Sometimes, the state is simply a coercive force upholding colonial and class interests (e.g., El Salvador). Building on Weber's analysis of short-lived charismatic regimes one can identify a state that is autonomous from class interests but serves the personal interests of the dictator (e.g., Somoza in Nicaragua, the Shah in Iran). And some autonomous states play a wider role in balancing competing interests and steering their respective societies.[35] In future pages we will come across examples of all types of economies, states, and revolution in the Third World.[36]

Current Efforts To Modernize

Many of the world's new countries are using variations on the above routes to modernity. If one thinks of a modern society as a society with a state, then much of the efforts of modernizing elites (often the military is the only structure stable and disciplined enough to undertake the effort) have been devoted to building state machines (to bring about nationhood and prepare for economic growth). The paths to modernity are marked by violence in yet another sense—many times a society attempting social-system change or threatened by it, will seek internal scapegoats, especially ethnic or racial groups. Indeed one of the overlooked features of modernization in general is the pervasive (though varied) pattern of large-scale violence that accompanies it. The English Civil War, the French Revolution, the American Civil War, along with pogroms in Czarist Russia, civil strife in Mexico, genocide against the Armenians by Turkey, the Spanish Civil War in the 1930s, and so on. Even Nazism and the Holocaust visited on Europe's Jews and other minorities can be better understood if seen as part of Germany's difficulty in modernizing (developing evenly). The millions of victims of Stalin's attempt to modernize on the left can also be added to this pattern. To this pervasive pattern of civil strife and genocide can be added large-scale population expulsions and the attempt to build social solidarity through political witch trials.[37]

The three routes to modernity are abstract formulations. Future chapters will provide case studies of all three, but it is doubtful if the enormous diversity of modern history can be captured by such large abstractions. Many societies are unique variations on these themes, while others are exceptions. Revolution from below, for example, varies considerably not only in Russia and China but say in Cuba (a mixture of radical leadership, middle-class disaffection, and peasant-worker support) as opposed to Vietnam (Western-educated leadership using vast peasant disaffection, a native anticolonial tradition, traditional religion, foreign sponsorship).

Some developing countries are having difficulty in modernizing—even large and potentially wealthy societies such as India,

---

[35]For an analysis of these three types of authoritarian Third World polities, see Manus I. Midlarsky and Kenneth Roberts, "Class, State, and Revolution in Central America," *Journal of Conflict Resolution* 29 (June, 1985): 181–3. For details and an extension of these three types to other parts of the world see What Types of Polity Are There? in Chapter 20.

[36]In an important comparative analysis, Misagh Parsa, "Economic Development and Political Development: A Comparative Analysis of the United States, Russia, Nicaragua, and Iran," *Theory and Society* 14 (September, 1985): 623–75, has argued that unstable states are those that are visibly implicated in the economy—when the economy falters or is threatened, the state serves as a lightning rod. Societies that diffuse the responsibility for economic failure and success and that can convince people that state and economy are separate (like the United States) are the most stable.

[37]For an analysis of the rate of political witch hunting in 39 widely different countries, see Albert James Bergesen, "Political Witch Hunts: The Sacred and the Subversive in Cross-National Perspective," *American Sociological Review* 42 (April, 1972): 220–33. For a surprisingly unsociological collection of essays on genocide (but with much useful material), see Irving Louis Horowitz, *Taking Lives: Genocide and State Power* (New Brunswick, N.J.: Transaction Books, 1980; augmented 3rd ed., 1982). Horowitz's attempt to derive eight social types on a continuum ranging from genocidal to permissive (see Chapter 4) is more properly called a spectrum of social control. For a valuable historical and sociological discussion of genocide, which relates it to social structure, especially the segmented societies produced by colonialism, see Leo Kuper, *Genocide: Its Political Use in the Twentieth Century* (New Haven, Conn.: Yale University Press, 1981).

Brazil, Mexico, and Nigeria while achieving nationhood, have yet to cross the threshold of industrialization, raise living standards, control population growth, or overcome dependency. Some developing societies are coming into the modern world via monarchy (Saudi Arabia) while others have stepped into it and are trying to "head back" (Iran). Some Muslim countries are badly handicapped by religious traditionalism and many societies are badly handicapped by their horticultural past (Africa) or simple feudal past (Latin America).

Scholars differ about the reasons for social-system change, revolution, and development. Theories stressing the role of economic and material factors, religion, state, and intersocietal factors will be explored when we analyze individual countries. There are also differences about the best way to develop once nationhood is achieved. Some follow import-substitution policies while others gear their economies to export manufactured goods. Some export food, staples, minerals, or oil in order to develop their economies. Some have little room to maneuver and must rely on outside sponsors. Only one thing is clear—the turbulence that marked the "modernization" of the West has and will continue to characterize the rest of the planet. And each country has its own unique traditions, assets, and liabilities and each will confront the modern world differently.

THE WORLD SYSTEM: STRATIFICATION AMONG SOCIETIES—A SUMMARY

Relations among societies are characterized by domination, conquest, exploitation, and dependence, in short, by stratification and imperialism.

Leaving aside the discredited folk theories based on biology, theorists tend to agree that imperialism occurs for economic reasons. Liberal (capitalist) theorists argue that imperialism is unnecessary and should be curbed as a barrier to competition and efficiency. Marxists, following Lenin, argue that imperialism is a necessary stage of mature

capitalism and will lead eventually to vigorous competition from colonies and the downfall of capitalism. Dependency theorists, also influenced by Marx, also argue that imperialism is necessary for capitalism to continue but say that it creates long-term if not chronic dependency among colonies and former colonies.

Empire imperialism is characteristic of agrarian society and consists of conquering other lands and peoples. *World-market* imperialism is when *core* societies exploit their economic superiority toward *peripheral* societies. *Semiperipherial* societies, while economically backward, manage to avoid being turned into underdeveloped countries. Some become core societies (Russia and Japan) while others develop but remain in a state of dependent development (for example, Brazil and South Korea).

Under empire imperialism core societies tend to turn colonies and dependencies into exporters of food, labor, and raw materials while they diversify and upgrade their economies.

Under world-market imperialism the above pattern persists but core societies also locate factories and offices in developing countries to take advantage of their cheap labor.

The world market has now reached a stage where capital moves easily and quickly to all corners of the First and Third Worlds and increasingly to the Second World.

Nationalism in the West emerged as part of the surge of the middle class to power. Nationalism destroyed feudal particularism and resulted in central government (common currency, taxation, laws, transportation) and large domestic markets. Nationalism outside the West is often part of a liberation movement directed against subservience toward imperialist powers.

In its present development the world market is characterized by geocentric corporations (multinational corporations) that operate in many countries either duplicating products and services or using the globe to rationalize their products and services through a multicountry division of labor. These huge corporations have also begun to undertake joint ventures with each other and to own parts of each other, further concentrating the world economy.

The international system from 1450 to 1950 was marked by acute rivalry among the capitalist countries of the West and the dominance of these countries over most of the world. Since 1950, the *First World* (the developed capitalist societies) have united under American leadership because of challenges from the *Second World* (the developed socialist countries).

The United States's clear dominance between 1945 and 1970 declined for various reasons:

1. Its relative economic position declined as other countries developed.
2. It has had to contend with the problems created by European (and its own) imperialism.
3. Its economic interests are so diversified that it has difficulty fashioning a coherent foreign policy.

There is no one modern society and no one route to modernity. Even the West modernized differently—England and France were modernized by a middle class that bent both the aristocracy and the masses to its values and interests (bourgeois revolution). Germany experienced a *revolution from above*—the aristocracy bent the middle class and the masses to its values and interests (this pattern is found in Japan and is being attempted in much of the Third World). A third pattern is found in partially Westernized Russia and in China—*revolution from below,* or entry into the modern world through the elimination of private property, a radical transformation to socialism based on widespread peasant discontent (made possible by defeat of their authoritarian systems in war). Variations on this pattern may be found in Cuba and Vietnam.

All in all, countries are modernizing in very different ways, and relying on the way in which one's own country modernized is a poor guide to understanding the world one lives in.

PART II The United States: Case Study of a Developed Capitalist Society

CHAPTER

6

THE ECONOMY AND PROFESSIONS

THE AMERICAN ECONOMY

Land and People

The United States has 3 million square miles of land, making it the third largest country in the world. Its natural environment has many positive features: rich soil, abundant rainfall, timber, iron, coal, oil, and other resources. For this and other reasons it has one of the most diversified and self-contained economies in the world. It grows wheat and corn but also cotton and oranges and its manufactured goods range from steel to electronics, from textiles to jetliners. Its unusually rich natural environment provided the American people with the base for spectacular economic growth. By 1986 its gross national product (GNP) was $4.2 trillion yielding a per capita income of $15,368.

The American population grew from about 4 million in 1776 to about 245 million in 1988. Abundant, and thus cheap, labor was an important element in the United States's eco-

nomic growth. Through natural growth, but also through the importation of slaves, 40 million immigrants (who were especially valuable because they were young and healthy and brought considerable capital with them), subjugated peoples (especially Mexican Americans), illegal and legal aliens, and child and female labor, the United States successfully supplied itself with its varied labor force needs.

The Liberal Monopoly

The people of the United States embody a unique amalgam of ingredients from European culture. American leaders defined the identity and destiny of the United States by relying on individualistic natural law, Protestantism, imperial expansion, cheap energy, technological innovation, cheap labor, ad hoc state action, and images of society, including ideas of natural harmony and natural conflict, derived from Newton and Darwin.

American culture is fairly homogeneous having somewhat more pluralism than say the Soviet Union and less than its kindred capitalist societies in Europe. Unlike Europe, where feudal groups fought the introduction of liberal institutions and profoundly influenced them, the United States was established on a relatively pure set of liberal institutions. American elites defined both nature and human nature as abstract forces whose real uses and identities could be established only by private property, freedom, and competition. Abstract equality of opportunity and competition, abstract individualism, and the abstract, absolute right of private property, all derived from an allegedly natural domestic and international exchange economy, were the doctrines that American elites used to establish and consolidate American society.

The Puzzling Economy

The capitalist societies of the West became extremely productive from the early nineteenth century on. From 1850 down through the 1950s they experienced rising standards of living. In this relatively short period, despite depressions and various financial panics, goods and services poured out of capitalist farms, factories, offices, hospitals, and schools. Recently, however, productivity rates have declined and the industrial countries have found it difficult to raise living standards.

The United States is no exception to this pattern. In the 1970s it suffered from stagflation (low growth and high inflation) a condition that violated alleged economic principles. The deep recession of 1981–82 wrung the inflation out of the economy through high unemployment and bankruptcy rates but new problems appeared. Inflation was held in check in good part because of a large volume of cheap imports. In 1985, the United States had a trade deficit of 150 billion dollars (it was buying more from abroad than it was selling) and had become a debtor nation (it owed more to foreigners than they owed it). Between 1980 and 1984, the national debt doubled (and grew 33 percent more by 1986). The reason was the huge budget deficit of

approximately 200 billion dollars for each of those years (the government was spending that much more than its income). And both the trade and budget deficits appeared to be chronic, that is, structural or built into fundamental power relations.

Stumped by stagflation in the 1970s, analysts had new puzzles to worry about by the mid-1980s. The United States appeared unable to raise its productivity despite huge tax supports for capital investment. The American economy was creating new jobs but unemployment was high and over 30 million people were living in poverty (one out of every four children in the country was living in poverty). After some improvement in the 1970s, poverty levels became as high in 1985 as they had been in 1960. The new economy showed up in comparisons of age groups. In 1973, the average 30-year-old earned $23,580—by 1983 the average 30-year-old earned $17,520 (in inflation-controlled dollars). Young people, even with good jobs, found housing in the 1980s far less accessible than their parents had found it. For the first time in American history the upward thrust of the economy had faltered, not from a temporary recession, but from what appeared to be long-term structural factors.[1]

The Crisis in Economics

From the early nineteenth century until 1929, Americans developed a great faith that theirs was an economy based on natural principles. They believed that if left alone (laissez-faire economic theory), an economy inherently seeks equilibrium and brings about the most rational use of human and material resources. This faith was shattered by the Great Depression of the 1930s that left 25 percent of the American labor force unemployed and devastated farmers and business. It also broke the consensus among property owners and professionals about the existence of a natural economy.

---

[1]The apparent stagnation of living standards has enormous implications for American society and forms a main theme of future chapters.

During the 1930s Americans looked to government to help them. Much of what government did was hit-and-miss since government had had no direct experience in managing the economy. Gradually, however, a theory developed by the English economist John Maynard Keynes was adopted. Keynes argued that the economy is not governed by an inherent process of equilibrium. The economy contains no principles that will produce full employment (the full use of material and human resources). Economic groups, especially business firms, but also labor unions, professions, and so on) seek security and control, not competition. Thus the economy as a whole lacks the flexibility (markets) that insures adaptation to new conditions. Overtime, the various elements that make up an economy can become unbalanced and unintegrated, for example, savings do not all go into productive investment, demand can falter and snowball into recession and depression as business cuts back production. Thus, argued Keynes, the government has a continuous and legitimate role to play in directing the economy.

Though never clear on what the government's role is, Keynes suggested that government could keep the economy growing in a balanced manner (full employment with price stability) in three ways: by acting as a consumer itself (government spending for housing or public works, etc), by cutting taxes to give private consumers or producers more money to spend (even if it means a public deficit), and by adjusting interest rates (the price that consumers and producers pay for credit) to either stimulate or slow down consumption and investment.

The two dominant American political parties have both adopted Keynesianism, but they interpret it differently. The Democratic party emphasizes government spending and giving tax cuts to individual consumers to stimulate the economy (demand-side economics) while the Republican party rejects government spending and emphasizes giving tax cuts to business to stimulate economic growth (supply-side economics). However, the United States's experience with a *mixed economy* (a private economy dependent in important ways on government activity) is not overly positive. Democratic administrations have had some success in stimulating the economy by enhancing consumer demand but have been unable to control inflation. The Republican administration of 1980 inaugurated an approach emphasizing tax cuts for producers. Almost all analysts agree that tax cuts for business and well-to-do individuals did not succeed in producing more capital investment and thus economic growth.

The record is clear: capital investment, both public and private has declined since 1977.[2] It continued its decline after the enormous tax cuts of 1981 (favoring the wealthy) because the tax cuts were not targeted to produce productive investment. In 1981, the industrial sector of the American economy (for example, the steel industry) showed evidence of decay and decline, and home construction was far below need levels. Deep tax cuts had been made to stimulate investment but the United States Steel Company, rather than modernize its plants, bought an oil company, Coca Cola bought a movie studio, and Holiday Inn announced a program to build luxury hotels. The improved economy after 1982 was led by consumers (who went heavily into debt), by cheap imports (which led to trade deficits and debt to foreigners), and by government deficits—that is, the present American economy is being buoyed by debt.

A major reason for the United States's inability to guide its economy is that economics has failed to provide a reliable picture of economic behavior. Economists cannot provide even gross predictions about the economy's general direction let alone how fast or how slowly it will move. Actually, economists are no better at forecasting economic behavior than noneconomists. The reasons for their failure are: the use of false analogies with nature, especially the concept of equilibrium, an excessive use of deductive reasoning, especially mathematics, and the distortion of

---

[2]Congressional Budget Office, Congress of the United States, "Trends in Public Investment" (Washington, D.C.: December, 1987).

facts through inappropriate abstractions.[3] From being the preeminent social science over the past century, economics is now in crisis.

Clearly something is amiss with both the American economy and our thinking about it. The situation is serious enough to warrant a deep look at our fundamental beliefs about how an economy works. The best way to bring our economic thinking into creative focus is to put economic institutions into comparative perspective.

Comparative Economic Systems: Use and Exchange Economies

Economic systems are quite diverse and not easy to compare. The purpose of comparison is to understand and evaluate, and the latter requires subjective value judgments. It is not enough, therefore, to say that a given society is more productive than another—the other society may be striving for full employment (which so far has been associated with inefficiency). In comparing economic systems (or anything else), therefore, it is best to state the criteria that will be used.

Historically the most important distinction among economic systems is between use and exchange economies. *Use* economies do not produce for profit nor are they characterized by investment in productive facilities (capital formation). Use economies tend to produce for direct consumption and are characteristic of hunting-gathering, horticultural, and agrarian societies. An *exchange* economy (also called a market, free enterprise, or price economy) is characteristic of commercial and industrial capitalist societies. Under a capitalist (exchange) economy, the bulk of productive property (land, animals, factories, offices, and so on) is in private hands. Producers sell their products and services and derive income (profit) directly from the use of their property. Under capitalism, work is

performed by legally free individuals who sell their labor time and skills. In the classic capitalist tradition (entrepreneurial capitalism), it is assumed that economic units are small and competitive and that the free exchange of goods, services, and labor is the most rational way to allocate resources and promote economic growth.

The basic assumption of capitalism is that the best economy and society will result if people are allowed to pursue their economic interests under conditions of freedom and competition. The pursuit of self-interest is not new—what is new is capitalism's assertion that *all* should pursue their self-interests and that this pursuit is compatible with equality, justice, stability, social integration, and material progress.

In the modern world, socialists and socialist societies reject the assumptions on which capitalism is based. Since both capitalist and socialist societies have track records, the next task is to compare their performance.

Comparative Economic Systems: Capitalist and Socialist Economies

Theory aside, capitalist and socialist systems are actual historical systems and can be analyzed empirically. In both cases, the reality is quite different from theories about them. In making comparisons one should be explicit about criteria and analytical terms. But the first step is to be wary of separating economies from their sociopolitical, historical, and global contexts and relying on inappropriate abstractions. After that one can ask the following questions:[4]

1. How are economic decisions made and by whom?
2. How is the economy coordinated?
3. What is the nature of the property system?
4. How is the general labor force motivated?

---

[3]For a succinct analysis, see Melville J. Ulmer, "Economics in Decline", *Commentary* 78 (November, 1984): 42–6. For an earlier discussion of how all social scientists are fond of using images from nature to think about human behavior, see Box 1-2. For a discussion of other professions, see below.

[4]The following questions are derived from Paul R. Gregory and Robert C. Stuart, *Comparative Economic Systems*, 3rd ed. (Boston: Houghton Mifflin, 1989), Chapter 1. However our answers, though informed by these authors, are somewhat different.

Despite the ideals of pure market or entrepreneurial capitalism (small economic units engaged in fair competition to yield a rational allocation of resources), the trend has been in the opposite direction, toward a corporate capitalism in which most sectors of the economy are dominated by large corporations. Thus the first thing to know about capitalist societies is that they have highly concentrated economies (that is, ownership is in the hands of a few). Thus basic decisions about capital investment are made by a small number of individuals and organizations, mostly private but also public. Decisions about ongoing economic activities rely on feedback from markets (markets heavily managed in various ways), and from governments, voluntary organizations, and churches (professional associations and labor unions are part of labor markets). Coordination of the economy is largely by government (the Keynesian-intervention state that monitors the economy and seeks to promote growth and control inflation through various means: overall guidelines, taxes, interest rates, subsidies, spending). Private groups (e.g., chambers of commerce, associations of manufacturers) also monitor the economy and let their wishes be known. Government intervention also occurs to help weak economic units or sectors, protect the environment, defend the country, and incorporate minorities into the mainstream. The general labor force is motivated by material incentives, moral imperatives (the Protestant-bourgeois ethic), insecurity, and fear (of failure, poverty, unemployment).

Capitalist societies vary among themselves. Countries like Canada, Great Britain, France, and the Federal Republic of (West) Germany have public ownership of many basic industries and services while the United States has little in the way of public ownership. The developed capitalist societies outside the United States have national health insurance (socialized in the case of Great Britain) while the United States relies heavily on private health systems, and the European capitalist societies have governments that extract a much larger percentage of the gross national product than either the United States or Japan to support extensive social services. Nonetheless the United States has an active government that intervenes in the economy and also has a welfare state.

Socialist societies also have highly concentrated economies, with ownership completely public in some societies and a mixture of public and private in others. Capital investment, decisions about consumption, and overall coordination are made by explicit public authorities in terms of a written plan (in the case of planned socialism such as the U.S.S.R.) or by a combination of national plan and reliance on markets (Hungary). A further distinction among socialist economies is the market socialism of Yugoslavia where considerable economic decision making occurs through worker councils who own factories and must respond to market conditions.

Evaluating economic outcomes is difficult because societies face unique circumstances. Economists agree that no one criteria should be used and that ultimately subjective value judgments must be relied on. Economies can be judged by:

1. gross national product and per capita income.
2. income distribution.
3. standard of living.
4. capital investment and growth rates
5. efficiency (productivity).

Comparative economists also agree that exact comparisons among economies, especially capitalist and socialist economies, cannot be made, and that there are no clear superiorities among the various systems (not even when two societies that are similar in most respects, capitalist West and socialist East Germany, are compared).[5]

Finally, we must recognize that we do not have more than a rudimentary grasp of how economies work or even what makes people

---

[5]Paul R. Gregory and Robert C. Stuart, *Comparative Economic Systems*, 3rd ed. (Houghton Mifflin, 1989) and Andrew Zimbalist, Howard J. Sherman, and Stuart Brown, *Comparing Economic Systems: A Political-Economic Approach*, 2nd ed. (San Diego: Harcourt Brace Javanovich, 1989).

work. Much more is needed along the lines of deep culture analysis, the investigation of how the deepest, often unstated values and beliefs of a culture affect behavior.[6] Clearly there is much hard work and deep thinking that must be done to understand the mainspring of modern society, its economy.

The Sociocultural Nature of Economic Behavior

Early capitalist theorists such as John Locke, Thomas Malthus, Adam Smith, and Herbert Spencer all assumed that the basic economic unit is the individual human being. The individual, they argued, is characterized by concrete, self-evident drives, needs, and skills (see Box 6-1, Rescuing the World from Robinson Crusoe Economics). Many theorists also assumed that individuals were rational, and that the sum of individual actions would lead to a rational economy. Using models from nature, especially Newtonian mechanics, theorists said a natural economy worked like a machine in perpetual equilibrium. The master idea that eventually emerged was that something called *markets* (transactions among individuals in given areas using an agreed-upon unit of exchange) would balance out the supply and demand of raw materials, labor, money, goods, and services. The role of other institutions, said early classical economists, is to allow this naturally self-balancing system to work.

Since the early days of classic capitalist theory, economists, sociologists, political scientists, and anthropologists have struggled to overcome these assumptions. Some have recognized that the self-interested, rational individual and self-equilibrating markets were

cultural fictions that emerged during the early stages of capitalism to help thinkers make sense of and feel at home in the novel and uncertain world of an expanding capitalist economy. And most social scientists have discarded the theory of human nature on which early capitalism was based. Human beings are not driven by instincts of hunger and gain. And they are no more driven by self-interest than by altruism, and no more oriented toward work and success than the opposite. The human being that early economists talked about is, like Robinson Crusoe, already a highly socialized being complete with acquired motives, expectations, interests, and skills. The individual's personality reflects the general socioeconomic level of his or her society. The fiction of the rational individual who pursues self-evident economic values has given way. Humans must learn how and what to eat, when and how to work, what to need, and what to value.

The sociocultural perspective has redefined other aspects of the economy. Nature is not a ready-made entity waiting to be utilized by ready-made individuals. Familiar aspects of nature such as land, water, animals, and timber do not exist as economic values until they have been culturally defined. Serfdom, slavery, "free" labor, ambition, strikes, greed, profit, slow-downs, property, money, contract, work-to-rule, and absenteeism do not exist in human nature—all must be created and institutionalized by given sociocultural systems. No conception of human nature, therefore, can explain the sharp variations in economic behavior in history or the spectacular economic growth in the West in the past few centuries. Far from being self-evident and natural, economic behavior is culturally directed and thus open to choice. How and why humans pursue economic values depends on religious and family values, on tax codes and military expenditures—it is neither a matter of obeying technical economic laws nor a matter of obeying principles laid down by nature.

There is no better example of the role of culture in economic behavior than the contrast between the way in which the native Indian inhabitants of North America utilized

---

[6]For an invaluable analysis of a survey of employees in 40 developed and developing countries representative of each country's middle class (and a compilation of all existing related studies), see Geert Hofstede, *Culture's Consequences: International Differences in Work-Related Values* (Beverly Hills, Calif.: Sage, 1980). Hofstede's findings are that the organization of work (the behavior of people in an organization and organizations as a whole) and the theories about work and management, including advice about management, are all relative to specific cultures.

BOX 6-1. Rescuing the world from Robinson Crusoe economics

Daniel Defoe's story of a shipwrecked sailor, *Robinson Crusoe* (1719), became a runaway best seller and an enduring part of popular culture. Crusoe's adventures on a remote island and his success in building a comfortable way of life had, and still has, a broad appeal. Beneath the surface of the adventure lay a world view and a hero that the rising middle class could identify with. Crusoe represented a hero new to Western literature. Unlike the aristocratic heroes of agrarian feudalism, Crusoe did no battle with other heroes or with supernatural forces. Crusoe did not serve lofty ideals or save his community from the forces of evil. Crusoe fought his battles against nature and loneliness. He is the entrepreneur as hero, the literary culmination of the individualism implicit in the invention of the horse harness (see Box 4-1, Technology and the Rise of Capitalism). Defoe's theme is clear: the individual who does not succumb to panic and is willing to work and improvise cannot only survive but can be the master of nature. The individual *does* count and must therefore be included in any thinking about the fundamental units of social organization.

In a sense, it is not much of a jump from Robinson Crusoe economics to Adam Smith's *The Wealth of Nations* (1776). But unfortunately, an individualist, market economics cannot be based on Robinson Crusoe, certainly not on the notion that Crusoe succeeded as a (natural) individual and that he can serve as a model for the organization of the economy and society. Crusoe arrived on his deserted island carrying in his nervous system (personality) the skills and motives of the world's most developed country (England). He also had a large chest of tools and considerable supplies such as lumber, rope, and pulleys that he salvaged from his ship. Without this personality and without these tools and supplies, he could never have succeeded as he did in creating a comfortable life on his island home.

Crusoe's personality also contained a developed self and an individualist religion (Protestantism), which held him in good stead in his struggle with loneliness, insecurity, and panic. But even these considerable cultural assets were not enough—Defoe also provides Crusoe with an all-purpose friend-companion, servant, laborer, and ward (Friday).

Robinson Crusoe economics had some validity in Defoe's day. Economic life was characterized by small economic units and the individual was a relevant economic actor. But its relevance declined rapidly during the nineteenth century with the rise of corporate capitalism. But Robinson Crusoe economics struck deep roots among the middle class and economists, becoming part of the mores and a major reason for our inability to think clearly about our economy.

---

the natural environment and the way it was utilized by early Europeans. For over ten thousand years the North American Indian made use of the natural environment in a static hunting and gathering economy (often augmented by fishing and horticulture). Europeans with the same natural environment developed first a systematic exploitation of timber, fish, and fur resources and then, in the relatively short expanse of two or three centuries, developed an economy that could actively identify, extract, use, and transform a host of natural resources (coal, minerals, oil). In the process, European settlers created a material standard of living that would have been incomprehensible to the original inhabitants of North America. The central variable that explains this difference is the complex sociocultural system of Europe (its imperial appetites, luxury economy, mathematics, missionary zeal, apprentice system, technology, individualism, and so on) that European settlers brought with them to the New World.

The reasons for the United States's successful industrialization include a uniquely favorable natural environment—good climate and soil, abundant rainfall (that produced huge food and staple surpluses for export), navigable rivers, and abundant resources, especially the sinews of early industrialism, coal and iron, in close proximity. Also important in American economic history is an abundant supply of cheap labor, especially imported slaves, 40 million immigrants, subjugated people (especially Mexican-Americans), illegal and legal aliens, and, of course, women and children. The export of food and staples and the import of cheap labor allowed the American colonies, and later the United States, to import European, especially English, technology, another important factor in the successful industrialization of American society.

Government policies also furthered economic expansion. The federal government established land grant programs to settle the West and paid for the canals, railroads, and highways that made it possible for people to get there and send their products back East. Schools provided the literacy, the manual and mental skills, and the character traits needed by an expanding economy. Beyond government, the Protestant religion helped supply the individualist character and explanation that a capitalist economy needed. Even sports played a role in the development and maintenance of a capitalist economy and society. Sports values and norms are explicitly designed to identify a small elite of superior individuals, which, of course, is what the economy, the professions, the polity, and education are alleged to do. As in society at large the rewards of sports are high and unevenly distributed. The big rewards go to the owners of the teams, television networks, sports executives, announcers, advertising firms, auxiliary suppliers, and a few thousand athletes while millions of youngsters labor in vain and tens of thousands more provide modestly paid support services.

Of all the distortions of how our economy and society work, perhaps none is as damaging as sports. Sports are played according to detailed rules and competition is carefully refereed. Sports highlight the efforts of individuals and present a clear hierarchy of scores, records, winners and losers. But are sports a good way to think about the capitalist economy? In sports only teams that are relatively equal ("in the same league") are allowed to play (in professional football, the last place team is given first choice of the talent emerging from college football). The players in the economy and professions are quite different. Most sectors of the American economy are marked by unequal competition, as winners consolidate and extend their advantage by monopolistic pricing, buying out competitors, and by buying the best talent from other companies or from elite business, engineering, law, and other schools. The laws designed to regulate the activities of businesses and professions (for example, anti-trust, environmental, and consumer protection laws) are not strictly enforced, sometimes not enforced at all. In short, sports is not a good model to use when thinking about the economy, professions, or society-at-large.

THE AMERICAN ECONOMY: BASIC STRUCTURAL FEATURES

The Nature of Capital (Productive Property)

The concept *capital* refers to anything that is used for economic production. Capital includes tools, land, animals, buildings, and patents as well as human labor (human energy, skills, knowledge, and motives as embodied in serfs, slaves, legally free labor, crafts persons, and professionals). The economic meaning of most forms of capital are easy to understand: bow and arrow, hoe, plow, herd of sheep, watermil¹, lathe, dock, grazing meadow, timberland, airport. Less easy to understand, but important to know, is that socially generated human energy, skills, knowledge, and motives are also part of the productive process.

Economic Groups

Economic activity is not conducted by abstract capital or abstract individuals. The reality of economic behavior is *the group organized for economic action*. Profit-oriented groups, especially corporations, dominate the American economy. A corporation is a legal entity, administered bureaucratically, that allows large numbers of people to pool their resources and thus engage in a scale of economic behavior they could not do as solitary individuals. The result is a responsive chain of command that allows the owners or controllers of the corporation to amass and focus large amounts of capital to produce desired outcomes. The responsibilities and liabilities of corporations are spelled out in legal norms— a key provision protects the owners' other property in case the corporation fails (law of bankruptcy). In addition, the corporation enjoys legal immortality and continues even though individual owners change hands or die.

Though the corporation is the dominant economic group, the economy has other groups: partnerships, family businesses and farms, labor unions, cooperatives, and professional and trade associations. Numerous other groups also have a large economic impact even though they are not always thought of as being economically relevant: sports clubs, hospitals, schools, newspapers, publishing firms, broadcasting companies, the military, prisons, and other governmental bodies.

Economic Concentration

The most striking feature of the American economy is the pronounced cleavage between dominant and weaker groups: a small number of corporations dominate all sectors of the economy and a small number of groups dominate economically related activities (professional associations, elite hospitals, universities, law firms, newspapers, and so on).

The size of dominant American corporations defies comprehension. A United States Senate study reports that the 122 largest corporations from all sectors of the United States economy had 41 percent of the market value of all outstanding common stock in 1976.[7] The same study found that voting rights in large American corporations are concentrated among a relatively few firms.[8] A recent United States Senate study of 100 large corporations across the top of the business spectrum (banking and insurance, automotive industry, energy, telecommunication and information processing, office equipment, retailing, twelve industry leaders) also found extensive economic concentration. The United States's largest companies each have concentrated ownerships and extensive participation in each other's governing boards (interlocking directorships).[9]

Control Mechanisms

The centralized capitalist economy is coordinated and controlled through a number of intercorporate mechanisms. These are:

1. The ownership by one corporation of part of another corporation. Significant voting power can come from as little as 5 percent ownership, and control is assured usually at 10 percent.

2. Interlocking directorates among corporations. Coordination and control are assured when the same people serve on the governing boards of various corporations. When interlocked corporations are in the same field, the threat to competi-

---

[7]U.S. Senate Committee on Governmental Affairs, *Voting Rights in Major Corporations*, (Washington, D.C.: U.S. Government Printing Office, 1978), p. 1; derived from *Forbes*, May 15, 1977.

[8]*Ibid*, p. 1.

[9]U.S. Senate Committee on Governmental Affairs, *Structure of Corporate Concentration: Institutional Shareholders and Interlocking Directorates Among Major U.S. Corporations* (Washington, D.C.: U.S. Government Printing Office, 1980).

tion is much higher. The span of control through interlocking directorates extends far and wide to link business corporations with hospitals, universities, foundations, and charitable organizations.

3. Debtholding. A creditor can exert considerable influence over debtors, allowing banks, for example, to control and coordinate the policies of a wide assortment of companies.

4. Specific product or service associations (such as the American Banking Association), wider associations (such as the American Manufacturers Association), or entities that represent the entire area of business (such as the American Chamber of Commerce).

Other control mechanisms are price fixing, patent control, and coordination through legal, management, personnel, consulting, and advertising services. In addition, interfamily marriages, along with friendships established at home and at school and maintained through common club membership and socializing are important links among property groups. There are also reciprocal supports between the corporate world, on the one hand, and voluntary organizations, universities, research foundations, and government on the other. Some of the most powerful concentrations in the American economy stem from a virtual merger of business and government, for example, the Federal Reserve System and banking; the Department of Agriculture and farmers; the Department of Labor and labor.

Clearly, the American economy diverges from our ideals about it. The American economy is characterized neither by individual nor group competition. Most of it is not subject to the play of market forces. The term *equal opportunity* does not fit it, and terms like *merit* and *achievement* probably obscure more than they reveal. Perhaps the best overall characterization of the American economy is high concentration in almost all sectors (including the professions, for which see below) with considerable cooperation and support from other institutions. The dominant groups of American society make up a unique structure of power. Some have even gone so far as to call the economy monolithic but this idea should probably be resisted (see Box 6-2, Is There a Monolith Called Business?).

The Shift to a Service Economy

Manufacturing pushed farming aside during the nineteenth and early twentieth century only to see the rise to prominence of the service sector. Services now make up a dominant portion of the gross national product and approximately 70 percent of the labor force is engaged in providing them. The economy's shift to services has caused many dislocations and requires a big change in how we think of American capitalism. The decline of manufacturing in some basic industries such as automobiles, steel, and textiles (during the 1970s and early 1980s) is a continuing source of misery for the American Mid-western and East-central states. The rise of new occupations has put pressure on educational institutions to offer new programs and reorganize old ones. Changes in the nature of work mean that American youth must develop skills and have aspirations that are vastly different from those of their parents.

The service sector has overshadowed the rest of the economy, but what exactly is it? Doctors and lawyers are certainly part of it. So are physicists and chemists, professors, economists, and public policy analysts. The service economy includes large numbers of service professionals who are better thought of as skilled workers rather than professionals: nurses, school teachers, computer programmers, police officers, and so on. And it includes semiskilled clerical workers and salespeople, professional athletes, religious workers, prostitutes, criminals, advertising personnel, financial specialists, and entertainers.

The Advent of Postindustrial Society?

Some have referred to the shift to a service economy as the decline of a property-based economy and the emergence of a postindustrial society (also referred to as a high information society). Some theorists say a managerial revolution has occurred in which educated managers have replaced property owning entrepreneurs as the central force in capitalism. The basic image proposed by postindustrial

BOX 6-2. Is there a monolith called business?

The United States is characterized by an oligarchic economy, but it cannot be conceived of in the same terms used to understand agrarian oligarchies. A feudal elite is relatively undifferentiated. Most of the elite is made up of hereditary landlords though there is some differentiation—there are large landlords and smaller landlords and some of the nobility specialize in government or military service, others in religion or scholarship. On the whole, however, a serf or slave faces a monolithic entity called the nobility.

Power in an industrial society is different. Aside from abstract capitalist values and beliefs there is no all-embracing business interest that unites small manufacturers and big manufacturers, small banks and big banks, or small anything versus big anything. The economy also has divergent interest groups within big manufacturing, for example, steel, aluminum, plastics, glass, and lumber all compete for the same customer. The same is true of big service industries, for example, railroads, airlines, and truckers. Small farmers do not have the same interests as the large agribusinesses. Established firms, big or little, are threatened by the emergence of firms riding the crest of new technology, for exam-

ple, the "free" television networks versus cable, direct satellite television, or home videotape machines. And some businesses fear foreign competition and want protection, and some do not, for example, textile, automobile, and steel manufacturers versus the manufacturers of medical technology and airplanes.

Just as there is no business or farm bloc, there is no labor bloc aside from broad groupings with broad interests. Some labor is committed to technological innovation while other labor fights it. Labor solidarity among different occupations is weak. Some occupational groups, such as doctors and lawyers, have more in common with business interests than with other workers, including their own nurses, aides, technicians, and secretaries.

All in all, the economic and professional groups of capitalist society are not united or homogeneous. It is a dynamic oligarchy in which economic loyalties and interests are not easy to establish or maintain. Though the "haves" have common interests vis a vis the "have nots," they appear to spend as much time fighting among themselves as asserting their interests over the bottom reaches of the economy.

---

theorists is a knowledge-based, bureaucratically administered society presided over by highly educated managers and professionals. But this image is faulty. Far from becoming a knowledge-based economy, corporate capitalism gives every indication of separating the American people into a small number of highly skilled and a huge mass of low-skilled workers. The facts about the American labor force are clear—highly educated professionals still make up only a small percentage of the American labor force and there is no indication that its relative size is grow-

ing. It is a mistake, therefore, to think of the service-centered economy as one characterized by reduced drudgery and the growth of challenging mental work. And it is certainly premature to think that the United States is under the direction of educated elites who know what they are doing or where they are headed.

The idea of a postindustrial society shares a basic kinship with functionalist stratification theory and is also an aspect of the liberal ideology of convergence: the belief that society is leaving behind the period of ascription, property, factory work, and centralized power and entering an era of achievement, administration, "strategic" elites, and a pluralist power structure.

The best known version of the postindustrial society is Daniel Bell's.[10] We are witnessing, Bell claims, a shift to a knowledge-centered economy, which is in turn creating unique problems for society to solve. The ultimate shape of the new society cannot be predicted because each industrial country (the United States, Germany, the Soviet Union, and Japan) will handle its problems in terms of its own traditions and political institutions). Essentially, Bell is arguing that the economic system needs political direction: indeed, that the shift from an economy-centered to a politically-centered society has already occurred and is a key aspect of the postindustrial age.

Bell's argument is also framed in terms of the decline of industrial workers relative to service workers, which is the equivalent of the growth of theoretical knowledge as the "axial" principle of society. The empirical support for Bell's views is derived from census data on the changing composition of the labor force. In 1947 goods-producing jobs accounted for 51 percent of the total; in 1968, 35.9 percent; and in 1980 such jobs will account for only 31.7 percent of the total. The service-producing totals for the same years are 49, 64.1, 68.4 percent respectively. Accordingly, argues Bell, "If industrial society is defined as a goods-producing society—if manufacture is central in shaping the character of its labor force—then the United States is no longer an industrial society."[11] Bell acknowledges that service work is not always white collar work, including as it does transport workers and automobile mechanics and that much of it consists of minor clerical and sales jobs. But, he argues, the male labor force has also been transformed in the direction of white collar work. Whereas in 1900 only 15 percent of American men (mostly independent small businessmen) wore white collars,

in 1970 almost 42 percent of the male labor force held white collar jobs. Of these almost 60 percent were managerial, professional, or technical workers, "the heart of the upper middle class." Blue collar workers were 35 percent of the total labor force in 1900, 40 percent in 1920 and 1950, 36 percent in 1968, and will be only 32.7 percent in 1980).[12]

Bell's reference to managerial, professional, and technical workers as the heart of the American upper-middle class is both correct and misleading. While these workers include the upper-middle class, a very large percentage of these categories is composed of teachers, nurses, dental assistants, entertainers, and the like. But even if we focus exclusively on the upper-middle class, it is not easy to depict it as signifying a break with the fundamental values and beliefs of capitalism. One has only to list some of its members—doctors, lawyers, engineers, business executives, scientists, college professors—to realize that it is anything but revolutionary.

Bell is mistaken in many of his assumptions. It is far from certain that property is divorced from management, that the property owners have lost control of their property, or that there is any significant tension between property owners and those who manage their property. Secondly, it cannot be said that the economy is declining vis a vis the state, but only that we are now more aware of the role of the state and the shortcomings of the economy. The economy and state have always served each other, and the former has always been the obvious pacesetter and beneficiary. Also, Bell implies that theoretical knowledge (a new intellectual technology) has emerged but he fails to cite any empirical evidence suggesting a consequent or eventual transformation of society. All in all, the new white collar occupations appear to be firmly embedded in bureaucracies oriented toward private property and a market economy and society.

Bell's prophecy that a postindustrial society is upon us appears to be another variation

---

[10]*The Coming of Post-Industrial Society* (New York: Basic Books, 1973).

[11]*Ibid.*, pp. 132–33.

[12]*Ibid.*, pp. 134–35.

on the technocratic theme in liberalism, which has its sources in the views of Condorcet, Saint Simon, and Comte. To his credit, Bell avoids the easy optimism of early liberalism. Instead, he stresses the inchoate nature of social change and is willing to predict only that the future will pose unique problems to tax humanity's political and moral capabilities. Despite his caution, however, Bell endorses many liberal myths: he believes that equality of opportunity is a feasible ideal; that meritocracy (rule by a trained, natural elite) is possible and is at odds with substantive equality; that prosperity has reduced inequality; and that the power of bureaucracies has been curtailed by committees and the popular demand for participation. These beliefs supplement his overriding belief that property and management have been divorced and that knowledge (embodied in upper middle class managers and professionals) has replaced property and economic entrepreneurialism as the "axial" principle of society.

In sum, the best interpretation of the growth of white collar occupations has been undertaken outside the liberal tradition. Though many questions are still unsettled, it seems best to think of the growth of white collar occupations as a change *within* industrial (liberal) society. The classic analysis along these lines remains C. Wright Mills'.[13] Leaving aside many of Mills's tendentious conclusions, the basic thrust of his argument is sound. The new service or white collar or professional occupations represent a change *within* the middle class. Far from transcending class or industrial society, the new occupations are firmly embedded in economic, political, and social structures based on private property, managed markets, upper-level coordination, and bureaucratic administration. That significant portions of the new middle class are propertyless does not dilute their commit-

---

[13]Mills's theory is presented in what should be viewed as two volumes in a single study, *White Collar: The American Middle Classes* (New York: Oxford University Press, 1951) and *Power Elite* (New York: Oxford University Press, 1956).

ment (unconscious as well as conscious) to a property-oriented market society.

PROFESSIONS AND OCCUPATIONS

The American Occupational Structure

Initially, industrialization transforms a labor force away from *primary* occupations (agriculture, fishing, lumbering) and toward *secondary* occupations (manufacturing, mining, processing). Mature industrialization produces a further decline of primary occupations, a stabilization of secondary occupations, and a large growth in *tertiary* occupations (services, white collar work, professions, semiprofessions). The trend toward service occupations is clear in all industrial countries.

Significantly, the American labor force is made up mostly of employees who work for bureaucratically organized corporations, schools, hospitals, voluntary organizations, churches, and governments. Americans no longer work for themselves and no longer work directly with or against nature. The intimate meshing of character, property, work, family, religion, and local community that was characteristic of rural, small-town America (entrepreneurial capitalism) has long disappeared. The contemporary economy separates the labor force from property ownership, family, and residential, religious, and political values and groups.

The United States makes little effort to manage its labor force. It tolerates considerable unemployment, on the average, more than other industrial countries. Some of its labor force is carefully trained but most worker-skill levels emerge haphazardly. Efforts to match the *quality* of man- and womanpower to the economy have failed totally. In the early 1980s, for example, as unemployment reached 10.5 percent, there were shortages of many types of skilled workers and professionals. There are other mismatches between the economy and the labor force. There appears to be a growing dissatisfaction with work, especially among young workers, including the educated. And, ominously, for young workers and today's college students the economy appears no longer capable of generating large numbers of middle-level jobs— most new jobs appear to be low skilled and low paid.

The main reason for all these mismatches and the failure to develop overall employment-labor policies is America's deeply ingrained laissez-faire tradition and fierce resistance to economic planning by almost all professions and economic elites. Accordingly, the American labor force is characterized by chronic oversupply especially at the lower levels. Among the professions and some skilled workers there is considerable control over jobs (with a pronounced tendency to keep both good jobs and qualified people artificially scarce). The overall picture for the rest of the labor force is too many people chasing too few jobs.

The Professions

The hallmarks of a profession are a high knowledge base, lofty service standards, control over entrance qualifications, control over the jurisdiction of the occupation, high income and prestige, and high-quality service to the well-to-do with relative indifference to the needs of the general public. In the modern world, the professions are connected to a dynamic science that spews forth a steady stream of knowledge and technology, indeed some important professions are sciences themselves. Given the power of science, professionalism has begun to permeate all sectors of society.[14]

Given the rapid growth of knowledge, the professions are also characterized by tension. There is tension between the scientific and the prescientific professions (science is seen as a threat by some clergy, some philosophers, some humanistic scholars). There is tension among the professions themselves as they quarrel over new and old knowledge, and over professional jurisdictions. There is

tension between the professions and other economic elites as they quarrel over cost and performance (for example, economic elites have become concerned over the exploding costs of the health care industry and professions). There is tension between professionals and their customers as a better educated citizenry has demanded more control over services rendered. Many of these tensions can be summarized as the tension (not always recognized) between the professional ideology of value neutrality in the name of objectivity and the inescapable fact that everything the professions do has value consequences.

The professions are legal monopolies, which means that they have succeeded in persuading the state to turn their skills and knowledge into private property.[15] An essential link in this process is the profession of higher education. Organized as a college or university, the academic profession is sanctioned by the state as a private or autonomous public "corporation" with the right to decide on the qualifications for entry into the other prized professions. The professions are also characterized by formalism (loss of touch with reality). In recent years considerable criticism has appeared about problem-solving elites, and they appear to have suffered a declining legitimacy.

The Semiprofessions

Beneath the professions is a sizeable contingent of semiprofessions: teachers, librarians, social workers, nurses, technicians, personnel officers, firefighters, police officers, and so on. Members of the semiprofessions behave toward their occupations in the same way as the incumbents of higher-level occupations. Turning an occupation into a profession requires control over entry and the semiprofessions have sought to limit their numbers by emphasizing quality through education and professional

[14]For information along these lines, see Helena Z. Lopata, "Expertization of Everyone and the Revolt of the Client," *Sociological Quarterly* 19 (Autumn, 1976): 435–47.

[15]Carolyn J. Touhy, "Private Government, Property, and Professionalism," *Canadian Journal of Political Science* 9 (December, 1976): 668–81.

training. As in the professions, *there is no discernible relation between the amount and type of education and occupational performance.*[16] Unlike the professions, however, the semiprofessions have had only limited success in gaining control over their respective occupations.

The semiprofessions coordinate and control their interests as best they can through "professional" associations and "professional" journals. They work hard to achieve legal control over entry into their occupations. They seek certification and licensing by the state and endorse civil service examinations for entry to and promotion in public service positions. The semiprofessions have also resorted to unionization. White collar unions have been the most dynamic force in the trade union movement since World War II. The semiprofessions resist absorption into blue collar unions, though some are organized by the more traditional trade union organizations, for example, teachers have been organized by the American Federation of Teachers, which is affiliated with the C.I.O./A.F.L.

The economic autonomy of the semiprofessions is compromised by their inability to establish high-level educational credentials for entry and by the fact that many of them work for local, state, and federal governments and often do not have the right to strike. Many of the semiprofessions are made up mostly of women (for example, teachers, nurses, social workers, and librarians) and this may have hampered solidarity and militancy. Subordination to the professionals above them and by the bureaucratic context in which they work may also have undermined the power of semiprofessionals.

The General Labor Force

The most significant fact about the American labor force (except for the professions and a small portion protected by trade unions) is that it is always (save during wartime) in oversupply. The lack of economic planning, along with immigration, illegal aliens, restrictive labor practices among the professions, semiprofessions, and skilled workers, and economic pressures that induce the young, women, and some of the old to join the labor force, all insure a chronic oversupply of workers. The most important point to make about the American economy, therefore, is that it rests on a very sandy foundation—the one-third or more of its labor force that is permanently unemployed, temporarily unemployed, underemployed, or poorly paid and insecure. Less than 20 percent of the American labor force is organized as trade unions and the percentage is declining. Many workers in trade unions are poorly paid (for example, hospital workers) while some are highly paid (especially the unionized workers of the great oligarchic industrial corporations—which until recently had assured markets and could therefore buy labor peace and cooperation with high wage and fringe benefits).

The history of America's industrial labor-management relations is filled with violence and conflict. A relative peace occurred (strikes rather than violence) after the Wagner Act of 1935 legalized collective bargaining. One of the serious institutional inadequacies in the United States is the absence of a comprehensive labor relations law. While the federal government is acknowledged to have general jurisdiction over the economy (and can influence it in regard to taxation and monetary policy, labor power policies, and immigration), it has no acknowledged authority over labor as such. State governments exert great influence over their labor forces, especially through boards that control entry into the professions and skilled labor. There can be little doubt that the ability of both the economic and the political spheres to perform their functions is seriously impaired by the lack of a workable national labor code.

The general working class of the United States is not politically conscious or active. The middle- and upper-classes have hammered into the national consciousness a pervasive individualistic ethos. Schools, churches, the mass media, voluntary organizations, government, and the law have all supported the

---

[16]For a fuller discussion, see Chapter 8.

entrepreneurial ethic. For most of American history economic elites fiercely resisted all measures to improve the lot of workers, including the legalization of labor unions and elementary man and womanpower planning. The basic structure of power in the United States creates an oversupply of labor at the lower levels,[17] not least by creating an artificial scarcity of labor at the top.

The abstract right of property owners and professionals to use their property for profit affects American workers adversely. Elites are free to send capital to other parts of the country or abroad, leaving communities stranded. The bias toward technology (supported by the tax code and government research and development funds) is a constant source of labor insecurity and labor market softness. Chronic poverty and near poverty along with underfunded social service programs force many into the labor market. Ineffective measures to prevent illegal immigration also work to depress some labor markets. The flood of aliens could not be stemmed as long as those who employed them were not held legally responsible (whether the new Immigration Law of 1987, which does hold employers responsible, will have much effect remains to be seen). All of the above has created a large and relatively chronic supply of depressed labor. The structure of power outlined above has also produced another feature of depressed labor—it is disproportionately composed of minorities.[18]

---

[17]The official unemployment rate (like any scientific statement) is based on assumptions about what facts count. It undercounts the unemployed because it omits the millions who have given up looking for work and includes anyone who worked as little as one hour in the survey week as employed. The unemployment rate of the 1980s would also be appreciably higher if adjusted for age—the declining numbers of young people make the rate appear lower than previous periods.

[18]For two arguments that depressed minorities are integral parts of the capitalist economy, see Edna Bonacich, "Advanced Capitalism and Black/White Race Relations in the United States: A Split Labor Market Interpretation," *American Sociological Review* 41 (February, 1976): 34–51, and Albert Szymanski, "Racism and Sexism as Functional Substitutes in the Labor Market," *Sociological Quarterly* 17 (Winter, 1976).

AMERICAN URBANIZATION IN A COMPARATIVE CONTEXT

Comparative Urbanization

The emergence of cities was a profoundly important event for the human race. Human beings wandered the earth as hunter-gatherers for hundreds of thousands of years before there were cities. Settlements appeared with horticultural society but a city way of life appeared only with the agricultural revolution, that supremely important transformation of human social life. The development of agriculture (or the ability to cultivate large fields through the use of new technology and a serf-slave labor force) yielded a considerable surplus of food. Freed from the need to grow their own food, people grouped in villages that grew in size. Above all, village dwellers expanded their activities. Their increased leisure led to new occupations and to creativity in many new fields: metal working, astronomy, commerce, and so on. The expansion of specialized activities led to more intense and varied forms of social interaction. Thus emerged the *city:* a social setting in which a large and varied population, freed from the endless drudgery of having to produce its own food, can create new technology and symbols and engage in more intense and varied social relations than villagers and nomads.

The first cities emerged in the fertile river valleys and deltas of the Tigris-Euphrates, Nile, Indus, and Yellow rivers. Above all, the city results from plentiful water. The earliest cities flourished between 5,000 and 3,000 years ago and then declined. Cities rose again in Greece and Rome about 2,500 years ago. Eventually other cities grew in North and West Africa, Mexico, Central America, and Peru, again largely in response to plentiful water and thus food surplus. Indeed, the challenge of managing water (irrigation, flood control, drainage) is directly linked to the development of the first bureaucracies and to centralized political control.

Cities are intimately related to the societies of which they are a part. But the relationship between city and society has never been without tension. Cities are strongholds of economic and political power. In them, religion flourishes and so do art and science. But cities are difficult to run. They experience riots and revolts. City streets have barricades thrown across them and blood spilt on them. Cities always make elites uneasy—they seem to be filled with unruly people and to be inherently unstable.

The ancient Greeks made the first scientific attempt to understand the city. No other serious study of the city occurred until recent times—somewhat tentatively during the nineteenth century and then more systematically in the opening decades of the twentieth century. Today urban sociology is an important sociological field that has built up important knowledge about how cities work. But the real future of urban sociology lies ahead since the city is still generating disorder, disease, and misery. The United States faces a formidable challenge—the heart and soul of civilization lies in the city yet American elites no more understand their cities than their counterparts in ancient Mesopotamia, Rome, or China understood theirs.

The Preindustrial City

The preindustrial city was small by modern standards. With some exceptions, early cities were ruled by hereditary, landed elites and monarchs. Early cities were organized on the basis of kinship and there was little spatial segregation by function—people conducted commercial and artisan activities out of their homes, in the streets, and in other parts of the city.

It was not unusual for cities to be parts of large empires and to contain conquered peoples or foreigners who had been invited to come because they had skills that the empires needed. The preindustrial city was segregated along ethnic lines and in terms of estate-caste distinctions. Unlike modern cities, however, segregation was established openly (not disguised as zoning laws, for example). However, unlike modern cities, the populations of early cities were not physically separated by well-defined residential areas or by districts devoted to economic functions.

The Industrial City

The modern city had its origins in the economic expansion of Europe and ultimately the rise and development of capitalism. The medieval cities grew along the trade routes of Europe and flourished as commercial centers linking Europe to the Mediterranean basin. Supplied with food from the outside, the city developed specialized trades in response to a variety of markets. From that point on, the Western city was marked by a growing, sustainable economic base—a productive agriculture to supply it with food, commercial and industrial expansion, and a large variety of special activities with important economic consequences: transportation, banking, retailing, research, education, medical care, and the arts.

The Industrial Revolution began the process of urbanization. The concept *urbanization* refers to the proportion of a given population that lives in cities and, in a broader sense, the proportion who live a city way of life wherever they live. Today, most industrialized countries have up to 80 percent of their populations living in urban centers, a point at which the curve of urbanization seems to flatten out.

Starting in the late nineteenth century, Western societies ceased being agrarian societies with cities and became the first urban societies. Today they are urbanized to such an extent that one can alternately call them industrial or urban. An urban society, however, is far more than a society with a majority of its members living in cities. The special culture of the industrial city has now reached out to bring the whole of society within its orbit. The suburb, the farm, the town and village, and the small city are now deeply imbued with industrial, or conversely, with urban values, ideas, and behavior.[19]

---

[19]A general perspective on the contrasts in the development and nature of the city may be obtained from Lewis Mumford, *The Culture of Cities* (New York: Harcourt, Brace, 1938) and *The City in History* (New York: Harcourt, Brace and World, 1961); Gideon Sjoberg, *The Pre-Industrial City* (New York: Free Press, 1960); *Cities: A Scientific American Book* (New York: Alfred A. Knopf,

Urbanization Outside the West

The process of urbanization is now world-wide with the proportion of urban dwellers as opposed to farm dwellers rising almost everywhere in the world. But there is no uniform pattern to this development: significant variations in city development exist among the First, Second, and Third Worlds[20] (and even among the capitalist countries of the West,[21] a matter to which we will return). But the greatest contrast in urbanization is between the developed and developing countries.[22] Western urbanization was accompanied (and one can say, caused) by economic growth, especially industrialization. In developing countries urbanization is taking place much faster than economic growth and is not supported and paced by industrial development—cities there have grown because the death rate has been lowered by more food, modern medicine, and sanitation, and because rural populations have been displaced by mechanized export agriculture. While cities in the capitalist world have stabilized their growth through suburbanization and the development of smaller cities, the Third World suffers from overurbanization in a few colossal cities and underurbanization in rural areas. For example, Bangkok, Thailand, is more than 25 times larger than the next largest Thai city and similar ratios can be found in the Philippines, Brazil, Burma, India, and China.

Historically, urbanization in the developing world, whether in Eastern Europe or the contemporary Third World, has reflected Western imperialism.[23] City growth in many Third World countries reflects the cash-crop agriculture, the settlement patterns, and the centralized control emphasized by former colonial powers. The vast displacement of rural populations continued after independence reflecting the continued shift from subsistence to cash-crop farming (see Box 1-1, The Green Revolution: Progress or Disaster?). In contrast to the West, cities in the Third World have yet to shake off agrarian influence. Some are mere clusters of different ethnic groups living adjacent to each other almost as separate societies. Third World cities are packed with the unemployed and underemployed. They lack transit, water, and sewerage systems. Many of them lack the vital ingredient of city life (besides water): a dependable supply of food. Many are political or health disasters waiting to occur.

There are two patterns in Third World urban development. The developing capitalist countries have given their overall economies a relatively free rein and their cities have grown in a spectacular but helter-skelter manner. As a result, cities segregated by race and ethnicity by former colonial powers have begun to

1965); and Irwin Press and M. Estellie Smith, eds., *Urban Place and Process: Readings in the Anthropology of Cities* New York: Macmillan, 1980). For a fascinating contrast between the preindustrial and industrial city, see Lyn H. Lofland, *A World of Strangers: Order and Action in Urban Public Space* (New York: Basic Books, 1973).

[20]For a valuable reference work on urban patterns in all parts of the world, see the two-volume work by Mattei Dogan and John D. Kasarda, eds., *The Metropolis Era: A World of Giant Cities* and *The Metropolis Era: Mega-Cities* (Newbury, Calif.: Sage, 1988). This collection suffers from not putting cities in the framework of domestic and international power relations and from not highlighting the enormous difference between urbanization in the developed and developing worlds. Nonetheless, these volumes contain analyses and meaty descriptions of cities in all parts of the world, including New York and Los Angeles (United States), Tokyo, (Japan), Delhi (India), Lagos (Nigeria), Sao Paulo (Brazil), Cario (Egypt), and Mexico City (Mexico).

[21]For a valuable analysis of the ways in which urbanization reflected contrasting forms of economic growth in Great Britain, continental Europe, and the United States, see Bryan R. Roberts, "Comparative Perspectives on Urbanization" in David Street *et al.*, *Handbook of Contemporary Urban Life* (San Francisco: Jossey-Bass, 1978), pp. 592–627.

[22]For informative discussions of this contrast, see Dennis McElrath, "The New Urbanization" in Irwin Press and M. Estellie Smith, eds., *Urban Place and Process* (New York Macmillian, 1980), pp. 214–23; Stanley D. Brunn and Jack F. Williams, eds., *Cities of the World* (New York: Harper & Row, 1982); and John Agnew, John Mercer, and David Sopher, eds., *The City In Cultural Context* (Boston: Allen & Unwin, 1984).

[23]For this perspective on world urbanization, see Byran R. Roberts, "Comparative Perspectives on Urbanization" in David Street *et al.*, *Handbook of Contemporary Urban Life* (San Francisco: Jossey-Boss, 1978), pp. 592–627.

disperse and to rearrange themselves along economic (class) lines. In cities oriented toward development under capitalist auspices, there are now marked contrasts between the gleaming skyscrapers and fashionable shops on the one hand, and the sweatshops, street stalls, and the large numbers of unemployed and underemployed on the other. Perhaps the sharpest contrast, however, is between luxurious residential areas (often walled in with private security forces) and vast squatter neighborhoods without running water or sanitation. Perhaps the best example of runaway, uncontrollable urban growth in the Third World is Mexico City.

The other pattern in Third World urban development is found in the socialist countries (both in the Second and Third Worlds). Here the state exercises control over the city's growth both by controlling population movement and by supporting the farm economy and the growth of smaller cities in the rural hinterland.

The network of cities linking the imperial powers to their colonies and to their dependencies is an important part of the history of the world system. Each stage of imperialism (both in the modern and premodern periods) can be told in terms of the city. The latest phase is the emergence of so-called global cities, though it is not always clear which cities belong in this category (London, New York, and Tokyo surely if one focuses on global financial markets).[24]

The American Urban Experience

Haphazard development is the American city's most characteristic feature. The settlement of North America was profoundly affected by geographic, climatic, and technological variables (and obviously reflected imperialist appetites). Cities developed because they had good ports and could serve as commercial, communication, transport, and military centers.[25] Later, the railroad helped to determine urban development and land settlement across the continent. Still later the trolley, the automobile, the airplane, and the elevator, along with other technology, further determined the shape and quality of city life.

In colonial times only a small percentage of the American population were city dwellers. That percentage grew somewhat up until the time of the Civil War, but the real spurt took place during the industrial boom from the Civil War to the 1960s (interrupted only by the Great Depression). The early urban period was characterized by industrial cities that were far from livable, boom towns thriving on manufacturing, transportation, and cheap labor (the flow of immigrants, but also migrants from the American countryside).

From the turn of the century the densely packed city was affected by another trend that has continued ever since—suburbanization. The advent of the automobile was one of the chief reasons for suburbanization. Cities that developed after the automobile, for example, Los Angeles, never developed as core, industrial cities. In any case, suburbanization soon blurred the identity of core cities throughout the country. To help understand the suburbanized city, the Bureau of the Census developed the concept *metropolis*. The Standard Metropolitan Statistical Area (SMSA) refers to a city or suburb of at least 50,000 people. The United States has almost 300 SMSAs comprising 73 percent of the population. Continuing urbanization has blurred the identity of the metropolis as well, and the Bureau of the Census has developed the concept *megalopolis* or Standard Consolidated Area (SCA). This refers to the interconnected cities and suburbs that run into each other. There are 13 of these at present with the largest being Boswash (Boston area to the Washington, D.C.

---

[24]For a discussion of investment and production patterns in localities, nation states, and in the world economy as they shape and use the city see Michael Peter Smith and Joe R. Feagin, eds., *The Capitalist City: Global Restructuring and Community Politics* (New York: Blackwell, 1987).

[25]For an interesting example of urban development that resulted in underdevelopment and stagnation, see David A. Smith, "Dependent Urbanization in Colonial America: The Case of Charleston, South Carolina," *Social Forces* 66 (September, 1987): 1–28.

area) which runs through 10 states and has over 40 million people.

Urban Problems, Urban Impotence

The problems of the American city stem largely from the fundamental thrusts of the American economy. The right of private capital to determine where profit can be made means that business firms can relocate, thus leaving cities without adequate employment, credit, or tax bases. The right of professionals to practice how and where they please also causes problems. Large sections of American cities, for example, lack doctors (as do many rural areas) because doctors tend to concentrate in wealthier districts. In addition, a long-term shift in the American economy from manufacturing to services has had an adverse impact on the city, as has the shift of manufacturing from the Northeast and Midwest to the South, Southwest, West, and to other countries. Much of the decay and ungovernability of American cities reflects not only the value-free rootlessness of propertied and professional groups, but their ability to escape taxation, public regulation, and public direction. Capital is not only free to exploit opportunities for profit but it can evade costs and responsibilities in various ways. The decay of Northeastern and Midwestern American cities, for example, reflects the flight of capital to cheap labor areas in the Sunbelt and abroad, protected and furthered by its political power at suburban, state, and federal levels.

In the development of American society, the American economy gained the right to be left alone or to be affected by politics only on its own terms.[26] It is interesting that, unlike England, France, and Germany, the United States separated its economic and political capitals. American social theorists developed a purer distinction between economy and society than the capitalist societies of Europe, something that was symbolically and physically reflected in the decision to transfer the federal legislature and government from New York to Washington, a new city created for that purpose. The artificial divorce between economic life and politics that is such a profound and unique feature of American society was thus given physical embodiment early in American history. The net effect of this separation was to make it easier for business and professional elites to use the state for their purposes while simultaneously denouncing politics and government.

All in all, the failure to represent urban populations fairly in state and federal legislatures had an adverse effect on the American city. Those who made their money in the city have tended not to live in the city. Starting with the wealthy Dutch families who moved out of New York City to develop feudal-like estates in the Hudson Valley, there has been a continuous exodus of the propertied from the American city. Throughout American history the city's masses have been disenfranchised by unbalanced and gerrymandered electoral districts. The reforms in the system of representation of the 1960s (one person, one vote) came too late to help the city, since the process of suburbanization had already depleted it of economic power as well as large portions of the middle and upper classes.

By stressing geographic and rational market variables, early urban sociologists overlooked the real dynamics at work. They, and all those concerned about urban problems, failed to see that the key variables affecting the city are economic (especially the profit-oriented firm) and political (especially a legal system that protects property and a legislative and governmental system responsive to property interests). The early commercial city was a hodgepodge of social relations. Central urban areas were a locus for small independent business people, workers, and professionals who often lived and worked in close proximity. The future growth of cities in grids, concentric circles, and functional zones was

---

[26]The unique autonomy and dominance of the American economy, led by propertied and professional groups, will also be highlighted in Chapters 7–10. For a detailed picture of the urban-based American upper class, see Frederic Cople Jaher, *The Urban Establishment: Upper Strata In Boston, New York, Charleston, Chicago, and Los Angeles* (Urbana, Ill.: University of Illinois Press, 1982).

no natural, spatial, ecological development, but was guided explicitly by land speculators who wanted to exploit the urban land boom.

The industrial city, from the Civil War until World War II, developed because manufacturers needed a large pool of cheap labor. The core of the city became the center of manufacturing, a basic split between work and residence began, and cities expanded both in population and geographically as they annexed surrounding areas. In time, labor unrest made the city less attractive to business firms and two related developments occurred: industry began to move out of the city and the older cities stopped annexing adjacent areas as power shifted to the suburbs.[27] Older cities are still useful, however, as corporate headquarters and general service centers. As such they are "redeveloped"—small businesses and the working and nonworking poor are dispossessed to make room for hotels, office buildings, convention halls, civic centers, research institutes, university and hospital expansion, and middle- and upper-class housing. However the old pattern persists—powerful economic groups continue to use the government for their own ends while a disorganized and apathetic electorate finds it difficult to confront and control the forces that determine their lives.[28] As such, the cities of the United States, says Katznelson, exhibit a "politics of dependency" in which the main objective of economic and political elites is not to solve problems but to control discontent and manage failure.[29]

---

[27]For a study showing a direct relation between unionization and capital flight, see David Jaffee, "The Political Economy of Job Loss In The United States, 1970–1980," *Social Problems* 33 (April, 1986): 297–318.

[28]For an insightful analysis of the development of the American city from a Marxist perspective, see David M. Gordon, "Capitalist Development and the History of American Cities" in William K. Tabb and Larry Sawers, eds., *Marxism and the Metropolis*, 2nd ed., (New York: Oxford University Press, 1984). pp. 21–53.

[29]Ira Katznelson, "The Crisis of the Capitalist City: Urban Politics and Social Control" in Willis D. Hawley *et al.*, *Theoretical Perspectives on Urban Politics* (Englewood Cliffs, N.J.: Prentice-Hall, 1976), pp. 214–29.

INTERRELATIONS BETWEEN DOMESTIC AND FOREIGN ECONOMIES

No economy or society stands alone; all are subject to the world market (see Chapter 5). The developing capitalist societies upgraded their occupational system by importing labor both unskilled and skilled (including professionals[30] and by exporting machinery to have unskilled, dirty work done by foreign labor. Historically, human capital of both high- and low-level productivity has been able to move freely. Today, only the more productive levels of human capital can move easily from one country to the next as countries exercise more and more control over immigration (and even migration). However, large numbers of unskilled workers still move from country to country either as temporary or illegal workers. It is estimated, for example, that the United States has anywhere from 5 to 15 million illegal aliens, most of them from Mexico.

A dramatic example of the interdependence between the American economy and those of foreign countries is the automobile industry. To remain competitive, American automobile companies are now producing or buying many of their parts in foreign countries with cheap labor and raw materials. In the meantime, America's midwestern cities decay as parts factories close (See Box 6-3, Is Ford's World Car Un-American?).

The United States's economy has relied heavily on foreign trade, investment, resources, and labor, and even territorial expansion throughout its history. Today, it depends heavily on overseas trade and investment to protect its internal markets and ensure its supply of raw materials. An important reason for the United States's spectacular economic growth in the past was its abundant supply of cheap fossil fuels and other raw

---

[30]For data showing a substantial brain drain from less developed countries into the United States, the United Kingdom, Canada, and Australia, see Jagdish Bahagwate, "The Brain Drain," *International Social Science Journal* 28:4 (1976): 691–729.

BOX 6-3. Is Ford's world car un-American?

The automobile is highly prized all over the world and car manufacturers have long hoped to build a car that is suitable for all countries. Standardization is one of the keys to successful manufacturing and the ability to supply cars for the world market would be the ultimate in standardized manufacturing. In 1980 the Ford Motor Company announced its world car, the Escort. The car is not only designed to function all over the world but it is made of parts that have been manufactured all over the world:

Taiwan—wiring
Mexico—door lift assembly
Brazil—rear brake assembly
Japan—transaxles
Spain—shock absorber struts

Britain—steering gears
France—clutch assembly
West Germany—valve bushings
Italy—cylinder heads

The use of parts from abroad reflects the lower cost of labor and materials in other countries. It also reflects the emergence of a world automobile industry and dealer network. It is part of a world economy that makes it difficult for workers to control their economic lives. It also makes it difficult for societies and national governments to direct their affairs. The contradictions of all this are exemplified in the request by American car manufacturers to restrict the import of foreign cars while they themselves were busy importing foreign car parts.

---

materials. Table 6-1 illustrates contemporary America's large dependence on foreign sources for most basic raw materials. Projections for the future indicate that by the year 2,000 the United States will be dependent on foreign sources for more than half of all basic industrial minerals except phosphate.

THE ECONOMY AND PROFESSIONS: A SUMMARY

The American economy has lagged in recent decades, and the United States no longer has the world's highest standard of living. During the 1970s the American economy experienced the puzzling phenomenon of stagflation (low growth and high inflation). Stagflation contradicted basic economic principles, and it was clear that economics was in crisis.

The United States appears unable to live within its means. It has run a large budget deficit domestically for many years and (in 1985 it became a debtor nation). Much of the prosperity of the 1980s was buoyed by personal, business, and governmental debt and masked a declining standard of living. The much vaunted American standard of living will continue its downward course unless the United States finds the political will to bring its affairs into order.

Since 1982 the American economy has continued its slow growth but has had little inflation thanks to unemployment, bankruptcies, cheap imports, and debt. Productivity rates have continued to decline. Much of the improvement in the economy rests on debt: the United States government, corporations, and the American consumer are living on money borrowed at home and abroad. And neither Democrats nor Republicans, using a variety of government policies (Keynesianism), have been able to achieve full employment and price stability. Young people face a future filled with chronic trade and budget deficits and an employment outlook and standard of living considerably lower than their parents.

Recent decades have also witnessed a serious indictment of America's professions.

TABLE 6-1. Percent of Minerals Imported by the United States: 1950 and 1978.

Minerals	1950	1978
Columbium	100	100
Mica (sheet)	98	100
Strontium	100	100
Manganese	77	98
Cobalt	90	97
Tantalum	99	97
Platinum—group metals	74	91
Bauxite and Alumina	55	93
Chromium	95	92
Tin	82	81
Asbestos	94	84
Fluorine	35	82
Nickel	90	77
Potassium	9	61
Gold	25	54
Zinc	41	62
Antimony	33	48
Cadmium	17	66
Selenium	53	61
Mercury	87	57
Silver	66	41
Barium	8	40
Tungsten	80	50
Titanium	33	39
Vanadium	4	27
Gypsum	28	34
Iron Ore	11	29
Copper	31	19
Lead	40	11

Source: Department of Interior, *Mining and Minerals Policy* (Washington, D.C.: U. S. Government Printing Office, 1979), Table 3–1.

Highly educated managers, doctors, lawyers, economists, and policy makers seem unable to supply satisfactory services or to solve social problems. It is clear that the United States needs to reexamine the foundations of professionalism.

Comparative analysis reveals different economic systems (use and exchange economies). The wide variety of economic behavior makes the idea of the self-driven, rational economic individual suspect. Individuals do not have self-evident economic needs or interests and are not equipped with a built-in mechanism for rational economic calculations. Economic actors are social beings who internalize the economic values and norms of time and place.

Human beings need food, water, air, clothing, and shelter to survive. However, there are no self-evident economic needs in the sense of specific foods or forms of shelter. There are also no natural entities that lend themselves to self-evident uses. All economic activity and all economic values and norms are sociocultural creations. The American economy creates wants, and above all, it supplies a motive for living, for accepting discipline, and for enduring hardship.

Like all industrial economies, the American economy is oligarchic, that is, it is highly concentrated and does not function according to its legitimating norms. Economic concentration has many implications and presents many complicated problems of analysis. A concentrated economy may be a threat to efficiency if it leads to monopolistic practices (like managed prices, or low production and high prices) or it may be more efficient than small-scale business if it results in a high ratio of capital to labor or a successful coordination of raw materials, research, manufacturing, and marketing. Even if efficient, however, a concentrated economy presents a further problem—it constitutes a political threat in that it reduces a vital element of social pluralism, economic competition.

Another major feature of the American economy is its long-term shift away from manufacturing (and farming) to services. Understanding the service economy is difficult and the image of a knowledge-based postindustrial society is not helpful. The relative number of professional jobs has not increased and the relative number of skilled jobs has decreased with the decline of manufacturing. All indications point to a growing division in the American occupational structure between a small and static number of highly educated and well-paid professionals and a growing mass of low-skilled workers whose wages are under constant pressure from the unemployed, new workers, legal and illegal aliens, and Third World labor.

The American labor force is extremely diverse. The upper occupations are well organized, secure, and highly rewarded. The bottom levels are unorganized, insecure, and poorly rewarded. In between is a diverse group of employees, some organized as trade unions and "professional" associations, some well paid and some not. There is little evidence of a positive relation between how the United States trains its upper occupations (including education) and actual performance. The United States lacks a national labor policy, a comprehensive man- and womanpower policy, and does not engage in open economic planning.

Economic concentration and widespread bureaucratization, whether supported for reasons of efficiency or national strength, are also producing a new mode of experience for large numbers of Americans. Bureaucratization contains important implications for the middle and upper-middle classes, the classes which, despite their smaller size, set the tone of American society and make most of the basic decisions affecting its life. No longer are American elites primarily individual entrepreneurs (farmers, business people, professionals)—most are now the hired hands and brains of large bureaucratic structures. Thus an ironic aspect of the concentrating surge of bureaucratization is that it has undermined individual private productive property in favor of corporate private property.

Cities emerged from the economic surplus of agriculture. The industrial city is a unique Western phenomenon that reflected the surging economy of capitalism. The industrial city was created by the actions of various power groups and does not have a basis either in nature or the logic of markets.

The non-Western city was massively shaped by imperialism and export agriculture. The rationalization of agriculture dispossessed rural labor and they huddled in cities unable to provide them with work.

The American city grew haphazardly as the locus of a dynamic capitalist economy. The American city has never had enough political power for its population to control the activities of propertied and professional groups. American cities undergo ups and downs largely in terms of the behavior of capital aided by its political power at the state and federal levels.

The United States's economy is deeply dependent on foreign trade and investment. The United States is increasingly dependent on foreign countries for raw materials. It has profited from being able to import cheap, unskilled and skilled labor (the brain drain). It profits from being able to export capital to use cheap labor abroad. Today the United States profits from cheap imports and the import of foreign capital but this has also made it a debtor nation. These and other trends in the economy raise serious questions about the ability of the United States to bring minorities into its mainstream, its ability to protect the environment, and its ability to direct itself.

7

POLITICS, GOVERNMENT, AND LAW
The American Polity

COMPARATIVE POLITICAL SYSTEMS

The Polity: A Definition

The polity refers to the struggle (politics) by power groups to control the public mechanisms (legislature, government, courts) that decide, in Laswell's famous phrase, "who gets what, when, and how".[1]

Legitimate and Illegitimate Polities

In his towering masterpiece, the *Politics*, Aristotle classified polities by whether power relations were legitimate or illegitimate. Legitimate power is when ruler and ruled agree on the relationship. A monarchy is a legitimate form of power; so is an aristocracy, and so is "constitutionalism" (government by established law). A monarchy that no longer serves the common interest and relies on co-

ercion rather than consent is a *tyranny* (illegitimate power). So, too, an aristocracy that ceases to rule in the common interest becomes an oligarchy and a failed constitutionalism degenerates into "democracy" (mob rule).

The reason why polities succeed and fail, argued Aristotle, lies in the relation between a society's economy and its political institutions. Realistically, monarchy and aristocracy are government by and for the wealthy while democracy is government by and for the poor. Constitutionalism is government by middle-level property groups. The best and most stable form of polity, argued Aristotle, is the latter because the wealthy and the poor tend to become extremist and cannot help but govern in their own interest. The only viable, enduring polity is one in which large numbers of relatively equal citizens of moderate wealth control the rich and the poor while balancing each other.

Aristotle's views are no idle echo from the ancient world. The historic basis of American

---

[1] Harold D. Laswell, *Politics: Who Gets What, When and How* (New York: McGraw-Hill, 1936).

democracy has had the same center of gravity: a large mass of small property owners (and middle-income earners). As we will see, all this may be changing.

Types of Authority

Max Weber developed a slightly different typology of legitimate power than Aristotle; it is widely used by sociology and political science. Weber refers to his three forms of legitimate power as types of *authority*:

1. One is *traditional* authority, where a static agrarian society is governed according to customary, ascriptive principles (age, birth, race, religion). Traditional rulers have power because they represent the ways things have always been.

2. Another is *charismatic* authority—power goes to individuals whose personal qualities attract followers. This form of power is essentially emotional and arises when society is experiencing disorder, change, and uncertainty and is usually shortlived.

3. A final form of authority is *rational-legal* authority, where political and social problems are tackled rationally and legally by individuals who reach positions of power through a selection process based on achievement criteria. This type of authority predominates in both state capitalist societies like the United States and state socialist societies like the Soviet Union. The exercise of power is defined carefully (in law) in terms of offices held. Thus a police officer, a judge, the tax collector, a member of Congress, and the president can do some things and not others.

Representative Government: Parliamentary and Presidential Variants

Representative government in the United States has taken the form of a presidential system as opposed to the parliamentary variant found in Great Britain, Canada, and much of Europe. Under the parliamentary system, electoral districts choose among candidates representing political parties (themselves not actually part of the state but voluntary organizations). Those chosen assemble as a lawmaking body. The party with a majority forms a government that can use its majority to enact laws binding on the population at large. The American presidential system separates executive and legislative functions, and a president and a legislature (Congress) are elected separately. The result is often a stalemate since the president and the Congress can represent different political parties and thus a different mix of economic and social interests. The American polity is complicated further by its federal nature—though the constitution has a clear function for strong, central government, the 50 states also perform important political-legal functions. These states vary widely in their socioeconomic development, and this is reflected in their legislatures, governments, and laws.

Comparative Legal Systems

Law refers to a special body of norms designed to uphold or realize a variety of social purposes. Law serves to integrate society by establishing public order and by maintaining rights and duties. It also facilitates interaction between diverse groups by enforcing rights. Law expresses a society's moral and ethical ideals and confers legitimacy on the holders of power insofar as it seems to pinpoint responsibilities and provides some measure of benefits to all.

In premodern society, legal and other norms openly enforce a *consensus* about the world. In premodern societies, law and morality, law and religion, law and philosophy are not easily distinguished. In these societies disputes are often settled by mediation or by open forums in which all values and beliefs are allowed free rein. Modern society separated law from other norms and made it society's ultimate boundary. Law became extremely complex and required special people and groups to embody it and give it life. As Durkheim pointed out, law in modern society no longer enforces consensus (mechanical solidarity) but must continuously restore and recalibrate rights and interests (organic solidarity).

Law also varies among modern societies reflecting a society's level of industrialization and the route it took toward industrialization. Western societies, for example, developed over a long period of time and experienced a protracted struggle among nobility, religious groups, and the middle class, followed by a long period of struggle among property groups and among property groups, workers, and minorities. Out of these conflicts emerged a rich body of law, intricate legal practices, professions and professional associations concerned with law, and public agencies assigned the task of adjudicating and enforcing the law. In contrast, Japan's development was imposed from above and its people and culture remained homogeneous—in consequence there was little need to develop elaborate legal solutions to problems of social integration and adjustment.[2]

Three major legal systems have emerged among the developed countries:

1. Romano-Germanic law—following Roman law, continental European countries have tried to develop an integrated, comprehensive code of law based on legal principles.

2. Common law—emerging in England and spreading to the United States and other former English colonies, the law in these countries is thought to be the result of individual court decisions.

3. Socialist law—developed in the U.S.S.R. to promote a socialist society.[3]

The developed capitalist and socialist (U.S.S.R. and Eastern Europe) nation states have many similarities in their legal systems. Czarist Russia was deeply influenced by Roman law and today the Soviet legal system still shares many features with Romano-Germanic law. But the Soviet legal system is also different. Socialist law does not accept "bourgeois" concepts of ownership (property) nor does it accept the sharp distinctions made in Western law between private and public spheres or between individual and society.

---

[2]For a case study of Japanese society, see Chapter 18.

[3]For a good classification and description of these and other legal systems in the developing world, see Rene Dair and John E. C. Brierly, *Major Legal Systems In The World Today: An Introduction To The Comparative Study of Law*, 2nd ed., (New York: Free Press, 1978).

The Uniqueness of Western Political Institutions

The capitalist democracies have a number of unique features:

1. The idea of the *public interest*—this is a powerful and highly functional convention to which all appeal but which no one can define.

2. The distinction between *delegates* (those who carry out the wishes of others) and *representatives* (those who act on behalf of others but who are permitted to think and act as they think best). The concept, "representative," which is related to the idea of a public interest, allows for political behavior and thought that is not rigidly and narrowly bound to the service of a particular group, locality, or interest. Representative government encourages mental flexibility, promotes political creativity, and makes compromise morally acceptable (as does majority rule). The principle of representation emerges from complexity and change and is also a way to cope with complexity and change.

3. The liberal democracies have also sought to solve the problem of economic and social conflict with other norms and practices: constitutionalism (a basic code standing above positive law or legislation), responsible government, majority rule, a neutral speaker of a legislature, government officials who are not political partisans, and an independent, impartial judiciary.

The Special Nature of Urban Life in the West

Early cities were feudal theocracies; power was in the hands of a priest-king (often a god-king) and a hereditary aristocracy. The uniqueness of the Western city derives from the Greek city-state and its successful break with the theocratic feudal tradition. The distinctive feature of the Greek city-state is that it was not derived from large-scale agriculture and thus was not part of a large feudal-authoritarian empire. Ancient Greece had its share of feudalism and oligarchy but it was also unique because its rocky, thin soil could support only small-scale farming. The social base of the Greek city-state was the small, independent farmer. Together with the freer atmosphere of maritime commerce, this social base developed the historically unique ideal of a *self-governing community*.

Since the time of the Greeks, the Western city has always had a freer, more secular intellectual and political atmosphere then the non-Western city. Above all, the Western city pioneered self-governance and stressed its autonomy from outside forces. The Greek ideal of self-governance was continued by Rome. After the fall of Rome, the ideal was revived by the medieval Western city. The West's self-governing city is a vital part of modern industrial Europe and the United States (as we will see shortly, it is more an ideal than a reality in the United States). The city is thus almost synonomous with the West's unique political tradition.[4]

THE AMERICAN POLITY: BASIC STRUCTURAL FEATURES

Rational-Legal Public Power

Public power in the United States is rational-legal rather than traditional or charismatic:

1. By and large, political power is obtained peacefully through discussion, persuasion, and elections.
2. American law is rational and universalistic as opposed to legal systems based on privilege, custom, and arbitrary decrees.
3. The American civil service is a rational or bureaucratic structure of behavior as opposed to administrative systems based on patrimony (heredity) or patronage (the spoils system).

The United States' Static, Negative View of Government

The American constitution is essentially a static document (despite amendments). It emerged in the agrarian-commercial capitalism of the eighteenth century and was deeply influenced by the static Newtonian (mechanistic) world view of that era. Despite two centuries of profound economic and social change, it is still regarded as an unchanging

reference point (for an earlier discussion of how models derived from nature mislead us about the nature of social institutions, see Box 1-2, Can Thought About Society Model Itself on Anything in Nature?).

Perhaps the most striking feature of the American constitution is its presumption that government is the enemy of the people. Understandable in the eighteenth century (the Age of Absolutism), this presumption is false and has badly handicapped efforts to modernize American society. Unlike other capitalist democracies, Americans can never discuss problems and solutions in a straightforward manner but must first debate (often unproductively and always with a great waste of time) whether government can do the job.

The static nature of the American constitution and its negative view of government are clearly indicated in James Madison's *Federalist Paper #10*, in many ways the metaphysical charter of representative government in the United States. The central American myth that inequality comes directly from the unequal nature of individuals (the biopsychological explanation) forms the heart of Madison's brief essay. Madison's argument (like that of Karl Marx's) is that economic conflict is at the heart of politics. Unlike Marx, however, Madison argued that differences in the types and amounts of property owned by individuals are due to "diversity in the faculties of men." Since economic differences and the conflicts that ensue from them have this natural basis, they cannot be changed without doing violence to nature. "The protection of these faculties is the first object of government," concluded Madison, and the proper role of government is to contain or soften the effects of natural economic differences and conflicts, not to change or eliminate them.

Madison's general position that unequal property groups should compete to control government but never use it to change the natural economic order is still the basis of the American polity. The most important thing about the American polity, therefore, is not that it is a democracy but that it is a *capitalist*

---

[4]For the indispensable contrast between Western and non-Western cities, see Max Weber, *The City* (New York: Free Press, 1958).

democracy. Public power in the United States rests on the fundamental premise that the people-at-large will be better off if the polity (and society) favor private property and private professional groups. While all of the developed capitalist societies routinely put a large percentage of their telecommunication, railroad, airline, electricity, steel, shipbuilding, and even automobile industries in government's hands, the United States uniquely leaves them in private hands.

Politics and Interest Groups

While agrarian societies obviously have internal conflicts, on the whole, they are characterized by widespread communalization—that is, by virtual universal acceptance of specific ways of believing and acting. Industrial society, on the other hand, is characterized by a complex and changing social division of labor, and the motivation to perform its myriad activities takes the form of "individualism," especially in the Anglo-American world. An intricate division of labor means that disputes and conflicts are almost routine occurrences and modern society has developed specialized groups—especially the state—to keep order and resolve conflict. The trend away from communalization toward "societalization" is everywhere accompanied by the growth of political parties and interest groups.

The right to associate for common purposes independently of government is fundamental to liberal democracy. The number and types of associations related to the political process are enormous. Political parties, for example, are voluntary associations and bear an intimate and unique relation to the liberal system of government and, of course, to the group or power structure of liberal society. Churches may be nonvoluntary in the sense that one is born into a church but, politically speaking, they are free, private associations, that is, a church cannot use the state to punish or coerce a member. Churches, labor unions, trade, business and professional associations, universities, in-

deed all interest groups are voluntary organizations that maintain continuous relations with legislatures and governments in an effort to control or influence public policies.

In addition to "bread and butter" groups a new type of interest group has emerged, the ideological group, or *single-interest* group based on principle. These groups are interested only in a single issue and make no attempt to relate it to other interests. Whether interested in gun control, evolution, abortion, saving the whale, nuclear energy, school prayer, or stopping communism, such groups run counter to the tradition of political compromise and represent an ominous development in American public life.[5]

Political Socialization and Legitimacy

Like other societies the United States socializes its members to accept the legitimacy of the American political-legal system and the social order it serves. The family, school, the mass media, religion, social science, and political participation itself all serve to bring new generations into the American way of life and to keep them there. Americans may ask for constitutional amendments or for new ways to finance political parties but the overall sociopolitical order is taken for granted, and Americans rarely raise questions about it or consider alternatives to it. Social science, schools, the mass media, and religion promote a take-for-granted attitude about public power and the social order, each in its own way (for the role of supernatural and civil religion in putting the American social order beyond conscious reflection, see Chapter 8).

The American social order is a particular version of liberalism (readers will remember that liberalism refers to the thoughtways and practices of capitalism—the equation of private property and private interest with the public good). The forces of socialization in the United States have succeeded in making

---

[5]For a classic statement, see Richard Revere, "Single-Issue Politics", *New Yorker* 54 (May 8, 1978): 139–46; widely reprinted.

liberalism a monopoly (Democrats and Republicans are both variations on liberalism) and in preventing alternatives from arising. The very success that American power groups have had, however, in establishing liberalism (especially its negative view of politics and government) has led to some important deficiencies in political socialization—America's socializing agencies have not been able to inculcate positive civic attitudes or behavior, overcome widespread political apathy, or prevent what appears to be a steady erosion of public confidence in politics, government, and law.

All this leads to the question, why? How do all of the above elements in the American polity and society actually work? What is their direction? What reality lies behind American political ideals? Let's start by asking, what does government do?

THE POLITY AS GOVERNMENT: WHAT DOES IT DO?

The Functions of Government

Government provides security against external enemies by maintaining armed forces and a variety of intelligence and espionage networks. Government also promotes foreign trade, scientific exchanges, tourism, and so on, and this requires a large and complex set of civilian agencies at home and abroad.

Government provides security against internal enemies whether they be criminals, terrorists, or rebels. To this end the United States has a large network of police forces (with the military always on standby) and a complex network of courts, jails, and law enforcement agencies.

Government provides education, both in schools and through a wide range of research activities (for example, the Census Bureau, the Bureau of Labor Statistics) and publications (the federal government publishes thousands of pamphlets giving advice on everything from raising babies to canning food and curbing house pests). Government facilitates communication and furthers commerce

by providing a comprehensive mail delivery service (public telephone and television systems are common in other capitalist societies).

Government provides drinking and irrigation water, highways, bridges, canals, airports, dams, and flood-control systems (comprehensive public transportation systems are common in other capitalist societies). Government inspects food products, restaurants, public toilets, automobiles, and airplanes to insure the public's health and safety. Government is a public health service that compiles data on disease, conducts, coordinates, and approves medical research, and promotes health standards. Government protects against fire and promotes health and safety in the workplace and in consumer products. Government takes measures to protect the natural environment. It also provides parks and other recreational facilities.

Government provides relief for those affected by disaster. It provides money, food, and other services for the destitute.

Government provides security in old age and health care for the needy, veterans, and the elderly (national health insurance for all is common in other capitalist societies).

Government endorses the activities of private individuals (by granting research funds or honoring public service) and of private groups (for example, by not taxing churches and nonprofit organizations). Of special significance is the growing practice of directly subsidizing voluntary organizations or of buying their services. Nursing homes, university budgets and university research, public television, the arts, hospitals, children's aid societies, political candidates, and so on, all receive public monies either for their operating expenses or for the direct provision of services to the public.

Government requires certification of and adherence to rules on the part of occupations, professions, and voluntary bodies: plumbers, doctors, lawyers, universities, political parties, charities, foundations, and so on. An important public practice gives private bodies quasipublic standing, including the power to determine who can enter valued occupations.[6]

Government coordinates "public" and "private" operations. In addition to influencing (exhorting, regulating, coordinating) economic bodies (farmers, management, labor, banks, and so on), government has had to pay more and more attention to the way in which other types of private bodies are discharging their public functions (for example, charitable organizations, hospitals, universities, professional associations, political parties). The role of government in assessing performance by such bodies is a delicate one. Sometimes government will meet a growing demand or need for a service by buying it directly from a private organization (for example, ambulance or adoption services), sometimes it will subsidize services by private bodies (for example, by contributing to university budgets), and sometimes it will operate competing services (by operating power plants or by starting public universities when private universities cannot expand or adjust rapidly enough to meet educational needs).

Central government also oversees the performance of state and local governments—many central government programs have stipulations requiring states and localities to provide matching funds and to meet federal standards.

In recent decades government has also undertaken perhaps its most important and sensitive task: the explicit guidance of the economy. Despite their ideology of weak government, American power groups have always sought and obtained political-governmental remedies for their economic problems (the Great Depression of the 1930s simply involved more groups in this process). Regardless of which party is in power, the central government is always active in bolstering sectors of the economy, providing currency, stimulating demand, regulating credit, and

maintaining income levels. Governments in a wide variety of industrial societies, including the United States, have become *welfare states* (an active interventionist state that attempts to provide minimal levels of employment, income, housing, health care, and old age security).

Functional and Conflict Images of Government

Functionalists think of government as society's way of integrating itself and adjusting to new conditions. They take it for granted that government is neutral and results from a valid pluralistic political process.

Conflict theorists (liberal and Marxist) see government as a partisan on the side of the powerful. The electorate is dominated by powerful economic groups and government expresses their wishes. Behind it all is a conflict between the interests of the economically powerful (business and professions) and ordinary people.

THE POLITY AS LAW: HOW DOES IT WORK?

The American Legal System

Americans have great respect for the law and associate it with fundamental values such as personal liberty and social unity. They also associate it with orderly change and social adaptation. To serve these important values the American legal system rests on a number of basic premises: (1) Americans distinguish between ordinary laws and constitutional law with the former subject to the latter; (2) all laws can be changed should the need arise; (3) conscience and intellect are respected against law in that individuals can speak against laws they don't like and are protected against self-incrimination or arbitrary acts by the state.

The American legal system has a number of other distinguishing features. The United States has far more lawyers per capita and far more of them employed in private practice than other countries. American law is subject

---

[6]"Public" licensing and certifying bodies are invariably dominated by the occupations or businesses being licensed or certified.

to the power of money probably far more than any other developed society. Private groups with money exert a powerful influence on the creation of law by legislatures and government officials. The services of lawyers must be purchased, which means that those with more money get more and better legal services.[7] And while Americans respect the law in the abstract, they are also great lawbreakers, and they dispute the law in great numbers both in and out of courtrooms.

All of the above is understandable given the main thrust of America's social development, which include:

1. an unprecedented commitment to individual rights.
2. an unprecedented incitement to material gain through competition.
3. a dynamic economic development that quickly outgrew custom and religion as sources of dispute resolution.
4. slavery and immigration that diversified the American population and further undermined customary sources of social control and conflict resolution.
5. the inexpensiveness of law (the loser pays nothing in court or legal fees).
6. lofty, expansive constitutional ideals and a difficult and expensive to influence political system have prompted Americans to turn economic and political grievances into legal issues.

Functional and Conflict Images of Law

Functionalists regard law as the product of a society based on consensus. Law, they argue, reflects the considered judgment of the community and is thus binding on the community. Functionalists emphasize the contribution of law to social stability, justice, and adjustment. Despite faults, law embodies our highest moral values and maintains goals that most agree on. Law as a set of procedures guarantees everybody a fair hearing and pro-

---

[7]For a fuller discussion of the relation between socioeconomic status and the administration of law, see Chapter 9.

tects us against arbitrary state action. When law breaks new ground it does so in terms of values that people accept. True, there are many conflicting opinions about laws and the judicial process, but this is because law is in the thick of things busy solving problems and helping individuals, groups, and society adapt to new conditions. The law may lag behind society but that is not necessarily bad since it forces people to think before they act. The established classes and most lawyers accept this view of law.

Conflict theorists agree that the law is a stabilizing, integrative force, but, they argue, this serves to protect both the good and the bad in the status quo. Law is always and everywhere primarily an instrument for legitimating and supporting existing power groups, be they priesthoods, landed aristocracies, business people and professionals, or dictatorships. The development of American law during the late colonial and early republican period (to cite one conflict legal theorist) clearly reflected the interests and needs of America's emerging commercial and industrial classes. American law has been intimately associated with their interests ever since (see Box 7-1, The Partisan Nature of Objective Law).

Americans break the law in large numbers and engage in litigation far more than other people, argue conflict theorists, precisely because the law does *not* rest on consensus. Legislatures enact ambiguous, vague, and contradictory laws, not because legislatures cannot write clearly but because legislatures themselves are not founded on consensus. Law, argue conflict theorists, is an expression of power. While it may sometimes express the common interest, law mostly expresses the interest of the strong and neglects the interests of the weak.

All this leads to poor law enforcement. Laws expressing a consensus often lack enforcement teeth (for example, fair employment and occupational safety laws). Though there is consensus on the need for law and order, the most important forms of criminal behavior cannot be controlled because they are being done by powerful business and

BOX 7-1. The partisan nature of objective law

Legal historians and philosophers have portrayed American law as an objective, apolitical, and autonomous code of norms. Despite disagreements, say between Roscoe Pound and Oliver Wendall Holmes, American jurisprudence has argued that the development of American law is marked by consensus, and that its outcome serves the common good. Even when legal analysts have seen the law in relation to economic and political developments, they have tended to adopt a functional and consensus approach in their interpretations. However a minority of legal historians has argued that law is better seen from a conflict perspective. M. J. Horwitz,[1] for example, argues that American law was drastically altered during the formative years of the republic, primarily through judicial interpretations. The eighteenth century regarded law as stemming from community customs derived from natural law. Property meant the absolute right to enjoy something and to be able to prevent others from interferring with that enjoyment. From 1780 to 1860, argues Horwitz, the legal conception of property was drastically altered to mean that one had the right to develop and use property *regardless of injuries to others.*

Not surprisingly, argues Horwitz, the changed meaning of property was accompanied by a change in the meaning of a contract. In the eighteenth century a contract had to be fair and could be set aside if it wasn't. By mid-nineteenth century, a contract was enforceable *even it its provisions were patently unfair.* The law was simply reflecting a fact of economic life: strong commercial and industrial interests were using their competitive advantages to exploit smaller businesses, consumers, and workers, and they legalized their exploitation by putting it in the form of a contract. They also protected their economic power by getting the courts to reduce their responsibility for damages (in keeping with the new dictum that the central meaning of property was the right to develop it) and juries gradually had their power to make judgments and award damages on the basis of fairness curtailed. Once all this had been accomplished, legal philosophers who earlier had argued in the name of utility and progress, then obscured the resulting changes by arguing that law is neutral, objective, and apolitical.

Why was all this permitted by a people who thought of themselves as living in a democracy? For one thing, the United States did not introduce universal male suffrage until the 1850s, that is, until *after* the new legal structures had been established. But perhaps the best explanation lies in the fact that the law was being shaped to benefit the dynamic property groups in the American economy. It suited the needs of an industrial capitalism and it was difficult to argue against the seemingly plausible assumption that economic growth was good for everyone. And those for whom it wasn't good—small manufacturers, small retailers, small farmers, consumers, and workers—were too weak and disorganized to do much about it.

[1]*The Transformation of American Law, 1780–1860* (Cambridge, MA: Harvard University Press, 1977).

professional groups often in conjunction with public officials.

Many of the deficiencies of the American legal system have been summarized by Derek C. Bok.[8] Bok charges that American law (for example, labor law, antitrust law, workplace safety regulations) cannot be related to the public interest (to verifiable results in each specific area). Legal scholars do little research into the legal system as such. The legal field, like medicine, is succumbing to bigness. The United States, says Bok, has far more lawyers than any other industrialized society, not only channelling huge numbers of able people away from fields in which they are needed, but once in place these lawyers (like surplus surgeons) create work whether needed or not. The legal system caters to the rich and powerful and neglects the interests of the middle class and the poor. The law schools have done little to counter all this—legal education, or learning how to think like a lawyer, means memorizing unique cases and knowing how to find variations in detail. Teaching students to think like lawyers, argues Bok, "has helped to produce a legal system that is among the most expensive and least efficient in the world." Ironically, concludes Bok, "the blunt inexcusable fact is that this nation, which prides itself on its efficiency and justice, has developed a legal system that is the most expensive in the world, yet cannot manage to protect the rights of most its citizens."

THE AMERICAN POLITY: PROBLEMS AND PROSPECTS

The United States' Immobilized Polity

In recent decades Americans have asked government to do more and more for them. The overall consequence appears to be a growing dependence of interest groups and citizens at all levels of society on government and the immobilization of the American political system (see Box 7-2, Is the Welfare State Making Wards of Us All?).

Myths About the Federal Government

Many Americans believe that

1. the federal government is getting bigger.
2. federal spending is increasing.
3. federal taxes are increasing.
4. the federal debt is growing larger.

None of these beliefs, however, is true. The federal government had fewer civilian employees per 1,000 population throughout the 1970s than it had through most of the 1950s and 1960s. There has been no significant change in federal spending as a percent of gross national product through much of the post-World War II period. Federal taxes as a percent of gross national product have remained largely stationary. And government debt as a percent of the gross national product (GNP) declined steadily for most of the post-World War II period and even after the rapid rise in debt under the Reagan administration stands at less than 50 percent of GNP (the same people who complain about government debt think nothing of giving loans to individuals and businesses for more than their annual worth or accepting such loans). It is also widely believed that federal programs transfer wealth from the better off to the poor. This too is not true.[9]

The United States' Unrepresentative Government

The American people have never been accurately or fairly represented in state or federal legislatures. Until the United States Supreme Court ruled in 1963 that one-person, one-vote (or numerically equal electoral districts) was the basis of representative government in the United States, state and federal legislatures were heavily slanted in

---

[8]Derek C. Bok, "A Flawed System", *Harvard Magazine* (May-June 1983):38ff. Bok, President of Harvard University, is a former Dean of Harvard Law School.

[9]For a full discussion of government, taxes, spending, and public debt, see Chapter 9.

BOX 7-2.   Is the welfare state making wards of us all?

John Earlylife knows that social security payments are indexed for inflation, that social security protects against disability at any age, that it protects spouses and children against premature death, and that it pays for a good part of medical care after 65. John has ignored warnings that he should not expect to live on a social security check. Rather than save for the future, he trades in his two-year-old car for a new one. His wife, not wanting to be left out, buys a new set of furniture when she learns that the bank is willing to lend them money for that too.

James Hearth finds the demand for his steel declining in the face of cheaper imported steel. Working through his trade association and a network of congressional representatives (who were elected with the help of funds raised by steel industry PACS or Political Action Committees), he gets the federal government to establish limits on imports, in effect subsidizing his inefficient mills. Satisfied that his mills are safe, Hearth invests his profits in an oil company rather than a new mill, in effect guaranteeing his dependence on government. Hearth supports a political party that promises "to get government off the backs of the people" but he gives money (tax deductible) to both parties just to make sure.

Robert Cornbloom's farm is bursting with cotton, wheat, beets, oranges, milk, cheese, and vegetables. Using the political power of rural voters (which far exceeds that of urban voters), he gets the federal government to pay him for his products at prices far above the world price. To make sure that individual enterprise, competition, and efficiency don't lead to chaos, he also gets the federal government to pay farmers *not* to grow food. With the help of government, some surpluses are allowed to rot in the sun, some of them are stored at taxpayers expense, and some are sent abroad to feed the hungry (the latter often has the latent function of supporting right-wing dictatorships).

Truckers, airlines, banks, and so on have all made similar arrangements to have government cushion them against competition and assorted adversities, including their own mistakes. Parents know that government has made it possible to borrow money for their children's education at heavily subsidized rates. Medical schools, hospitals, and nursing homes are financed with tax money with few questions asked. Defense contractors with no plans to convert to civilian production become heavily dependent on government contracts, and they get sour stomachs at signs that peace might break out. Discouraged workers who have exhausted their unemployment benefits go on "welfare." Abandoned wives and their children go on "welfare." Eventually John Earlylife and his wife go on welfare.

In the next general election, many candidates denounce "welfare bums," high taxes, and excessive government spending. The candidate who promises to get the government off the people's back defeats the candidate who gives examples of how this should be done.

favor of numerically smaller, rural, small-town populations. Despite this ruling and the enlargement of the suffrage to include hitherto excluded minorities, the *gerrymander* still prevents an accurate reflection of the number and composition of the American people in the political life of the nation. To gerrymander is to bunch up your op-

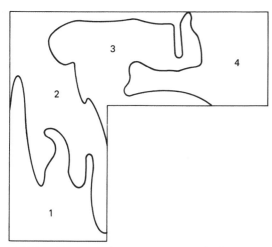

FIGURE 7-1. The Gerrymander, or Stilling
The Voice of the People

In 1812 Governor Gerry of Massachusetts devised an electoral pattern which enabled the Republican Party to elect 29 members to only 11 members for the Federalist party even though they got a smaller popular vote than their opponents (50,164 to 51,766). Simplified, the basic process is as follows: voters are arranged so that Party A wins narrow victories in, say, 3 districts and loses big in one. The result is three members elected to one loss even though the other party got more votes.

Party A	Party B
55	45
55	45
55	45
10	90
175	225

ponent's voters in electoral districts, where they win overwhelming victories (thereby wasting votes), and to spread your own supporters over a number of districts to insure smaller majorities for your party—the result is to neutralize your opponent's numerical strength and magnify your own (see Figure 7-1). The gerrymander is possible because income, ethnicity, and race are fairly good indicators of how people will vote, and those who draw electoral lines know where such differences exist thanks to the Census Bureau and other research agencies.

The Burden of Powerful Interest Groups

Interest groups have power far beyond their numbers. A small minority can thwart a large majority. For example, large majorities of the American people support national health insurance, gun control, and a nuclear freeze but the American medical establishment, the National Rifle Association, and the proponents of nuclear arms buildup have prevailed, each in its own sphere, to prevent any of the above from occurring.[10]

Many different interest groups have entrenched themselves at the public trough and their combined effect is to produce what appears to be chronic deficits and a mounting federal debt. American corporations, professions, farmers, students, retirees, the poor, and so on receive huge amounts of money, the total exceeding public income. On top of this is the special burden of the military-industrial complex (see Box 7-3, The Iron Triangle, or Blurring the Lines Between Public and Private, and Figure 7-2, Defense Expenditures and Lagging Productivity, 1960–79).

Creative Politics

The creative process in politics consists of separating concrete issues from all-embracing ideological programs and solving each one on a piecemeal basis. It is unlikely, for example, that the United States would have been established in the first place if the founders of the nation had not side-stepped the issue of slavery. The extension of suffrage from the 1850s into the 1960s, the rise of the great regulatory agencies from the last decades of the nineteenth century on, the Wagner Act of 1935, which established collective bargaining, the Social Security Act of 1935, the War on Poverty, and the Great Civil Rights Acts of the 1960s are milestones of creativity in American history. From the 1930s to 1968, reform-minded business people, professionals, and voluntary groups, members of both major political parties, intellectuals, labor leaders, and leaders of racial and ethnic groups developed a working, elite consensus about how the United States should be run.

---

[10]For a good overview of interest group politics, see Ronald J. Hrebenar and Ruth K. Scott, *Interest Group Politics In The United States* (Englewood Cliffs, N.J.: Prentice-Hall, 1982).

BOX 7-3. The iron triangle, or blurring the lines between public and private

The interrelations among the Department of Defense, Congress, and giant defense contractors has been called an *iron triangle*.[1] Adams's case study of eight of these contractors reveals a world in which the federal government and Congress enjoy a tight, often secretive relation with each other and with military contractors in violation of basic American norms and values. Defense contracts are noncompetitive and, in addition to their wasteful cost-plus basis, they include many hidden subsidies. There is a revolving door of personnel from the Pentagon to defense contractors and vice-versa. There is a questionable emphasis on high-tech-

nology weapon systems and a neglect of conventional weapons and combat readiness. And the general public is excluded from participation in the formulation of defense policy.

Not only does this concentration of power not yield adequate defense but it is a huge drain on national resources and a contributor to America's declining productivity (see Figure 7-2). And, of course, declining productivity further weakens the United States's ability to defend its interests.

[1]Gordon Adams, *The Iron Triangle: The Politics of Defense Contracting* (New York: Council on Economic Priorities, 1981).

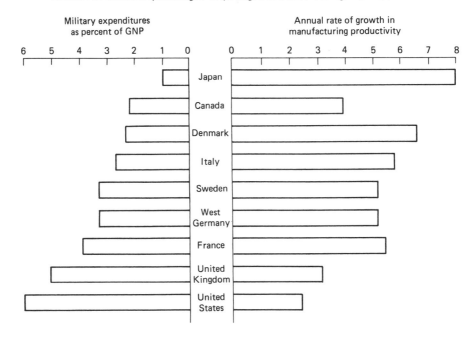

FIGURE 7-2. Defense Expenditures and Lagging Productivity, 1960–79. Source: U.S. Congressional Budget Office, *Defense Spending and the Economy* (Washington, D.C.: U.S. Government Printing Office, 1983), p. 40. The burden of defense spending, if anything, increased during the 1980s.

The Decline of Creative Politics

Something new may have appeared on the American political scene—a decline of creative politics. Creative politics in American history reflected the dominance of a fairly homogeneous collection of property and professional groups. Today, dominant property and professional groups are far more complex and fragmented than they were before World War II. Farm, manufacturing, and service interests along with a wide variety of professions are extremely heterogeneous. It is doubtful if they could escape stalemate even if they had no other groups to contend with. But, of course, America's property and professional groups no longer have a clear predominance of power. In recent generations single-interest groups based on principles derived from morality, religion, or secular philosophies have appeared: the working class and the elderly (since the 1930s), blacks, Hispanics, women, the handicapped, and other minorities (since the 1960s). And for the first time in its history the United States is shouldering a huge peace time military burden (and is aiding a variety of foreign countries) as it struggles to defend its many and varied interests around the globe.

Each of the above groups—professional, ideological (single issue), labor, blacks, Hispanics, women, handicapped, and other minorities—is diverse. Combined, they make a bewildering array of forces pulling and pushing the polity in all directions at once. Combined, they have become a heavy burden for American political institutions to carry. The reason America's political system exhibits rigidity and irrelevance may well be that it is overloaded by excessive and irreconcilable demands about how the country should be run and how the nation's resources should be allocated. Should the American people be thinking of the need to "get off the government's back" rather than vice-versa?

The failure of American capitalism in the Great Depression of the 1930s led to the creative politics of the 1930–60 period. But the period since the late 1960s is marked by a growing tangle of postponed problems and half-solutions. Poorly framed legislation, the very expensive manned moon shot in the 1960s (whose primary purpose was prestige since the same knowledge could have been obtained through inexpensive machines), the very expensive and unpaid-for Vietnam war, the dramatic increase in claimants on social resources during the 1960s and 1970s, the end of the era of cheap resources, the expense of protecting the environment, and the relative decline of the United States in world affairs all came together during the late 1970s to create a noticeable inability to solve problems. Each problem area and each proposed solution affects the others, making for a politics of drift and stalemate. Perhaps the best index to the United States's loss of adaptive capacity is the steady decline of the political party.

The Decline of the Political Party

The political party is a prime mechanism for reconciling sociocultural conflicts and contradictions.[11] When political leaders compete for election in a constituency of mixed economic, religious, ethnic, or racial groups, they are likely to search for common denominators and to pay attention to the problems of all voting segments. Political relations characterized by competition for support in a diverse electorate are likely to be both more creative and more responsive to public need. When like-minded leaders come together to combine their strength in order to win majorities at various electoral levels, the political party is born. The party that garners a majority forms the government and can be held accountable by lay citizens. *Putting political leaders in this relation to each other and to the general citizenry is the major achievement of Western political life.*

---

[11]For an incisive analysis on which much of this is based, see Morris P. Fiorina, "The Decline of Collective Responsibility in American Politics," *Daedalus* 109 (Summer, 1980): 25–45.

When parties are viable there is a tendency to worry about the quality of candidates. Elected officials are eager to compile a good party record. Party leaders have the organizational strength and resources to discipline wayward members and protect creative mavericks. Strong parties prevent the fragmentation of the political public into rigid factions and groups based on absolutist principles. Strong parties help prevent personal characteristics (charisma) from being the main factor in elections. A strong party can force those with a point of view or an interest to relate it to other points of view and other interests—interest groups that fail to do this have little hope of success.

American political parties have never been strong. The antipolitical tradition in the United States has not made politics an attractive arena for most members of the middle and upper classes. Civil service reform, the emphasis on nonpartisan politics and government, and the general rise of the welfare state have robbed the party of its patronage, its reputation, and its ability to do favors and deliver benefits. Party reforms in the 1970s helped bring the political party to its knees. The party's control over candidates declined as the nominating process was opened up and many more states conducted primaries to determine who should run for office.

The financing laws of the 1970s curtailed contributions to the overall party organizations but allow uncontrolled contributions to specific individuals (through political action committees or PACS). The decline of the party has also been furthered by the cumulative results of gerrymandering, which homogenizes electoral districts, by technological changes, especially in mass communications, and by the growth of professional political services performed outside the party by media, advertising, and polling specialists and groups.

The demise of the political party is reflected in and reinforced by a decline in voter identification with a particular party (the rise of the undecided, the independent, the apathetic), by an increase at the state and federal level of split-party control of the executive and legislative branches, and by the growing practice of holding separate state and federal elections.

The demise of the party means a loss of problem-solving ability at the political level. Public life becomes fragmented and stalemated as it dissolves into single-issue groups, campaigns based on empty rhetoric and personality, and a divorce between political life and social problems. The overall trend also reflects and contributes to a significant new trend, the growth of mass political apathy. Since 1960 voter participation has declined almost steadily, reaching a low of 49.1 percent of the eligible electorate in 1988 (see Figure 7-3). Strenuous efforts by both parties to involve more voters in the 1984 election succeeded only in stabilizing voter turnout at 53 percent. Voter turnout in the United States remains far below that of the other developed capitalist societies (with the exception of Switzerland whose low turnout is due to the unimportance of central government).[12]

The decline of the political party has not led to the decline of politics but if anything the reverse. More time and money than ever are being pumped into political campaigns. The bulk of the money comes from conservative groups, from the extreme right to moderate Republicans. The essence of the new political campaign is to sell an image through mass marketing techniques. The explicitly arranged package is the candidate who says little, and thus offends as few as possible, who projects a *pseudo-Gemeinschaft* personality and who can disguise nineteenth-century norms and values with twentieth-century words. The ability to produce this sterile form of interaction between leader and follower has been enhanced by new audio-visual and computer technology.

Technology and the New Politics

Technology's impact on politics is large and varied. The printing press, for example, did much to change Europe's politics by bring-

[12]Robert W. Jackman, "Political Institutions and Voter Turnout In The Industrial Democracies", *American Political Science Review* 81 (June, 1987).

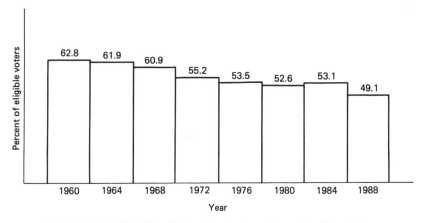

FIGURE 7-3. Political Participation in American Presidential Elections, 1960–1988.
Source: U.S. Bureau of the Census, *Statistical Abstract of the United States: 1988* (Washington, D.C.: U.S. Government Printing Office, 1987), Table 419; CBS News estimate, *N.Y. Times*, November 10, 1988, p. B6.

ing about, first a literate middle class, and then a literate citizenry. In the United States mass literacy (through mass education) and universal male suffrage both emerged in the 1850s. Newspapers and magazines became important political forces during the nineteenth century. In the 1930s President Roosevelt used the radio to galvanize the American people to overcome the Great Depression.

Technology's impact on politics has continued in the age of television. The advent of television (along with other technology) may actually have introduced new and dangerous levels of control over American political life. For one thing the dominance of television has turned politics away from written to oral discourse. No sane business person or professional would dream of conducting business primarily through verbal discourse. But first radio and now television has steered the American political world away from writing to audio-visual interaction. The new audio-visual technology in combination with other technology actually makes it possible for people to see and believe in things that don't really exist. The carefully arranged studio setting, the live shot in shopping malls and residential areas, and the staff of advertising experts, media consultants, pollsters, and psy-

chologists allow political elites to package and *sell* a candidate.[13] What is sold is an image, an individual larger than life, one who appeals to the public's hunger for a leader of heroic, unblemished stature. With careful editing, the leader always has a word of wisdom to offer. There is no fumbling or hesitation. With careful attention to props, the leader is associated with God, the flag, children, books, a fireplace, and the current fashion in dress. The leader is against evil, is generous to the needy, and verbalizes society's highest values. The result is not politics but a civil religious ceremony.[14]

The mobilization of opinion and voters takes place through political commercials and films that present an abstract political point of view. The selling of the candidate is supported by film shots of the candidate on the campaign trail. These are supplied free to the news bureaus of television stations. But the clips are carefully edited so that the candidate's mistakes and hesitations are omitted. Editing allows the candidate to appear

---

[13]For a classic analysis of the 1968 presidential campaign on behalf of Richard Nixon, see Joe McGinniss, *The Selling of the President, 1968* (New York: Trident, 1969).

[14]For the United States' civil religion, see Chapter 8.

with famous people—even when the famous people do not support them—and with large adoring crowds (sparsely attended rallies and opposition heckling are carefully edited out). Film clips are carefully geared to play on regional biases. Not only are commercials and news clips indistinguishable from each other but seeing is no longer believing. Technology and its owners have created a vivid, plausible but false reality.

The Captive American City

By common agreement, cities in capitalist Canada, Europe, and Japan are much better run (and much safer) than American cities. Why? One obvious reason is that the other capitalist societies have accepted government as a necessary and even primary factor in running society. Toronto, Canada, for example, is a thriving, clean, and safe city, on the whole. It has no slums like the notorious South Bronx in New York City and one is hard put to find even rundown areas. Why? One reason is that Toronto developed a federated metropolitan government to tackle the obviously related problems of the region. Another, and perhaps more important reason, is that the wealthy, the upper middle class, and the broad middle class all live in the metropolitan area. Toronto's elites, therefore, are subject to any and all policies adopted to solve problems. They have immediate feedback on failed programs because they and their families also experience the failure. And they can also see more clearly how policies adopted at other levels of government impact on cities because they also impact on them.

American elites, on the other hand, do not experience their policies first hand. It is much easier, therefore, for them to develop policies based on naturalistic, abstract, market conceptions (for example, the ecological-functional approach in sociology). American elites approach the city with the same ad hoc skills and practices that they use elsewhere (reliance on technology, management controls, public relations). But improved efficiency in administration, labor practices,

budget controls, spending, and welfare expenditures have not arrested the decline of America's great cities—all such improvements do is to slow the rate of decline. What they amount to is the energetic "management of failure."

The United States does considerable planning but it largely benefits the middle and upper classes.[15] Planning to help the working and lower classes is woefully incomplete, underfunded, and fitful; all in all, it compares very unfavorably with the capitalist democracies of Europe. American welfare programs also lag badly behind those in Europe. Neither in urban-housing planning nor in welfare do the European countries deprive the upper classes while benefitting the lower. Their planning is better; they get more for their money and consequently the poor, though still poor, are better off.[16]

The American reform and planning tradition has always been elite run and elite bounded. Policy debates about the city have taken place largely among rival elites. Without questioning the basic thrust of American economic expansion (our heavy reliance on private initiative and private profit), American elites have struggled to control the city. Subject to a laissez-faire national and international economy, cramped by a fragmented governmental system, lacking a vital economic and tax base, the urban center can neither control itself nor be controlled from the outside. Perhaps most striking is the way in which the urban center responds to all forms of technology, giving the technology of the past as well as the technology of the present and the future an equal and unexamined home. Thus the city is shaped to suit the needs of maritime technology, the railroad, the auto-

---

[15]Anthony Downs has analyzed the federal government's highway and subsidized housing programs that enabled the middle and upper middle classes to leave the city and thus erode its tax base; see "The Impact of Housing Policies on Family Life in the United States Since World War II," *Daedalus* 106 (Spring, 1977): 163–80.

[16]For an informative argument along these lines, see Susan S. Fainstein and Norman I. Fainstein, "National Policy and Urban Development", *Social Problems* 26 (December, 1978): 125–46.

mobile, the airplane, and construction technology (for example, the elevator). In the recent decades the computer, satellites, and the airliner have made possible the multinational corporation, the world market economy, and mobile, value-free, nonnational capital.[17] The result is not shape but shapelessness, at once short-term economic rationality and political-social disorder. Huddled close to take advantage of the division of labor, city elites and others radiate out to find suitable places to live, city mortgage money and its construction technology making the "suburban society" possible, those shapeless, problem-ridden agglomerates of better housing that are mere phases in the sprawling process of urbanization.[18] The overall thrust of the economy not only undermines community but makes politics, government, and citizen action difficult (see Box 7-4, Technology and the Decline of Community).

The American city reflects national life—the unprecedented privatization of society that has absorbed political institutions at federal and state levels has also absorbed them at the local level. The United States lacks a viable public sector composed of a national civil service, explicit functions, and capital resources. Political and administrative functions and jurisdictions are badly fragmented, the antigovernment, antipolitical tradition is as strong as ever, and American governments can never use capital directly (and thus plan) but must always distribute capital indirectly through tax laws, subsidies, or bond issues. Federal economic policy and most federal legislation simply channel public money to private groups to use as they think best. The absorption of public functions by private

bodies not only leaves the United States with many of the marks of an underdeveloped nation-state, but like many new countries its political life is deeply marred by corruption (see Chapter 20). Whether the United States can bring its cities under control is problematic. The city is a creature of the national and international economy and polity. Only when they are brought under control by a viable public will the city fulfill its promise.

PROPOSALS FOR REVITALIZING THE AMERICAN POLITY

Electoral Reform

The stalemate of the American political process is evident to all. There has been an ominous drop in political participation. People may have lost their sense that they have power to influence government. Many are aware of and often cynical about the way government works to help the strong, the wealthy, and the educated more than their opposites.

Proposals to revitalize the American polity include the following:

1. Abolishing the gerrymander to force candidates and parties to compete in mixed electoral districts.
2. Financing all elections with tax money thus curbing the special power that goes to those with money.
3. Making it easier to register and vote.

The overall thrust of electoral reform is to make politics more meaningful and to make political actors accountable and their discourse clear and relevant.

The prospects for electoral reform do not look good. Those who benefit from existing arrangements are the same ones who must make the reforms and that is asking a great deal. Existing arrangements fragment the electorate and allow entrenched power groups to veto electoral and other reforms. The gerrymander separates the population into relatively homogeneous enclaves of people who elect candidates tied to narrow interests. The

---

[17]For the new international context that explains why some American cities decay and some prosper, see Norman J. Glickman, "International Trade, Capital Mobility, and Economic Growth: Some Implications For American Cities and Regions In The 1980s," in D. A. Hicks and N. J. Glickman, eds., *Transition To the 21st Century: Prospects and Policies For Urban-Regional Transformation* (Greenwich, Conn.: JAI Press, 1983), pp. 205–39.

[18]For an excellent analysis of suburbia, see Robert Fishman, *Bourgeois Utopias: The Rise and Fall of Suburbia* (New York: Basic Books, 1987).

BOX 7-4. Technology and the decline of community

Downtown Anycity, U.S.A. began its decline with the giant surge of prosperity after World War II. The automobile made it possible for people to live in suburbs. People found it more convenient to drive to giant shopping malls on the outskirts of cities than to downtown stores. The automobile also led to fast-food outlets on the highways of America. Places like MacDonald's exude an air of prosperous hustle and bustle but critics charge that 83 percent of their revenues are siphoned out of the local community.[1] Community decline amid prosperity seems impossible. But faith in progress and in the automatic value of technology has begun to wane. The impact of technology (and other forces) on the common standards (moral norms and values) that make up a community has also been noticed. The story of John Moviehouse is a case in point.

John Moviehouse's father had prospered in downtown Anycity, U.S.A. as the owner of a movie theater. John did well for a while but in 1963 a shopping mall outside the city constructed a theater with three showing rooms. Since then two other theaters have opened at suburban malls and John was threatened with bankruptcy. But John was 43 and had no prospects for earning a living in a different way. John decided to show X-rated films.

John's decision created an uproar. Church groups denounced his move and picketed his theater. The PTA passed a resolution condemning it. The city council discussed ways to stop "the flow of filth." A representative of a national women's group visited Anycity to speak against pornography. John's lawyer argued that any attempt by the city to stop his client from showing whatever films he wanted violate the first amendment and its guarantee of free speech. Civic leaders were firm though since the U.S. Supreme Court had ruled that it was permissible to stop the expression of things that violated community standards. John was indicted and brought to trial.

The town was in an uproar about the case for a week until John's lawyer realized something that brought the agitation to an end. Four local appliance stores sold X-rated video tapes and film for private collectors, a cable television company was beaming X-rated programs to Anycity, and the city had two adult motels. The case was dismissed once it became apparent that, at least in this regard, there were no community (common) standards.

[1]For a radical indictment of fast food chains as detrimental to both human and community health, see Peter Barry Chowka, "Hamburger's Last Stand" *East West Journal* (June, 1979); discussed in Box 18-4.

---

financing and running of campaigns tends to emphasize candidates' personality, not issues or overall policy programs. Laws to control contributions to political parties and to limit campaign expenditures have not been effective—power groups ignore them for the most part or find it easy to get around them. In addition, the United States Supreme Court has declared that property interests (corporations) have the right to free speech (on ballot issues) thereby loosening the limits that reformers had hoped to place on the power of corporations to influence politics.[19]

The flow of money directly to candidates frees them from party discipline and makes them the agents of the suppliers of money.

[19]This continues the nineteenth-century legal fiction that corporations are persons entitled to constitutional rights.

Public money to help finance presidential campaigns has been a step toward reforming elections but Congress has refused to finance congressional elections with public money (for the obvious reason that incumbents have a huge advantage over challengers). The present arrangements benefit business and professional interests, and it is doubtful if their power over elections and candidates can be curtailed without strenuous effort. An aspect to this problem that is also detrimental to creative, pluralist politics is that over 90 percent of the money contributed to candidates goes to incumbents and it is not uncommon for private power groups to contribute to *both* Republican and Democratic candidates. No wonder then that three-quarters of the seats for the U.S. House of Representatives are noncompetitive!

Reformers argue that curtailing the power of private money will force interest groups to argue their positions on their merits. Forcing power groups to explain why what they want is good for all is the meaning of a democratic polity. Reformers argue that Great Britain puts very strict limits on how much can be spent on elections and no harm has come to their democratic processes. Great Britain also allots free time on television for political parties (after all, the air waves are public property). This reduces the party's need to solicit funds from private groups and it curtails the use of political commercials focused on irrelevant slogans and images.

Economic and Social Planning

The American polity, argue reformers, must play a bigger role in explicitly guiding the development of American society. Our present policy is not working. Calling all this free enterprise and democracy obscures the issue: the lack of policies to run the country is itself a policy and deserves to be evaluated as such. The American economy must be directed, if not actually planned, so that recessions, unemployment, and bankruptcy can be prevented. Explicit government direction can help modernize and adjust the economy to new conditions—at present threatened businesses dig in and use government to protect obsolete ways. Explicit government direction can help the professions evaluate their performance according to their own achievement criteria—at present threatened elites dig in and use government to protect the incompetent and preserve obsolete practices. Once this process is started labor unions, farmers, and other groups can afford to follow. The main objective is to make it possible for groups to adjust to new conditions. An important condition for developing adaptive personalities and an adaptive society is to create public confidence in which all have faith that losses and gains will be shared equitably.

Strengthening Social Policy Research

Social policy research has emerged in recent years as an encouraging development both in sociology and American public life. Despite impressive beginnings much remains to be done. Relations between social researchers and government data-collection agencies must be improved. A wide range of data must be recast to make fact gathering relevant to policy formation. Relations between fact collectors and policy makers must be improved. And evaluation must be carefully built into our public policies and programs to make sure that they have their desired effects.

The use of advisory committees and consulting firms to formulate reports and make policy recommendations to our legislatures and political leaders must be reexamined. Such bodies are widely used and enjoy quasi-public standing. But, charge critics, such bodies help to disguise the exercise of power, allow partisan powerholders to appear disinterested and objective and block or mismanage needed reforms.[20]

---

[20]For an indictment of the federal government's use of private advisory and consulting bodies, see Daniel Guttman and Barry Willner, *The Shadow Government: The Government's Multi-Billion-Dollar Giveaway of Its Decision-Making Powers to Private Management Consultants, 'Experts,' and Think Tanks* (New York: Pantheon Books, 1976).

Public policy educational programs must address the issue of how to infuse the exercise of power with knowledge, imagination, flexibility, and responsibility. At both the undergraduate and graduate levels, education for the professions must deal with the real world faced by problem solvers. They must recognize that running public affairs is neither a matter solely for technical knowledge, nor a matter to be approached only in a value-neutral way. Ultimately, problems make sense only if they are put in a sociopolitical context and solved through a mixture of cognitive and value judgments.[21]

THE POLITY: A SUMMARY

The concept *polity* refers to politics, government, and law. The polity (or the state) is the major way in which citizens and groups resolve their differences and try to achieve both their separate and collective interests. The polity's basic functions are to protect a society against foreign enemies, maintain internal order, help society adapt to new conditions, and give legitimacy to power relations.

The American polity is based on constitutionalism, the rule of law, and representation through elections. American government has undertaken many new functions, especially the task of guiding the economy, since the Great Depression of the 1930s. The basic reason for the growth of explicit government is that various groups, especially the middle and upper classes, have demanded it.

The American polity displayed a creative politics for much of its history. But in recent decades it seems to have lost its ability to solve problems. Interest groups have become so specialized, complex, and intertwined that it is now difficult to solve any one problem

without arousing a large number of interest groups who benefit from the conditions creating the problem. New and old economic groups, the growth of political consciousness in minorities, the decline of the political party, and the growth of political apathy and disenchantment have produced what appears to be a stalemated politics and a remote and unresponsive government.

Part of the problem with the American polity is that it originated in the static, rural world of the eighteenth century. Over time, it has been depicted in both Newtonian and Darwinian terms and surrounded with myths, especially about the federal government. Thus while functionalists focus on the reality of constitutionalism, the rule of law, the extension of civil rights, and creative, political problem solving, conflict theorists focus on a different reality—politics, government, and law, argue conflict theorists, are dominated by the upper classes who use them to solve their own problems first and those of the people second (and sometimes not at all).

The tangle of interest groups under corporate capitalism means that it is difficult to develop coherent governing majorities. Power groups have searched for consensus by becoming more formalistic, by skillfully appealing to the public with broad abstractions. One result has been to transform two-way interaction between the seekers and holders of power, on the one hand, and the electorate, on the other, into one-way interaction.

One result of the cleavage between leaders and followers and the resulting emergence of ineffective government is to raise questions about the alleged rationality of voters and the alleged harmony of interest among self-interested segments of the population.

Proposals to revitalize the problem solving capacity of the American polity are: a more positive attitude toward government; electoral reform to neutralize the power of private money, curb the gerrymander, and strengthen political parties; a more explicitly planned economy and society; and continued efforts to improve policy research and policy making.

---

[21]For an indictment of Harvard's Kennedy School of Government (which can also stand for most public policy programs in the United States) along these lines, see Jonathan Alter, "Harvard vs. Democracy" *Washington Monthly* 15 (March 1983): 32–39.

8

FAMILY, RELIGION, AND EDUCATION

COMPARATIVE FAMILY FORMS

Most societies define marriage carefully to specify such things as the rights and responsibilities of spouses and the "ownership" of and responsibility for children. Marriage is, as is all behavior, a cultural act, as is reproduction. Sexual intercourse is mediated by a host of values and norms—it is never (in or out of marriage) a simple biological act. The emotions, the values, and the purposes associated with sex vary enormously from culture to culture. Depending on time and place, sex has been associated with religion, family honor, love, politics, economic values, and state policy. Birth and fertility rates,[1] therefore, are not a direct function of either sexual energy or sexual intercourse.

The family does more than replenish population. Its members are deeply implicated in the economy. It is the medium through which property is transmitted. It is the seat of religious values. And, as the most important mechanism of socialization, it is central to personality formation.

Basic Family Types: Extended and Nuclear

There are two basic types of family, *extended* and *nuclear*.[2] The *extended family* is a

---

[1]The *birth rate* is the number of births per 1,000 people in the population; the *fertility* rate is the number of births per 1,000 women in the childbearing ages (for example, 15 to 44 years old).

[2]For basic readings on the family, see Arlene S. Skolnick and Jerome Skolnick, eds., *Family In Transition: Rethinking Marriage, Sexuality, Child Rearing and Family Organization*, 5th ed., (Boston,: Little Brown, 1986) and James M. Henslin, ed., *Marriage and Family In A Changing Society*, 2nd ed., (New York: Free Press, 1985). For national family policies in 14 capitalist and state socialist societies, which includes a discussion of the United States, see Sheila B. Kamerman and Alfred J. Kahn, eds., *Family Policy: Government and Families in Fourteen Countries* (New York: Columbia University Press, 1978). For a

household composed of a number of married couples and their children and can include a variety of relatives from grandparents to cousins. The *nuclear family* is a household composed of a married couple and their children.

There are so many subtypes and variations of these two basic family structures, depending on the type of society, that it is probably best to think of family behavior in terms of a continuum. At one end, in hunting-gathering and simple horticultural societies, the extended family is often a central institution, and occasionally, coextensive with society itself. In agrarian and early industrial societies, the nuclear family predominates. In an advanced industrial society, the nuclear family is still primary but appears to enjoy the least support from other institutional structures. As a general type, therefore, the nuclear family clearly predates industrialization.

The contemporary American nuclear family, however, is not the same as the nuclear family in the American past, the nuclear family in feudal China, India, and Europe, or the nuclear family in preindustrial Ireland, France, or French Canada. While the preindustrial nuclear family had a monogamous pair who lived in a separate household with their immediate children, it often had more in common with the extended than the industrial nuclear family. The term *extended stem family*, which is sometimes used to describe such families, denotes the strong continuity that exists among generations. In the agrarian nuclear family, there are deeply implanted obligations whose force is to insure the immediate and the long-range integrity and survival of the bloodline and its means of sustenance.

The industrial nuclear family is always monogamous and the husband, wife, and immediate children live independently of relatives (neolocal). While the family name is taken from the husband, authority, privileges, property, and duties are shared by the husband and wife and the children are treated equally and share the family legacy equally regardless of age or sex (in the ideal middle-class family).[3]

Capitalism and Family Structure

The rise and subsequent development of capitalism had an enormous impact on family life. The development of commerce and industry during the early stage of capitalism meant a drift from the countryside into urban centers. Gradually, the factory system undermined cottage industry. With fuller industrialization, a vast structure of specialized occupations grew outside of farming, handicrafts, and small businesses. The movement from farming to factory and office work represented a massive shift away from the family as an economic unit. Indeed, the new economy undercut the family by hiring individuals as individuals. It also undercut it as an economic unit by providing it with many of the things that family members once produced for themselves, for example, food, clothing, furniture, entertainment. Professionalization also stripped the family of some of its former functions. Today, the family depends on outside experts in the realms of religion, schooling, medicine, conflict resolution, and even child raising. Government also took away some family functions. Indirectly, it did so by stimulating economic and professional development. Directly, it reshaped the family by making provisions for the elderly, the sick, the abandoned, and those in economic distress—all formerly done (when it was done) by the family.

Many contemporary family values and practices make sense if seen as an accommodation to the needs of capitalism. The changed attitude toward sex that accompanied the rise and development of capitalism is a case in

---

magnificent reference book covering every conceivable aspect of family life, see Marvin B. Sussman and Suzanne K. Steinmetz, eds., *Handbook of Marriage and the Family* (New York: Plenum Press, 1987).

[3]For a fascinating set of readings on the American family, see Michael Gordon, ed., *The American Family in Socio-Historical Perspective,* 3rd ed., (New York: St. Martin's Press, 1983).

point. The medieval church's acceptance of sex as a natural function was part of its broad familistic orientation and its broad acceptance of a static agrarian world. Capitalism represents an attempt to master the world, to bring nature under human control. To further its goal of mastery of nature, capitalism, aided by Protestantism, drastically devalued sex as it sought to bring all irrational and nonrational forces under its control. Like the other passions, sex is unpredictable and has consequences that can divert time, energy, and resources away from work and thought. The strong emphasis on controlling sexual expression, ranging from Puritan inhibitions and taboos to the growth of contraceptives and family planning, is part of capitalism's attempt to either curtail passion or harness it to the conquest of nature.

New attitudes about and practices concerning children are also related to the capitalist economy. The "invention of childhood" during the nineteenth century stemmed from the need to regulate the flow of family members into the work force (child labor laws can certainly be interpreted in this way). Concern about and love for children are also necessary to provide the emotional commitment needed to see parents and children through the long years of dependence (childhood) mandated by industrial society and to compensate for the impersonality of capitalist society.

Capitalism also penetrated the home directly with consequences for sex roles. The introduction of new technology into the home between 1860 and 1960 was a vast and complex process of industrialization. The new household devices required electricity, oil, municipal water and sewerage systems, and continuous maintenance and repair by skilled workers. This new technology drastically reorganized work inside the home. Whereas the preindustrial home required extensive sharing of the heavy manual work with little differentiation of labor, the industrialization of housework led to a sharp division of labor: women stayed home ("the invention of housework") and men went out to earn the money to pay for the new technology and services.

Technology's impact on the family was to segregate the sexes and to separate the home from "work" (housework was no longer considered work despite its similarity to other forms of industrial-service work).[4]

The Functions of the Industrial Nuclear Family

Despite the decline of familism, the family is functionally important to industrial society. It is still the major source of population replenishment. It socializes each oncoming generation, though much of its socialization function is now shared with outside groups. The family also provides emotional support and reinforcement for the personality of parents as well as children. By and large, the bulk of the population enjoys family life—most Americans spend a great deal of time with their families, and, on the whole, children value and appreciate their parents. Interaction with a wider circle of kin (either because of close proximity or because the telephone and easy travel make it possible) is quite common (aided by the United States's many family-centered holidays).

The motives for having children have changed over the past 50 to 100 years. Today, there is less emphasis on having children to serve God or to maintain the family bloodline. Parents no longer think of children as an insurance policy against old age. By and large, parenthood is now associated with personal fulfillment. In line with the new emphasis on personal fulfillment, there is also a small trend toward marriage without children.

FAMILY IN THE DEVELOPING WORLD

The American nuclear family is a unique historical phenomenon. The developing world is experiencing economic change differently

---

[4]For a fascinating contrast between the preindustrial and industrialized household, see Ruth Schwartz Cowan, *More Work For Mother: The Ironies of Household Technology from the Open Hearth to the Microwave* (New York: Basic Books, 1983).

than the West and the family there is adapting differently. As we will see, the Third World is still largely rural and the family is still a central institution, especially in economic terms and for the care of the elderly. Kinship relations are extremely important even when Third World peoples move into cities. Politics in the Third World are often based on kinship or kin-like relations (patron-client or clientelism). And the position of women has not changed nearly as much in the Third World as it has in the United States (except in some communist countries such as Cuba, Vietnam, and China).

FAMILY, MODERNIZATION, AND POPULATION

Population Analysis: The Essentials of Demography

The intimate relation between modernization and population dynamics requires a word about *demography*, the analysis of population. Demographers are sociologists who try to determine how population characteristics have come to be what they are and how they will develop in the future. Understanding population characteristics and trends is important to policy makers and holds special interest for our policy theme.

In addition to size, demographers want to know how fast a population is growing, how many males and females there are, marriage rates, and what the age distribution is. Demographers are also interested in patterns of internal and international population movement (see earlier references to the importance of slavery, immigration, illegal aliens, and the brain drain to the economic development of the United States).

Many factors explain the quantities and qualities in any given population. Religious variables, contraceptive technology, political-military policy, nutrition and sanitation, employment opportunities, and health-care systems all affect human reproduction and help decide who lives and for how long. The impact of these variables is not always easy to understand. Improved nutrition, for example, not only allows people to live longer but hastens the onset of puberty for teenage girls, making them susceptible to pregnancy at earlier ages. As in other areas of sociology, there are no simple, monocausal explanations in demography. Indeed, the causes behind population characteristics are so numerous and so subject to change that a leading demographer has warned against assuming that the causes of population change are permanent or universal.[5]

Comparative Population Dynamics

World population size has grown very unevenly. From paleolithic times until the middle of the twentieth century, the world's population grew slowly. Since 1950 it has accelerated enormously and poses a problem or, rather, a series of problems. It took tens of thousands of years to reach the present world population of 5.5 billion—in 20 years it will grow by approximately 50 percent to stand at 7.5 billion. Some countries (basically the more-developed countries) have undergone what is called the *demographic transition*— they have crossed the threshold into low death and low birth rates. The less-developed countries are marked by high population growth because they have drastically reduced their death rates while maintaining high birth rates.

Lowered birth rates in the developed countries stem from changes brought on by industrialism, the rationalization of life, and individualism. A large family is no longer an asset supplying labor on the farm or support during times of crisis, especially old age. On the contrary, a large number of children is a burden. Individuals today expect personal satisfaction from their marriages and families, and frame their lives accordingly—one result is a limitation on children (parents also want their children to be happy and this is another reason for birth control and small families).

---

[5]Nathan Keyfitz, "Causes and Consequences of Population Change" in Amos H. Hawley, ed., *Societal Growth: Processes and Implications* (New York: Free Press, 1979), pp. 76–95.

In less-developed countries population has soared. The introduction of Western medicine and improved sanitation have drastically lowered death rates. But high birth rates have continued because of the persistence of traditional religious and family values. Strenuous efforts at family planning have helped curb runaway population growth in some countries but headway is difficult because the values family planning represents run counter to tradition.

Societies experience other kinds of population problems besides overpopulation. A society can have a relative decline in population vis-a-vis its enemies. It can have a burdensome mix of people: too many young or old. It can have the "wrong" mix of ethnic groups (the Soviet Union at 286 million people is the third largest nation in the world but it faces a labor shortage and an internal political problem in the near future because the Russian segment of its population is growing at a much slower rate than its non-Russian ethnic groups). In a totally different sense, the developed countries are the ones that are overpopulated if one judges population size by pressure on the environment. One American, for example, consumes, on average, 50 times as much as one Chinese.

Characteristics of the American Population

The American population grew from approximately 4 million in 1790 to approximately 246 million today. Population growth is caused by the surplus of births over deaths, immigration (legal and illegal), and peoples acquired through conquest, purchase, and annexation (Native Americans, Mexicans, Eskimos, Hawaiians).

The main cause of population expansion is the American family. Over time the American fertility rate has declined (interrupted by the baby boom of 1945–65) and now stands near the replacement level. It is clear that middle-class "rationality" has permeated family life and that all economic levels, regardless of religion, have begun to restrict birth, primarily through the prevention of concep-

tion but also through abortion. It is also clear that women are having their children early and spacing them. In addition, their ability to free themselves from child care in their thirties and forties, combined with a life expectancy in the upper seventies, means that women are now capable of pursuing lives outside the home and beyond child raising.

Life expectancy has more than doubled since colonial times, going from roughly 35 years to more than 75 during the 1980s. However, women live significantly longer than men—the average male lives into the low 70s while the average female lives almost to 80. Life expectancy also varies depending on race and economic background. Caucasians live to an average of 74 years while non-Caucasians (mostly black Americans) live to 69.[6]

Changes in age structure are important to policy makers in all areas of social life. An aging population has implications for health care policy, housing, and so on. Changes in the number of young people are important in many ways. Young people go to the movies more often than older people, commit more crime, are less interested in politics, and have higher unemployment rates. Unless policy makers take age into account they will get misleading pictures of what is going on. Today, young people make up a smaller, and older people a larger, percentage of the population, a trend that is pronounced in all industrial societies. The reverse is true in the developing world.

THE AMERICAN FAMILY

Households: Types and Trends

A *household* is any living arrangement of people under one roof and comes in two basic forms: the *family* household (two or more persons related by marriage, blood, or adoption) and the *nonfamily* household (persons

---

[6]U.S. Census Bureau, *Statistical Abstract of the United States, 1988* (Washington, D.C.: U.S. Government Printing Office, 1987), Table 108.

living alone or with unrelated individuals). One important trend in the composition of households has been the growth of non-family households as a percentage of total households, a reflection of the aging of the American population.

Analysts also distinguish between two types of family household, the married-couple family (72 percent) and other families (28 percent). Here another important trend has emerged—the married-couple family has declined as a percentage of *all* households (to 58 percent in 1987 down from 71 percent in 1970) while other families (composed primarily of one-parent families headed primarily by women) has increased to 14 percent of all households. Given the crucial role of the family as a socializing agency, it is important to know the types of households that children grow up in. One-parent homes, especially those headed by women, increased significantly between 1970 and 1987. By 1987, 24 percent of all children were living in one-parent homes.

The typical American family is still composed of two parents and immediate children, though the two-parent family with one breadwinner has declined significantly. The Census Bureau reports that, in 1987, both spouses were working in 50 percent of all married-couple households. When looked at in terms of *all* households, the traditional nuclear family of one male breadwinner, one homemaker, and dependent children makes up a mere 10 percent of the total. American families are still nuclear-neolocal—adult children typically still leave home to work or marry (although they are often forced to stay at home or move back in during times of economic recession). Though the average age of first marriage has risen, marriage is still very popular—95 percent of the population marries at one time or another and Americans remarry at high rates after divorce.

Marriage and Parenthood

Societies sanction marriage in many different ways. In the United States (and other industrial countries) the sentiment that legit-imates marriage is romantic love. Romantic love may or may not be an innate drive but it seems to flourish only under certain social conditions. Romantic love suits the economic, political, and religious traditions of the United States insofar as these stress individualism and equality. In an individualistic-equalitarian society, it would be contradictory to have arranged marriages or spouses for sale. Romantic love, on the other hand, allows both individuals entering a marriage to remain individuals. Love is also important after marriage. The stripped-down nuclear marriage-and-family requires partners who can provide each other with a wide range of emotional, physical, and intellectual supports and services. Love is an open ended sentiment that facilitates a complex and demanding marital status. American marriage, no less than economic and political statuses, requires the versatile, all-purpose individual.

The American emphasis on romance may prevent young people from understanding that most of married life is quite prosaic—a matter of hard work, often boring, always time consuming. Marriage and parenting require many skills ranging from empathy to plumbing, from budgeting to sex. Raising children is of preeminent importance to society but parenting has been devalued by major forces in American society. Consider, too, that much of the socialization for marital status takes place *after* marriage, that is, at the same time that the marriage partners are searching for emotional fulfillment. In addition learning how to be a parent must be done *after* children have arrived. And all this learning must go on as young couples struggle to establish careers and often merely to make ends meet.

Clearly, the pervasive individualism of American society is not a good preparation for marriage or parenthood. The United States has no structured courtship practices. Males and females are still segregated in the socialization process, and many teenagers and young adults find dating difficult. Often dates are exchange relations (a mutual calculated search for tangible benefits) not a search for friendship and love. Young career and working singles find it difficult to meet members of the opposite sex. Clearly growing up in America is not a realistic preparation for marriage and the assumption of family responsibilities.

Marriage is still popular with Americans although some new marriage arrangements have appeared along with some alternatives to marriage. "Partnership" marriages (with or without separate careers) are probably increasing. Occasionally such marriages even include a contract spelling out rights and duties. Childless marriages by design have also made their appearance. There is a small tendency for couples to live together without marriage and a small number prefer to remain single. However, despite the emergence of new living arrangements, Americans remain overwhelmingly agreed that marriage and children are preferable to remaining single, living together, or being childless.

Working Wives and Mothers: The Triple Burden

Women have worked outside the home throughout American history. What has changed is that women no longer work for a short period before marriage and then settle down at home to a life as a wife and mother. Women now work throughout their adult years: before and after marriage, before and after children. The reason that women work is that their families need the money—most women work to make ends meet, not for luxuries and not for fulfillment.

The entry of women into the labor force accelerated after World War II. Many think of this as women's liberation, the desire of women to lead more satisfying, fuller lives. This may be true of the small numbers of educated women who have spearheaded the women's movement. The period since 1945 brought a unique and misunderstood prosperity to the United States. For a majority of households, keeping up and sharing in prosperity was possible only with double breadwinners. This period saw an end to the idea of the husband as sole breadwinner, an idea that had only partial validity even during its heyday between 1860 and 1940. The truth of the matter

is that the American economy was no longer generating the well-paid jobs that had given this concept its limited validity. The working American woman is largely the story of the decline in good jobs for males.

Working women now bear a heavy burden. Child-care facilities, babysitting relatives, flexible hours, paid maternity leaves, and so on have helped a few working wives and mothers assume new responsibilities. In some cases, husbands have made adjustments. By and large, however, working women (in the United States as well as other countries) have merely assumed more responsibilities, not a new and fulfilling package of statuses. They still seem to do the shopping, cooking, cleaning, and parenting as well as bringing home some of the bacon. When marriages fail, they often have to bring home all the bacon as well.

European countries have a far more comprehensive set of public services and subsidies for working women than the United States. These include maternity care, paid maternity leave, government income support for families, government support for housing, government support for flexible hours, child care, and job training. The European countries have a much higher acceptance of the role of government, and help for working women was simply taken for granted as part of their citizenship and as a way to overcome labor shortages.

Divorce

Divorce became more accepted legally and morally after World War II, and the divorce rate has gone up.[7] Divorce is a painful experience for both spouses and children and usually results in a loss of economic status for women and children and a gain for men. It tends to occur among those who are young, nonreligious, and of average or lower economic prospects. Most divorced people re-

---

[7]The United States has the highest divorce rate among developed societies, 4.9 per 1,000 (followed by the Soviet Union's 3.4); see United Nations, *Demographic Yearbook, 1984* (New York: United Nations Publishing Division, 1986), Table 4.

marry and it is now common to have households with a stepparent. The effects of divorce on children can be shattering and while the evidence is not conclusive, divorce is yet another way in which America is failing its children.

The Pathology of the American Family

The pathology of the American family is hard to imagine. For obvious reasons, there are few reliable figures on violence in the home, the destructive force of loneliness, the number of runaway fathers, children, and even mothers, or the impact of mental illness and alcoholism.[8] Family instability through divorce and separation, a deep estrangement between the sexes, and some estrangement between age groups ("the generation gap") are well known. A conservative estimate places the number of children subjected to physical injury by parental violence in one year (1975) at somewhere between 1.4 and 1.9 million.[9] In 1972, a Senate subcommittee estimated that between 500,000 and one million children run away from home every year.[10] Conservative estimates place the number of physically-abused wives at one million for 1972.[11] Surveys also suggest that between 1.5 and 5 percent of individuals and one family in ten may be involved in some form of incest.[12] And, in 1978, the Department of

Health, Education, and Welfare, in mounting a computer search for runaway fathers, estimated that there were 8 million men who had abandoned their families. In 1984 a U.S. Justice Department report by its Task Force on Family Violence estimated that there are 8 million acts of violence committed in the American home every year: husbands against wives, parents against children, adult children against elderly parents. A recent summary of research concluded that family abuse is higher in lower socioeconomic groups and among families suffering from unemployment, economic privation, and lack of attachment to community, friends, or organizations.[13]

America's high divorce, separation, and desertion rates take a heavy psychological toll on spouses and children, lead to economic loss, create unexpected housing demands, inflate the welfare rolls, and contribute to individual deviance and the formation of unlivable communities.

Supports for the American Family

New supports for the family have appeared in recent years. A wide variety of books and professions advise parents on how to raise their children. Charities, foundations, and even governments have begun to treat the family as a unit rather than concentrating solely on individuals. And mental health and alcoholism experts have begun to ask that families be treated, not just individual family members. The growth of no-fault divorce has also helped to reduce messy family disputes (though women tend to lose out on economic settlements). Also of help is an interesting and somewhat effective new procedure for settling family disputes, mediation.

---

[8]A Gallup Poll revealed that 33 percent of American families said alcoholism had caused trouble in their family; *The New York Times* (November 16, 1982), p. A16.

[9]Richard J. Gelles, "Violence Toward Children in the United States" in Richard Bourne and Eli H. Newberger, eds., *Critical Perspectives on Child Abuse* (Lexington, Mass.: Lexington Books, 1979), p. 60.

[10]Christine Chapman, *America's Runaways* (New York: William Morrow, 1976), pp. 31–32, 255. For evidence of a dramatic rise in runaway wives, as well as for runaway husbands, children, and elderly parents, see Myron Brenton, *The Runaways: Children, Wives and Parents* (Boston: Little Brown, 1978).

[11]Del Martin, *Battered Wives* (San Francisco: Glide, 1976), pp. 11–15, and Murray A. Straus, Richard J. Gelles, and Suzanne K. Steinmets, *Behind Closed Doors: Violence in the American Family* (Garden City, N.Y.: Doubleday, 1980).

[12]Blair and Rita Justice, *The Broken Taboo: Sex in the Family* (New York: Human Sciences Press, 1979).

[13]David Finkelhor, "Common Features of Family Abuse," D. Finkellor *et al.,* eds., *The Dark Side of Families: Current Family Violence Research* (Beverly Hills, Calif.: Sage, 1983), Chapter 1. The rest of this volume updates our understanding of the varieties of family abuse and the progress being made in analyzing it. For comparative material showing that family abuse is a problem for all industrial countries, see Richard J. Gelles and Claire Pedrick Cornell, eds., *International Perspectives on Family Violence* (Lexington, Mass.: D.C. Heath, 1983).

Other "solutions" to family problems are homes for battered wives and hot lines for runaways. In 1984, legislation was passed establishing a national clearing house on runaway children modelled on the computerized system for keeping track of stolen cars. But all of the above responses are focused essentially on symptoms. The best ways to support and stabilize the American family are to provide full employment for the American people, targeted housing, and child-care programs. Ways must be found to provide a better transition from school to work and a better relation between residence and work. And there is no reason why many of the skills that the new family professions are selling cannot be learned in school as part of the normal curriculum. The United States has double the teenage pregnancy rate of other industrial societies, for example, and experts have concluded that the main reason is the lack of sex education and readily available birth control devices.

The Durable But Dependent Family

The American family reflects profound long-range causal processes in the American economy and overall power structure. To the extent that we focus on the family as an autonomous cause and confuse myths with reality in this area, we obscure the power of the American economy and its auxiliary institutions: government, education, religion, and voluntary groups. Here, as in most problem areas, the United States lacks an explicit, openly discussed and agreed-upon policy. The lack of consensus is understandable. There are conflicts about sexuality, birth control, abortion, and family values in general among religious groups and between feminist groups and assorted traditionalist groups. Given the differences in their socioeconomic development, the various states have conflicting definitions of minors, runaways, and the rights of husbands and wives. Against this background, legislators and family professionals are far from agreed on what should be done. Given deep conflict and stalemate, it is no wonder that vague abstractions, unfounded faith, and empty ideals are the order of the day.

Despite its many and varied pathologies, the American family is amazingly durable. Though no one can be certain, it will undoubtedly be with us for some time. It is not even possible to say that it will undergo a slow, long-term decline. But one thing is certain—the deep diversity, nay cleavages, in American society, including its multiple moralities and stalemated political system, will make it heavy going for those who want the United States to develop a meaningful family policy.[14] For the immediate future, therefore, the American family will sputter along, performing its functions inefficiently, and for many, not at all.

AMERICAN RELIGION IN COMPARATIVE PERSPECTIVE

Religion has been hard hit by modernization all over the world. In the West, religion is on a 500-year decline. Even in the United States, the most religious society in the West, membership in religious bodies slipped drastically during the 1970s. But even as religion declines, religious themes and values find new expression: in personalistic Protestantism, in youth-oriented cults, in the use of the supernatural to explain and justify American society, in right-wing political movements, and even in rackets that line the pockets of self-appointed religious leaders.

Outside the West, religion has had a varied fortune. Communist countries openly suppress and discourage its expression (though changes are taking place). The Roman Catholic Church is influential and politically engaged in Poland, Africa, Latin America, and the Philippines. The Muslim world is currently undergoing a vast religious revival, in

---

[14]For background on the ill-fated attempts by both Republican and Democratic administrations to develop a national family policy, see Gilbert Y. Steiner, *The Futility of Family Policy* (Washington, D.C.: The Brookings Institution, 1981).

many places seeking to stem the tide of secularism. And throughout the world, in places as varied as Northern Ireland, Lebanon, India, and Sri Lanka, conflict among religious groups has led to bloodletting and social stalemate.

THE SOCIOLOGY OF RELIGION

Religion consists of values, beliefs, and practices that assume a supernatural or sacred realm of being and causation. When sociologists study religion, they are interested in its social origins and functions, not its validity or truth. Their focus is on religion as a cultural phenomenon that energizes behavior and helps populations to survive (or hinders them from surviving and adapting). Whether declining or reviving, whether thriving or in crisis, religious behavior is an important indicator of what is happening to society.[15]

The Functional View of Religion

Stemming from the work of Durkheim, functionalist sociologists have stressed religion's positive contributions to society. It promotes social solidarity, gives life meaning, and helps people adjust to new conditions. Religion provides ideals that people can use to direct, evaluate, and reform their behavior. It provides an element of social pluralism. It stabilizes society by diffusing anxiety and conflict. It provides reform initiatives by criticizing the treatment of the poor and the weak, fighting racism, upholding the rights of homosexuals, and so on. Perhaps most important, it constitutes a reservoir of moral capital to sustain people and their institutions in an impersonal market society (which, at least to some, seems unable to generate its own morality).

The Conflict View of Religion

Conflict theorists look on religion differently. For them, present day religion is opposed to the main interests of humanity. Religion's main consequence is to justify an obsolete system of power. Religious leaders are depicted as members of a ruling class and religious values and norms are seen as a way to deceive the masses and divert them from the true causes of their troubles: the unequal distribution of power and property. Evil is real, say conflict sociologists, but it has nothing to do with human nature and everything to do with the way in which society is organized. While acknowledging the often progressive role of religion in American history, conflict sociologists also point to its conservative and reactionary actions. It has justified racism and sexism. It has substituted pie-in-the-sky for work and income. Today, well-organized religious groups are fighting hard to block the extension of rights to blacks, Hispanics, women, homosexuals, and other minorities and they are supporting questionable foreign policy initiatives including an excessive reliance on military force.

COMPARATIVE RELIGIOUS SYSTEMS

The Variety of Religious Expression

The unstructured nature of human nature has made possible a wide variety of secular as well as religious behavior.[16] At one time or another, humans have defined almost the entire range of animate and inanimate nature as sacred: bears, snakes, birds, the sun, stars, the moon, mountains, rivers, the wind, and so on. The sacred can also be a collection of human-like gods, or a single god. Religious symbolism can be diffused and particular (irrational, magical, nonrational), or highly

---

[15]For valuable source books, see H. Paul Chalfant, Robert E. Beckley, and C. Eddie Palmer, *Religion in Contemporary Society*, 2nd ed., (Palo Alto, Calif.: Mayfield, 1987) and Kenneth D. Wald, *Religion and Politics In the United States* (New York: St. Martin's, 1987).

[16]For comparative studies in religion, see William A. Lessa and Evon Z. Vogt, eds., *Reader in Comparative Religion: An Anthropological Approach*, 2d ed., (New York: Harper & Row, 1965) and John B. Noss, *Man's Religions*, 6th ed., (New York: Macmillan, 1980).

abstract and universal (rational, philosophical). Religious organization can be embedded in the family, in individual choice, in specialists, in loosely organized groups (sects), or in highly organized, bureaucratic groups (churches). Religious worship can be emotional or sedate, simple or elaborate. It can be a frenzied attempt to escape from the workaday world or a soothing, meditative break from the world's frenzy.

Type of Society and Type of Religion

Sociologists explain religion by relating its forms and functions to the type of society. Early sociological theorists, for example, Saint Simon and August Comte, gave considerable attention to religion, and their attempt to correlate religious and social evolution is a prominent feature of their sociology. Some examples of theorists who have interpreted religion in evolutionary terms are Guy Swanson,[17] Robert N. Bellah,[18] and Anthony F. C. Wallace.[19] Basically, the sociologists of religion have established a rough correspondence between the development of society and the development of religion.

All societies distinguish between the profane and the sacred but in many different ways. Belief in one god, a hereafter, eternal punishment or reward, and so on, are by no means characteristic of the religions of human beings. In simple societies, religion is *particularistic*, imparting a discrete form of sacredness to each institutional area. Simple societies are *zoomorphic* (the worship of animals, plants, or entities such as the sun, moon, or stars). Each sacred force has a function in a particular area: the hunt, fertility, war, and so on. In simple societies, the characteristic religious norm is the *taboo*, a norm that controls behavior in regard to a particular action, thing, time, or place.

Complex society develops a *universalistic* (broadly abstract) way of expressing religious norms and values. With the rise of agriculture, religion changes from zoomorphism to *anthropomorphism* (the worship of superhuman men and women). Complex agrarian society eventually leads to full universalism or the emergence of *monotheism* and the elaboration of a body of abstract ethical norms to cover a wide variety of situations. The characteristic religious norms of complex society are abstract goals (for example, ethics, brotherhood, love, peace, duty) and absolute, abstract morality (for example, the Ten Commandments).

A society's economic base also affects the form and content of religion. Herding societies tend to be warlike and to have war-oriented religions. Pastoral or herding societies often translate their economic experience (shepherding flocks) into monotheism and conceive the relation between God and humans along the lines of a shepherd and his flock.[20] The watchful, concerned God of Christianity had its origin in the pastoral life of the ancient Jews. Lenski also notes that herding societies practice bride purchase and require couples to live with the husband's kin. Such practices are extensions of the strong male principle that emerges in herding-military societies. It probably also explains why, in those societies, God is conceived of as a male and why clergy (high and low) are male.

Modern society has also profoundly affected religion. The rise of capitalism promoted individualism and thus helped turn some Christians into Protestants. Eventually, the emergence of representative government forced the Roman Catholic Church to sever its connection to feudal absolutism and endorse liberal democracy. Contemporary technological and economic forces continue to shape religion, for example, contraceptives are altering the relation of Roman Catholics to their church.

---

[17]*The Birth of the Gods* (Ann Arbor: University of Michigan Press, 1960).

[18]"Religious Evolution," *American Sociological Review* 29:3 (1964): 358–74.

[19]*Religion: An Anthropological View* (New York: Random House, 1966).

---

[20]For an interesting compilation of ideas and data along these lines, see Gerhard Lenski and Jean Lenski, *Human Societies: An Introduction to Macrosociology*, 5th ed., (New York: McGraw-Hill, 1987), pp. 214–15.

Major Religions in the Contemporary World

Christians taken as a single group make up the largest body of religious adherents in the world (est. 1.1 billion). The main divisions in Christianity are Roman Catholics, Protestants, and Eastern Orthodox. The Muslim and Hindu religions are the next largest (est. 555 million and 460 million respectively) followed by Buddhist and Confucian (est. 250 million and 158 million respectively).[21]

Religion, Reform, and Social System Change

Religion is often conservative but it also initiates reform, that is, changes within a given social order. These include defending the rights of the weak, opposing the exploitation of children, and promoting civil rights for all. In addition, religion supplies energy for social system change, that is, for establishing or pioneering a new social order. One example is the role of the medieval Christian Church in the modernization of the West. Its important role in pacifying and "civilizing" barbarian Europe is often overlooked. The medieval church was the preserver of Greek and Arabic philosophy, mathematics, and science. As the center of intellectual life, the church preserved Greek social theory and Roman law, cultural ingredients that played a significant role in the modernization of the West.

The role of a dynamic Protestantism in the creation of modern society is better known. The Reformation stemmed the flow of resources both to the national churches and to Rome. Confiscation of church properties freed them for purely economic exploitation. Above all, perhaps, Protestant religious individualism supported the capitalist impulse. The Protestant Reformation was a religious purification and mighty revival, a protest against the worldliness of the medieval church. Protestants wanted salvation but they could no longer seek it through the

magic and routine of the church's sacraments and they could not believe that it was possible to understand God through deductive teleological analysis (Thomistic philosophy). Cut off from the traditional avenues to God, Protestants experienced considerable anxiety about the proper road to salvation. By and large, Protestants found relief in the belief that they had a calling to do God's work in this world. The burgeoning capitalist economy was there to provide a ready outlet for their pent-up energies and anxieties. Their value to capitalism was twofold: they worked without consuming the full fruits of their labor (the result is saving and capital formation) and their stern religious character provided the moral relations (trust, predictability) needed for social interaction in an anonymous, impersonal capitalist economy.

Christianity also played a large role in the development of political individualism and constitutionalism during the early centuries of the modern West. Both Protestant and Roman Catholic theorists contributed to the conception of a people defined as the possessor of natural rights. The Roman Catholic Church has served to moderate the politics of industrial society starting with the papal encyclical, *Rerum Novarum* (1891). Though hampered by its long association with feudalism, the Roman Catholic Church has been liberal in the United States, revolutionary in Ireland, has spawned worker priests in France, and has been a moderating, sometimes critical force in some of the Latin American dictatorships. In 1986 it helped remove Haiti's dictator and openly campaigned against the Marcos dictatorship in the Philippines (and is credited with much of the success in bringing about its downfall).

American religious history bears a broad resemblance to the history of European religion during the postmedieval period. The tensions between otherworldly and worldly values and beliefs that marked other countries also appeared in the United States. Similar religious organizations and doctrines appeared in the United States, Great Britain, and Canada. As in other countries religious developments in the United States were both

---

[21]*Britiannica Book of the Year*, 1985, p. 365.

cause and consequence. And finally, as in other industrialized nations, there is a pronounced trend in the United States toward the supremacy of secular over religious values.

Religion and Nationalism

Religion is not only a prime force in the making of the modern state but it has also promoted nationalism. *Nationalism* is the love of country: its geography as well as culture. Religion helped the modern nation state emerge by acquiring an ethnic-linguistic flavor and by taking sides in political and economic rivalries. Ultimately, French Roman Catholics found it easy to war against German Roman Catholics and vice-versa. Religion also became the vehicle for expressing the aspirations of oppressed ethnic groups (for example, the Roman Catholic Church in Ireland or Poland and Zionism among European Jews). In more recent times religion has provided some Third World peoples with a means of expressing their national identity against imperial powers. Confucian scholars provided leadership for Vietnamese resistance to French imperialism. Ho Chi Minh, who led Vietnam's drive to free itself from foreign control, was himself much influenced by these Confucian "freedom-fighters." Confucianism is also useful in modernization since its principles of hierarchy and authority have helped Japan, South Korea, Taiwan, Hong Kong, Singapore, and more recently China to industrialize. And religion can be traditionalist even as it promotes nationalism as witness Islam, the Ayatollah Khomeini, and Iran.

RELIGION IN THE UNITED STATES

The Historical Context

Despite the United States's sharp separation between state and church, religion has played an important role in American history. The Pilgrims thought of themselves as free individuals bound in service to God—thus making an individual-centered society possible. Protestantism was powerful if not predominant in the English colonies and the early period of the American republic. Religion sanctioned slavery but also led the fight against it. Religion opposed American imperialism but also imparted a divine purpose to the continental and overseas expansion of the United States. Religion opposed America's wars but also declared them righteous because they were also being fought to realize God's purposes.

At the end of the nineteenth century, religion opposed secular progress but it also elaborated the social gospel (the use of religious values to solve social problems rather than for individual salvation alone) and thus helped the United States make the transition from an agrarian to an industrial society. Religion has fought the march of science (for example, by opposing the scientific theory of evolution), but other Protestants supported the scientific impulse. The black American's struggle for civil rights in the 1960s would be inconceivable without the leadership and help provided by black (and white) churches.

Protestants, Roman Catholics, and Jews mounted strong protests against the Vietnam war. In 1981 the Council of Protestant Churches joined the American Roman Catholic Church in opposing President Reagan's policy of sending military aid to the government of El Salvador claiming that an unjust, exploitative economy and a repressive government were the problems, not outside forces. In 1982, the American bishops of the Roman Catholic Church announced that nuclear war and preparations for it could never be justified, thereby putting pressure on the Reagan administration to seek arms reduction and moderate its military buildup. In 1985, the bishops issued a pastoral on the American economy that demanded corrective action to eliminate poverty and unemployment (in effect amounting to a severe criticism of the free enterprise system). Side-by-side with these religious impulses, a number of fundamentalist Protestant sects and groups strongly support the nuclear arms buildup and endorse the free enterprise system.

Religion has been an important force in creating and sustaining a unique secular society. Alone of the emerging capitalist societies, the United States had no established aristocracy experienced in governing society. One of the latent, that is, unintended functions of religion has been to supply the United States with the functional equivalent of a governing class and with much of its legitimating ideology.

Religious Belief and Practice Today

Americans are among the most religious people in the world when judged by belief in God and in an afterlife. The United States's strong religious beliefs makes it unusual among industrial countries. The European industrial countries have experienced marked declines in church attendance and in religious belief. The reason for this remarkable difference is that Christianity in the United States was an energizing force in the *creation* of American society. Christianity in Europe, however, is identified with *opposition* to modernization. The Roman Catholic Church, for example, was massively identified with feudalism and as an open enemy of the emerging liberal nation-state. Similarly, Lutheranism in Germany and Calvinism in Geneva were identified with absolutism and theocracy. Actually, the Christian churches of many countries in Western Eastern and Mediterranean Europe were associated with monarchy, reaction, and fascism well into the twentieth century. Even in England, where many of the liberalizing forces were religious, it was apparent to many that religion, from the established Angelican Church on down, was political in nature.

It should be noted, however, that American church attendance is not high and appears to be declining. Overall church membership also underwent a drastic decline in the 1970s with most of the losses taking place among traditional churches—fundamentalist, politically conservative Protestantism actually enjoyed a revival in the 1970s.[22]

The United States' Civil Religion

The rationale for establishing a capitalist society (the liberal nation-state) in the United States was supplied, to a large extent, by Protestantism. Setting up a society based on the free individual is not an appealing prospect to elites anywhere including Protestants. Individuals are likely to choose their self-interest over the social good, likely to go in different directions rather than toward common goals, likely to quarrel rather than work in harmony. Protestantism reconciled the public good with the free individual by assuming that individuals were in the service of God. It declared the new world the promised land, Protestant New Englanders were chosen people, and society was at once a covenant among believers and between believers and God.

The affinity between the Protestant world view and the liberalism of Jefferson and Madison is apparent. In the years after the American Revolution the Puritan image of society was secularized and blended with liberalism. The reverse was also true: liberalism was sacralized. The tension between religion and secular society remained but was transmuted, by and large, into the service of liberalism, providing what one author calls a "Christian industrialism."[23] Eventually, the free individual was reconciled with the social order and the welfare of society, not only by Providence, but by the providential market.

The intertwining of religion and liberalism eventually became what Bellah has called a *civil religion,* the celebration of Americanism using vague religious terminology.[24] Through its civil religion, the United States seeks to identify itself with both the natural and supernatural worlds. Through civil religion

---

[22]For an invaluable source and analysis of data about religion in the United States, see Jackson W. Carroll, Douglas W. Johnson, and Martin E. Marty, *Religion in America: 1950 to the Present* (New York: Harper & Row, 1979).

[23]For a fascinating picture of the organization of an early industrial town in Pennsylvania and of the role of Christianity in helping the propertied classes fight socialism and in providing religious support for the expansion and consolidation of American capitalism, see Anthony F. C. Wallace, *Rockdale* (New York: Knopf, 1978).

[24]Robert N. Bellah, "Civil Religion in America," *Daedalus* 96 (Winter, 1967): 1–21.

much about the United States passes beyond conscious thought into the taken for granted world.

Civil religion has a number of sources. Christianity supplied the concept of a single God with special plans for the United States. The early secular leaders of the republic turned this into deism (religion and morality based on reason rather than revelation, on an image of a finished universe no longer needing the intervention of the Creator) and evoked the concept of a detached yet concerned God to buttress the American social order. The Civil War spurred the development of civil religiosity. Memorial Day, Arlington and local cemeteries, and a variety of public monuments imparted sacredness to the Civil War effort. Today, Washington's and Lincoln's birthdays, Veterans's Day (Armistice Day), along with the Fourth of July, and Memorial Day celebrate America and promote its solidarity. American exceptionalism rests in large part on Americans' belief that God has specially favored them and their way of life.

Civil religion in the United States is a pervasive auxilliary to secular institutions, a celebration and reinforcement of the American way of life. Public bodies and artifacts (for example, legislatures, courtrooms, coins) and public occasions of all sorts from Presidential inaugurals to baseball games evoke the sanction of the divine. In effect, American institutions are made divine by clothing them in vague, nondenominational religious terminology. Americans are the most religious of all the industrial nations if judged by church attendance and beliefs in God and an afterlife. However, it is clear that Americans do not take religion seriously enough to let it interfere much with the pursuit of liberal (secular) values. What Americans worship, in short, is Americanism.

The Personal and Social Functions of Religion

Religion has long provided Americans with ways to discuss their personal and public problems and with resources to comfort them in their troubles.[25] Contemporary developments continue this tradition. Religious groups are now active in a variety of right-liberal, left-liberal, and radical political causes. Some have spoken out against investment in racist South Africa and have taken action to withdraw their own investments from that country. Other groups strongly opposed the Reagan's administration's policy of overthrowing the government of Nicaragua. Others oppose the Reagan administration's cutbacks on spending for the needy.

Some religious groups defend and others deny the rights of homosexuals and some accept and some deny the right of women to abort pregnancy. Women have joined the ranks of ministers and rabbis (as yet there are no female Roman Catholic priests). Some religious groups have threatened to boycott the major networks unless they reduce the amount of violence and sex on television. And religious groups continue to provide fellowship and sources of personal identity in an impersonal, trouble-filled world. American religiosity is probably best understood as a culturally approved way for Americans to express their secular concerns and to realize their secular interests.

Religion also reflects new currents of social development. Benton Johnson argues that the new religions and the new secular therapies of recent years have a common thrust—they address the problems of personal life. Our new preoccupation with self, says Johnson, comes from the gap between our growing expectations for fulfillment in work and in intimate personal relations, and the inability of the corporate economy and contemporary family life to provide it. The insecurities, dependencies, inequalities of the new corporate economy are out of kilter with the individualism spawned by the small-scale capitalist economy of the American past (entrepreneurial capitalism). Americans find it difficult to

---

[25]For an analysis of American religious history within the framework of modernization and social change theory, see Peter W. Williams, *Popular Religion in America: Symbolic Change and the Modernization Process in Historical Perspective* (Englewood Cliffs, N.J.: Prentice-Hall, 1980).

achieve a sense of self-worth in an economy they don't understand and over which they have little control. Americans also find it difficult to find self-fulfillment in love. They are distracted and confused by values that take them beyond traditional norms about marriage, love, sexuality, and parenthood. In addition, self-hood at home is difficult because home is where Americans act out the frustrations and disappointments of work. And the rise of new expectations by women has added to the problem.

The new religions and the new secular therapies are a response to this new stage of American social development, argues Johnson. The new religions tend to be more successful than secular therapies because they absorb the self in a common ethic. But both the new religions and the self-fulfillment therapies are politically conservative. Rather than tackle corporate capitalism as the source of problems, the new religions (like most of the old) frame problems in personal terms. By and large, this brings religion into line with secular traditionalism. American culture emphasizes the autonomy of the individual, the voluntary nature of behavior, and places the source of good and evil, success and failure, in the individual. It is understandable that the religious approach to social problems is in line with what Americans believe about themselves and their society.[26]

COMPARATIVE EDUCATION

Education in Agrarian Society

Education in agrarian society is usually controlled by a priesthood and access to education is openly restricted to the children of

the landed nobility. This educational monopoly is really a monopoly over the creation and definition of reality and goes far in explaining the power and durability of landed elites. The content of feudal education bears little practical relation to the problems and challenges that face feudal society (though occasionally some of the elite are trained in warfare). Aesthetics dominated the curriculum in ancient Greece, China, India, Japan, and medieval Europe—the dominant classes used poetry, the dance, art, and the science of lovemaking to distinguish themselves from the lower classes.[27]

Education in Industrial Society

From the advent of complex society some 7 or 8 thousand years ago until recently only a tiny fraction of society could read or write. Starting about 125 years ago in the West, a relatively abrupt and seemingly revolutionary change began—ever larger numbers of each new generation were separated from their family for a good part of the day to attend school.

Industrial societies (capitalist and socialist) stress the personal and social utility of education with particular stress on intellectual and scientific achievement. Formal education is free in socialist societies, and in capitalist societies, free through "secondary" school and, for many, heavily subsidized through college and graduate-professional training. An urban industrial society needs citizens who can act as responsible selves in a world of secondary interaction. It needs to develop symbolic skills so that its members can participate in an economy and polity based on writing and other forms of complex communication. And it needs to instill discipline among its working and professional classes and the ability to act in terms of abstract time, schedules, authority, hierarchy, and goals.

---

[26]Benton Johnson, "A Sociological Perspective on the New Religions," in Thomas Robbins and Dick Anthony, eds., *In Gods We Trust: New Patterns of Religious Pluralism in America* (New Brunswick, N.J.: Transaction Books, 1981), pp. 51–66. For an analysis of self-awareness and self-help groups as ideologies that put the blame on individuals for their troubles, see Edwin Schur, *The Awareness Trap: Self-Absorption Instead of Social Change* (New York: Quadrangle Books, 1977).

---

[27]For a valuable comparative analysis of education, see Randall Collins, "Some Comparative Principles of Educational Stratification," *Harvard Educational Review* 47 (February, 1977): 1–27.

While all industrial societies now place almost all their young people in schools, there is considerable variation in their philosophy of education. Broadly, Japan and the European liberal democracies are relatively elitist in their educational practices while the United States and the Soviet Union stress broad participation in schooling for as long as possible. However, beneath their egalitarian rhetoric, the American and Soviet educational systems are also deeply elitist.[28]

Almost all industrial countries (capitalist and socialist) report difficulties with student motivation, teacher training, school discipline, or lack of educational resources. All countries have difficulty translating their educational practices into positive outcomes in the wider world. This is true even of the socialist societies that explicitly seek to achieve social purposes through education.

EDUCATION IN THE UNITED STATES

Free, Compulsory, Equal Education

The most striking feature about American education is the great faith that Americans put in it. In a real sense the United States is much closer in this respect to the communist countries than to its kindred capitalist democracies. The United States pioneered the idea and practice of educating the masses through public schools. Starting in the 1850s in Massachusetts, the United States developed a vast system of public education based on the principle that education was an individual right and a social good. By the end of the nineteenth century the age-graded, school-centered sequence of primary, secondary, and higher education was in place. By the 1930s the bulk of teen-age Americans were enrolled in high schools. Starting in the post-World War II period a vast expansion of higher ed-

ucation began and by the 1960s approximately 50 percent of high school graduates were in college. And starting in the 1960s graduate education became the increasingly important gateway to high-level positions in business and the professions.

Throughout this development public education was funded by *general* taxes, which means that everybody pays them whether they have children in the public schools or not. American public schools are strictly separated from religion by constitutional law that prohibits government from establishing any form of religion. Public schools are also coeducational. Both boys and girls are deemed eligible for education in the same classroom and increasingly in the same subjects. The separation of the sexes is more likely to be found in private schools (religious and secular) but the pattern of sex segregation, especially in terms of single-sex schools has declined rapidly in recent years.

For most of its history the United States provided either no education for its racial minorities (it was even illegal to teach slaves to read) or education that was segregated and inferior (in the case of America's native peoples, education in white schools was deeply destructive of native cultures). America's racial practice of "separate but equal schools" (which were far from equal) was overturned by the United States Supreme Court in *Brown* vs. *Topeka* (1954), and an effort to incorporate minorities into mainstream education began. More than 35 years after *Brown* vs. *Topeka*, the United States is still struggling to reach its traditional goal of equal educational opportunity (for a further discussion of race and education, see below).

Local Funding and Control

The United States is relatively unique in that its national government provides little money and little direction for education. With some exceptions, the United States places the responsibility for education with local governments (each of the 50 states and each of 15,000 or so school districts). For most of American history, local school districts paid

[28]For a comparison of American mass education with England's elitist education, which concludes that these two systems produce the same results, see Alan C. Kerckoff, "Stratification Processes and Outcomes in England and the United States," *American Sociological Review* 39 (December, 1974): 789–801.

the largest amount for education but this has changed somewhat in recent decades. In 1985–86, local school districts paid 41 percent, state governments 53 percent, and the federal government 6 percent of the total cost of elementary and secondary education. The federal government contributes money for specific purposes (science, mathematics, programs for the poor or handicapped) but, by and large, American schools are run by state-certified personnel using state-approved curricula. State legislatures often specify how much history, English, and science that students should study and they are not above specifying concrete topics such as free enterprise and programs condemning communism.

The tradition of local control keeps education close to the wishes of parents but it also results in disparities in the amount of money spent on individual schools. One of the main outcomes of the heavy emphasis on the local control of public schools is that America's various income levels pay taxes only for the education of their own children.

Public and Private Schools

Most education in the United States takes place in public schools. But there is a vigorous and important private system of education, which is paid for with private money. The private school system has two components: religious schools, run directly by religious organizations, and private secular schools. The largest network of religious schools is run by the Roman Catholic Church (it has over 2,000 primary, secondary, and higher schools enrolling over 3,000,000 students). There are many Protestant colleges and universities and in recent years conservative Protestant schools have expanded at the primary and secondary level (largely to avoid racial integration). The private secular system of education is composed of elite preparatory schools at the primary and secondary levels and a wide array of elite and nonelite schools of higher learning.

Ninety percent of children are in public elementary and high schools and 70 percent of college students are in public colleges. The trend toward public colleges has been accelerated in recent years by economic pressures and demographic changes. Significantly, by 1983 half of all undergraduates were in two-year (public) community colleges.

THE FUNCTIONS OF EDUCATION

Transmitting the Culture

The first function of education is to transmit the cultural system from one generation to the next.[29] In the United States this means that children must be socialized into literacy rather than illiteracy, science as opposed to magic, individualism and equality rather than feudalism, fascism, or socialism, and that they must be socialized to accept the authority of (prevailing liberal definitions of) achievement statuses as opposed to ascribed statuses.

Schools transmit culture (and behavioral skills) in a variety of ways. All students learn some things in common, like arithmetic and elements of American history, while some learn specialized things such as physics, Byzantine history, medicine, and marketing (students also learn to respect the authority of those who have this knowledge). Students are ranked impersonally against classmates in a way that the family cannot do. They learn that the female can be both mother and teacher, that is, perform achieved as well as ascribed roles. As teachers are changed and as children experience a plurality of teachers, they learn to respond to statuses rather than to persons; that is, they learn to live in an impersonal industrial society.

Schools also stress punctuality, methodical diligence, orderliness, and personal responsibility in an impersonal atmosphere. They impart a hierarchical value scheme that places symbolic mastery and skill (especially outside of music and art) above other values (such as the validity of immediate experience, mystical states, or immediate and con-

---

[29]The following relies heavily on Talcott Parsons, "The School Class as a Social System: Some of Its Functions in American Society," *Harvard Educational Review* 29 (Fall, 1959): 207–318.

tinuous gratification). And individualism and competitiveness prevail over group goals and cooperation.

Promoting Social Solidarity

The American school was framed from the start to provide a shared experience and a "common faith" with a view toward making democracy work. Much of the American effort to build a viable society through education consists of imposing homogeneous practices and standards on each generation. By imposing things in common (school day, school year, so many years of the national language and literature, national history and geography, and science and mathematics, school rituals and ceremonies), the school promotes social solidarity through homogenization.

Assuring Personal Development and Selection by Merit

The American school is also a place for personal development. Schools provide a wide range of opportunities for individuals of all ages to stretch their minds and develop a variety of interactional skills. As students display their abilities and develop their potential, they separate themselves into better and worse. The school is seen as a place where individuals are nourished into becoming what nature intended them to be. (The school selects and ranks individuals, so goes the prevailing belief, according to abilities established by nature.)

Generating Knowledge and Updating Society

Schools also generate culture by producing new knowledge, technology, aesthetic creations, and political and moral perspectives. University research supplies new knowledge in the natural and social sciences and new artistic experiences in literature and music. In addition, colleges and universities help farmers and business people to modernize their work practices. Academics have also taken the lead in the environmental movement and

have played a conspicuous part in the issues arising from nuclear energy and nuclear arms.

Reproducing Class Inequality

The sociology of education has uncovered a deep pattern of hidden "class" inequality in American education (the term *class* refers to the general economic status of the household that students come from—for a fuller discussion, see Chapter 9). Many studies have shown that schools have a pronounced bias in favor of the values, norms, and skills of the upper classes and that they either overlook or discriminate against the values and skills of the lower classes.

Schools require character and cognitive skills (for example, punctuality, self-discipline, the ability to manipulate symbols) that correspond to those found in the middle and upper classes and which are difficult for the lower classes to acquire. Subject matter also favors the upper classes, and teachers and textbooks rarely discuss the world in conflict terms or from the viewpoint of the lower classes. Instead, schools teach a complacent nonideological subject matter that suits children from the upper classes and ignores the conflicts and deficiencies in American life that children from the lower classes can relate to. Teachers also overlook assets and skills associated with the lower classes and frown on behavior and values that would be easy to include in the educational process. Students from the upper classes arrive in school already housebroken and teachers can concentrate on academic work. In schools populated by the children of the lower classes much of the time is spent on fostering obedience to rules. Not surprisingly, the ability to do well in school and on IQ and other tests correlates strongly with social class.

Perpetuating Racial Inequality

Segregating the races legally was ended by the United States Supreme Court in 1954, but the races are still separate and unequal because of the dynamics of income, work, and residence. The American tradition of local schools means that education reflects local conditions. Most black-American children go to all-black schools because they live in all-black neighborhoods. All-black residential areas reflect a long history of racial discrimination in housing. In addition, the movement of business to the suburbs and the sunbelt has left many blacks high and dry in decaying inner cities.

Like white working- and lower-class children, black youngsters are not prepared for the demands of middle-class education. The problem for black students is magnified because most of them are from working-class families and a disproportionate number of them come from lower-class or poor families (especially one-parent homes). The result is a cycle of failure—parent "failure" in the economy leads to children "failure," first in school and then in the economy, and so on.

Victimizing Both Sexes

Many school norms and values do not harmonize with the personalities of incoming students. The character traits that schools inspire and favor are punctuality, diligence, obedience, passivity, neatness, and cleanliness—character traits that characterize girls rather than boys. Boys are also penalized because their vocabularies develop more slowly than girls (probably because the latter spend more time with adults at home) but they are still subject to comparison with girls their own age.

Later, the situation is reversed, especially as the number of male instructors increases (male teachers are more noticeable in high school and predominate in college). Here forceful, assertive masculine behavior is favored and female students are at a disadvantage. And female students are subject to another form of discrimination. More college instructors do not call on female as often as male students and these teachers respond differently and less favorably to their answers.[30]

AMERICAN EDUCATION: PROBLEMS AND PROSPECTS

Most of the conventional problems of education are due to a fairly simple cause—education has always tried to impose *one type of schooling on a highly diversified student body.* Critics and reformers have recognized this at various stages in the history of education. The progressive education movement early in the century stressed the need to improve the fit between schools and students. Only by tailoring the school to student interests and capabilities, argued progressive educators, such as John Dewey, could the school involve the student as an active participant in the learning process. The progressive movement waned in the 1930s and the problem of student diversity was "solved" through testing and grading, tracking, and educational "choice."

In recent decades, the problem of student diversity has appeared in new forms. Black, Hispanic, and Asian minorities now make up larger proportions of student bodies. Schools must now educate handicapped children and cope with children from poverty backgrounds, especially those from one-parent families. And students attending institutions of higher education are also more diversified. As the number of 18-year-olds drops, the two- and four-year colleges are increasingly made up of ethnic and racial minorities and the average age of college students has gone up.

The new diversity has created problems for educators. The story of how the United States has tried to deal with these problems is largely the story of federal initiatives (spawned by the great reform movements of the 1960s).[31]

Compensatory Education for the Poor

The War on Poverty in the 1960s spawned a number of federal education programs to

---

[30]For studies showing that boys get "more attention, encouragement, and airtime than girls," see Myra Sadker and David Sadker, "Sexism in the Schoolroom of the 80s," *Psychology Today* 19 (March, 1985): 54–57.

[31]The following sections draw on an excellent survey and analysis of federal reform efforts by Paul E. Peterson, "Background Paper," *Making The Grade: Report of the Twentieth Century Fund Task Force on Federal Elementary and Secondary Education Policy* (New York: Twentieth Century Fund, 1983).

help poor students. Given the federal system, and especially the tradition of local control of education, federal programs are administered by the states. The general initiative on behalf of the poor from the mid-1960s on had few positive results because, for one thing, state and school districts used the money that Congress had earmarked for the poor on behalf of *all* students. Thus by benefitting all equally, relative differences remained. But the money did help shore up poor schools and helped hard-pressed urban schools to at least not fall even farther behind.

Busing

Even after the U.S. Supreme Court struck down the practice of establishing racially segregated schools by law, white and black students remained segregated on a de facto basis, and the same pattern of differential academic achievement continued: Black students did less well on all standardized tests that educators used to measure achievement.

One of the devices that reformers felt would improve the problem was busing. Research had suggested that students from the lower classes do better if they attend predominately middle-class schools. Busing students to school was well established in rural and suburban American education and reformers felt that this device could be used to improve the educational experience of *both* white and black students.

Busing worked well in school districts where advanced planning took place. However, most busing was introduced hastily, often because of court-ordered integration and aroused strong political opposition. The Republican Party's strategy of courting the South, the Southwest, and the better-off suburbs also undermined busing. On the whole, busing appears to have been abandoned as a solution to racial inequality in education. But busing did not work for another reason—it dodged the real issue, racial inequality in the economy and (through gerrymandering) in the polity. Black children do poorly in school because they are poor, because they live in racially segregated neighborhoods separated from the mainstream economy, and because their political strength is diluted by rigged electoral districts.

Bilingual Education

Evidence that Mexican-American and Puerto Rican-American students were lagging in school because of difficulties with the English language prompted Congress to set up a program of bilingual education. The strategy behind bilingual education is to allow youngsters from Spanish-speaking backgrounds to use Spanish (or other languages depending on their ethnic background) in order to make progress in English. The strategy, it must be stressed, is to foster assimilation, not to develop bilingual citizens or ethnic pluralism.

Bilingual education was adopted on an experimental basis. However, the evaluation of the program has been inconclusive because of suspected faults in research design. By 1983, more than 10 years after their start, only a fraction of American youngsters from non-English-speaking homes were in bilingual educational programs.

Education for the Handicapped

Mounting pressure by interest groups and educators and court decisions ordering full and free education for all children, regardless of handicap, prompted Congress to pass the Education for All Handicapped Children Act of 1975. The unmet need in this area is enormous, covering millions of youngsters who have handicaps ranging from speech impairment to mental retardation, from deafness to emotional disturbance. Though Congress appropriated major sums of money they fell short of need, and local governments have complained that they are being asked to achieve the aims of the federal law without being given the money.

Improving Professional Schools

Perhaps the most devastating criticism of American education is its failure to train effective professionals. In recent years even educators have become aware that something is wrong with the way in which the United States educates doctors, lawyers, business executives, professors, and other professionals. Our graduate schools train our future professors without requiring training in education and teaching. In medical school, the faculty is oriented almost totally toward research. Medical students receive a long, arduous, and systematic introduction into specialized medicine that neglects the patient as a whole person and that is indifferent to health. Law schools teach students to memorize legal materials while neglecting almost all the things that real-life lawyers do. Business schools teach their MBAs to manipulate symbols and analyze financial data while failing to stress that the world of business means negotiation, personnel evaluation, product development, labor relations, marketing, sales, and so on. And none of these graduate and professional programs has valid admission standards, and none has any evidence that graduates perform better for having attended its program.[32]

Why does all this take place and why does it endure? A clue lies in the acknowledged fact that all these programs are too long. America's elites have succeeded in putting into practice their self-serving values and beliefs. All tolerate a failed system because it succeeds in curbing labor flows into top jobs. Through a prolonged and irrelevant system of obtaining credentials, American education perpetuates the myth that good jobs are naturally scarce because, for one thing, goes the circular argument, good people are hard to find.

What does all this mean? Schools, it seems, do not cause cognitive growth. Students learn *in* schools, not because of them, and they learn depending on how well they are prepared for school by their economic and family background. Second, what is learned seems not to be related to the basic purposes of courses—indeed, learning seems not be re-

lated, in any positive sense, to the world that students must live in. And finally there is little evidence that achievement in schools is positively related to occupational achievement. One reason perhaps is that the business world shows little interest in cognitive achievement. The United States will do little to improve itself through education if it continues to base it on faculty assumptions. As long as education fails to prepare people for work, politics, and personal living, it will function inefficiently for most, and for many, not at all.

FAMILY, RELIGION, AND EDUCATION: A SUMMARY

Marriage and family are socially defined in keeping with historical variables and the type of society.

The *nuclear family* (parents and immediate children under the same roof) is the basic family type in most societies. Less frequent is the *extended family* (related nuclear families under one roof or working together).

The preindustrial family reproduces, socializes children, performs important economic functions, and often has explicit functions in the realms of politics and religion. The industrial family has been shorn of many functions. It is now primarily a reproductive, socialization, and consumption unit.

Demography is the study of the causes of population changes both in numbers and composition. Population is affected by economic, political, religious, and other variables in changing patterns. The characteristics of a population (demographics) are important for understanding social change, modernization, and for formulating economic and social policies.

Population analysis reveals that the American family continues to supply the vast bulk of replacements for those who die and even for additions to the population. Like other developed countries the United States has made the *demographic transition* to a slowly growing, aging population because of low

---

[32]For a convincing, well-written indictment of medical, legal, and business education, see Andrew Hacker, "The Shame of Professional Schools," *Harper's* 263 (October, 1981): 22–8.

birth and low death rates. The developing countries have lowered their death rates but their high birth rates give them fast-growing young populations.

The American *household* (living arrangements under one roof) has changed its composition. Among family households (two or more individuals related by marriage, blood, or adoption), 28 percent are now single-parent families. *Nonfamily* households (individuals living alone or unrelated individuals living together) have also increased, reflecting a change in age distribution, especially the aging of the American population.

The American family suffers from a large assortment of problems largely associated with unemployment, economic insecurity, poverty, and individualism.

The family seems not to be declining despite recent revelations about its pathologies. The family has probably always had serious troubles and it is only recently that sociology (and other groups) has uncovered them.

The United States is deeply divided on most issues concerning family life and has no national family policy. America's prospects for developing solutions to its family problems are not encouraging.

Religion is a social phenomenon that varies with type of society. It assumes a supernatural or a sacred realm of being and causation. Religions are extremely diverse ranging from *zoomorphic* (the worship of natural entities) to *anthropomorphic* (the worship of superhuman men and women) and from *polytheistic* (many gods) to *monotheistic* (one God).

Religion tends to protect the status quo. But religion has also helped to produce social system change (for example, it helped bring about capitalism) and it has furthered social reform (for example, against slavery, for public help to the needy, for civil rights for minorities).

Organized religion in the United States is very diverse. Americans attend church and believe in God and in an afterlife far more than people in other industrial societies. However, membership in religious bodies underwent a drastic decline in the 1970s.

Christianity, especially its Protestant variant, helped to establish the central liberal myth that the sources of behavior and the explanation for success and failure lie within the individual (human nature). In this sense, religion is a servant of secular power groups and the unwitting supporter of American ideology (liberalism).

The United States also has a civil religion in which it celebrates itself (vague, nondenominational religious practices, beliefs, and artifacts that sanctify the American social order). New forms of personal religion have also appeared in recent years to help Americans cope with the insecurities and dependencies of an impersonal, corporate economy and society.

By and large, America's religious forms and practices tend to depoliticize social problems. By stressing themes of original sin, personal responsibility, and redemption, religion diverts attention from institutions and social groups as the source of problems even as it provides personal comfort and supports social stability.

Educational values, norms, and practices reflect the society in which they occur. Under feudal society, education is restricted to an hereditary elite. Modern society (capitalist and socialist) demands literacy from all and has placed its young people in school for a good part of the day for a long number of years. However, education still reflects the interests of power groups—in the United States, access to education and achievement in it are largely a matter of social class.

Functionalists think of education as a positive force performing a number of social functions: education promotes good citizenship, it provides economic skills and virtues, and helps society adapt to new conditions through research and the creation of new knowledge and technology.

Conflict theorists argue that research has failed to show that education has positive results outside itself. Education, they argue, is largely geared to serve the interests of the upper classes. American education has a number of latent functions. Experiences in school develop character traits and behavioral skills appropriate to industrial society. By and large, schools do not impart a critical intelligence, and cognitive skills are not valued anyway by employers.

The key variable in education is the personality of the student. Success in school and the success of the school are largely a function of the character and cognitive skills provided by the social class-family background of students. Basic improvements in education are possible only when improvements are made in the experiences of young people *outside* of school.

Elementary schools have an impact on young children (both retarding and promoting learning depending on how the school is run) because children tend to conform to what is expected of them, but high schools and colleges have little independent effect on learning or on society once social class-family background is taken into account.

Americans are not better educated today than they were in the past despite a steady rise in the number of years of school completed by the average American. The main criterion for judging education is whether or not it prepares elites and nonelites for social roles. On this count, education in the United States is a failure.

The great stress on education and on educational reforms that promote abstract academic learning and skills are really ways for elites and power groups to turn young people into scapegoats and evade responsibility for solving economic and political problems.

CHAPTER
9
THE AMERICAN CLASS SYSTEM

Social stratification in modern society takes the form of a class system.[1] The owners and controllers of property in general (whether land, factories, office buildings, hospitals, airports, or knowledge and personal skills) control the generation and distribution of all values.

Stratification theorists ask: how does it come about that some members of society labor in fields or tend furnaces while others sit at desks and earn their living writing and talking? Why do some live routine lives while others enjoy a varied life style? Why are some economically insecure while others have iron-clad job guarantees? Why do 15 percent of the American people live in poverty while many earn their livings creating luxuries for the idle rich? These questions are important because how we work and the rewards we get for it have a profound effect on our lives

outside of work. Socioeconomic or class position affects all aspects of behavior—our image of ourselves and others, whom we date and marry, the size and stability of our family, our physical and mental health, who succeeds or fails in school, what politics we prefer, and who gets justice and who does not. The goal of stratification analysis is to understand the causal system that creates and distributes all these economic and social benefits over time.

In pursuing their analysis, stratification theorists often run counter to the explanations offered by society's elites. Both in agrarian and industrial society, elites claim that inequality represents forces beyond society (God, history, nature, and human nature). These explanations of inequality are false and self-serving. Elites have a stake in freezing society as it is. Invariably, they resort to naturalistic models to explain inequality because nature appears fixed (see Box 1-2, Is There a Model in Nature On Which Thought

---

[1] For an earlier discussion, see Chapter 4.

About Society Can Be Based?). In the final analysis, both feudal and industrial elites explain inequality by referring to human nature, the former by referring to family birth, the latter by referring to individual ability by birth.

COMPARATIVE ECONOMIC CLASSES

The concentration of power over productive property is a standard feature of all industrial societies regardless of past history, type of culture, or whether those societies have capitalist, fascist, socialist, or communist governments. The techniques of concentration and control vary considerably and include interlocking directorships, intercorporate stockholding, favorable tax laws, private corporate concentration, nationalized industries with private managerial control, public corporations, and governmental ownership and supervision by monopolistic political parties.

The distribution of material culture (wealth and income) is also roughly similar in all industrial countries. Despite minor variations, the outstanding characteristic of the material culture of industrial society (aside from the dramatic increase in the standard of living in the capitalist systems) is its radically unequal distribution.

Economic inequality is also remarkably *stable*. It should be emphasized that the long-term rise in the absolute standard of living has not changed the relative economic status of the various classes of any given industrial population. Modern structures of stratification are like a fleet of ships in a harbor—an incoming tide (economic expansion) does not diminish the relative difference among row boats, cabin cruisers, cargo vessels, and giant ocean liners, though all are higher than they were at low tide.

Comparative Wealth Distribution

The ownership of wealth is and has been extremely concentrated in all capitalist societies. This is especially true if one focuses on the ownership of productive property and excludes automobiles, appliances, homes, and liquid assets.

Scholars across a wide variety of capitalist countries have found a decline in wealth concentration during the twentieth century or at least the first three-quarters of it.[2] However, wealth concentration at its lowest was still very high, and there appears to have been a resurgence of concentration starting in the 1970s and accelerating in the 1980s.[3]

Comparative Income Distribution: Developed Capitalist and Socialist Societies

All developed countries, capitalist and socialist alike, are very unequal and reveal no trend toward equality when looked at broadly. Under closer scrutiny, however, a number of variations appear. The developed capitalist countries that have had long-term socialist governments or sustained welfare states (for example, Sweden) have more income equality than the more market-oriented societies (for example, the United States). In addition, it is clear that capitalist countries with more income equality (because of their commitment to full employment and their more developed public service sectors) than the United States have not suffered economically. On the contrary, the economies of West Germany, Norway, Sweden, the Netherlands, and Japan have outperformed the American economy.[4] The European capitalist countries also have a better record of curbing poverty.[5] Not only is it possible to reduce income inequality and alleviate the hardships

---

[2]Edward N. Wolff, ed., *International Comparisons of the Distribution of Household Wealth* (Oxford: Clarendon Press, 1987).

[3]This is certainly the case with the United States as we will see shortly.

[4]Malcom Sawyer, *Income Distribution in OECD Countries* (Paris: Organization for Economic Cooperation and Development, 1976). The data in this work are from the 1960s and early 1970s. There is little reason to assume that any changes have taken place in recent years.

[5]Vic George and Roger Lawson, eds., *Poverty and Inequality in Common Market Countries* (London: Routledge & Kegan Paul, 1980).

of poverty without curtailing economic growth, but, on the contrary, the commitment to full employment seems to lead to a more productive economy!

One of the reasons for the steep inequality among capitalist countries and for higher and lower levels of inequality is income from property (rents, interest, dividends, profits). If one focuses on income from employment alone (setting aside income from the ownership of property), income distribution is remarkably similar, for example, in Denmark, the United Kingdom, Sweden, Yugoslavia, Poland, the Federal Republic of Germany, Canada, Belgium, the United States, and Austria, though there are variations in particulars. On the same basis, it appears that New Zealand, Australia, and most communist countries have less income inequality than the Western capitalist countries.[6]

By and large, the greater actual equality of income in the Soviet bloc countries is because they have eliminated the significant income that goes to the capitalist upper class (and others) from the ownership of property. Also important in producing greater income equality is the open promotion of full employment. Though this leads to some inefficiency in the use of labor, it curbs the surplus labor that is such a chronic condition in the capitalist countries.

Occupations and Professions

The emergence of industrial society everywhere reduces the number of people engaged in farm work and increases those in manufacturing and services. Good jobs for skilled workers are small in number in relation to semiskilled and unskilled workers, and the people in the good jobs tend to keep them scarce by inflating entry requirements beyond functional requirements (excessive education, certification and licensing, labor law, collective bargaining). Over time skill levels have increased but there has been no equalization of occupations. The resulting hierarchy of occupations generates sharp differences in income and prestige and is an important determinant of social class.

SOCIAL MOBILITY

Social mobility means movement from one social class to another (for example, a manual worker becomes a business person). Social mobility should not be confused with rising living standards and should be carefully distinguished from horizontal mobility (often accompanied by geographic mobility), which is a change (usually of occupation) *within* a social class (a professor becomes a government scientist or a business executive is transferred to another city).

Analysts of social mobility distinguish between mobility during an individual's lifetime, mobility of a family over time, and social origins mobility (or the social class that incumbents of various occupations have been recruited from). To help them analyze social mobility, sociologists also distinguish between *structural* or "forced" mobility (when economic expansion moves everybody up) and *equal opportunity* or "circulation" mobility (when mobility can be attributed to institutions that promote equal competition and opportunity).[7]

The analysis of mobility (in the United States and other industrial societies) reveals a basic pattern of structural (or forced) mobility. Most social mobility takes place because of economic expansion, and mobility rates are not much different among capitalist and socialist societies. Mobility analysis also reveals that there is much less movement *between* classes than is popularly thought. Mobility between class levels is mostly from adjacent classes and mobility rates are, on the whole, more alike than different across the

[6]Harold Lydall, *The Structure of Earnings* (London: Oxford University Press, 1968), pp. 156–62; Jerry Cromwell, "The Size Distribution of Income: An International Comparison," *Review of Income and Wealth*, Series 23: 3 (Summer, 1977): 291–308; Gerhard Lenski, "Marxist Experiments in Destratification: An Appraisal," *Social Forces* 57 (December, 1978): 364–83.

[7]Leonard Broom and F. Lancaster Jones, "Father-To-Son Mobility: Australia in Comparative Perspective," *American Journal of Sociology* 74 (January, 1969): 333–42.

entire industrial world. What all this means is that the United States is not *the* land of opportunity; like all expanding capitalist and socialist systems, it is *a* land of opportunity.

ECONOMIC CLASSES IN THE UNITED STATES

Analyzing the United States in terms of its contrasting social classes introduces us to a world not easily accessible through ordinary experience. Typically, Americans think of inequality as something that emerges from individual competition and equal opportunity. How can that image be squared with the fact that major portions of the American economy are inherited? Americans think that inequality derives from individuals and that it serves social needs. But don't humans acquire their personalities from their socialization experiences? Many argue that equality is opposed to efficiency. But how efficient is it to have an economy in which millions are idle? What right has government to take from some to give to others? How would Americans frame this question if they knew that government spending and taxation favored the upper classes by a wide margin? Our analysis will address these and other questions. Is equality increasing or decreasing? Is the United States still a land of opportunity? Is upward mobility through hard work a feasible dream for the majority of Americans? Is the United States a meritocracy?

The elements that make up an economic class are wealth, income, occupation, and education. Uncovering the hierarchy of economic classes means grouping American households in terms of their relative standing on these four dimensions.

The Distribution of Wealth

The first question about an economy is, who owns it? Finding an answer, however, is not easy. The upper classes of all societies are secretive about many things, including their wealth. Scholars agree that the basic pattern

in the distribution of American wealth is high and relatively steady concentration.

The concentration of wealth is apparent in Table 9-1. Far from being a people's capitalism, the economy of the United States is owned by a tiny handful of households. In 1983, the super-rich (one-half of one percent or about 400,000 households) owned 35.1 percent of the total wealth (net worth or assets minus liabilities). The richest 1 percent owned 41.9 percent of the total personal wealth, and the richest 10 percent owned 71.8 percent of the total. This left the remaining 90 percent (about 72 million households) with 28.2 percent of the total wealth. Significantly, commercial real estate, corporate stocks, bonds, and business assets are even more highly concentrated. This means that investment decisions (where and when factories, offices, and stores will be built, and the amount and nature of jobs available to Americans) are in the hands of a small fraction of the total population.

As Table 9-2 indicates, a dramatic increase in the concentration of wealth took place between 1963 and 1983. The top 10 percent of households had an 8.8 percent increase in their net worth, the top 1 percent, a 24.3 percent increase, and the top one-half of one percent saw their holdings swell by a whopping 34.5 percent. The bottom 90 percent obviously lost, falling 16.8 percent.

Much of the change in wealth concentration between 1963 and 1983 came from changes in the stock market value of holdings, but it was also caused by explicit government policies: tax laws favoring the upper classes, antilabor policies, a relaxation of antitrust law enforcement, and a sizable cut in social services. The trend toward more concentration in personal wealth has undoubtedly continued since 1983 since the same policies have remained in effect.

Two things more are important about wealth: one, the large majority of those who are wealthy either inherited it or used an inheritance to make money.[8] And two, the

---

[8]"The Richest People in America," *Forbes* 136 (October, 1985): 108–330.

TABLE 9-1. Concentration of Personal Wealth, The United States, 1983 (Amounts in Billions of Dollars)

	All Households		Richest 10%		Richest 1%		Richest 5%	
	Amount	%	Amount	%	Amount	%	Amount	%
Real Estate	5362.3	100.0	2632.6	49.1	1048.4	19.6	821.8	15.3
Home (gross)	3585.5	100.0	1251.1	34.9	300.8	8.4	189.1	5.3
Other (gross)	1776.8	100.0	1381.5	77.8	747.6	42.1	632.7	35.7
Corporate Stock	981.7	100.0	876.5	89.3	588.8	60.0	456.6	46.5
Bonds	329.6	100.0	297.7	90.3	168.2	51.0	143.6	43.6
Savings Bonds	28.9	100.0	11.8	40.8	4.7	16.3	4.0	13.8
Other Federal Bonds	93.8	100.0	87.5	93.3	36.6	39.0	32.2	34.3
State and Local Bonds	163.7	100.0	159.8	97.6	114.8	70.1	101.6	62.1
Corporate Bonds	43.2	100.0	38.6	89.4	12.1	28.0	5.8	13.4
Checking Accounts	115.8	100.0	52.3	45.2	20.3	17.5	12.0	10.4
Saving Accounts	189.2	100.0	11.8	6.2	4.7	2.5	4.0	2.1
Certificates of Deposit	385.7	100.0	193.9	50.3	43.7	11.3	20.6	5.3
Money Market and Call Accounts	265.8	100.0	163.5	61.5	65.8	24.8	46.5	17.5
IRAs and Keogh	142.6	100.0	95.9	67.3	31.6	22.2	21.1	14.8
Trusts	491.6	100.0	467.8	95.2	402.9	82.0	378.4	77.0
Business Assets (net)	3272.0	100.0	3065.7	93.7	2168.1	66.3	1904.9	58.2
Management Interest	2903.1	100.0	2724.3	93.8	1977.5	68.1	1753.2	60.4
No Management Interest	368.9	100.0	341.4	92.5	190.6	51.7	151.7	41.1
Insurance Cash Surrender Value	260.8	100.0	80.2	30.8	26.0	10.0	16.9	6.5
Land Contracts	111.2	100.0	56.6	50.9	18.4	16.5	15.6	14.0
Miscellaneous	157.9	100.0	84.2	53.3	43.7	27.7	25.9	16.4
GROSS ASSETS	12066.2	100.0	8078.7	67.0	4630.6	38.4	3867.9	32.1
DEBT	1479.0	100.0	481.1	32.5	202.2	13.7	153.8	10.4
Consumer Debt	327.1	100.0	108.7	33.2	48.6	14.9	31.2	9.5
Real Estate Debt	1151.9	100.0	372.4	32.3	153.6	13.3	122.6	10.6
NET WORTH	10587.2	100.0	7597.6	71.8	4428.4	41.9	3714.1	35.1

Source: James D. Smith, *The Distribution of Wealth* (Ann Arbor, Mich.: Survey Research Center, University of Michigan, 1986), Table 2.

TABLE 9–2. Trends In Wealth Concentration, 1963–1983.

Percent of Households	Percent 1963	Share 1983	Absolute Change	Percentage Change
Richest:				
10%	66.1	71.8	+5.8	8.8
1%	33.7	41.9	+8.2	24.3
.5%	26.1	35.1	+9.0	34.5
Lowest:				
90%	33.9	28.2	-5.7	-16.8

Source: James D. Smith, *The Distribution of Wealth* (Ann Arbor, Mich.: Survey Research Center, University of Michigan, 1986), Table 5.

wealthy get most of their income from property ownership, setting up a relationship that goes far in explaining class maintenance and continuity over time. (And the share of income from rents, dividends, and profits has been rising in relation to income from wages). The ability to save leads to the high concentration of wealth; in turn, the high concentration of wealth helps to explain high income (dividends, interest, capital gains, stock appreciation), which in turn promotes the unequal ability to save, and so on. This has been called the Matthew Effect—"For to everyone who has will more be given" (Matthew 25:29, RSV).

Income Distribution: Unequal and Increasingly So

Income distribution has been unequal since 1947 when exact records first began. And until recently income inequality has remained fairly similar (see Figure 9-1 for current levels by fifths). In recent years income inequality has increased as measured by the gap between the richest fifth and the poorest fifth.

Inequality of income continues after taxation (see Figure 9-2). As we will see later, in the section, Stratified Politics, it is also true before and after government spending.

New Income Trends: The End of a Growing Standard of Living?

The United States experienced a much higher growth in living standards in the 1950s and

1960s than from 1970 on. One way of measuring standard of living is by median family income (the point at which 50 percent of families are above and 50 percent are below). As Figure 9-3 shows, median family income

FIGURE 9-1. Percentage Share of Total Income by Fifths of Families, 1987.

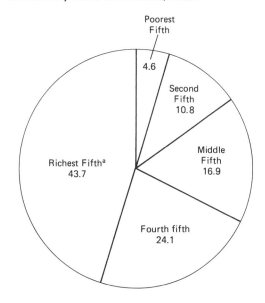

[a]The top 5 percent of families received 16.9 percent of total income. Income inequality among unrelated individuals is even more pronounced than among families.

Source: U. S. Bureau of the Census, "Money Income of Households, Families, and Persons in the United States: 1987," *Current Population Reports*, P-60, No. 162 (Washington, D.C.: U. S. Government Printing Office, 1989), Table 12.

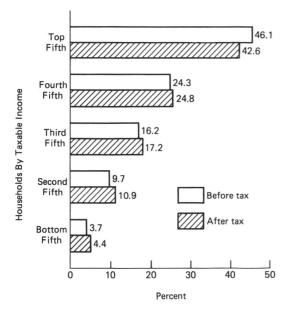

FIGURE 9-2. Distribution of Before-Tax and After-Tax Household Income, United States, 1986.
Source: U. S. Census Bureau, "Household After-Tax Income: 1986," *Current Population Reports*, Series P-23, No. 157 (Washington, D.C.: U. S. Government Printing Office, 1988), Table C.

grew strongly in the 1960s but remained fairly stationary after 1970.

The slowdown in economic growth is reflected in (and caused by) declining productivity, personal savings, and skill levels, and by rising social overhead (crime, pollution, welfare, military expenditures, debt service). Expressed in more personal terms, the average 30-year-old male earned $25,580 in 1973 compared to $17,520 for a 30-year-old in 1983. The same male had to pay 44 percent of gross earnings to buy a median-priced house in 1983 compared to 21 percent in 1973.[9]

The period since 1970 affected families differently than Figure 9-3 suggests. The Congressional Budget Office computed an Adjusted Family Income (using family size and a different inflation index) and found that all living standards increased after 1970 (though not as much as in previous decades). Elderly families and individuals had a strong growth (50 percent), all families had a low growth of 14 percent, and single-mother families had a very low 2 percent growth over the space of these 16 years. Significantly, the Adjusted Family Income of families varied by age. Families headed by 65 year olds rose 54 percent while young families under age 25 had a drop of 18 percent.[10]

The American standard of living, when computed as above, does exhibit growth but a number of things should be noted. One, it grew at a much lower rate than in previous decades. Two, it grew because families got smaller. Three, households had more workers. Four, it grew because the elderly received substantial sums of non-means-tested Social Security increases. And five, it grew because all sectors of the society (individuals, business, and the federal government) went deeply into debt.

New Income Trends: A Bipolar America?

The 1970s saw a new trend in income distribution. Reversing its previous history, the United States appears no longer able to provide an expanding number of middle-income households. The new household income structure is moving away from the big bulge in the middle that was once characteristic of the United States and toward a bipolar (hour glass, two-tier) shape (see Figure 9-4). The United States may or may not be generating as many good paying jobs as in the past. But even assuming that it is, the crucial question to ask is, how are these jobs distributed by households? Double earners are now common at all levels but better-paid individuals marry each other

[9]Frank S. Levy and Richard C. Michel, "Economic Future of the Baby Boom," Report, Joint Economic Committee of Congress (Washington, D.C.: U. S. Government Printing Office, 1985).

[10]Congressional Budget Office, "Trends In Family Income: 1970–86" (Washington, D.C.: U. S. Government Printing Office, 1988).

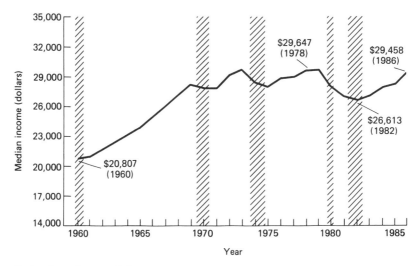

FIGURE 9-3. Median Family Income: 1960–1986 (In 1986 dollars)
Source: Bureau of the Census, "Money Income and Poverty Status of
Families and Persons In the United States, 1986," *Current Population Reports,*
P-60, no. 157 (Washington, D.C.: U. S. Government Printing Office, 1987),
Figure 1.

FIGURE 9-4. The Trend Toward A Bipolar
Distribution of Household Income, 1960s to
the 1980s

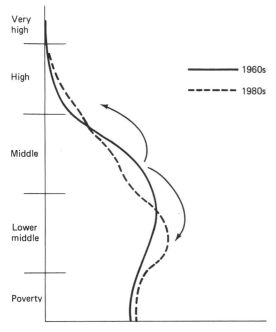

and this means that middle-income jobs are
no longer held by single breadwinners. In
addition, the lower classes have more single-
income households largely because divorced
mothers pile up at that level.

The structural reasons for the new distribution of household income are the surge
toward service industries, the movement
of capital to low-wage, nonunionized sections of the United States and abroad, the
decline of trade unions, and active support
of these trends by government (deregula-
tion, the large tax cuts of 1981, the curtail-
ment of public services and benefits, and
antiunion rulings by the National Labor
Relations Board). The women's movement
and the rising divorce rate also contributed to the new trend toward bipolar family incomes. The women's movement has
essentially opened up opportunities for
the daughters and wives of the upper classes.
But the general surge of civil rights, individualism (laissez-faire American liberalism), and an erratic economy have also
led to a high divorce rate—the major cas-

ualties of divorce are women and thus the swollen ranks of lower-level, one-parent female households.

Occupations: Quantity and Quality

Sociologists have determined that occupation is a powerful determinant of behavior. Occupational trends and the hierarchy of jobs, therefore, are central to understanding the formation and maintenance of social classes. Four facts stand out about the American occupational system:

1. The type of work that Americans do has been shifting away from farm work and manufacturing to services (for a previous discussion, see Chapter 6).
2. The inequality of jobs, already steep, seems to be getting more unequal with the bulk of new jobs coming in semiskilled and unskilled occupations.
3. Reflecting the surge toward corporate capitalism, recent decades have seen a steady decrease of self-employed individuals and the rise of salaried professionals and managers.
4. Though the number of people working continues to grow, the number of jobs always remains smaller than the number of people who want to work. Unemployment in the United States is chronic and large, significantly larger than official rates would have it.

Occupational Prestige

The first scientific study of occupational prestige was conducted by the National Opinion Research Center in 1947. Americans were asked to rate ninety occupations as "excellent," "good," "average," "somewhat below average," "poor," or "don't know where to place." The results were clear and unequivocal. Americans consistently accorded highest prestige to occupations characterized by highly specialized training and high responsibility for the public welfare. Other studies since 1947 have revealed a remarkable stability in Americans' views of occupations. Though some titles have been changed, the hierarchy of occupational prestige has remained essentially the same for almost 40 years (see Table 9-3).

The Distribution of Education

Despite the advent of mass public education, there has been relatively little equalization of educational status in modern society. Like the rise of wealth, income, and occupational skill levels, it is best to think of the rise of educational attainment as resembling the rise of a fleet of unequal-sized ships during an incoming tide.

Americans have completed more years of school and more Americans have completed high school and college than in the past but absolute figures such as these are not useful. The meaning of a high school and college education has declined and graduate degrees, the road to the better jobs, are still quite scarce.

Economic class is important because it causes the distribution of a great many values outside the economy. Let's begin with the relation between economic class and access to education.

CLASS AND ACCESS TO EDUCATION

Researchers have found that educational achievement of every kind—scores on IQ and all forms of achievement tests, attendance, years of school completed, grades, prizes, degrees, types of programs taken— all correlate with class background.[11] By and large, the American school is designed to produce middle and upper middle class personalities and it is not surprising that students who come from the middle and upper classes do better in school than those who don't. A key outcome of all this is that success during early schooling determines who goes on to higher education. It is clear that access to higher education is class based (see Figure 9-5). The type of

---

[11] For a summary of the literature on inequality and education, see Caroline Hodges Persell, *Education and Inequality: A Theoretical and Empirical Synthesis* (New York: Free Press, 1977) and Richard H. Delone, *Small Futures: Children, Inequality, and the Limits of Liberal Reform* (New York: Harcourt Brace Jovanovich, 1979), a study for the Carnegie Council on Children.

TABLE 9-3. The Relative Occupational Prestige of 50 Occupations In the United States

Occupation	Prestige Score	Occupation	Prestige Score
Physician	82	Secretary	46
Professor	78	Air Traffic Controller	43
Lawyers/Judges	76	Fireman	44
Dentist	74	Mail Carrier	42
Bank Officer	72	Restaurant Manager	39
Airplane Pilot	70	Building Superintendant/Manager	38
Clergyman	69	Automobile Mechanic	37
Engineer	67	Airline Stewardess	36
Registered Nurse	62	Brick/Stone Mason	36
Dental Hygenist	61	TV Repairperson	35
Officials, Administrators,		Hairdresser	33
Public Administration	61	Bulldozer Operator	33
Elementary School Teacher	60	Bus Driver	32
Union official	58	Truck Driver	32
Accountant	57	Cashier	31
Actors	55	Retail Sales Clerks	29
Dietician	52	Gas Station Attendant	22
Funeral Director	52	Taxi Driver/Chauffeur	22
Social Worker	52	Bartender	20
Editor/Reporter	51	Waiter	20
Locomotive Engineer	51	Farm Laborer	18
Sales Manager	50	Household Servant/Maid	18
Electrician	49	Garbage Collector	17
Machinist	48	Janitor	16
Policemen and Detectives	48	Bootblacks	09
Insurance Agent	47		

Source: Adapted from James A. Davis and Tom W. Smith, *General Social Surveys, 1972–1986: Cumulative Codebook* (Chicago: National Opinion Research Center, 1986), Appendix F. Missing from the general social survey are titles such as U.S. Supreme Court Justice, federal cabinet member, U.S. Representative in Congress, mayor of large city, and state governor, which had appeared in earlier surveys and received high prestige scores.

higher education that Americans attend also corresponds to social class. Youngsters from the lower middle and working classes tend to go to junior and lower-prestige four-year colleges while the upper classes attend the "better" four-year colleges.

The importance of education in the overall class system is easy to see. Educational credentials are used by employers, professional associations, and trade unions to distribute occupations in various labor markets. The hierarchy of occupations results in healthy differentials in income. In turn, occupational and income differences emerge as class differences as family units undergo different life experiences and degrees of consumption. Class differences also emerge as differences in the ability of the next generation of children to succeed in school.

CLASS, SEX, MARRIAGE, AND FAMILY

The broad upper and lower classes behave differently in regard to both premarital and marital sex.[12] Age of marriage also differs by class, the children of the upper classes marrying later largely because of the education required for adult economic roles. Another class-related aspect of marital behavior is that Americans tend to marry within their own class (as measured by residential propinquity, education, or occupation of bread-

[12]Martin S. Weinberg and Colin J. Williams, "Sexual Embourgeoisment? Social Class and Sexual Activity: 1938–1970," *American Sociological Review* 45 (February, 1980): 33–48; James M. Henslin, "Sex and Marriage" in James M. Henslin, ed., *Marriage and Family In A Changing Society*, 2nd ed. (New York: Free Press, 1985), p. 344–47.

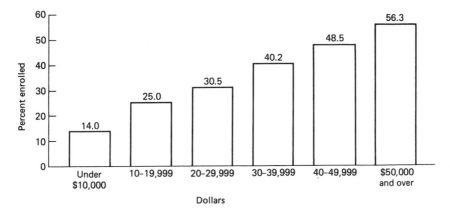

FIGURE 9-5. College Enrollment of Dependent Family Members 18 to 24 Years Old by Family Income,[1] 1986.

[1]College enrollment refers to junior as well as four year colleges and family income includes households with more than 1 earner. Class differences in college attendance would be far more pronounced if only 4-year colleges were included.

Source: U.S. Bureau of the Census, Current Population Report, Series P-20, No. 429, "School Enrollment—Social and Economic Characteristics of Students, October, 1986" (Washington, D.C.: U. S. Government Printing Office, 1988), Table 12.

winner in family of origin and occupation of spouses), and to marry within their own religion, ethnic group, and race.

Birth rates are related inversely to social class (using family income and woman's education). Class differentials also appear among black and Spanish-origin Americans.[13] There appears to be no deviation from national class-related patterns in fertility among religious groups.[14]

LeMasters and Rubin have provided rich (and disturbing) portraits of working-class marriages, ranging from those among higher-skilled, better-paid, and more work satisfied construction workers to those among lower-level, blue collar workers.[15] The lives of working class spouses are differentiated by sex. Men lead their lives largely outside the home (at work and with male friends) while women lead their lives largely inside the home and with relatives. All this may be changing as more wives are forced into the labor market. Middle-class spouses may also lead differentiated lives, especially when only the husband works, but they have far more in common (about sex, raising children, planning for the future) than working-class spouses. In another study, Halle has provided a variation of working-class marriage. He too found much that LeMasters and Rubin had found. But because his study group consisted of well-paid workers at an automated chemical plant, the cleavage between the sexes and differences with white collar workers were not as extreme as those found by LeMasters and Rubin.[16]

[13]Donald J. Bogue *et al., The Population of the United States: Historical Trends and Future Projections* (New York: Free Press, 1985), Table 6–23A.

[14]*Ibid,* pp. 659–62.

[15]E. E. LeMasters, *Blue Collar Aristocrats* (Madison, Wisc.: University of Wisconsin Press, 1975) and Lillian Breslow Rubin, *Worlds of Pain: Life in the Working Class Family* (New York: Basic Books, 1976).

[16]David Halle, *America's Working Mass: Work, Home, and Politics Among Blue-Collar Property [Home] Owners* (Chicago: University of Chicago Press, 1984), Chapter 3.

CLASS AND CHILDREARING

Classes raise their children differently. Elkin and Handel summarize our knowledge of class-based childrearing by contrasting the socialization environment of an upper-middle-class family with that of the working class.[17] The upper-middle-class child grows up according to the *deferred gratification* pattern in which daily life, while enjoyable, is always pointed to the future. Youngsters receive a far more varied experience in school and in other areas and interact more with adults who provide upper-middle-class role models. By and large, upper-middle-class children are trained for independence, something that corresponds to the type of occupations held by their parents. By and large, the working class provides a more limited range of interaction experiences and socializes its young for conformity.[18]

CLASS AND HEALTH

Capitalism has provided conditions and facilities for a dramatic improvement in health and longevity (perhaps including even mental health insofar as this can be determined). Interestingly, improvements in health and longevity have stemmed primarily from a more plentiful supply of nourishing food and from more sanitary ways of obtaining water, disposing of garbage, and maintaining personal hygiene, and not from the practice of medicine. However, despite the general rise in health and life expectancy, the distribution of health values is still markedly unequal. Class location determines your chances of becoming sick or disabled either on or off the job and of receiving medical treatment (including type and quality of treatment). Birth into a class also affects your chances of being biologically deformed or retarded. Needless to say the upper classes have markedly better experiences in all these regards. It should be noted that while the lower classes have a lower life expectancy than those above them, the difference appears to be significantly less than in the past.

Despite affluence, many Americans go hungry[19] and many must live in unsanitary conditions. Health is also undermined unequally by the type of work done by the various classes—occupational hazards are concentrated among the working classes (little effective protection is afforded by government, despite explicit occupational health and safety laws, for the simple reason that such laws are not enforced). Members of the lower classes are also more likely to be victimized by crime, suffer from family violence, and are more prone to mental illness.

CLASS AND CONSUMPTION

Many believe that Americans consume a great deal in common. A further myth is that Americans are largely middle-class consumers. The truth is that Americans consume both equally and unequally in keeping with the thrust of a mass production economy and the distribution of wealth, income, and education. The mass production economy of capitalism spews forth huge amounts of standardized products and services, and Americans are socialized to want ("need") them. Food, beverage, household products, appliances, clothing and footwear, sporting goods, plus a variety of services such as entertainment and transportation, are consumed in common by most Americans. Americans also use many public facilities and

---

[17]Frederick Elkin and Gerald Handel, *The Child and Society: The Process of Socialization* (New York: Random House, 1984), Chapter 4.

[18]The general proposition that parents who associate self-reliance and independence with their own success also value the same traits in their children, and that those who are closely supervised at work and in life tend to value conformity in their children was found across 122 cultures by Godfrey J. Ellis, Gary R. Lee, and Larry R. Petersen, "Supervision and Conformity: A Cross-Cultural Analysis of Parental Socialization Values," *American Journal of Sociology* 84 (September, 1978): 386–403.

[19]In its report, *Hunger in America: The Growing Epidemic*, the Physicians Task Force on Hunger, headed by J. Larry Brown, Harvard School of Public Health, estimates that in 1984–85, 20 million Americans were adversely affected by hunger (as reported in *The New York Times*, February 27, 1985, p. A12).

services in common and have the legal right (as consumers) to use privately owned facilities such as housing, restaurants, hotels, theater, stadiums, and so on.

But consumption is also very unequal. Upper-class families routinely spend more on personal adornment and leisure activities than millions of families spend on food, clothing, and shelter. Millions of Americans own two homes while millions find it difficult to own one and hundreds of thousands go without shelter. Even when they consume things in common, class differences are often pronounced—there are budget, moderately priced, and luxury hotels, public eating places within everybody's income and places where a meal costs $125 without a drink or tip. All in all, the culture of capitalism has established the legitimacy of wide differences in consumption. Americans accept even lavish consumption amidst poverty because they believe that consumption is related to what individuals earn through their own efforts and is thus deserved.

CLASS AND INTERACTION: HOW AMERICANS ASSOCIATE

Americans do not associate at random with anyone. Basic forms of interaction such as friendship, marriage, socializing, club membership, and participation in voluntary groups are deeply structured by social class. Whether the focus is on *primary* groups (marriage, family, friendship, clubs, socializing groups) or *secondary* groups (charities, reform, fraternal, professional, trade, political, service groups), researchers have found that Americans behave and interact according to class.[20] A class hierarchy of primary prestige groups and primary interaction results because families in different economic classes do not socialize either at home, clubs, or in resorts, and as a rule their members do not intermarry. Economic classes are also separated by the *kind* of primary interaction they engage in. Working-class Americans tend to have fewer friends,

entertain less, and belong less to clubs and other organizations devoted to entertainment and companionship than the classes above them. And working-class marriages and family life provide fewer and lower-quality satisfactions than middle- and upper-class marriages. Below the working class lies an underclass (the homeless, skid row people, bag ladies, or elderly poor) that experiences deep social isolation since its members do not engage much in either primary or secondary behavior.

The evidence also reveals a pronounced correlation between economic class and participation in voluntary groups. Especially significant is the sharp split in the behavior of the middle- and upper-classes, on the one hand, and the working- and lower-classes on the other. Far from being a nation of joiners, most working- and lower-class Americans do not participate much in voluntary groups. Individuals from the upper levels of the economy and the professions dominate the boards and staffs of all sectors of the voluntary realm: research and reform groups, foundations, hospitals, museums, symphony orchestras, charitable groups, universities and colleges, and so on.

STRATIFIED POLITICS

Social actors engage in political action to control the enactment and enforcement of a special body of norms called *law*. The purpose of politics is to influence or control the polity (or state)—the military, police, tax collector, courts, schools, and so on. *Stratified politics* means that social classes have different access to and different control over the state and thus get different benefits from it. Following Max Weber's usage, *political-legal power* refers to only one form of social power, the state, or the political-legal forces that promote or reduce social inequality.[21]

---

[20]Participation in social groups is also differentiated by religion, ethnicity, race, and by sex and age.

[21]For Weber's discussion of law and politics in relation to social stratification, see his "Class, Status, Party" in *From Max Weber: Essays in Sociology*, ed. and tr. H. H. Gerth and C. Wright Mills (New York: Oxford University Press, 1946), Chapter 7, Sections 1, 10.

Many believe that representative government (or political democracy) marks an advance in equalizing political-legal power. Here again, as in so much about modern society, the realities are otherwise. Under feudalism, only landed property owners can turn economic power into political power. Under representative government, property groups *in general* (including the owners of managerial and professional skills) are able to translate their economic interests into political-legal power. All that political democracy means, therefore, is that a wider range of propertied-professional groups have political power. The dominance of American political life by the diverse property groups that we call the middle and upper classes has been confirmed by research.

Class Representation

The United States has never had an effective one-person, one-vote system of representation. It was not until the 1850s that the property qualification was lifted for white males. Women did not receive the vote until 1919 and blacks did not receive an effective vote until the 1960s. The formal equality of the vote was offset until the 1960s by the fact that electoral districts throughout the United States were grossly unequal in size of population. Today the gerrymander, or drawing electoral lines to reflect class, ethnic, and racial lines, still thwarts the principle of one person, one vote.[22]

Voting and Other Forms of Political Participation

Participation in elections follows class lines: the higher one's education, income, and occupation, the more likely one is to vote.[23] Other forms of participation in politics are also class based. A small group of Republican and Democratic activists from upper socio-

economic levels dominate political participation other than voting: campaigning, contacting government officials, contributing money, attending rallies, and so on.

Voting Preference

Americans tend to support political parties and political programs according to class. Upper- and middle-class individuals (professionals, managers, proprietors, college graduates, and individuals with high incomes) largely support the Republican party. Members of the working class and those with low prestige status regardless of class (manual workers, laborers, blacks, Roman Catholics, Jews) have tended to support the Democratic party. On economic matters, the upper classes support a hands-off stance toward government (though in practice the upper classes demand and get government support on things that matter to them) while the lower classes stress the need for government to intervene in the economy on their behalf. On issues concerning civil rights, toleration of dissent and minorities, and foreign policy, the reverse is true: the lower classes are less tolerant and less interested in aiding foreign countries than the upper classes (though there are obvious exceptions by issue).

The class basis of American politics is not accompanied by militant class cleavage and conflict. The American class system is so diverse and contradictory that it is difficult for Americans to formulate distinct, unambiguous class interests. The United States has three basic economic (class) markets: labor, commodities, and credit. Americans often find themselves in more than one market and often have conflicts in their overall economic (class) interests. In addition, each market has a different economic over- and underdog and it is difficult for the diverse underdogs to unite (and the same is true to a lesser extent for overdogs). For example, American farmers and workers are both underdogs but they cannot easily come together to take joint political action since farmers' class interests lie in high prices for food and low

---

[22]For a discussion of the gerrymander, see Chapter 7.

[23]U. S. Bureau of the Census, Current Population Reports, Series P-20, no. 370, "Voting and Registration in the Election of 1984" (Washington, D.C.: U. S. Government Printing Office, 1986), Tables 10, 12, 13.

prices for manufactured goods, the opposite of the class interests of workers.[24]

Political Parties and Interest Groups

The two major American political parties (and most third parties) are derived from and dependent on the upper reaches of the American class system. Organized, politically relevant interest groups also come primarily from the upper classes and all tend to develop ideologies in keeping with their location in the class system. Politically relevant groups include learned societies, civic betterment associations, groups concerned with particular problems (such as taxation, foreign affairs, veterans' affairs, or abortion), professional associations, labor unions, trade associations, and governmental units themselves (associations of civil service employees, including teachers, and even associations of elected officials).

Whether measured in terms of rates of participation by members, the credentials of staff members, or effectiveness, America's political parties and other politically active groups reflect the interests and power of the middle and upper classes. Pressure groups from the lower classes are highly visible but their effectiveness is much exaggerated. By and large, economic strength is the telling force in American politics and so far all efforts to curtail the power of money have failed (for an earlier discussion, see Chapter 7).

Elected and Appointed Officials

Elected and appointed officials in the United States are drawn overwhelmingly from the upper classes. Both at the state and federal levels the pattern is clear: the middle and upper classes predominate among elected officials and high appointed civil, military, and political offices. Another pronounced feature of American political life is the large flow of traffic between the upper levels of private and public life. Banks, universities, and especially law firms and large corporations supply a steady flow of personnel to staff the 2,000 to 3,000 political positions at the apex of the federal government and the various regulatory commissions. Such traffic provides valuable political experience for the future leaders of the private economy and professions and of course gives them and the organizations they represent direct control over policy making. Traffic between private and public life (the revolving door) is limited to some extent by professional ethics, conflict of interest laws, and technical occupational requirements.

Class, Legislation, and Government

No area or type of legislation is nonpartisan or classless. Legislation biased in favor of or against certain classes is a fundamental feature of American political history. Banking policy has been a tug-of-war between creditors and debtors since the beginning of the American Republic. High tariffs favored manufacturers and penalized farmers during the nineteenth century. Energy, transportation, and natural resources policies all have serious implications for broad class interests. The Selective Service System during the Vietnam war discriminated deeply among the classes: working class males were far more subject to the draft and to combat than the sons of the middle and upper classes.[25]

Representative government and universal suffrage, therefore, do not result in laws or governments that favor the mass of the people.[26] No matter what area is examined, taxation, support for farmers, highway legislation, housing, urban renewal, support for

---

[24]For a sophisticated analysis and background on class politics in the United States, see Norbert Wiley, "America's Unique Class Politics: The Interplay of the Labor, Credit and Commodity Markets," *American Sociological Review* 32 (August, 1967): 529–41.

[25]James W. Davis, Jr. and Kenneth M. Dolbeare, *Little Groups of Neighbors: The Selective Service System* (Chicago: Markham, 1968), and M. Zeitlin, K. A. Lutterman, and J. W. Russell, "Death in Vietnam: Class, Poverty, and the Risks of War," *Politics and Society* 3 (Spring, 1973): 313–28.

[26]For an analysis similar to the one that follows, see Benjamin I. Page, *Who Gets What From Government* (Berkeley, Calif.: University of California, 1983).

the humanities and arts, funds for pre- and post-doctoral faculty research in science, funds for medicine and mental health, disaster aid, small business loans, the enforcement of safety and antipollution standards, labor legislation, or minimum wage laws, the result is the same—government spending heavily favors the middle and upper classes. And nothing at the local and state levels runs counter to this pattern; if anything, the class nature of government is even more pronounced at these lower levels.

American public policy is largely based on the trickle-down theory—help the rich, the educated, the better-off and they will produce so much that eventually benefits will trickle down to the rest of the population. The evidence strongly indicates that the trickle-down theory is wrong.

The Stratified Welfare System

Many believe (falsely) that government spending favors the poor, and that *transfer payments* (such as welfare checks for the poor, medicaid, workmen's compensation, unemployment insurance, food stamps, social security, school lunch and other nutrition programs) equalize the classes. In truth, government spending does the opposite— far from equalizing wealth and income, government spending helps the upper and middle classes far more than the poor.

It is not easy to see government spending on behalf of the upper classes because of bias and selective perception. The federal tax code, for example, is a form of government spending that analysts call *tax expenditures.* Every decision to forego taxes on certain income or to allow deductions and credits is considered government spending. The vast bulk of such benefits go to upper-income groups.[27]

---

[27]One analyst for the *Wall Street Journal* has put public welfare for corporations at $140 billion; Gregory Fossedal, "Corporate Welfare Out of Control," *The New Republic* 192 (February 25, 1985): 17–9. In contrast welfare checks for dependent mothers amount to less than $10 billion.

Direct public spending also favors the upper classes. The class nature of education means that money spend on elementary and high schools and on higher education represents vast subsidies to the middle and upper classes. Aid to college students from the 1970s on has widened the disparity in benefits since most aid goes to the upper classes. Consider public benefits for farmers. As embattled middle-class property owners, farmers have received large amounts of public assistance in the form of interest rates, price supports, cheap electricity, and so on. Today, the federal government still spends huge sums on price supports and subsidized loans for farmers but now most of this welfare goes to agribusinesses since farming, like most of the American economy, is highly concentrated (12 percent of American farms generate 63 percent of farm sales).

Myths About the Poor

Many Americans believe that the welfare rolls are filled with deadbeats and cheats, able-bodied individuals who do not want to work. They believe that welfare makes people dependent and that people do not want to get out of poverty. Many believe that welfare spending is the reason for their high taxes. Many Americans are afraid to provide help to the poor because of the belief that it will attract the poor to their city or state. The truth contradicts all these beliefs. People on welfare are almost all children, mothers, and the elderly. Most poor people are poor for a short while and all would work if work were available or possible. Able-bodied men cannot get welfare checks regardless of how poor they are (they can get food stamps). People do not move to get higher welfare. The amount of money spent on welfare to mothers with dependent children is very small and even the highest amounts represent a very low level of living. Food stamps make up a more sizable amount but this helps to dispose of surplus food that the federal government buys from farmers and that would rot if not given away. As for cheating and waste, experts agree that there is very little and that most of the waste and fraud is due to poorly researched laws, government confusion and incompetence, and corrupt administrators.

Beeghley, a leading expert on poverty, says we must distinguish between antipoverty programs and public assistance. The antipoverty programs of the 1960s and '70s were designed to help the poor become self-reliant, productive members of society. These now have been largely abandoned (because they threatened the interests of the classes above the poor). Assistance for the poor, on the other hand, is basically institutionalized pauperism—one has to be destitute to receive aid and aid levels are pitched at subsistence and subsubsistence levels. In addition, the overall amount for public assistance is far lower than people think. In 1982 the total federal outlays for public assistance of all kinds amounted to 8.2 percent of the federal budget.[28]

Structural Poverty and the New Poor

The United States has generated a new mix of poor people in recent decades. The poor are still disproportionately made up of racial and ethnic minorities, but the poverty group now includes a large number of female-headed households and this means that children are disproportionately poor (almost 25 percent of America's children live in poverty). There are one to two million full-time workers and their families that are poor. And there are the hundreds of thousands of deinstitutionalized mentally ill who are poor (and homeless).

Structural poverty means that basic institutions and power relations are causing poverty. Specific causes are chronic unemployment, unnecessary qualifications for occupations, poor management, the cultural bias toward technology and against labor, the movement of capital abroad, antifamily

bias in welfare programs, the lack of public programs fostering birth control, the separation of work and residence, the irrelevance of education to work, and in general the absence of socioeconomic planning.

AND JUSTICE FOR SOME: CLASS AND LAW

Does the law affect the American population uniformly? Does obeying or disobeying the law have anything to do with social class? Does the state—represented by police officers, prosecutors, juries, defense attorneys, judges, court officers, prison officials, and professional auxiliaries—treat individuals equally? Are the agencies of power that specialize in maintaining the law and administering justice impartial in their treatment of the American people? In short, is there equality before the law?

Class and the Definition of Crime

One of the most dramatic effects of social class is that the law breaking activities of the middle and upper classes are not characteristically thought of as criminal—crime in the popular mind is law breaking by the lower classes. Edwin H. Sutherland made a great contribution to criminology by simply pointing out that when high-level people break the law they should be called criminals.[29] In thinking about crime, therefore, we must imagine a hierarchy of classes committing different kinds of crime. Business executives, bankers, lawyers, doctors, and other elites who conspire illegally to set prices on goods, interest rates, or services, or who embezzle or commit fraud steal more money by far than all the lower classes put together. And, morally, their crimes are far more damaging to society than crime by ordinary people. Below them are small business people, semiprofessionals, and salespeople who break the law in various ways (misgrade products, commit

---

[28]For perhaps the best single book on poverty, see Leonard Beeghley, *Living Poorly In America* (New York: Praeger, 1983).

[29]*White Collar Crime* (New York: Holt, Rinehart and Winston, 1949).

arson, shortweight, accept bribes, pilfer). At the bottom of our hierarchy of class crime are burglars, robbers, and muggers.

In an indictment written from a radical conflict perspective, Reiman charges that the American criminal justice system is largely organized (unintentionally) to perpetuate crime and to create the impression that the poor are the main criminal threat to society. What this does, says Reiman, is to focus the attention of the broad middle classes on the poor and away from the crimes of the powerful.[30]

Legal Services and the Administration of Justice

Legal services in the United States must be bought just as most other things. Money buys the services of a lawyer, pays bail, and can be used to pay a fine to avoid prison. By and large, legal services go to the middle and upper classes, especially the most wealthy and powerful. Judicial outcomes depend on the skills of lawyers, and merely having a lawyer does not ensure justice. Providing lawyers free for poor defendants appears to be largely a way to finance the court system and to expedite "negotiated convictions." By and large, the lower classes do not use the machinery of law though they have many legal problems. American legal institutions assume middle-class status: to benefit from the law in practice requires money, education, information, and middle-class assertiveness. Federally funded legal aid has helped but so far has made only a dent in the problem because of opposition by conservatives.

THE CLASS POSITION OF AMERICAN MINORITIES

The term *minority* was first used in the peace treaties of World War I to refer to ethnic groups in Eastern Europe that needed protection against dominant ethnic groups. Today the term refers to a wide variety of groups

and aggregates that want a change in power relations: ethnic, racial, and religious groups as well as aggregates such as women, the aged, youth, the handicapped, the overweight, and those with different life styles, especially homosexuals (who prefer to be called gays).

Ethnicity and Race in Comparative Perspective

Science tells us that human beings have the same mental and moral capacity regardless of skin color, sex, or other physical features. The fact that all must learn how to behave is of the greatest importance in establishing human equality. Most observable differences among human beings are due to *what* they experience (learn), and differences become pronounced if human beings in different cultures are compared. When the human beings of different cultures meet, their interaction cannot be the same as that between members of the same culture. In the latter case, behavior is smooth and predictable, almost unconscious, like putting on an old pair of shoes. But when members of different cultural groups meet they are strangers and cannot take anything for granted. Language, dress, food, and so on are all different. Given time, newcomers will *acculturate* (take on the characteristics of their new society). But if they are thought of as belonging to a different category of being (that is, if differences are attributed to some permanent or relatively permanent feature such as race, sex, religion, or nationality), and all members of that group are treated as inferiors, then a minority has been created. Thereafter interaction between socially dominant and socially created inferior groups will reinforce and consolidate differences and the social distance between them will make it difficult for the dominant to see qualities that they share with the dominated.

In the great agrarian empires of the past different ethnic groups lived together as separate societies within a larger imperial whole. The relations of these groups were sometimes peaceful, sometimes turbulent, but there was no effort to mingle or assimilate the

---

[30]Jeffrey H. Reiman, *The Rich Get Richer and the Poor Get Prison,* 2nd ed. (New York: John Wiley, 1984).

various ethnic or racial groups into a greater whole. All this was changed by the rise of capitalism. The dynamic capitalist economy moves people around to suit the needs of commerce and industry and this tends to bring ethnic groups into contact with each other. The capitalist economy is powered by cheap labor and capitalist societies import labor, often diversifying their ethnic and racial makeup. The United States imported a large number of slaves to labor on the cash-crop plantations of the American South. It imported 40 million immigrants during the nineteenth century to work in its cities and factories. Also important in the development of the United States is the wide use of female labor outside the home. One consequence of all this was the emergence of themes of ethnic, racial, and sexual inequality. Often this inequality took on the force of law as well as well-established practice.

Capitalism also had a countercurrent. As it developed in England, France, and the United States, it declared all eligible for participation in the main benefits and positions in society. The rising middle classes argued that all human beings had the right and the duty to develop their brains, morals, and tastes. This could best be done by participating in a free and rational division of labor. In keeping with this argument, capitalism transformed its members into a legally free, all-purpose labor force (possessive individualism, or the doctrine that individuals own themselves and are free to work for themselves or sell their labor to others). All this runs counter to racial and ethnic beliefs and practices that keep some people ignorant, idle, and apart.

The clash of these two traditions is the heart of America's majority-minority relations. To state the conflict concretely: early (entrepreneurial) capitalism developed racist-ethnic-sexist norms and values to justify the cheap labor it needed, but it also established values declaring all humans eligible for full membership and participation in the life of society. When beliefs that ethnic newcomers, nonwhites, females, and others were innately inferior crumbled in the face of experience and science and when economic need required

a more fluid, flexible (efficient) use of labor, a later (corporate) capitalism changed the legal and political statuses of minorities in an effort to create an abstract labor force, that is, a labor force made up of all members of society.

Societies in the contemporary world are filled with the tension and conflict of opposing ethnic-racial groups. Majority-minority relations occur, however, in two fundamentally different types of society: the *segmented* and the *associational*. Segmented societies (also known as multicommunal or multiethnic societies) result from empires that do not assimilate conquered peoples or from peace settlements that put different peoples inside arbitrary national boundaries, for example, Canada, Northern Ireland, Belgium, Switzerland, Cyprus, Lebanon, Sri Lanka, Malaysia, and the Union of South Africa. These societies are openly and explicitly organized around ethnic and racial values and all (with the exception of Switzerland) have serious disputes between dominant and minority groups. In contrast, there are associational societies such as the United States, much of Western Europe, the Soviet Union, Australia, and others, where ethnic and racial groups are at least nominally free to participate in the basic institutions of society and associate freely with members of the dominant groups.

Ethnic and Racial Minorities in the United States

The United States has had a continuous wave of newcomers from different ethnic and racial backgrounds.[31] Though some came willingly and others by force, newcomers were largely thought of and treated as inferiors. Over time, some newcomers managed to attain full membership in American society. By and large, Roman Catholics (from Europe and Canada but not Latin America) have been culturally assimilated (though not in terms

---

[31]For a comprehensive reference book with good thematic essays on American ethnic and racial groups, see Stephen Thernstrom, ed., *Harvard Encyclopedia of American Ethnic Groups* (Cambridge, Mass.: Harvard University Press, 1980).

of associational patterns) and are well represented at all income, occupational, and educational levels. Roman Catholics from Spanish-speaking countries (with the exception of Cubans), however, are still minorities and differ markedly from mainstream Americans on all counts. Greek-Americans have also assimilated and can no longer be considered a minority. Japanese, Chinese, and Jewish Americans have enjoyed notable success in educational and occupational achievement but are still minorities in some important respects.

The groups that have fared the worst are racial groups. Race, as such, has no scientific standing since no causal relation between behavior and skin color (or hair texture, eyelids, or other such physical attributes) has ever been established. But to its enduring shame, white America has been openly racist in its treatment of all nonwhites and, at one time or another, has made black Americans, native American Indians, Hawaiians, Aleutians, Chinese, Japanese, and Filipinos into distinctly depressed racial minorities.[32]

Ethnic and Racial Demographics

Minority groups vary considerably in size (see Table 9-4). Black Americans are the largest minority group forming 11 percent of the total population. Latins or Hispanics, most of whom are Mexican American, are the next largest. Excluding Jewish Americans, approximately 17 percent of the American population is made up of deeply disadvantaged minorities. Ethnic and racial minorities are younger than dominant groups. Their birth rates are higher and they have a shorter life expectancy than majority Americans. And they have a higher dependency ratio (the number of those not likely to work in relation to those that are).

Comparative Sex Statuses

Racial and ethnic groups can be radically stratified because they are composed of households. Female inequality (along with age inequality) must be conceptualized differently since females (and different ages) are found in most households high or low in the ladder of social class.

Men and women seem to be unequal in almost all societies. Even among the Arapesh in which men and women both have nurturing personalities, men have more privileges and authority.[33] But the inequality of females, even though universal, varies considerably depending on the type of society. One need only compare women among the Tiwi[34] (where they are essentially the property of older men) to middle- and upper-class women in the United States (who have considerable independence and achievements in a variety of fields) to appreciate the sociocultural basis of gender identity. Women and men are unequal in hunting and gathering societies, but, on the whole, are far more equal than in any of the complex societies. The most sexual inequality occurs in agrarian societies where most of the ideology about women's innate inferiority was developed as part of the great universal, patriarchal religions. The basic variable associated with more equality for women, argues Blumberg (on the basis of the anthropological-historical evidence), is not work or economic participation but control over productive property and its surplus.[35] Marvin Harris argues that male supremacy stems from warfare and the male monopoly over weapons.[36] Though social scientists

[32]Prentice-Hall's Ethnic Groups in American Life Series, edited by Milton M. Gordon, provides excellent case studies of major ethnic and racial minorities, including a study of white Protestant Americans. Harry H. L. Kitano and Roger Daniels, *Asian Americans: Emerging Minorities* (Englewood Cliffs, N.J.: Prentice Hall, 1988) updates our picture of Chinese and Japanese Americans and provides a valuable picture of other Asian Americans as well as Pacific Islanders.

[33]Margaret Mead, *Sex and Temperament In Three Primitive Societies* (New York: Dell, 1935).

[34]C. W. M. Hart and Arnold R. Pilling, *The Tiwi of North Australia* (New York: Holt, Rinehart and Winston, 1979).

[35]Rae Lesser Blumberg, *Stratification: Socioeconomic and Sexual Inequality* (Dubuque, Iowa: W. C. Brown, 1978).

[36]Marvin Harris, *Cannibals and King: The Origins of Culture* (New York: Random House, 1977), Chapter 6.

TABLE 9-4. Racial and Cultural Minorities in the United States.

Total American Population	245,807,000 (1988)
Blacks	30,072,000 (1988 est.)
Hispanic Origin (Total)	9,431,000 (1988)
Mexican	12,110,000
Puerto Rican	2,471,000
Cuban	1,035,000
Central or South American	2,242,000
Other Hispanic	1,573,000
Jews	5,814,000 (1986 est.)
Native Americans	800,000 (est.)
Asian Americans (Total)	5,147,900 (1985 est.)
Chinese	1,079,400
Filipino	1,051,600
Japanese	766,300
Vietnamese	634,200
Korean	543,400
Asian Indian	525,600
Laotian	218,400
Kampuchean	160,800
All other	169,200
Pacific Islanders (Total)	259,566 (1985)

Source: *Statistical Abstract of the United States, 1989* (Washington, DC: U. S. Government Printing Office, 1981), Tables 2, 15, 78; U. S. Bureau of the Census, *Current Population Reports*, Series P-20, No. 431; "The Hispanic Population in the United States" March 1988 (Washington, D.C.: U. S. Government Printing Office, 1988), Table A and Robert W. Gardner, Bryant Robey, and Peter C. Smith, "Asian Americans: Growth, Change, and Diversity", *Population Bulletin* 40; 4 (October, 1985), Table 1.

continue to disagree about causes, most have discarded human-nature explanations as the reasons for sexual inequality.

Comparisons among contemporary countries (developed and developing) do not reveal any real break with the pervasive pattern of sexual inequality. Developing socialist societies bring about dramatic changes in the position of women but seem only to incorporate them into more up-to-date, male-dominated family, educational, and political-economic institutions. Women in some countries are better off in some ways because of local policies (for example, better maternity or child-care facilities) or they may be more equal to men because the entire society is more equal (for example, Sweden, a highly unequal capitalist society, has more overall equality for all including women than the United States). On the whole, however, women in industrial societies are very unequal to men regardless of the ideology of their respective societies and regardless of whether they live in capitalist or socialist societies.[37]

America's Minorities: Running Hard and Standing Still

The federal government did not collect meaningful and useful data about American minorities until well after World War II. Its growth in data-gathering capability about minorities was climaxed by the 1978 publication of the United States Commission on Civil Rights, *Social Indicators of Equality for Minorities and Women*.[38] The Commission's report is particularly valuable since it contains data on both large and small minorities: women, blacks, American Indians, Alaskan natives, Mexican Americans, Japanese Americans, Chinese Americans, Filipino Americans, and Puerto Ricans.

Minorities, said the Commission, are concerned about the following:

1. underdevelopment of human skills through delayed enrollment or nonenrollment in secondary education, and nonparticipation in higher education;

2. lack of equivalent returns for educational achievement in terms of occupational opportunities and earnings;

3. discrepancies in access to jobs, particularly those having greater-than-average stability, prestige, and monetary returns;

4. inequality of income, relatively lower earnings for equal work, and diminished chances for salary and wage increases;

---

[37]For a superb comparative-historical analysis of gender inequality in terms of specific types of society (forager, horticultural, pastoral, agrarian, and developed and developing capitalist and socialist), see Charlotte G. O'Kelly and Larry S. Carney, *Women and Men In Society: Cross-Cultural Perspectives on Gender Stratification*, 2nd ed. (Belmont, Calif.: Wadsworth, 1986).

[38]United States Civil Rights Commission; Washington, D.C. 20425.

5. a high likelihood of being in poverty;
6. and a proportionately higher expenditure for housing, less desirable housing conditions, restricted freedom of choice in selecting locations in which to live, and greater difficulty in attaining homeownership.[39]

The thrust of its analysis is to establish equality ratios between majority males and minorities over time. Assembling data from 1960, 1970, and 1976 to see if there has been movement toward equality, the Commission's finding are clear and unequivocal—minorities and women are grossly unequal (even when achievement is held constant!) in 21 measures in the above areas. Even more important, their position has not improved since 1960, and in some areas has not even kept pace with majority males!

The Civil Rights Commission's report along with other evidence raises disturbing questions about the nature of minority inequality and what to do about it. *Of the greatest importance is the fact that the United States' minorities have made no relative advance toward equality despite considerable legal and political help during the greatest and longest period of economic expansion in American history.*[40] *The highly stable and unequal position of ethnic and racial minorities (and women) raises these questions:* do civil rights and other minority-oriented legislation have any effect on economic inequality? The answer appears to be no. Should minorities make a greater effort in education? The answer appears to be no. Are the civil rights laws and programs mostly a way for corporate capitalism to modernize its labor force? Over the past 600 years capitalism has developed a labor force composed of legally free indi-

viduals. In the United States it also developed first a slave and then a segregated labor force. Are the civil rights laws merely a way to turn minorities into legally free individuals who can then be held responsible for failure?

All evidence points to systematic and stable injustice for large portions of the American population. The evidence again points not only to the failure of American society to live up to its norms and values but to what appears to be an inherent inability to do so. The evidence suggests that American society cannot hope to achieve its values as long as the nature of its economy remains unproblematic. Giving minorities their civil rights may actually be more a process of legitimating their exploitation than a real improvement in their relative social position.

CLASS AND CLASS CONSCIOUSNESS

Karl Marx saw class consciousness as the awakening of the working classes (the great majority of the population) to their exploitation by a small group of big property owners. Marx felt that class consciousness was a natural by-product of class struggle in which first the middle class rises against the feudal lord (in the name of liberty, equality, and representative government) and then the working class rises against the now obsolete middle class (in the name of humanity and the classless society).

Are the American people conscious of social classes and class exploitation in the way Marx predicted? Are they aware that the American class system has many illegitimate elements? Are they aware that their society has a deeply rooted system of advantage and disadvantage based on family birth? Are the American people class conscious in any sense, Marxian or otherwise?

Class Self-Identification

In a recent study the Jackmans found no class consciousness along the lines that Marx

---

[39]*Social Indicators of Equality for Minorities and Women 1978*, p. 3.

[40]L. Paul Metzger argues that the traditional assimilationist perspective of sociology (and of left and right liberals) was shattered by the events of the 1960s—see his "American Sociology and Black Assimilation: Conflicting Perspectives", *American Journal of Sociology* 76 (January, 1971): 627–47. The events of the 1970s and 80s have done little to restore faith in it and if anything have undermined it further.

predicted. What they discovered, though, is that Americans are very much aware of classes. Americans, argue the Jackmans, perceive classes as a graded series of social communities, which they define in economic and cultural terms. In a national sample, Americans were asked to place themselves in the following hierarchy of five classes: upper class, upper middle, middle, working, and poor. Ninety seven out of one hundred respondents indicated that they knew which class they belonged to and they used the basic components of class such as income, occupation, and education in defining class.[41]

Americans' self-identification did not exhibit a sharp difference between blue and white collar workers or between the propertied and nonpropertied. Americans also failed to carry their awareness of class into the arena of politics. This is not surprising, say the Jackmans, because American political institutions, including our political parties, consistently deny the existence of class-based interests.

Why the Lack of Awareness About Class Stratification?

Americans are somewhat aware of the meaning of class but they are not aware of class structure in sociological terms—that is, as a comprehensive social system that determines the distribution of opportunities and other social benefits. They have little awareness, in other words, of a highly organized system of social power connecting the economy, the professions, education, family, health, consumption, interaction in primary and secondary groups, politics, government, and law.

The main reasons for the lack of a deeper understanding of class in the United States are:

1. Economic expansion has diversified the economic interests of Americans, often giving them contradictory and crosscutting interests. Economic growth has provided economic mobil-

ity for many and has raised living standards (remember that a general rise of living standards is not the same thing as social mobility or movement across class lines but can easily be misinterpreted as such).

2. Immigration and migration (along with the aftermath of racial slavery) have diversified economic classes on ethnic, religious, and racial grounds, making it difficult for those in similar economic positions to develop an awareness of their common class identity.

3. Sexual inequality has also contributed to diversity among those in similar economic statuses and has also made it difficult to think in terms of common class interests and grievances.

4. The steady extension of legal and political rights encouraged Americans to feel that equal, individual competition was either a reality or could become one. However, American political institutions have always reflected the interests of property and professional groups—not surprisingly, political parties and the politically powerful rarely present the problems of American society in class terms.

5. American popular and intellectual culture, including social science, has a pronounced tendency to formulate goals and to explain success and failure in individualistic (biopsychological) terms and to assume that social problems are temporary and correctable (evolutionary liberalism).

IS THE UNITED STATES A MERITOCRACY?

The concept of a meritocracy refers to a society in which material, psychic, and power rewards are distributed according to merit. The idea of merit is easy enough to define when contrasts are made with systems of the past in which privilege or ascription are dominant. It is more difficult to define what merit means in today's society. Two positions on merit are found in the United States. A large majority of the population defines merit (and success) in terms of moral qualities, especially hard work, ambition, and perseverance. Ability is also mentioned but, by and large, Americans seem to believe that ability is widely distributed and that moral traits are not. Success, they believe, goes to those who

---

[41]Mary R. Jackman and Robert W. Jackman, *Class Awareness in the United States* (Berkeley, Calif.: University of California Press, 1983), Table 2.1.

help themselves.[42] This picture of a meritocracy, however attractive, does not explain
success and failure since the possession of
moral qualities does not insure success nor
their lack prevent it. But more important,
moral qualities must themselves be explained. The sociology of socialization
clearly indicates that the accident of birth and
socialization by social class is how individuals acquire their character traits.

Another view of merit defines it as cognitive ability. This view is found among educators, social scientists, and the testing
establishment. Those who emphasize cognitive ability think of it both as an ideal to be
achieved and as a statement of fact—individuals with brains will and do rise to the top.
Grades in school, scores on tests, and years of
schooling completed are usually associated
with cognitive ability, merit, and success. In
an interesting study, little positive relation
was found between IQ and economic success.[43] There is also no evidence that grades
in school correlate with economic success.

Educational standards are largely irrelevant to behavior outside school. Their latent
purpose is to control labor flows into prized
occupations. The recent emphasis on raising
standards will serve only to keep down the
numbers of those who allegedly qualify for
the better jobs. Americans who believe they
are making it on their own will resent affir-
mative action programs as violations of the
meritocratic ethic (and this could be a cause
of the increased amounts of campus racism
and rape in recent years as resentful individuals blame minorities for declining opportunities instead of the power groups who

control access to occupations through the im-
position of nonfunctional qualifications).

The United States cannot be called a meritocracy, therefore, using either a moral or
cognitive definition of merit. A meritocracy
should specify what kinds of abilities make
people happy and contribute to concrete, socially valuable behaviors. Simply trying to
generate abstract moral qualities or cognitive
skills will not add up to a satisfactory society.
The truth of the matter is that the United
States relies on abstractions such as these
because it does not really know what qualities its citizens should have. The matter of
specifying what personalities the United
States should promote in its economy, polity,
schools, families, and churches remains an
open question and a largely unfinished task.

THE AMERICAN CLASS SYSTEM: A SUMMARY

Comparative-historical analysis reveals that
all societies are unequal. Of all the types of
social inequality—age, sexual, ethnic, racial,
and socioeconomic—the most important is
the socioeconomic. As we saw in Chapters 2
and 4, socioeconomic inequality or social
stratification varies by type of society.

The heart of social stratification is the difference between those who control or own
property and those who do not. Actually,
economic classes derive from gradations in
economic assets: the ownership of physical
assets and the ownership of personal traits
and labor skills deemed economically valuable—both can be fruitfully understood as
property.

In an agrarian society, the most important
property is agriculturally productive land,
followed by political-military-economic
skills, tools, and human and animal muscle
power. In industrial society, property means
industrially productive technology, facilities,
patents, legal rights, money, land, water, raw
materials, air space, professional skills, and
skilled and unskilled labor.

Achievement and social mobility are best
explained by economic expansion (structural

[42]Joe R. Feagin, "Poverty: We Still Believe That God
Helps Those Who Help Themselves," *Psychology Today* 6
(November, 1972): 101ff; Joan Huber and William Form,
*Income and Ideology: An Analysis of the American Political
Formula* (New York: Free Press, 1973); Michael Lewis, *The
Culture of Inequality* (Amherst, Mass.: University of Mas-
sachusetts Press, 1978).

[43]Michael R. Olneck and James Crouse, "The IQ Meritocracy Reconsidered: Cognitive Skill and Adult Success
in the United States," *American Journal of Education* 88
(November, 1979): 1–31.

mobility) rather than by innate ability or abstract rights or opportunities (equal opportunity mobility). Some mobility up and down across class lines occurs but such mobility is largely due to economic factors (along with political, religious, and other factors). Social mobility is far more limited than most people think and far more similar in all industrial countries (capitalist and communist) than different.

The basic pattern of mobility is a rise of the entire society with no equalization—most people in modern society experience a rise of benefits but no change of class. The "mobility" of society (as opposed to movement by social actors within a society) with no reduction of inequality is one of the most difficult concepts in stratification analysis. The image of a fleet of ships of varying sizes rising during an incoming tide is helpful in understanding this process.

The United States is characterized by a pronounced class system and one must resist the false doctrines that depict the United States as individualistic, *the* land of opportunity, functionally differentiated, or in a postindustrial stage.

A social class is an aggregate of households that share similar material, interactional, and psychic benefits across various institutional sectors. Class inequality in the United States is a mixture of illegitimate (ascribed) and legitimate (achieved) elements difficult to disentangle. It is not a meritocracy (inequality by moral or cognitive achievement), and there is no trend in this direction.

Wealth and income inequality are pronounced and have increased significantly in recent years (both before and after taxes and government spending).

Occupations in the United States have shifted away from farming and manufacturing and toward services. Skill levels have risen and the number of jobs has expanded with the growing economy. But good jobs are as scarce as they have ever been, and the number of jobs has always been and will remain (unless changes are made) far smaller than the number of people seeking work. Ominously, the United States may have reversed past trends—

most new jobs appear to be low skilled and low paid and the percent of middle-income jobs appears to be shrinking. In any case, a bipolar household income distribution has appeared in recent years.

Education has also increased, as measured by years of school completed, but it cannot be said that the American people have become better educated if that means they are better able to perform social roles. By and large, education cannot be related to performance in economic or political roles.

Educational success is strongly related to class background. Though irrelevant to performance outside of school, educational credentials control access to good jobs and thus high class standing. Ominously, the United States may have reversed past trends and for the first time has begun to exhibit a growing separation between those with more and those with less education.

The scarcity of property is a striking feature of American society. Despite the astonishing rise in the productive power of the American economy and the standard of living that it provides (especially between the 1850s and the 1960s), economically valuable property, that is, property from which high and steady income can be derived, is so highly concentrated that it is scarce relative to the American population.

The concentration of property takes two forms: one, the ownership of the economy itself, and two, the ownership of economically valuable personal skills (the latter is highly concentrated among college graduates, especially those with graduate and professional degrees). Overall the concentration is even more pronounced if one realizes that concentrated ownership of material property and of property in valued skills is often lodged *in the same people and families*. Indeed, one leads to the other in a reciprocal relation with far-reaching consequences. Those with high income from material property (profit, dividends, capital gains, interest, rent, royalties) or from occupation (salaries, bonuses, pensions, fringe benefits) can save, which leads to more income from the work of property, and so on.

Over time, differentials in wealth, income, occupation, and education lead to differentials in family stability, family health, and in the ability of families to secure a good education and good jobs for their children.

Prestige distinctions are a vital feature of the American class system. Prestige hierarchies based on occupation, consumption, voluntary groups, race, religion, and ethnicity, all serve to reinforce the legitimacy and primacy of economic class. America's many forms of prestige inequality help to diffuse class-and-prestige struggles thus helping to stabilize American society. Through its prestige forms, including minimum levels of political-legal-moral prestige, American society helps to defuse the tension between its deep economic inequality (much of it ascriptive) and its universalistic achievement ethic.

All available evidence about the distribution of political and legal benefits points in one direction—those who are higher up in the class system have more access to the state and benefit more from its actions. Politics and law reflect the class system and appear to have little independent power against it.

Economic concentration among the tiny upper and upper middle classes means that decisions on how material resources, and therefore human resources, will be developed and used are in the hands of a small number of Americans. The upper classes also have power over the voluntary and political-legal sectors and the result is a national power structure that not only exhibits illegitimate and unnecessary inequality but may be increasing it.

So far all efforts to provide equal education, equal access to political power, or equality before the law have failed. So far, all efforts to provide a better economy have failed.

All reform efforts appear doomed unless they confront the essential structure of social power in the United States—the highly concentrated corporate capitalist economy and the influence of the upper classes over the rest of society. Perhaps the essential thing for reform groups to focus on is *unnecessary* and *illegitimate* economic and political-legal inequality (hereditary wealth, unnecessary qualifications for jobs, the power of money over politics and law, and gerrymandering, to name the most important).

CHAPTER
10
FOREIGN POLICY, SOCIAL CHANGE, AND ADAPTIVE CAPACITY

THE SEAMLESS WORLD OF SOCIAL AND INTERSOCIETAL RELATIONS

Americans have come to realize that they cannot explain what is happening to them without placing events in a wider intersocietal setting. Imagine closed shoe factories in Maine, unemployed textile workers in South Carolina, rusting steel mills in the valleys of Pennsylvania and Ohio, farm foreclosures and auctions in Iowa and Nebraska, declining lumber towns in Oregon, and a depressed oil economy and bank failures in Texas. None of these can be understood by studying only the United States.

Think of the decline of the American middle class, the reduced economic opportunities for young people, and the emergence of the United States as a debtor nation. Think of the growing concentration of wealth and the growing inequality of income. Here again, one needs to place social trends in an intersocietal setting to understand them.

THE UNITED STATES IN THE WORLD SYSTEM

Functional, Interactionist, and Conflict Theories of the International Economy

Theories about the international economy are similar to theories about the domestic economy. Liberal (capitalist) economists argue that the emerging world economy is best understood as a rational system of comparative advantage in which nations specialize in what they do best. Liberals believe that a pure system of competition and specialization has already been partially realized and that we should work to realize it fully. Individuals and groups will act rationally if left alone. Though they are aware that actors deviate from this rational system of comparative advantage, liberals continue to believe that a free market in the international flow of goods, services, labor, and capital is the best way for humanity at large to prosper and improve itself. By and large, they reject the idea that the international economic system is exploitative and imperialist.

Conflict theorists argue that free trade and the overall idea of international specialization through market mechanisms is the ideology of economically powerful societies. The only strong believers in free trade have been Great Britain (in the nineteenth century) and the United States (in the twentieth). The actual practice of nations (including Great Britain and the United States), they argue, is far different than the ideal of universal competition and freedom of trade. Even the strongest societies rely on political, military, moral, religious, and ideological institutions to achieve their economic ends. Nations may know that it is in their interest to specialize in what they do best and that all will be better off if an international division of labor occurs. But each is subject to strong internal political pressures from threatened businesses and other interests. Each knows that the pure world of competition and the free flow of resources toward their best use is a long way off. In the meantime, they all take steps to avoid competition or to press advantages unfairly. By and large, conflict theorists conclude, the powerful take advantage of the weak leading to the imperialism of the world-market economy.

The Outward Thrust of the American Economy

The major economic units that carry on class relations beyond America's national boundaries are corporations engaged in manufacturing, agriculture, mining, timber, construction, and in various services such as banking, insurance, law, publishing, research, journalism, entertainment, and sports. Professional associations and labor unions also operate abroad in pursuit of class interests.

The United States was openly protectionist until the 1930s when the Great Depression forced it to liberalize its international trade in conjunction with other countries. At the end of World War II, from which it

emerged with by far the world's strongest economy, the United States embarked on a philosophy of free trade. From the late 1950s on, American corporations began their spectacular surge of direct foreign investment. This unique historic process was part of the shift from empire imperialism to world-market imperialism: instead of owning countries and then lending them money (the British Empire), the United States adopted the practice of direct foreign investment—the ownership and management of businesses in foreign countries.

Most international trade takes place among the developed capitalist countries and most of that is done by a small number of giant multinational corporations (of which a large number are American). Significantly, the majority of American overseas trading has shifted to Asia in recent years. Another significant aspect of the growing internationalization of the American economy is an increase of direct investment in manufacturing in Third World countries. Still another significant development (representing movement away from entrepreneurial to corporate capitalism) is the gradual shift from ethnocentric and polycentric to geocentric organizations. Huge corporations, operating in as many as 60 nations, are each administered from a central command post, thanks to advances in transportation and communication technology, especially the computer.

Most international economic transactions are among the developed countries. However, developing nations attract considerable investment because they have important resources and cheap labor. The freedom of capital to move from Detroit, Cleveland, and other areas of the United States to utilize cheap skilled and unskilled labor in Taiwan, the Philippines, or South Korea is one of the reasons for unemployment and decay in America's Midcentral and Northeastern cities (and for a decline in good-paying, skilled jobs). Oftentimes capital movement is aided by tariff laws that allow United States companies to send parts abroad for assembly, import the finished products to the United States, and pay a tariff on the "value added" overseas (which is very little when computed on the basis of the low wages paid abroad).

The 1980s have witnessed new developments in the international trading status of the United States. The ominous shift to a debtor nation has already been noted. The internal shift of the American economy to services has been matched by a growth in the service share of American exports but America's advantages here have not borne fruit because of foreign protectionism and because American corporations do not know how to deliver services in other cultures.[1] The failure of the United States to regulate domestic and international banking led to bank failures (and fraud) at home and huge bad loans to foreign countries. The giant federal deficit in the domestic budget of the United States was matched by a huge balance of payments deficit, *both of which appear to be deeply rooted in how the American economy is organized.*

By the late 1980s, it was clear that the United States was living beyond its means. One reason was that the huge, untargeted tax cuts of 1981 had deprived Uncle Sam of revenues without making the United States more productive or competitive (large portions of the tax cuts went abroad, into luxury goods and services, or corporate mergers). The American deficit kept interest rates high because the federal government had to borrow huge sums putting pressure on limited savings. High interest rates attracted large flows of capital from abroad helping to finance large portions of the American deficit but depriving other countries of needed capital. The rise of interest rates aggravated the debt problem of Third World countries, which, in turn made it difficult for American firms to sell abroad. During this time the United States cut spending on the poor and working class, dramatically increased military spending, preached free trade, practiced selective protectionism, and refused to cooperate with other societies since the major demand from

other societies was that the United States live within its means.

While experts argued that the United States was better off as a whole under a system of free trade, hardpressed owners and workers in textiles, shoes, steel, copper, tractors, and automobiles fought hard to protect themselves. By the 1980s a variety of devices were in place to cushion American industry. A new device called "voluntary restraint" under which foreign countries agree to limit their exports has a special importance. If imports are restricted by taxation (tariffs), the tax goes into the public treasury. Under voluntary agreements, private domestic and foreign companies are dividing up a market allowing them to raise prices to make the least efficient profitable. Both sides are happy and the consumer pays (for example, Americans have paid $1000 extra for their automobiles during the 1980s because of the voluntary agreement of the United States with Japan on its automobile exports).

By the 1980s it was clear that the mass-production economy of the United States had not responded to global competition and needed to emphasize quality production, specialty products, and a quick response to new opportunities. American corporations had become *pure* multinationals (exporting capital to make sure they had the resources and the markets for their ever higher levels of high-technology, high-skill production. It was clear that a large percentage of America's best talent and of its large corporations were engaged in "paper entrepreneurialism," making money from the rearrangement of existing assets (mergers, arbitrage, speculation, litigation, manipulating tax laws) rather than from producing more assets.[2]

The Outward Thrust of the American Polity

The United States government maintains a vast military establishment both at home and around the globe to protect and further

---

[1]Dorothy I. Riddle, *Service-Led Growth: The Role of the Service Sector in World Development* (New York: Praeger, 1986), Chapter 7.

[2]For a full analysis, see Robert B. Reich, *The Next American Frontier* (New York: Times Books, 1983).

American interests (by latest count it has 389 military bases abroad). Often framed in moral terms, the display of military might and alliances such as NATO, SEATO, and the Organization of American States are essentially ways to protect and enhance the United States's position in the world-market economy. The United States is massively dependent upon foreign resources to run its industrial economy and it needs overseas markets for its goods, capital, services, and surplus food and staples. Like all modern societies the United States cannot exist without relatively continuous economic growth, and economic growth is not possible unless its access to world markets is unhampered. In short, it is vital to American society that international trade is unhampered, that sea lanes are kept open, and that many diverse societies remain friendly and compliant to its wishes.

The most dramatic examples of the class basis of the policies of the United States government are its efforts (often secretive and illegal) to influence the internal politics of friendly countries (for example, the U.S. Central Intelligence Agency has a long history of contributing money to Italy's capitalist political parties) or to prevent the establishment of socialist and communist societies as witness its actions in Russia (1917), China, Cuba, and Chile.[3] Less well known and often misunderstood are the elaborate tax and tariff laws that facilitate the penetration of American capital abroad, and the foreign aid programs that tie other countries to American technology and services. Very little of American foreign aid is given away as a gift though there is a widespread impression that this is so. American foreign aid is primarily a subsidy to American business and professions (the impact on labor is mixed because jobs are won and lost through foreign aid) and a way for American capital to trade and invest abroad.

Foreign aid invariably stipulates that foreign countries must buy American products and use American services such as engineering firms. This not only promotes sales on a long-term basis, since replacement parts must come from the United States, but prevents recipient countries from developing their own engineering and other skills.

Foreign aid also consists of providing money for various international lending agencies. The United States government participates in and is a preponderate influence in a number of international agencies such as the World Bank, the International Monetary Fund, and the Asian Development Bank. Essentially capitalist institutions, these agencies promote development along capitalist lines in Third-World nations by lending money primarily to finance the construction of ports, electric power plants, highways, and other facilities essential to trade and investment.

American immigration policies also reflect class interests. The United States imported approximately 40 million people during the period between its War of Independence and World War I to staff its developing industrial economy. The large flow of illegal aliens since World War II may be curbed by the Immigration Act of 1986, which will penalize employers who use them. The United States also imports large numbers of professionals, relying, for example, on doctors trained abroad to make up significant portions of its hospital staffs.[4]

The United States also encourages exports, for example, through low-cost government loans (Export-Import Bank), government insurance against investment loss, and its tax laws. Aid to investment abroad is explicit American policy. An empirical analysis has largely substantiated the radical claim that private investment by American companies and economic and military aid by the American government have a common feature: the

---

[3]For the actions of the United States Government (in conjunction with major American corporations), which helped to overthrow socialism in Chile, see James Petras and Morris Moreley, *The United States and Chile: Imperialism and the Overthrow of the Allende Government* (New York: Monthly Review Press, 1975).

[4]For data showing a substantial brain drain from less-developed countries into the United States, the United Kingdom, Canada, and Australia, see Jagdish Bhagwate, "The Brain Drain", *International Social Science Journal* 28; 4 (1976): 691–729.

recipient countries have compliant right-wing governments.[5] The United States also has developed some (small) payment and retraining programs to cushion American workers against the loss of jobs due to foreign competition. It also protects a large number of American industries, not so much through tariffs but through voluntary agreements, in effect, allowing private corporations in foreign countries and the United States to divide up markets, raise prices, and keep the gains at the expense of American consumers.

A basic theme in the United States's foreign policy since World War II is its unwavering support for Great Britain, France, and Portugal as these nations struggled in vain to suppress independence movements in their colonies. To a considerable extent the United States has succeeded in replacing British power in Canada, Egypt, and Saudi Arabia. It is struggling with only mixed results to replace British power in Greece, Turkey, and Palestine. It has failed in Iran, has been relatively unsuccessful in Africa, and suffered a heavy defeat trying to replace France in Vietnam. In addition to its huge military establishment, the United States conducts elaborate programs both at home and abroad to train the military and police forces of compliant and friendly countries. The United States also participates in the United Nations but no longer finds it the compliant instrument of Western interests that it was before the 1960s.

The basic dilemmas of American economic and foreign policy stem largely from its own actions (and from those of other Western countries). The instability of most Third-World countries stems from economic change induced by the impact of Western capital. The development of a cash-crop economy dispossesses people from the land and leaves them easy preys for radicals. When landed and other oligarchies refuse to institute political and economic reforms, regimes become unstable and the United States rushes in (claim-

ing that Soviet communism is to blame). To soothe public opinion and to keep American aid coming, regimes promise reforms but few are delivered.

American foreign policy in the 1980s veered to the right. The Reagan administration began a massive military buildup, which, combined with large tax cuts, is a primary cause of the abnormal federal deficit. The military buildup had no coherent policy behind it and consisted of buying and developing every conceivable weapon system to cope with every contingency (this is a policy, of course, but not very practical since no nation is wealthy enough to afford it). America's military buildup also meant a reduction in the use of economic and political means to bolster our allies and sway the uncommitted. In addition to its refusal to cooperate with our friends, the Reagan administration conducted economic warfare against the Soviet Union, in effect, escalating the economic embargo we had in place against Cuba and Vietnam. This served only to harm American businesses and to outrage our European allies, who were being asked to bear the burden against their wishes (they were especially incensed by our efforts to force the European subsidiaries of American corporations not to trade with the U.S.S.R.).

The ineptness of the Reagan administration led to a major political defeat in the Middle East when the United States acquiesced in Israel's invasion of Lebanon in 1982. Our isolation in the world increased because of our policies in Central America, our failure to sign the Law of the Sea Treaty, and our continued toleration of South Africa's stalling in regard to its illegal occupation of Namibia. The success of the United States in placing first-strike missiles in Europe was a defeat for the Soviet Union but it only highlighted our reliance on military force, our reluctance to negotiate arms control, and the American government's disregard for the majority of the American people who wanted a nuclear freeze (the United States and the U.S.S.R. agreed to eliminate intermediate missiles in 1987). The Reagan administration's open policy of trying to overthrow the government of Nicaragua was a continuing source of embar-

---

[5]Steven J. Rosen "The Open Door Imperative and U.S. Foreign Policy" in Steven J. Rosen and James R. Kurth, eds., *Testing Theories of Economic Imperialism* (Lexington, Mass.: Lexington Books, 1974), Chapter 6.

rassment to the United States. In 1984 the Reagan administration announced that it would restrict population planning funds to private international organizations that perform or promote abortion (all this was done without Congressional approval and in violation of American public opinion, done largely to court favor with powerful domestic groups). The Reagan administration argued that economic growth through private enterprise was the solution to population problems. All population experts agreed that this policy would be disastrous and would undo years of effort to bring world population under control.

In 1987 the United States suffered a major foreign policy disaster when the full details of the Reagan administration's illegal, hypocritical, and ill-advised sale of arms to Iran and the use of profits to fund illegally the opposition to the government of Nicaragua were revealed.

Cultural Imperialism: Education, Churches, Foundations, and Mass and Elite Media

Political action is rarely suspected in the activities of educational groups, churches, foundations, philanthropies, news media, and so on because such groups are generally regarded as nonpartisan. Critics have argued, however, that the extension of American (or Western) educational principles to other societies amounts to neocolonialism.[6] Colonial nations such as England and France have a long tradition of educating at home the leaders of their colonies. Today the United States edu-

cates large numbers of foreigners: in 1985–86 it had 343,780 foreign students, approximately 80 percent of the total enrolled from developing countries.[7] The major suppliers of foreign student in the United States are Iran, Taiwan, Malaysia, South Korea, India, Canada, Iraq, China, Nigeria, Japan, and Hong Kong.

Cultural imperialism takes many forms. The role of missionaries, technical aid teams, exchange programs, foundations, philanthropies, and the news, publishing, and entertainment media are undoubtedly supportive of class values but their impact has not been studied systematically. There is little question that the United States has a large impact abroad through its entertainers, films and other mass-media materials, novelists, and athletes, and that it dominates global trade (outside the socialist countries) in television programs, films, books, magazines, and scholarly journals.[8] The content of American books, films and television programs is often nationalistic and racist but such biases have declined as foreign sales have become more important to media producers. American publishers, however, continue to print books in languages and about subjects that correspond to the interests of privileged native elites.[9]

Cultural imperialism takes place in unsuspected ways. Textbooks and the media distort our image of foreign nations and people. Western literature has promoted ethnocentrism in the West and has created myths about the white man's burden.[10] American best sellers about Asia in the twentieth century have

---

[6]For general background, see Martin Carnoy, *Education as Cultural Imperialism* (New York: David McKay, 1974), and Ali A. Mazrin, "The African University as a Multinational Corporation: Problems of Penetration and Dependency," *Harvard Educational Review* 45 (May, 1975): 191–210. For a history of the Ford, Rockefeller, and Carnegie foundations educational policies toward Africa and a charge that they furthered American corporate rather than African interests, see Edward H. Berman, "Foundations, United States Foreign Policy, and African Education, 1945–1975," *Harvard Educational Review* 49 (May, 1979): 145–79 (with brief but vigorous responses from foundation officials: pp. 180–84).

[7]*The Chronicle of Higher Education* 30 (October 22, 1986): 34.

[8]Richard P. Nielsen, "International Trade and Policy in Mass Media Materials: Television Programs, Films, Books, and Magazines," *Cultures* 3: 3 (UNESCO, 1976): 196–205.

[9]Philip G. Altbach, "Literary Colonialism: Books in the Third World", *Harvard Educational Review* 45 (May, 1975): 226–36.

[10]Jonah Raskin, *The Mythology of Imperialism: Kipling, Conrad, Forster, Lawrence, Carey* (New York: Random House, 1971).

given Americans a twisted view of all Asian peoples and societies.[11] The Western scholarly tradition has also biased the West's perception of other peoples, and, in turn, its perception of itself. Anthropology supplied information that furthered the ends of colonial administrators.[12] The West's main scholarly tradition, especially in England, France, and the United States (claims Edward Said) also created a fictitious oriental world (encompassing the Middle East, parts of Africa, and all of Asia), which served largely to further the ends of colonialism.[13] The late nineteenth century also witnessed the spread of ethnocentrism to the general public through the medium of ethnographic exhibits,[14] the spread of mass education, and the rise of the yellow press. Even today, argues Edward Said, the mass media have a narrow and biased view of the world, as witness their handling of the Iranian crisis, especially from 1979 to 1981.[15]

The Rockefeller Foundation's sponsorship of agricultural research to spur food production in Third-World countries illustrates how "objective" research sponsored by "public interest" foundations can create more problems than it solves. The Rockefeller Foundation's agricultural research centers developed high-yield hybrid plants, the basis of the Green Revolution in the developing countries. High-yield plants require fertilizer, irrigation, and considerable technology; as a result, the Green Revolution has everywhere led to high land concentration, the displacement of millions of families, massive Third-World unemployment, hunger, and dependence.[16] For a discussion and other positions, see Box 1-1, The Green Revolution: Progress or Disaster?

A number of private voluntary groups exercise considerable influence in foreign affairs: the Council of Foreign Relations, The Committee for Economic Development, and a number of research corporations and institutes. All are basically financed by large corporations, their membership is drawn exclusively from the world of big business along with a few lawyers and university presidents, their members have often served in government foreign policy posts, they recruit candidates for government service, and their research reports and research grants play an important role in shaping public policy.[17]

INTERRELATIONS BETWEEN DOMESTIC INEQUALITY AND FOREIGN POLICY

The United States does not have a coherent and effective foreign policy. The reasons for this are clear enough. The various groups within the United States that have interests abroad are too diverse and contradictory to yield a coherent policy. The outer world is also too diverse and contradictory to yield a coherent policy. The result is moral posturing, abstract ideology about freedom, free

---

[11]Daniel B. Ramsdell, "Asia Askew: U. S. Best-Sellers on Asia, 1931–1980", *Bulletin of Concerned Asia Scholars* 15 (October–December, 1983): 2–25.

[12]Talal Asad, ed., *Anthropology and the Colonial Encounter* (New York: Humanities Press, 1973); Roy F. Ellen, "The Development of Anthropology and Colonial Policy in the Netherlands: 1800–1960." *Journal of the History of the Behavioral Sciences* 12 (1976): 303–24; and Gerrit Huizer and Bruce Mannheim, eds., *The Politics of Anthropology: From Colonialism and Sexism Toward a View From Below* (The Hague: Mouton, 1979).

[13]Edward W. Said, *Orientalism* (New York: Pantheon, 1978).

[14]William Schneider, "Race and Empire: The Rise of Popular Ethnography in the Late Nineteenth Century," *Journal of Popular Culture* 11 (Summer, 1977): 98–109; and William Schneider, "Colonies at the 1900 World Fair," *History Today* 31 (May, 1981): 31–6.

[15]Edward W. Said, *Covering Islam* (New York: Pantheon, 1981).

[16]For background on the widespread misery produced by Western, especially American agricultural aid, and for a critical analysis of the rationalizations that cover American policies, see Susan George, *How the Other Half Dies* (Montclair, N. J.: Allanheld and Osmun, 1977). George shrewdly notes the connection between fertilizer and the Rockefeller oil interests.

[17]For an analysis from a conflict perspective, see G. William Domhoff, *Who Rules America Now?* (Englewood Cliffs, N.J.: Prentice-Hall, 1983).

trade, and interdependence, and a huge reliance on military force.

If one assumes that the best long-term interests of the United States are to work hard and openly to transform the dictatorships of the developing world into middle-class democracies (even social democracies if necessary), then the United States does not know its own interests. Very little of its foreign policy can be characterized as preventive—most of it is defensive and negative. American foreign policy energies are devoted almost exclusively to damage control and countering the Soviet threat both real and imaginary.[18]

Why is this? Is it because the United States considers itself a model for the world and thinks all societies should be judged by its own values? Is it that right-wing dictatorships are much closer to American values and interests than left-wing dictatorships? Does the United States deal with so many different kinds of countries that it cannot afford to do or say anything in the concrete for fear of offending an ally, a friendly government, a hanger-on regime? A human rights policy was advanced by the Carter administration and downplayed by the Reagan administration, but our focus was on abstract legal and political rights when it is clear that these are being violated because oligarchies refuse to share power with their own people. It is clear that the American government is aware of this because it says precisely this about the Soviet Union but fails to say it about the dozens of right-wing dictatorships that it supports in a variety of ways.

An important new condition that the United States and other societies face is that the era of cheap resources may be drawing to a close. What this portends for the future is not easy to say but no aspect of American society,

either internally or externally, can be understood unless its dependence on foreign resources and markets is understood. American foreign policy analysis will continue to lack relevance and effectiveness until it is grounded in the knowledge that the United States has massive investments in and economic dealings with regimes of every conceivable type: fascist, liberal, racist and white-settler minority regimes, military dictatorships, religious-nationalist one-party states, decaying former colonies led by native elites, and even absolute monarchies.

Deeply dependent on military dictatorships, absolute monarchies, and a racist regime, the United States is also subject to deep internal pressures by its own ethnic groups to follow one or another policy: Jewish Americans, Greek Americans, Italian Americans, Polish Americans, and so on.

Unable to say or do anything because of its complex tangle of foreign interests, the United States finds it easier to translate all foreign affair issues into one issue, the threat of communism. The Soviet threat is real enough. But if there is one issue, it is the danger to world peace presented by oligarchies that refuse to share power with their people.

COPING WITH SOCIAL CHANGE

The Reality of Change

Change is everywhere and unstoppable. Our bodies change and so do the seasons. Our attitudes change and so do mountain ranges. Friendships wax and wane and so do civilizations. Less than a hundred years ago Americans used cow manure to cure tuberculosis and stove soot mixed with molasses to cure pleurisy. Today hearts are transplanted and a promising beginning has been made on developing antibiotics that can be targeted to kill cancer cells. Medicine is on the verge of discovering how to eliminate a wide range of diseases and birth defects by engineering hi-tech fetuses. Computers are rearranging how we work and learn. Satellites can beam programs around the world. Jet planes can whisk us to any point on the planet in a

---

[18]For a detailed analysis of Soviet world power (judged by the number of countries in the Soviet camp, their share of world population, and GNP), which concludes that it is quite small and that it has declined since its highpoint in 1958, see Center for Defense Information, "Soviet Geopolitical Momentum: Myth or Menace?" *The Defense Monitor* 15: 5 (1986).

matter of hours. Men and women can now go into space, walk on the moon, and return safely. In the past 100 years more technological change has occurred than in the previous 2,000–3,000 years.

But all changes are not for the better. Thirty years ago the South Bronx was a thriving, family-centered community. Today it is a social wasteland known around the world. Women are now beginning to commit more crime, contract more lung cancer, and make up the bulk of single parents, many living in poverty. Old people are more likely today to be picked up for shoplifting than in the past. Twenty-five percent of American children live in poverty.

Change is also not easy to interpret. Is the multinational corporation a force for modernizing the planet or an instrument of imperialism? The control of disease means one thing in the West (an aging population) and something else in the developing world (overpopulation). The elimination of disease (a real possibility) has staggering implications for every society. For the first time in its history the United States has a large peacetime military force that appears to have put down deep roots in the economic and political systems of the country. What does this development mean? As we will now see, there are real changes, apparent changes, and no changes where there should be changes. How to develop an eye for understanding social change is one of the biggest changes we need.

Identifying and Interpreting Social Change

What exactly is it that changes? How real are changes? Is there a direction in change? Many changes are hidden or not easily perceived—how can they be detected? Others, like an assassination or a stock market crash, are dramatic and inescapable—how can they be anticipated or prevented? Some changes take place slowly over a long time period while others move quickly; some accelerate their movement while others decelerate. A change can affect a limited area or a whole society or even the planet. An ordinary person dies or is married and only a few are affected. On the other hand, industrial fumes that block the escape of heat into the atmosphere or the actions of international banks affect the entire planet.

A social change can take place in how people relate to each other, how they perceive nature and technology, or how they feel about themselves and each other. A basic social change refers to deep changes in these areas. But how does change take place? Does it take place by design or by drift? The study of history suggests that most social change occurs through drift rather than design, more by half-understood changes in behavior (new roles, new technology, unintended consequences) than by foresight or by a redefinition of statuses and deliberate planning (manifest functions).

Social change is not inevitable like the biological process of aging. Social change comes from social causes. How did a healthy, ethnic community in New York City become a desolate wasteland (known throughout the world as the South Bronx) in less than 30 years? Did humankind's 3,000 years of experience with cities teach them nothing? Why did American productivity decline from the mid-1960s on. No one paid much attention at first. Then people began to notice it. Now we are aware of what happened. American capitalists found they could make money without investing in new technology by buying up undervalued companies. American business schools turned out MBAs skilled in finance but not in production. The United States' production of engineers slumped along with the decline in manufacturing. At the same time the number of lawyers soared. The United States was failing to produce people who make the pie grow larger (productive entrepreneurs, engineers) and producing more people skilled in carving it up (lawyers). At what point will the decline of productivity change the United States into a zero-sum society (a society in which gains for some represent losses for others)?

Humans have struggled to understand change since the beginning of conscious thought. Until the modern period most people and, particularly, thinkers disliked change. The ancient Greeks could think of change in biological and botanical terms only—things develop or change in terms of their intrinsic natures: acorns to oak trees, puppies to dogs, babies to adults—although sometimes they thought of social change in terms of cycles like the seasons.

Modern elites, tied to science, trade, industry, technology, and government are much more positive about change—they accept qualitative changes and breaks with the past. For modern elites, change means doing something new and creative even if all its consequences are not known. All in all, however, it cannot be said that there is much agreement about how to analyze change.

Liberal and Socialist Images of Change

Challenged by the problem of change in the eighteenth century, creative capitalist theorists "solved" it with the idea of progress. Capitalist thinkers, including functionalist sociologists, defined progress as the development of individualism, private property, free markets, research, science, and representative government. They assumed, too, that once in place these institutions would yield more progress. In the nineteenth century capitalist thinkers developed evolutionary theories of social change modelled on Darwin's discovery of evolution in nature.

Conflict thinkers (both capitalist and socialist) are more apt to portray social change as a haphazard process in which society is moved by half-understood changes in technology, property, and power relations. Humans will never master change until they accept economic and social planning, that is, until they come to realize that the multiple conflicts of complex society do not always result in justice or rational adaptation.

The Unique Human World

Most theories of social change have tried to interpret social change like that found in nature. These theories failed largely because they ignored the uniqueness of the human world. Humans are cultural creatures who live in a world of almost infinite complexity. Human behavior does not obey principles or natural laws—humans are subject to configurations of power, and power systems vary greatly. Understanding social change, therefore, means understanding the power structure of concrete historical societies.

The search for a unified theory of change should continue. Certainly we need to know more about change. But we should not put off acting on the knowledge we have. Clearly we do not know how to arrange all the variables of social life to see the total causal process at work in the United States. But we do know that enormous power is exerted by a small number of corporations over how American resources (including human resources) are invested. We know that the professions are powerful and that they are difficult to evaluate and reform even when they fail to cope with change or solve problems. We know that government reflects the structure of power and that it is not always the referee it pretends to be. The search for the abstract laws of social change should not divert us from acting now.

THE UNITED STATES AND SOCIAL ADAPTATION

Societies do not unfold naturally nor do they improve (or decay) naturally. If we want a society to work, we must design it to work. Ultimately, the sociologist must have an image of a workable society: one composed of groups and institutions that foster creative, competent, adaptive personalities.

The Ideal of an Adaptive Society

An adaptive or functional society (not to be confused with functionalist social theory) is a problem-solving entity not a problem-free utopia. The members of a functional society can feed themselves, reproduce, settle disputes, and adjust to new conditions. Adaptive power groups are able to develop the motives, ideas, and skills needed for replenishing, sustaining, and adapting a given way of life to both old and new circumstances.

A functional society has *legitimacy*, which means that people take it on faith that power groups deserve their power. Hierarchy, laws, taxes, unequal wealth and income, discipline, high standards, and competition are not suspect because ordinary citizens see direct and beneficial consequences flowing from them. Setbacks and failures are not resented because they appear to occur in a *just* society. A functional society has statuses and norms that, by and large, produce intended and desired results. The adaptive society is an ideal but it is not beyond reach—to repeat, it is a problem solving society rather than a utopian one.

Americans have always taken it on faith that they live in a functional society. Americans have used various terms to express this faith (democracy, laissez-faire, achievement ethic) but the main concept used to justify faith in the adaptive capacities of the status quo has been *pluralism*. What does this term mean and how well does it stand up when measured against America's record?

Pluralism: The Ideal of a Moving Equilibrium

Pluralist theorists believe that American society is adaptive because it is characterized by creative competition among relatively equal social actors. Pluralists argue that competition among individuals and groups (within the framework of free markets, law, toleration, and professionalism) transforms group diversity and conflict into social integration, stability, harmony, justice, and progressive adaptation.

Pluralists argue that social differentiation has led to a society whose various parts check and balance each other. They argue that American society is open and fluid, allowing individuals and groups to rise and fall according to ability. Pluralists see society as a natural, objective system, and oppose views suggesting that society has to be explicitly managed. When "artificial" human actions are taken, argue pluralists, they should be directed toward helping the natural society struggling to emerge from history.

American pluralists allege that no single group or combination of groups can dominate the others. America's wide variety of groups makes for overlapping group membership, which in turn inhibits groups from acting unilaterally. Our pluralist group structure, they argue, avoids cleavage between large contending blocs—there is stability if religious disputes occur among 200 denominations as opposed to 2. A pluralist society produces "strange bedfellow" relations. Those who want to ban abortion do not agree on the need to ban nuclear energy. Those who want gun control do not necessarily agree that school prayer is a good thing. The insurance company that argues against government interference in its investment policies wants the government to control hospital costs or require safer automobiles. Segments of Protestantism and Roman Catholicism oppose gay rights, but other segments join secular groups to support them. This crisscrossing of interests and values makes it impossible, argue pluralists, for arbitrary and unilateral power to emerge. In this world power groups are forced to make alliances with one another and to learn the arts of negotiation and compromise. Given a pluralistic power structure the public is always provided with alternatives to choose from and is constantly supplied with a wide variety of information to help it make up its collective mind about public issues. Under pluralism the public interest is guaranteed, or at least is being pursued and approximated.

Pluralist theorists defend both elites and ordinary people. American pluralism, they argue, allows the talented to rise to the top. Each area of human endeavor gradually develops standards to insure competence, and society is led by its true aristocracy: the achievers in science, business, medicine, law, art, and so on. Ordinary people have their rights, including the right to compete for high positions, and indirect rights as consumers, voters, or volunteer workers to influence how society works.

Pluralists argue that the United States is ruled by a shifting coalition of elite groups that comprise a moving equilibrium not a unified upper class. Elites can get their way only in certain areas and have to yield to other elites on other issues. In addition, professionalism has made many elites competent and responsible. Ordinary Americans have at least some power to influence events in their everyday lives, but their real power derives from elite competition to gain their support, especially in economic and political markets. American society, pluralists argue, is flexible enough to achieve reforms when needed and no group will remain powerless or be victimized over the long run.

Semi-Pluralism: The Reality of Oligarchy

Twenty years of research has undermined pluralist theory. While no definitive opposing theory has been established, sociologists (at least judging from introductory textbooks) no longer claim that the United States is characterized by a relative equality of power, by responsible (professionalized) elites, or by a relative equality of opportunity and competition. Some argue that the United States is run by a power elite, a tiny group of corporate elites, which, in conjunction with the federal executive, make all the important policy decisions. C. W. Mills pioneered this concept and William Domhoff continued it.[19] Power elite theorists point to research exposing the small elite astride the apexes of American society. They point to the enormous evidence of economic concentration (see the section, The American Economy: Basic Structural Features in Chapter 6). They point to evidence of how difficult it is to get into the system of power. There is much evidence, in other words, of a power elite. And, argue power elite theorists, to all this we must add evidence that the elites of various countries have also joined hands to unify their efforts and enhance their power.

Most sociologists would characterize the American power structure as *semi-pluralistic*

(shying away from its synonym, *oligarchy*) and reject the power elite image. The evidence against pluralism (and a power elite) is large. In every sector of American society, there is competition but also hierarchical power. Business firms compete but the economy is also deeply concentrated and excludes many from effective power and renders many powerless. The professions are based on significant competition and have developed achievement standards, but are also deeply marked by artificial scarcity and incompetence and by significant amounts of unethical and criminal behavior. The American polity is competitive but the economically powerful prevail. Government officials and legislators are drawn from the upper classes. Legislation and the law in general favor the powerful. Three-quarters of the seats in the U. S. House of Representatives are noncompetitive. Almost half of the eligible voters stay away from elections, many undoubtedly because they believe that they are powerless to influence events. The free press is useful in clarifying issues and protecting the rights of some, but it is also a powerful force in favor of the upper classes and the status quo. Education is not a fair contest to determine the natural elite, but deeply biased in favor of the upper classes and the status quo. Voluntary groups perform many functions and help to disperse power, but their policy-making boards and committees are dominated by the upper classes.

No matter what process, issue, or outcome is analyzed, the pattern is clear. The benefits of American life (income, wealth, occupation, education) are distributed unequally with no close, positive relation to merit or functional outcomes. The lower classes bear the brunt of unemployment, insecurity, and occupational disease and disability, and it is their sons that bear the burden of war. And the government supports this overall process through its taxes, spending, and other policies.

No assessment of power in the United States, therefore, can ignore three basic aspects of American life. They are as follows:

---

[19]G. William Domhoff, *Who Rules American Now? A View for the 80s* (Englewood Cliffs, N.J.: Prentice-Hall, 1983).

1. the existence of significant amounts of powerlessness, exploitation, and privilege,
2. the fact that these phenomena are deeply institutionalized and thus not easily eradicated, and
3. oligarchic relations are *systemic*, that is, they characterize all aspects and apexes of American society.

Has The United States Become a Stalemated Society?

Something new may have emerged to reduce the adaptive capacity of the United States. Semi-pluralism has its drawbacks but it is not incompatible with a certain measure of adaptive behavior. The most significant change in American society may be the decline of whatever pluralism the United States has had and the emergence of a stalemated society. At present many, if not most, sociologists would agree that much of the following is true about the United States:

1. No power group or combination of power groups has enough power to run society unilaterally. But coalitions of power groups that can solve problems are also scarce.
2. America's diversified oligarchy appears stalemated, adrift in a world it appears not to understand. Within a system of very unequal power, no one appears to be in charge, no one appears able to take charge.
3. The basic dynamic in the American power structure is rivalry among the very rich, and among the rich and their powerful auxiliaries, the near-rich and the well-to-do upper-middle class.
4. Many American policies are made through an elaborate process of non-decision.[20]

There is more than a little evidence that the United States is not making progress against its problems. For over a decade the United States has no longer enjoyed the world's highest standard of living, and many countries now have better health care, far less crime, and much more livable cities. Under the joint pressures of economic and political rationalization and reform, the general nature of group life has become even more hierarchical as more of life is run by professions embedded in bureaucratic structures. Almost no sphere of life has remained immune from this process, though the results are not unilaterally bad or easy to evaluate. Workers and professionals alike find themselves earning their livelihoods in vast impersonal structures. Political parties find it hard to build political followings as government welfare agencies and direct-action groups steal their former supporters. Volunteers find themselves drawn into bureaucratic structures run by career professionals. Voluntary organizations find themselves drawn into orbits controlled by governments. A large network of interest groups, many of them single-issue groups that practice a paranoid style of politics, clog up public life. And everyone finds a bureaucratic rationality substituted for individual rationality.

With the rise of a complex and interdependent economy and social system ever on the threshold of stalemate and conflict, economic power groups have resorted to political means to achieve economic and social objectives even as they continue to denounce politics and government, uphold the virtues of self-reliance, and affirm the vitality of grass-roots politics. Faced with the need to plan, American society has undertaken a considerable amount of "public" planning often using personnel whose experience and outlook have been derived from a lifetime of affirming anti-planning, entrepreneurial values and ideas. When policymakers attempt serious planning or reforms, they find themselves deadlocked by an interlocked structure of veto groups that makes it difficult to enunciate any policy unless it is so abstract or compromised as to be virtually meaningless. Given the experience of much of its personnel and given the "veto" power structure contained in a mature industrial economy, the remorseless trend of turning politics into administration grows apace.

The irrelevance of American political institutions to social problems is now widely acknowledged. The ideology of relying on

---

[20]In this latter respect, see Peter Bachrach and Morton S. Baratz, *Power and Practice* (New York: Oxford University Press, 1970).

private actions to solve public ills is so deeply planted that no effective urban, state, or national politics or planning appears possible. The United States has no coherent and effective economic, energy, transportation, health, educational, housing, urban, family, or youth policy. Its system of taxation is inequitable and badly related to public purposes. The problems of retirement and the elderly are far from met. It has no meaningful, reality-oriented foreign policy, relying largely on anticommunism, military force, and the abstraction of a laissez-faire, world-market economy. From the late 1970s on, huge, chronic domestic and foreign trade deficits began to appear, indicating not only that the United States was living beyond its means but that it lacked the capacity to stop.

Failure can be measured on many dimensions: the United States has been unable to provide full employment or equal competition and opportunity. There appear to be sizable amounts of poverty with no advances in reducing it since 1960. Minority groups have made no relative economic advances since they acquired their civil rights over two decades ago. The economy and the environment are still on a collision course, despite a quarter-century of warnings and efforts. The United States has a poor health care system, perhaps the worst in the capitalist world. Its private and public educational system is largely irrelevant to the needs of contemporary citizenship and fails to provide skilled workers or competent professionals.

Few can argue that the natural and social sciences have produced the knowledge needed to run an advanced industrial system. Certainly the news media have not provided the knowledge or awareness needed by modern publics. And, despite their profession of rationality and commitment to knowledge, American elites deviate considerably from the reality of the known world (see Box 10-1, How Widespread Is Resistance to Knowledge Among American Elites?).

The image of a stalemated society may not be accurate; it is perhaps too static to capture the hustle and bustle of American society. But the image of incremental adaptation through pluralism and professionalism seems to be even further from the reality.

Were the 1960s a Watershed?

Our major concepts for understanding social change in the United States have been entrepreneurial and corporate capitalism. Within an unchanged capitalist society, the United States has moved from a small-scale entrepreneurial to a large-scale corporate economy and society. Has a further change occurred implicit in the concept of a stalemated society? The 1890s are usually cited as the watershed of change from entrepreneurial to corporate capitalism. Do the 1960s constitute a new watershed and do they herald a stalemated society? The post-1945 era produced a unique social tempo and a unique set of social expectations. America was suddenly saddled with world leadership and after notable victories (for example, the Marshall Plan and the creation of a capitalist Japan) it was severely shaken by its defeat in Vietnam. Domestically, it found itself beset by novel problems. The costly Vietnam war had not been paid for—indeed was actually accompanied by a surge of domestic spending in an effort to build support for the war. The result was serious inflation, indeed novel stagflation. The United States also found itself having to make good on meaningful social membership for its entire population. For the first time in their history American propertied and professional groups faced having to run a society in which all participate on an equitable basis, and it may well be that such a society is not compatible with a private economy.

The slowdown in the American economy and the relative stagnation in living standards from the 1970s on are unique occurrences in American history. Are they temporary or do they herald a more permanent condition? The easy optimism that has marked America's past, an optimism derived from unprecedented economic growth, may be a false guide. The United States may be facing a future that its past does not prepare it for. Not only are energy sources dwindling

BOX 10-1. How widespread is resistance to knowledge among elites?

The list of resistance to knowledge by elites is long. Here is a partial list:

Government has not acted on the knowledge that smoking is a menace to health.

Knowledge that education can be improved significantly only by improving the class conditions that students come from has been ignored.

Elites have not changed their belief that tax cuts improve savings and capital investment despite overwhelming evidence to the contrary.

Corporations do not reduce prices when demand slumps but raise them, giving the lie to ideas of market rationality and the alleged law of supply and demand.

The United States Air Force still believes in strategic bombing even though four of its own studies have found no strategic value in bombing.

Groups resist knowledge because they have interests that knowledge threatens. Resistance to knowledge in medicine provides details of this process. Mechanic reports that research findings in biomedical research and technology tend to get accepted since they do not interfere with the interests of professionals and actually complement and extend them (and of course generate profits for business firms). Research in the area of health care and services tends to be neglected and, when done, ignored. Mechanic cites an example from a study at Yale/New Haven (a Yale University teaching hospital). Children scheduled for tonsillectomies were randomly divided into an experimental and control group. The control group received the normal care. Mothers of the children in the experimental group were admitted to the hospital and given a realistic picture of what to expect. The mothers in this group experienced less stress and their children had much better medical readings, made better adaptations to the hospital, and experienced a more rapid and better recovery after leaving the hospital. These findings are of added significance because tonsillectomies are widely performed and psychological problems are known to have important adverse effects on health. Neither Yale/ New Haven nor other hospitals acted on the findings.[1]

[1]David Mechanic, "Sociological Critics Versus Institutional Elites in the Politics of Research Application: Examples from Medical Care" in N. J. Demerath *et al.*, eds., *Social Policy and Sociology* (New York: Academic Press, 1975), pp. 99–108.

---

but all planetary resources are going to become increasingly scarce. The United States may no longer have the flexibility it once had as a white, Protestant, middle-class male monopoly. Today a vast new array of groups are clamoring for their share of America's benefits, and the American polity appears overloaded with demands. For the first time in its history, the United States cannot buoy its fortunes on a dependable supply of victims: the poor, racial and ethnic minorities, women, the young and the old, the handicapped, and those different in other ways.

Has the United States lost its enchanted world of manifest destiny and inevitable progress, its sense of being in tune with the cosmos? Forty years of prosperity seem to have created rather than solved problems. Not only have the consequences of prosperity contradicted basic American beliefs, but little has been done to prepare Americans for coping with what may be a no-growth future. Instead of a creative set of elites able to deal with problems one by one, the United States has an interlocked set of power groups that seem unable to tackle the deep tangle of intertwined social problems.

The elaborate welfare state erected during the past century is no doubt a source of stability for American society and has helped to correct some injustices and prevent some hardship and suffering, but the welfare state has also locked all power levels of American society into a structure of dependency and immobilization.

The basic group dynamic in American society is competition among the various levels and types of propertied groups to maintain or increase relative advantage. The higher morality guiding rivalry among the haves in an exchange economy is economic growth in the abstract (GNP, profit margin, Dow-Jones index), not as measured by meaningful work, healthy consumption, or husbandry of resources (use economy). Ominously, economic growth is no longer easily equated with rising levels of social welfare. Ever larger portions of our gross national product are going into unproductive, unsatisfying social overhead: military preparations, fighting crime, repairing the physical and human costs of pollution, unsafe workplaces, and unhealthy life styles, and welfare subsidies for unproductive people at all class levels.

The 1960s may be a watershed by another criterion—it may mark new heights of formalism and reliance on myth. Our assorted indices and theories do not provide meaningful categories for judging economic and social outcomes. Expectations soar beyond what society can deliver, and widespread deviance is the order of the day. Absolutist, single-interest groups multiply as demands are unmet. Meanwhile elites orient themselves to vague, often empty abstractions: freedom, excellence, research, economic growth, and so on. Far from being tied to social functions, elites have given themselves the right to look after their own interests and provide solutions to their own problems, under the master myth that self- and public interest are the same.

America's Alienated Electorate

Most analysts agree that portions of the American electorate find the political realm alien and beyond control. One response is mass political apathy both at the ballot box and in civic organizations: another is to use the vote to punish political figures who look as if they are agents of the status quo. Much of the difficulty that political experts and pollsters have had in recent years in predicting political behavior is due to their failure to take into account the alienation of many sectors of the electorate.

Functional theorists explain alienation in terms of the decline of intermediate organizations such as local political parties, neighborhood associations, newspapers, racial and ethnic associations, and reform groups. These groups are needed, say functionalists, because they involve and inform citizens and create the feeling and the reality of power for ordinary citizens.

Conflict theorists tend to agree with all this but point to the growth of corporate capitalism as the problem. Economic and political concentration (engendered by technology, rationalization, and bureaucratization), they argue, is the main reason why local groups have declined. If we are to understand our alienated electorate, we must see its roots in remote national and multinational corporations, national business and professional associations, large-scale churches, charities, foundations, research, and reform groups, and nationwide film, publishing, newspaper, and television corporations.

Declining Legitimacy?

A society rests on faith that its norms are fair and effective. There is considerable evidence that this faith has eroded in the United States. The United States has a huge underground illegal economy made up of many respectable people. In Chapter 7 we found considerable political apathy. Ominously, tax evasion is on the rise and seems to be feeding on itself. Public opinion polls reveal that half of the American people do not believe that they will ever collect their social security benefits. A Yankelovich poll in 1981 revealed that 83 percent of Americans agreed that rule breakers are rewarded while rule observers go empty-handed.

The erosion of faith in our leaders comes from concrete examples of deviance visible to all. Who is not aware that the F.B.I. has been used to harass and undercut legitimate political groups? Who cannot be aware that the Environmental Protection Agency has dragged its feet on enforcing environment laws. In 1983 banks across the nation mounted a campaign against a law to enforce an *old* tax by withholding taxes on interest and dividends (large tax revenues are lost because the well-to-do and rich do not voluntarily report such income). The banks printed cards for their customers to mail to Congress and ran advertisements against the new law making it appear that it was a *new* tax. They also argued it would be a hardship on the poor and the elderly knowing full well that these groups were exempt from the new enforcement provision. Congress knew that the effort to repeal the law was based on deception but repealed it anyway. Is it any wonder that the public is apathetic and cynical?

The trend toward an *alienated* public appears to be paralleling the rise of a stalemated society. Public opinion polls have shown a steady loss of confidence by the American people in their leaders. Americans from all income levels and in all other social categories are disenchanted with the elites who serve them. On a scale measuring powerlessness, cynicism, and alienation (disenchantment), Americans registered 55 percent in 1973 up from 29 percent in 1966. Americans felt that the quality of life in the United States had declined and, on the average, only 33 percent of the American people expressed confidence in its leadership (only two functional areas still enjoy majority support: medicine and local trash collection). All areas fell in public confidence except for television news and the press.

The American elite (as represented by public officials) disagreed sharply with these views and expressed considerable satisfaction in American achievements as well as confidence in the future. Particularly striking was the cleavage between the people and public officials over television news

and the press—public officials were far more critical of the news media than the general public.

The Survey Research Center and the Center for Political Studies (of the Institute for Social Research at the University of Michigan) have studied the attitude of trust in government for over two decades. Significant declines in trust in government began in the early 1960s and plunged during the 1970s. In tracing this development, Arthur N. Miller points out that "analysis conclusively demonstrates that the current, widespread political distrust of government is rooted in attitudes that are more generic than evaluations of the incumbents."[21] In short, American distrust of leaders is so profound that it seems to be undermining their faith in *institutions*. Widespread apathy toward elections can certainly be interpreted in this way. Trends in confidence toward institutional leadership rise slightly from time to time as presidents are elected or if the economy improves. But the long-term trend from the 1960s to 1982 clearly indicates a decline in confidence by the American people in its leadership. As such it poses a distinct threat to the legitimacy of American institutions.[22]

The cleavage between the elites and other people extends to policy matters. The American people clearly want a strong federal government to solve the problems of war and peace, the economy, and quality of life. Nine out of ten Americans believe that the federal government is responsible for seeing to it that no one goes hungry and that every person achieves a minimum standard of living. They also clearly express a preference for wage and price controls to fight inflation. The American people support the right to have abor-

[21]Arthur H. Miller, "The Institutional Focus of Political Distrust" (paper delivered at the 1979 Annual Meeting of the American Political Science Association), p. 46.

[22]For a comprehensive review of the many polls tapping public confidence and an analysis of the relation between declining confidence and the legitimacy of American society, see Seymour Martin Lipset and William Schneider, *The Confidence Gap: Business, Labor, and Government In The Public Mind* (New York: Free Press, 1983).

tions and favor a curb on handguns. Seventy-five percent of the American people express a clear preference for jobs as the best way to curb crime, a preference that runs counter to elite beliefs.[23] The American people express clear support for national health insurance.[24] Their attitudes toward nuclear arms and foreign policy are also at variance with those of American elites, most preferring a nuclear freeze and a less belligerent foreign policy.

Another index of disenchantment with public authority is the growth of direct-action groups, not only self-help programs, neighborhood organizations, communes, public-interest firms, and malpractice suits (by individuals) against a wide range of professionals, but direct-action groups aimed at corporations and other private groups. Many of these direct-action groups are political but there appears to be less of a trust in government and legislature than in the past and more emphasis on self-reliance and direct action.

The decline in legitimacy appears real. By and large, it stems from the deep cleavage between the interests and values of American elites and those of the American people. In another sense, it reflects a decline in the adaptive ability of American elites. Again the master problem seems to be a social system whose basic institutions separate elites from direct experience with the problems of ordinary people. Elites are separated from ordinary people because institutions allow them to solve their own problems under the false faith that by doing so they are also serving the public.

Is Directed Change Possible?

Human beings have long dreamed of a society subject to human control and direction. Auguste Comte, a founder of sociology, thought of knowledge as scientifically determined prediction about, and thus control, over collective existence. Despite disagree-

ments on other matters most sociologists agreed with Comte in this respect. Whether functional, conflict, or interactionist, whether pure or applied in orientation, most sociologists have always thought of sociology as a way to help individuals and groups take conscious charge of their collective affairs. In adopting this outlook, sociology has been at odds with the main current of American society. By and large, American elites have argued that society needs no explicit direction. Our knowledge, they argue, should help us understand and conform to society's basic principles.

Today we know that the alleged principles of society are merely misplaced analogies between nature and society. All groups have used government to overcome problems despite their theories. Nonetheless, government intervention and social planning remain dirty words in the United States. Today the United States is the only developed country in the world that has no open, officially acknowledged planning process. But the United States has always been planned—by Congress, corporations, professional associations, local governments, commissions, and institutes. All policy making is an attempt to predict the future. *The choice is not between planning or not planning but between good and bad planning.* Perhaps things are changing—certainly policy occupations, policy research, and policy programs are booming.

Social planning gained some respectability in American history thanks largely to wars and depressions. During the Great Depression of the 1930s the United States actually committed itself to a limited form of planning. Since the '30s the federal government has tried openly to direct the economy by using its monetary, tax, and spending policies to balance supply and demand (Keynesianism). Democratic administrations have favored stimulating consumer demand while Republicans favor producers. But Keynesianism appears to have failed. The reason is not difficult to undercover. Like so much else in American society the Keynesian state is abstract to a fault. Its purpose is economic balance and growth in the abstract, leaving all the major decisions about how and where to

---

[23]As reported by Elliott Currie, "Fighting Crime," *Working Papers* 9 (July–August 1982): 22.

[24]*Public Opinion Quarterly* 45: 179–98.

invest resources up to private, self-interested groups. Reliance on broad abstractions is formalism not policy.

Lifetime habits are not shed easily. Freedom from government interference (free enterprise economics) and survival of the fittest (social Darwinism) have been the dominant philosophy of American elites for almost a century and a half. But the relative economic decline of American society, its apparent inability to make headway against its problems, and its frustrations abroad may be leading to changes. In the late 1970s some American leaders called for the United States to explicitly give its economy some direction. The term used was *industrial policy*. The United States has always had an industrial, that is, economic, policy but it has always been secretive, implicit, and on a backdoor basis. Now American leaders, especially in the Democratic party but also in the business world, are beginning to call for an explicit public policy to revitalize the American economy.

So far however, American leaders have shown little interest in social planning in the full meaning of the term. Meaningful social planning would require control over the basic investment process by the organized public. It requires fresh approaches to basic questions. Can we achieve full employment *and* price stability? Can public investment make the economy more efficient and equitable? How should human resources be developed? What proportion of the economy should go into health services, education, recreation, food, clothing, housing, the military, research?

Improving Policy-Making Institutions

Planning requires knowledge about how society works. But knowledge is acquired and used by social groups. People must do the planning but people see the world from their location in groups. Above all, directed change and better policy making means structuring groups so that they can function better.

The major change needed is to put less faith in nonexistent market solutions. Basic decisions about the economy must be made by a public organized for that purpose. The second major change is to improve our political institutions, especially by freeing them from the power of private money (see Chapter 7). The third is to transform education to emphasize applied knowledge from kindergarten on with a view toward generating competent, adaptive citizens and improving our professions and occupations. And all reform must be guided by the overriding principle that policy groups are effective if they have heterogeneous memberships and are operating in a genuinely pluralistic system of power. Only when all social groups are adaptive will the Owl of Minerva fly by day instead of by night.

FOREIGN POLICY, SOCIAL CHANGE, AND ADAPTATIVE CAPACITY: A SUMMARY

The United States has struggled since 1945 to build an alliance of developed capitalist societies (the First World), stabilize the new nation states, and stem the tide of revolution in the developing world (the Third World).

American society is deeply dependent on the world market to invest capital, sell goods and services, and import raw materials, manufactured products, and capital. Its economic and political relations with the outside world stem from and are consistent with the American class system.

The internationalization of the American economy reflects the same trends that have changed its domestic economy and polity from entrepreneurial to corporate capitalism. Direct investment abroad by private geocentric corporations has yielded considerable profit for these corporations and their stockholders, but the United States as a whole has recently become a net debtor nation. Direct investment abroad and competition from other countries are also part of the explanation of the decline of good paying, skilled jobs in the United States.

The United States has difficulty developing a coherent and effective foreign policy because it has relations with a very diverse set of countries and because its own interests are diverse and contradictory. By and large, however, the actions abroad of American power groups (both public and private) tend to serve the interests of the upper classes of the United States (as well as the upper classes of other non-communist countries).

Nature and society are characterized by change. Some change is recurrent and predictable (a seed becomes a plant, a baby becomes an adult, night follows day) while other changes bring about new things and are difficult to predict (revolution, urbanization, technological inventions). Some social changes are minor and take place within an unchanging society while others spread to affect a host of other variables and can even change society itself.

Interpreting change is very difficult. Until recently most interpreters saw progress in change. Today radicals and even some liberals have questioned the American faith in progress. However, liberals and radicals still have very different views about such things as individualism, the market economy, private property, private investment, technology, modernization, and whether the United States is a postindustrial society.

Social change in the United States has changed the labor force, the middle class, the status of minorities, our attitude toward technology and the environment, and the activities of government. Again, liberals and radicals differ about the meaning of these changes.

Pluralism, or competition among private individuals and groups refereed by government and law, is how Americans think of a healthy, adaptive society. Considerable evidence has appeared that the United States is *oligarchic* rather than pluralist. More evidence suggests that it is a *stalemated society* (one unable to solve its problems) and that it is losing its *legitimacy* (people no longer take it on faith that power groups deserve their power).

Directed social change is an old idea but realizing it has eluded human beings. Whether the United States can control and direct social change depends largely on whether it can bring its economy under the direction of a public organized for adaptation. This requires a change in the American power structure, less faith in nonexistent market solutions, revitalizing political institutions, especially freeing them from the power of private money (see Chapter 7), and an educational system geared toward developing competent, adaptive citizens and professionals.

CHAPTER

11

SOVIET SOCIETY

THE HERITAGE OF ABSOLUTISM[1]

The great land expanse on which Czarist
Russia and the Soviet Union emerged has
few natural barriers against invasion except for sheer space and the severity of its
winters. Subject to constant invasion, Russia

---

[1]Soviet society is changing rapidly and general sources
become dated quickly. *The U.S.S.R.: A Country Study* (Washington, D.C.: U. S. Government Printing Office, 1971),
part of the comprehensive series on contemporary countries prepared by Foreign Area Studies of the American
University, is outdated but nonetheless provides valuable general information in the usual bland, nonpolitical
manner of this series. For a fine, comprehensive source,
kept reasonably up-to-date with new editions, see Vadim
Medish, *The Soviet Union*, 3rd ed. (Englewood Cliffs, N.J.:
Prentice-Hall, 1987). For a valuable series of articles designed to puncture the largely false picture that Americans have of the Soviet Union, written for the *Nation* by
an American Soviet specialist and especially suitable for
students, see Stephen F. Cohen, *Sovieticus: American Perceptions and Soviet Realities* (New York: W. W. Norton,
1986).

centralized under a czar who was theoretically omnipotent vis a vis nobles and clergy
as well as peasants. Russian feudalism lacked
the decentralized institutions that made rivalry between monarchy and nobles such a
vital feature in the rise of Western constitutionalism. All land belonged to the czar who
assigned it to those who performed state functions. Christianity (Greek Orthodox Church)
in Russia also developed as an agency of the
state. Missing from Russian history are the
conflicts between Caesar and God, state and
church, and society and individual conscience,
which played such fruitful roles in the development of Western ideas of pluralism, toleration, and individualism. In short, Russia never
developed a distinction between state and
society or the society and the individual. It
was an oriental despotism or, perhaps better,
a despotism derived from and legitimated by
need. In this sense the highly centralized Marxist system after 1917 continues the main thrust
of Russia's historical development.

Russians are only one of many ethnic groups in the U.S.S.R. The expansion of Czarist Russia incorporated many radically different ethnic groups into Russian society. Czarist Russia's pressure against its neighbors has continued under Communist rule as well. Here again there is no break with the past—the pursuit and enhancement of national interests would find czar and commissar (and even a liberal government) in agreement on many things.

While ethnic diversity has led to distinct ethnic political entities in the Soviet Union, including the legal right to their own languages, there is also an insistence on the sovereignty of the national state. The Soviet Union is an *integrated* nation state which also means that Russians who make up a bare majority of the population are the dominant ethnic group.

LAND AND PEOPLE

Geography

The Soviet Union has 8 million square miles of relatively landlocked territory, much of it worthless. Much of its agricultural land is poor and its good soil suffers from frequent droughts. Soviet rivers often run the wrong way, and its resources are not located in close proximity to each other. The country's economic problems are further aggravated by the need to disperse its industry as a defensive measure. Nonetheless, the U.S.S.R. is fabulously rich in natural resources and is largely self-sufficient except for tin, rubber, and coffee. Recently, it has also become aware that some resources are being depleted and that it must protect its natural environment. There is some evidence that planning includes environmental concerns and long-range energy conservation.

Population

The CIA places the Soviet population in 1988 at 286 million.[2] Population size and composition are important to a nation's economy

and military strength. The population of Soviet Russia was not known, indeed kept secret, for a number of years following World War II. Soviet losses in World War II were so large (estimates place war dead at 20 million compared to 300 thousand for the United States) that the country understandably did not advertise its weakness.

The Soviet Union has pursued both anti-natalist and pronatalist policies. Currently, it is concerned about prospective labor shortages and would like to increase its low birth rate, especially among its Slavic peoples. But here, as elsewhere, there are no easy answers. A growth of population would yield a dependent population group for the next 20 years. The extra cost of housing, child care, education, and loss of female labor would not bear fruit for two decades. For this and other reasons, one expert doubts that the Soviet Union will take further steps to increase the birth rate.[3]

Nationality Groups

A distinctive feature of the Soviet population is its racial, ethnic, and linguistic diversity. There are approximately 100 distinct "nationalities" and a wide range of linguistic groups, most of them very small. Russians make up only 53 percent of the population though they are clearly the dominant ethnic group. The major difference in the Soviet population is between the Westernized achievement-oriented European peoples, making up approximately 85 percent of the population and the traditionalist rural people, largely Muslims, found in the Soviet Union's Asian republics (see Table 11-1). Given their higher birth rate, Asians have increased their relative size and Russians will drop to a bare 50 percent of the total and Europeans to 71 percent by the year 2000.[4]

---

[2]U. S. Central Intelligence Agency, *The World Factbook 1988* (Washington, D.C.: U. S. Government Printing Office, 1988), p. 216.

[3]David M. Herr, "Population Policy", in Jerry G. Pankhurst and Michael P. Sacks, eds., *Contemporary Soviet Society* (New York: Praeger, 1980), Chapter 3.

[4]Jeremy R. Azreal, "Emergent Nationality Problems in the U.S.S.R." in Jeremy R. Azreal, ed., *Soviet Nationality Policies and Practices* (New York: Praeger, 1978), p. 381.

The Soviet Union has pursued a policy of Russianizing its population, which means not only attempting to make Russian the primary language but also bringing non-Russians into the achievement-oriented world of industry and science. A number of the smaller "nationalities" have disappeared but the Soviet Union is not a melting pot. Russification has led to a smaller number of ethnic groups but these are now larger and more self-conscious and continued integration will no doubt become more difficult, indeed has already become more difficult, with the liberalization of political expression under Gorbachev. The number of Russians in non-Russian areas has increased but the competition for jobs, housing, and other benefits, especially with the economic slowdown from the 1970s on, will accentuate ethnic differences rather than resolve them.[5] An idea of the language problem faced by the Soviet Union can be seen in the fact that only 59 percent of the population have Russian for their mother tongue, although an additional 17 percent know it fluently enough to call it a second tongue.[6]

Population, including rate of increase, is an important element in a nation's economic strength. One of Russia's economic achievements (and one of the reasons for its economic success) is that it has fully engaged its European population, both male and female, in its economy. Given a declining birth rate among its European population, the Soviet Union faces labor shortages in the 1990s and beyond. Unlike the industrial countries of the West, the Soviet Union is not likely to benefit from an inflow of professionals, immigrants, guest labor, or illegal aliens.

Ethnic and racial diversity are common features of societies. Each society faces both unique and similar problems in managing ethnic diversity. All have found that ethnicity

TABLE 11-1. The Ethnic Diversity of the Soviet Union, 1979.

Ethnic Group	Percent of Total
Russians	52.42
Ukranians	16.16
Uzbeks	4.75
Byelorussians	3.61
Kazahks	2.50
Tatars	2.41
Azeri	2.08
Armenians	1.58
Georgians	1.36
Moldavians	1.13
Tadzhiks	1.11
Lithuanians	1.09
Turkmens	.77
Ethnic Germans	.74
Khirgiz	.73
Jews	.69
Chuvash	.67
Latvians	.55
Bashkirs	.52
32 Other Groups Less Than .5 percent	5.13

Source: Derived from Ralph S. Clem, "The Ethnic Factor in Contemporary Soviet Society" in Michael Paul Sacks and Jerry G. Pankhurst, eds., *Understanding Soviet Society* (Boston: Unwin Hyman, 1988), Table 1-1. Used with permission.

is reviving not declining. Most experts agree that the Soviet Union faces a considerable drag on its future because of its multiethnic population.[7] The open restiveness of ethnic groups in Lithuania, Georgia, and elsewhere since the liberalization of life under Gorbachev confirms their forecasts.

THE SOVIET ECONOMY

The Command Economy

The most notable features of the Soviet economy are that it is totally planned from by the central government and the basic resources

[5]Richard Pipes, "Introduction: The Nationality Problem" in Zev Katz *et al.*, eds, *Handbook of Major Soviet Nationalities* (New York: Free Press, 1975), pp. 1–5.

[6]Jonathan Pool, "Soviet Language Planning: Goals, Results, Options" in Jeremy R. Azreal, ed., *Soviet Nationality Policies and Practices* (New York: Praeger, 1978), p. 224.

[7]Ralph S. Clem, "The Ethnic Factor In Contemporary Soviet Society" in Jerry G. Pankhurst and Michael Paul Sacks, eds., *Understanding Soviet Society* (Boston: Unwin Hyman 1988), Chapter 1. For a collection of essays that sees multiethnicity as a major Soviet weakness, see S. Enders Wimbush, ed., *Soviet Nationalities in Strategic Perspective* (New York: St. Martin's Press, 1985).

and productive capital of Soviet society are publicly owned. In short, economic growth follows the priorities laid down by government planners, which ultimately means the Communist party. Other economies are based on public ownership (for example Yugoslavia) and others receive considerable direction by government (most developed nations). However the Soviet model is distinctive in that public ownership is accompanied by central planning in the form of directives from a government bureau and compliance from below—a command, nonmarket economy. The U.S.S.R. State Planning Committee (Gosplan) develops plans for the entire economy for a given period (usually five years), which formally adopted have the force of law. Whatever its defects, centralized planning (as a type of centralized power) transformed the U.S.S.R. into a superpower in less than half a century. Soviet centralized planning gives priority to industrial growth (and military preparedness) and has clearly sacrificed living standards in favor of capital formation.

The Soviet command economy is a success in a number of respects. Under socialist auspices the Soviet Union industrialized in a relatively short time. Accordingly, it has served as a model for some Third-World countries providing a significant counter to liberal images of development. State socialism has also been a success if the Soviet economy is compared to other economies. Measured in terms of output growth the Soviet economy is in select company.[8] In any case, the Communist party's single-minded emphasis on heavy industry has made the Soviet Union the world's leading producer of a wide range of basic industrial products, for example, coal, oil, steel, and a number of basic chemicals.

The Soviet Union commits far more of its annual production to capital investment than the United States and even surpasses Japan's rate. Soviet GNP rose from 40 percent of the U.S. level in 1955 to 60 percent in 1977 and then fell to 55 percent in 1985 (GNP in 1986 was $2,357 billion and per capital income was $8375[9]). The investment rate had to be cut in the late 70s because of mass discontent with consumption levels and for this and other reasons the Soviet growth rate has slowed considerably.[10]

The Economic Slowdown

The Stalinist model of economic growth (deliberate sacrifice of consumption in favor of investment) succeeded in establishing the Soviet Union as an industrial superpower. Central planning and direction must clearly receive some credit for the Soviet Union's spectacular economic growth. Clearly, an economy without private property and market mechanisms can succeed—indeed it took less time to industrialize than the capitalist countries.

However the command or Stalinist model may be suitable only for the initial stage of industrialization. During the 1970s the Soviet growth rate slowed considerably and is now on a par with that of the United States. From a broad perspective the slowdown represents the other side of the coin of economic growth. Initial economic growth, regardless of the type of system, appears to be largely the result of employing unused, readily available resources: labor, land, raw materials, waterways, easily obtainable

[8]Paul R. Gregory and Robert C. Stuart, *Soviet Economic Structure and Performance*, 3rd ed. (New York: Harper & Row, 1986), Chapter 11; Joint Economic Committee, Congress of the United States, *U.S.S.R.: Measures of Economic Growth and Development, 1950–1980* (Washington, D.C.: U. S. Government Printing Office, 1982), Part I.

[9]U. S. Central Intelligence Agency, *The World Factbook 1988* (Washington D.C.: U. S. Government Printing Office, 1988), p. 217.

[10]For a good comparison of the U. S. and Soviet economies, see Andrew Zimbalist, Howard J. Sherman, and Stuart Brown, *Comparing Economic Systems: A Political-Economic Approach*, 2nd ed. (San Diego: Harcourt Brace Jovanovich, 1989), pp. 151–74. For a full picture of the Soviet economy, see Paul R. Gregory and C. Stuart, *Soviet Economic Structure and Performance*, 3rd ed. (New York: Harper & Row, 1986). An overall assessment of the Soviet economy and comparison with other countries may be found in Chapter 11.

coal, oil, and other energy sources. Between the 1920s and the 1970s Soviet Russia succeeded in transforming its people and natural resources into economic forces. Now it faces the problem of maintaining productivity without being able to bring low-cost resources on line. Soviet oil production, for example, is the highest in the world but its new fields cost considerably more to develop than its older ones.

The Soviet labor force is already fully utilized and there are no prospects for fresh additions from immigrants, illegal aliens, women, or births. In all areas the Soviet economy faces the problems of mature industrialization: how to maintain growth in the face of markedly more expensive costs for all economic factors in the context of rising consumer expectations and rising social overhead such as crime, alcoholism, broken families, absenteeism, and military expenditures. How much of the country's economic difficulties are due to the maturing of its economy and how much to its commitment to centralized planning is not easy to determine. A leading expert on comparative economies argues that centralized planning has inherent operational problems in the areas of "the transmission of user demand, quality, innovation, initiative, long-term responsibility, misleading prices, lack of objective criteria for choice."[11] Feedback from operational situations, especially from lower-level experience, is poor in a centralized system because of fear, careerism, and the dogma that the center knows best. Centralized planning makes it difficult to identify and replace incompetent personnel. Socialist full employment policies lead to an inefficient use of labor and inefficiencies have a way of multiplying—for example, the shortage of consumer goods means that a significant amount of time is lost by people standing in line waiting to shop.

Central planning, says Nove, also has good features: a steady rate of investment, environmental planning, and a more effective control of wages and prices, which provides stability and channels resources and labor into social objectives and full employment. These virtues are to some extent due to the superior long-range time perspective that is inherent in centralized control and planning.[12]

Most experts on comparative economic systems agree that different economic systems, especially market capitalist and planned socialist economies, cannot be fully and precisely compared (the variables are too complex) and cannot be judged scientifically because at some point value judgments must be used.[13] Both systems have impressive advantages and defects. While market economies are more adaptive, more technology oriented, provide high levels of quality consumption, and utilize labor more efficiently, they also suffer from inflation, wide income differentials, unemployment, economic ups and downs, economic insecurity, large amounts of frivolous consumption, and a significant neglect of basic needs (avoiding these defects is the good feature of the socialist systems). Some similarities between capitalist-market and socialist-command economies, however, can be noted. Both are highly concentrated and both stress achievement as a qualification for occupation. Also both use political means to achieve economic ends and both have developed welfare states to tie their populations into their respective ways of life.

The ascension to power of Mikhail Gorbachev in 1985 may be a new beginning for the Soviet economy. The three leaders prior to Gorbachev had been elderly and ailing. Gorbachev, relatively young and vigorous, appears to be astute and capable. Domestically, he has launched a campaign to reinvigorate the economy including some distinct moves toward market mechanisms and decentraliza-

[11]Alec Nove, *The Soviet Economic System* (London: George Allen and Unwin, 1977), p. 377.

[12]Nove may be idealizing here somewhat—the Soviet Union is handicapped by a pervasive focus on short-term goals (the five-year plan) and its superior environmental record appears to be largely a function of low consumption.

[13]For an earlier discussion see the section, Comparative Economic Systems: Capitalist and Socialist Economies, in Chapter 6.

tion. Clearly aware that the Soviet Union has failed to match the West's ability to grow through increased efficiency, Gorbachev has exhorted workers to work harder, has made it easier to voice grievances about incompetence, and has undertaken a campaign against the economic scourge of alcoholism. But there is no evidence that he is willing (or able) to decentralize the economy fully to permit greater on-the-spot decision making, give managers greater power to utilize labor more efficiently, and provide enough consumption incentives to spur work and performance.

Gorbachev's major thrust to invigorate the economy has been to liberalize political expression so that popular demands can put pressure on the Communist party hierarchy and the managers of state industries and services. Another major initiative by Gorbachev to reduce pressure on the Soviet economy has been to purchase consumer goods abroad and to borrow money abroad to purchase factories that produce consumer goods. Still another initiative to spur the economy has been in the area of foreign affairs. Heavy military expenditures are a drag on the Soviet economy and Gorbachev has worked hard to achieve arms control and/or reduction with the United States and to lessen tension with Western Europe and China although Western experts do not see much gain resulting from even a significant reduction of military expenditures.

Gorbachev has also intensified the U.S.S.R.'s entry into the world market that began on a large scale during the 1970s. In 1986 the Soviet Union applied to GATT (General Agreement on Tariffs and Trade) for observer status and two years later applied for membership. Since GATT is mainly an organization of capitalist countries, the Soviet Union's request for membership signifies that it wants to become more involved in trade outside the Soviet bloc. It has also raised the possibility of joint ventures with capitalist companies and free-trade zones. The one remaining large stumbling block is the failure to make Soviet currency freely convertible, that is, to allow foreign companies to remove their profits.

Whether any of the above will revive the Soviet economy is problematic. The U.S.S.R. will certainly benefit from exposing its economy to popular demands and world competition. But all these initiatives are probably no substitute for opening its domestic economy to more competition, innovation, and on-the-spot decision making.

Clearly, centralized planning is not a pure economic act but is inextricably intertwined with political institutions and goals. The Soviet Union can be seen as a huge corporation in which the same president and board of directors simultaneously govern a total economy and use it to provide for defense, art, schools, sports, and justice, as well as food, housing, and clothing. Ultimately, the effective center of the Soviet economy is found in Soviet political institutions, especially the dominant Communist party.

THE SOVIET POLITY

From Totalitarianism to Rational-Legal Authoritarianism

The Soviet Union is a centralized, autocratic one-party state. As such it is clearly distinct from the presidential and parliamentary systems of representative government in the West. But comparisons among countries are difficult to make without slipping into moral judgments and empty abstraction. In analyzing a society one must clearly distinguish between an analysis that treats a society on its own terms and analysis that treats it in terms of differences and similarities with other countries.

Czarist Russia was only beginning to develop liberal political institutions when it suffered a crushing defeat in World War I. A small Marxist party, brilliantly led by Vladimir Lenin, seized power and managed to consolidate its grip on Russian society against considerable odds. The monopolistic one-party system that Lenin established was consistent with his aristocratic conception of socialist tactics and strategy (the party is the vanguard of the prolatariat). It was also consistent with the enormous problems that Soviet Russia faced and with Russian absolutism.

Soviet society is essentially an attempt to industrialize rapidly in order to build the economic abundance necessary for socialism. The only way to achieve rapid industrialization is through state action. The success of Germany and Japan in the nineteenth century (and, say, France in the twentieth century) in transforming themselves into industrial societies is largely because of state action. State action was also important for that matter in the industrialization of England and the United States, although obscured by liberal ideology.

Lenin's aristocratic style was transformed into one-person rule after his death. Soviet political development has two distinct periods: an initial phase of totalitarianism (largely under Joseph Stalin) that lasted until the 1960s and its current phase of rational-legal authoritarianism.

Totalitarianism means systematic, explicit, total control from above by a willful leader. Totalitarian rule is unique to industrial society because only it has the technology that makes total political control possible. Totalitarian rule appears in twentieth century societies when power groups are determined to destroy one order of society and replace it with another.

Totalitarianism was used by the Communist party to establish and consolidate power. Its essential ingredients are physical and psychic coercion. Enemies and even potential enemies of the socialist order were neutralized by executions, labor camps, or exile. Just as important was psychic control, not merely in the sense of propaganda and education, but through the cultivation of suspicion and distrust. Ultimately totalitarianism must use terror to prevent the formation of solidarities that could oppose the central power. Terror is a social form that undercuts predictability and trust—its most obvious mechanism is the secret police who can arbitrarily invade the home or office, imprison, and punish. Its ultimate form is the civilian spy or informer—people become afraid to speak or act for fear of being betrayed by coworkers, friends, or relatives.

Totalitarian rule, however, cannot be used to manage and direct a complex industrial system. Undermining the predictability of social relations to forestall opposition also undermines the essence of society. To cow people into submission means that personality features essential to industrialization will not be forthcoming: initiative, personal responsibility, methodical reasoning, ambition, and a concern for the future. Soviet totalitarianism must be sharply distinguished from Nazi totalitarianism. The Nazi party was not oriented toward building a new social order—at best it was a nonrational, at worst, an irrational movement whose only future lay in war and conquest. Marxism is a rational social philosophy that seeks to build on and perfect the world mastery orientation begun by liberalism. Its social goals and time perspective are abstract but also concrete. To reach its goals the Communist party must create a viable industrial society and that means it must establish predictability, initiative, and voluntary commitment to the social order.

It was not surprising, therefore, that the various groups that make up the effective power hierarchy of the Soviet Union took the death of Stalin as an opportunity to curb the secret police and to curtail the power of the party's head to act arbitrarily. Both because Soviet Russia's internal enemies had been silenced and because of the need to develop a more positive institutional system, the 1960s saw a shift from totalitarianism to rational-legal authoritarianism.

Russian authoritarianism is somewhat different from authoritarianism in Bismarckian Germany, Franco Spain, fascist Italy, the Muslim monarchy in Saudi Arabia, the Muslim one-party rule in Libya, Syria, or Iraq, or the civilian or military authoritarianisms of such countries as Chile, Peru, Brazil, or Mexico. Soviet Russia is an industrial society and authoritarianism at this level of social development requires the systematic cultivation of dynamic, advanced skills on the part of ordinary citizens, including the ability to critically examine social problems. As we examine the political institutions of the Soviet Union, readers should anticipate a major theme that will emerge—the fundamental similarity to systems of representative government, especially in the United States. Similarities are not always apparent and analysts must learn to think in terms of functional equivalents—for example, one-party rule in the U.S.S.R. and two-party rule in the United States both function to preserve a given social order and to prevent alternatives from arising.

Perhaps the simplest way to distinguish between totalitarianism and authoritarianism in Soviet Russia is to see it from the standpoint of the ruling party. To achieve a dynamic, expansionist economy the Communist party must allow structured groups to develop: government, factories, schools, labor unions, occupational communities, especially in the professions, and so on. The existence of such groups curtails the party's power; to coordinate them means political control rather than control through hierarchy, edict, and coercion. The most the party can hope for is authoritarian oversight. In turn, authoritarian oversight leads to explicit organization, in short, to bureaucracy or rational-legal administration, and that curtails arbitrary, willful, total power by a charismatic leader.

The Soviet Union has also been called *corporate pluralism*[14] and *welfare-state authoritarianism*.[15] The central insight behind any characterization, however, is that the dominant Communist party has so far been able to combine monopoly power with enlarged opportunities for policy input by outsiders, while at the same time delivering on its overall promise that its rule is ultimately in the interests of the masses.[16] It has also succeeded

by providing tangible benefits (housing and consumer goods) to its "middle class" of industrial managers, scientists, engineers, and civil-military administrators, a process going back to the 1930s but accelerated in the post–World War II period.[17] The story of recent years is that the Communist party has been forced to enlarge the opportunities for policy input by, and to deliver material benefits to, those below the "middle class."

Soviet Political Institutions

The Soviet Union is governed by a constitution and by a legal order. As in all complex societies, both feudal and industrial, the "people" are alleged to be the source of power, the legitimating force behind institutions. The various legislative levels or soviets are made up of individuals "elected by the people." Until the Gorbachev reforms there was only one slate of candidates and their fitness for office was debated during the nomination process. Elections were a formality and the Soviets did not spend a great deal of time discussing policy. Legislative power was delegated to executive committees and ultimately to government departments. In early 1989, however, voters were given a choice of candidates representing different policy stances and a number of high-ranking party officials suffered defeat. The election's main result was to support Gorbachev's reform program by officially registering significant popular discontent. A few months later, in yet another demonstration of his power, Gorbachev peacefully retired 74 old line members of the 301-member Central Committee of the Communist party.

The Soviet political system is a federation of member republics but, in reality, is a highly centralized system. The Soviet state runs everything: the economy, education, arts, the press, television, publishing, and so on. Ultimately, all activities are in accord with the

[14]Samuel Huntington, "Social and Institutional Dynamics of One-Party Systems" in Samuel Huntington and Clement H. Moore, eds, *Authoritarian Politics in Modern Society* (New York: Basic Books, 1970), p. 35.

[15]George W. Breshauer, *Five Images of the Soviet Future: A Critical Review and Synthesis* (Berkeley, Calif.: Institute of International Studies, University of California, 1978), Chapter 2.

[16]For perhaps the best analysis of pluralism at the top in the Soviet Union (which he refers to as *institutional pluralism*), see Jerry Hough, *The Soviet Union and Social Science Theory* (Cambridge, Mass.: Harvard University Press, 1977), Introduction and Chapters 1–7.

[17]For this implicit covenant, called the *Big Deal* by Vera Dunham, see Terry L. Thompson and Richard Sheldon, eds., *Soviet Society and Culture: Essays in Honor of Vera S. Dunham* (Boulder, Colo.: Westview Press, 1988).

plan developed by the U.S.S.R. State Planning Committee (Gosplan), which has the power to oversee ministries.

The Communist party is the reality or energizing force behind Soviet politics, overseeing nominations to legislatures and making appointments to the various government departments. It is a hierarchical organization much on the order of any bureaucratic group: the Roman Catholic Church, General Motors, the Chase Manhattan Bank, and so on. Western scholars have misdefined the Communist party's relation to Soviet society by thinking of it as a small, homogeneous entity separated from the Soviet people and imposing its will on them. In one sense this is true—the party has a Central Committee of 301 members from which a smaller group, the Politburo is derived. The Politburo is nominally controlled by the Central Committee but the reverse is true. In turn the Politburo is headed by a single leader who also controls the party bureaucracy.

There is no doubt that the leader, presently Gorbachev, wields great power (as do presidents and prime ministries in the Western liberal democracies), but there is far more to this picture (as there is in the West). The Communist party is actually very large, enrolling a considerable percentage of the adult (male, over 30) population. It is also far more representative of the broad mass of the Soviet people than the Democratic and Republican parties in the United States combined are representative of the American people. The Communist party is quite heterogeneous internally. It contains cleavages along generational, ethnic, educational, and, above all, along lines created by functional specialization. The internal politics of the party reflect these differences as the various levels of the party with their various economic, political, and social specialists push and pull to establish their claims on resources and their sense of priorities. In a real sense, the party is the primary medium through which the various economic and professional interests of the Soviet society, along with the various interests of women, consumers, environmentalists, and others, exert and coordinate

themselves. Thought of this way the one-party Soviet state is not different from political processes in the West.[18]

Participation in policy debating and policy making institutions by the Soviet population has increased significantly since the 1950s. One major reason for the increase is the Communist party itself. For many reasons the party needs public participation; it can keep power only if its links to the population are strong and positive. It needs to know how its policies are working and what the various factors are in any policy area. In this sense, the single party in the Soviet Union performs the same vital role played by multiple political parties in the West—keeping the political elite in touch with other elites and with the masses, allowing the differentiated population of industrial society a channel to voice grievances and become a part of national life.[19]

The Communist party also needs links to the masses as a counterweight to the power of bureaucrats and professional groups. As such it is continuously urging vigilance by ordinary citizens against red tape, corruption, nepotism, and incompetence. And in a more abstract sense the Communist party's very legitimacy depends on its ability to show that it is derived from the people and is in tangible ways serving their interests. Again, this need also exists in the West and underlines many of the practices of Western political parties.[20] The need is present in all polities for that matter—the Saudi absolute monar-

[18]For an analysis along these lines, see Jerry Hough, *The Soviet Union and Social Science Theory* (Cambridge, Mass.: Harvard University Press, 1977), Chapters 3 and 5.

[19]For a case study of the party's success at establishing a dense network of local political-voluntary channels for citizen mobilization, see Theodore H. Friedgut, "Community Structure, Political Participation, and Soviet Local Government: The Case of Kutaisi" in Henry W. Morton and Rudolf L. Tokes, eds., *Soviet Politics and Society in the 1970s* (New York: Free Press, 1974), pp. 261–96.

[20]For an analysis along these lines, see Jerry Hough, *The Soviet Union and Social Science Theory* (Cambridge, Mass.: Harvard University Press, 1977), Part I, especially Chapter 4. For an interesting analysis claiming that there is wide popular participation in all aspects of power in the Soviet Union because under socialism there is no need

chy, for example, has a network of open-house hearings in which individuals voice claims and complaints, in effect, providing the monarchy with feedback and legitimacy.

The Soviet population is expected to engage in free and full debate on public issues and problems (but without criticizing the principle of Communist party leadership or maligning the top leaders). By and large, the populace is free to discuss and even criticize policies of any and all kinds, including ideas or policies of the party or leaders.

Most observers agree that there is considerable popular support for the Communist party, a testimony to its success in forging a superpower in its first half century of power. To appreciate the achievements of the Soviet Communist party is not to condone its excesses—but by any reckoning, its achievements rank with those of any of the great ages of social reconstruction.

The great similarity between Soviet and American political institutions should also be noted. Both are rational-legal systems of authority at least formally and to some extent in practice. The power of leaders allegedly derives from their ability to perform social functions and their recruitment to office is allegedly based on merit. In both countries the effective flow of power is from the top down. Making allowances for differences in socioeconomic development, the effective holders of power are those at the apex of the economy (including the professions) and the state.

Considerable public discussion and citizen action takes place in both countries, but the formation of policy positions is conducted by those at the top and these policy positions do not challenge the constituent principles of each country's social order. The power groups of each country also dominate the political process. Only a handful of people are effective participants in the nomination of political candidates, in the day-to-day po-

litical process, and elections do not provide the broad public with clear policy choices. And in both societies a welfare state has been developed to provide ad hoc solutions within the system of society and to undercut and immobilize opposition. Despite their differences, therefore, political institutions in the Soviet Union and the United States are in many ways similar (even many of the differences are functional equivalents) yielding an identical result: an oligarchic polity in which the interests and ideology of the upper levels of power prevail over those of the lower levels.

In recent years the similarities have increased. Gorbachev's reforms have produced what appears to be a significant step toward representative government. Elections in 1989 had rival candidates and some high-ranking Communist party officials were defeated. However representative government is not necessarily the same as or even the road to democracy (a society based on and for the benefit of ordinary people and the poor, that is, those without much economic power under all known forms of complex society)—it can also be thought of as a substitute for or a barrier to democracy.

The Legal System

Law varies with the type of society. Above all, it reflects a society's level of industrialization and the route it took toward industrialization. Western societies, for example, developed over a long period of time and experienced a protracted struggle between feudal-religious groups and the middle class, followed by a long period of struggle among property groups and between property groups, workers, and minorities. Out of these conflicts emerged a rich body of law, intricate legal practices, professions and professional associations concerned with law, and public agencies assigned the task of adjudicating and enforcing the law.

The West's conception of law, therefore, reflects its unique history and should not be used in an unqualified way to think about law elsewhere. In contrast, for example,

---

for power groups to exploit nonpower groups, see Albert Szymanski, "The Class Basis of Political Processes in the Soviet Union", *Science and Society* XLII (Winter 1978–1979): 426–57.

Japan's economic and social development were imposed from above and its people and culture remained homogeneous—in consequence, there was little need to develop elaborate legal solutions to problems of social integration and adjustment.

Having noted the importance of historical and sociocultural contexts one can still distinguish three major legal systems among the various developed countries:

1. Romano-Germanic law—following Roman law, continental European countries have tried to develop an integrated, comprehensive code of law based on legal principles.
2. Common law—emerging in England and spreading to the United States and other former English colonies, the law in these countries is thought to be the result of individual court decisions.
3. Socialist law—developed in the U.S.S.R. to promote a socialist society.[21]

Early Soviet thinkers saw the state and law as the instruments of coercion and exploitation characteristic of feudal and capitalist societies. Many of them thought that state and law would be unnecessary to socialism and would wither away. Today, Soviet thinkers have fully accepted the idea that the state and law are necessary to the formation, guidance, and day-to-day operation of even an (alleged) nonexploitative, nonantagonistic socialist society.

The developed capitalist and socialist (U.S.S.R. and Eastern Europe) nation states have many similarities in their legal systems. Czarist Russia was deeply influenced by Roman law and today the Soviet legal system still shares many features with Romano-Germanic law. But the Soviet legal system is also different. Socialist law does not accept "bourgeois" concepts of ownership (property) and it does not accept the sharp distinctions made in Western law between private and public

spheres or between individual and society. There is also a separate "legal" system for handling political cases—actually, a system in which arbitrary power is exerted against those who are seen to threaten socialism and Communist party dominance. But, in all other matters, the Soviet Union, by virtue of being a complex (developed industrial) society has all the earmarks of legal systems in other developed societies.[22]

Mass and Elite Media, Sport, and Civil Ceremonies

The Soviet Constitution promises freedom of the press but actual practice produces a press that is far different than what Westerners understand by a free press. Newspapers, magazines, radio, television, and books are all published by the government, which tightly controls all information. Journalists are government employees, more public relations experts than dispensers of independently collected information. Radio, television, theater, and film are also government run, and like the print media are openly designed to glorify the nation and celebrate the achievements of the Communist party.[23] Under Gorbachev's reforms, the press, book publishing, and mass and elite media have blossomed to express a much wider range of opinion than has hitherto been allowed.

---

[21]For a good classification and description of these and other legal systems, see Rene Dair and John E.C. Brierly, *Major Legal Systems In The World Today: A Introduction To The Comparative Study of Law*, 2nd ed. (New York: Free Press, 1978).

[22]For a classic study, see Harold J. Berman, *Justice in Russia* (Cambridge, Mass.: Harvard, 1950). For a general introduction, see E. L. Johnson, *An Introduction to the Soviet Legal System* (London: Methuen, 1969). For a collection of essays on contemporary legal developments, see F. J. M. Feldbrugge and William B. Simons, eds., *Perspectives on Soviet Law for the 1980s* (The Hague: Martinus Nijhoff, 1982). For a comprehensive reference work, see Donald D. Barry et al., eds., *Soviet Law after Stalin*, Vols. 1 and 3 (The Hague: Martinus Nijhoff, 1977, 1979) Vol. 2 (Alphen aan den Rijn, The Netherlands: Nijhoff and Noordhoff, 1978). For an informative analysis of one aspect of the legal profession, see Louise I. Shelley, *Lawyers in Soviet Work Life* (New Brunswick, N.J.: Rutgers University Press, 1984).

[23]For a good description, see Vadim Medish, *The Soviet Union*, 3rd ed. (Englewood Cliffs, N.J.: Prentice-Hall, 1987), Chapters 9 and 10.

Sports are also state sponsored—the Soviet Union has made the availability of free sports to the masses an integral part of a socialist society. Sports are promoted through the workplace and labor unions as a way of acquiring good health and socially valuable skills, of integrating the various nationalities, and even of emancipating Muslim women. Since it is free, it is also free of the class and commercial character of Western sports (although the stress on professionalism and mass spectator sport is somewhat contradictory of stated intentions).[24] The above advantages of sports to a power structure can also be framed somewhat differently. Fascist, capitalist, and communist countries all promote sports. The reason is simple: the discipline and morality of sports blend easily with any type of power structure. Especially valuable is the ability of sports to create the false impression that all society is governed by rules and that all society is a competitive race to uncover human nature's aristocracy.

Since the 1960s the Soviet Union has made a strong effort to develop a comprehensive set of social rituals to replace religion and to help socialize its citizens into socialism. These include family life-cycle rituals, initiation into political and social groups, and celebrations of the seasons, military-patriotic traditions, and political traditions. The Soviet Union's commitment to rituals as a way to socialize its members appears to be the largest in history. However, all countries make extensive use of rituals, and it is not at all clear, for example, that the United States, does not have a comparable commitment to "political" rituals (for example, public holidays).[25]

THE SOVIET FAMILY

The Soviet Union's typical family structure is similar to that of other countries in a similar stage of social development. Marxism has a specific stance toward the family and in the early years of communist rule the Soviet government attempted to create a new socialist marriage and family. By and large, Marxism sees the family as an inhibitor of the free personality, and early Soviet legislation sought to loosen marital and family ties. But the family performs vital social functions and the Soviet government soon began to support the family: divorce was made more difficult, abortion was banned (now legal), and in general the importance of family life was emphasized. Since the 1930s the Communist party and the Soviet state have emphasized the socialization responsibility of the family, especially mothers, and linked it to responsibility to the wider national community. Tangible support for the family has taken the form of child support payments and child care for working mothers.[26]

The Soviet family is nuclear neolocal. As in other industrial countries the family consists of parents and children; when children become adults they tend to leave home and establish their own families. This ideal varies, of course, by class level, nationality, and is profoundly affected by the availability of housing. The extreme shortage of housing until the 1970s no doubt contributed to the low birth rate among the European portion

[24]For a sophisticated analysis, see James Riordan, "Sport in Soviet Society: Fetish or Free Play?" in Jenny Brine *et al.*, eds., *Home, School, and Leisure in the Soviet Union* (London: George Allen and Unwin, 1980), Chapter 10.

[25]For an analysis of and a comparison of Soviet rituals with the United States and other countries, see Christel Lane, *The Rites of Rulers: Ritual In Industrial Society—The Soviet Case* (New York: Cambridge University Press, 1981).

[26]H. Kent Gieger, *The Family in Society Russia* (Cambridge, Mass.: Harvard University Press, 1968) and Vladimir Shlapentakh, *Love, Marriage, and Friendship in the Soviet Union: Ideals and Practices* (New York: Praeger, 1984) provide basic introductions to the Soviet family. Shlapentakh emphasizes the divorce of personal, microlevel behavior from official Marxist morality and sociopolitical goals because of the anomie induced by the decline of communist ideology and repression. Most observers would probably refer to Soviet developments as normal to industrialization. For a richly detailed historical picture of Soviet women, and thus the Soviet family, in the context of Soviet economic, political, and ideological development, see Gail Warshofsky Lapidus, *Women in Soviet Society: Equality, Development, and Social Change* (Berkeley, Calif.: University of California Press, 1978).

of the Soviet population. But the fall in the birth rate is not abnormal—all industrial countries have experienced similar declines (it should be noted that Muslims in the Soviet Union have a high birth rate).

As in liberal society, the family is the transmission belt for class status over the generations.[27] Unlike the United States, the upper classes of the Soviet Union do not own the economy and, therefore, cannot pass it on to their children in the form of private property (stocks, corporate bonds, real estate holdings). But the upper classes control the economy of the nation and control is passed on largely through education, the gateway to occupations with power and to valued group memberships. The upper classes also pass on significant amounts of money and personal property to their children.

Marxist ideology is somewhat ambiguous about sexual inequality and places far more emphasis on matters of class inequality. In a vague way, the ideal family is conceived as a cooperative venture by free individuals. In practice, however, the sexes are rather sharply differentiated. While Soviet women participate fully in the economy, unlike men, they must also work at household and childraising tasks. In imposing this burden the Soviet Union is similar to other industrial societies. The burden borne by women (and the Soviet family) is inherent in the primary economic goals established by Stalin. By stressing heavy industry and neglecting consumer goods and services the family was forced to perform many economic functions that other industrial countries perform outside the home and to engage in many wasteful practices (such as standing in long lines to shop).

Despite the power of its highly centralized state it cannot be said that the Soviet Union's family policies have been more successful than those of other countries or that it even exercises much control over the family. As in other countries the Soviet family is a refuge from the world's troubles and the Soviet people insist on using it to pursue interests as they see them. The Soviet family is where resistance to government policies develops, not in the sense of politics or subversion, but in the demand for better food and housing, grumbling about long lines at the stores, and the need for more day care centers. The Soviet Union appears not to have had any unusual success in curbing domestic problems, juvenile delinquency or in controlling the decline in the birth rate. Its very success in mobilizing both men and women for work outside the home has no doubt contributed to its limited successes in family policy.

RELIGION IN THE SOVIET UNION

Marxism is thoroughly naturalistic and thus opposes supernaturalism in any form. On the whole, the Soviet government's policy toward religion is one of discouragement rather than persecution. Churches still function openly but attendance seems to be low and mostly by older people, especially women. Christianity is the major religion with the Greek Orthodox Church, Roman Catholicism, and Baptists as major denominations. There is also a significant number of Muslims in the Asian republics. After more than 70 years of Communist party rule and hectic industrialization approximately 45 percent of the population remain believers.

During the early decades of Communist rule religion was openly attacked and discredited as "the opiate of the masses" and many churches were destroyed or allowed to fall into disuse. Official policies also led to a shortage of clergy and in many new cities there are no churches at all. Religion has come into greater favor in recent decades, especially since it appears too weak to offer any serious resistance to the Communist social order. Both because it feels more secure and as part of its effort to enhance national strength and sentiment, the regime has not harassed religious worship and has even restored many old churches now considered part of its architectural heritage and as tourist attractions.

---

[27]For an analysis of social stratification in the Soviet Union, see Chapter 12.

The decline of religion has also occurred because the Soviet state has actively promoted atheism and sought to substitute its own practices for those of religion. It has developed a comprehensive set of rituals for the major "crises" of life: birth, coming of age, marriage, and death. The heroic figures of Marxism have been canonized, especially Marx, Engels, and Lenin. Soviet education glorifies Soviet history and its successes. World War II and the monumental effort and victory over fascist Germany are an everpresent reality for Soviet citizens because of their commemoration in word and marble.

The decline of religion in the Soviet Union has no doubt been accelerated by official policies, but the decline of religion is found in all industrial countries and the major reason for its decline in the Soviet Union is undoubtedly the multiple attractions of secular life. Large portions of the Soviet population have experienced a spectacular growth in their life fortunes and the heady excitement of occupational mobility along with a steady growth in the standard of living (at least up to the 1970s) have diverted Soviet citizens from religious to secular values.[28]

SOVIET EDUCATION

Marxism stresses the social nature of personality and this has been reflected in Soviet educational policy. Marxism also stresses technical, scientific knowledge as the basis of economic growth and social self-direction and this too has been reflected in Soviet education. After an initial period in which educational policy stressed the free, spontaneous unfolding of the personality, Soviet education restored the authority of the teacher and school, established classroom and academic discipline, and stressed personal responsibility.

Western countries have autonomous educational institutions that are assumed to be performing positive social functions (as we saw, this is far from being the case). The Soviet Union has no such tradition—education is clearly a department of government and is organized to serve social purposes. It openly espouses values and seeks to create good character, and it openly glorifies the nation, socialism, and the Communist party.

The Soviet educational system is highly centralized and carefully monitored to ensure conformity with established programs. The Soviet Union has invested considerable sums in education. One out of three individuals is enrolled in some form of education. Like all power groups, the Communist party is aware that control over the development of youth is the key to its power and to its ability to shape the development of Soviet society.

The Soviet educational system also has other purposes besides training compliant citizens and trained workers. Nursery schools and child care centers help to free mothers for work. Educational opportunities help to integrate Asian minorities into the achievement ethic. But above all, the Soviet mass educational system (as in other countries) helps to legitimate power. The schools emphasize the central role of the Communist party and instill patriotic values. Power is legitimized in yet another, perhaps more fundamental, way. Like the United States, the Soviet Union claims to be classless. Because of its mass educational system the Soviet Union, like the United States, can claim that those at the top are a natural elite recruited from the people in open, fair competition.

Finally, education is openly used for more sophisticated political purposes than mere patriotism. The Communist party promotes educational opportunities for the lower classes as a way of keeping families in the upper classes (high managerial, governmental, and professional groups) on their toes, and it has openly worked to ensure a large flow of individuals from working and peasant backgrounds into the upper reaches of the party and other elite groups. In the early years of Communist rule this was done to counterbalance the need

[28]For background on religion in the U.S.S.R. including details on the emergence of religious interest groups, see Jerry G. Pankhurst, "The Sacred and the Secular In The U.S.S.R." in Michael Paul Sacks and Jerry G. Pankhurst, eds., *Understanding Soviet Society* (Boston: Unwin Hyman, 1988), Chapter 8.

to rely on trained personnel in government, the economy, and the military whose origins lay in Czarist Russia. In recent decades, however, the policy of promoting upward mobility has also had as one of its purposes to offset the traditionalism inherent in elite positions that are not subject to competitive recruitment.

12

DOMESTIC INEQUALITY, FOREIGN POLICY, AND ADAPTIVE CAPACITY

SOCIAL, RACIAL, ETHNIC, AND SEXUAL INEQUALITIES

Is the Soviet Union a Class Society?

Class inequality (as opposed to social stratification by estates and castes in agrarian society) is an outcome of industrialization and appears in a variety of forms in all kinds of industrial society, capitalist and communist alike. Whether communist countries—also called *socialist, state socialist, state capitalist, classless,* and *elite versus mass societies*—are class societies is not settled, but our best analysts say yes.[1] The essentials of class so-

ciety appear when science and human effort make mastery over nature feasible and turn it into a supreme value. The depiction of human destiny as inextricably bound up with the mastery of nature is common to liberal and Marxian thought, and both liberals and Marxists claim that the ideal society is classless—that is, unequal because of functional differentiation.

Stanislaw Ossowski was perhaps the first to note the similarity among apologists for different social systems (for example, John of Salisbury, Adam Smith, James Madison, fascist corporate theorists, Joseph Stalin, and some contemporary functionalist sociologists).[2] Yanowitch has traced the development of the functionalist position in Soviet theory since

---

[1]For a judicious examination of the various positions on this issue, which concludes that the key question about socialist society is whether it can maintain its openness in the long run, see Frank Parkin, *Class Inequality and Political Order* (London: MacGibbon and Kee, 1971), Chapter 5. For an analysis that finds the similarities between systems of stratification in different industrial societies to far outweigh the differences, see David

Lane, *The End of Inequality?: Class, Status, and Power Under State Socialism* (London: George Allen and Unwin, 1982).

[2]*Class Structure in the Social Consciousness,* trans. Sheila Patterson (New York: Free Press, 1963), pp. 172–80.

the original Stalinist conception. In the Soviet Union, says Yanowitch,

The vision of society as a set of functional, non-antagonistic social groups remains intact as an underlying conception. The distinct social groups, however, now include not only two classes and a stratum employed in mental labor but a multiplicity of "socio-occupational strata" within and overlapping the larger social groups. It has become a common practice for studies of social and cultural differentiation in the 1970s to encompass a variety of distinct strata (seven to nine seems to be a typical number), ranging from unskilled laborers to managerial personnel and technical specialists. Inequalities are seen as a function of location in social structure rather than as reflections of individual merit. The differential contributions of the various strata to the system's economic and cultural growth are the basis for (declining but still significant) inequalities in rewards, opportunities, and public esteem. Economic and technological change make for an increasingly "complex" social structure, and thus the precise boundaries of social groups are less clear-cut than formerly. The political dimension of stratification and inequalities in the distribution of power—unlike economic and cultural inequalities—remain largely ignored.[3]

Lane has also noted that

the "official" description of Soviet society is similar to the description that many structural functionalist sociologists make of Western liberal-democratic societies. Marxism-Leninism is a central value system rather than a "dominant" ideology as conceived of by Marxists. There is no fundamental conflict which could tear apart the society, though there are "deviations" from the central value system. The need for "politics", in the sense of making social arrangements or mobilizing people and resources, continues. The social system depicted in Soviet theory is very similar to Parsons' "ideal type" of industrial society. One might draw attention to the fact that the Soviet Marxist view of the U.S.S.R. and the Parsonian approach to the structure of American society are similar and might be conceived of as providing a kind of ideological "convergence".[4]

Despite the ideology of classlessness, the central aspect of class—significant economic inequality and its transmission through the family—is present in all industrial societies. Despite historical variations in the emergence of industrialization, the overall impact of sustained economic growth is relatively uniform. State socialist societies may be under more direct political control (though the difference between them and liberal democracies in that respect should not be exaggerated), and may reveal more social mobility and less extreme cleavages between the various strata, but these characteristics are probably due to the rapidity of industrialization and the urgency of eliminating vestiges of the past. High technical and occupational competence is rewarded handsomely in all communist countries (as it is in capitalist countries), and managerial and professional groups have established themselves and developed considerable autonomy vis a vis the party machinery. Also noteworthy is the fact that both capitalist and communist countries have a high concentration of economic *control* despite their contrasting forms of property ownership and control.

We must assume, therefore, that regardless of previous cultural tradition or present ideology, any country that successfully industrializes has by definition changed its principle of stratification from caste or estate to class. Industrial countries also reveal marked similarities, again despite ideology and previous cultural tradition, in the relationship between class status (occupation, income, education) and responses to questions of belief and value.[5]

Despite obvious differences, the Soviet Union is similar to the United States in a number of fundamental ways. Both have a family system that is characteristic of other industrial countries at similar stages of development.[6] Both rely heavily on laws and lawyers, al-

---

[3]Murray Yanowitch, *Social and Economic Inequality in the Soviet Union* (White Plains, N.Y.: M. E. Sharpe, 1977), p. 19f.

[4]David Lane, *The Socialist Industrial State: Toward a Political Ideology of State Socialism* (Boulder, Colo.: Westview Press, 1976), p. 28.

[5]For a classic compilation of cross-national data, see Alex Inkeles, "Industrial Man: The Relations of Status to Experience, Perception and Value," *American Journal of Sociology* 66: 1 (July, 1960): 1–31.

[6]See H. Kent Geiger, *The Family in Soviet Russia* (Cambridge, Mass.: Harvard University Press, 1968).

though the Soviet Union has adopted European rather than Anglo-American legal practices.[7] Similarities also exist in their medical establishments.[8] Both recognize and encourage achievement by *all* citizens in the struggle against nature and in the management of society. There are striking inequalities in economic, prestige, and power statuses in both countries, related (at least ideologically, and to some extent in practice) to functional achievement. In contrast to preindustrial society, and insofar as it can be measured, the two nations have considerable social mobility and similar problems of motivation, rigidity, and privilege. Both have pronounced tendencies toward the transmission of occupational (and, in general, stratum) position by means of the family and education. Both have extensive job dissatisfaction and many workers who are educated beyond what their occupations require.[9] In addition, both have inequalities by sex and among ethnic-racial groups.[10] And finally, both are living beyond their means, experiencing sluggish economic growth, and finding it difficult to maintain living standards, let alone raise them.

Once these fundamental similarities are noted, their differences should also be highlighted. The Soviet Union does not have a capitalist class that derives large amounts of income from its property—thus income distribution in the Soviet Union (and all Eastern European communist countries) is significantly more equal than in most capitalist societies (Sweden, Australia, New Zealand, all with strong socialist movements, also have more equality than the typical capitalist society).

Lenski cites the greater income equality of the Soviet Union as one of its successes (another success is successful economic growth without private productive property or free enterprise ideology). Lenski also suggests that when both privileges and free public services are taken into account, living standards are also more equal in the Soviet Union than in capitalist societies. The Soviet elite (along with elites in other countries) receives more income than ordinary citizens. But while it lives well, the ratio of its income to ordinary workers is far smaller than in capitalist countries. Lenski estimates that the ratio of highest to lowest wages (that is, excluding income from property in the United States) in the early 1970s was 50 to 1 in the Soviet Union and 300 to 1 in the United States (other ratios in communist countries were 40 to 1 in Poland and China, and 7.3 to 1 in Cuba). Putting Lenski together with other analysts, one can say that Soviet manual workers receive more income in relation to nonmanual workers than in capitalist countries and living standards between elite and nonelite and among the nonelite tend to be more equal.[11]

The Soviet Union (and other Soviet bloc countries) also differs from the United States and most other developed capitalist countries in according manual workers more occupational prestige.[12] Social mobility is also high in the U.S.S.R., perhaps overall, even higher than in the United States. Especially

[7]For an earlier discussion, see the section, The Legal System, in Chapter 11.

[8]Vicente Navarro, *Social Security and Medicine in the U.S.S.R.: A Marxist Critique* (Lexington, Mass.: Lexington Books, 1977).

[9]Murray Yanowitch, *Work in the Soviet Union* (Armonk, N.Y.: M.E. Sharpe, 1985).

[10]Seymour M. Lipset, "Commentary: Social Stratification Research and Soviet Scholarship" in *Social Stratification and Mobility in the U.S.S.R.*, ed. and trans. Murray Yanowitch and Wesley A. Fisher (White Plains, N.Y.: International Arts and Sciences Press, 1973), pp. 355-391; Murray Yanowitch, *Social and Economic Inequality in the Soviet Union* (Armonk, N.Y.: M. E. Sharpe, 1977); Alastair McAuley, *Economic Welfare in the Soviet Union* (Madison, Wisc.: University of Wisconsin Press, 1979); and David Lane, *The End of Inequality? Class, Status, and Power Under State Socialism* (London: George Allen and Unwin, 1982).

[11]Gerhard Lenski, "Marxist Experiments in Destratification: An Appraisal," *Social Forces* 57 (December, 1978): 364–83. Lenski's position was anticipated (in an extended way) by Frank Parkin, *Class Inequality and Political Order: Social Stratification in Capitalist and Communist Societies* (London: MacGibbon and Kee, 1971) and Murray Yanowitch, *Social and Economic Inequality in the Soviet Union* (Armonk, N.Y.: M. E. Sharpe, 1977), Chapter 2.

[12]Murray Yanowitch, *Social and Economic Inequality in the Soviet Union* (Armonk, N.Y.: M. E. Sharpe, 1977), p. 105. For similar differences in Czechoslovakia and Poland, see Roger Penn, "Occupational Prestige Hierarchies: A Great Empirical Invariant?" *Social Forces* 54 (December, 1975): 352–64.

noteworthy is the fact that mobility from the lower classes to managerial and professional ranks and into the elite is higher in the Soviet Union than in the United States.

The major reasons for these similarities and differences are essentially structural, that is, rapid industrialization. Manual workers make more and have more prestige because they are central to industrialization (and there are some labor shortages). Whether manual workers can maintain their position if and when the Soviet economy shifts to services remains to be seen. But a good part of the greater income, prestige, and mobility of the lower classes, and thus the greater overall equality in the Soviet Union, is due to socialist ideology and practice.

Ethnic Inequality

Inequalities of income, education, prestige, and political power exist among Soviet ethnic groups. But these inequalities do not appear to be severe or immune to social policy. Russians are clearly the dominant group in all Soviet republics but ethnic groups outside the European Republics of the U.S.S.R. have benefited from the industrialization of the Asian Republics, and income levels are not markedly different from one republic to another. The major reason for this is the deliberate dispersion of industrial development (and Russian migration). Another is that the government sets aside educational quotas for non-Russian minorities. And non-Russians, though not too well represented in central political positions, have done well at local levels.[13]

The Position of Women

Sexual inequality in the Soviet Union requires a separate word. Readers will remember that sexual inequality is different from social stratification. In the latter, some men and women and their male and female children are better off than both males and females in other families. In addition, parents tend to transmit their benefits and social rank to offspring of both sexes. Women may be unequal in important respects to men but some wives and daughters are better off than other females and many males.

The Soviet Union has made impressive gains in freeing women from their complete segregation from social life in Czarist Russia. Significantly more women work, especially at full-time jobs, in the Soviet Union than in the United States. In addition, they make up large portions of many important professions (though occupations in general are segregated by sex). Their representation in the professions (and their heavy representation at the lower levels of the Communist Party hierarchy) may give them more political power than their absence at the upper reaches of political power may suggest.[14] All of these developments are the result of industrialization, not Marxist ideology. Indeed, others argue that the position of women in the Soviet Union is strikingly similar to that of women in the capitalist countries: they are increasingly absent as one goes up the ladder of power and they bear the heavy burden of working and also running a home.[15] As in all developed countries, women have simply been mobilized for work outside the home. By and large, women's civil rights serve to legitimate their pursuits outside the home. Because their rights are neither enforced nor operational, the vast majority of women in all industrial countries provide a huge pool of cheap labor.

[13]Ralph S. Clem, "The Ethnic Dimension" in Jerry G. Pankhurst and Michael P. Sachs, eds., *Contemporary Soviet Society* (New York: Praeger, 1980), Chapter 2; David Lane, *The End of Inequality? Class, Status, Power Under State Socialism* (London: George Allen and Unwin, 1982), pp. 82–95; and Nancy Lubin, *Labor and Nationality in Soviet Central Asia: An Uneasy Compromise* (New York: Macmillan, 1984).

[14]Michael Paul Sacks, "Women, Work, and Family in the Soviet Union" in Michael Paul Sachs and Jerry G. Pankhurst, eds., *Understanding Soviet Society* (Boston: Unwin Hyman, 1988), Chapter 4.

[15]Dorothy Atkinston, Alexander Dallin, and Gail W. Lapidus, eds., *Women in Russia* (Stanford, Calif.: Stanford University Press, 1977) and Gail W. Lapidus, *Women in Soviet Society* (Berkeley, Calif.: University of California Press, 1978).

DEVELOPMENTS IN THE SOVIET CLASS SYSTEM

Communist thought and policy in the first decade after the Russian Revolution tended toward substantive egalitarianism.[16] But by the early 1930s a systematic policy of encouraging social differentiation (by means of such practices as the increasingly precise definition of occupations, the establishment of piecework, large differentials in income between salaried and wage workers, and bonuses) led to a definite hierarchy of social classes. Inkeles distinguishes ten such classes, ranked in the following order:

1	Ruling elite
2	Superior intelligentsia
3	General intelligentsia
4	Working class aristocracy
5.5	White collar
5.5	Well-to-do peasants
7	Average workers
8.5	Average peasants
8.5	Disadvantaged workers
10	Forced labor

During and immediately after World War II, the process of formalizing the class system continued. Especially significant was the widespread adoption of civilian uniforms, the practice of awarding prizes and honors for outstanding achievement, and a tax system that allowed high-income groups to keep most of their money and even to pass it on to their children.

No exact picture of the contemporary class structure of the Soviet Union can be drawn. The general dichotomy of nonmanual versus manual work has some reality across a number of dimensions including income, occupational prestige, and access to and success in school.[17] Recognizing that many nonmanual positions are unskilled and poorly paid, Yanowitch has proposed a three-tiered grouping of income groups:

Managerial personnel (plant directors and department heads) and senior scientific workers.

Skilled workers, technical workers (engineering-technical personnel below top management and higher-ranking office staff (economists, accountants).

Low-skilled manual workers and those in routine clerical and office jobs not requiring extended training.[18]

Both Lane and Yanowitch stress that differentials are accentuated by numerous hidden class perquisites: shopping privileges, use of cars, and above all housing subsidies. Most of these go to the top managerial and professional occupations. As in other industrial countries there is also considerable class ascription—children tend more or less to follow in the class steps of their parents. As in the United States and the other capitalist democracies, the crucial link in the chain of class ascription is the superior access to education by the upper classes. Class factors are also at work in consumption and in the choice of friends and marriage partners.

To the broad three-tiers proposed by Yanowitch—a small "upper middle class," a heterogeneous middle tier of skilled manual and nonmanual workers, and a low unskilled group of manual and nonmanual workers—should be added a sizable poverty group, a distinct "lower class." Though not numerous there are also a small number of highly paid and privileged entertainers, sports figures, artists, and intellectual-scientists.[19]

Another aspect of the development of the Soviet class system has been apparent since the 1950s. Leadership and brainwork cannot

[16]For Soviet developments up to 1950, see Alex Inkeles, "Social Stratification and Mobility in the Soviet Union: 1940–1950," *American Sociological Review* 15 (August, 1950): 465–79.

[17]David Lane, *The End of Inequality? Class, Status, and Power Under State Socialism* (London: George Allen and Unwin, 1982).

[18]Murray Yanowitch, *Social and Economic Inequality in the Soviet Union* (Armonk, N.Y.: M. E. Sharpe, 1977), p. 47.

[19]For additional details, see Merwyn Matthews, *Privilege in the Soviet Union* (London: George Allen and Unwin, 1978). Caution should be exercised in reading Matthews; his concept of *privilege* creates the impression that all inequality in the Soviet Union is illegitimate and that Marxism in practice is a thorough fraud.

be emphasized in a universalistic achievement-oriented society without risking demoralization and deviance at the bottom levels. The position of the upper range of occupations cannot be shored up without risking the development of caste-like obstructions to competition and achievement. And it is dangerous to monopolistic political power to allow a rigid hierarchical system to develop or to permit social groups to become too structured and thus somewhat autonomous. Recognizing all this, the Communist party has deliberately sought to prevent such developments by asserting the fundamental class principle of individual achievement.[20] It has appealed for "popular participation" to curb administrative incompetence and nepotism; abolished many civilian uniforms; upheld the dignity of manual work; modified income structure in favor of lower income groups (though differences in the distribution of economic values are still considerable and equalitarianism is still denounced); and increased opportunities for the lower classes, especially through educational reform.[21] Indeed, many of the internal political events in the Soviet Union since the 1950s bear striking resemblances to political struggles and reforms in the United States such as the war on poverty, federal aid to education, and the like.

The similarities between the U.S.S.R. and the United States are also striking in another respect. Like their counterparts in the United States, Soviet policy makers do not understand how their society works. Based on false images, their policies have resulted in serious failures though they have continued to experiment and improvise. As in the United States, the attempt to define social problems

in technical and administrative terms has run aground on political reefs. For example, to increase the opportunities of the poor in the United States or to alleviate their suffering means helping black Americans, but helping black Americans often entails depriving racists of their values or reducing opportunities for whites; understandably, the powerful white majority has made reform slow and difficult. In the Soviet Union helping the poor often means helping the non-Russian ethnic groups, which runs counter to the interests of the dominant Russian majority.

The reformist ferment within the Soviet Union (and in the United States) is best understood as an attempt to maintain the momentum of industrial expansion by means of a differential reward system while preventing the least privileged from dropping behind or other levels from losing pace. As is true of the United States, internal reform in the Soviet Union appears not to have lessened the overall structure of social inequality or to have threatened the ability of the privileged strata to transmit their positions to their children.

COMPARING THE UNITED STATES AND THE SOVIET UNION

In discussing developments in the Soviet class system, similarities between the United States and the Soviet Union were emphasized. These similarities indicate that many conditions and problems are common to all urban-industrial social systems. They do not imply that the United States and the Soviet Union are identical or that either has created a classless system of individual merit and functional differentiation. Seeing the similarities is important to Americans because it enables them to view their own society better (that is, to see it in structural terms rather than in terms of the ideology of classlessness). It is also important to note differences, although here great caution must be exercised. The United States has an independent judiciary system and equality before the law, but do the majority of the American people

[20]And, of course, by the systematic undermining of such groupings, in the earlier years of communist rule, through the use of terror, forced labor camps, and the like and, since the 1950s, through censorship and harassment as well as positive economic and social programs.

[21]For general background on the Soviet Union's struggle to deal with poverty and welfare, see Alaistair McAuley, *Economic Welfare in the Soviet Union: Poverty, Living Standards, and Inequality* (Madison, Wisc.: University of Wisconsin Press, 1979).

enjoy benefits from these differences? The United States has a strong civil rights tradition but has the possession of these rights helped American minorities and are they substitutes for good government and social justice?

In turn, the Soviet Union has free medical care, but has this improved the health of the Soviet people very much? What the Soviet people need for better health is better food, safer work, and less stressful lives. Does it prevent the upper levels of Soviet society from getting superior medical care?

There is another similarity between capitalist and socialist societies that must now be raised—the way in which domestic pressures resulting from institutions and social classes (both their legitimate and illegitimate aspects) spill out into foreign relations.

SOVIET FOREIGN POLICY

The Continuity of Russian National Interests

All countries pursue national objectives, determined by the exigencies of geography, power, history, and internal pressures. Considerable continuity exists between Czarist Russia and the U.S.S.R. in so far as certain national interests are concerned.[22] For one thing, both Czarist and Soviet Russia have had much to fear from aggressive neighbors. Early Russian history saw continuous problems with the nomadic herding peoples of the Asian steppes. In more modern times Russia suffered major invasions from Sweden, France, and Germany (twice).

After a period of almost complete withdrawal from world affairs between 1917 and the death of Stalin in 1953, the U.S.S.R. has become active in all parts of the world. In many ways Soviet foreign policy during the period between the world wars reflected Soviet isolation and weakness. World War II changed the U.S.S.R.'s relative world status. With the defeat of Germany, the Soviet army occupied Eastern Europe and the U.S.S.R. installed communist governments in Poland, Rumania, Bulgaria, Hungary, Czechoslovakia, and East Germany. This enlarged Soviet influence considerably and gave the U.S.S.R. a buffer against the developed industrial capitalist nation states of Western Europe, which Leninist theory and Russian experience had defined as inherently expansionist.

The Soviet Union, like all nation states, pursues policies to serve its interests. A nation state has many interests but none can be furthered without strength. Unlike the United States, which has no powerful neighbors to threaten it and is surrounded by stable societies, the Soviet Union has always had unstable neighbors.

The Soviet government has achieved a number of Czarist Russia's historic objectives besides establishing a deep buffer zone between it and Western Europe. Long a landlocked giant, Russia searched for warm water ports to enhance its naval power and to provide maritime transport to link its vast internal spaces. The Trans-Siberian Railroad was a spectacular achievement by Czarist Russia, although it could not prevent Russia's defeat by Japan in 1905. Still, without warm water ports Soviet Russia has used modern technology and its economic strength to build large merchant, fishing, and naval fleets, and is now a global maritime and naval power.

Domestic Pressures and Constraints

Like all complex societies the Soviet Union has conflicting domestic interests and problems that spill over into its foreign policy.[23]

---

[22]For valuable background, see Alvin Z. Rubinstein, *Soviet Foreign Policy Since World War II: Imperial and Global*, 3rd ed. revised and expanded (Glenview, Il.: Scott, Foresman, 1989).

[23]For an interesting collection of essays on how domestic groups and needs (for example, the military, nationalities, the economy, Eastern Europe) influence Soviet foreign policy, see Seweryn Bialer, ed., *The Domestic Context of Soviet Foreign Policy* (Boulder, Colo.: Westview Press, 1981).

One observer says that the Soviet Union is "totalitarian" and that its freedom from internal pressure gives it an advantage in foreign policy.[24] Most other observers say that it is not as open to public pressure as the United States and the other liberal democracies (this may be based on an exaggerated sense of how open the American foreign policy-making process is). Nonetheless, Soviet foreign policy is (like all countries) subject to a wide variety of domestic pressures and is used (as in other countries) to further domestic interests. For example, during the initial stages of Soviet development, Joseph Stalin rallied the Soviet people by denouncing "capitalist encirclement." Stalin also conducted well-publicized political show trials to purge Soviet society of "subversives," an activity common to many types of society, including the United States.[25]

Russia's Changing Position in World Affairs

Soviet foreign policy is still determined by some of the constraints faced by Czarist Russia. Most of the Soviet Union's attention and foreign aid are focused on its immediate neighbors: Turkey, Iran, Afghanistan, Pakistan, India, and China (and of course Eastern Europe and NATO). But as the world's second largest economic power and a coequal in military power with the United States, the Soviet Union is also different from Czarist or Stalinist Russia. Its only military threat is from the United States and it has exerted itself considerably (at the expense of both its productive capacity and living standards) to match American military efforts. The dramatic increase in the Soviet Union's relative world position has brought about significant changes in both its foreign and domestic policies.

Since the death of Stalin the Soviet Union has developed a far more pragmatic outlook on foreign relations. It now trades and has dealings with all types of regimes. Its need to trade abroad is deeply rooted in the imperatives of its economy—to maintain any pace of industrial expansion it must buy food and advanced technology from abroad. Until the death of Stalin the Soviet Union emphasized self-sufficiency and the need for internal discipline and vigilance because of "capitalist encirclement." Growing Soviet economic and military power have led to growing confidence in its relations with the rest of the world. From its inception, the U.S.S.R. also proclaimed itself as the leader of the working classes and socialist movements everywhere in the world. Ironically, its new industrial economy has made it less able to identify with the developing countries. And the steady pursuit of national self-interest has alienated even other socialist countries and movements. In 1953 Yugoslavia defected from the Soviet camp; in the late 1950s a serious split developed with the People's Republic of China; and in the 1970s the large communist parties of France and Italy asserted their independence from Moscow and their commitment to the political traditions of their respective countries.

The Soviet Union does not have relations or dealings with other countries through private firms or professional groups or through voluntary groups. Internally, the Soviet class system is more like the capitalist countries than different, but externally the Soviet Union's policies and relations are all official and coordinated. Nevertheless, a major thrust of Soviet foreign policy has been to mesh its economic needs (and those of the East European bloc) with the economies of developing nations. It has stressed mutual benefit but its policies toward Third-World countries are very similar to those of the West—what it wants from

---

[24]Leonard Schapiro, "Totalitarianism in Foreign Policy" in Kurt London, ed., *The Soviet Union in World Politics* (Boulder, Colo.: Westview Press, 1980), Chapter 1. Most observers would reject Schapiro's use of the term "totalitarian" (and would note that he fails to appreciate the pronounced pragmatism and flexibility of Soviet foreign policy in recent decades). The concluding essay by Kurt London is useful mostly as a good example of how right-wing (right-liberal) Americans view the Soviet Union.

[25]Albert James Bergesen, "Political Witch Hunts: The Sacred and the Subversive In Cross-National Perspective," *American Sociological Review* 43 (April, 1977): 220–33.

these countries is increased raw material production, on-the-site processing of raw materials, light, labor-intensive industry, especially types related to staple production, and long-term credit and supply agreements.

The Soviet Union's overall relations with developing countries, therefore, are largely the same as the capitalist countries. Marxist ideology denounces First-World policies as imperialist and dependency-creating, but the same policies are described as an international division of labor based on mutual benefit and respect when engaged in by the Second World. The Soviet Union has also rejected the notion that it has an obligation to aid Third-World countries, arguing that such countries have problems created by the colonialism of capitalist nation states. Socialist ideology aside, the Soviet Union has adopted a stance toward the rest of the world that is in its national self-interest, and like the United States and other First-World societies, it has studiously rejected attempts by Third-World countries to reorganize power relations in the world's economy. Soviet economic self-interest also coincides with its political-military interests—the bulk of its foreign and technical aid has gone to a narrow band of countries on its borders (though considerable aid has also gone to Cuba and Vietnam).

In recent years the Communist party and the Soviet government have downplayed ideology in their foreign relations. They are now the pragmatic managers of a vast corporation. Their focus is on their own economic problems and development and their foreign policy is designed with this in mind. A considerable trade has grown between the U.S.S.R. and developed nations. The Soviet Union buys food and imports the latest technology and engineering-managerial skills that it can buy (or steal). Interestingly, its partners in Eastern Europe have piled up considerable debts to First-World banks in their effort to keep up with the Western economies. All in all, there is little doubt that the Soviet Union and Eastern Europe are deeply implicated in the world-market economy.

It is also clear that Soviet theorists, researchers, and planners look upon the world in the above terms. Soviet paranoia, revolutionary rhetoric, and universalist propaganda still persist but these are no longer characteristic of Soviet leadership.[26] Soviet economic thinkers now classify countries much on the order of Western economists, paying much less attention to a country's political forms or to its ideology. Soviet theorists now recognize a global or one-world economy with specialized subsystems.[27] Gorbachev's speech to the United Nations in 1989 disavowing class struggle in the international arena and citing the need for all countries to cooperate to solve common problems simply climaxed trends that began much earlier. The U.S.S.R. has sidestepped the demand by the Third World for a new international order. Its basic philosophy is similar to that of the United States: all countries should promote international trade through cooperative efforts each doing what it does best—in effect asking Third-World countries to remain suppliers of raw materials. The Soviet Union no longer espouses self-sufficiency and no longer holds up its own path to development as a guide for other countries. By and large, both in theory and practice, the Soviet Union has shifted from promoting revolution abroad to a world-market form of imperialism. Even its revolutionary efforts appear not to be aimed at promoting socialism abroad but as efforts to destabilize capitalist dependencies and cut off sources of raw materials to the West, thus enhancing its own relative power position.

---

[26]For a digest of how the Soviet Union views world developments on a daily basis, see *World Affairs Report* published quarterly by The California Institute of International studies, Stanford University.

[27]For a comprehensive analysis of the shift from the Khrushchev era when the Soviet Union thought of itself as the defender of the Third World (who could also provide guidance and aid for a quick transition to socialism) to the present one-world outlook, see Elizabeth Kridl Valkenier, *The Soviet Union and the Third World: The Economic Bind* (New York: Praeger, 1983).

Soviet Foreign Policy Strategies and Priorities

Soviet foreign policy is debated continuously and there are distinct and conflicting orientations in the upper levels of the Soviet power structure just as there are in all countries.[28] One basic division is between those who take a hard line against capitalism and imperialism and those who argue that detente and the liberalization of trade and cultural exchange are necessary and in the best interests of the Soviet Union. Much of this debate revolves around interpretations of the "scientific-technological revolution." The Soviet elite believes that the world at large is being revolutionized by the advance of science and technology. It very much wants to be part of this revolution and to bend it to serve traditional Marxist-Leninist goals. But there are disputes about how to go about this, with some emphasizing self-sufficiency and military strength and others pushing for detente and participation in the world economy.[29] As Hough points out, the Soviet leadership has even been told that the Brezhnev policy of relying on imported technology is a failure. Soviet experts have stated that the Soviet Union can learn from the export-oriented countries of the Third World. Only if Soviet industry tries to compete in the world market can it upgrade quality and lower costs and thus gear Soviet industry to meet domestic needs. Adoption of such a policy, argues Hough, will further the already distinct movement of the Soviet Union toward being a "normal" member of the international community.[30]

Soviet military and foreign policy toward the West is heavily influenced by its relations with China. In recent years it has made a serious effort at reconciliation with China with growing but still limited success. It must also deal with many complex issues of a more concrete nature—how to cope with separatist tendencies among some of its nationalities, how to maintain stability among its Eastern Europe satellites (many of which not only have higher living standards than it has but are more politically sophisticated and open to Western influence than it is), and how to relate to many diverse communist/Marxist/radical nationalist movements around the world.

The Soviet Union relies heavily on military strength for its foreign policy, as does the United States, but there is a clear and often creative, practical strategy in its dealing with other countries. While the United States supports the status quo in the Third World (many of whose members are run by unstable, undemocratic, and often oppressive regimes), the Soviet Union's policy is to destabilize such regimes. American foreign policy is often badly handicapped by America's ahistorical, metaphysical outlook, by its economic power groups, and by its ethnic blocs. In some ways the Soviet Union's sociocultural, historical outlook is an advantage.

Soviet presence in the Middle East, Africa, and Asia has not been translated into influence or control.[31] Despite its heavy presence in Iraq, Egypt, and Afghanistan, for example, it has had no success in turning these nations into compliant allies. Iraq is continuously purged of communists and pursues policies often favorable to the West. Egypt renounced its Friendship Treaty with the Soviet Union and ousted Soviet advisors. Afghanistan's many tribal groupings remained stubbornly non-Marxist and politically unstable despite huge aid and even a Marxist central govern-

---

[28]For a comprehensive analysis, see Jerry F. Hough, *The Struggle for the Third World: Soviet Debates and American Options* (Washington, D.C.: The Brookings Institution, 1986).

[29]For a full discussion, see Erik P. Hoffmann and Robbin F. Laird, *"The Scientific-Technological Revolution" and Soviet Foreign Policy* (New York: Pergamon Press, 1982).

[30]Jerry Hough, *The Struggle for the Third World* (Washington, D.C.: The Brookings Institution, 1986), pp. 284–86.

[31]This is the conclusion reached by the various essays in Robert H. Donaldson, ed., *The Soviet Union in the Third World: Successes and Failures* (Boulder, Colo.: Westview Press, 1981).

ment; both to protect its investment and to protect itself from Muslim revivalism, the Soviet union invaded Afghanistan in 1979 but had to withdraw in defeat in 1988-89. The U.S.S.R. has been successful in its policies toward India largely because both share a deep interest in restraining China and Pakistan.

The Soviet Union, however, has learned to get maximum use out of limited commitments and assets, something no doubt prompted by its various failures. The use of Cuba as a surrogate in Africa has been extremely successful. It is a major seller of arms, thus reducing the cost of its defense establishment while making allies abroad. Its worldwide fishing fleet no doubt brings home needed protein but also serves as an intelligence network and gives it vitally needed contacts with foreign ports and governments. Its presence in various countries or on the open seas gives it potent political and psychological power in the abstract. It also enhances its image abroad through sports, space exploration, and artistic-educational exchanges.

In any case, the Soviet Union clearly supports a policy designed to take as many countries out of the First-World orbit as possible, assuming, probably correctly, that autonomous self-sufficient countries (such as Iraq, Syria, Libya) though not necessarily Marxist or Soviet satellites, are nonetheless more of a danger to the West than to it. And there is little doubt that it has pursued (even as an alleged socialist society) an expansionist foreign policy of both empire and world-market forms.

Marxist theory holds that socialist society has no need to dominate or exploit either at home or abroad. In 1988 the Politburo's head of ideology, Vadim Medvedev, in a published speech, called for more experimentation with markets at home and rejected the idea of a world struggle between communism and capitalism. "Universal values such as avoiding war and avoiding ecological disaster must outweigh the idea of a struggle between classes," he argued.[32] But theory aside, the same question we asked of the United States arises: does the internal structure of power in the Soviet Union impel it toward foreign expansion and adventures? The two superpowers have each other as an excuse not to democratize their societies. The ultimate question that must be asked of any society is, are its power groups willing to improve the lot of the masses, both materially and in terms of participation in policy making, and thus lose power? Neither the power groups of the United States nor those of the Soviet Union show any signs that they are willing to go as far as is necessary to do this (though each has some who understand that their rivalry postpones the day of peace through plenty).

CORPORATE PLURALISM AND ADAPTIVE CAPACITY

The concept *adaptive capacity* refers to a many-sided, complex phenomenon—all the mechanisms and processes that enable a society to solve its problems. People will disagree often when discussing adaptive capacity and it is important to state what one means by the concept, essentially, it means the ability of a society to generate leaders and citizens who can solve problems and adjust to new conditions.[33]

A society's adaptive capacity reflects its power structure. The most relevant image, therefore, for capturing the problem-solving capacity of the Soviet Union is one that analyzes power relations. Policy makers must have a wide range of information to be successful. They must have a sense of the multiple values implicated in every problem. They must be aware of the different possible perspectives on every problem. They must have a channel that brings problems to their attention and feedback mechanisms to tell them how well policies are working. In short, a pluralistic social structure creates problems and a pluralistic power structure is the ideal way to solve them. A first question to

---

[32]*New York Times*, October 6, 1988, p. 1.

[33]For a fuller definition, see the section, The Ideal of an Adaptive Society in Chapter 10.

ask, therefore, is, how pluralistic is the Soviet Union's power structure? As we saw earlier, the best assessment appears to be that the Soviet Union has a fairly pronounced pluralism-at-the-top or corporate pluralism. The second and most important question is, can the Soviet power structure solve problems and direct Soviet society? Here it is important to focus separately on changes in the policy-making process (the power structure) and substantive issues, policies, and implementation.

In tackling these questions no attempt will be made to analyze the adaptive or problem-solving capacity of the Soviet Union in depth or in the same terms as the United States. Our knowledge of the Soviet Union is quite extensive and many generalizations can be made about its past record and many about its future, at least for the short to medium term, but we have almost no knowledge about the opinions, attitudes, and expectations of the Soviet people and we lack reliable data about the incidence of many important social problems: nationality unrest, family instability, crime, alcoholism, deficit spending, and so on (though Gorbachev's reforms have led to many new insights into Soviet social problems).

The Communist party's problem-solving record since 1917 must be characterized as outstanding, the equal of any power group in history, including those of Periclean Athens, Elizabethan England, Revolutionary America, or Bismarckian Germany. Its record is also unique because the problems it faced are not comparable to other times. And its past record is not a sure guide to how it will perform in the future because the problems it faces in the next 10 to 50 years will be different from the problems of the past.

The Communist party has its dogmas and its metaphysics, which are sources of both strength and weakness. Of special note, however, is the fact that in recent decades it has become more explicitly pragmatic and political rather than ideological and dogmatic. Also of interest is the fact that Communist party members are carefully recruited and apprenticed, yielding a political elite with no

parallel in the Western liberal democracies. Internally, the Communist party is a congeries of "interest groups" rather than a monolithic, rigid hierarchy of similar-minded individuals—some segments of the Communist party favor heavy industry, others the military, others detente, others the consumer, and so on. It is also representative of the major powers outside the party. Above all, it appears to enjoy solid popular support.

Corporate pluralism encompasses "interest groups" outside the party and above the masses: the military, scientific establishment, high civil servants, managers, conservationists, ethnic groups, historical preservation associations, and so on. These groups all make claims on Soviet resources and the Communist party must coordinate, integrate, and ultimately make the compromises necessary to prevent conflict, stalemate, or drift. The general stance taken by the Communist party along with its actual interaction with Soviet society has led to impressive achievements. That same relation may not work too well in the future since Soviet problems have changed. The most important problem area is economic performance and here the traditional posture of the Communist party, while successful for over half a century, seems to be failing.

ECONOMIC PROBLEMS

All problem areas are interrelated but perhaps the most difficult one and the one most likely to cause problems (or have good effects) in other areas is the problem of the Soviet economy. Under Stalin the Soviet Union gave top priority to heavy industry and defense and neglected light and heavy consumer goods industries, service industries, transportation, and agriculture. In recent decades more emphasis has been placed on improving the levels and the quality of consumer goods and on increasing agricultural productivity. The Soviet Union has achieved a notable success in housing (which is still in very short supply) and there has been a slow but steady increase in the standard of living.

Policy changes have no doubt been prompted to forestall mass unrest. However, we do not know what ordinary Soviet citizens expect from their society—expectations are relative to experience, and living standards that Americans or Czechs might find burdensome could well be seen as improvements by the average Soviet consumer.

Today's stagnant command economy is a result of past success. Like the United States, the Soviet Union succeeded in building a mass production economy. Like the United States, it assembled cheap resources via large bureaucratic structures and out poured huge amounts of steel, chemicals, energy, and so on. But it has been unable, again like the United States, to reorient its mass production economy to changing domestic and world conditions.

Policy changes, therefore, have been prompted by the need for a more efficient program of economic development. Modern economies interrelate in many ways and neglected areas have a way of curbing development in emphasized areas. The Soviet failure to develop rail and truck transportation is now causing serious delays in industrial production. The failure to develop retail trade causes a huge loss of time spent waiting on long lines to shop. The failure to insist on quality housing construction will plague the Soviet economy with costly maintenance problems for decades.

A notable change since the death of Stalin has been a relatively full acceptance of the need to trade abroad. In effect the Soviet Union has abandoned the concept of national self-sufficiency in favor of an international division of labor. It is more efficient for the Soviet Union to import food and advanced technology than to provide them for itself. It is also aware that it cannot hope to keep pace with the capitalist societies unless it participates fully in the world economy. Its application for observer status with GATT in 1986 and for membership in 1988 are evidence that it wants to participate more fully in the world economy.

The key to a more productive economy, however, is decentralization. In 1987 Gorbachev proposed a set of wide ranging reforms in the direction of a more market-oriented economy. Today, the Soviet Union allows cooperatives in many service businesses and will scrap collective farming to spur food production. It has admitted that its economy has experienced inflation and that its political economy has budget deficits, it has also put state businesses and factories on notice that those not making the grade will be closed. It has invited foreign investment allowing majority ownership and is on the verge of allowing foreign companies to take profits out of the country. In 1988 the Soviet Union took out large loans from capitalist countries, in effect, asking them to build consumer-oriented factories and services in the U.S.S.R. In 1989 it gave (government-controlled) labor unions the legal right to strike. Whether vested interests will allow these various reforms to take hold remains to be seen. In any case, lagging economic growth will make it difficult to solve or mitigate problems in other areas. Here is another similarity with the United States.[34]

POLITICAL PROBLEMS

Succession to Power

Transferring power peacefully is important to social systems. The liberal democracies use elections to transfer power and have provisions for succession in case leaders die or are incapacitated. So far the Soviet Union has been successful in transferring power after the death of its leaders and in one case from one holder of power to another (Khrushchev to Brezhnev).

Reviving Political Vitality and Legitimacy

That the Communist Party enjoys wide support is undoubted. Nonetheless, the party

---

[34]For an analysis of Gorbachev's economic reforms by a leading Soviet economist who helped formulate them, see Abel Aganbegyan, *The Challenge of Perestroika*, ed. Michael Barratt Brown, intro Alec Nove, tr. Pauline M. Taffen (Bloomington, Ind.: Indiana University Press, 1988).

is aware that its power is threatened by the long economic slowdown. To counter threats to its legitimacy, the party, under Gorbachev, has made some far-reaching reform proposals in regard to political institutions. Hand-in-hand with efforts to spur economic growth through more economic freedom, Gorbachev has proposed that the Soviet people have more say in choosing their leaders. He suggests that terms of offices should be limited and there must be a scrupulous regard for law even as personal rights and freedoms are expanded. The law must be changed to foster social development and everything not prohibited by law is to be allowed. The functions of the party and government must be carefully outlined so that they can always be seen as instruments of government by the people. And everything must be done to strengthen the self-regulation and self-government of society, and the initiative of citizens and social groups.[35]

Gorbachev's economic and political reforms are attempts to modernize the U.S.S.R. or, rather, to bring its institutions abreast of the far-reaching changes that have occurred since Stalin. It would be a mistake, though, to think of the reform ferment of the Gorbachev era as an impulse from below or by civil society against an oppressive polity. The Community party and society are intertwined and the new Soviet "civil" society is largely the creation of a dynamic party, building on an advanced feudal-authoritarian system. Today, the Soviet people are urbanized, educated, and highly political. The party, as always, is promoting reforms to keep power—but it is also doing so because the reforms are in line with the basic values of socialism. As always, the party is urging the people to support its fight against inefficiency and privilege. Thus two perspectives on the reform ferment in the Soviet Union should be kept in mind:

1. As a rational authoritarian society (that is, a society in which the state has clearly established functions for the direction and welfare of society), the Soviet Union is further

politicizing itself in response to the qualitative increases in the complexity of its problems, in other words, nonfunctional bureaucratic routines are no longer tolerated. The shift toward representative government here has parallels with how representative government evolved in England and the United States and is evolving today in say Brazil and South Korea.

2. The reforms may be leading to a greater degree of Western-style representative government and reliance on market mechanisms, but they are basically attempts to shift from a socialist command to a socialist market society. It should be clearly noted that economic and political markets neither rest on equal power nor do they equalize: their main function in all countries is to provide intelligence to the assorted power groups that run society, and economic and political feedback to enable policy makers to make needed adjustments. In short, economic and electoral markets are ways to prevent social system change. They should be viewed in this manner in the Soviet Union or elsewhere.

The Problem of Nationalities

Integrating its ethnic, religious, and linguistic minorities into its urban-industrial system will no doubt be a continuing problem for the Soviet Union into the foreseeable future. The Eastern European countries will also require considerable attention—much of the political future here depends on whether their economies can be wedded to the Soviet Union's. These countries have experienced a nationalist resurgence in recent years (except for Bulgaria and East Germany) and clearly belong in our next category as a foreign policy problem for the Soviet Union.

Foreign Policy

Foreign policy problems will continue to loom large for the Soviet Union. On its immediate borders, it still faces an unreconciled China (despite the recent warming of relations), a restive Poland and Czechoslovakia, Muslim fundamentalism in Iran, and Turkey, a member of NATO and a military ally of the United States.

---

[35]*New York Times*, June 29, 1988, p.1.

The Soviet Union has some important allies beyond its own borders. Vietnam helps it to outflank China and gives it access to Southeast Asia and the South Pacific. Cuba gives it presence in the Western hemisphere and has proven an effective agent in Africa. But on the whole, it cannot be said that the Soviet Union has had any great success in foreign policy, something that no doubt accounts for the extraordinary emphasis it has placed in recent years on military preparedness. Its presence in the Middle East, Asia, and Africa is more appearance than substance. It has no control over the countries it deals with and even the ones it favors, such as Iraq, Syria, and Libya, are far from being compliant allies or peripheries. Its invasion of Afghanistan was more an admission of failure than success and has proven costly in terms of economic, political, and moral values.[36]

Gorbachev has taken a number of initiatives to ease foreign pressures on the Soviet Union. During 1986 he put the United States on the defensive by proposing a series of arms control and reduction measures across a wide variety of areas including both missile and conventional arms. He also called for a moratorium on nuclear testing and stopped Soviet testing for extended periods. His unilateral reduction of the conventional arms facing NATO (small in number but large psychologically) and his repeated request for negotiations to reduce short-range nuclear weapons in Europe has appealed to continental West Europeans and separated them significantly from Great Britain and the United States. Gorbachev has also made overtures to China on easing border tensions and on establishing better relations, and his visit to China in 1989 was of great symbolic importance. Clearly, having an able and energetic leader is a valuable addition to the Soviet Union's adaptive capacity.

Is Corporate Pluralism Enough?

The Communist party has succeeded in building a superpower for many reasons. One of these was its success in developing feedback systems so that it could tell how well its policies were working. It has permitted, even encouraged, the development of many political mechanisms that are functional equivalents of Western political institutions. The ultimate political problem it faces is whether corporate pluralism provides the party with what it needs to solve social problems. Apparently, the party does not think so, at least judging from the recent liberalization of political expression and the significant steps taken to provide the Soviet people with political choice. And this raises another question: can the Communist party keep diversifying and then liberalizing the Soviet social system without losing control of it?

SOCIAL PROBLEMS

The Soviet Union is beset with the usual array of social problems found in all industrial societies. The exact nature and extent of these problems are difficult to determine because of the lack of research and reliable data. Leaving the future aside, analysts agree that Soviet problem solving up to the 1970s was impressive.[37] The story since the 1970s has been different. An important perspective on Soviet social problems is gained if one compares living standards there with other countries. Soviet living standards are still far below American, European, and even Eastern European standards. The Soviet standard of living is roughly one-third that of the United States and half that of France and the Federal Republic of Germany. And not only have there been no gains since the 1970s but, if anything,

---

[36]The Center for Defense Information, "Soviet Geopolitial Momentum: Myth or Menace?" *The Defense Monitor* 15:5 (1986) argues that Soviet world power is quite small and has been in decline since its high point in 1958 (for an earlier discussion, see Chapter 10).

[37]Vic George and Nick Manning, *Socialism, Social Welfare, and the Soviet Union* (Boston: Routledge and Kegan Paul, 1980) and Gordon B. Smith, ed., *Public Policy and Administration in the Soviet Union* (New York: Praeger, 1980).

the Soviet Union is losing ground in one area after the other.[38]

Poverty

Poverty is an obvious place to start in discussing Soviet problems. With its heavy emphasis on capital formation and its burdensome military spending, it is not surprising that many Soviet citizens are poor. Since the death of Stalin a variety of antipoverty measures have been taken, in many ways resembling measures taken in the United States. On the whole, however, the Soviet Union cannot hope to make much headway against poverty unless it makes radical changes in its economic priorities.

The abstract problem of poverty (and near poverty) manifests itself in a number of concrete ways: housing hardships, family instability, alcoholism, delinquency among the young, and crime.

Cities and Housing

Soviet leaders have declared their intention to provide housing and to design cities so that egalitarian ideals can be achieved. They have deliberately spread industrialization into regions beyond European Russia in order to prevent regional imbalances or sharp differences between urban and rural areas and also for purposes of national defense.

Soviet urban planning has had some success in preventing the marked segregation of life styles by class and income that marks Western cities. However urban planning as such has not succeeded in establishing itself. State economic ministries still control a great deal of the investment in housing, transport, child care, schools, and medical facilities, and these often violate urban plans. In addition, Soviet citizens are

not free to live where they want and an elaborate system of domestic passports controls their movement in an effort to ration labor and housing, both of which are in short supply. This control has helped to protect older cities, which are relatively free of some of the pathologies that plague Western, especially American cities (for example, crime—the newer cities with larger numbers of young males tend to have higher crime rates).[39]

Health

The Soviet Union has free health care for its citizens. Soviet leaders recognize that a healthy population is more productive and have stated their commitment to preventive medicine. The reality of Soviet medicine, however, reflects the scarcity of resources that is found everywhere outside heavy industry and the military. Here, as elsewhere, the Soviet elite enjoy a higher level of benefits. This is similar to other countries, including the United States. Actually, the Soviet health care system has many similarities to the United States: reliance on doctors, technology, and large hospitals to take care of people *after* they become ill or disabled.

The Soviet Union registered significant gains in health after the Revolution. In recent years, however, not only have there been no gains, but ominously, reversals have appeared. Infant mortality has increased and life expectancy for men has declined (and remained stationary for women).[40] The Soviet health care system, say Davis and Feshbach, has not deteriorated, but they are unable to pinpoint the reasons why the earlier drop in infant mortality reversed itself in 1971. However, it now appears that no increase in infant mor-

---

[38]For a comprehensive analysis of Soviet living standards (goods and services, poverty, medical care, housing, education, and work), with extensive comparisons with other countries, see Horst Herlmann, ed., *Quality of Life In the Soviet Union* (Boulder, Colo.: Westview, 1987).

[39]For a fairly positive picture of Soviet urban achievements, see, James H. Bater, *The Soviet City* (Beverly Hills, Calif.: Sage, 1980). For a less positive picture, see Henry W. Morton and Robert C. Stuart, eds., *The Contemporary Soviet City* (Armonk, N.Y.: M.E. Sharpe, 1984).

[40]For an analysis of the latest data, which stop early in the 1970s, see Christopher Davis and Murray Feshbach, *Rising Infant Mortality in the U.S.S.R. in the 1970s*, (U. S. Bureau of the Census: Washington, D.C., 1980).

tality took place, once attention is paid to differences in data collection and better reporting in the Asian republics.[41] The U.S.S.R. has made mistakes in its medical investment strategy (more instead of better facilities, for example) and the proportion of GNP spent on health care has declined. Alcoholism is rampant in the U.S.S.R. and this no doubt has contributed to the drop in male life expectancy (for example, drunkenness on the job and while driving has led to a large increase in deaths). Food supply seems adequate but whether the population is eating the dull diet is another matter. And there appears to be a widespread indifference to risks from industrial wastes, pesticides, and other hazardous materials. In any case, if the reversal in Soviet health statistics after the early 1970s continues it will be a unique case of a developed nation heading back toward the health levels characteristic of developing nations.

Crime

Although no exact data are available, a significant amount of crime takes place in the Soviet Union (though much less than in the United States). It is also clear that crime can no longer be explained as a vestige of Czarist Russia but clearly stems from contemporary Soviet society. It is also growing. There is much ordinary crime, especially by young males in the developing cities of the Far East and Far North. A great deal of it is associated with alcoholism. Of greater significance is crime by individuals in positions of power.[42]

Ordinary crime in the Soviet Union is largely a matter of society's raising expectations and then not satisfying them. In this, it resembles

crime in the capitalist world. And the most important types of crime, those committed by individuals in positions of power, also resemble those in capitalist societies. Because curbing crime means that power groups have to curb their own crime (and thus their own power), the chances of reducing crime in the Soviet Union are as small as they are in the United States.

SOVIET SOCIAL SCIENCE AND ADAPTIVE CAPACITY

The social sciences in the Soviet Union are embedded in Marxism. Partly because Marxism is a rational philosophy committed to science and partly because all power groups in complex society, especially its industrial variant, need information about how society is working, the Soviet Union has developed an empirical sociological tradition similar to that in the United States.[43] In addition, there is considerable evidence that Soviet economists and foreign policy analysts are now primarily pragmatists and empirical realists rather than dogmatists. The recent official abandonment of class struggle as the key relation in international relations and acceptance of state-centered political relations has antecedents in Soviet foreign policy theory.[44] And considerable discussion has taken place about improving policy-making organs and administration.

Soviet thinkers have an overall image of Soviet society as a sound functional system that requires time and research to solve its problems. The similarity to how American theorists see the United States is startling. Also startling is the pronounced tendency to concentrate on deviance among the lower classes and to blame the victim for problem behavior. Because the system is fundamen-

[41]Ellen Jones and Fred W. Grupp, "Infant Mortality Trends in the Soviet Union," *Population Development Review* 9 (June, 1983): 213–246, and Barbara A. Anderson and Brian D. Silver, "Infant Mortality in the Soviet Union: Regional Differences and Measurement Issues" *Population Development Review* 12 (December, 1986): 705–38.

[42]Louise I. Shelley, "Crime and Criminals In The U.S.S.R." in Michael Paul Sacks and Jerry G. Pankhurst, eds., *Understanding Soviet Society* (Boston: Unwin Hyman, 1988), Chapter 9.

[43]For a depiction of Soviet sociology by two leading Soviet sociologists, see G. V. Osipov and M. N. Rutkevich, "Sociology in the U.S.S.R., 1965–1975" *Current Sociology* 26: 2 (Summer, 1978): 1–60.

[44]Allen Lynch, *The Soviet Study of International Relations* (New York: Cambridge University Press, 1987).

tally sound, pathological behavior must stem from the willful irresponsibility of the individuals involved.[45] The Soviet Union is no more likely than the United States to make inroads into its social problems as long as it fails or refuses to link them to the basic processes of industrialization and concentrated power.

Solving social problems requires considerable resources. Given the Soviet Union's present allocation of resources, it is unlikely that the resources needed to solve social problems will be forthcoming. Solving such problems also entails prevention and social reorganization. Given the present Soviet power structure these too are unlikely. It is already clear that Soviet ideologists, including Soviet social scientists, have developed the same orientation toward social problems that is found in the United States. Like mainstream American social science, Soviet social science is unlikely to connect social problems directly to Soviet institutions or to the power groups that create and benefit from them.

Soviet leadership from Brezhnev on has emphasized the need to master the revolution in science and technology and bring it to bear on the overall management of society.[46] Soviet leaders and thinkers now talk of Soviet society as "developed" or "mature socialism." There is an urgent need to develop "scientific management" and to incorporate the latest findings in science and technology into the productive process. While affirming the continuing validity of political direction by the Communist party, the Politburo has widened elite participation in policy making and encouraged mass participation in administration. But, as Hoffmann and Laird point out, the call for new ideas and innovative practices exceeds the actual development of policies, and far exceeds the development of new

institutional arrangements. The Soviet leadership, they argue, is not committed to a democratization of Soviet society, which would bring goals and institutions into question, but, instead, is committed to a more efficient, productive "technocratic socialism," which the Soviet leadership claims is a preparation for democracy (communism). The similarity with mainstream social science and mainstream professionalism in the United States (technocratic liberalism) is striking with one exception—American elites believe they are already in a democracy.

THE U.S.S.R. AS AN OLIGARCHY

The high adaptive capacity of the Communist party and other Soviet power groups is beyond question. It is also unquestionable that the Communist party, along with the military, high government officials, the managers of industry, the scientific establishment, and the aesthetic and sports establishment enjoy considerable popular support and that they have considerable operational control over the institutions of Soviet society. The adaptive capacity of the Soviet Union is no doubt enhanced by the fact that its various elites find it much easier than their counterparts in the United States to think and act in terms of an interrelated whole.

Soviet elites also enjoy high material and psychic benefits. To think of their unequal rewards as forming a system of privilege is a mistake. The Soviet Union has an explicit and open justification for inequality, one that is identical to the United States: those who do more for society deserve to get more. The question is, to what extent are the unequal rewards undeserved? The Soviet elites are secretive about their rewards and observers must conclude that they are higher than can be easily justified. Beyond that it is not possible to investigate since there is very little hard data about how ordinary Soviet citizens feel about the hierarchy of rewards or how much they know about it. Our most important source of how ordinary citizens feel is the large number of emigres (mostly Jewish) who report

[45]Walter D. Conner, *Deviance in Soviet Society: Crime, Delinquency, and Alcoholism* (New York: Columbia University Press, 1972), Chapter 10.

[46]For a full discussion, see Erik P. Hoffman and Robbin F. Laird, *Technocratic Socialism: The Soviet Union in the Advanced Industrial Era* (Durham, N.C.: Duke University Press, 1985).

that there is considerable resentment and cynicism among the Soviet people.[47]

The hierarchy of reward is also based on illegal activities, everything from a flourishing black market and an underground economy to outright theft, bribery, and other criminal acts. There is also evidence of considerable sluggishness in the Soviet lines of communications, something not unrelated to the hierarchical command structure and the partially illegitimate hierarchy of rewards.

In short, the U.S.S.R. does not operate in the way in which its power group(s) says it does—in this sense it is oligarchic in the classic meaning of the word: the rule by the few is not totally in the interests of the many.

The Soviet Union may develop in a number of directions: toward liberal or market authoritarianism, social democracy, or toward reactionary authoritarianism. At present it appears committed to "technocratic socialism," the development of better, scientifically based techniques for running society from above complemented by new forms of political expression. From 1986 on, under the leadership of Gorbachev, a new openness in the arts and the mass media appeared—citizens are freer to express their views and to voice grievances. Government and party officials are openly criticized and even the Red Army

has not escaped censure. A more liberal policy in regard to civil rights and dissidents has appeared. And far-reaching practices have been put into effect that have taken the U.S.S.R. a good way toward representative government. Where all this will lead is not clear. It does indicate, however, that the Soviet leadership is aware of how stagnant the Soviet economy and polity have become.

Nonetheless, its initiatives for reform are careful not to question the essentials of Soviet-style socialism. In this sense, it shares much with the value-neutral social science, public and business administration, and public policy programs in the United States. However, the various forces that make up Soviet society are so numerous and so complex that it is not possible to form definitive judgments as to the country's future.

Like all complex societies, the Soviet Union is a prisoner of its history (both before and after the Russian Revolution) and subject to outside forces over which it has even less control. As in all other complex societies, it is unlikely that Soviet power groups will enact policies that will undermine their power. Like all complex societies, the Soviet Union will more than likely remain an oligarchy, a permanent half-way house, a menace both to its own people and to others.

---

[47]In this regard, see Mervyn Matthews, *Privilege in the Soviet Union* (London: George Allen and Unwin, 1978).

CHAPTER

13

REPRESENTATIVE CAPITALIST DEPENDENCIES

Greece, Peru, and the Republic of (South) Korea

INTRODUCTION

Parts II and III were case studies of the two most powerful countries in the world, the United States and the Soviet Union. The United States also served as an example of an integrated capitalist nation state while the Soviet Union illustrated the integrated socialist nation state. Neither the United States nor the Soviet Union is self-sufficient; both are deeply dependent on the outer world to keep their economies going and for protection. However, as large industrial nation states they tend to get the most out of their relations with other countries and tend to have more room to maneuver and initiate actions.

Part IV will present case studies of nation states that are dependent in two senses of the word:

1. Like all other nation states they could not exist without participating in the world economy.

2. Unlike the industrial nation states, these societies were massively influenced by other countries (all have been part of another country's empire and have had to throw off foreign rule, while many of them have had their lands ravaged by wars of liberation, civil wars, or the wars of other countries). And, though formally sovereign states, all are still very much influenced by other, more powerful countries.

The countries in Part IV have also been selected to represent different kinds of preindustrial economies, different cultural traditions, and the problems that such differences produce for developing countries. A key question underlying all others, however, is, can any of these countries ever become developed?

A major difficulty in analyzing the various types of countries in the contemporary world is that they have cultures markedly different from the liberalism that characterizes the English speaking nations. These differences in culture, or basic outlook on the world, are especially difficult to capture because oftentimes there are superficial similarities, say between the United States (or the modern West) and the country being studied. American foreign policy makers have made avoidable blunders because often they simply did not understand the country they were dealing with. Because various peoples look on human nature, the sexes, the family, work, time, causality, and so on differently, countries have to be evaluated on their own terms and not simply as deviations from the allegedly natural and, thus valid, American way or the allegedly natural Western way.

A particular caution is necessary about the analytical framework employed in the following studies. Institutional areas are separated and behavior is impersonalized, segregated, and specialized in mature industrial society to a degree that is absent in preindustrial society. Not only are institutional priorities different; for example, family, religion, and military values may take precedence over other values, but preindustrial institutions interpenetrate and mix in ways unfamiliar to industrialized Westerners. Every effort must be made, therefore, to avoid ethnocentric arrogance and misperceptions when dealing with the world outside the industrialized West.

Part IV will present brief discussions of seven Third-World countries: three capitalist, Greece, Peru, and the Republic of Korea, and four socialist, Cuba, Tanzania, the Socialist Republic of Vietnam, and the Republic of Iraq. Perhaps the most important fact to remember about the countries of the world is that they vary in ways that appear much closer to utter diversity and irreducible uniqueness than to unified, generalizable uniformity. The variety of ecological habitats of the earth's various populations would by itself make for extreme diversity. Human agency within given societies has also developed in an amazingly diverse manner. And human agency denoted by the terms "imperialism" and "cultural diffusion," the impact of one type of society on another, has also helped to produce a wide and unique spectrum of societies and intersocietal systems.

One need only compare the thin and rocky soil of Greece with the rich alluvial plains of the Tigris and Euphrates of Mesopotamia (present-day Iraq) and the Red River Delta of Vietnam to appreciate the impact of the natural environment on human behavior. One need only compare the different impact of imperialism on Greece, Peru, Korea, Cuba, Tanzania, Vietnam, and Iraq to appreciate the importance of intersocietal relations in the development of internal social systems.

The seven societies of Chapters 13 and 14 have been chosen to represent the widest possible set of variables at work in the Third World (here defined to mean the integrated societies that have emerged in the past few centuries, especially under the stimulus of Western expansion). A list of the major variables that are at work may help to guide the reader through the maze of countries that will be analyzed. The variables are as follow:

1. Ecological variables such as soil, water, minerals, and other natural resources as well as geographic location and other natural variables.

2. Distinctive economic variables, especially the type of rural economy.

3. The influence of different institutional and normative traditions on the premodern society in question and on its overall ability to adapt to imperialism and the problems of nation building.

4. Population characteristics, especially composition and growth. Some of the societies we will analyze have homogeneous populations: Greece, Korea, Cuba, and Vietnam are societies with homogeneous linguistic and ethnic populations. The other societies are more diverse but have not become segmented (segmented societies are discussed in Chapters 15 and 16). Peru thoroughly subordinated its Indian population, Tanzania's multiplicity of ethnic groups and the relatively equal number of Christians and Muslims has yielded no dominant group and thus no ethnic problem. Iraq has been troubled by a division between Sunni and Shia Muslims and between Arabs and Kurds but so far the dominant Arab Sunni have managed to develop an integrated nation state. Also important is population growth and whether or not a country exports its labor either to its advantage or disadvantage.

5. The influence of various kinds of imperialism—not only the difference between the imperialism of empire and that of the world-market economy but differences within each (England, France, and Spain developed distinctive empires; England, the United States, and the U.S.S.R. developed distinctive forms of world-market imperialism).

To represent the Third World, these seven countries must be supplemented by other variations in social type (it is important to keep in mind that segmented societies in the First, Second, and Third Worlds are studied in Chapters 15 and 16). The claim that the societies being studied are representative must be judged by the major purpose of this study, to provide an analysis of the basic types of societies and their interrelations at a useful level of abstraction.

GREECE[1]

Land and People[2]

Modern Greece is a nation of almost 10 million people with a linguistic, literary tradition that goes back 3,500 years and a homogeneous religious tradition that dates back to the missionary work of Paul. Ethnically, 98 percent of the population is Greek.

Politically, Greece was absorbed by Rome in 146 B.C., became part of the Byzantine Empire after the fall of Rome, and was part of the Ottoman Empire until 1825 when it became an independent nation state. Economically, Greece is essentially a rural society with an interesting mix of market institutions that have also pointed Greeks toward the outer world. Greeks have left Greece and prospered in other lands; some left for good, some worked as guest workers, some returned voluntarily, and some were forced to return.[3] But throughout Greek history there has been an abiding constant to its economy and thus to the Greek character and society; its ecology. Greece has a climate and land that are hospitable in many ways but it is also very hot and dry in the summer and uncomfortably cold and damp in winter. All in all, the soil is thin, the terrain is mountainous and lacks large open land areas, only 30 percent of the soil is arable, there is an overall shortage of water, and there are few significant deposits of raw materials.

Economy

The outstanding feature of ancient and modern Greece is the prevalence of small landowners. Greece's natural environment is not suited to large-scale landholding or to large-scale irrigation. Greek agriculture did not spawn centralized feudalism; neither did it generate a decentralized, natural (or self-sufficient) manorial economy. The Greek ecology forced specialization, especially olive oil, wine, and herding, and Greeks were forced to develop market relations with each other and with foreigners.

Greece's small-scale, cash-crop economy had profound effects on the Greek mentality, family, and polity. Unlike serf or slave families tied to the soil of a landlord, where income is directly tied to production, the Greek

---

[1]For a previous discussion of ancient Greece as a seedbed society, see Chapter 3.

[2]*Greece: A Country Study*, 3rd ed. (Washington, D.C: U. S. Government Printing Office, 1986), part of the comprehensive series on contemporary countries prepared by Foreign Area Studies of The American University, is an invaluable source of information about Greek geography, population, history, and society. For an analysis of Greece's social development since World War II, see William H. McNeill, *The Metamorphosis of Greece Since World War II* (Chicago: University of Chicago Press, 1978). For an analysis of Greek society as a function of outside forces, see Nicos P. Mouzelis, *Modern Greece: Facets of Underdevelopment* (New York: Macmillan, 1978) and Jon Kofas, *Intervention and Underdevelopment: Greece During the Cold War* (University Park, Penn.: The Pennsylvania State University Press, 1989). For essays on all aspects of contemporary Greek society, see Richard Clogg, ed., *Greece In The 1980s* (London: Macmillan, 1983). For a current picture of Greek society, see George A. Kourvetaris and Betty A. Dobratz, *A Profile of Modern Greece* (New York: Oxford University Press, 1987).

[3]The historic exodus of Greeks to other countries was reversed in the 1970s by Greece's economic development and by the slowdown in economic growth in other countries—by and large, more Greeks are returning to Greece than leaving.

also gained or lost income from bargaining and from the vagaries of the market. Shrewd bargaining not only became characteristic of economic transactions but of the organization of the family, village, and Greek polity.

Ancient Greece prospered because olive oil and wine were scarce and easily stored whereas foreign wheat was relatively plentiful and difficult to store. Selling in domestic and foreign markets led to commercial and other skills, especially trading, banking, insurance, pottery making, shipbuilding, and shipping. From ancient times well into the modern era, and in some respects to the present, the Greek mentality was permeated by the spirit of competitive commerce. The mentality of the trader is common to both the Greek peasant and the urban middle class—only the military and some professions do not share this character and value orientation. It is vital to understanding Greek history to know that the Greek businessperson is an active capitalist entrepreneur but in commerce rather than in manufacturing.

The commercial-capitalist spirit did not lead to American-style individualism or to the impersonal, achievement ethic. The entrepreneurial spirit was firmly embedded in the Greek nuclear family. The multipurpose Greek family (which has its counterparts in other countries, especially those with a similar ecology) is the key to understanding Greek history and Greek accomplishments and failures. Greece's farms, almost all its commercial enterprises, and a substantial percentage of its industry are family owned and operated. Equal inheritance has worked to prevent land (and other forms of economic) concentration. Equal inheritance (also with migration) also prevented the growth of a body of landless laborers. The family nature of economic activity also worked to retard impersonal capital formation and large-scale enterprises (the corporation).

The modern Greek economy (as well as the entire Mediterranean basin) developed as an underdeveloped, nonindustrial economy based on cash-crop agriculture and a large rentier-service sector (banking, law, retailing, insurance, shipping, and tourism). Modern Greece's underdeveloped economy was considerably affected by industrialization in northern Europe. In the nineteenth century the fledgling Greek textile and shipbuilding industries, for example, were ruined by the more advanced English economy. Western European demand for agricultural products (often under exploitative arrangements) channelled Greece (and the energies of the entire Eastern Mediterranean) into agriculture.

Greece's "industrialization" after World War II has also been marked by dependence on foreign countries. Greece's contemporary position in the world market will be easier to see after we discuss the Greek polity. In 1986, its GNP of $39.5 billion yielded a per capita income of $3,950.[4]

Polity

The basic pattern in Greek political life after it became an independent nation state in 1825 was authoritarianism. The Greek monarchy, army, government, and civil service were all, either separately or in combination, independent of popular control (though parliamentary elections often provided a facade of popular control). Greece did not achieve a system of representative government similar to those in the other liberal democracies until 1975.

Authoritarianism (or any cultural practice or element) has a different meaning depending on social and historical context. The small-scale Greek rural and urban economy produces a self-sufficient, family-oriented individualism and equalitarianism and poses a different political problem than a serf- or slave-based agrarian society. The essential power relation in Greek society has always been between the small farmer and small business person, on the one hand, and larger property owners, merchants, bankers, shipowners, the professions, higher civil servants, including university faculty, the military, and the upper clergy, on the other. This power

---

[4]Central Intelligence Agency, *The World Factbook 1988* (Washington, D.C.: U. S. Government Printing Office, 1988), p. 91.

relation was legitimized (and thus obscured) in some ways while also remaining a source of transparent exploitation and political tension in other ways.

Perhaps the outstanding feature of modern Greek history is the relative absence of agrarian protest or revolutionary movements. Rural society is often marked by considerable unrest, sporadic violence, organized political movements, and even by revolution in all kinds of horticultural and agricultural economies, including the free-holding farm economy of the United States. An exception to this pattern (besides Greece) was French Canada before 1914, but here the reason was apparent: the French-Canadian family was anchored in a free-holding farm that was organized for rural self-sufficiency.

There are a number of reasons for the relative peace in the Greek countryside. Greek farmers have a long tradition of coping with market relations and have long since been absorbed into a competitive system, which isolate families from each other. Greek surplus population was siphoned off to the cities, the merchant marine, or overseas (either as merchants, brokers, immigrants, or guest laborers). Greece achieved independence early, and economic grievances could not be inflamed and multiplied by political-nationalist grievances. And, having achieved independence, Greece developed a pronounced system of patronage politics, which also helped to stem agrarian unrest even as it promoted the authoritarianism of the state and the interests of the commercial middle class.

Patronage politics (also referred to as patron-client politics or clientelism) is found in all political systems (it is the heart of feudal political relations). Under this system of personal relations, a political leader dispenses favors (jobs, contracts, licences, food) in return for favors (money and other support, campaigning and getting out the vote). While present in the developed capitalist and socialist societies, patronage politics supplement rather than dominate politics (which are carried out by large organizations mobilizing a mass electorate). Patron-client relations are characteristic of the politics of all less devel-

oped countries. While these personal relations provide a thick density of interaction leading to many useful results (stability, for one thing), they also make it difficult for broad political coalitions to emerge, coalitions that can enact reforms and promote change.[5]

Modern Greece has lacked both an industrial middle class and a working class to diversify its politics and to make it necessary to develop the political institutions found in the industrial West. Greece developed authoritarian political relations but without a bureaucratic (efficient, honest, impartial, impersonal) civil service (the authoritarian pattern, for example, that characterized pre-World II Germany). Greek politics and government reflected the values of the Greek economy and family—it was based on personal contact, influence, and patron-client relations. This pattern has persisted despite urbanization for a simple reason. Greek city dwellers are actually displaced peasants who depend for survival in nonindustrial cities on the same personal characteristics and the same family values that served them in the countryside. A similar pattern (with variations) is found throughout the Third World.

Greece's first genuine parliamentary system emerged in the election of 1974. The struggle for liberal democracy not only ended the Greek monarchy but established that the military was subject to the government, which in turn must command a majority in parliament. The authoritarian state that ruled Greece from independence until the 1960s gave Greece's commercial property class relatively full rein. The emergence of parliamentary government reflects the emergence of a more industrialized and urbanized economy. The Greek polity must now service the needs of a broader, more diversified property

---

[5]For pioneering analyses of patronage politics in the developing world, see Steffan Schmitt, James Scott, Carl Lande, and Laura Guasti, *Friends, Followers, and Factions* (Berkeley, Calif.: University of California Press, 1977); Samuel Eisenstadt and Rene Lemarchand, *Political Clientelism, Patronage, and Development* (Beverly Hills, Calif.: Sage, 1981); and Lucian W. Pye, *Asian Power and Politics* (Cambridge, Mass.: Harvard University Press, 1985).

class as well as workers and ordinary citizens. In the 1980s a socialist government was elected and Greece's polity had to balance a large capitalist and a large socialist party.

Family, Religion, and Education

The family is supremely important to Greek society as it is in preindustrial society in general. The family, especially in rural areas, is nuclear-patrilocal. However, it also extends outward to include other relatives and invariably includes an outside sponsor of a child (the godfather). The family is tightly knit under the authority of the father and is essentially an economic unit geared for survival over the generations. The family openly provides emotional support for all members. The sexes are segregated and children are carefully raised but there is also a substantial amount of equality. In practice wives have power, children are included in family activities at all times, and children of both sexes inherit equally.

The dowry system tells us a great deal about the traditional Greek family and, for that matter, Greek society in general. The dowry is much misunderstood. For example, a dowry is not property used to purchase a husband but a daughter's share of the family inheritance that provides an economic base for women in general. Actually, the dowry has many uses: it promotes marriage between equals; it both prevents and permits social mobility; it guarantees the stability and vitality of family values; it provides economic and other guarantees for all the affected parties (including females and the aged); it prevents property from becoming rigidly tied to family values, thereby promoting (sometimes) a more mobile and rational utilization of resources (the dowry system, in effect, sometimes gives preindustrial societies a functional equivalent of the market system found in the more economically developed societies); and it facilitates social interaction between villages and between villages and urban centers.[6]

The Greek family was a product of agrarian conditions. Given the economic growth of the post-World War II period, the Greek family has changed both in practice and in law to resemble the system in the more industrialized societies. In 1983 the socialist government made basic changes in family law: the dowry as a legal requirement for marriage was abolished, divorce by mutual consent was made much easier, and official discrimination against illegitimate children was ended.

Greece has an established church, the Eastern Orthodox Church of Christ, to which over 95 percent of the population belongs. The Orthodox Church is deeply intertwined with the secular and political life of Greece. The church served to preserve Greek culture and Greece's ethnic and political identity during foreign rule. Between 1825 and 1975 it was part of the authoritarian state. Today it is less central to Greek life and serves as a teacher and moral guide.

Greek orthodoxy is heavily ritualistic and does not stress personal knowledge or conviction in religious matters. The ordinary clergy are not people apart and are not regarded as the bearers of a special morality. In rural areas religious rituals play an important part in the social life of the people but, as has happened elsewhere, church attendance and religious ritual have declined in the cities.

Greeks place a high value on education and families are willing to save and sacrifice to get their children, especially sons, into higher education. The educational system is highly centralized, free, and compulsory to the age of 15. Historically, its basic orientation was toward literature, philosophy, theology, and the law. In addition, higher education (and government) required knowing a variant of the Greek language that was difficult to acquire. The result was to make education in-

---

[6]In these respects, see Elinor G. Barber, "Changing Patterns of Mobility" and Conrad M. Arensberg, "The Irish Countryman" in W. J. Goode, ed., *Readings on the Family and Society* (Englewood Cliffs, N.J.: Prentice-Hall, 1964), Chapters 8 and 9, and Ernestine Friedl, *Vasilika: A Village in Modern Greece* (New York: Holt, Rinehart and Winston, 1962), Chapter 4.

accessible to most of the population and largely irrelevant to the needs of Greek society. However significant changes have occurred especially under the socialist government of the 1980s. The power of university faculties has been curtailed and a much greater emphasis has been placed on technical and scientific education. The socialist government has made the popular tongue the language of Greek society (except in religion). And by equalizing the rights of women and promoting their education, the reforms of recent years have helped to increase access to education for all and to democratize Greek society.

Class and Dependency

Until the 1960s the Greek class system had two poles: small landownership and commerce. By and large, social power lay in the hands of a commercial middle and upper class. Disputes between commercial capitalists, who dominated the national (nondemocratically elected) legislature and the monarchy, which controlled the military, were insubstantial, intrafamily squabbles. However they appeared, they were not conflicts between a popular, democratic force and authoritarianism. This deeper conflict was between the two basic social classes of modern Greece (down to the 1960s when industrial activity began to spawn a working class and manufacturers): the great mass of the Greek people who consisted of marginal peasant families and a commercial bourgeoisie. The latter benefited enormously from a monarchy, a military, and a civil service that (at least until 1975) were clearly not under popular control. Parliamentary institutions obscured rather than expressed class relations. The overgrown civil service tied the peasantry into a system of dependence based on patronage and credit arrangements. Formalistic, irrelevant politics and education, including a variant of the Greek language that the masses could not master, effectively insured the dominance of a mercantile middle class, as well as the autonomy of monarchy and military.

With the growth of industry and urbanization in the 1960s and 1970s a new dimension was added to the Greek class structure—the dominant mercantile class now included an industrial sector and the dominated now included a propertyless urban proletariat. The development of Greek politics has reflected this new reality—Greek power groups can no longer assume the subservience of the masses and contentedly squabble among themselves. From the 1960s on it became clear that Greece's power groups would have to fight for the support of the Greek people.

In many ways modern Greece is a creation of outside forces. The rise of capitalism in Western Europe inaugurated an international division of labor. The Eastern Mediterranean became a supplier of food and agricultural staples. From the seventeenth century on, Greece (along with contemporary Turkey, Egypt, and others) developed as an underdeveloped country. Greek agriculture was commercialized and Greek traders prospered both in and outside Greece. The Greek economy developed some important handicraft and shipbuilding sectors during the eighteenth century only to have them destroyed by competition from industrialized England.

Greek independence in 1825 was largely due to English, French, and Russian imperialist actions against the Ottoman Empire. From 1825 until after World War II Greece was subject to British influence. The characteristic pattern of British imperialism was portfolio investment: loans to governments who would use it to build the infrastructure of nationhood: roads, railroads, generating plants, communications, a military-police force, and a civil service. The classic British pattern was to develop a state strong enough to repay loans and to develop the country for its role in the international division of labor. British portfolio investment effectively suited the mercantile character of Greece's property classes and gave added impetus to Greece's development as an underdeveloped society lacking an industrial sector.

After World War II the United States replaced Britain as the major outside power in Greece's internal development. The Truman Doctrine proclaimed in 1947 was an economic and military aid program to Greece (later extended by the Marshall Plan). The Truman Doctrine also set the stage for the United States' foreign policy in the period after World War II: bypass the United Nations, rely on military aid and political support to compliant right-wing governments, give economic aid that prevents industrialization and facilitates raw material exports, set favorable conditions for American investment, promise open-ended support against radicalism or Communism to prevent collapse in whatever part of the world is involved (the domino argument that if one country "falls" surrounding countries will also fall), and frame all actions in the language of universal values and democracy. American military aid to right-wing forces helped to defeat Communism in the chaos after the withdrawal of German occupation forces but it also ensured the emergence of a right-wing dictatorship. Humanitarian aid steered Greece toward its traditional economy. By the 1960s the classic American pattern of imperialism was in full view: direct investment, especially in industry, and direct involvement in the modernization of the military, the police, and the civil service. American imperialism has led to an industrial sector not linked organically to Greek society. Given the highly favorable terms arranged with the Greek state, the main benefits of Greek industrialization flowed abroad. An unintended result of American investment has been the creation of an urban working class and a new mood of popular militancy.

Greece has been subject to outside forces in many other ways. Not only did it have a German monarch imposed on it in the nineteenth century (which helped make its internal politics irrelevant and obscure) but its military has had more in common with first the British and now with the American governments than with its own people. Greece's internal political and social development was also profoundly affected by the Greek tradition of "exporting" its surplus population either as traders, immigrants, or guest workers. And the Greek diaspora has furthered Greece's development as an underdeveloped nation by providing it with foreign capital for education, village development, commerce,

but not for industry. And the many Greek communities abroad, especially in the United States, have given modern Greece important spokespeople for the defense of its interests in international affairs.

Greece's current foreign policy concerns involve disputes with Turkey over Cyprus (Turkey invaded Cyprus in 1974 and occupies one-third of the island in response to what it perceived as a threat to the island's Turkish-Cypriot minority of 18 percent) and over the Aegean Sea (Turkey has made new claims to air rights and undersea rights to the Aegean and so far has refused to allow the World Court to adjudicate the dispute). Both of these issues affect the performance of Greece and Turkey in NATO and at present Greece is blocking Turkey's request to enter the European Community. And both parties feel that the United States has sided with the other.[7]

Greece's economic growth in the period from the end of World War II to 1980 was one of the highest in the world. Its gross national product of U.S. $39.5 billion and per capita of $3,950 (1986) put it well below the more industrialized countries but well above most of the Third World. Its growth, especially in manufacturing, is impressive, but Greece has moved from underdevelopment to dependent development. It is now better able to direct its affairs but cannot escape dependence on the world market and has been unable to live within its means.

The socialist government of the 1980s has sought to redirect Greece's foreign policy away from its alignment with the United States and to direct more explicitly the Greek economy. The goal of Greek socialism is a more democratic society through increased economic growth and public participation in decision making. To accomplish these goals, the socialist government has asserted government control over some basic industries, promoted development outside the Athens area, decentralized decision making, and promoted economic deci-

---

[7]For a balanced analysis, see Theodore A. Couloumbis, *The United States, Greece, and Turkey: The Troubled Triangle* (New York: Praeger, 1983).

sion making through boards composed of workers, consumers, and government representatives. During the 1980s the government found that Greece's maneuvering is limited by its position in the international economy and that it had raised expectations higher than it could satisfy. When the world economy slowed in the mid-1980s the socialist government's austerity program (plus corruption) led to electoral defeat in 1989.

PERU

Peru represents a particular variation of a capitalist dependency, one that emerged from the imperialism of a backward monarchy, Spain. What is true of Peru is also true of most of Latin America and the Philippines. The study of Peru, therefore, should be placed in a wider Latin American context. Here as elsewhere, we will try to let voices from the area being analyzed speak for themselves.

Land and People[8]

Ecological factors are always important in social structure and process but perhaps more so in the case of Peru. Peruvian society has been massively influenced by its three distinct geographical zones: the coast, the sierra, and the jungle. Peru's major development has occurred on the coast, which contains half of its population of approximately 21 million. The Selva or jungle region is still sparsely settled.

One-third of the Peruvian population is Indian, one-half *mestizos* (descendants of Spaniards and Indians), and one-seventh is white, mostly descendants of Spanish colonists. Most of the population speaks Spanish, although Indian languages are still common. Roman Catholicism is the religion of 95 percent of the population. Population growth is a burdensome 2.5 percent.

Spanish imperial expansion, in the person of Pizarro, brought Peru (then Inca society) into Spain's orbit in 1532. Inca society was quickly and ruthlessly subdued and the agrarian autocratic, feudal practices of Spain blended easily with the autocratic feudal practices of Inca society (based on advanced horticulture).[9] Colonization from Spain soon led to a variant of the white settler form of colonial society—a tiny elite from the outside superimposed on a large native population. Unlike English white settler colonialism, however, Spanish rule did not bifurcate the population by race. The whites and native Indians blended to form a large group of mixed-blood Peruvians.

Economy

Peru's coastal plain is arid because the cool Peruvian or Humboldt current dries the air before it reaches shore. The desert plain supports a rich agriculture, however, because of the many rivers that flow to the sea from the Andes. The coastal plain is also the center of the world's largest fishing industry. The same cool current that shapes the rainfall pattern of Peru churns up nutrients in the ocean creating one of the world's most valuable fishing areas. A small industrial sector is tied to Peru's agricultural strengths and to its mineral resources: food processing, beverages, textiles, clothing, farm and mining machinery. Peru is also rich in minerals, with most of its mining located in the sierra. Peru's extensive forests are potentially valuable but remain largely untapped.

---

[8]*Peru: A Country Study*, 3rd ed. (Washington, DC: U. S. Government Printing Office, 1981), Foreign Area Studies, The American University, provides valuable information about all aspects of Peruvian society. David Scott Palmer, *Peru: The Authoritarian Tradition* (New York: Praeger, 1980) provides a brief but meaty history. Three valuable compilations covering almost every aspect of Peruvian society are Abraham F. Lowenthal, ed., *The Peruvian Experiment: Continuity and Change Under Military Rule* (Princeton, N.J.: Princeton University Press, 1975); David Chaplin, ed., *Peruvian Nationalism: A Corporatist Revolution* (New Brunswick, N.J.: Transaction Books, 1976); and Cynthia McClintock and Abraham F. Lowenthal, eds., *The Peruvian Experiment Reconsidered* (Princeton, N.J.: Princeton University Press, 1983).

[9]For a previous discussion of horticultural society, see Chapter 2.

The Peruvian economy is unusual in that it is a diversified export economy, though ups and downs in the international economy often force reliance on one or two of its products.[10] Historically, Peru was sharply divided into an export-oriented, land and capital intensive agro-extractive-urban sector, on the one hand, and subsistence farming by large haciendas in the Sierra (employing serf-like labor), along with small marginal holdings, on the other hand (the sierra has recently developed a significant export crop in coffee). It is a distinctly dual economy in which the bulk of national income is generated by the modern export sector employing only one-third of the work force. In 1986 its GDP of $19.8 billion yielded a per capita income of $980.[11]

From independence in the early nineteenth century until 1968, Peru developed as a relatively static export-oriented, oligarchic society. Its tiny oligarchy had two wings: the owners of large haciendas in the sierra (comprising a relatively self-sufficient manorial economy) who lived on the coast, especially Lima, and an export-based elite who ran the sugar and cotton estates on the coast and the copper and other mines in the sierra. The oligarchy also included auxiliary groups: bankers, merchants, insurance companies, professionals, and government officials.

Most significant about Peru's economic history, therefore, has been its inability to break away from an export economy. With its resources in the hands of a tiny handful of families and its dependence on outsiders for markets and capital, Peru's economy has a long history of small growth and extreme economic inequality. The little growth that has taken place in recent decades has been accompanied by more economic inequality and greater poverty. The absence of growth, even economic decline in recent years, has caused widespread misery and shaken its newly acquired system of representative government.

Polity

Peru's political institutions are a combination of Inca and Spanish absolutism: the Spanish Conquest caused essentially the replacement of one elite by another. The social base of Peruvian absolutism or *caudillista* (strongman) rule is the landowning oligarchy. While Peru's oligarchy has had its differences, especially between the export-oriented, agro-extractive property interests and the absentee landowners of the upland haciendas, by and large, they have cooperated to maintain a united front against the vast majority of the population. The working alliance among landowners encouraged localism, especially between coast and sierra and produced a deep cleavage between Peru's cities and its rural hinterland. The feudal-bourgeois oligarchy also retarded the growth of a civic or public culture. Until the military takeover in 1968, Peru had only the rudiments of nationhood. With the great mass of the population tied to subsistence agriculture, there was little need to develop political institutions. In addition, the rugged and difficult terrain made transportation and communication difficult and helped to retard political as well as economic development.

Peru's strongman-weak state polity is endemic to Latin America and to many parts of the developing world. Until World War I, the Peruvian state simply reflected the various factions in the oligarchy. It had no independent power to force settlements on any part of the oligarchy. There was no army loyal to the state or nation but rather a series of private armies loyal to local strongmen. The state had no autonomous sources of money since it could not tax the wealthy—most of its meager revenues came from customs duties and a few other indirect taxes. The state had some police duties, especially in the cities, but provided little in the way of education, social security, health care, sanitation, fire protection, or transportation.

---

[10]For a detailed history and analysis of the Peruvian economy, see Rosemary Thorp and Geoffrey Bertran, *Peru 1890–1977: Growth and Policy in An Open Economy* (New York: Columbia University Press, 1978).

[11]Central Intelligence Agency, *The World Factbook 1988* (Washington, D.C.: U. S. Government Printing Office, 1988), p. 189.

Between 1968 and 1980 Peru witnessed an attempted revolution from above[12] by a military government (for an assessment, see below). During this period Peru acquired the rudiments of a modern state. For the first time in Peru's history, an autonomous state emerged, that is, a state not tied to or representating a single interest. Further, the state, at least for a time, was able to force concessions from the various sectors of Peruvian society. The government developed its own staff to match its new role as both an owner of economic properties and as an economic regulator. And the state began to provide a wide range of public services, especially in the areas of education, health, transportation, and police.

The military dictatorship from 1968 until the return to an elected civilian government in 1980 was essentially a nation-building effort. Reflecting and furthering the diversification of Peruvian society, the military reform movement helped prepare Peru for representative (civilian) government. It promoted economic diversification, essentially capitalist in nature, and a more diversified foreign policy, largely to escape dependence on the United States. In 1985, a second elected civilian government replaced the civilian government elected in 1980—this was a first for Peruvian politics. The new government inherited an extremely depressed economy and a festering guerrilla movement. The new left-of-center government took action to stimulate the economy but only made problems, including the guerrilla movement, worse. The dependence of Peru on the world market and its inability to transcend class cleavage at home had again become clear (for an analysis of the domestic power structure in relation to Peru's dependence on the world market, see below).[13]

---

[12]For a discussion of revolution from above and the various routes to the modern world, see Chapter 5.

[13]For a straightforward, if perhaps overly optimistic, picture of Peru's political development toward democracy (representative government), see Paul P. Saba, *Political Development and Democracy In Peru* (Boulder, Colo.: Westview Press, 1987).

Family, Religion, and Education

Like all preindustrial societies Peru places great stress on family values. The family is the key institution for most of the population regardless of its ethnic background or its position in the economic or political hierarchy. However, unlike societies characterized by freeholding farmers (for example, Greece and French Canada), the Peruvian family is not an autonomous, self-sufficient unit with its own economic base.

Roman Catholicism is the religion of 95 percent of the Peruvian people. Ethnically, the Peruvian population contains a fairly rigid hierarchy. Until recently, a small white Spanish-origin elite dominated the vast bulk of the population. Located primarily in Lima, the tiny white Spanish-origin oligarchy formed a tightly knit group bound by kinship, intermarriage, elitist Spanish-based sociocultural traditions and forms of association, leisure, and consumption.

In the absence of an impersonal market economy and an electoral politics, Peru has a well-defined agrarian sense of individuality and self-sufficiency, which in the Spanish tradition is known as personalism (*personalismo*). Normative traditions that stress personal qualities are common to all agrarian societies. As we saw earlier, individuality, a stress on seeing other individuals as persons, self-sufficiency, and personal honor were norms and values common to Greek society. Also common to Greece, Peru, and other agrarian systems is a focus on seeing people in terms of kinship, friendship, or other ascriptive relations, especially male and female statuses. As is common in almost all complex preindustrial systems, the sexes in Peru are sharply differentiated. In ways common to much of the agrarian world, the male is defined as superior to females and acquires a distinctive male personality. In Peru and the Latin tradition male personality traits stress self-confidence, action, virility, and daring (*machismo*).

A distinctive feature of established "feudalized" agrarian systems is a stress on social status. Unlike Greece, Peru developed as a pronounced landowning oligarchy. Peru's normative system includes, therefore, a well-developed sense of the behavior appropriate to rungs in the social hierarchy. Ideally, all individuals should be treated well as persons but always in keeping with their station in life.

Peru's Indian population is also family oriented and segregated by sex but as a conquered and subjugated people it understandably lacks the aggressive individuality of the Spanish *machismo* tradition.

Education is valued in all complex societies but for different reasons and in different ways. Peru had no mass educational system until the revolutionary military regime of 1968 inaugurated educational reforms as part of its effort to incorporate the masses into Peruvian society. There was relatively no need for a literate or technically skilled population under the landowning oligarchy. University education was valued largely because it validated social status (and offered some social mobility). The landed oligarchy actually had negative views about intellectual activity.

The emergence of a middle class after World War II invigorated the universities and today university education is seen more widely as an avenue to social mobility and as a means of achieving self-directed nationhood. The new military government stressed more programs in the natural sciences and in occupationally related subjects and has reformed the universities to neutralize the political power of students. The stress on an up-to-date education, more accessible to the entire population, has continued under the elected civilian governments of the 1980s.

Class and Dependency

The distribution of economic wealth and income is very unequal in all complex societies though in some, such as Peru, economic inequality is perhaps more extreme than most. The dual or feudal-bourgeois oligarchy that dominated Peru until the 1960s concentrated economic, social, and political resources in a handful of families and, by and large, saw to it that a disproportionate share of economic growth remained at the top. Peru's income distribution is similar (perhaps a little more unequal) to that found in most developing nations. The highest 10 percent of households had 42.9 percent of income (1972) while the top 20 had 61 percent of the total. The lowest 20 percent had 1.9 percent while the bottom 40 percent received 7 percent of the total.[14]

Given the sources of their economic strength, the Peruvian oligarchy had little need of a strong state (as opposed to strongman rule) during much of Peru's history. A strong state is needed to integrate a nation through communication and transport networks. A strong state provides education and directs the economy to provide balance and exploit strengths. A strong state controls currency and credit to serve economic development needs. And a strong state remains strong if it can distribute the benefits of society in ways deemed fair and just.

The traditional Peruvian oligarchy was not oriented toward an internal market and it had no need to mobilize the masses since it lived off either an inert mass of peasants or through export trade. Members of the oligarchy did not even like to talk of a Peruvian nation since it implied that they had something in common with the masses. By the 1960s, however, an important industrial sector had emerged in Peru together with a significant urban middle class. The strongman-weak state that had served the export-hacienda oligarchy was no longer in keeping with the thrust of the Peruvian economy. By the 1960s Peru had a number of disaffected groups, including a guerrilla movement in the countryside. The Peruvian oligarchy lacked the mechanisms to crush or coopt the various disaffected groups. It was also clear that the new middle class was not strong enough to achieve a bourgeois revolution. The only modernized sector of the state was the military, which had developed (with American help) largely in response to internal disorder (and disputes with neighboring countries). In 1968 the military stepped in to modernize Peru's antiquated state and its disjointed institutions.

---

[14]World Bank, *World Development Report, 1986* (New York: Oxford University Press, 1986), Table 24.

Revolutions from above are not uncommon (see the section, The Preparatory Period in Chapter 3, and the section, Revolution From Above, in Chapter 5). In thinking about revolution (the movement from one type of society to another) one must focus on power. Slaves, serfs, and peasants often revolt but because they lack power they rarely succeed. Revolution occurs when power groups decline and new power groups arise. A revolution may occur when a given power group is smashed by military defeat (Russian Revolution) or where war so enervates a defunct and corrupt system that newcomers can seize power (Chinese Communist Revolution). Revolution should not be thought of as the masses (who by definition are weak) rising against those in power.

Even the bourgeois revolutions of England and France were struggles among power groups, not uprisings by the people. Peru's "revolution" in 1968 was by a military that used the term revolutionary to describe its aims.[15] The Peruvian military's success in achieving power was due to a number of factors: the military was disciplined and could act as a unified force; it was recruited from the middle and lower middle classes and had no ties to any of the wings of the oligarchy; its morale was high because it had been successful against a guerrilla uprising in 1965; and its tours of duty throughout Peru gave it an all-Peruvian perspective. By 1968 the strongman-weak state oligarchy was obviously not capable of running the country or even maintaining public order for very much longer and the military acted.

The military regime that took power in 1968 did so to modernize Peru and build a national state. Its basic reforms have been extensive. It destroyed the hacienda system and affected a significant redistribution of land. Water was nationalized to ensure equitable access. It created many of the mechanisms of the modern state to service a more complex economy. Government agencies and departments were established to guide and stimulate all areas of the once totally private economy. The government took direct control of the central bank and now controls a large majority of direct bank business. It also established an agency to finance economic development. The government established its own marketing boards, and fishing, the railroads, and the telephone system are now government owned. The military also acted to reduce foreign holdings in the Peruvian economy and took a tougher line in negotiating contracts with foreign firms and governments. It proposed ambitious plans for industrial development including direct state investment. And it insisted that the larger business enterprises still in private hands develop worker-participation, cooperative schemes.

The military government also acted to induce participation at the local level and to extend education. Its explicit purpose was to incorporate workers, including the large Indian population, into the life of society. And it committed Peru toward providing "health for all."

Despite these initiatives the military had only limited success. Essentially, it promoted a fuller, broader-based capitalist society. Almost all of the new benefits have gone to the upper 25 percent of the population. Peruvian health care remains lopsidedly urban. Unlike socialist governments (and some capitalist), which concentrate on primary care and reach out to rural areas, Peru's health care system is inefficient and geared to the upper classes. As such the health of Peru's population does not compare well even with other Latin American countries with its per capita income.[16] The worker participation schemes have created a coopted worker elite and diffused class awareness. The modern agro-extractive sector still received the most attention and the most capital, leaving a badly skewed income distribution, a poor internal market, a back-

---

[15]For a comparative discussion, see Ellen Kay Trimberger, *Revolution from Above: Military Bureaucrats and Development in Japan, Turkey, Egypt, and Peru* (New Brunswick, N.J.: Transaction Books, 1978).

[16]For a superb set of essays on Peru's health care system, including reform proposals, see Dieter K. Zschock, ed., *Health Care In Peru: Resources and Policy* (Boulder, Colo.: Westview Press, 1988).

ward subsistence farm economy, and a continuing exodus from the land to the city. The military government could not hope to redistribute resources or balance the economy without taking from the urban middle and upper classes. To do this would have required a radicalization of the masses; instead its basic strategy was to coopt the masses and to diffuse their aspirations.[17]

The reforms of the 1970s did little to alter Peru's dependency on the outer world. Dependency theorists range from those who see outsiders as the main cause of dependency to those who stress the interaction of outside forces with local forces.[18] So far the evidence supports the latter interpretation. A careful study by Goodsell of American business and governmental forces in Peru indicates no preponderant American influence on Peruvian politics. American corporations in Peru with the help of the American embassy were active and eager to have their wishes satisfied in Peru but they were not always successful. Since 1968 the Peruvian government has taken

steps to reduce foreign penetration.[19] Goodsell does not address the major issue, however. British and American investments in Peru may not have been of large magnitude in relation to Peru's overall economy. But the impact of even small amounts of foreign investment was and is considerable because it coincided with the basic structure of the Peruvian economy and polity. Whatever the intentions of foreign investors, what count are consequences. Peru's economy is still deeply dependent on its past and on outside forces: foreign markets, foreign capital, and loans (from governments and the World Bank). Peru's polity is also dependent on American government and foundation help in developing its police and armed forces, education, and civil service. All in all, the basic changes in Peruvian national life have so far been cosmetic: a national state led by a reformist military has simply facilitated a change from visible control by an internal oligarchy and external companies to the invisible control of the world market economy securely anchored in the main power structure of Peruvian society—its export sector serviced by a modernized state.[20]

Peru's system of representative government seemed well planted in the mid-1980s. Whether elected civilian government can continue and whether it can make a difference remain to be seen. The left-of-center Garcia government has acted to assert limits on Peru's debt (it declared that payments on its debt to foreigners cannot exceed 10 percent of its export earnings).[21] It has also acted to direct

---

[17]For these developments, see E. V. K. Fitzgerald, *The State and Economic Development: Peru Since 1968* (New York: Cambridge University Press, 1976) and *The Political Economy of Peru, 1956–1978: Economic Development and the Restructuring of Capital* (New York: Cambridge University Press, 1979), George D. E. Philip, *The Rise and Fall of the Peruvian Military Radicals, 1968–1976* (London: Athlone Press, 1978), David Booth and Bernardo Sorj, eds., *Military Reformism and Social Classes: The Peruvian Experience, 1968–80* (New York: St. Martin's Press, 1983), and Cynthia McClintock and Abraham F. Lowenthal, eds., *The Peruvian Experiment Reconsidered* (Princeton, N.J.: Princeton University Press, 1983).

[18]Latin America has generated the main bulk of dependency theory. The basic pioneering works, either by Latin Americans or about Latin America, are Andre Gunder Frank, *Capitalism and Underdevelopment In Latin America* (New York Monthly Review Press, 1967) and *Lumpenbourgeoisie and Lumpendevelopment* (New York: Monthly Review Press, 1972); Rodolfo Stavenhagen, *Social Classes In Agrarian Societies* (Garden City, N.Y.: Doubleday, 1975); a valuable comparison of Latin American and African developments; Fernando Henrique Cardoso and Enzo Faletto, tr. Marjory Mattingly Urquidi, *Dependency and Development in Latin America* (Berkeley, Calif.: University of California Press, 1979); and Peter Evans, *Dependent Development: The Alliance of Multinational, State, and Local Capital In Brazil* (Princeton, N.J.: Princeton University Press, 1979).

[19]Charles T. Goodsell, *American Corporations and Peruvian Politics* (Cambridge, Mass.: Harvard University Press, 1974). For a general history of the relation of the United States to three Andean societies, see Frederick B. Pike, *The United States and the Andean Republics: Peru, Bolivia, and Ecuador* (Cambridge, Mass.: Harvard University Press, 1977).

[20]Cynthia McClintock and Abraham F. Lowenthal, eds., *The Peruvian Experiment Reconsidered* (Princeton, N.J.: Princeton University Press, 1983).

[21]For a careful history and assessment of Peru's debt, which blames Peru but mostly the IMF (seen as an instrument of the developed world), see Thomas Scheetz, *Peru and the International Monetary Fund* (Pittsburgh: University of Pittsburgh Press, 1986).

the Peruvian economy, at first with more skill than previous governments but recently a number of innovative policies have failed and failed badly. But civilian government, no less than the reformist military government of 1968–80, cannot transcend the internal deficiencies generated by Peru's history: conflict of interest between rural and urban areas, between workers and propertyowners, a weak entrepreneurial class, insufficient internal savings, inadequate tax base, and heavy foreign debt. A move to favor rural development means higher prices for urban consumers and less capital for industry and public services. Rural development is hurt if the government acts to aid urban consumers. Helping workers alienates business and retards entrepreneurial activity. These class cleavages lead to a stagnant economy and it in turn aggravates class cleavage. The traditional way out is to borrow from abroad and invite foreign investment. This leaves Peru prey to the volatility of foreign markets and a further loss of social self-determination.

By the late 1980s, Peru's intrinsic problems, worsened by poor government economic policies, had reached crisis proportions. Runaway inflation, unemployment, a growing guerilla movement, and inability to borrow because of a boycott by international lenders had narrowed Peru's options and were even threatening its system of representative government.

THE REPUBLIC OF (SOUTH) KOREA

Land and People[22]

Korea (formerly called Chosen, the land of the morning calm) occupies a peninsula on the Northeast coast of Asia. Korea has a distinctive language and culture though it has been massively influenced by its giant neighbors, China and Japan.

The population of South Korea in 1988 was 42.7 million.[23] The religion of South Korea is primarily Buddhist but Confucists and Christians represent sizable minorities. South Korea is not well endowed with natural resources. It lacks minerals and fuels, its topography is mountaineous, its soil poor, and overcutting has denuded it of trees. Aside from its hardworking, disciplined people, perhaps its most valuable resource is its fishing waters.

Korea has a continuous history of settlement that stretches back into paleolithic times. The various groups on the Korean peninsula were united in the seventh century and Korea remained a unified kingdom until 1905 when it was occupied by Japan (formally annexed by Japan in 1910). Feudal Korea was similar to Imperial China and in general conformed to authoritarian or state feudalism rather than manorial, decentralized, stateless feudalism.[24]

Land is the basis of power under all forms of feudalism. In advanced agrarian systems large landowners supplement their local power by participating in a central power structure. Under the Chinese system the gentry prepared their sons to take rigorous examinations in the classics, the gateway to highly prized positions in the Emperor's civil service. Confucianism supplied the legitimating ideology for China's power structure. Though it has distinctive nuances, Confucianism has many similarities with other feudal symbolic forms. As is common in feudal symbolic systems, Confucianism gave a central position

[22]*South Korea: A Country Study*, 3rd ed. (Washington, DC: U. S. Government Printing Office, 1982), Foreign Area Studies, the American University, provides invaluable background on all aspects Korean history, culture, and society, including the separation of North Korea after

World War II. An indispensable companion to this volume is *North Korea: A Country Study*, 3rd ed. (Washington, DC: U. S. Government Printing Office, 1981). Further studies and contrasts between the two Koreas may be found in Young Whan Kihl, *Politics and Politics in Divided Korea: Regimes in Contest* (Boulder, Colo.: Westview, 1984) and Donald Stone Macdonald, *The Koreans: Contemporary Politics and Society* (Boulder, Colo.: Westview, 1988). David I. Steinberg's focus on South Korea, *The Republic of Korea: Economic Transformation and Social Change* (Boulder, Colo.: Westview, 1989) reflects the growing scholarship in the United States on Korea but (as is true of the other general works cited above), fails to interpret Korea in terms of dependency and world system theory.

[23]The population of North Korea in 1988 was an estimated 22 million.

[24]For a discussion of agrarian society, see Chapter 2.

to the family or, rather, the patriarchal family. The authority of the father and thus the superiority of males is the linchpin of the entire system. Filial piety is the most important obligation, and the hierarchical family is the model for thinking about society. The ultimate image in Confucian as well as feudal thought in general is of a harmonious, finished hierarchy that extends from one end of human nature to nature at large. The essential value for all to seek, in keeping with their station in life, is the world's harmony.

Feudal Korea was a highly concentrated society dominated by a handful of large landowning families. The concentration of power continued under Japanese rule and has continued into the present despite Korea's independence and industrialization.

With the defeat of Japan in World War II, the U.S.S.R. occupied the Northern half of the Korean peninsula and the United States occupied the Southern half. Contemporary Korea is divided into the Republic of (South) Korea and the People's Republic of (North) Korea.

Economy[25]

For various reasons, including influence and pressure from the outside, Korea's economy and polity tended to promote concentrated landholding. For much of its history feudal Korea was subsistence oriented. Perhaps the chief activity beyond its rural economy was moneylending. There is evidence of increased market activity in the nineteenth century as Korea experienced other foreign influences besides China, most notably Japan and Western countries.

Under Japanese rule Korea developed as a typical colonial economy. Japan treated Korea as booty—it took over all land, businesses, and government and colonized it with a thick strata of Japanese who occupied all important positions. The Korean agricultural sector became export centered to supply Japan with food and staples while Japan supplied Korea with manufactured products.

World War II and the Korean War of 1950–53 brought new forms of economic devastation to Korea. After the stalemate and negotiated peace of 1953 massive American aid and investment (matched and then surpassed by Japanese investment in the 1970s) wrought a significant transformation in the Korean economy. During the 1960s Korea had one of the highest economic growth rates in the world. Essentially its economy was oriented toward exporting from a labor-intensive manufacturing sector. Using imported capital, Korea also imported most of its raw materials and exported them in the form of finished goods.

Korea's agricultural sector was bypassed by its industrial boom. Land reform after World War II had ended Korea's long history of large feudal landholding. Korea took back its economy after the defeat of Japan and redistributed the large Japanese-held lands to its own people. The effect, however, was not to produce a balanced economy or a greater equality of political power. Korean autocracy and elitism switched from agriculture to industry and services. As always Korea was dependent on outsiders. The impact of China during Korea's early history had helped to produce a hierarchical, concentrated bureaucratic agrarian economy and society. The Japanese reinforced this structure by deliberately using it to dominate and exploit Korea between 1910 and 1945 (the United States also relied on the feudal-authoritarian tradition during its occupation between 1945–48 thereby giving it added legitimacy). Korea's modernization after 1948, based on its own efforts, massive American aid and military protection, and American and Japanese investment, took place within this feudal-authoritarian system.[26]

---

[25]For indispensable background and analysis of all of Korea's institutions, see Norman Jacobs, *The Korean Road to Modernization and Development* (Urbana, Ill.: University of Illinois Press, 1985).

[26]For a brilliant analysis of how and why Korea modernized without developing (a useful distinction), see Norman Jacobs, *The Korean Road to Modernization and Development* (Urbana, Ill.: University of Illinois Press, 1985). By modernization Jacobs means adopting new ways of achieving old values and by *development* he means maximizing the potential of a society regardless of existing values or organizational structures (one has to conclude that what Jacobs means by this is development into a capitalist democracy).

Korea's economic development deviates considerably from other Third-World countries. Significant steps toward industrialization have been taken; its standard of living has shown a steady increase; and its inequality, while considerable, is more in line with developed rather than developing countries. Its GNP of $118 billion in 1987 yielded a per capita income of $2,800.[27] Korea's economic success is due to a number of factors. Japan's occupation from 1905 to 1945 and land reform, thanks to the American occupation after World War II, left Korea without a landed oligarchy to oppose modernization and industrialization. In addition, an uprooted population fell back on a cultural tradition that stressed discipline, hierarchy, state service, and respect for education. And Korea's government has provided a wide variety of support facilities and services, including reliable statistics and planning services.

In an important sense, like Japan and Germany (and perhaps the U.S.S.R.), Korea derived significant benefits from the devastation of war (and in Korea's case from colonial exploitation). The destruction of Japanese and German industry during World War II allowed both countries to build the world's most modern factories. Together with guilt and shame over their defeat, a traditional sociocultural system that stressed discipline, employee loyalty, and a hierarchical world, in addition to massive American aid, including military protection, Japan and Germany channelled their efforts into industry. Much the same can be said of the Republic of Korea.

It should be noted that Korea's economic success since the 1960s is no miracle of free enterprise and should not be considered to result from Korean efforts alone. Korea's economic success should also not be attributed to abstract forces like Confucian values or education. Korea (like any society) is a product of history.

Chinese hierarchical feudal forms certainly played a part, but Korea is also a result of Japan's imperial expansion from the late nineteenth century through World War II. The Japanese conquest and colonization provided Korea with much of what it needed to become part of the capitalist world. And Korea is also a result of American policy since World War II. The United States' major foreign policy goal in Asia has been to contain and rollback Communism. To that end it fought the Korean war and it supported Korea with massive economic aid of various sorts including making its own giant market available to Korean exports.[28]

A World Bank analysis attributes Korea's competitive edge to private-public cooperation, or rather to the Korean government's skill in providing incentives to private producers oriented toward export markets. The analysis stresses the importance to these producers of being able to rely on long-term government support of the export-oriented manufacturing sector. It also cites the importance of Korea's work force, with its Confucian-derived beliefs in loyalty, punctuality, hard work, and respect for authority, and of foreign capital. The report fails to note that the Korean government is authoritarian, that Korean labor is managed in a military manner, works a 55–60 hour week, and is consistently repressed and unable to organize. The World Bank also fails to note that Korea's export-centered economy has made it vulnerable (dependent) to the world market, put it deeply in debt, and is not connected to, and thus not producing benefits for, Korean society in general. Needless to say, the report fails to place Korea in history or in the context of Japanese and American imperial expansion and policies.[29]

---

[27]Central Intelligence Agency, *The World Factbook 1988* (Washington, D.C.: U. S. Government Printing Office, 1988), p. 131.

[28]For a valuable analysis placing the economic success of Korea (as well as Taiwan and Japan) into its historical context, including the role played by Japanese and American imperialism, see Bruce Cumings, "The Origin and Development of the Northeast Asian Political Economy: Industrial Sectors, Product Cycles, and Political Consequences," *International Organization* 38 (Winter 1984): 1–40.

[29]Yung Rhee, Bruce Ross-Larson, and Garry Pursell, *Korea's Competitive Edge: Managing The Entry Into World Markets* (Baltimore: The Johns Hopkins University Press, 1984), a World Bank report.

A number of other liberal analyses have also failed to explain Korea's economic "miracle." In addition to specific deficiencies, these studies also fail to place Korea in history or to cite the enormous impact that Japan and the United States have had in preparing Korea for economic expansion (and dependency).[30]

There can be little doubt about one thing, however: Korea's economic success is real and puts it in a select group of Third-World countries that have managed to achieve significant economic growth, *including relative gains against the developed world*. By the late 1980s its consistent trade surpluses and overseas assets had made its foreign debt a negligible factor. As is true of many developing capitalist countries, however, Korea's industrial sector is not organically linked to Korean society and its benefits do not flow evenly or equitably to the Korean people. In Korea, as in Greece and Peru (and throughout the developing capitalist world), American and First-World aid and investment have promoted a highly concentrated dual economy and an authoritarian political regime.

Polity

Korea's political institutions, like its economy, have been massively influenced by outsiders.[31] Korea did not develop as a decentralized, self-sufficient feudal society. The landed elite of a self-sufficient manorial economy fears the state and retards its growth even as it develops enough state power to maintain the status quo. A good part of England's political development, for example, is explained by the successful resistance of its landed nobility to royal power. The Magna Carta is essentially a feudal document in which a landed nobility curtailed the growth of a central power. In France the landed nobility neglected their estates and allowed themselves to be drawn to the royal court. As a result, royal power not only grew but became arbitrary, autocratic, and corrupt. In the modern world oligarchies whose power is based on self-sufficient estates behave much on the order of Peru's hacienda owners. The owners of Peru's self-sufficient agricultural sector, it will be remembered, cooperated with the owners of Peru's agroextractive sector to retard the development of nationhood and to create a strongman-weak state polity.

Political institutions in China, Korea, and Japan, as well as in Prussia, Russia, and the Ottoman Empire were ideally based on the absolute authority of the ruler. The absolute power of the ruler, it must be noted, extended over the nobility and not just the masses. Korea, following China's practice, developed an employee mentality among its entire population—the elite prepared for examinations for state service while the remainder of the population worked for their superiors in a hierarchy that ended in a supreme ruler.

The most successful modernizers among the above group were Prussia and Japan. Both countries developed an efficient, centralized, bureaucratically organized system of state power in the service of feudal values, and both countries managed to escape dependence on outside powers. In both countries modernization led to movement away from feudal values and into liberal democracy only through defeat in war.

[30]L. L. Wade and B. S. Kim, *Economic Development of South Korea: The Political Economy of Success* (New York: Praeger, 1978) provides a useful analysis of Korea's economic "miracle," including invaluable comparisons with other developing countries but it too fails to mention Korea's authoritarian-repressive political regime and the major handicap such a regime presents for coping with economic difficulties. The volume by Edward S. Mason *et al., The Economic and Social Modernization of the Republic of Korea* (Cambridge, Mass.: Council on East Asian Studies, Harvard University, 1980), which summarizes seven studies of Korea's modernization, is another example of the complacent liberal view of modernization. Relying on scanty, biased data and ignoring dependency theory, this book exaggerates Korean income equality, the spread of benefits to the population at large, and the role of education, and has few misgivings about the export economy (no mention is made of Korea's huge debt) or the repressive political system.

[31]For analyses of Korean political institutions that provide valuable historical contrasts and continuities, see Gregory Henderson, *Korea: The Politics of the Vortex*

(Cambridge, MA: Harvard University Press, 1968), Edward Reynolds Wright, ed., *Korean Politics in Transition* (Seattle: University of Washington Press, 1975), and especially Norman Jacobs, *The Korean Road to Modernization and Development* (Urbana, Il.: University of Illinois Press, 1985).

Korea has also modernized successfully due in large part to its authoritarian experience.[32] Korea's social order and political system came largely from its giant neighbor China. That system was reinforced by Japan and the United States. Korea's status as a Japanese colony reinforced the authoritarian system and deprived Korea of valuable political experience. The Japanese monopoly of all important positions also meant a lack of Korean administrators, though Japan established Japanese-oriented schools and Korean military figures went to Japanese military schools.

The American occupation after World War II did not alter the feudal-authoritarian system. Independence led to a liberal political constitution and land reform (similar to the pattern that occurred in the American military occupation of Japan). But land reform had no real significance (except perhaps to facilitate the neglect of the agricultural sector) and the liberal political constitution became a dead letter thanks to the Korean war and to the fact that electoral politics threatened the power of Korea's tiny elite.

The net impact of American influence (and the United Nations' military effort during the Korean War) has been to prevent both a communist dictatorship and a liberal democracy from developing in Korea. By the early 1970s Korea had crystallized into a authoritarian-police state. Backed by the military and the police, a lifetime president, heading a government derived from an unrepresentative legislature, outlawed political opposition and repressed dissidents. When it came to the economy, the Korean state was no passive night watchperson. From the end of the Korean war on, the state actively undertook the development of the economy—indeed there is an explicit political economy in Korea complete with national state planning. Despite considerable direct economic activity by government, however, the economy has become more and more concentrated in private hands.

Korea has an extremely large military-police establishment. With considerable American aid and with huge expenditures of its own, the Korean military defends Korea against North Korea as well as its own people. Violent political protests in 1987 finally forced the government to agree to genuine elections. Whether and how soon Korea develops a viable system of representative government remains to be seen. In 1988, the right-wing (authoritarian) party won the presidential election by a plurality but lost control of the legislature.

Family, Religion, and Education[33]

As is common in countries with a well-established agrarian tradition, the family has first claim on the energies, time, and resources of Koreans. The Korean family is male oriented and is explicitly conceived as the permanent foundation of society over time. In the ideal agrarian Korea, the household is a three-generation extended family. In practice the eldest son and his family (as the eventual inheritors of the family property and authority) continue to live with his parents while other sons establish separate households (primogeniture). Further reflecting Confucian values and beliefs, age and sex were carefully delineated as forms of super- and subordination: grandparents received considerable respect while elder brothers had authority over younger brothers, brothers over sisters, and husbands over wives.

Given the large concentration in landholding in feudal Korea, the hierarchical, ascriptive family form was generalized into a model for all social relations. Confucian religion and philosophy stressed filial piety and argued that all social relations must be modelled on authority relations derived from a father-headed family. Social harmony would ensue

---

[32]Norman Jacobs argues that this is so because Korea, like China, is a patrimonial society, something distinct from feudal society. It seems best, however, to maintain a different and more fruitful distinction among agrarian societies: those that were feudal (decentralized) and those that bent their populations, including the nobility, into the service of a state headed by a supreme ruler (feudal-authoritarian).

[33]Both for this and the concluding section, the key source is still Norman Jacobs.

if all obeyed the obligations of their ascriptive stations in life.

Korean family forms, though more formalized, are similar to those we encountered in Peru, forming at once an internal group hierarchy and a model for society-at-large (Peru's Spanish corporatism is not as explicit or formalized). In Greece (and in other small landholding societies), the family is also vitally important but does not become a model for hierarchical social relations.

In today's Korea the family has changed in keeping with urbanization and industrialization. As in other countries experiencing economic growth, Korea's urban families have become nuclear, neolocal, smaller, and the position of Korea's urban women has been changing, though slowly.

Korea's religious institutions are relatively diverse ranging from shamanism and nativist eclectic forms to Buddhism, Confucianism, and Christianity. While the largest group of religious adherents belong to Buddhism, the most influential religion has been Confucianism. Since the end of the nineteenth century a significant Christian sector has established itself largely because Christianity brought with it Western values that Koreans wanted.

Like Greece, but unlike Peru, education was highly valued by Korea's elite, and Korea has made striking gains in mass literacy and university education in recent decades. The Chinese practice of gearing education to the development of officials has been a burden. Confucian educational precepts emphasized memorizing classics and acquiring basic ethical forms. The goal of education was wisdom and it was assumed that wise officials could solve problems through the application of what they had learned from the classics.

Christian influences widened educational opportunities for ordinary people (including women) and, along with American secular influences, have stressed an education that is more scientific and critically analytical. After 1945 Korea witnessed an extraordinary development of education leading to mass literacy. The educational system is no doubt part of the explanation for Korea's economic success. Education is highly graded and extremely competitive with a pronounced emphasis on credentials. It is still deficient in scientific and vocational programs. The emphasis on academic learning has had two consequences: one, it cut back on the supply of qualified (that is credentialled) job applicants since it is easier to inflate academic, as opposed to technical, requirements and, two, it created a reservoir of politically active students who brought an end to one government and has challenged others from the 1970s on.

Despite Korea's traditional preference for the classics (which has been carried into the present), it has not lacked trained technical personnel. Whether derived from training in the United States or Japan, from American technical training programs in Korea, or through its own efforts, Korea's economic success is in no small measure due to its supply of trained economists, civil servants (including military, intelligence, and police), engineers, and technically oriented business leaders. It is also important to note that Korea appears far more successful than other countries in getting its citizens to extract meaning and benefits from utilitarian, lower-level schooling.[34]

Class and Dependency

Korea is an unequal country with a considerable disparity among the upper and lower reaches of its system of social stratification. Analyzing inequality even when quantitative income distribution data are used is very difficult unless reference points are clear and explicit. Thanks to its unusual history (Japanese occupation, the ouster of Japan and land reform in the post-World War II period, and the Korean war), Korea began its development as a relatively more equal society than most other Third-World countries. Economic expansion has raised living standards but has also led to a considerable amount of income inequality.

[34]R. P. Dore, "South Korean Development in Wider Perspective," *Pacific Affairs* 50 (Summer, 1977): 196–98.

Perhaps the most remarkable thing about Korean inequality is the ease with which authoritarian-feudal forms have transferred themselves to urban-industrial conditions.[35] In any case, neither have the fruits of economic growth been distributed evenly to the Korean people nor has economic growth equalized income and wealth. This pattern is not uncommon, especially in capitalist countries, both developed and underdeveloped—economic expansion sometimes raises general living standards but never produces more equality.

Korea is one of the few developing countries whose class system has been studied in some depth.[36] In making this study, Hagen Koo has argued that we cannot simply use Marx's central criterion of property owner versus nonproperty owner and purchaser versus seller of labor power to understand social stratification. One must also analyze the occupational system, especially nonmanual versus manual statuses. Combining these criteria, Koo argues, yields five social classes: capitalist and state elite, new middle class, petty bourgeoisie, working class, marginal class, plus farmers (who are relatively equal). Between 1965 and 1975 the new middle class (white collar), petty bourgeoisie, and the marginal class all grew while the working class expanded rapidly and farmers declined significantly.

The inequality of household income declined during the 1960s (largely because manufacturing reduced the number of unemployed and underemployed) but increased during the 1970s. The top 20 percent of households increased their share of the total from 41 to 45 percent while the bottom 40 percent declined from 19 to 16 percent. Beyond income inequality, Korea's class structure went from one that was relatively fluid and amorphous to one with more clearly defined boundaries

and overall hierarchy. First, there is an extremely wealthy and politically powerful capitalist class—anchored in highly concentrated economic groupings called Jaebols (the largest 20 Jaebols, for example, control 33 percent of manufacturing). By and large, the capitalist class refers to large industrialists as well as the political elite both of which are joined at the hip. Koo notes that there is considerable resentment of this class by the Korean people, more than any resentment of foreign capital. The people resent this class because they know it has received its wealth through political favoritism. Second, there is now a distinct working class. By and large, Korean workers receive higher wages than their counterparts in other developing countries but there is still considerable resentment about the injustice of its relative share in Korea. The white-collar class has enjoyed a good share of economic growth along with small business people. Farmers, marginals, and especially industrial workers have lost out.

Koo argues that while Korea is a case of dependent development, it is different from such dependency in other countries, most notably in Latin America.[37] Korea's development is a result primarily of state action, with foreign capital and mutinationals playing only a small role. The other difference with dependency elsewhere is that development has not led to a dual economy and the marginalization of significant portions of the population. The benefits of economic growth have been distributed widely though not fairly or equally (Koo focuses on 1960 to 1980 and cannot be completely faulted for failing to put Korea's development in deeper historical context, including the role of Japanese and American imperialist expansion and policies).

Korea's dependency takes a number of forms. One, it is dependent on world markets and has accumulated considerable debt (which its

---

[35]This has parallels in the West; see the section, Agrarian Feudalism and the Modern World, in Chapter 2.

[36]Hagan Koo, "Transformation of the Korean Class Structure: The Impact of Dependent Development" in Robert V. Robinson, ed., *Research in Social Stratification and Mobility*, Vol. 4 (Greenwich, Conn.: JAI Press, 1985), pp. 129–48.

[37]For an original contribution to the theory of dependent development, see Peter Evans, *Dependent Development: The Alliance of Multinational, State, and Local Capital In Brazil* (Princeton, N.J.: Princeton University Press, 1979).

economy can service as long as its exports remain strong). And it is dependent in the sense that it is still subject to what outsiders do. Dependence on outside powers is such a marked feature of Korean history that it is remarkable that it has developed as a distinct ethnic-linguistic group. American policy since 1945 has openly supported South Korea's survival and development as part of larger American interests in the Far East.[38] Though President Carter was on the verge of removing American troops in 1977, the step was never taken and the United States is still directly tied to Korea's military security.

Historically, South Korea's own foreign policy has been simply a reaction to the initiatives taken by China, Russia, Japan, or the United States. However in recent years, perhaps dating from its participation in the Vietnam war as an ally of the United States, and certainly because of its growing economic strength and the complexity of its economic problems, South Korea has begun to assert itself in foreign affairs. Security against North Korea (which is supported by the Soviet union and the People's Republic of China) is still South Korea's primary concern. And its relations with the United States, from which it receives military protection and economic and political support, are still its number one priority. But the Vietnam war also revealed the limits of American power. Korea also knows that the United States needs it if it is to project its power and presence into the Asian world. For these and other reasons, South Korea has become a more sophisticated negotiator with the United States. It has also broadened its contacts with Southeast Asia, the Third World in general, and, more recently, the Second World, in order to keep pace with the changing needs of its export economy. Its relations with Japan remain volatile and troublesome despite Japan's heavy investment in and considerable aid to Korea. And South Korea has been at pains to show that it is willing to talk

about how the two halves of Korea can be united peacefully.[39]

South Korean governments have worked hard to promote national pride and have even begun to purge the Korean language of Chinese characters and of loan words from China, Japan, and the United States. But dependency is structured deeply into the fabric of Korean life. Despite its highly centralized political tradition and its explicit intertwining of state and economy, Korea's radical dependence on world markets makes it extremely vulnerable to ups and downs in the world economy. The political turbulence of the late 1970s, climaxed by the assassination of President Park Chung Hee in 1979, is directly linked to the painful recession that accompanied the dramatic rise in oil prices after 1973 and the surge in world prices for raw materials. Efforts to intensify exports to pay for higher cost imports left Koreans with fewer consumer goods and high inflation. A government-promoted recession further violated domestic expectations. Korea's internal political instability is directly linked to its economic dependency.[40]

During the late 1970s, Korea's efforts to develop heavy industry was not as successful as its earlier investments in light industry. By the 1980s, the economy was back on track and Korea, somewhat chastened, was now a producer of steel, automobiles, ships, and other products that directly competed with even mighty Japan. Korea's main problem, however, is still political. Its internal political instability is unlikely to end as long as an authoritarian government is geared to the defense of an economy that does not benefit the Korean people directly and equitably. Authority is undermined when followers can no longer see the connection between the actions of powerholders and their own inter-

---

[38]For background on American foreign policy toward Asia and Korea, see Frank Baldwin, ed., *Without Parallel: The American-Korean Relationship Since 1945* (New York: Pantheon, 1973).

[39]For a valuable set of essays on all aspects of Korean foreign policy, see Youngnok Koo and Sung-joo Han, eds., *The Foreign Policy of the Republic of Korea* (New York: Columbia University Press, 1985).

[40]Chong-Sik Lee, "South Korea 1979: Confrontation, Assassination, and Transition", *Asian Survey* 20: 1 (January, 1980): 63–76.

ests. The flow of benefits from economic expansion and the manner in which economic troubles and political protests have been handled have made it clear whose interests Korean society serves. The first steps toward representative government in 1987 were followed by considerable labor union activity, including strikes, demanding better wages and working conditions. A new, more ideological anti-Americanism has appeared among Korea's influential students. Whether these significant events will give the Korean people more influence over their society remains to be seen.

14

REPRESENTATIVE SOCIALIST DEPENDENCIES
Cuba, Tanzania, Vietnam, Iraq

INTRODUCTION: THE VARIETY OF SOCIALISMS

There are many forms of socialist theory and socialist practice. One classification distinguishes between socialism in developed countries and in nondeveloped. Most socialist movements in the developed liberal (capitalist) West oppose the private ownership of the means of production. Here socialists believe that a private economy is associated with exploitation, injustice, waste, and social disorder. Western socialism fights against the equation of private interest with the public good. Socialists believe that the abstract right of capitalists to use the means of production for maximum profit or to send it to areas of maximum profit will lead inevitably to the separation of elites from the performance of social functions. The socialists of the West direct their fire primarily at capitalists and their auxiliaries in government, education, religion, and the military. The main figure in

Western socialism is Karl Marx and two general orientations can be associated with his work: one, the authoritarian socialism found in the Soviet Union and, two, the democratic socialism found in Germany (democratic socialism, derived from a variety of other sources, including Christianity, is also strong in France, Great Britain, and Scandinavia[1]).

Democratic socialism in the developed capitalist countries (of whatever variety and source) has tended to adopt an evolutionary, peaceful, parliamentary stance toward the problem of how to transform capitalism to socialism. It thinks in terms of building on capitalist achievements. By and large, democratic socialism, whether Marxist or non-Marxist, has more or less accepted the essential nature of the bourgeois nation state. New, creative currents in socialist thought have occurred on

---

[1]The basic thrust of Sweden's socialist governments is to leave the economy in private hands but to promote equality through taxation and public services.

the rim of developed Europe (Vladimir Lenin in Russia, Georges Lukacs in Hungary, and Antonio Gramsci in Italy) and in peasant China (Mao Tse-tung).[2] Other creative developments have occurred especially in the post-World War II period in response to movements of national liberation.[3]

Socialism in the developed countries of the Second World tends to stress the Soviet model of development and expansion: centralized command economies explicitly directed by a party-dominated government. Hungary is an exception, having instituted a considerable reliance on market mechanisms. Yugoslavia is also an exception to Soviet-style socialism; it has combined a party-dominated polity with a "market" economy and worker participation and control to yield a unique brand of "market socialism."[4] The emergence of free trade unions and the solidarity movement in Poland, along with the elections of 1989, herald changes away from Soviet-style socialism in that country too.[5]

While sharing similarities with the socialism of the developed West, Third-World socialism has distinctive components and is, on the whole, different. Socialism in the West emerged in the nineteenth century, either after or during the economic breakthrough into industrialism and the establishment of the liberal nation state. As such, Western socialists could take nationhood for granted. Third-World socialism (like Third-World capitalism) faces the job of building a modern state as well as a modern economy. It must struggle not simply for economic and political development but must overcome the heavy burden of economic and political *under*development. In the West socialists fought against landed aristocrats and capitalists both of whom were tangible, easily recognizable internal enemies. In contrast, Third World socialism has fought primarily against foreigners who controlled their country through some mixture of force, settlement, inequitable trade relations, or an alliance with native elites.

The inspiration for socialism in various parts of the world is both similar and different. Western socialism is largely secular and humanistic. It takes for granted the association of reason, science, technology, and human effort with progress and happiness, and ultimately with justice and equality. The Western socialist image of an organic, collective whole (to combat the atomistic, mechanistic imagery of capitalist theory) derives from Greece and Rome, from Judaism and Christianity, and from agrarian commercial-corporate traditions. Chirot has even found a parallel between corporate fascist theory and practice, and the theory and practice of Eastern European socialism (and of many developmental theories both on the right and left).[6]

Third World socialism derives much of its inspiration from the West (many elites in the Third World received their education in the West) as well as from agrarian, national, and religious traditions.[7] But in all instances the results are considerably different. As in the West, agrarian communal traditions inspire an image of a cooperative agricultural and, ultimately, an industrial society. Many African societies, Tanzania, for example, are still close to horticultural tribal life and have used imagery from that way of life to help them modernize. As we will see a society's traditions can be both a help and a hindrance.

---

[2] For developments in Europe, see Lewis A. Coser, "Marxist Thought in the First Quarter of the Twentieth Century," *American Journal of Sociology* 78 (July, 1972): 173–201.

[3] For a valuable compilation of the ideas of the leaders of the Third World in the immediate post-World War II period, see Paul E. Sigmund, Jr., ed. and intro., *The Ideologies of the Developing Nations* (New York: Praeger, 1963).

[4] For an analysis of Yugoslavian socialism, see Chapter 15.

[5] The Soviet Union and (especially) China are also introducing market mechanisms into their state-controlled economies.

[6] Daniel Chirot, "The Corporatist Model and Socialism", *Theory and Society* 9 (March, 1980): 363–81.

[7] For two important comparative works on socialism with special reference to the Third World, see Rene Dumont with Marcel Mazoyer, Jr., tr. Rupert Cunningham *Socialisms and Development* (New York: Praeger, 1973); originally published in 1969 and Helen Desfosses and Jacques Levesque, eds., *Socialism in the Third World* (New York: Praeger, 1975). For a valuable reference work on societies with Marxist governments, see Bogdan Szajkowski, ed., *Marxist Governments: A World Survey* (New York: St. Martin's Press 1981), 3 vols.

The part played by nationalism in socialist theory and practice has also varied. Western socialism emerged after the creation of capitalist nation states. For one thing socialists could take national identity for granted; for another, they had to fight narrow nationalism as an enemy of socialism (for example, the French and German socialist parties supported the war efforts of their respective societies in World War I). Third-World countries have had to face the enormous problem of building viable nation states, often out of artificially created colonies or from a population that had been divided and pitted against itself by colonial overlords eager to retain control. Third-World countries have faced many and varied problems. Some lack central powers, others have central powers dominated by outsiders or by corrupt native elites. Some are desperately poor while others are fairly well off. Some are blessed with valuable resources while others live in a sparse environment and face a bleak future. Some Third-World countries are more developed than others but have had their development spearheaded by settlers from the outside (for example, the French in Vietnam and Algeria and the British in Kenya and Zimbabwe). Some new nations have a homogeneous people and settled boundaries while others have been constructed with arbitrary boundaries that include different ethnic and racial groups. Understandably, socialism in the Third World has been deeply absorbed in fighting imperialism and in nation building as well as socialist revolution. By and large, its focus has been on international "class" struggle rather than on domestic class struggle.

Religion is still a powerful force in the Third World and has had a significant impact on some forms of Third-World socialism. Religion can both retard and promote change. Christianity's role in furthering capitalism and nationalism in the West is well known. Its role in helping to generate the heavenly city of the French (liberal) Enlightenment is also known. Judaism and Christianity also played a role in furthering the apocalyptic vision of Marx and in promoting Christian socialism. Christianity's role has varied depending on historical context. In Greece and Ireland Christianity formed the center of resistance to an occupying imperial power. In Korea it was a liberalizing force; in Lebanon it has allied itself with Israel; and in South Africa it has formed an important part of Afrikaner ideology and has helped to promote a racially based society.[8]

Christianity in Latin American was largely a conservative, imperialist force though in recent years the Roman Catholic Church has begun to criticize and even oppose some Latin American dictatorships. The role of the Roman Catholic Church in Latin America varies according to the social development of the various countries. Both the church hierarchy and church-sponsored local Christian fellowship-political groups have supported insurrection against blatantly oppressive regimes in Nicaragua, El Salvador, and Guatemala. In Brazil the Roman Catholic Church (the most progressive in the world where segments openly espouse Liberation Theology or linking Christianity to the secular redemption of the poor from capitalism and imperialism) has also sponsored local fellowship-political groups and involved itself in the ongoing political process. The Roman Catholic Church has been active on the reformist left (which in the context of Latin America often means revolution) in Argentina and Chile. In the more paternalistic and progressive Latin American countries, such as Mexico, Costa Rica, and Venezuela, it has been less active. In Colombia the Roman Catholic hierarchy has a long history of conservatism and its sponsorship of local religious groups and other mass organizations has promoted authoritarianism in the Church (which coincides with a general dislike of grass-roots organizations in Colombia's secular life despite its relatively open politics).[9]

---

[8]Randall G. Stokes, "Afrikaner Calvinism and Economic Action: The Weberian Thesis in South Africa," *American Journal of Sociology* 81 (July 1975): 67–80.

[9]For essays on variations in the relation between Roman Catholicism and politics in Latin America, see

Third-World religious traditions have also had a varied impact. Islam has had a profound affect on the development of Arab (and other forms of) socialism in the Middle East, Asia, and North Africa. Though there are similarities, each country professing an Arab socialism has been different because of radically different local conditions: Nasserism in Egypt, Baath socialism in Syria and Iraq, Qaddafi socialism in Libya, and the mixed Marxist-Muslim socialism of Algeria. The role of Islam in developing socialist ideologies in sub-Sahara Africa and in Asia must also not be overlooked.

Other Third-World religions have also played a role in the development of socialism. Confucianism appears to suit the needs of modernization under both Chinese socialism and Korean capitalism. In Vietnam Confucian scholars formed an important center of resistance to French colonialism, and their example had a direct influence on the development of revolutionary socialism in that country. However, Hinduism in India has probably been a brake on both capitalist and socialist development because of its pronounced otherworldliness.

The socialisms of the Third World vary considerably because of the strikingly different conditions, experience, and needs of various Third-World countries. Understandably, socialist theory outside (and even in) the West is vague and moralistic though in some cases there have been attempts to spell out practical implications. Socialist leaders as varied as Mao and Qaddafi, for example, have developed socialist catechisms to guide their people. Like all societies faced with internal differentiation and complex problems, Third-World socialism has stressed unity and integration through central authority. Like most Third-World countries, socialist societies are authoritarian and some are outright repressive dictatorships. In Sri Lanka, however, a socialist government was voted out of power in 1977 and in Jamaica a socialist government was voted out of power in 1980.

Perhaps the major similarity among the socialist countries is their conscious attempt to escape the lure of the capitalist world-market economy. In one way or another, all have stressed withdrawal from the capitalist world economy and have developed programs to promote self-sufficient, balanced socioeconomic development. As a result, a broad difference has emerged between Third-World capitalist and Third-World socialist societies. The latter have less income inequality and less imbalance between rural and urban sectors.[10] In addition they tend to have better records in employment, health care, and education, and have done a better job of overcoming absolute poverty. Actually, the socialist countries that I will deal with in this chapter are small and have had severe disabilities to overcome—as a result they only approximate the success of Third-World socialism in each of these areas. The most spectacular success story of Third-World socialism, the People's Republic of China, will be treated in Chapter 18.

Despite these successes Third-World socialist societies have been unable to insulate themselves from the capitalist world-market economy (or its politics). For one reason or another all must participate in world trade and investment patterns (something that is also true of the socialist countries of the Second World).[11] Whether they can succeed in maintaining both their autonomy and their socialism remains to be seen.

Daniel H. Levine, ed., *Religion and Political Conflict In Latin America* (Chapel Hill, N.C.: University of North Carolina Press, 1986). For a brilliant and wideranging analysis of the compatibility of Marxism and Christianity, providing a valuable history of the Roman Catholic Church's sociopolitical history since the French Revolution and a sympathetic picture of Liberation Theology, see Arthur F. McGovern, *Marxism: An American Christian Perspective* (Maryknoll, N.Y.: Orbis Books, 1980).

[10]Taiwan is almost alone among the capitalist Third-World countries in having a strong rural economy; for an analysis and the special reasons for this, see Guistav Ranis, "Equity With Growth in Taiwan: How 'Special' is the 'Special Case'?" *World Development* 6: 3 (Fall, 1978): 397–409.

[11]Steven Steiber, "The World System and World Trade: An Empirical Exploration of Conceptual Conflicts," *Sociological Quarterly* 20 (Winter, 1979): 23–36.

One scholar has argued that socialist countries have been unable to develop genuine socialist modes of production because they must function in a powerful and still dominant capitalist world economy. Until there is a socialist world economy, individual socialist countries (from the Soviet Union and China on to smaller countries) are essentially forms of capital accumulation and thus essentially capitalist societies.[12] From a similar perspective another scholar argues that the first and second worlds are now simply different manifestations of capitalism. No real Arab socialism, he argues, can develop until the Arab nation (all Arab countries) frees itself both from the private capital of the First World and the state capitalist orientation of Moscow.[13] Other critics to the left of socialist practice will be encountered as we survey the four countries chosen to represent Third-World socialism.

CUBA

Land and People[14]

Cuba is an island nation state (746 miles long and approximately 60 miles wide) lying 90 miles south of the United States. Its popu-

lation is approximately 10 million and characterized by low growth. Its birth rate is lower than many Third-World nations and it has not felt the population pressures of other Caribbean nations. The size of its population was also affected by the relatively large exodus of people (to the United States) after the socialist revolution in 1959. Like other Third-World countries its population is young, though in Cuba's case this is also due to the emigration of large numbers of adults in the post-revolutionary period.

Unlike many other Latin American countries Cuba is marked by a division between Caucasians and blacks rather than whites and Indians. The Indians native to Cuba were cruelly exploited by the Spanish and did not survive the diseases introduced after the Spanish conquest. Cuba's blacks are descendents of the numerous slaves imported from Africa to work the land. Racial characterizations are officially decried in (socialist) Cuba but, nonetheless, are important. Estimates place the number of blacks at between 30 and 40 percent of the population with whites and *mestizos* (mixed) making up the rest.

Despite "racial" diversity, Cuba is a relatively homogeneous nation—it does not have tribal, ethnic, religious, or linguistic cleavages and has no leftover colonial settlers or imported middlemen important to its economy to contend with.

Economy

Cuba's economy and thus its social structure reflects outside forces. From 1511 to 1898, Cuba was a colony of Spain, which used it as staging area for imperial expansion into the new world. The other outside force to affect Cuba was the world market for sugar. The growing value of sugar in the world market from the nineteenth century on tipped the island's economy toward sugar cane production. As a colony of Spain, under occupation by the United States (1898–1902), as an American protectorate (1902–34), as a nominally independent country (1934 to 1958), and under a socialist regime (since 1959), the underlying economic reality of Cuban society is sugar.

---

[12]Christopher K. Chase-Dunn, "Socialist States in the Capitalist World-Economy," *Social Problems* 27 (June, 1980): 505–25.

[13]Samir Amin, *The Arab Nation*, tr. Michael Pallis (London: Zed Press, 1978); first published 1976.

[14]The *Area Handbook for Cuba,* 3rd ed. (Washington, D.C.: U. S. Government Printing Office, 1987), part of the comprehensive series on contemporary countries prepared by Foreign Area Studies of The American University, is an invaluable source of information about Cuban geography, population, history, and society. Other valuable general sources are Jorge I. Dominguez, *Cuba: Order and Revolution* (Cambridge, Mass.: Harvard University Press, 1978), Irving Louis Horowitz, ed., *Cuban Communism,* 6th ed. (New Brunswick, N.J.: Transaction, 1987), Sandor Halebsky and John M. Kirk, eds., *Cuba: Twenty-Five Years of Revolution, 1959–1984* (New York: Praeger, 1985), and Tad Szulac, *Fidel: A Critical Portrait* (New York: William Morrow, 1986). For a comprehensive and balanced appreciation and criticism of all aspects of Cuban society, see Juan M. del Aguila, *Cuba: Dilemmas of a Revolution,* rev. and updated ed. (Boulder, Colo.: Westview Press, 1988).

Changes in regime and social structure have been important to Cuba but no changes have affected its dependence on sugar.

Much of Cuba is arable and rainfall is fairly good. Though its land and climate are assets, these have helped to slant Cuba's economy toward agriculture. Other important economic products are cattle, fruit, tobacco, fish, and lumber. Cuba has the world's fourth largest deposits of nickel and nickel exports provide significant foreign exchange. With almost no source of energy Cuba is unable to use its abundant iron ore and cannot sell it because it is too mixed with other minerals to make it attractive to foreign buyers.

The Castro regime pursued a policy of economic diversification after 1959 but ideological enthusiasm was no match for hard economic realities. After some serious mistakes in the 1960s, Cuba's economy, while remaining state controlled, came under more pragmatic and professional management. The Soviet Union has provided massive economic (and military) aid,[15] and Cuba has pursued trade relations with a wide variety of non-socialist societies despite the economic embargo by its former major trading partner, the United States, and by Latin America (the Organization of American States, which lifted its embargo in 1972).

Cuba is an example of a centrally planned economy, more like the Soviet Union than Hungary. Many of its economic problems are due to central planning, something the Cuban leadership is aware of, but the Cuban leadership believes central planning is necessary to its still largely agricultural economy and has not followed the Soviet Union toward decentralized economic decision making. It also feels that centralized economic

planning is the only appropriate way to remain politically alert to American hostility.[16]

The CIA estimates Cuba's 1987 GNP at $18.7 billion yielding a per capita income of $1800.[17] Cuba's general standard of living was relatively high in comparison to other nondeveloped countries even before the socialist revolution and it has remained higher than most Third-World countries. The socialist regime succeeded in replacing the huge loss of trained personnel who emigrated (mostly to the United States) after 1959. The gross poverty and the large unemployment amidst affluence by the few that is typical of developing capitalist countries has been eliminated by rationing[18] and full employment policies. Indeed labor shortages are short-term problems and the number of women in the labor force has been encouraged and now stands at 10 percent.

By the 1980s Cuba's economy, though still heavily dependent on the export of sugar, was more diversified than it had been before the revolution. Cuba is less vulnerable to the world market than it was earlier and, while heavily dependent on Soviet aid, the Soviet Union does not own investments in Cuba and does not withdraw profits. By and large, Cuba's economic growth in the past decades has matched that of other Latin American countries, most of which received at least as much outside aid as Cuba did.

Perhaps the major economic difference between socialist Cuba and the developing cap-

---

[15]Total Soviet assistance between 1962 and 1976 totalled approximately $11 billion ($8.2 billion economic and $2.8 billion military aid). In the same period the United States' total aid to Israel was $7.7 billion and to South Korea $7.9 billion (plus other aid through the World Bank and other international organizations). In this connection, see Table 2.3 in Cole Blasier, "The Soviet Union in the Cuban-American Conflict" in Cole Blasier and Carmelo Mesa-Lago, eds., *Cuba in the World* (Pittsburgh: University of Pittsburgh Press, 1979), pp. 37–51.

[16]For recent analyses, see Susan Eckstein, "State and Market Dynamics in Castro's Cuba" in Peter Evans *et al.*, eds., *States versus Markets In The World System* (Beverly Hills, Calif.: Sage, 1985), pp. 217–45; Andrew Zimbalist, ed., *Cuba's Socialist Economy Toward the 1990s* (Boulder, Colo.: L. Kienner, 1987); and Andrew Zimbalist, ed., *Cuban Political Economy: Controversies In Cubanology* (Boulder, Colo.: Westview Press, 1988).

[17]Central Intelligence Agency, *The World Factbook 1988* (Washington, DC: U. S. Government Printing Office, 1988), p. 58.

[18]For socialist Cuba's success in eliminating hunger, see Medea Benjamin, Joseph Collins, and Michael Scott, *No Free Lunch: Food and Revolution In Cuba Today* (San Francisco, Calif.: Institute For Food and Development Policy, 1984).

italist economies has been income redistribution away from the wealthy to the poor. Economic growth under socialism has produced dramatic gains for the poor, unlike, for example, in Brazil and Peru.[19]

Polity

Cuba has had an authoritarian regime since it became a Spanish colony in 1511. After the defeat of Spain in 1898 by Cuban insurgents and the United States, Cuba struggled futilely to develop responsible government. Lacking a large middle class, subject to outside forces (first Spain and then the United States), and heavily dependent not only on large landowners but on widely fluctuating world prices for sugar, Cuba could develop neither a responsible government nor even the semblance of political stability.

The revolution that brought Fidel Castro to power in 1959 had unique elements. The Batista regime of 1952 to 1959 was openly repressive and hugely inept. It also had a very narrow social base and its opposition included substantial elements of the Cuban middle class as well as workers and peasants.

The reality of political life since 1959 is complete power by the Communist Party and the armed forces, both under the personal leadership of Fidel Castro. It has produced almost thirty years of political stability because the government openly redistributed wealth and opportunities to favor the masses and inaugurated social services to improve the standard of living. Stability has also stemmed from the regime's willingness to allow large portions of the middle and upper classes (almost 10 percent of the population) to leave, leaving their wealth behind, and by comprehensive rationing, which insures an equitable sharing of whatever is in short supply.

The politics of the 1960s were marked by personalism and revolutionary fervor as the

ruling party and the masses exerted themselves to build a socialist society. Personalism and top-heavy central authority led to many mistakes. Since the 1970s a clear trend toward developing a more technocratic and pragmatic approach to economic and social development is discernible.

The other significant (internal) political development is continued political mobilization and a cautious extension of local political participation. The revolutionary party governs in the name of revolution and does not claim to reflect the will of the people. The aims of state power and political mobilization are to channel mass energies into socially constructive activities. The almost universal literacy achieved after the revolution has not meant increased power by the masses but an increase in their skill in responding to the government-controlled mass media. In a similar vein the extension of voting for local officials and the emphasis on public participation is primarily on the level of the implementing, not making public policy. Nonetheless, the revolution has put down deep roots among the people and Cuba now has the first polity in its history that can claim legitimacy.

Family, Religion, Education, and Health

Family, religion, and education followed traditional agrarian lines before the socialist revolution of 1959. In the absence of public and professional services, the family was a central institution for all. Family forms varied by social class—a leisure and consumption-oriented upper class stressed continuity of bloodline, links to Spain and Hispanic culture, tasteful consumption, chastity by and subordination of women, and personalism. The lower classes also relied heavily on family values but often without marriage or through matriarchical forms.

Roman Catholicism arrived with the Spanish conquest and, by and large, supported the status quo. It played almost no role in either the struggle for reform or revolution siding with whatever group(s) was in power, including the repressive Batista regime of the 1950s. On the eve of the revolution the church's social base was narrow, consisting primarily of the small upper classes. Unlike the Roman Catholic church in Ireland and Poland, it could not claim to represent Cuban nationalism and thus had little political power.

Education in prerevolutionary Cuba was primarily for the well to do. Efforts to enlarge educational services after Cuba's independence floundered because there was no middle class to give it impetus and purpose—indeed much of the money for education went into the pockets of officials.

The socialist revolution has dramatically altered family and educational institutions. The upper-class family has disappeared (both as a form and because its members left Cuba)—a consumption-leisure class is not compatible even with a capitalist society and is openly attacked under socialism. Without income from property, a large home with servants, exclusive (racially and sexually segregated) clubs, and the ability to consume and travel, the upper-class Cuban family is no more.

Family life at the lower levels has been strengthened largely through full employment, housing, rationing, and public services, especially education and health care. The socialist regime enacted a Family Code in 1975 to strengthen family life by basing it on mutual respect, cooperation, and equality. The new code runs counter to the male superiority (*machismo*) theme in Cuban culture and has encountered resistence. The divorce rate has risen but so has the marriage rate. All in all, the position of women has been radically altered. The socialist regime is solidly supportive of women's rights, has sponsored coeducation and, above all, has encouraged women to enter the labor force.

The socialist regime has invested unusual resources in education. As in the Soviet Union youth is favored. The basic goals of Cuban education after the revolution were to provide education where none existed, to eliminate illiteracy, break down disparities in education between rural and urban areas, gear education to building socialism, avoid the separation of school and work, and to relate education to the overall economic and technical needs of Cuban society. Success in these goals cannot be measured precisely. Certainly the results are spectacular when judged against the prerevolutionary period.[20]

Certainly it is healthy to gear education to social needs. It is interesting to note that a wide variety of countries have stressed similar goals and made education an agent of development: Greece, a capitalist country with a socialist government, Peru, a capitalist country under a military government, and the Republic of (South) Korea, an authoritarian capitalist country, have all worked hard to develop an educational system geared to national economic, professional, and technical needs.

Cuba's health record is a good one. The socialist system of free comprehensive health care (along with Cuba's food policy) has made dramatic extensions of what was already a good health record. Cuba participated in the improvement of health found throughout the developed world during the twentieth century. The first dramatic steps toward a healthier Cuba occurred during the American occupation after the Spanish-American War (1898–1902); other improvements occurred before the revolution. The socialist revolution made a concerted effort to improve sanitation, to immunize the population, and provide health care, especially in rural areas. Today Cuba's population has a health record that compares favorably with the developed countries.[21]

Religion has been left alone by the Cuban regime. The main challenge to religion has been the quasireligious fervor with which the regime sought to build a socialist social order. Never very popular, religion and church

---

[20]For two accounts of Cuban education, both of which stress the use of education to create a new society, see Jonathan Kozol, *Children of the Revolution: A Yankee Teacher In The Cuban Schools* (New York: Delacorte Press, 1978) and Theodore MacDonald, *Making a New People: Education in Revolutionary Cuba* (Vancouver, Canada: New Star Books, 1985).

[21]Sergio Diaz-Briquets, *The Health Revolution in Cuba* (Austin, Tx.: University of Texas Press, 1983).

attendance have declined. In recent years the Roman Catholic church has pursued with vigor a policy of dialogue and cooperation with the government letting it be known that much of socialism coincides with Christianity. The government has responded positively to the Church's overtures.[22]

Class and Dependency

Cuba's inequality before 1959 was severe and lacked legitimacy. Racial inequality was pronounced (white and mixed blood over black) as was sexual inequality. Class or economic inequality was also pronounced and somewhat different from most other Latin American countries. Cuba's independence from Spain came much later than other Latin American countries and one result was to retard the development of self-sufficient haciendas on which a landed class had legitimated power over a dependent peasantry. Spanish colonialism fostered an export economy. Cuba developed a stratum of cane growers who sold their cane to American-owned mills. Many cane growers were tenants but managed to gain some security of tenure and some stabilization of "prices" for their cane. Often they acted as bourgeois nationalists seeking to defend Cuba (and their interests) against the United States. Both cane growers and mill owners used wage labor and there was a large surplus of unemployed rural labor.

Cuba's upper class was largely urban and oriented toward Spain. After independence American influence accentuated the pattern of looking abroad for guidance and well-being. Cuba's upper classes of business people, bankers, merchants, and professionals were increasingly tied to American business and to North American values. Cuba's small middle class was also urban and also dependent on foreign, mostly American business.

Thus the two basic property classes of Cuba had weak roots in Cuban society and lacked legitimacy because they performed no visible, positive social functions.

Cuba's workers were relatively well organized before the revolution of 1959 and some were relatively well off. Organized and unorganized labor had organic links with Cuban society, which combined with the foreign orientation and the urban, impersonal, market orientation of the middle and upper classes gave Cuba's workers considerable power. The remainder of the population was relatively depressed: a rural and urban population of unskilled, uneducated laborers who also lacked links with Cuban society. Most were unorganized farm laborers (frequently migratory); others were squatters, sharecroppers, and renters. Others lived at the margins in cities. Unemployment and underemployment were high.

The socialist regime has equalized the population in many ways. Two-thirds of Cuba's professional and semiprofessional workers left after 1959 creating a vacuum at the top. Large estates and foreign businesses were expropriated and exclusive clubs, resorts, and schools were abolished. Equality was further augmented by rationing and by the establishment of a large variety of free goods and services. A major housing program was launched including efforts to distribute it equitably. A large part of the equalization process has come about because of the deliberate emphasis on improving conditions in rural areas and downgrading the role of Havana in Cuba's national life.[23]

In the 1960s the regime relied on moral exhortation to build a classless society. Its initial efforts were successful largely because it redistributed available values and met relatively little opposition. However, production

---

[22]For a history of Cuba's Roman Catholic Church, both before and after the socialist revolution, which argues that a rapprochement between the church and socialism is occurring, see John M. Kirk, *Between God and the Party: Religion in Revolutionary Cuba* (Tampa, FL: University of South Florida Press, 1989).

[23]Susan Eckstein, "The Debourgeoisement of Cuban Cities" in Irving L. Horowitz, ed., *Cuban Communism*, 5th ed. (New Brunswick, N.J.: Transaction Books, 1984), pp. 91–112; David Barkin, "The Redistribution of Consumption in Socialist Cuba," *Review of Radical Political Economics* 4 (Fall, 1972): 80–102.

declined since wasteful economic practices developed. Neither capitalist nor socialist societies have yet mastered the problem of combining efficiency and full employment. In the 1970s Cuba began to rely less on moral exhortation and voluntary labor and more on material incentives to spur its people. The socialist regime and the population still value education, and differential rewards for differential work has remained a strong tradition. Compared to the prerevolutionary period, present-day Cuba has been radically equalized. For various reasons, it is still far short of a classless society.[24]

Cuba after the revolution is a more autonomous society than it had been earlier. Its dominant classes before the revolution were deeply dependent on Spain and the United States—Cuba's heavy reliance on the sale of sugar in foreign markets was both the reality and symbol of its dependence. Its inability to harvest its rich nickel deposits was another important indicator of its dependence on both American markets and technology and the international nickel monopoly.[25] Today Cuba's rulers, while still dependent on outsiders, especially the Soviet Union, have more room to maneuver and have taken foreign policy initiatives even against Soviet opposition. Cuba's foreign policy since the revolution lies between the poles of a new found freedom of movement and a new dependence.[26]

To some extent the spectrum of foreign relations parallels the spectrum of internal politics. The personalism and revolutionary ardor of the 1960s are reflected in Cuba's support of revolution throughout the world (Algeria, Vietnam, Angola, Central America, and elsewhere). In some respects this reflects the need to build internal support for the revolution (and its genuine commitment to socialism) and, in another, it reflects a need to increase its allies abroad. Foreign adventurism has also been matched by a pragmatic program of diversifying its trading partners. Cuba is heavily dependent on the Soviet Union for aid and for purchasing sugar. However, it has successfully pursued a policy of establishing relations with a wide variety of socialist and nonsocialist societies. The American trade embargo has been a significant burden but Cuba has succeeded in mitigating its impact somewhat by trading with Western Europe, Canada, and Japan. It has also moderated its earlier attempt to export its revolution to Latin America and has succeeded in establishing relatively good relations with a number of Latin American countries, especially Venezuela and Mexico.

It remains, however, an example of a pioneering and successful native-grown revolution and a native-grown socialism that is certainly of interest to many societies (like Nicaragua in Central America and Angola in Africa) that are trying to develop in a socialist mode. Cuba's pragmatism in foreign affairs has had its parallel in its internal affairs. Since 1970 the ruling regime has downplayed socialist heroism and has begun increasingly to staff government and other positions with technically qualified personnel. By the 1980s Cuba had diplomatic ties and friendly relations with a growing number of Latin American countries. The United States government remained hostile but was losing support among Cuba's neighbors. American hostility, ostensibly because Cuba is a Soviet ally, also stems from the threat posed by an example of a successful socialist revolution. The cost of America's hostility in political and moral credibility is matched by the loss of a valuable economic market.

---

[24]Joseph A. Kahl, "Cuban Paradox: Stratified Equality" in Irving L. Horowitz, ed., *Cuban Communism,* 3rd ed. (New Brunswick, N.J.: Transaction Books, 1977), pp. 241–64.

[25]Theodore H. Moran, "The International Political Economy of Cuban Nickel Development" in Irving L. Horowitz, ed., *Cuban Communism,* 5th ed. (New Brunswick, N.J.: Transaction Books, 1984), pp. 135–56.

[26]For the analysis of Cuba's foreign relations, see Cole Blasier and Carmelo Mesa-Lago, eds., *Cuba in the World* (Pittsburgh: University of Pittsburgh Press, 1979); William M. Leogrande, "Foreign Policy: The Limits of Success" in Jorge I. Dominquez, ed., *Cuba: Internal and International Affairs* (Beverly Hills, Calif.: Sage, 1982), pp. 167–92, and H. Michael Erisman, *Cuba's International Relations: The Anatomy of a Nationalistic Foreign Policy* (Boulder, Colo.: Westview Press, 1985).

THE UNITED REPUBLIC OF TANZANIA

Land and People[27]

Tanzania (now joined with the island of Zanzibar) is a relatively large country (approximately 365,000 square miles) in eastern equatorial Africa. Its population is black, approximately 24 million, and the birth rate is high. Tanzania's population has no significant cleavage either of race or ethnicity (there are approximately 120 ethnic groups with none politically or socially predominant). Swahili is the national tongue though English is used at the university level and for international transactions.

Tanzania is a very poor country. Its soil is not uniformly good, water supply is uncertain, minerals and energy sources are not abundant, and health conditions are poor. Its GDP in 1987 was $4.9 billion. Its per capita income of $240 ranks it among the bottom 20 of the world's 165 or so nation states.

Economy

Tanzania's economy is overwhelmingly pastoral, horticultural, and in the hand-tool stage of technology. It is also formally committed to achieving economic growth, self-

---

[27]*Tanzania: A Country Study*, 2nd ed. (U. S. Government Printing Office, 1978) prepared by the Foreign Area Studies, The American University, though dated, is still a valuable reference work on all aspects of Tanzania. Also valuable are Kwan S. Kim, Robert B. Mabele, and Michael J. Schultheis, eds., *Papers on The Political Economy of Tanzania* (Nairobi, Kenya: Heinemann Educational Books, 1979), and Bismarck U. Miwansasu and Cranford Pratt, eds., *Toward Socialism in Tanzania* (Toronto: University of Toronto Press, 1979). For a Marxist critique of Tanzanian socialism, see Issa G. Shivji, *Class Struggles in Tanzania* (London: Heinemann Educational Books, 1976). Also valuable are Idrian N. Resnick, *The Long Transition: Building Socialism in Tanzania* (New York: Monthly Review Press, 1981) and James H. Mittleman, *Underdevelopment and the Transition to Socialism: Mozambique and Tanzania* (New York: Academic Press, 1981). For the best overall account, see Andrew Coulson, *Tanzania: A Political Economy* (Oxford: Clarendon Press, 1982). Also quite good is the shorter account by Roger Yeager, *Tanzania: An African Experiment* (Boulder, Colo.: Westview Press, 1982). For basic data on Tanzania, see Central Intelligence Agency, *The World Factbook, 1988* (Washington, D.C.: U. S. Government Printing Office, 1988), p. 230.

sufficiency, and "socialism." Tanzania's socialism is an outgrowth of its family and tribal heritage—the Swahili word for its socialism is *ujamaa* or familyhood. The socialism of Tanzania is not directed at class enemies and does not postulate a dialectic of struggle and a sequence of social stages. Tanzania was once a colony (first of Germany and then of Great Britain) but unlike Kenya and Rhodesia (now Zimbabwe) was subject neither to significant settlement from the outside nor to large flows of outside investment. The basic economic history of Tanzania consists of subsistence farming combined with a cash crop sector (cotton, sisal, tobacco, coffee) that has struggled against declining prices on the world market. As is typical of Third World countries, Tanzania's economic woes are aggravated by the fact that imported goods have to be paid for in terms of rising prices.

Tanzania has borrowed abroad and has allowed foreign investment. One result is that debt service is heavy (since its economy has not grown sufficiently to support its debts). Another has been that the government has not been able or willing to control multinationals, therefore, the result is that profits are sent abroad through indirect means and Tanzania lacks the means to produce capital goods. In effect, therefore, there is no internal capital accumulation, a continued need to import technology, and foreigners are determining the direction of the economy.[28]

Unlike socialism in Cuba (and elsewhere), which resulted because of severe exploitation from abroad, Tanzania's socialism derives somewhat from the relative lack of influence from abroad. Its colonial economy was not massively developed in the direction of export agriculture or minerals and thus its social

---

[28]For a careful analysis, see C. E. Barker, M. R. Bhagavan, P. V. Mitschke-Collande, and D. V. Wield, *African Industrialization: Technology and Change In Tanzania* (Hants, England: Gower, 1986). For another careful analysis, which stresses internal deficiencies as the cause of Tanzania's economic woes, but which does argue that Tanzania would be greatly helped if world commodity prices were stabilized, see C. George Kahama, T. L. Maliyamkono, and Stuart Wells, *The Challenge For Tanzania's Economy* (London: James Curry, 1986).

structure never developed a native power structure oriented to the outside world. Tanzania also lacked a feudal system based on large holdings serviced by serfs, tenants, or slaves. As such, it was able to build its socialism on a heritage of tribal cooperation and relative equality.

Tanzania has pursued the same goals of social self-direction as socialism in other countries. Self-reliance has meant an emphasis on food crop production and by and large Tanzania has succeeded in feeding itself despite an increase in population. Second, socialist self-reliance means industrialization in an effort to reduce dependence on consumer goods and technology from abroad. To achieve self-reliance the government has encouraged rural settlements, food crop production, and has provided health and educational services (again the basic socialist pattern of providing services on a broad, nonmarket, nonelitist basis). Future growth in the agrarian sector will require irrigation, control of disease, and mechanization. Tanzania's stress on rural development and the utilization of labor is a strategy common to Third World socialist societies (for example, Cuba, the People's Republic of China, Vietnam, and Iraq). The stress on full employment is a related strategy. Tanzania's record in this latter regard seems to be relatively less successful with significant urban unemployment, especially among women.[29]

To ensure self-reliance in other sectors the government bought out the small manufacturing and commercial sector and has since provided public investment capital for new industry. The government met little opposition from the tiny white and Asian economic groups that dominated these sectors. Using a national banking-credit system and a national development agency, the government has pursued a strategy of making Tanzania as self-sufficient as possible in consumer goods and light technology. In a related strategy the government has set up an agency to develop mineral resources both for export and to provide the base for future industry.

The history of economic and social development policies since independence has been one of fits and starts, lacking clear direction. The reality of socialism has been one-party government whose rural and industrialization policies have largely failed. The reality has been a failure to create wealth at home for investment and a massive reliance on outside aid and investment. Despite its ideology and considerable effort, therefore, Tanzania remains a deeply dependent society. It must earn foreign exchange in a world of soft commodity prices (which means that it must buy the things it needs from industrial nations that have the means to keep their prices up). The steep rise in oil prices after 1973 was a major setback. The groups tied to capital inflows, especially from Scandinavia and the World Bank group, have consistently tried to promote antisocialist policies. The World Bank initially opposed the cooperative village program and stressed help for efficient farmers. In recent years the World Bank appears to have reconciled itself to Tanzanian socialism. Anxious to prevent the political instability that comes from an exodus from the countryside, the World Bank has supported broad rural development even if it means helping poor, i.e., inefficient, farmers. Nonetheless, Tanzania has piled up a sizable external debt and its room for maneuvering is bound to be further curtailed as it struggles to service its debt costs.[30]

Polity

Tanzania is a republic governed by a single party that is constitutionally supreme. The Revolutionary Party (CCM), a merger of the Tanzanyika African National Union (TANU)

---

[29]R. H. Sabot, "Open Unemployment and the Employed Compound of Urban Surplus Labor" in Kwan S. Kim et al., eds., *Papers on the Political Economy of Tanzania* (1979), pp. 261–71.

[30]James H. Mittlemen, "International Monetary Institutions and Policies of Socialism and Self-Reliance: Are They Compatible? The Tanzanian Experience," *Social Research* 47 (Spring, 1980): 141–65. Issa G. Shivji, *Class Struggles in Tanzania* (London: Heinemann, 1976) argues (from a Marxian standpoint) that the "socialist" regime has done little to change Tanzania's dependence on outside capital.

and Zanzibar's Afro-Shiraze Party (ASP), is above the government. Supreme power is held by Julius K. Nyerere, who as chairman of the CCM is also President of the Republic. Other party officials hold parallel positions in government. Under Tanzania's formal political institutions Zanizabar is given considerable autonomy and a share of power larger than that warranted by its size.

The stress on equality and the call for participation in decision-making has not led to much de facto sharing of power. It is clear that workers' councils are mainly instruments to control workers.[31] All in all Tanzania has developed a strong central authority and policies are imposed from above.

Tanzania pursues a foreign policy of nonalignment, maintaining a friendly but formal relation with both the United States and the Soviet Union. It has had strong ties with the People's Republic of China, which has supplied it with economic and military aid. Tanzania openly supported black liberation movements in Rhodesia (now Zimbabwe), Southwest Africa (Namibia), the Republic of South Africa, and in Portuguese Mozambique (now independent).

Family, Religion, Education, and Health

Kinship ties are central to Tanzanians (and Zanzibaris). An individual's rights, duties, and opportunities are largely fixed by kinship status. Given the complexity of local conditions and the variety of ethnic groups, there is no uniform family system. Individuals often have a choice as to which kin ties to stress and, of course, kinship is diffused by economic mobility. However, the basic thrust of Tanzanian socialism, which is to develop cooperative rural villages, has done little to undermine family ties. The overall equalitarianism of Nyerere's socialism has altered the

status of women somewhat. However women are still sharply segregated in occupational status, and are still overworked, under rewarded, and underappreciated in the farming economy.[32]

Approximately one-quarter to one-third of the Tanzanian population is Christian and another number of approximately equal size is Muslim. For the remainder the concept of a high God is common. However, there is considerable belief in witchcraft, and the government has continued the efforts of British colonial administrators to curb its use.

Education is geared for use and complete in itself rather than a preparation for the next level up to the university. The government has pursued an antielitist educational policy and has put most of its educational resources into preparing youth for the agricultural life they will actually live. Education is also available to women and has helped to equalize their status somewhat. An important reality beyond egalitarian ideology, however, is that university education is far beyond the reach of ordinary citizens.

The health of a people derives from a mixture of causes. A sociology of health and health care emphasizes socioeconomic conditions. Tanzania's experience as a colony had a major impact, most of it negative, on the health of the population. The development of a plantation labor force meant malnutrition and poverty. The movement of people and wide new contact among natives and whites led to large outbreaks of diseases both old and new. Western-style medicine was imposed, which meant a curative approach dependent on hospitals located in urban centers, especially the capital. Traditional medical practices were ignored and no effort made to connect health to the living experiences of ordinary Tanzanians.

Health care after independence changed somewhat—more attention was given to rural

---

[31]Goren Hyden, " 'We Must Run While Others Walk': Policy-Making for Socialist Development in the Tanzania-Type of Polities" and Henry Mapolu, "The Organization and Participation of Workers in Tanzania" in Kwan S. Kim et al., eds., *Papers on the Political Economy of Tanzania* (1979), pp. 5–13; 272–77.

[32]M. A. Bienefeld, "Occupational Structure and the Distribution of Wage Earners" and Louise Formann, "Women and Tanzania [sic] Agricultural Development" in Kwan S. Kim et al., eds., *Papers on the Political Economy of Tanzania* (1979), pp. 245–52; 278–87.

areas, prevention of disease has been stressed, and an effort made to supply medical personnel more in keeping with the actual medical needs of Tanzanians. But the reorganization of health has lagged for two reasons: one, the colonial legacy left behind powerful medical interests that continue to insist on centralized health care by specialists and, two, because Tanzania has been unable to develop enough wealth to pay for needed health services.[33]

Class and Dependency

Tanzania's class structure is similar to but also distinctly different from that of most black African states (and from other developing societies). Most black African countries were more massively penetrated by the colonial powers and had more developed food-staple export economies at the time of independence. As a result, their class structures have a large number of white settlers or foreign propertyowners and professionals (these countries are often referred to as *white settler* societies). The other African states are therefore capitalist and the African-controlled polity has become a heavy player in the economy. State power is used for the enrichment of individual Africans and the overall short-term orientation of political figures is not conducive to long-term economic development (for a discussion of Nigeria's class system, see Chapter 16). Tanzania's class system, on the other hand, reflects its horticultural past, its less distorting colonial past, and the socialism of those who led it to independence.

None of the above should be construed as denying inequality in Tanzania (by virtue of income, wealth, occupation, and education). However the range of differences among Tanzanians has been reduced by government policies and services: an effective system of

progressive taxation,[34] ceilings on salaries, minimum wages, and by limiting government officials to their public salaries. Income figures are far from the full story of the range of inequality because Tanzania's economy is heavily slanted toward subsistence agriculture—people grow and eat their own food and make many of the things they need. In addition, the government's commitment to equitable sharing has resulted in many equalizing public services such as health care, sanitation, water, and education. Disparities between rural and urban dwellers are still marked but the disparity is lessened by the fact that urban workers transfer money to their families in the countryside. One reality is that the real incomes of most Tanzanians declined throughout the 1970s with no discernible improvement in the eighties.

Tanzania's class system (a hierarchy of households with different economic benefits, higher and lower prestige, and more and less political-legal power) is not derived from the private ownership of the means of production. Tanzania does not have a significant property-owning entrepreneurial group. Nor is the society dominated by small property owners such as peasants, shopkeepers, or business people. Labor is not a source of social power. The class system in Tanzania is anchored in state power (the dominant "class" has been referred to as a *bureaucratic bourgeoisie*).

State power, or the ability to decide how a country is to be run and who gets what, is important in all countries. Tanzania's ruling elite, including Julius Nyerere, who has led Tanzania since 1961, derives from chieftain families, and from a university system which produces technocrats for the government and state-owned corporations. By and large, it is not a dynamic ruling class able to create wealth or to innovate, as is the Communist party in the Soviet Union or the feudal-authoritarian leadership of the Republic of Korea (and Japan, the Republic of China, and the People's Republic of China).

---

[33]For a full-scale sociology of health that connects disease and inappropriate and inadequate health care in Tanzania to colonialism, Western medicine, and dependency after independence, see Meredeth Turshen, *The Political Ecology of Disease In Tanzania* (New Brunswick, N.J.: Rutgers University Press, 1984).

[34]Yukon Huang, "Distribution of the Tax Burden in Tanzania" in Kwan S. Kim et al., eds., *Papers on the Political Economy of Tanzania* (1979), pp. 155–63.

Tanzania's power structure is largely continuous with its horticultural past. Here it has something in common with the nondynamic rulers of Peru who derived from a simple feudal system. Tanzania's nondynamic rulers preside over a society in which new wealth comes largely from the outside. In this sense its dependency is both large and unique. Unlike capitalist dependencies such as Greece, Peru, and the Republic of (South) Korea, Tanzania's internal power structure is not derived from a property system shaped and maintained by outsiders. Tanzania's power structure is derived from its static horticultural past (in which those who hold political power are consumers and distributors of wealth in a particularistic world) and maintained by outsiders, each of whom has various reasons for helping it. Tanzania's dependency is no less real because it is camouflaged by socialist ideology or because its power structure has produced over 25 years of political stability. By the early 1980s those years of stability had produced no strategy for achieving the economic growth needed to improve the standard of living, much less for producing socialism. In the late 1980s, Tanzania was given a three-year moratorium on debt payments (a crushing 65 percent of its export earnings), and the government adopted a series of policies toward letting some market forces determine prices, motivate people, and allocate resources. The stagnant economy revived and, at least for the short term, Tanzania's future is brighter.

THE SOCIALIST REPUBLIC OF VIETNAM

Land and People[35]

The Democratic Republic of Vietnam is situated south of the People's Republic of China along the east coast of the Indochina peninsula that also includes Laos, Cambodia, Thailand, Burma, Malaysia, and Singapore.

Vietnam is essentially a series of fertile coastal plains with a rugged mountainous interior. Its climate is tropical monsoon although there is considerable variation from the coast to the highlands. Its population is approximately 65 million (1988) and the government has taken vigorous action to curtail population growth with some success. Its GNP in 1986 was $12.4 billion and its per capita income of $240 made it one of the poorest countries in the world.[36]

Vietnam is an old culture dating back to centuries before the birth of Christ. The people are Mongoloid and probably originated from China. For 1000 years Vietnam was ruled by China and massively influenced by it. Its primary religions are Buddhism, Confucianism, and Taoism, with a significant number of Roman Catholics, a legacy of French colonialism. Like Korea, which was also heavily influenced by China, Vietnam retained a distinct ethnic (including linguistic) identity. From the tenth to the nineteenth century it was an independent feudal-authoritarian society. The ancient seat of Vietnam is the fertile Red River delta in the North. From there historic Vietnam expanded south absorbing smaller societies, at Cambodia's expense, until it reached the fertile Mekong delta in the south. In the nineteenth century, from the 1860s to the 1880s, Vietnam gradually suc-

---

[35]Melanie Beresford, *Vietnam: Politics, Economics, and Society* (New York: Pinter, 1988) stands alone as a richly detailed synthesis of Vietnamese history and present

society (and includes a valuable bibliography). The *Area Handbook for South Vietnam* and the *Area Handbook for North Vietnam* (Washington D.C.: U. S. Government Printing Office, 1967), Foreign Area Studies, The American University, contains useful information despite being badly dated. For a full-length analysis of Vietnam before the socialist victory in 1975, see Samuel L. Popkin, *The Rational Peasant: The Political Economy of Rural Society In Vietnam* (Berkeley: University of California Press, 1979). For treatments of presocialist Vietnam in a comparative context, see Eric R. Wolf, *Peasant Wars of the Twentieth Century* (New York: Harper, 1968), Chapter 4; Jeffery M. Paige, *Agrarian Revolution: Social Movements and Export Agriculture in the Underdeveloped World* (New York: Free Press, 1975), Chapter 5; and James C. Scott, *The Moral Economy of the Peasant: Rebellion and Subsistence in Southeast Asia* (New Haven: Yale University Press, 1976), pp. 105–56.

[36]Central Intelligence Agency, *The World Factbook 1988* (Washington, D.C.: U. S. Government Printing Office, 1988), p. 252.

cumbed to French imperial forces and became a French colony.

After the defeat of Japan in World War II France attempted to reassert its colonial dominion over Vietnam but to no avail. A liberation movement led by Ho Chi Minh defeated France in an armed struggle that ended in 1954. Vietnam and the socialist North immediately pressed to undermine the South, which was still characterized by the highly exploitative export agriculture established by the French. The French were too weak to sustain South Vietnam and the United States, which was busy trying to bolster the decaying empires of a Europe exhausted by war, became South Vietnam's main sponsor. By the mid-1960s the United States had a large expeditionary force in Vietnam fighting the North Vietnamese who were being supported by the People's Republic of China and the Soviet Union. In 1975 South Vietnam collapsed and the United States was forced to withdraw. Since then a united socialist Vietnam has struggled to incorporate elements in South Vietnam that had developed in a profoundly antisocialist direction, repair a war-devastated economy, and cope with foreign hostility, especially from China and the United States.[37]

Economy

French imperialism in Vietnam was similar, at least on the surface, to the imperialism we encountered in Greece, Peru, South Korea, Cuba, and Tanzania. All countries were shaped at one time or another to be exporters of food and raw materials. But beneath the surface French imperialism was also quite different. Of the countries that we have studied, Cuba's history is closest to that of Vietnam—but Cuba and Vietnam are also different in many ways. Spain settled Cuba and conquered a simple people, largely extinguish-

ing the native culture. In Vietnam, the French settled and conquered a large and complex agrarian society and actively worked to subdue and shape it to suit its own needs and interests.

French colonial rule was extremely burdensome to the Vietnamese people. France imposed forced labor (to work on the rubber plantations) and extremely high taxes (including the corvee or taxes paid in labor). Taxes were used to pay for the infrastructure of transportation needed to orient Vietnam to the outside world. Taxes also supported a parasitic French colonial administration at very high salaries.

The agrarian base of Vietnam developed in two very different ways after the French occupation. The northern part of Vietnam had developed the classic agrarian pattern of feudal-authoritarianism. China's thousand-year control of Vietnam had led to a centralized bureaucracy (to administer the water control system) that rested on a landlord base. The central authority could not pay its supporters with money but instead used land and the rights to local taxes to secure its political base. The classic tension between emperor and landlords ensued with the central authority constantly struggling to limit the power of local landlords. By various means, for example, limiting the size of holdings and insisting that communal lands be maintained for the support of the poor and luckless, a strong central power established its authority by the eighteenth century.

The French occupation did not change much in the thickly settled subsistence agricultural economy of the delta portions of north and central Vietnam. These sections resisted French power especially in regions where the environment was harsh and unpredictable. The Vietnamese had a tradition of resisting Chinese pressure and control and they now directed toward the French their painfully acquired skills at resisting foreign penetration. Vietnamese resistance was greatly aided by skills and values acquired serving in the French Army in Europe during World War I and by education in France (the same process was at work in French-occupied Algeria). Nonetheless,

---

[37]For a history of the United States' political and military involvement in Vietnam, see Stanley Karnow, *Vietnam: A History* (New York: Viking Press, 1983) and George McT. Kahin, *Intervention: How America Became Involved In Vietnam* (New York: Knopf, 1986). For a superb 13-hour visual account, see Richard Ellison, *Vietnam: A Television History* (Chicago: Films Inc., 1983).

anticolonial leaders found it difficult to mobilize mass resistance in northern and Central Vietnam because of its intricate, graded,
and individualistically oriented social and
stratificational structures.

The situation was quite different in the
South, especially in the Mekong Delta. The
fertile land of the South was relatively un-
populated when the French seized it in 1859
and did not have the serious water control
problems of the North. To establish political
control and to pay for its occupation, the
French followed the classic pattern of distributing land and encouraging the export of
rice. From 1860 to the 1930s the agricultural
system of the South developed in sharply
opposed ways to that of the rest of Vietnam.
Most of the land went to Vietnamese supporters of the colonial regime, though approximately 11 percent went to French nationals.
Two characteristics of landownership stand
out: there was a heavy concentration of landownership and the owners were not settlers
but rather people who had urban-bureau-
cratic backgrounds. What emerged was a
deeply exploitative, unworkable, and ultimately fatal pattern of absentee landlordism.

Absentee landlordism can be stable when
combined with a manorial or subsistence
agriculture. The great latifundia of ancient Rome
and Eastern Europe suffered because landlords were not present to enforce their rights
and perform social functions, but they generated ad hoc uprisings rather than chronic
mass rebellion. Landlords who stay on the
land, for example, the classic Chinese or English gentry, were far better able to achieve
stability than landlords who were drawn to
court circles (like the French aristocracy) or
who came to live in urban centers (as happened gradually to many of the Chinese gentry).

The absentee landlord in a market, export-oriented agricultural economy becomes
a capitalist rentier. The labor force is turned
into tenants and returns are calculated precisely rather than embedded in and diffused
by custom and services. With a growing

population (that is, labor is becoming cheap)
and a growing rice yield (the land is growing
in value), the landlord can charge high rents
(the average was 50 percent but 70 and 80
percent was not unusual). Under Vietnam's
system of landlordism, however, work was performed by tenants not serfs, slaves, laborers,
or employees. In point of fact, the Vietnamese tenant was really an entrepreneur in
charge of all phases of cultivation. Tenants
took the risks, had the skills, and could easily compute the value of what they were
producing. Not only did they have to turn
over 50 percent to landowners who did no
work and performed no functions but the
peasant was also exploited by moneylend-
ers and by Chinese middlemen who milled
and exported the rice at Saigon.[38] What had
emerged was a nonworkable society, one that
could stay in place only with military force.
The radical anticolonial forces had no trouble mobilizing the peasants of the south since
they all had the same enemies and the same
interests.

After the unification of North and South
Vietnam in 1975 the victorious Communist
party committed Vietnam to socialism. Vietnam is the result of a twofold revolution:
national liberation from French colonial status (and the attempt by the United States to
prop up the unworkable South) and a socialist revolution superseding both feudal and
capitalist economic forms. As in China, the
Vietnamese socialist forces wisely stressed
national aims during their anticolonial struggle in order to unite the various class levels
in the Vietnamese population.

But after 35 years of armed struggle (against
the Japanese, 1940–45, and then against the
French and Americans (1945–1975), the Vietnamese have found that establishing a society,
and a socialist one at that, extremely difficult.
The Vietnamese economy was badly damaged by over 25 years of heavy fighting and
much of the time since 1975 has been spent

---

[38]A similarity between Cuban tenants and American
mill owners can be drawn up to a point.

in rebuilding wartorn areas and rehabilitating supporters of the South Vietnam regime.

The South presented a serious problem. It had bloated cities with large numbers of idle people. The government estimated that Southern cities had 100,000 war invalids, about 1 million orphans, and that about 5–6 percent of the population had venereal diseases. In addition, there were many who had long served the South Vietnam regime or who had been part of the commercial prosperity induced by the large influx of American aid between 1965 and 1975. The socialist regime undertook treatment and rehabilitation programs for addicts and prostitutes, sought to shelter orphans, and instituted public health measures. It also developed programs to resettle urban populations into new lands and to rehabilitate members and supporters of the South Vietnamese regime. But resources were scarce and habits die hard and all these programs lagged. The expulsion (and flight) of large numbers of Chinese "middlemen," in an effort to curb and eliminate capitalist trade, aggravated Vietnam's relations with the People's Republic of China (of which more below).

The second five-year plan inaugurated in 1976 (the first five-year plan was in 1961–65 before unification) was predicated on large amounts of foreign aid and these did not materialize. The second five-year plan failed for other reasons—natural disasters, an American embargo, the difficulty of integrating South Vietnam, and the burden of Vietnam's invasion of Kampuchea (Cambodia) with the subsequent military incursions and pressure by China. Beginning the 1990s, Vietnam remains a very poor country.

Always resourceful and pragmatic, the Vietnamese Communist Party has laid much of the blame for failure on itself and from 1979 on has adopted a variety of reforms that look encouraging. Essentially, it has improved incentives for agricultural production (within a system of cooperatives and collective farms) and has allowed a private enterprise sector to emerge in the South and Ho Chi Minh City (formerly Saigon) has boomed. Given contin-

ued experimentation, significant Soviet aid, and the possibility of substantial off-shore oil deposits, the future is not without hope.[39]

Polity

One of the lessons of history is that exploitation is successful more often than not. Social stability is often a sign (and a euphemism) for processes that have succeeded in channelling unearned values upward into the pockets of exploiters. The economic conditions of agrarian revolt (which are common throughout Southeast Asia) were outlined above in our discussion of the absentee landlord as capitalist rentier. A successful peasant revolution, however, requires other elements besides a transparent system of exploitation and open polarization between over- and underdogs. If the threats to peasant survival (posed by the commercialization of land, labor, commodities, and obligations) are to be countered, the peasant must be organized. This requires intellectuals and an organization, which also means that the peasant must be linked to an urban base.[40]

In addition to these outside forces, revolutionary socialism in Vietnam also relied on communal agrarian traditions (whose power should not be exaggerated) and affinities be-

---

[39]For general accounts, see G. Ngugen Tien Hung, *The Economic Development of Socialist Vietnam 1955–1980* (New York: Praeger, 1977), William S. Turley, ed., *Vietnamese Communism in Comparative Perspective* (Boulder, Colo.: Westview Press, 1980), William J. Duiker, *Vietnam Since The Fall of Saigon*, rev. ed. (Athens, Ohio: Center For International Studies, Ohio University, 1985), and Melanie Beresford, *Vietnam: Politics, Economics, and Society* (New York: Pinter, 1988).

[40]For the roots of revolutionary socialism in Vietnam to Confucian scholars and French-educated Vietnamese and the links between the countryside and urban centers, see Christine Pelzer White, "The Vietnamese Alliance: Intellectuals, Workers, and Peasants" in John Wilson Lewis, ed., *Peasant Rebellion and Communist Revolution in Asia* (Stanford, Calif.: Stanford University Press, 1974), pp. 77–95. For a general discussion of rural-urban relations and revolution, see Charles Tilly, "Town and Country in Revolution", *Ibid*, pp. 271–302. Eric Wolf's *Peasant Wars of the Twentieth Century* also provides case studies of rural-urban relations under unstable conditions.

tween Confucianism and Marxism to appeal to peasants and others. Its strategy for revolution and for governing has stressed Lenin rather than Marx and the Soviet model of development rather than the Chinese. Vietnamese socialism (like all Third-World socialism) has stressed human volition, character, and the efficacy of political struggle and has downplayed economic causation.

As in other socialist societies the party is supreme and dominates the government as well as the people. Vietnam's polity is highly centralized—despite influences traceable to the French, the U.S.S.R., and China, the Vietnamese have built their polity on their own traditions and stressed bureaucratic and legal forms. Historically these traditions came from the thousand-year impact of China on Vietnam. In relying on them, Vietnam, at least at first, ironically followed the Soviet model of development rather than that of communist China. The party also stresses party and state contact at the local level and is making serious efforts to revitalize and expand the party in the south. Thanks to the tradition established by Ho Chi Minh, leadership at the top has tended to be collective but that may be changing.

The formal Vietnamese political system openly gives the Communist party monopoly power. It also has extensive formal institutions to create the impression that the system of political power rests on and derives from the people. In this latter respect, it is similar to other authoritarian systems and for that matter to the liberal democracies. Politically, the party recognizes that in reality there is no unified monopoly power. It openly acknowledges that peasants are in conflict with government policy (and are often willing to blame government policy). They are aware of regional and urban-rural differences. They also denounce bureaucratic obstructionism and waste but this reflects conflict within the party. All in all, there is a lively contest among interest groups (just as we saw in the Soviet Union). The dominant party, to remain dominant, must respond to articulated interests outside the party and government, recognize the legitimate differences inside the party

and government, and bring about negotiated settlements. While the trappings are different, all this is not so different from what occurs in the liberal democracies. When dealing with complex societies one must always separate out real differences from their functional equivalents.

By the late 1980s the ever pragmatic Vietnamese socialists had committed themselves to a younger leadership with more technical training and to a liberalization of the economy. They have welcomed foreign investors and many developed countries (with the conspicuous absence of the United States) have responded eagerly. The Vietnamese have worked hard to better relations with the United States but to little avail. The United States' interest in this part of the world is to counter Soviet expansion into the South Pacific and, in addition to its objection to Vietnam's occupation of Cambodia, continues to use the feeble but politically popular excuse that its missing servicemen must be accounted for before normal relations can begin. The economic consequence of this political decision is similar to American policy toward Cuba—to give over an important market to foreign competitors. In 1988 Vietnam announced it would withdraw from Cambodia. Here again the Vietnamese had decided to cut their losses. No matter what their intentions or hopes, the occupation of Cambodia was costly in both money and adverse world opinion. It also announced again that it was willing to cooperate in the search for missing American servicemen.

Family, Religion, Education, and Health

The traditional Vietnamese family is similar to that found in complex agrarian society—the similarity with Korea is quite pronounced thanks to the influence of China and Confucianism in both countries. The family was central to the individual in traditional Vietnam and ancestor worship was an important aspect of family life. Large families were desired and marriage was a social contract not a personal relation. The male was formally dominant and the family strove for harmony through a practical ordering of relationships under the eldest male.

The socialist regime has worked hard to downgrade the family (unlike Cuban socialism which has worked hard to strengthen it since it posed no threat to party dominance). Vietnamese are told that their loyalty is to the nation and socialism. The party has championed the rights of women and declared them equal to men. It has advocated a simple marriage ceremony and strongly urges a small family to ensure enough time and energy for work.

The traditional Vietnamese were heavily immersed in the Confucian ideal of an ordered and harmonious universe. Most were formally Buddhists but Buddhism was mixed with Confucianism and other religious elements to yield a distinct Vietnamese blend. The Communist party has given constitutional guarantees of religious freedom but in practice it has transformed pagodas and temples to other uses and has harassed worshipers and religious staffs including the once sizable Roman Catholic population. Confucianism with its emphasis on discipline and ordered, hierarchical relations blended well with the needs of the embattled Communist party and is still central to the Vietnamese value system, though the words now used are those of Marx, Lenin, and Ho Chi Minh.

Education in Vietnam is openly used for constructing a new society. Women have made dramatic strides in education including higher education. The party has a steady emphasis on promoting literacy, adult education, and technical training. There is a heavy emphasis on political indoctrination and relatively little choice of educational program. The rigors of Confucian, French, and Soviet education have all had their influence—at present Vietnam relies heavily on educational aid from the Second World and sends sizable student contingents to Eastern Europe and the Soviet Union to acquire technical training.

Vietnam has struggled to improve the health of its people but has faced formidable odds. Persistent food shortages have weakened resistance to disease; malaria has been difficult to control because, for one thing, tens of thousands of bomb craters have provided water for breeding mosquitoes; venereal diseases and crippled children and adults are legacies of the war; and the American embargo has made it difficult to import medical supplies. Nonetheless, the Vietnamese life expectancy of 60 years for males and 63 for females places Vietnam much higher on this scale than most poor countries.

Class and Dependency

There is little data about inequality in Vietnam. Scanty information provided by journalists indicates that Vietnam's commitment to socialism includes keeping incomes relatively equal. Equality is further augmented by a wide range of free public services.

The major internal problem for Vietnam has been the integration of the North and South. South Vietnam had a relatively advanced capitalist agricultural economy and well-developed capitalist commercial and light manufacturing sectors. Differences in the "class" interests between the victorious socialist North and the capitalist South were large and extreme. The ban on private trade resulted in the exodus to China and elsewhere of large numbers of Chinese business people, which slowed the economy and which helped to sour relations between Vietnam and China. In the mid-70s the economy of the South was stagnant with idle capacity in all phases of trade and manufacturing and with agricultural production down.

Food production faltered because of the shortage of fertilizer, machinery, and other needed capital. But it lagged also because the former tenant farmers were not prepared for socialism. They had fought against a concrete enemy, the parasitic landlord, largely in the name of national liberation and with the hope that they would get control of their own land and thus their own labor. This was not forthcoming under socialism.

In recent years the government has stimulated economic production in the South by allowing private enterprise in a number of selected areas. Presumably this is an expedient and will be terminated once the economy is on its feet again. Vietnam's internal economic difficulties were worsened because of difficulty in obtaining foreign loans. The United States has organized a trade embargo against it and has used its power on the International Monetary Fund to curb loans.

Vietnam's internal difficulties have also spilled over into foreign affairs in another way. Border disputes developed with Kampuchea despite the fact that both countries were ruled by communist parties. Vietnam invaded Kampuchea in January, 1979, perhaps to divert attention from its internal problems, perhaps to consolidate one of its flanks. The Khmer Rouge communists of Kampuchea had instituted a barbarous return to subsistence agriculture (opponents were simply killed; huge numbers were doomed to starvation) and their unpredictability and difference with the growth-minded Vietnamese may have provided further incentive for Vietnam's invasion.

China has also become hostile to Vietnam; it supports the Pot Pol guerrillas in Kampuchea and has kept troops massed on Vietnam's Northern border (it mounted a 17-day military incursion in 1979 to punish Vietnam for its invasion of Kampuchea a month earlier). China's interest in joining the United States, Japan, and ASEAN (the Association of Southeast Asian Nations—Brunei, Thailand, Malaysia, Singapore, Philippines, and Indonesia) in pressuring Vietnam is essentially related to its hostility to the Soviet Union. As this hostility has eased so has hostility to Vietnam. Vietnam's dominance of Laos and Kampuchea threatens Thailand, Malaysia, and Singapore who also occupy the Indochina penisula but the major incentive for the United States and China (and Japan) is their determination to block the Soviet Union from expanding its influence in Southeast Asia.

Given its various problems since 1975 Vietnam has become more and more dependent on Moscow. Vietnam is a member of the Soviet-Eastern European economic bloc, CMEA (Council of Mutual Economic Assistance). It sends large numbers of students to the Soviet bloc countries. And it receives large amounts of foreign aid. In return it has reluctantly given the Soviet Union military bases on Vietnamese soil (especially naval ports). Given this course of events, China feels encircled by the Soviet Union while the United States, ever ready to give containment of the Soviet Union first priority, has joined China and the Association of Southeast Asian Nations, ASEAN, in pressuring Vietnam. While this pressure forces Vietnam into the arms of the Soviet Union, its real purpose is to increase the cost of Soviet penetration into Southeast Asia. Thus having waged a long and costly war to rid itself of great power domination, Vietnam's fortunes are still embroiled with those of the great powers.[41]

THE REPUBLIC OF IRAQ

Land and People[42]

Iraq is a country of 17.5 million (1988) people about the size of California. Like many contemporary nation states its boundaries were constructed rather arbitrarily and it has

---

[41]Gareth Porter, "The Great Power Triangle in Southeast Asia" *Current History* 79 (December, 1980): 161 ff. For further background, see Gavin Boyd, "East Asia" in Werner J. Feld and Gavin Boyd, eds., *Comparative Regional Systems: West and East Europe, North America, the Middle East, and Developing Countries* (New York: Pergamon Press, 1980), Chapter 7. For Soviet perceptions and policies in Asia, see Gerald Segal, "The U.S.S.R. and Asia in 1987: Signs of a Major Effort", *Asian Survey* 23 (January, 1988): 1–9.

[42]*Iraq: A Country Study*, Foreign Area Studies, The American University, 3rd ed. (Washington, D.C.: U. S. Government Printing Office, 1979), though dated, is a valuable sourcebook on all aspects of Iraqi society. Hanna Batatu, *The Old Social Classes and the Revolutionary Movements of Iraq* (Princeton, N.J.: Princeton University Press, 1978); Abbas Kelidar, ed., *The Integration of Modern Iraq* (London: Croom Helm, 1979); and Tim Niblock, ed., *Iraq: The Contemporary State* (New York: St. Martin's Press, 1982); and, above all, Phebe Marr, *The Modern History of Iraq* (Boulder, Colo.: Westview, 1985) provide valuable background analyses on all aspects of Iraq's history and society. For an analysis of the unique nature of Arab society, see the section, Preindustrial Hybrids: The Unique Arab World, in Chapter 3.

little in the way of natural frontiers. Many societies have existed and flourished on the soil of present-day Iraq, sustained and nourished by the waters of the Tigris and Euphrates Rivers. Modern Iraq is the Mesopotamia of old, site of the world's earliest agrarian society, Sumer. While plentiful water is the reason behind the continuous settlement of Iraq for 8,000 years, oil has loomed large in its fortunes in the past few decades.

Iraq is an Arab nation and it looks back, not to Sumer and Babylonia for its roots, but to the seventh century A.D. when Mesopotamia was conquered by Arabs and brought under the Islamic religion. Soon after the conquest, the land of the Tigris and Euphrates became the center of Arabic and Islamic culture, while Baghdad (especially under the Abbasid Caliphate) was the leading city of the world for 500 years.

Over 90 percent of Iraq's population is Muslim and of these (70 percent) speak Arabic as their first tongue (and most of the remaining population is familiar with it). Despite this, Iraq is not fully homogeneous. Its first division is among Muslims themselves. The Muslim population is divided by the great schism that runs through all of Islam, the Sunni versus the Shia (commonly but incorrectly referred to as Shiites). The differences between these two wings of Islam are many and often subtle. The Sunni (or orthodox) are numerically dominant in the Islamic world. In the schism that developed after the death of the prophet Mohammed, the Sunni accepted the traditional method of electing the caliph and it accepted the traditional ruling family. The Shia (from Shiat Ali, the Party of Ali) supported Ali, Mohammed's son-in-law as the successor to Mohammed and as leader of the Muslim community.

The Sunni tend to have a more pragmatic approach to the relation between religion and the secular world. A just and moral society must be Muslim but the means for achieving such a society need not entail a merger of clergy and secular power. The Shia tend to stress the role of the Imam, the descendant of the House of Ali, thus designated by God as the spiritual authority at any given time or place. The Imam is not only a spiritual leader but as the concrete spokesperson for God, a political leader as well. With no established method for ascertaining the identity of an Imam, the Shia have themselves split into factions.

The Sunni make up approximately 40 percent of the population and the Shia make up approximately 50 to 55 percent. Thus Iraq is the only Arab nation with a Shia majority. To further complicate matters, only 25 percent of the Sunni are Arab—approximately 18 percent are Kurds. The significance of all this is that the Arab Sunni who dominate politically must contend with actual and potential social cleavages running along religious and ethnic lines. The separation of the population goes beyond religion—the Sunni tend to live in Northern and Central Iraq and tend to be urban, while the Shia live in Southern Iraq and tend to be a depressed rural population. The Kurds also inhabit a distinct geographic area and until the late 1980s had been granted a semiautonomous status.

Economy

The basis of settlement in Iraq for over 8,000 years has been a plentiful supply of water. The land between the Euphrates and Tigris rivers is enormously productive, provided the waters are tamed and distributed by human agency. The enormous agrarian surplus of this region allowed a rich culture to develop and a complex social organization emerged over 5,000 years ago (Sumer) to generate and administer the rich yields of wheat, barley, and other crops.

Large-scale water control is the basis of all the mighty civilizations that arose from agriculture.[43] Taming and harnessing a large volume of wild water require centralized government and such a government is a mixed blessing. The centralized government needed to maintain the irrigation, drainage, and flood control systems in the Tigris-Euphrates region yielded sociopolitical problems as well as food—the large network of government

---

[43]For a discussion, see Chapter 2.

officials and landlords absorbed large amounts of the surplus and quarrels about its distribution created tensions among the upper classes. The Laws of Hammurabi speak both of the achievements of the Sumerian people in building a viable and just society and of the problems their complex and centralized society was generating.

The riches of the region also made it a prey for outsiders. The history of the entire Middle East is filled with the conflicts between settled and nomadic peoples, and with the conflicts among diverse peoples who were brought into contact with each other for one reason or another.

Iraqi territory has flourished for periods through agriculture and trade (for example Sumer, Babylonia, and the Assaid Caliphate from eighth to the thirteenth centuries) and has languished at other periods because of internal dissension, neglect of the water control systems, and war.

Iraq was a stagnant backwater under the Ottoman Empire, as a British Mandate after World War I, and as an independent monarchy between 1932 and 1958. After the emergence of a republic in 1958 and the gradual seizure of power by the Arab Socialist Baath (Resurrection) Party (climaxed by a bloodless coup in 1968), Iraq's economic fortunes improved dramatically, much of it due to the dramatic rise in oil prices after 1973. Whatever the reasons, Iraq has exhibited considerable dynamism in recent decades. Since 1958 it has been ruled by a centralized, one-party government committed to economic reform and growth in the name of an egalitarian, democratic, socialist Iraq.

Land reform was undertaken in 1958 (largely to undermine the power of local landlords who dominated the central government). Though landlords were powerful, Iraq did not have a deep rooted and developed feudal system. Agriculture was important because of water from the Tigris-Euphrates but modern Iraq never developed a landlord government that could control both people and the flow of water. In 1958 large landholdings were expropriated and after some compensation was paid for redistributed

land, the government announced that peasants need pay no more and that the remaining land would be redistributed free. In the name of socialist equality, landholdings were limited and the state attempted to create cooperatives and collective farms. But the agricultural sector stagnated (for various reasons, including lack of irrigation, lack of managerial and farm skills, land fragmentation, shortage of water) and by 1980 Iraq had gone from an exporter to an importer of food.

In 1965, most of the large firms in manufacturing, banking, insurance, and foreign and wholesale trade were nationalized. In addition, the transportation (by railroad, airline, or marine shipping), communication, electric power, water, and tobacco sectors of the economy are state monopolies. In the early 1970s Iraq finally nationalized the oil industry giving the government full ownership and control.

The dictatorship under the Baath Party is consistent with Iraq's history. Iraq was a poor country with no tradition of self-rule and little cohesiveness based on tribal identity. The basic agricultural economy, whether oriented toward export or subsistence, required a central authority to achieve and maintain a complex network of water control. As such, Iraq's agriculture has always oscillated between being a centralized "hydralic civilization" and a relatively poor, decentralized, rainfall-based subsistence economy.

The Baath Party committed Iraq to agricultural improvement to insure self-sufficiency in food, to maximize gains from the sale of its considerable oil resources, and to industrialize. Overall, it pursued a typical Third-World socialist economic and social policy—balanced growth to insure self-sufficiency and internal stability. Again, typically, the government managed to prevent inflation and unemployment, though again typically there is inefficiency because of overstaffing and lack of managerial and other skills.

Iraq's economic growth during the 1960s and 1970s was managed fairly well, yielding both a rising standard of living and the capital investment needed for future growth. Its GNP in 1987 was $40 billion (est.) and per capita income was $2400.[44] In 1980, Iraq, ostensibly hoping to take advantage of Iran's internal revolutionary turmoil, seized full control of the waterway to the Persian Gulf that had formerly been half-held by Iran. But the deeper reason was Iran's open call to all Shia to rise up against their governments, a clear violation of the 1975 accords between Iraq and Iran. The result was a costly eight year war that brought Iraq's social progress to a halt, indeed, has brought about decline.

Polity

Iraq has always had autocratic, authoritarian government though its forms and purposes have varied. Under the Baath Party, Iraq has developed the rudiments of the modern state—bureaucratic administration and a variety of social services to incorporate its citizens into society.

In most complex societies, the present, status quo, is protected by reference to either the past, agrarian society, or to the future, industrial or expanding society. Iraq's rulers refer to their polity as transitional—the future, they claim, will usher in a socialist, democratic, and Islamic society. In the meantime, the origin of government and its derivation from the will of the governed are ignored. And Iraq's rulers even evoke Iraq's strong tradition of pan-Arabic unity in which Iraq is seen as merging with other Arab countries in the Arab Nation.

Before the war with Iran, the ruling Baath party and its leader Saddam Husayn enjoyed considerable popular support and legitimacy. Husayn had full control of the military, the civil service, and the economy. Thanks to Iraq's oil wealth, the party and government were putting down deep roots among the Iraqi people by improving basic living conditions at all levels. Here Iraq had the unique advantage of being an Arab society, or rather, the unique advantage of not having a power-

ful entrenched landed oligarchy to resist modernization and development.[45]

If anything the war has proven the competence of the ruling party and the viability of the institutions it created. After all, war is the supreme test of a social system and Iraq outfought and outlasted a larger and determined foe. Though the country's material progress was halted by the war and the human casualties were high, Iraq may have achieved through war what its oil wealth might not have purchased, nationhood.

Family, Religion, Education, and Health

Iraqi family life is fundamentally similar to that of agrarian societies. The family is the basic unit of society (not the state or the individual) and family members tend to look to relatives for help or to mount economic or political activities. The senior male dominates the family and women are largely confined to household tasks. Elders, especially uncles, are given respect and precedence over those who are younger. Again, as in other societies regardless of type, the centrality of the family has declined in Iraq in response to urbanization, occupational differentiation, and the state's assumption of many functions hitherto performed by the family. Urbanization, economic mobility, and war have also undermined tribal identity throughout Iraq.

Islamic religion is divided by the cleavage between Sunni and Shia. The Sunni approach God directly and there is no elaborate network intermediate to the worshipper and God. The Sunni have clergy who occupy a status much like Christian clergy. Sunni Muslims believe that society should reflect Islamic law but this does not mean that there should be a merger between the civil and religious spheres or that civil society should be subject to a religious leader. The Shia are more mystical in their version of religion and stress the need for an Imam, a specially designated religious

---

[44]Central Intelligence Agency, *The World Factbook 1988* Washington, D.C.: U. S. Government Printing Office, 1988), p. 113f.

[45]For more on the unique nature of Arab society (excluding Egypt), see Chapter 3.

leader who is free of sin and error and can lead and even redeem society.

Religion is potentially important to Iraq because Sunni Arabs dominate the society. Long an urban-oriented ruling class engaged in civil and military administration, the Sunni rule a rural-oriented Shia Arab group, who form a numerical majority, and a sizable group of Sunni Kurds. The advent of a Shia-led revolution in Iran, the spread of religious fundamentalism during 1979–80, and the call to Iraq's Shia by Iran's Imam, the Ayatollah Khomeini, to overthrow the Sunni regime, undoubtedly did much to prompt the Iraqi government to invade Iran in September of 1980.

Educational changes in Iraq follow the pattern of all developing (perhaps especially socialist) countries. Education is free from primary grades through university; an effort has been made to extend education outside the cities; vocational education has been stressed; and educational opportunities have been extended to women.

Health care is socialized and free. Like other socialist societies Iraq has stressed the right to health and has recognized the economic value of a healthy population. Sanitation measures and other forms of disease prevention have been stressed along with the provision of primary care facilities, especially in rural areas.

Class and Dependency

Iraqi society never developed (except for brief periods) as a peasant or feudal system. Its system of stratification does not fit the usual pattern of either caste or estate stratification. Even with its potentially rich agricultural base, Iraq never became an agrarian society with an articulate stratum of hereditary landlords and a well-defined stratum of serfs. The essential basis of Arab society (with the exception of Egypt) was trade not agriculture.

The apex of historic Arab society was composed of diverse elites: merchants, urban-based administrators and warriors, landlords, and tribal chiefs. Below them were other diverse groups in ill-defined relations.[46]

Changes in Iraqi society occurred with the end of the Ottoman Empire and the impact of British imperialism.[47] By and large, British policy led to a coalescence of Iraqi elites into a static upper class of landlords and traditional political leaders.[48] By the time of the 1958 revolution Iraqi society was extremely unequal with a tiny handful of families owning most of the land. The Iraqi ruling class was out-of-step with the growing urban "middle class," the new oil wealth, and with Arab nationalism.[49] The 1958 Revolution destroyed the power of landlords and created a modern state. The outstanding change within socialist Iraq is the enormous growth of the public sector. The essence of class in contemporary Iraq is largely a function of state employment. The upper class of Iraq is made up of high party and governmental-military officials, upper-level civil servants and professionals, and so on down the ladder to other occupational levels. Of great importance is the fact that Iraqi class relations do not depend on squeezing a surplus out of the lower classes. Oil revenues have provided the wherewithal for job creation, upward mobility, and a wide range of public services.

---

[46]C. A. O. Van Nieuwenhuijze, *Social Stratification and the Middle East* (Leiden: E. J. Rill, 1965) and Samir Amin, *The Arab Nation*, tr. Michael Pallis (London: Zed Press, 1978; originally published 1976), Chapter 1.

[47]For the relation between internal and external developments in Iraq, see Edith and E. F. Penrose, *Iraq: International Relations and National Development* (London: Ernest Benn, 1978) and Christine Moss Helms, *Iraq: Eastern Flank of the Arab World* (Washington, D.C.: The Brookings Institution, 1986). For background on the contemporary Middle East as a regional system, see James P. Piscatori and R. K. Ramazani, "The Middle East" in Werner J. Feld and Gavin Boyd, eds., *Comparative Regional Systems: West and East Europe, North America, the Middle East, and Developing Countries* (New York: Pergamon Press, 1980), Chapter 8.

[48]David Pool, "From Elite to Class: The Transformation of Iraqi Political Leadership" in Abbas Kelidar, ed., *The Integration of Modern Iraq* (London: Croom Helm, 1979), pp. 63–87.

[49]For a richly detailed history and analysis of Iraq, especially in the pre-1958 period, see Hanna Batatu, *The Old Social Classes and the Revolutionary Movements of Iraq* (Princeton, N.J.: Princeton University Press, 1978).

The new inequality of Iraq may not stem from private property, but it is also not due to socialism say critics. What has emerged, critics claim, is a "bureaucratic bourgeoisie," a state capitalist society. Similar criticisms from the left have been levelled against Cuba, Tanzania, and other socialist societies both developed and developing. State ownership of the economy, in other words, is not necessarily socialism.

Iraq's upper class and its other classes are dependent on the export of oil and ultimately on their success in translating oil revenues into industry, self-sufficiency in food, and public services. It is also dependent on how well it can use its oil revenues to lubricate the relations among its religious-ethnic groups and defend itself from a variety of forces inside (pan-Arabic, communist) and outside (Iran, Syria, and others). Like other countries it is dependent on an export economy. Unlike other developing countries that must sell sugar, coffee, or bauxite in a soft market, Iraq and other oil-rich countries have a product that may experience low prices for a time (as it did during the 1980s) but whose future worth is assured.

Iraq's foreign relations before 1980 placed it in the revolutionary Arab camp along with Algeria, Libya, and Syria. It was anti-Israel and anti-United States. It was hostile to the "conservative" Arab countries such as Egypt, Saudi Arabia, and the smaller Gulf oil states, such as Kuwait, for trying to reach a settlement with Israel under the good offices of the United States. During this time Iraq accepted the support of the Soviet Union, which became its biggest supplier of arms (along with France).

During the war with Iran, Iraq became a favorite of the "conservative" Arab nations because of their fear of the revolutionary religious fervor of Iran. It received considerable aid from Saudi Arabia and the Gulf Emirates and moral support from Egypt. The United States has adopted an official policy of neutrality. Its public stance was that the Iraq-Iran war should be brought to a negotiated settlement with no winner or loser. The United States' overall interest was to prevent Iran from overturning the conservative Arab societies, especially Saudi Arabia. But it also wanted Iran's favor on a long-term basis as a counter to Soviet influence in the region. Through its naval actions in the Persian Gulf and working through the United Nations (with Soviet help), it helped to bring about a cease-fire between Iraq and Iran in 1988.

PART V *Case Studies of Developed and Developing Segmented Societies*

CHAPTER

15

CANADA AND YUGOSLAVIA
Developed Segmented Societies

INTRODUCTION: THE UNIVERSE OF SEGMENTED SOCIETIES

The United States and the Soviet Union are associational societies. The bulk of societies in the world, however, are segmented (or multicommunal). Part V explores a representative variety of segmented societies. This chapter examines two developed societies, one capitalist (Canada) and one socialist (Yugoslavia). Chapter 16 examines three developing capitalist societies that are segmented (Nigeria, Malaysia, and Sri Lanka).

A segmented society is one in which different ethnic or racial groups either want or are forced to live separately. In an associational society all ethnic-racial groups share much in common and are expected to participate fully in the values, beliefs, and group-life of society (realistically, as defined by a dominant group).[1]

Segmented societies are not always successful in accommodating their various groups, for example, civil war breaks out, repression and even genocide are resorted to, societies are split up, or chronic political instability occurs. Successful accommodation takes a number of forms. Switzerland is the preeminent case of success among multicommunal societies. The Swiss solved the problem of segmentation fairly simply (with the aid of geographical isolation, economic expansion, and neutrality in Europe's wars): they instituted one citizenship, one foreign policy, and one customs entity for all ethnic groups but otherwise gave each ethnic-linguistic group full territorially based freedom to practice their language and religion and to run their own educational system and local affairs. Switzerland's policy of linguistic-ethnic territoriality has resulted in 23 local units (cantons) of which 14 are German, 4 French, 1 Italian, 3 bilingual, and 1 trilingual.

Belgium has also opted for linguistic territoriality plus compromise in areas where sep-

---

[1] For a full discussion, see the section, Segmented Nation States, in Chapter 4.

aration is not feasible. In addition, linguistic groups are represented in the central government and tax money supports a variety of ethnically based services such as radio and television stations. There is also autonomy for religious groups.

Variations on Switzerland's and Belgium's practices are found throughout the universe of segmented societies. Major difficulties arise when one ethnic group tries to make one language or one religion the official language or religion, for example, when the Sinhalese made their language the primary tongue of Sri Lanka. Another source of difficulty is when ethnic separation masks the economic domination of one ethnic group over another, for example, Protestants over Roman Catholics in Northern Ireland.

CANADA: A SEGMENTED LIBERAL NATION STATE

Land and People[2]

Canada is the second largest country in the world, much of it vacant. Though inhospitable in great part for permanent settlement (most of Canada's population lives close to the American border), Canada's natural environment holds an abundance of resources.

Canada's population growth has fluctuated because of ups and downs in the birth rate, the ebb and flow of newcomers from abroad, and migration south to the United States. At present Canada's fertility rate is low and is tending toward the replacement

level. Nonetheless, population growth has continued and reached the 26 million mark in 1988.

The 1981 census was the first to recognize more than one ethnic origin for an individual. In 1981, 7.6 percent of the population (1.8 million) identified themselves as having more than one ethnic identity. Of these over three-fourths reported British as one of the sources of their ethnic identity. Of those who gave a single source 40.2 percent were British, 26.7 were French, followed by German (4.75 percent), Italian (3.1 percent), and Ukrainian (2.2 percent).

The 1986 census revealed that English was the mother tongue of 61 percent of the population and French the tongue of 24 percent. The number of people able to speak both English and French (Canada's official languages) in 1981 was 3.7 million, a significant increase since the 1971 census. The 1986 census revealed that the proportion of Francophones continued to decline in Canada (stationary at 80 percent in Quebec) and the proportion of Anglophones continued to decline in Quebec.

The Overall (Ideal) Social System

Expressed in ideal or formal terms the Canadian social system has the following features: a sovereign state and the sovereign individual; a rational (scientific), futuristic (progressive) and secular-humanistic (though not necessarily antireligious) value-norm or symbolic system; a pluralistic group or power structure (multiparty political system, contending economic often regional interests, a variety of business, professional, labor, ethnic, religious, fraternal, charitable and educational voluntary associations, and provincial and subprovincial governments); specialized institutional structures, all of which allegedly center around the values and norms of individual achievement as developed and expressed in the central concepts of a free-market structure, a free electoral structure, and a free or voluntary system of social groups; and a class system of inequality in which social benefits are distributed according to performance by

[2]Basic information on Canada is available from *Canada Yearbook: Review of Economic, Social, and Political Developments in Canada* (Ottawa: Statistics Canada, Annual). For general background, see Arthur R. M. Lower, *Canadians in the Making: A Social History of Canada* (Toronto: Longmans Green, 1958); S. D. Clark, *The Developing Canadian Community* (Toronto: University of Toronto Press, 1962); George Woodcock, *The Canadians* (Cambridge, Mass.: Harvard University Press, 1979); Richard A. Preston, ed., *Perspectives on Revolution and Evolution* (Durham, N.C.: Duke University Press, 1979); and Elliot J. Feldman and Neil Nevitte, eds., *The Future of North America: Canada, The United States, and Quebec Nationalism* (Cambridge, Mass.: Center for International Affairs, 1979).

individuals in the struggle against nature and in the rational management of society, and not according to birth, religion, ethnicity, or race.

Canada is a political democracy and shares the liberal or middle-class view of human nature and nature with other liberal democracies such as the United Kingdom, the United States, France, and Australia. In contrast to other views of human nature and nature, the liberal world view (still speaking in ideal terms) assumes that humans can achieve a mastery of themselves and of nature through human reason (science) and human effort (the Protestant-bourgeois personality).

Commentators have agreed that there is a particular Canadian variant of the liberal social system just as there are particular British and American variants. Like Britain, and unlike the United States, Canadian society is not based on a convenant derived from starkly stated social and philosophical principles. Canada represents an attempt to continue European culture in the New World (English and French) rather than to break with it. So too, no understanding of Canadian political and social institutions is possible unless one knows that Canada inherited rather than created its democratic values and ideas. Democracy in Canada began and has flourished more as a functional device and necessity (to better manage the sprawling diversity that was and is Canadian society) than as a revolutionary response to ideological and moral imperatives.

Given its unique natural environment, history, and American influence, Canada is alleged to be more equalitarian than Britain but less so than the United States; more achievement oriented and futuristic than Britain but less so than the United States; and more willing to define itself in spacious universalistic terms than Britain but less so than the United States. For a variety of reasons Canada has had a more explicit elitism than its fellow liberal society, the United States. The state (including the military) and the church (Anglican and Roman Catholic) were accepted by the Canadian people as part of a broad consensus about the value of authority structures, again in sharp contrast to developments in the United States. Canada's elitism has been counterbalanced somewhat by the egalitarianism of low-church Protestantism, the influence of the frontier, assorted types of radical movements, economic expansion, mass education, and mass immigration.

Unlike preindustrial societies, which have social functions performed by specialized groups, especially the family ranked by estates or castes, Canada, like all other industrial societies, relies (formally) on the versatile and yet specialized individual to see to it that its population is replenished and fed, the young motivated and educated, its internal disputes settled, and its boundaries and interests upheld. The use of the individual as a social type to perform social functions is part of the deep institutional specialization of industrial society. Unlike agrarian societies, distinctive institutional areas exist in Canada charged with the performance of specific functions.

Less formally speaking, Canada in fact relies on economic and occupationally specialized groups to make its society work. Though overshadowed by its reliance on private, specialized groups, Canada also has a significant corporatist tradition or tendency to hold private groups to public accountability.

Economy[3]

Though Canada has a private enterprise economy, it never made a radical commitment either to laissez-faire economic theory or practice. Its origins as a British colony subject to British imperial policy, its elitist parliamentary tradition, the obstacles encountered in settling a harsh Northern environment, and the danger of absorption by its giant neighbor to the south, all combined to bring about an explicit acceptance of the need for strong governmental direction of the Canadian economy.

---

[3]For two contrasting histories of the Canadian economy, see R. T. Naylor, *The History of Canadian Business, 1867–1914* (Toronto: James Lorimer, 1975) and William L. Marr and Donald G. Paterson, *Canada, An Economic History* (Toronto: Macmillan, 1980).

As an industrial society Canada ranks high among the world's economies in terms of gross national product ($412.8 billion, 1987) and enjoys one of the world's highest per capita incomes ($15,900, 1987).[4]

Canadian economic institutions contain a number of structural features and trends that are common to other industrial countries and a number that are unique. As in other countries, the steady growth of industry and urbanization has drastically altered its occupational structure: primary occupations (mining, fishing, lumber, especially agricultural) have declined drastically while secondary occupations (manufacturing) have remained stationary and tertiary or service occupations (professional, managerial, clerical, sales) have grown steadily. And, as in other industrial countries, most sectors of the Canadian economy are highly concentrated. Collective bargaining is fully established and approximately 37 percent of Canadian workers belong to labor unions (1986), somewhat down from previous years. Like other developed capitalist societies Canada tolerates considerable unemployment (9 percent during the 1980s). A unique feature of the Canadian economy and a source of chronic uneasiness among Canadians is the fact that significant portions of the Canadian economy (as high as two-thirds in manufacturing and mining) are owned and controlled by foreign firms, especially firms based in the United States.

The Canadian economy has long relied on the production and export of raw materials: fur, fish, grain, minerals, oil, gas, and timber. During the 1970s and 1980s Canada made an effort to diversify its economy, emphasizing more processing of its raw materials, and greater reliance on regional strengths. In 1988 its conservative government concluded a free-trade agreement with the United States indicating both that it felt that Canada was able to compete, and that it was necessary for it to learn how to compete in continental and world markets. Opponents of the free trade agreement

argued that, far from strengthening Canada's national identity, free trade would further the absorption of Canada by the United States.

Polity[5]

Formally speaking, Canada's political institutions are rational-legal in nature (as opposed to traditional or charismatic), a parliamentary variant as opposed to the presidential type in the United States. Under the parliamentary system, electoral districts (ridings) choose among candidates representing political parties (themselves not actually part of the state but voluntary organizations). Those chosen assemble as a legislature (the House of Commons) and the party having a majority, or occasionally the largest party, forms a government and is able (usually) to govern up to five years using its majority in the House to enact laws binding on the population at large.[6]

Unlike Great Britain, Canada is a federal state governed by a written constitution, the British North America Act (1867) and by the Canadian-constructed Constitution Act of 1982. The 1982 constitution formalized Canadian constitutional practices, established the division of powers between the federal and provincial governments, clarified the amending

[4]Central Intelligence Agency, *The World Factbook 1988* (Washington, D.C.: U. S. Government Printing Office, 1988), p. 42.

[5]For background on and various interpretations of the Canadian polity, see Donald V. Smiley, *Canada In Question: Federalism in the Seventies*, 3rd ed. (Toronto: McGraw-Hill Ryerson, 1980); Leo Panitch, ed., *The Canadian State: Political Economy and Political Power* (Toronto: University of Toronto Press, 1977); David V. Bell and Lorne Tepperman, *The Roots of Disunity: A Look at Canadian Political Culture* (Toronto: McClelland and Stewart, 1979); Garth Stevenson, *Unfulfilled Union: Canadian Federalism and National Unity* (Toronto: Gage, 1979); Hugh G. Thorburn, ed., *Party Politics In Canada*, 5th ed. (Toronto: Prentice Hall Canada, 1985); Ronald I. Cheffins and Patricia A. Johnson, *The Revised Canadian Constitution: Politics as Law* (Toronto: McGraw-Hill Ryerson, 1986); and Robert J. Jackson, Doreen Jackson, and Nicolas J. Baxter-Moore, *Politics In Canada: Culture, Institutions, Behavior, and Public Policy* (Toronto: Prentice Hall Canada, 1986).

[6]Canada's political system is male dominated. For an analysis, with valuable comparisons with other Western-style democracies, see Sylvia B. Bashevkin, *Toeing The Line: Women and Party Politics In English Canada* (Toronto: University of Toronto Press, 1985).

process, and formalized a list of fundamental rights and freedoms.

Unlike the American constitution, Canada's constitution is not permeated by a negative view of government; its main purpose is to distribute jurisdictions and functions between the federal parliament and government and the provincial parliaments and government. Within this framework each level of government is sovereign. Unlike the United States Supreme Court, therefore, the Canadian Supreme Court does not decide whether a legislature is entitled to act but rather *which* legislature can act.

The legal system of Canada is derived from two sources: English common law for English Canada and French civil law in Quebec.[7]

The Basis of Segmentation

The basis of segmentation in Canada is the existence of two large ethnic-linguistic groups, or rather one dominant and one subordinate ethnic-linguistic group. Some nation states developed in terms of definite geographical boundaries, a common political system capped by a sovereign state, a common legal system, a common citizenship, and a broad homogeneity in religion, ethnicity, and language. From its confederation in 1867, Canada has lacked the broad homogeneity of religion, ethnicity, and language characteristic of some other nation states. Other social systems, of course, have been marked by diversity and even with serious internal problems, but Canada's particular problem stems from the fact that much of its diversity is sanctioned legally and politically. It is not so much that Canada is officially a bilingual society or that it is ethnically diverse, but rather that it contains a large ethnic-religious minority, French Canadians, who have control of their own political-governmental system: the province of Quebec.

A segmented society is one in which a variety of power groups (located on one or a mixture of linguistic, religious, and national origin dimensions), remain ethnically, economically, politically, and racially distinct. Some segmented societies manage to function amidst such diversity and others are less successful. English-French relations in Canada were relatively successful when both groups were more diverse. As French Canada became more like the rest of urban-industrial Canada, French Canadians became more separatist and segmentation increased. Though French Canada has been economically dominated by English Canadians, French Canadians have been able to assert themselves politically. Canada's federal system gives each province considerable power and French Canadians not only have full control of Quebec's provincial government but have considerable leverage in federal politics since they provide the bulk of the elected members of Parliament for the party that has governed Canada the longest. In short, the facts of Canada's social development make it feasible for many French Canadians to think of themselves as forming a distinct and viable social system independent of the rest of Canada.[8]

---

[7]For a analysis of Canadian law, including valuable discussions on the nature of law, the position of the lawyer in Canada, and legal education, see Gerald L. Gall, *The Canadian Legal System*, 2nd ed. (Toronto: Carswell Legal Publications, 1983).

[8]E. C. Hughes, *French Canada in Transition* (Toronto: University of Toronto, 1963), though written in 1943, is still the best introduction to premodern Quebec and to the dynamics that changed it from a family-based, subsistence community to an urban-industrial province. Herbert F. Quinn's *The Union Nationale: A Study in Quebec Nationalism* (Toronto: University of Toronto Press, 1963) places Quebec politics in an indispensable historical and social context. For a fascinating collection of essays and extracts on concrete aspects of French Canadian life (land use, family, birth-rate, industrialization, class structure, the Roman Catholic Church, etc.), see Marcel Rioux and Yves Martin, eds., *French-Canadian Society* (Toronto: McClelland and Stewart, 1964), Vol. 1. For a collection of essays ranging from the evolution of Quebec to the separatist movement of recent decades, which provide a comprehensive and politically sophisticated sociology of Quebec and its relations with the rest of Canada, see Herbert Guindon, *Quebec Society: Tradition, Modernity, and Nationhood*, edited and introduced by Roberta Hamilton and John L. McMullen (Toronto: University of Toronto Press, 1988). For a valuable discussion of Canada as an approximation of a consociational society (over-

During the nineteenth century there emerged a definite ideology of biculturalism to parallel the bilingualism of the Canadian population. Until World War I, French Canadians maintained a coherent clerico-agrarian ideology in opposition to the industrializing, (liberal) democratizing currents in the rest of Canada. The Quebec government played a collaborative role for foreign capital (until 1960). Between 1920 and 1941 the percentage of Quebec's labor force engaged in agriculture declined from 37 percent to 10 percent and the percentage engaged in manufacturing rose from 38 percent to 64 percent. The pace of change has been even more dramatic since 1941. In regard to almost every type of behavior and condition Quebec has become almost indistinguishable from the rest of Canada. Since World War I French Canadians have become urban people and their birth rate has declined to a level below the national rate.

Quebec has changed in many specific ways. It has drastically revised its civil code that derived from the Code Napoleon. Especially important are the changes affecting women, changes which in effect have completed the transformation of the political-legal status of women, which started in 1945 when women were given the right to vote in provincial elections. In a wider setting, the Quebec Liberal party's victory in 1960 inaugurated a significant reform of Quebec's political system: a commitment to an honest and efficient civil service, a legislature committed to normal (liberal) democratic procedures, and the development of a public who now accepts political and governmental action as a legitimate way to realize their aspirations. The Parent Commission's Report on Education in 1963–4 was evidence of a widespread desire in Quebec to develop an educational system geared to the scientific-technological age (and one that could help Quebec assert its claims against the rest of Canada).

Although the long-range trend in Quebec's internal development indicates a growing similarity with the rest of Canada, French Canadian nationalism has also grown. The victory of Rene Levesque's separatist and left of center party (*Parti Quebecois*) in 1976 was a significant move toward bringing the issue of separatism and reform to a head. Not only did the separatist movement challenge the political status of the province within the federal union but it challenged the economic hegemony of the English-speaking capitalists who have dominated the province's economy (with the help of the Quebec government) up until 1960. The government's White Paper on language in the spring of 1977, which accompanied a bill to make French the primary language of Quebec's private and public life, including education, was clearly directed at achieving a new economic status for French Canadians within Quebec and a new political status vis a vis the rest of Canada. Hydro Quebec, a government energy corporation, conducts business in French. Significantly French Canadian universities have increased their output of graduates with business degrees.

The separatist government and movement suffered a severe setback in 1980 with the defeat of a referendum to authorize the Quebec government to negotiate a new status for Quebec. The 80 percent of Quebec's population who are French Canadians split 40/40 on a referendum to authorize the government to begin negotiations for "associate status" with Canada. Since English-speaking Quebecers voted en masse against the referendum, it lost, 59/41.[9] Separation faded and in 1987, Premier Bourassa of Quebec reached an agreement with the federal government and the other provinces to sign the Constitution Act of 1982.

---

coming segmentation based on language, religion, and regionalism), see Kenneth McRae, ed., *Consociational Democracy: Political Accommodation in Segmented Societies* (Toronto: McClelland and Stewart, 1974), Part Four, especially the essay by Kenneth McRae, "Consociationalism and the Canadian Political System."

[9]For a background and opposing views on contemporary Quebec, see Pierre Vallieres, *White Niggers of America: The Precocious Autobiography of a Quebec "Terrorist"* (New York: Monthly Review Press, 1972); Michael B. Stein, *The Dynamics of Right Wing Protest: A Political Analysis of Social Credit in Quebec* (Toronto: University of Toronto Press, 1973); Dale C. Thomson, ed., *Quebec: Society and Politics* (Toronto: McClelland and Stewart, 1973); Leon Dion, *Quebec: The Unfinished Revolution* (Montreal: McGill-

Family, Religion, and Education

Canada's family system is a monogamous nuclear system, that is, a family composed of husband, wife, and immediate children.[10] Not only is the nuclear family limited in number but it performs only limited functions. No longer an important productive, religious, educational, or recreational unit, the nuclear family is now primarily a reproductive unit, a center for the socialization of the young, a consumption unit, and the primary source of emotional gratification, stability, and refuge for adults. With Canada's transition to an urban-industrial society after World War I and the resulting separation of residence and work, it was inevitable that the nuclear family would emerge as the Canadian family type. Even in Quebec, the self-sufficient, multifunctional *habitant* family has been gradually transformed by the magnetic pull of industry and city. Family and kinship are still strong, especially among Canada's native peoples and among the relatively large number of South Mediterranean immigrants who came to Canada after World War II, but the trend toward the specialized and relatively unstable nuclear family is clear and pronounced.

In 1986 Canada had 8.9 million private households of which 73.8 percent were family and 26.2 percent were nonfamily. As is true of the United States and other developed societies the size of households has declined in Canada and the number of households occupied by one person (21 percent) or by unrelated persons (4.7 percent) has grown. Among family households, the number of one-parent households has also grown significantly (to 13 percent of family households).

Culturally defined age and sex attributes are used in Canada (as in all societies) to assign individuals to social functions. Age and sex definitions, perhaps necessary in an earlier age, linger on to become the basis of exploitation in a later age. Youth and vigor were once highly prized because they were needed in coping with a harsh nature. Today they are still prized though no longer so economically necessary and serve as an excuse to discard older members of the labor force that the Canadian economy has no room for. Women were restricted to home and hearth at one time and a distinct cultural definition of women as passive, inferior, and inherently feminine developed. While perhaps necessary to preindustrial society, this definition of women serves to restrict their access to the broader experiences made possible by industrialization and to make them an exploitable segment of the labor force.

Nonetheless women have entered the labor force and are now engaged in a wide variety of activities outside the home. Despite the law and despite self-help movements and organizations, it cannot be said that women in Canada, any more than women elsewhere, have made relative gains in the economy or society. A jump in the divorce rate after the new divorce law of 1968 probably represents a gain for women in that they can now escape from unhappy marriages (but at considerable cost since the women are the chief economic losers in divorce).[11]

Approximately 47 percent of Canadians are Roman Catholics and 41 percent are Protestants (7 percent report no religious preference). Essentially, however, Canada is

---

Queen's University Press, 1976); Pierre Fournier, *The Quebec Establishment: The Ruling Class and the State* (Montreal: Black Rose Books, 1976); Richard D. Basham, *Crisis in Blanc and White: Urbanization and Ethnic Identity in French Canada* (Cambridge, Mass.: Schenkmen, 1978); Henry Milner, *Politics in the New Quebec* (Toronto: McClelland and Stewart, 1978); and Kenneth McRoberts and Dale Postgate, *Quebec: Social Cleavage and Political Crisis*, rev. ed. (Toronto: McClelland and Stewart, 1980).

[10]For background, see K. Ishwaran, ed. and intro., *The Canadian Family* (Toronto: Holt, Rinehart and Winston, 1971); and "Family and Demography", ed. P. Krishnan, *Journal of Comparative Family Studies* VII (Summer, 1976), Special Issue.

[11]For background on women in Canada, see the *Report of the Royal Commission on the Status of Women in Canada* (Ottawa: Information Canada, 1970); MaryLee Stephenson, ed., *Women in Canada* (Toronto: New Press, 1973); Susan Mann Trofinenkoff and Alison Prentice, eds., *The Neglected Majority: Essays in Canadian Women's History* (Toronto: McClelland and Stewart, 1977); and Pat Armstrong and Hugh Armstrong, *The Double Ghetto: Canadian Women and Their Segregated Work*, rev.ed. (Toronto: McClelland and Stewart, 1984).

a Protestant country since the large Roman Catholic minority is concentrated in Quebec (and to a lesser degree in New Brunswick). Historically, religion has played a large role in the development of education (notably at the university level) though the control of education has gradually passed into the hands of the state, business leaders, and professionals, even in Quebec. Historically, the political impact of religion has been strong though varied. High church orientations (Roman Catholic and Anglican) have left a deep authoritarian imprint on Canadian public life, while low church or sect orientations have tended to pluralize and democratize Canadian life. Economically, both Protestant churches and sects and the Roman Catholic Church had a retarding effect on Canadian development.[12]

With the growth of industrialization and the emergence of universal suffrage, Canada (like other industrial societies) has developed a compulsory or mass educational system.[13] The same problems associated with public education in other countries have appeared in Canadian education. There is a wide disparity in per capita educational expenditure and in educational quality from province to province (the quality of education is especially uneven between rural and urban areas and provinces). Most elementary and high school educational systems are still dominated by university preparation curricula though significant attempts have been made in recent years to adopt curricula (and teaching as well) as to the diverse needs of an ever more specialized economy. The industrial boom in the post-World War II period created large gaps between Canada's economic needs and the education of its population. The serious need

for university trained personnel of almost every description, for example, brought about a dramatic expansion of Canadian higher education during the 1960s. Despite the delegation of jurisdiction over education to the provinces by Canada's constitution, the federal government now pays for 50 percent of postsecondary education (82 percent of higher education financing is public).

Canada's Colonial Heritage

Canada was settled as a colony of France but became a colony of England in 1760 with the defeat of French power in North America by British arms.[14] The basic thrust for the settlement of the New World was not only profit but also national glory and power, religious freedom, and religious missionary zeal. Canada was developed in terms of its salient geographic feature: the St. Lawrence River which allows access to the Great Lakes and the Mississippi River, and thus to the heart of the North American continent. As in the development of modern Greece, Canada's original development comprises largely the story of British mercantilist policy, a policy later adopted by Canada under confederation (National Policy). Mercantilism is a preindustrial political economy in which political and economic means are used to build up a society's net worth and to ensure its self-sufficiency. The main agencies of mercantilism are state-charted companies and the merchant-finan-

---

[12]S. D. Clark, *Church and Sect in Canada* (Toronto: University of Toronto Press, 1948) and *The Developing Canadian Community* (Toronto: University of Toronto Press, 1962), Part II.

[13]For background see George Martell, ed., *The Politics of the Canadian Public School* (Toronto: J. Lorimar, 1974); Thomas H. B. Symons, *To Know Ourselves: The Report of the Commission on Canadian Studies* (Ottawa: Association of Universities and Colleges of Canada, 1975), 2 vols.; and Alison Prentice, *The School Promoters* (Toronto: McClelland and Stewart, 1977).

[14]The standard histories of Canada have been found wanting mostly by theorists on the left: Arthur K. Davis, "Canadian Society and History as Hinterland Versus Metropolis" in Richard J. Ossenberg, ed., *Canadian Society: Pluralism, Change, and Conflict* (Scarborough, Ontario: Prentice-Hall, 1971), pp. 6–32; Gary Temple, ed., *Capitalism and the National Question in Canada* (Toronto: University of Toronto, 1972); H. Edward English, ed., *Canada-United States Relations* (New York: Academy of Political Science, 1976); Wallace Clement, *Continental Corporate Power: Economic Elite Linkages Between Canada and the United States* (Toronto: McClelland and Stewart, 1977); John Hutcheson, *Dominance and Dependency: Liberalism and National Policies in the North American Triangle* (Toronto: McClelland and Stewart, 1978); and Daniel Glenday, Hubert Guindon, and Allan Turowetz, eds., *Modernization and the Canadian State* (Toronto: Macmillan, 1978).

cier rather than the private, market-oriented firm and the industrial capitalist.

British imperialist penetration took two forms: the British merchant entrepreneur (often with a monopoly charter and favorable trading terms) and British loans especially to public authorities with the taxing power to pay their interest and repay their principal.

The fact that Canada was also largely settled by an imperialist power created an obvious but important difference with other colonial areas. The English-Canadian connection to London and Westminster could be far more complete and enthusiastic than say the relations between Britain and Greece or Britain and Turkey. And relations between Britain and Canada were far different than the relation of Britain to its other colonies where white English settlers superimposed themselves on native peoples of a different skin color and different sociocultural background (for example, Kenya, Rhodesia). Finally Canada is unique in that English settlers superimposed themselves not only over a small native population but over a sizable group composed of settlers from another imperialist power.

The early merchant capitalists, supported by English capital, markets, and monopolies, and by local English government officials, exploited Canada's fur, timber, land, grain, and fish. Profits were also made in banking, insurance, maritime shipping, railroads, and retailing. By 1867 Montreal was clearly the metropolitan center of Canada, which, along with important urban complexes in Halifax and Toronto, exploited a vast hinterland.

Confederation in 1867 marks the emergence of Canada as a nation state though full "autonomy" came in 1928 (in 1981 Canada petitioned the British Parliament and received the right to revise its constitution on its own, that is, Canada officially became a sovereign nation with the Constitution Act of 1982). But as R. T. Naylor points out, confederation was far different than is usually thought. Confederation also represented the emergence of Canadian mercantilism, which, hand-in-hand with British mercantilism, created the "Third Commercial Empire of the St. Lawrence,"

which lasted from 1867 to the decline of British imperial power after World War I.[15] According to Naylor, Confederation was the triumph of the English merchant-financial class over the remainder of Canada, in effect providing legitimacy for a Canadian core (metropole) to dominate a Canadian periphery (hinterland).

Confederation established a strong federal authority over all matters pertaining to economic development and gave it a base in the most important form of taxation in that day to insure the inflow of British portfolio capital. The basic source of taxes in 1867 was tariffs on imports. The federal government's early supremacy began to decline after World War II to some extent because the basic tax power had shifted to the provinces. Tariffs were no longer an important source of revenue—all direct taxes including the all-important income tax are reserved to the provinces.

The National Policy of high tariffs did not protect Canadian industry of which there was none but was designed by merchant capitalists to attract capital (supported by the Quebec clergy in hopes of keeping their flock home paying tithes and rents, and using the railroads of which they were major stockholders) and to expand overall absolute economic activity. Canada's entire industrial development was firmly based on the primacy of profits from high credit, transportation, and raw material costs. National Policy also meant a branch-plant economy owned and supervised from abroad—industry in Canada but no Canadian industry.

National Policy eventually brought the Liberal Party to power as direct American investment began to supplant British portfolio

---

[15]R. T. Naylor, *The History of Canadian Business, 1867–1914* (Toronto: James Lorimer, 1975), 2 vols. Naylor's thesis is also in two articles: "The Rise and Fall of the Third Commercial Empire of the St. Lawrence" in Gary Teeple, ed., *Capitalism and the National Question in Canada* (Toronto: University of Toronto Press, 1972), pp. 1–41, also reprinted, W. E. Mann and Les Wheatcroft, eds., *Canada: A Sociological Profile* (Toronto: Copp Clark, 1976), pp. 42–65; and "Dominion of Capital: Canada and International Investment" in Alkis Kontos, ed., *Domination* (Toronto: University of Toronto Press, 1975), pp. 33–68.

investment.[16] The mercantilist sector of the Canadian economy has also lost ground to the American dominated manufacturing and extractive industries sector.[17] American direct investment blurs a Canadian identity by promoting a "free trade continentalism" while at the same time enhancing provincial power by paying "direct taxes" and royalties on provincial extractive industry. In short American direct investment, promoted by the dominant Canadian political party, helps to undermine the power of the federal government and the emergence of an autonomous Canadian nation.[18]

The Canadian character has been affected by the fact that Canada did not derive the bulk of its capital from its own people. It was spared much of the laissez-faire, social Darwinist practices and ideology that plagued (and still do) English and American society. Its merchant-financial class gave it a positive image of government, which has held it in good stead in its struggle to solve problems of unemployment, poverty, urban blight, health, and education.

Canada has imported much of its labor (unskilled workers from Mediterranean countries, professional workers from England and the United States). Not surprisingly, Canada up to the 1980s was unable to gain a clear identity as a core state.[19] Canada's regionalism is a potent source of disunity with the federal government increasingly reduced to a collector and distributor of transfer payments, and a first among equals in relation to the ten provinces. Much of Canada's disunity is not due to the fact that Canadians have different values, attitudes, or behavioral patterns—*on the contrary, the more that Canadians have come to agree on the primacy of economic gain and self-interest, the more Canadian disunity has grown, especially when provinces want absolute and relative improvements vis a vis other provinces.*[20]

The development of Canada has produced marked regional economic disparities. Southern Ontario and the Montreal region have dominated in manufacturing, finance, and trade while the remainder of Canada has specialized in farming and extraction. As a result there is a marked disparity among and within the provinces in standard of living and amounts of unemployment and poverty. The Maritimes, rural Quebec, and much of the prairies are consistently depressed regions while Alberta and British Columbia have built up a relative prosperity because of their rich primary resources.[21] A long tradition of political protest against their "colonial" relation to the urban-manufacturing East increased as Alberta and British Columbia prospered (the clamor for separation abated during the 1980s).

Historically, a large part of federal politics and administration have been devoted to making this skewed economy work. The Maritime provinces receive transfer payments to bolster their economies while Quebec, Alberta, and British Columbia are mollified in various ways to forestall serious confrontation over the issue of whether staying in the Canadian union is worth the economic price of having to pay higher prices for services and manufactured goods obtained from On-

---

[16]American penetration has been facilitated, of course, by proximity and by the fact that there is no sharp ethnic, racial, or even personality difference between English Canadians and Americans. The only real difference between Americans and Canadians is that the latter are more sensible about all matters political.

[17]Canada is still a major exporter of staples (Western wheat, oil, gas, timber, potatoes, minerals, fish).

[18]Robert Gilpin, "American Direct Investment and Canada's Two Nationalisms" in R.A. Preston, ed., *The Influence of the United States on Canadian Development* (Durham, NC: Duke University Press, 1972), pp. 124–143.

[19]Canada has long had "imperial" interests in the Caribbean. It has substantial investments in the United States. In the late 1980s, it has exerted itself with commendable vigor on the international political scene, separating itself from the United States on a number of key issues and augmenting its already considerable activity in the United Nations.

[20]Walter D. Gainer, "Western Disenchantment and the Canadian Federation" in H. Edward English, ed., *Canada-United States Relations* (New York: The Academy of Political Science, 1976), pp. 40–52.

[21]Albert's oil riches have led to important petrochemical industries and to the growth of banking. The 1980s witnessed greater economic, including manufacturing, growth in Saskatchewan, Alberta, and British Columbia than in the rest of Canada.

tario as opposed to the lower prices that would prevail if such items were imported from the United States. Starting in the 1970s but getting worse by 1980–81 a major struggle developed between Alberta and the federal government over the price of oil. The federal government has kept the price of Alberta's oil considerably lower than the world market price in order to benefit the rest of Canada. The Constitution Act of 1982 gave the provinces full control of their primary resources.

The Liberal party has had the most success governing Canada espousing a vague free enterprise continentalism, a vague welfare state, a vague nationalism (that has somehow kept Canada's dominant capitalist classes of all stripes in line). The Liberal party derives its main electoral strength from Quebec (and has therefore been seen as able to keep the country united). But the 1970s and 1980s brought about vast changes in Canada's economic position in the world market. Gradually, the federal government shifted its primary focus from helping the "have-not" provinces to helping all provinces, especially the Western ones, to build their economies to compete in world markets. In 1988 the Conservative government signed a free-trade agreement signifying its belief that the already open borders with the United States could be opened still wider for mutual benefit.[22]

Is Canada a Dependent Nation?

Canada's historical development clearly establishes its origins and development as a colony and its coming to maturity under the influence of larger, more powerful outside societies. Levitt's argument that Canada's history and current status are that of a dependency[23] sparked a large number of studies in the 1970s in a similar vein and were part of a growing political consciousness that perhaps Canada was not an autonomous society.

Earlier historians (for example, Harold Innes[24]) and sociologists (for example, S. D. Clark[25]) highlighted Canada's success in forging a viable national identity. But concern for Canada's autonomy surfaced strongly after World War II from both right and left theorists. On the right, employing a Burkean perspective, George Grant has given foreign influence a conservative cast.[26] Grant has lamented the loss of Canadian nationhood to the forces of individualistic liberalism and runaway technology, both driven into Canada's heart by the United States. In their place he would prefer a Canada based on reverence for the past, firm principles that protected the public order against individual freedom, and that belonged to a vital British Commonwealth, the latter being the only way to protect Christian civilization and promote development in the world at large.

On the left, dependency theorists argue that Canada suffers at least relative dependency and underdevelopment because of high foreign ownership of mining, energy, and manufacturing. Direct investment, largely American, has taken the form of branch plants. This has been detrimental, argue critics, because research and development remain in the United States. Foreign ownership also means that money leaves Canada in the form of profits, royalties, and professional fees. Even retained earnings are bad because they lead to more investment in existing foreign companies and prevent Canadians from competing.

Dependency also stems from the loss of control over Canada's man- and womanpower development. Canadians, both skilled and unskilled, have left Canada to work abroad even as foreigners, both skilled and unskilled

[22]For a variety of views on this issue, see James Laxer, *Leap of Faith: Free Trade and the Future of Canada* (Edmonton, Alberta: Hurtig, 1986); Murray G. Smith and Frank Stone, eds., *Assessing the Canada-U.S. Free Trade Agreement* (Halifax, N.S.: Institute for Research on Public Policy, 1987); and R. M. Stern, P. H. Trezise, and John Whalley, eds., *Perspectives on a U.S.-Canadian Free Trade Agreement* (Washington, D.C.: Brookings Institution, 1987).

[23]Kari Levitt, *Silent Surrender* (Toronto: Macmillan of Canada, 1970).

[24]Harold Innes, *The Fur Trade in Canada* (Toronto: University of Toronto Press, 1930).

[25]S. D. Clark, *The Social Development of Canada* (Toronto: University of Toronto, 1942).

[26]George Grant, *Lament for a Nation* (Toronto: McClelland and Stewart, 1965; reissued with a new intro. in 1970).

have entered Canada. As John Porter and others have argued, Canada has failed to provide the education needed for developing Canada's labor.

Dependency theorists, along with middle-of-the-road liberals and right-oriented thinkers have also complained about foreign influence on Canada's culture (mass media, news, art and music, sports), an influence that contributes to Canada's inability to forge a national consciousness.

The concept of dependency is refuted by both mainstream liberals and orthodox Marxists. Liberals argue that there is mutual benefit in a continental and world market (this is the explicit direction taken in the late 1980s by Canada). Orthodox Marxists, continuing the elaboration of Marxian thought by Rudolph Hilferding and Vladimir Lenin (and others) have attacked dependency theory because it neglects the class nature of capitalist production and the worldwide power of monopoly capitalism. Carroll has rejected the dependency explanation of Canada's development and current status in a carefully written Marxian analysis.[27] Carroll argues that the distinction between commercial and industrial capitalists is false, that the Canadian economy is not truncated (or unusually unbalanced), and that Canadian capitalists are not dependent on American capitalists.

Hammer and Gartrell have tackled the issue of whether Canada suffers from dependency by arguing that what is needed is not cross-national but longitudinal analysis. There is little doubt that Canada developed as a staple-exporter, that its elites cooperated with foreign elites, and that there has been extensive foreign capital penetration of Canada. Indeed, Canada's history shows considerable parallels with Brazil (see Chapter 18). But Canada is different from Brazil, say Hammer and Gartrell. Unlike Brazil, it suffers from *mature dependency* rather than dependent development. A society characterized by mature dependency has a more balanced economy,

can generate its own capital, does not need to repress or exclude the masses, and can act to counter the negative effects of dependency (here Canada is a core country). Where Canada shows dependence, say Hammer and Gartrell, is that its gross national product has lagged because of American direct investment (allowing nine years for its full effects to take hold). In short, while it is a rich core nation, Canada would have been richer had it not relied so heavily on foreign capital for its development.[28]

Social, Cultural, and Political Links with Foreign Power Centers

Canada's dominant Anglo-Saxon elite has itself been subject to considerable foreign influence and control. Given Canada's development as a nation state while still a colony, given the existence of French Canada, and given the complex problems of conquering and settling a vast and hostile natural environment, it is not surprising that Canada's English elite failed to develop a vibrant and coherent national identity. Of course, nationalism and other homogenizing cultural elements are ways to disguise economic conflicts and differentials in opportunity and power, and their absence is not necessarily a bad thing. Indeed, Canada's heightened nationalism in recent years is probably best interpreted as a way for Canada's economic and political elites (both English and French-speaking) to gain more power vis a vis foreign elites without changing the internal power structure of Canada or Quebec.

One cannot separate economics from other institutions. Our focus here, however, is on lesser known aspects of Canada's dependence on foreign influence. Directly related to Canada's dependence on foreign capital and branch plants of foreign firms are collateral dependencies in economic services (research and development, marketing, advertising, and so on). Canadian workers have belonged to American-

[27]William K. Carroll, *Corporate Power and Canadian Capitalism* (Vancouver, B.C.: University of British Columbia, 1986).

[28]Heather-Jo Hammer and John W. Gartrell, "American Penetration and Canadian Development: A Case of Mature Dependency," *American Sociological Review* 51 (April, 1986): 201–13.

dominated trade unions (this has changed recently). Canadian professionals belong to international professional associations, many of which are American dominated.

In addition there are other links between Canadian power groups and foreign power groups:

Elitist capitalist economic institutions receive ideological support from elitist domestic sports. Internationally, Canada participates in American-dominated professional hockey and baseball networks.

Canada relies heavily on American television programs, films, books, and magazines. The United States dominates international trade in these areas and Canada's dependence in this regard is not unusual.[29] Canadian artistic talent is drained off to the United States or is often employed by Canadian firms owned by Americans. Understandably, Canada has taken steps to ensure Canadian content in its mass media and to support its arts.

It is not uncommon for American foundations and cultural groups to include Canadian residents as eligible for grants and fellowships along with Americans. Canadians are also educated abroad, especially in the United States, and remain oriented toward American standards of scholarship and professional prestige. Canadian postsecondary educational institutions have also relied heavily on foreigners (English-speaking) though they appear to have become more self-sufficient in this regard in recent years.

The Canadian government and military are deeply intertwined with American counterparts on a large number of intergovernmental agencies having to do with various matters of mutual concern.

Class, Dependency, and the Structure of Social Power

Canada (like other developed capitalist societies with representative government) is a highly stratified class democracy.[30] As in all industrial countries, liberal democratic or not, the distribution of social benefits in Canada (income, property, occupation, education, family stability, physical and mental health, prestige derived from occupation, associational membership, consumption, religion, ethnicity, race, and political, governmental, and legal benefits) is sharply graded into relatively distinct social classes. Unlike caste and estate systems of inequality, class systems allegedly distribute social benefits according to individual performance determined by a system of alleged equal opportunity and competition. In 1985 the top 20 percent of the upper income units in Canada received 43 percent of the national income while the bottom 20 percent received 4.7 percent of the national income (a similar ratio is found in all capitalist societies and if income from wealth is excluded the same general ratio probably holds for developed socialist societies). And there has been no significant change in this distribution of income for as far back as records have been kept (by and large, something which is true of all other industrial countries).[31] Thus neither a rising standard of living, progressive taxation, inheritance taxes nor the rise of the welfare state has altered the relative distribution of income in Canada.[32]

---

[29]Richard P. Nielsen, "International Trade and Policy in Mass Media Materials: Television Programs, Films, Books, and Magazines", *Cultures* 3:3 (Unesco, 1976), pp. 196–205.

[30]Social stratification in Canada is analyzed in the following books: J. R. Seeley, R. A. Sim, and E. W. Loosley, *Crestwood Heights* (Toronto: University of Toronto Press, 1956); John Porter, *The Vertical Mosaic: An Analysis of Social Class and Power in Canada* (Toronto: University of Toronto Press, 1965); James E. Curtis and William G. Scott, eds., *Social Stratification: Canada*, 1st and 2nd eds. (Scarborough, Ontario: Prentice-Hall, 1973, 1979); Wallace Clement, *The Canadian Corporate Elite: An Analysis of Economic Power* (Toronto: McClelland and Stewart, 1975); Peter C. Newman, *The Canadian Establishment* (Toronto: McClelland and Stewart, 1975), Vol. 1; Lorne Tepperman, *Social Mobility in Canada* (Toronto: McGraw-Hill Ryerson, 1975); Dennis Forcese, *The Canadian Class Structure*, 3rd ed. (Toronto: McGraw-Hill Ryerson, 1986); and Alfred A. Hunter, *Class Tells: On Social Inequality In Canada*, 2nd ed. (Toronto: Butterworths, 1986).

[31]*Canada Yearbook, 1988*, Table 5.30.

[32]For an up-to-date analysis of income distribution with comparisons showing Canada to be a typical devel-

Poverty in Canada is similar to poverty in the United States. It is composed of unattached elderly, low-income working poor, and is increasingly young and female. In one respect it may be different, however—there is more poverty in Canada than the United States (the differences may be due to differing definitions of poverty). Some statistics put 16.9 percent of all Canadian households under the poverty line while the Canadian Council on Social Development put the figure at 27.55.[33]

Inequality in wealth is even more unequal than income inequality. Data about wealth in Canada are not as precise as for the United States (or as recent) but it is known that the top decile of family income units in 1970 owned 69.1 percent of all financial assets (cash, deposits, bonds, stocks, and mortgages).[34] Occupations in Canada have followed the typical pattern in developed countries—a sharp decline in primary occupations, an overall rise and then "stabilization" and slow decline of manufacturing, and a steady rise of tertiary or service occupations. Canada also has an abnormality in its occupational structure—it has the smallest percentage of manufacturing jobs of any industrialized nation, a decline from 26 percent in the 1950s to 19 percent in 1978, and a striking 66 percent in service occupations.

Again, as in other industrial societies, there is a marked relationship in Canada between the class position of parents and the educational achievement of children (IQ, years of school completed, grades, prizes, diplomas and degrees).

In common with other industrial countries, Canada has a graded hierarchy of occupational prestige, a hierarchy that reflects the allocation of prestige according to education and skills allegedly useful in the control of nature and in the management of society. Prestige is also accorded by amount and quality of consumption. Though there is a pronounced moral equalitarianism in Canada, much of it derived from the Judaic-Christian tradition, religious prestige is also stratified, largely according to class status.

Ethnicity and race are also related strongly to class position. Native peoples and most other racial minorities have been heavily victimized by the development of Canadian society and they occupy the lowest rungs of the class ladder. Anglo-Saxons predominate in the economy and French Canadians are badly represented in the upper levels of income, wealth, and occupation.

Canadian society has a rich and complex group or associational structure, which provides differential prestige and other benefits. If used broadly, the term voluntary association best depicts the nature of this group structure, examples of which are political parties, farm, business and professional associations, labor unions, fraternal and ethnic clubs, charitable associations, reform groups, women's groups, universities, hospitals, churches, and sects. These varied types of nongovernmental groups perform various functions for Canadian society: as forms of participation they help to shape and stabilize the personality of Canadians, they provide mechanisms for innovation and criticism, and they provide the diffused, semipluralistic power structure that is the reality behind Canada's liberal democracy.

The amount of such participation should not be exaggerated, however. As in the United States, it is safe to assume that no more than 50 percent of the Canadian population is active in voluntary organizations and that participation is directly related to class (the higher the class, the more participation). Like

---

oped capitalist society, see Francois Vaillancourt, Research Coordinator, *Income Distribution and Economic Security in Canada* (Toronto: University of Toronto Press, 1985).

[33]David P. Ross, *The Canadian Fact Book on Poverty, 1983* (Toronto: James Lorimer, 1983), Table 2. The Canadian Council on Social Development's National Task Force on the Definition and Measurement of Poverty issued a report, *Not Enough: The Meaning and Measurement of Poverty in Canada* (Ottawa, Canada: CCSD, 1984), which greatly buttresses its case and makes a significant contribution to the understanding of poverty.

[34]J. R. Podoluk, "Measurement of the Distribution of Wealth in Canada," *The Review of Income and Wealth*, Series 20, no. 2 (June, 1974), p. 212, Table 6.

the United States and other mature industrial countries, the nature of participation has been affected profoundly in recent decades by rising levels of income, education, leisure, and life expectancy. Perhaps even more importantly, the process of bureaucratization is well advanced within the entire voluntary sector, something that means that the relations within and the relations among groups are increasingly conducted by professional staffs whose class background and experience not only separate them from rank and file members, but give them much in common with each other. And the interrelatedness of the problems that groups are concerned with and the need for adequate financing have brought voluntary groups increasingly into the political arena and within the orbit of governmental support and scrutiny.[35]

Canadian education neglects Canada and (along with magazine fiction[36]) tends to stress abstract middle-class values embodied in white males. Even universities in Canada fail to stress Canadian studies. In recent years an effort has been made by government to promote Canadian content in television and news magazines.

The skewed educational system favoring the middle and upper classes means that the professions are largely recruited from the existing class system and help to support it (with the help of the state). Canada's professions (though not as well studied as those in the United States and Great Britain) exhibit the same characteristics as professions in other countries: high, arbitrary, irrelevant standards, restricted entry, and superior service to the well-to-do and neglect of the lower classes.

The professions in Canada as elsewhere exhibit considerable amounts of deviance on both an individual and organizational basis. In their analysis of professional deviance, W. E. Mann and Allan Listrak discount professional claims for autonomy and argue that the public can and should set high standards for all the professions.[37]

One professional area in Canada that has received attention is the medical profession and health care. Hamowy has provided a picture of the historical development of Canadian medicine clearly showing similarities with medicine elsewhere. All in all, Canadian medicine succeeded in establishing itself as a monopoly (thus extending its jurisdiction unnecessarily, restricting entry, and preventing price competition).[38] For their part, David Coburn and his associates have provided a many-sided picture of health care in Canada.[39] Canadian medicine is almost exclusively curative and shows little interest in prevention. Despite public health insurance, medical care is still related to class. In all this, Canada's medical establishment is similar to that in the United States. In addition health statistics in Canada and the United States are similar, but Canada has a distinct edge because of national health insurance—because of government monitoring, its health care costs are at least 20 percent less than in the United States.[40]

Voting and other political activities, and political and governmental occupations are

---

[35]For an analysis of Canadian voluntary organizations, see Daniel W. Rossides, *Voluntary Participation in Canada: A Comparative Analysis* (Toronto: Canadian Association for Adult Education, 1966).

[36]For the way in which Canadian magazine fiction stresses middle-class values abstracted from nationhood (along with a stress on youth and negative stereotyping of women), see Elia T. Zureik and Alan Frizzell, "Values in Canadian Magazine Fiction", *Journal of Popular Culture* X (Fall, 1976): 359–76.

[37]W. E. Mann and Alan Listrak, "Deviance and the Professions" in W. E. Mann and Les Wheatcroft, eds., *Canada: A Sociological Profile*, 3rd ed. (Toronto: Copp Clark, 1976), pp. 296–308.

[38]Ronald Hamowy, *Canadian Medicine: A Study in Restricted Entry* (Vancouver, B.C.: The Fraser Institute, 1984).

[39]David Coburn, Carl D'Arcy, Peter New, and George Torrance, eds., *Health and Canadian Society* (Toronto: Fitzhenry and Whiteside, 1981).

[40]Theodore R. Marmor, "Canada's Path, America's Choices: Lessons From the Canadian Experience with National Health Insurance" in Peter Conrad and Rochelle Kern, eds., *The Sociology of Health and Illness: Critical Perspectives*, 2nd ed. (New York: St. Martin's Press, 1986), Selection 18.

not subject to formal property or birth criteria in Canada. In practice, however, the upper classes vote and participate in politics far more than the lower classes. Given the close ties among class, ethnicity, and education, Anglo-Canadians in the upper classes tend to dominate Canadian federal and provincial politics (save for Quebec and for the political necessity of having significant French Canadian components in federal governments) and the Canadian federal and provincial public bureaucracies (again with the exception of Quebec). Protest and radical movements in Canada emanate from exploited groups, primarily farmers but also workers (and even professionals).

Legislation and law in Canada are largely class related and tend to maintain the regional and class status quo. Most reforms should be thought of as modernization toward a more fully developed liberal society rather than a shift or change in essential power relations. Those who complain about the inadequacy or decline of Canada's political culture[41] should be aware that political institutions are a reflection of a society, especially its economy, and not of ideas and morality (education, the press, human nature).

Canada's class system is anchored in an economy that is deeply dependent on and in significant part controlled by the United States. Canada's political life is a continuing attempt to maintain easy access to foreign powers carrying capital and other gifts. Some gains have been made in recent years to heighten public awareness about Canada's dependence. Laws have been passed to increase Canadian ownership of energy and other firms and steps taken to cut down Canada's exposure to American mass media and its use of foreign professionals. But none of this is a threat to basic power relations. Canadian nationalism is primarily a way for Canada's elites to get more power away from

American elites without relinquishing any to the Canadian people.[42]

A number of related trends in the post-1945 period have served to create a national malaise about Canada's future. A greater self-conscious nationalism in Quebec, a decline in the authority of the federal government due to the postwar resurgence of provincialism, especially in Alberta and British Columbia, the difficulty that Canada has had in achieving majority, broad-based governments, and a concern about the effect of American ownership of large portions of the Canadian economy, all combine to raise Canadian doubts about Canada's viability as an autonomous society. No hairshirt is as satisfying to Canadians as a discussion about their identity or rather alleged lack of identity and about the dire consequences that this holds for their nation's survival.

It is difficult to identify the features in Canadian life that make for national unity and viability and those that disrupt and divide. Canadian society, for example, is held together by one of the world's finest civil services and by public systems of rail and air transport and radio and television communication, but these are also objects of jealousy and suspicion. National companies provide a network of national products and services and facilitate a national outlook by a mobile managerial elite, but they are also subject to attack as monopolies and as agencies of foreign penetration. There is little doubt that French Canadians are linked deeply to the rest of Canada by economic and political ties, just as there is little doubt that the pace of change in Quebec has sparked new forms and new heights of French Canadian self-centeredness. And while for some the adoption of a national flag in 1965 was a harbinger

---

[41]Steven Lewis, "The Decline of Political Culture", *Canadian Forum* 62 (May, 1977): 19–23.

[42]For an analysis of how Canada's political parties fail to provide the Canadian people with a full set of relevant choices, see Maurice Pinard, "Working Class Politics: An Interpretation of the Quebec Case," *Canadian Review of Sociology and Anthropology* 7:2 (1970) and Rick Ogmundson, "Party Class Images and Class Vote in Canada," *American Sociological Review* 40 (August, 1975): 506–12.

of unity, for others the protracted struggle to adopt was a source of pessimism. All in all, therefore, it is difficult to say how much of Canadian instability is real and how much is appearance, how much of it is due to the deep dynamism of Canada's institutions and how much of it due to disagreement about fundamentals and the mismanagement of problems.

Canadians may be unduly pessimistic about the future of their society. While Canada is a geographic monstrosity and an economic improbability, it is also a political triumph. By almost any standard Canadian society, at least until now, must be judged a success. Given the many difficulties presented by its natural environment, including the deep geographic pull to the South, Canada's successful settlement of Northern North America is no mean achievement. If one remembers that some of the deepest motivational urges to behavior center on language, religion, and ethnicity, then Canada's accommodation of not only its English and French cultures, but its absorption of other cultures, is an achievement of the highest order. If one recognizes the difficulties that stood in the way of a successful political confederation in 1867 (hostile economic regions, difficult transportation problems, and ethnic and ideological cleavages), then Canada's survival into the 1990s ranks high on the ladder of societal achievements. On yet another level, its efforts to cope with the divisive and disruptive effects of industrialization (while laboring under the continuing burden of linguistic, religious, and ethnic diversity) can stand comparison with any industrial nation. And finally if one thinks of war as the supreme overt test of a social system, Canada acquitted itself quite admirably in the two major military challenges that it faced in the twentieth century.

The crucial assumption that must be made if one is to find the virtues in Canada's defective national identity is that a fast-changing industrial society must be able to define and redefine its problems quickly and effectively. Thought of from this vantage point, a finely articulated symbolic world (or national identity) is a great disadvantage if it forces a population and its leaders to define new situations in terms of obsolete ideas and values. The coherent and valuable American identity, for example, can also be judged a heavy metaphysical burden if one considers the difficulties which the American population has experienced in trying to define the problems of industrialization and urbanization in terms of a symbolic culture forged under eighteenth-century agrarian conditions. Thought of in this light, Canada's diversity becomes a distinct asset: its provinces become experimental laboratories; its ethnic groups become repositories of personalized values; its interest-reform-charitable-fraternal groups identify problems, pioneer new approaches, and resist oligarchical-bureaucratic coordination; and its political parties provide a rich spectrum of economic, political, and even social alternatives. In a fascinating article,[43] Gad Horowitz has argued that socialism in Canada has established itself as a significant force (while failing completely in the United States) because (among other reasons) it had available to it both Tory and liberal symbolic elements (unlike socialism in the United States which could not establish itself against the monopolistic power of American liberalism).[44]

Questions of adaptation always come down to questions of power. What then is Canada's power structure and why has it so far succeeded in overcoming both the problems of industrialization and of segmentation? The answer is fairly simple but leads to another

---

[43] "Conservatism, Liberalism, and Socialism in Canada: An Interpretation," *Canadian Journal of Economics and Political Science* (May, 1966).

[44] For two good introductions to public policy issues in Canada, see M. M. Atkinson and M. A. Chandler, eds., *The Politics of Canadian Public Policy* (Toronto: University of Toronto Press, 1983) and Ronald Manzer, *Public Policies and Political Development In Canada* (Toronto: University of Toronto Press, 1985). For the politics of foreign policy, see Kim R. Nossal, *The Politics of Canadian Foreign Policy* (Toronto: Prentice-Hall Canada, 1985). For current issues in the relation between Canada and the United States, see *Canada and the United States: Enduring Friendship, Persistent Stress* (Englewood Cliffs, N.J.: Prentice-Hall, 1985); William T. R. Fox, *A Continent Apart: The United States and Canada in World Politics* (Toronto: University of Toronto Press, 1985); and David Leyton-Brown, *Weathering The Storm: Canadian-U.S. Relations 1980–1983* (Toronto: C.D. Howe Institute, 1985).

question. Canada has survived because it has an elitist, semi-pluralist power structure.[45] The question that this raises is, have there been trends in its power structure? Judging by a comparison of John Porter's findings about the Canada before 1960 and Robert Prestus' and Wallace Clement's findings about Canada after 1960, it appears that Canada's elites have become smaller and more coordinated.

The tendency toward a power elite (as opposed to a small, diversified, and competitive set of elites) cannot be proved. But if this trend has appeared, it is because Canada has tried to solve its segmentation along linguistic, religious, and regional lines by maintaining the appearance of being an integrated nation state. Beneath appearances, a small set of elites is busy brokering into being a Canada composed of disparite and unreconciled elements. The process, according to Prestus, has succeeded in overcoming segmentation, but at the expense of a fuller democracy.[46]

THE SOCIALIST FEDERAL REPUBLIC OF YUGOSLAVIA: A SEGMENTED SOCIALIST NATION STATE

Land and People[47]

Yugoslavia is in Southeastern Europe extending Northwest of Albania and Greece to borders with Italy, Austria, and Hungary. On its East lie Romania and Bulgaria and on its West, the Adriatic Sea. Yugoslavia's size is 99 thousand square miles, about two-thirds the size of California. Its terrain is two-thirds mountainous, one-third lowland hills and plains, and its climate is moderate.

Yugoslavia's population is multiethnic and numbered 23.5 million in 1988 with a low growth rate of under 1 percent per year. Yugoslavia's ethnic groups break down as follows: 40 percent Serbs, 22 percent Croats, 8 percent Slovenes, 8 percent Bosnian Muslims, 6 percent Macedonians, 6 percent Albanians, 2 percent Montenegrin Serbs, 2 percent Hungarians, and 1 percent Turks. Religiously, 40 percent are Serb and Macedonian Orthodox Christians, 30 percent Roman Catholic (including most Croats, Slovenes and Hungarians), and 12 percent Sunni Muslim. Yugoslavia's ethnic groups are associated with territorial areas and with separate languages and the result has been considerable tension and conflict over the terms of social organization during its history (both before and after the emergence of an independent Yugoslavia in 1918.) The present socialist regime has managed to contain ethnic cleavage by pioneering some interesting variations on Marxist philosophy.

Economy[48]

In 1986 Yugoslavia had a GNP of $145 billion and a per capita income of $6,220.[49] Yugoslavia has been classified as a developed society because a significant part of its annual production comes from its industrial

[45]For two critical analyses of the Canadian power structure across a wide range of social sectors, see Leo Panitch, ed., *The Canadian State: Political Economy and Political Power* (Toronto: University of Toronto Press, 1977) and Richard J. Ossenberg, ed., *Power and Change in Canada* (Toronto: McClelland and Stewart, 1980).

[46]Robert Prestus, *Elite Accommodation in Canadian Politics* (Toronto: Macmillan, 1973). For a more succinct and recent statement, see Robert Prestus, "Evolution and Canadian Political Culture: The Politics of Accommodation" in Richard A. Preston, ed., *Perspectives on Revolution and Evolution* (Durham, N.C.: Duke University Press, 1979), pp. 103–32.

[47]*Yugoslavia: A Country Study*, Foreign Area Studies, the American University, 2nd ed. (Washington, D.C.: U. S. Government Printing Office, 1982) is an invaluable source of information about Yugoslav geography, population, history, and society. For informative essays on various aspects of Yugoslav society, including politics, the economy, foreign policy, the press, feminism, religious policies, and the environment, see Pedro Ramet, ed., *Yugoslavia in the 1980s* (Boulder, Colo.: Westview Press, 1985).

[48]For general background on Yugoslavia's economy, see Martin Schrenk, Cyrus Ardalan, and Nawal A. El Tatawy, *Yugoslavia: Self-Management Socialism the Challenges of Development* (Baltimore: Johns Hopkins University Press, 1979), a World Bank report, and Fred Singleton and Bernard Carter, *The Economy of Yugoslavia* (New York: St. Martin's Press, 1982).

[49]Central Intelligence Agency, *The World Factbook 1988* (Washington, D.C.: U. S. Government Printing Office, 1988), p. 263.

sector and because of its high annual capital investment. Despite abundant natural resources Yugoslavia's economic development has been hampered by a history of war, conquest, and internal conflict. But its high rate of economic growth since World War II ranks with that of almost any country in the world and has changed Yugoslavia from an agrarian to an urban-industrial society.

Yugoslavia has two (interrelated) characteristics that make it almost mandatory to include it in an overall typology of social system types. The first is that Yugoslavia represents a unique attempt by power groups to industrialize a population composed of a multiplicity of distinct ethnic groups. It is thus an interesting variation of a segmented society. The second thing of interest about Yugoslavia is its attempt to industrialize under market socialism rather than planned socialism or market capitalism. These two features are related and market socialism is as much a political as an economic device. From still another perspective Yugoslavia is a unique attempt at participatory socialism.

Socialist guerrilla forces under Josip Broz (Tito) were the main Yugoslav resistance to German and Italian occupation during World War II and were in effective control of the country when the Axis powers fell in 1945. Yugoslavia was the only communist regime in Eastern Europe that was not installed by the military forces of the Soviet Union. Yugoslav socialists established a one-party polity and proclaimed Yugoslavia a Federal People's Republic (renamed later as the Socialist Federal Republic of Yugoslavia).

The means of production in all economic sectors were socialized and large land holdings were abolished. Yugoslavia's basic economic orientation in the first years emulated the centralized command economy of the Soviet Union. However, soon after the break with the Soviet Union in 1948, Yugoslavia embarked on a series of policies aimed at decentralizing its economy and orienting it as much as possible to market forces. It became a leader of the nonalignment movement and in general has opened its society to a variety of external forces.

It also adopted its unique worker management policies in which workers in given enterprises elect a council to formulate general policy. The workers' council also elects a management to assist the director in running the day-to-day operations of the enterprise. Productive resources in Yugoslavia are socially owned but managed by workers as trustees of society. Yugoslavs are relatively free to work where they want, including abroad (Yugoslavia is the only Marxist society that allows large numbers of its citizens to work abroad). Despite its "free" labor market, Yugoslavian Marxism does not accept the idea of buying and selling labor. In Marxist theory labor is not merely another commodity but the source of all value. Capital is not an entity with its own rights separate from productive labor but simply "surplus value" or unrewarded "past labor." Accordingly, workers should control the disposition of all that they produce. Worker income, therefore, is a share of the enterprise's income after production costs, depreciation, and social dues ("taxes") are paid. It is in this sense that Yugoslavia appears to be putting Marxism into practice and avoiding the Soviet practice of insisting on a period of development before self-management by workers becomes a reality.

Individual enterprises are free to determine what they will produce, where they will buy and sell, and what prices to charge. Worker self-interest is tied into the productive process by making worker income dependent to a considerable degree on the income ("profits") of the enterprise. The central government has given up the administration of the economy but retains considerable powers. The central government develops a plan for the economy as a whole (now drawn up for five-year periods) and local governments draw up their plans in keeping with the federal plan. The federal government uses a variety of fiscal, trade, price, and credit devices to implement its "planned market economy." The federal government also has considerable influence over the basic allocation of capital. A general investment fund is the source of considerable amounts of long-range credit for productive and auxillary facilities. Enterprises and auxillary groups such as local governments submit requests for investment credit and decisions are made about which projects are economically most desirable and in keeping with the federal plan.

Economic relations are not simply a matter of abstract government goals and individual enterprise initiatives. The commitment to market relations includes a full endorsement of negotiation among enterprises and other social groups. The Yugoslav commitment to market relations goes beyond Maoist China's antistatist policies. What the Yugoslav Marxists have attempted is a heavy dose of capitalism without private property.

The League of Communists (the current name of the dominant communist party) and the federal government and legislature have had open, frank discussions about these policies and have not hesitated to experiment or to scrap policies that weren't working. A considerable effort has been made to keep enterprises competitive in world markets, consumption has been allowed to rise to increase worker incentives, surplus workers have been allowed to go to other countries to work (and earn foreign exchange for Yugoslavia through their remittances), and tourism has been encouraged. The federal government also abandoned forced collectivization of agriculture when it became apparent that it wasn't working and a good part of Yugoslavia's agrarian sector is in private hands (holdings are limited). The government, however, has helped to modernize all agriculture and the state sector has grown in relative size and importance.

The Yugoslav experiment with market socialism has been a mixed success. Economic growth in the 1950s and 1960s was phenomenal, enough to transform Yugoslavia into an urban-industrial society. The large growth of industry and services under public ownership also meant that the socialist sector of the economy eclipsed the private agricultural sector (which itself shrank in relation to public agriculture). But a persistent balance of payments deficit from 1970 on caused a considerable drag on the Yugoslav economy. A failure to develop export markets, changing world economic conditions, such as the development of the Common Market and the spectacular rise in oil prices after 1973, and droughts all hampered economic growth. By the 1980s, Yugoslavia was using 20 percent of its export earnings to service its foreign debt and was experiencing considerable economic difficulties.

Market socialism in Yugoslavia has also developed a number of the undesirable features that are associated with market economies—inflation, unemployment, balance-of-payment deficits, and monopolistic practices. And despite considerable effort, Yugoslavia has not been able to make any significant changes in the uneven development of its regions. Regional economic imbalance also means continued disparities in the socioeconomic development of Yugoslavia's various ethnic groups. The numerically smaller Croats and Slovenes, for example, are more economically advanced than the politically dominant Serbs, a disparity that has caused considerable friction.

Polity[50]

The Communist party dominates political as well as economic and social life in Yugoslavia. Its rule is based on a constitution that it has not hesitated to change to meet new conditions. By and large, changes over the years have "liberalized" Yugoslavian political life, something that has come about not because of weakness or pressure from below—changes have come from strength (because of the enormous popular support for Tito and the party) and as policies designed to solve problems. Constitutional reform in a Marxist society also means economic and social reform—the steady enlargement of the scope

---

[50]For good analyses of the conscious attempt by the Communist party to build conflict resolution processes into both the Yugoslav political system and the party itself, see Steven L. Burg, *Conflict and Cohesion in Socialist Yugoslavia: Political Decisionmaking Since 1966* (Princeton, N.J.: Princeton University Press, 1983), Pedro Ramet, *Nationalism and Federalism in Yugoslavia, 1963–1983* (Bloomington, Ind.: Indiana University Press, 1984), and Jim Seroka and Rados Similjkovic, *Political Organizations in Socialist Yugoslavia* (Durham, N.C.: Duke University Press, 1986).

and meaning of worker self-management, or direct (participatory) democracy, is part and parcel of Yugoslavia's political and governmental institutions.[51]

The spirit and goals of the various constitutions have remained the same: to promote socialism (and thus the legitimacy of one-party communist rule); to integrate a multi-ethnic society that is divided not only by religion and language but by different socio-economic development (by emphasizing the equality of all nationalities); to promote the power of workers (which by and large means the people organized for self-rule in as literal and direct a manner as is feasible); to increase mass participation in public life; and to provide for an orderly succession of leadership. Analysts agree that Yugoslavia has indeed achieved a significant amount of pluralism in its basic power structure.

The 1974 constitution established a collective leadership that rotates the office of president but that also acts collectively (the presidency). The federal Assembly (or legislature) is composed of a Federal Council and a Council of the Republics and the Provinces. The Federal Council has 220 delegates: 30 from each of the 6 republics (Serbia, Croatia, Slovenia, Bosnia and Herzegovina, Macedonia, and Montenegro) and 20 from the 2 autonomous provinces inside Serbia. These delegates are elected indirectly from locally elected bodies. The other legislative body, the Federal Council of Republics and Provinces has 58 members: 8 from the parliaments of each republic and 5 from the parliaments of each province.

The basic logic behind Yugoslavia's latest constitution is to increase the power of ordinary workers vis a vis economic and political elites (managers, administrators) and to promote socialist democracy rather than state socialism, which Yugoslav Marxists tend to equate with state capitalism. Yugoslavia is also unique among Marxist societies in that it established a constitutional court in 1963, one of whose main purposes is to adjudicate disputes between the federal government and a republic, or between republics.

From another perspective, however, the entire process of decentralization is also a way to curb ethnic identity and dissolve inter-ethnic tension and conflict. By emphasizing occupational and economic interest groups, the Communist party weakens ethnic identification and helps prevent the federal system from segmenting along ethnic-religious-linguistic lines. Self-government also pinpoints responsibility for solving problems that arise in any kind of society and helps to prevent a divorce between the expectations of a better-educated citizenry and what society can afford (or a one-party government can yield).

Since Tito's death in 1980 the provisions for succession in the 1974 constitution have appeared to work. Yugoslavia has managed to transfer power peaceably and smoothly to a collective president. By and large, Yugoslavia has developed political institutions and a political culture that has successfully dislodged the traditional social order and has established deep roots in the Yugoslav population.[52]

Family, Health, Religion, and Education

The Yugoslav family has been transformed in the same general way as in every other

---

[51]William Zimmerman has highlighted the importance of international factors on the domestic political development of Yugoslavia in *Open Borders, Nonalignment, and the Political Evolution of Yugoslavia* (Princeton, N.J.: Princeton University Press, 1987). Zimmerman's analysis of the large, positive impact on Yugoslavia because of its policy permitting Yugoslavs to work abroad is especially valuable. Zimmerman's thesis that comparative politics and international relations are two sides of the same coin, and further, that when a plurality of external factors impinge domestically they can actually strengthen a regime's stability and autonomy of action is especially valuable.

[52]Two analysts, the first using a socialist and the second a liberal perspective, agree that Yugoslavia has successfully made the transition from a traditional multinational society to a working multicommunal, developed nation state: Bogdan Denis Denitch, *The Legitimation of a Revolution: The Yugoslav Case* (New Haven: Yale University Press, 1976) and Gary K. Bertsch, *Values and Community in Multi-National Yugoslavia* (Boulder, Colo.: Eastern European Quarterly, 1976).

society that has come out of a traditionalized horticultural or agrarian past. The self-sufficient peasant family engaged in subsistence or local-market farming has given way to the neolocal, nuclear family dependent on income from an occupation. Even the rather significant practice of extended family structure in less developed regions of Yugoslavia has succumbed to modernization.

The government actively promotes family planning (abortion is legal) and emphasizes sex education and the role of social services in maintaining a healthy, stable family life. Health care services are run on a cooperative, local basis and the improvement in the health of the Yugoslav people in the post-World War II period has been dramatic.

Yugoslavia is largely a Christian country with a sizable Muslim minority.[53] Before the socialist revolution religion in Yugoslavia took the usual agrarian form of a church (a hierarchy with elaborate theology and ritual, organically linked to the state) rather than a sect form of group structure (an egalitarian fellowship, informal, separated from the state). The largest church, the Serbian Orthodox, resulted from a unification of a multiplicity of Serbian churches during the 1920s (while Yugoslavia was a kingdom). The Roman Catholic Church is the second largest religious group and it too had various hierarchies based on nationality until a unified Yugoslavian church was negotiated with the Vatican by the prewar monarchy (never put into effect because of prewar political tensions). The Muslim communities were unified after 1918 as part of the emergence of a unified kingdom of Yugoslavia. Under the monarchy, the Serbian Orthodox Church was formally affiliated with the state, given subsidies, and exempt from taxation.

After 1945 the socialist government launched an attack on organized churches (which had been seriously weakened by wartime devastation). The extensive landholdings of the various churches were drastically reduced and churches and clergy were subject to taxation. Government subsides, especially for clerical salaries and insurance benefits, were funnelled through government-organized clerical associations. And the state took charge of marriage, divorce, family life, and statistical services, all formerly under the jurisdiction of churches.

The government and party have reduced their hostility to organized religion in recent years and the freedom and equality of all religions are guaranteed in constitutional law. The government's policies have no doubt changed because the various churches' power to influence the political and economic organization of society has been drastically reduced.

Education is favored under communist rule and two pronounced themes are apparent: (1) education is used to build a patriotic socialist citizenry and (2) training for positions in a modern economy is stressed. In Yugoslavia educational groups are also considered self-governing entities and are part of the general policy of emphasizing participatory democracy (within limits set down by the monopolistic Communist party).

Class and Dependency

Yugoslavia does not have social classes in the Marxian sense of the term since there is no structure of private property in productive facilities and no fully institutionalized labor market for buying and selling labor. But classes exist, not only because there is economic inequality among households, but because the source of inequality lies in the differential ability of parents to prepare children for success in school and the economy.[54] Further, there is a class structure because economic inequality stems from the explicit actions and policies of the state.

Yugoslavia's decentralized or market socialism has led to a number of similarities

[53]For background on Yugoslavia's religions and their relation to state and society, see Stella Alexander, *Church and State in Yugoslavia Since 1945* (New York: Cambridge University Press, 1979).

[54]For a previous discussion of social stratification under socialism, see Chapter 12, The Soviet Union, and the introduction to Chapter 14, The Variety of Socialisms.

with capitalist countries, including substantial income inequality. In addition, Yugoslavia experiences unemployment, inflation, balance of payments problems, heavy foreign debts, and monopolistic practices (enterprises expand to dominate areas, enterprises enter into noncompetitive agreements, workers vote to give themselves excessive incomes and neglect investment needs). And there is another similarity with capitalist societies—the Communist party and government actively guide, adjust, and correct the economy much on the order of capitalist governments.[55]

Yugoslavia also has internal cleavages along economic-regional grounds, which tend to coincide with ethnic cleavages. The party and government have done a skillful job of balancing Yugoslavia's multiple interest and ethnic groups and forging a common Yugoslav identity. Much of its success stems from its ability to define Yugoslavia in terms of its relation to outsiders. The successful struggle for national liberation is a source of pride for Yugoslavs of all nationalities. Another source of national identity is Yugoslavia's success in establishing and maintaining its independence from the Soviet Union. And still another source of pride is Yugoslavia's prominent role on the international scene in forging the Organization of Nonaligned Nations. The 1981 census revealed a surprising rise (to 5.4 percent) in the number who thought of themselves as Yugoslavs rather than as members of a particular ethnic group.

Social integration is maintained internally by directing Yugoslavs toward their immediate problems on the job and in their local communities. There is a consistent attempt (not always successful) to balance representation in the federal legislature, government, party, and army. Heavy emphasis is placed on the equality of all nationalities and there is a wide use of other languages besides the three official languages. And the freer atmo-

sphere in regard to personal freedom and access to books, newspapers, films, radio, and television (including those from abroad) undoubtedly helps to create a sense of contentment. In thinking of Yugoslavia's political stability, it is also important to note that having a multiplicity of ethnic blocs may be easier to handle than having two contending blocs (as, for example, in Canada, Belgium, and Northern Ireland).

Denitch argues that the regime is securely anchored in the basic classes that make up Yugoslavia. The peasantry is largely neutral, is shrinking, and has deep ties to the upwardly mobile urban-based working classes and others. The industrial working class is a main beneficiary of Yugoslavian socialism. The new technical intelligensia has also experienced upward mobility and is a positive supporter of Yugoslavian socialism. Marxist humanists and purists may grumble but there is positive loyalty to new social order. Only the traditional humanist intelligensia, often closely identified with nationality groups, drags its feet. Denitch also argues that Yugoslavia is closer to the type of society Marx and Engels had in mind, that not only does it represent an innovative route to modernization but that Yugoslavia has made creative thrusts at the problems facing socialism in advanced industrial societies.[56]

Yugoslavia forged its political and social autonomy both against external and internal threats by a skillful policy of stressing "direct democracy," including worker self-management, but its independence has been purchased in the coin of a considerable amount of dependence. Yugoslavia is now dependent on foreign markets and capital, on tourism, and on remittances from its citizens who work in other countries (down considerably from the 1970s on). Yugoslavia's dependency on the outer world was revealed during the late 1980s when its economic fortunes stalled and declined. The worldwide recession and Yugoslavia's failure to upgrade its manufacturing

---

[55]Harold Lydell argues that market socialism is fatally flawed because of ambiguity over the ownership of capital and advocates a full commitment to a market capitalism; see his *Yugoslavia In Crisis* (New York: Oxford University Press, 1989).

[56]Bogdan Denis Denitch, *The Legitimation of a Revolution: The Yugoslav Case* (New Haven: Yale University Press, 1976), Chapters 1 and 2.

competitiveness also aggravated ethnic relations internally. The serious ethnic hostilities that broke out in the late 1980s were no doubt due to the austerity forced on Yugoslavia by its loss of economic momentum.

Yugoslavia's troubles as well as its successes spring only partly from the policies of its socialist leaders—Yugoslavian society is also the result of its history and the world-market economy.

16

NIGERIA, MALAYSIA, AND SRI LANKA
Developing Segmented Nation Societies

NIGERIA[1]

Land and People

The Federal Republic of Nigeria is the largest country in Black Africa. Located in West Africa, Nigeria takes its name from the Niger River which combines with the Benue River to form a giant letter Y. This river system runs through the length and breadth of Nigeria and forms the basis of whatever geographical sense the country makes. Geographically, Nigeria has a hot, humid coastal area suitable for agriculture and a drier uphill region more suited to grazing and cattle growing.

Nigeria's population is about 110 million (no recent census exists) making it one of the world's most populous countries. It has a large growth rate of over 3 percent per year. Spread out over a large territory Nigeria's population is also segmented by a numerous assortment of tribal, religious, and linguistic groups.

Ethnic Composition

Nigeria probably has the most diverse ethnic composition in the world. No officially recognized census has been taken since 1963 so here too only estimates can be made.[2] There are approximately 300 ethnic (tribal) groups, many divided into subgroups. The number of languages (including dialects is between 350 and 400. English is the official language used in government, modern businesses, the mass media, and education beyond the primary grades.

---

[1]For a valuable, straightforward, apolitical description of all aspects of Nigerian society, see *Nigeria: A Country Study*, 4th ed. *(Washington, DC: U. S. Government Printing Office, 1982), Foreign Area Studies, The American University.*

[2]There is an unusual lack of reliable data about Nigeria, something that also badly handicaps its policymakers.

Of the many ethnolinguistic groups, a few major groups stand out:

Hausa—about 21 percent
Yoruba—over 20 percent
Ibo—over 16 percent
Fulani, Kanuri, Ibibio, Tiv, Ijaiv—about 16 percent

The main religions are Islam (Sunni), Christianity, and animistic native religions. Muslims make up almost half the population and Christians make up about 35 percent. The Hausa (who live in the interior) are Muslims and have their own language. Separated from the commercially active coast, the Hausa have remained traditional (feudal). The Yoruba (half Muslim, half Christian) and the Ibo (mostly Muslim with a substantial number of Christians) had a long exposure to European traders and British colonial rulers and are well adapted to modern ways. The acute differences among Nigerians are compounded by the fact that ethnic identity tends to coincide with geography, all in all, a classic recipe for segmentation.

The Colonial Heritage[3]

The Portuguese established contact with the West African coast in the early fifteenth century. The Dutch broke Portugal's monopoly on trade in the sixteenth century only to have its monopoly broken by France and England. By the eighteenth century Britain had established a trade dominance including the lucrative slave trade.

Britain became more and more involved in Nigeria in the nineteenth century, to some extent because of its efforts to stop the slave trade (the British Parliament passed a law in 1807 outlawing the slave trade). Gradually, it became involved in other forms of trade and by the end of the nineteenth century, its political control had grown over both the coast and the interior. From a loose series of protectorates Nigeria was united in its present boundaries as a colony in 1914. It became an independent nation state relatively peacefully in 1960.

Contact with Europe's colonial powers had a profound impact on the various peoples who make up presentday Nigeria. Essentially, the horticultural tribes of Nigeria were transformed from self-sufficient, subsistence farmers and herders into exporters. This pattern, which is common to Third-World countries, had some distinctive features in Nigeria. For one thing, Nigeria became deeply involved in the export of human beings as slaves. Slavery and the slave trade existed before the arrival of the European powers. While Nigerians were victims of the new traffic in slaves across the Atlantic, other Nigerians openly collaborated in the huge and lucrative business of supplying labor for the plantations of the New World (estimates place the number of slaves transported from Africa to the New World at eight million, a huge number both in absolute and relative terms).

The second distinctive aspect of Nigeria's development under colonial rule is that land was left in the hands of native Nigerians (and there was no great influx of settlers from the European world). This made Nigeria different from Rhodesia (Zimbabwe) with its large white settler population and from Ceylon (Sri Lanka) where the British took possession of the lucrative tea and rubber plantations.

A third distinctive aspect of Nigeria's export economy was that exports and imports were in balance during the colonial period. Nigeria has had balance of trade problems only since independence when it became deeply implicated in the world market economy thanks to a new export item, oil.

Economy

Nigeria is still predominantly an agricultural (horticultural) nation with a relatively low per capita income. Its GNP of $39.5 billion in 1987 yielded a per capita income of $370.[4] Manufacturing accounts for only 10 percent of its GDP and consists largely of

---

[3]R. Olufemi Ekundare, *An Economic History of Nigeria, 1860–1960* (New York: Holmes and Meier, 1973).

[4]The World Bank, *The World Bank Atlas 1988* (Washington, D.C.: The World Bank, 1988), p. 8.

import substitution products. Cocoa, cotton, groundnuts, edible oils, palm tree products, and rubber were major exports until the 1960s. By the 1980s only cocoa remained as a major export item. Starting in the 1960s farm production declined throughout the country and Nigeria not only had few farm products to export but had to import food.

In the 1960s Nigeria's oil production got underway and it soon became a major supplier of the world's oil (the United States receives a major share of its imported oil from Nigeria). Oil wealth has not only *not* helped Nigeria but has contributed to its economic shortfalls in other areas. Nigeria failed to use its oil wealth to improve its farm economy. It has sizable investments in hydrocarbon-related industries as well as steel production but on the whole it has failed to expand and diversify its economy, especially in manufacturing.

An economic problem that Nigeria faces (along with much of the Third World, especially African countries) is famine. Many interpret famine as an "act of God," a natural occurrence due to bad weather or a changing natural environment. Increasingly, however, environmentalists have called attention to some social factors that underlie food shortages and cause environmental changes. Nigeria, like other African countries, shifted to export crops only to find that they were degrading the environment. The spread of the Sahara Desert is partially due to a change in the uses to which land have been put, for example, the growth of groundnuts for export purposes on land unsuited for that purpose.[5]

Nigeria has made a major effort to bring its economy under its own control. Soon after independence it passed laws stipulating that Nigerians must own controlling interests in specified industries, declaring at the same time that the government would play a major ownership role in the economy. These laws have certainly created a climate of Nigerianization, but, in practice, most were easily circumvented. Formally (and using unreliable data at that), foreign ownership declined from the 1960s to the 1980s. But, in practice, foreigners continue to play a major role in the Nigerian economy.[6] And despite the fact that 60 percent of domestic spending is by government and that the government spends according to five-year plans, there is no suggestion of a socialist society. Quite the contrary; Nigeria is a free enterprise, private property society. Nigeria's government is not separate from or a referee of the private economy but simply its largest player.

Polity

Nigerians knew that independence was coming long before it took place in 1960 and extensive preparations were made for it. Special attention was paid to preparing Nigeria for self-government. The first period of civilian self-government in the 1960s took a parliamentary form, but no preparation could overcome Nigeria's severe ethnic segmentation and Nigeria's first attempt at self-government faltered and ended in a major civil war.

From 1967 to 1970 a section of Nigeria seceded to become the Republic of Biafra. The effort failed and after a bloodletting that cost between one and two million lives, Nigerian unity was restored under military rule. Military rule is common in Third-World countries but its nature varies. In Peru we saw that military rule was explicitly undertaken to better prepare Peru for civilian rule and liberal democracy (readers will recall the use of tyrants in ancient Greece to prepare society for popular government). Often, however, military rule exists for its own sake or for legitimating the power of property and status groups who fear popular government. Though military rule in Nigeria began be-

---

[5]For a discussion of this issue focused on Nigeria, see G. Jan van Apeldoorn, *Perspectives on Drought and Famine in Nigeria*, (London: Allen and Unwin, 1981). For a discussion of the environmental degradation of the planet at large due to social causes, see Lester Russell Brown *et al.*, *State of the World, 1986; A Worldwatch Institute Report on Progress Toward a Sustainable Society* (New York: W. W. Norton, 1986).

[6]Thomas J. Biersteker, *Multinationals, the State, and Control of The Nigerian Economy* (Princeton, N.J.: Princeton University Press, 1987).

cause of civil war, a new military government in 1975 openly committed itself to returning Nigeria to civilian, popular government.

The complex problem of Nigeria's political instability through ethnic segmentation can be seen by discussing it in terms of the mutual fears of two groups, the Hausa and Ibo. The Hausa feared that the Ibo, who were more attuned to and accomplished in the realms of education, business, and administration, would reap the major benefits of independence. The Ibo, in turn, feared that the Hausa would use the political preference given to them by the new constitution to hog the benefits of independence for themselves. This ethnic rivalry was multiplied manyfold by the existence of many other ethnolinguistic groups and made it impossible to develop national unity and common purposes through the use of political institutions, which to function properly had to have a broad consensus on goals and means in the first place.

The Nigerian military handled its victory over Biafra with great common sense. The Ibo rebels were not punished nor was property destroyed or confiscated. The military made it clear that it wanted the Ibo reintegrated into Nigerian society and this was accomplished to its enduring credit. Similarly, its preparations for a return to civilian life were also marked by a creative sense of what was needed if Nigeria were to become a viable nation state. It commissioned a group of 50 civilian experts to draft a new constitution. The result was a series of steps all designed to overcome ethnic segmentation. The new constitution had a strong president and it shifted many powers from the state governments to the national government. Nineteen states were created, which cut across ethnic boundaries in a conscious effort to separate political power from ethnic identity.[7] Ethnic

groups were forbidden to engage in politics and political parties and other private groups were required to have balanced ethnic representation in their governing structures.

Elections were held in 1979 and again in 1983, but by this time Nigeria was in deep economic trouble. However astute politically, the military had done a poor job of directing the economy. By the late 1970s Nigeria's oil-export economy had made it deeply dependent on the world market. The world recession of 1981–83 made a shambles of its economy and finished off any prospects for stable civilian rule. Ironically, the new constitution seemed to be achieving its purpose—in the election of 1983, the world's fourth largest liberal democracy (after India, the United States, and Japan) had a president elected by voters from a wide variety of ethnic groups and from most regions of the country. But the new government had no coherent, concrete mandate for action against the country's severe economic troubles. By year's end military rule had returned.

Domestic Inequality

Nigeria is a land divided by ethnic stratification, by male-female inequality and, increasingly, by economic divisions. Ethnic stratification has led to stalemates among its major groups (which may also turn out to be a beginning of toleration and equality).

Nigeria's emerging system of class stratification cannot be described in terms familiar to westerners. For one thing there are not reliable data on income, wealth, occupation, and so on. In addition, given Nigeria's horticultural past, it lacks a structured world of large landlords and a serf-slave work force. Given its dependence on foreign capital, it has only a small native capitalist class. Given its state-led economic growth, its middle class is heavily dependent on state employment. By and large, its class system, which is found in variations among all black African nations, is anchored in a concentrated private economy, still directed in good measure by outsiders, and in the large state-owned sector, which also employs foreign professionals.

---

[7]The same problem faced those who were preparing ancient Athens for self-government and they too drew political boundaries in such a way as to undermine tribal loyalties. Feudal kings try to achieve the same diffusion of power by granting scattered fiefs to each lord and by never assigning civil administrators to their own localities.

Nigeria's class system is heavily anchored in state power: as in much of the developing world there is an open and visible connection between the holders of political power and the acquisition of income and wealth through political means (legal and illegal). There are two terms for this phenomenon, *state bourgeoisie* and *bureaucratic bourgeoisie* and either will do. Whether the government is civilian or military, the pattern is the same (in much of black Africa and developing nations): there is a heavy emphasis on quick returns either in legitimate business or through corruption and a net loss to the country because large parts of the gains are transferred abroad.

Nigeria also has a private and public sector of small business, semiprofessionals, clerks, security personnel, and so on. It has only a small working class and there is no discernible trend toward an increase in its size or an upgrading of its skills. Nigeria's class structure includes a vast underground economy both legal and illegal, which undergirds its cities: street vending (especially food) services of all kinds, petty crime, smuggling, and illegal currency transactions. And beyond the cities lies a vast peasantry, squeezed (as in most of black Africa and most developing countries) by government policies that use food marketing boards to exact revenue (while failing to return it in forms that would increase productivity) and to keep food prices low for urban residents and workers (who are politically more potent and dangerous than peasants.) All of the above is modified and lubricated by a crisscrossing network of kinship and ethnic relations adding yet more particularism to an economic system already honeycombed with ad hoc personal relations.

Two facts stand out about the Nigerian class system: there is a small number of very rich and there is a vast gulf between them and the large number of those who are poor or of very modest circumstances. Some beginnings of a middle level have emerged but the future is uncertain because of the chronic ups and downs of the economy, corruption, and crime. The other thing that stands out is that government welfare policies have been directed at a general improvement, and as is well known, this tends to perpetuate and even create more inequality. The best way to prevent poverty or to keep people from falling behind is to develop welfare services and economic opportunities for the underclasses directly. This has not happened in Nigeria.[8]

Foreign Policy, Dependency, and Adaptive Capacity

Nigeria is conscious of itself as the most powerful of the black African states and is anxious to be its leader. Since 1960 it has taken the lead in helping other African countries throw off colonial rule and has become a determined foe of apartheid in South Africa and a champion of Namibian independence.

In global politics Nigeria pursues a pro-Western policy of nonalignment. By and large, its posture of nonalignment means that it wants to keep outsiders from interfering in Black Africa's affairs, including the United States, the Soviet Union, and North African countries.[9]

Nigeria is a country with abundant resources and an energetic, resourceful people. Its failure to become a viable nation is due to its history rather than to the specific faults of the Nigerian people, i.e., the period of colonialism, the artificial entity created in 1914, the failure to integrate the rival ethnic groups prior to independence (the British actually solidified feudal traditionalism among the Hausa), and the export-oriented economy in

---

[8]Henry Bienen and V. P. Diejomaoh, eds., *The Political Economy of Income Distribution in Nigeria* (New York: Holmes and Meier, 1981). Other useful books on inequality in Nigeria are Nina Emma Mba, *Nigerian Women Mobilized: Women's Political Activity in Southern Nigeria, 1900–1965* (Berkeley: Institute of International Studies—University of California, 1982), Bade Onimode, *Imperialism and Underdevelopment in Nigeria: The Dialectics of Mass Poverty* (London: Zed Press, 1982), and I. William Zartman, ed., *The Political Economy of Nigeria* (New York: Praeger, 1983).

[9]For a full background on Nigeria's foreign policy as well as a focus on domestic forces that influence it, see Timothy M. Shaw and Olajide Aluko, eds., *Nigerian Foreign Policy: Alternative Perceptions and Projections* (New York: St. Martin's Press, 1983).

addition to its horticultural past and the absence of a national tradition (language, civil service, and universalistic ideology), usually acquired through feudal-authoritarianism.

Its history also included the destructive civil war of 1967–70 and the corrosive, disruptive effects of abrupt oil wealth which propelled Nigeria into the turbulent world-market economy. In addition, its history included Nigeria's need to devote most of its valuable time, energy, and resources to developing institutions of self-government and its resulting inability to forge a government strong enough and skillful enough to guide its economic and social development.[10]

The strong central government of military rule during the 1970s, which coincided with Nigeria's oil wealth, did not direct oil revenues to social development: neither did the civilian government of 1979–1983. Both the military and civilian governments allowed (could not help?) a chaotic, free enterprise economy to engulf the nation. The large revenues from oil were squandered on prestige projects and developments of dubious economic value. Instead of subsidizing productive enterprises, the government gave untargeted money to various ethnic groups and state governments, in effect, buying political peace. How much different things would have been had the oil revenues gone to increase productivity in agriculture and to develop manufacturing. The government failed to manage its currency in even the most elementary manner. It allowed Nigeria's currency to become grossly overvalued which led to a huge influx of imports and a rising national debt (increased domestic consumption through "cheap" imports also helped to buy political peace). Corruption, both official and private, took place on a scale with few parallels in human history.[11]

Thus, well before the military coup at the end of 1983, the Nigerian economy was in shambles. Nothing symbolizes this failure better than the incredible fact that by the late 1970s Nigeria not only had to import food but also some of the staple products (for example, edible oils) that had sustained the country before independence. Successive governments allowed oil production to remain insulated from the rest of the economy, thus creating no spillover effects to diversify or upgrade manufacturing or labor skills. They allowed a great flood of foreign oil revenues to inflate Nigeria's currency spurring unearned consumption and foreign exchange corruption. Despite laws requiring substantial Nigerian ownership of businesses operating in Nigeria, Nigeria never developed its own capabilities in regard to one endeavor after another.[12] Foreigners run its airline, railroad, harbors, and inland waterways. Foreign firms are relied on for many construction projects, including mechanized farms. The country has a vast army of unneeded middlemen, brokers, and commission agents. And the unproductive nature of the Nigerian economy is symbolized by many who earn their living through crime, including pirates who prey on the ships lying helpless in Nigeria's clogged harbors and waterways.

Nigeria has been buffeted badly by the steep drop in the price of oil that began in 1985. Or rather, Nigeria's failure to manage its earlier oil wealth made it vulnerable, like most Third-World countries, to wild swings in the value of exports. Its failure to use its oil wealth wisely puts it in the company of other developing countries who have made serious miscalculations about the nature and uses of their oil wealth: Venezuela, Iran, Mexico, and Indonesia (but not Iraq or Saudi Arabia).

---

[10]For a dependency analysis of Nigeria's "second experiment with bourgeois democracy," see Toyin Falola and Julius Ihonvbere, *The Rise and Fall of Nigeria's Second Republic: 1979–1984* (London: Zed Books, 1985).

[11]Nigeria finally took control of its financial system in the 1980s.

[12]Attempts to control one's economy by requiring a certain percentage of local ownership have been tried in many countries (for example, Canada, Malaysia, Tanzania) but rarely succeed.

The military government has made preparations for a gradual return to civilian government by 1992. Elections are scheduled for state legislatures and governors in 1990. In 1991 a census will be taken, and in 1992 an election will take place for the federal legislature and president. On the economic front the military has worked to reduce the government's role in the economy in order to spur efficiency and curb corruption. By and large it has instituted a free-market economy and plans to sell many government corporations. It has allowed the Nigerian currency to fall in order to curb imports and spur exports and has invited foreign investment by reducing native ownership requirements. Agricultural marketing boards have been abolished. However, the only result of all this has been to lower the standard of living of the masses. By 1989 after three years of austerity, the economy remained limp. Without an economic recovery the military could well postpone the return to civilian rule. And the failure of free-market austerity in Nigeria poses a threat to the confidence with which 25 other African countries have embarked on a similar course. Nigeria's stagnant and inequitable economy only underscores its dependence on oil and the world market. Only time will tell if Nigeria will use the revenues from a rise in oil prices, if and when they occur, more wisely than in the past.

MALAYSIA[13]

Land and People

Malaysia is in Southeast Asia and is made up of two distinct geographical entities divided by hundreds of miles of ocean: penin-

sular Malaysia and Sarawak and Sabah on the Northeastern coast of Borneo. Malaysia's climate is hot and humid, it has abundant natural resources, and its soil, while not overly fertile, is good for trees. The bulk of its 15,700,000 people (1985 est.) live on the mainland and its settlement pattern follows geography: mountainous and densely vegetated interiors make the coastal plains preferred settlement areas and the location of tin and trading ports on the west side of the peninsular make that a favored settlement area.

Ethnic Composition

Malaysia is a segmented (or plural, multicommunal) society. Ethnicity is the center of how people live, work, play, and practice politics. Its three main ethnic groups are Malays (6.3 million who make up 48 percent of the total and 55 percent of the peninsular population), Chinese (3.8 million, who make up about 20 percent of the total and 33 percent of the peninsular population) and Indians (1.1 million who make up about 8 percent of the total and 10 percent of the peninsular population). The Malays have increased their share of the total since 1970 because of their higher fertility rate. However, Malaysia has a strong family planning program, and fertility rates have declined significantly among all ethnic groups.

Religion

Malays are Sunni Muslims, which is also the state religion (the constitution guarantees and, in practice, there is religious freedom). The Chinese practice an amalgam of China's three major religions: Confucianism, Taoism, and Buddhism. Indians (mostly Tamils) are Hindu. There are other religions, including Christianity.

---

[13]*Malaysia: A Country Study* (Washington D.C.: U. S. Government Printing Office, 1985), part of the American University Foreign Area Studies Series; C. M. Sturnbull, *A Short History of Malaysia* (Melbourne: Melbourne University Press, 1980); Kevin Young, Willem Bussick, and Parvez Hasan, *Malaysia: Growth and Equity in a Multi-Racial Society* (Baltimore: The Johns Hopkins Press, 1980); E.

E. K. Fisk, and H. Osman-Rani, *The Political Economy of Malaysia* (Oxford, England: Oxford University Press, 1982); and K. S. Jomo (Jomo Kwame Sundaran), *A Question of Class: Capital, the State, and Uneven Development in Malaya* (New York: Oxford University Press, 1986), which includes a superb bibliography.

Language

When Malaysia became independent in 1957, Malaysian became the official language for the conduct of government business and for education beyond the primary grades. (English is widely used in business and is a compulsory second language.) Language differences are a source of conflict in many segmented societies (for example, Canada, Belgium, Sri Lanka). On the whole, Malaysia's decision to make the language of a bare majority the official language has been successful—a large portion of young Chinese and Indian origin citizens are now fluent in Malaysian.

The Colonial Heritage

The Malay peninsula is situated at a major crossroads of sea traffic and has experienced wide contact with many peoples. The Islamic people came in the fifteenth century, carried by Arab traders, followed by Portuguese and Dutch traders who developed colonial enclaves. The British were latecomers but became the dominant colonial power during the nineteenth century and had a major impact on the shape of Malaysian society between 1870 and 1940. Britain's policy toward its colony followed a classic pattern: the development of an export economy (especially rubber and tin, which were valuable to industrializing Britain and the West, and lumber and palm oil), and a political policy of keeping the colonized population divided. The British supported the Malay aristocracy giving them pensions and a symbolic role but no real power. Malays stayed in rural areas while the rubber plantations and tin mines were developed with foreign labor (Indians and Chinese respectively). Each of these three ethnic groups were kept in distinct economic roles and the policy of allowing unlimited immigration changed the demography of Malay society toward its present composition. During this period, the Chinese began to dominate in the developing commercial and manufacturing world.

Malaysia became independent in 1957 quite peacefully. The colonial heritage included parliamentary government, English-style education, and of course the English language.

Economy

Malaysia's abundant natural resources, which include oil and natural gas, a hard-working population, including a segment that has entrepreneurial skills (the Chinese), and a directive, supportive government have all combined to produce an impressive record of economic growth over the past few decades. Its GNP in 1987 was $29.5 billion yielding a per capita income of $1800[14] (putting Malaysia well into the world's middle-income group).

Malaysia's government openly directs its economy. It has five-year economic plans, state enterprises, and the government directly intervenes in the economy in other ways, such as, by promoting commodity futures markets, establishing free-trade zones, starting new industries, protecting established industries, diversifying its trading partners, joining international producer organizations, and so on. Nonetheless, Malaysia has a capitalist economy: private entrepreneurial activity is encouraged, the government believes in free trade (and its practices are as good or better than most countries), and it encourages foreign investment. In recent years it has leaned toward Japan and South Korea and away from Britain both as trading partners and as economic models.

Manufacturing has steadily increased its share of the Malaysian economy with the government actively promoting industry both light and heavy. Foreign investors own 60 percent of its capital and Malaysian Chinese own 20 percent. The government is openly committed to increasing the Malay share and some progress has been recorded.

---

[14]The World Bank, *The World Bank Atlas* (Washington, D.C.: The World Bank, 1988), p. 8.

Polity

Malaysia's political system is a parliamentary form of representative government with a figurehead monarchy.[15] Since independence its system has worked well in many ways. For one thing, it has successfully transferred political power through peaceful elections. There have been no coup attempts and no need to call on the military to perform political functions. But its major achievement has been to make a multicommunal society work.

In the 1950s, in preparation for independence, the major ethnic groups (Malays, Chinese, Indians) made a compact that represents a unique political achievement. Acknowledging the political supremacy of Malays and the economic supremacy of the Chinese, the ethnic groups agreed that the political process would be used to increase the economic position of Malays and the political position of Chinese and other minorities. Deriving from this understanding, the Malays, who are a bare numerical majority, received a 2 for 1 preponderance of political power. In addition, the Malay language became the official language, Islam became the official religion, and Malays were to receive preference in the distribution of government positions, educational benefits, and business opportunities. In return, the Chinese and other minorities benefited by a liberalization of citizen status and a constitutional guarantee of free enterprise.

Some Chinese thought this arrangement unfair and some Malays thought that too much had been given to the Chinese and other minorities. But independence from British rule took place peacefully and Malaysia's power groups succeeded in avoiding the massive bloodletting that occurred when other multicommunal British colonies achieved independence (for example, India and Nigeria).

Intercommunal tension continued, however. Singapore (with its dominant Chinese population) withdrew from Malaysia in 1965 and there were ethnic riots in 1967 and 1969. The 1969 riots in Kuala Lumpur led to an addition to the ethnic compact, the New Economic Policy. The ruling coalition blamed poverty for the rioting and undertook a campaign to eliminate poverty among all ethnic groups. In 1974, the ruling coalition expanded to 10 parties to become the National Front. The United Malays National Organization is the dominant core of this coalition, which represents a wide spectrum of interest groups. In the years since 1974 the coalition has held roughly 130 out of 154 seats in the national legislature.

Domestic Inequality, Dependency, and Adaptive Capacity

Economic inequality in Malaysia coincides first with ethnicity: Malays have lower incomes and less wealth than the Chinese (and even Indians). The government's basic policy has been to change this relation and some success has occurred. Malays have increased their income and wealth relative to other ethnic groups though they still lag behind.[16]

Rural people (regardless of ethnicity are poorer than urban dwellers and here too some equalization has taken place. Women's income is very unequal to men's even when performing the same work. By and large, female inequality cuts across all categories of ethnicity, employment, and location.[17]

Income and wealth inequality are pronounced *within* each ethnic group and the wealthy of Malaysia get one of the highest shares of total income in the world.

Malaysia depends on foreign investment, and a great deal of its economy is owned by

---

[15]Lloyd D. Musolf and J. Frederick Springer, *Malaysia's Parliamentary System: Representative Politics and Policymaking In a Divided Society* (Boulder, Colo.: Westview, 1979).

[16]Donald R. Snodgrass, *Inequality and Economic Development in Malaysia* (Oxford, England: Oxford University Press, 1980); Charles Hirschman, *Ethnic Stratification in Peninsular Malaysia* (Washington, D.C.: American Sociological Association, 1975); Charles Hirschman, "The Making of Race in Colonial Malaysia: Political Economy and Racial Ideology," *Sociological Forum* 1 (Spring, 1986): 330–61.

[17]For a case study of Malay women in a rural village, see Heather Strange, *Rural Malay Women in Tradition and Transition* (New York: Praeger, 1981).

foreigners. It is also dependent on the world market, being very sensitive to price fluctuations for some of its commodity exports (tin, rubber, coconut and palm oils, and more recently petroleum).

However, Malaysia's long history of an export-skewed economy and foreign investment has not resulted in the marked dependence characteristic of many developing nations. It has not incurred a heavy foreign debt. And thanks to decades of political stability and the dominance of its ruling party and coalition, the Malaysian government has been able to monitor foreign investment, take some steps to moderate fluctuations in commodity prices, diversify its economy and trading partners, and participate in a variety of international arrangements to increase its flexibility and prevent costly foreign entanglements.

Malaysia, therefore, cannot be characterized by mainstream dependency theory, that is, as a society shaped for subordination by outside forces. There is little doubt that Malaysia is part of the world-market system. But, as Jomo Kwama Sundaram argues, internal class formation and contention (in conjunction with British rule and the general process of world capitalist accumulation) explains much of Malaysia's history. Since independence the various segments of the capitalist class (private entrepreneurs, representatives of foreign capital, and statist or bureaucratic capitalists) in contention among themselves, the peasantry, and workers have been dynamic enough to make Malaysia a partner in its own (uneven) development.[18]

Malaysia's record in establishing an independent nation, developing its economy, avoiding adverse foreign influences, and, above all, in managing its communal tensions and rivalries, at least until recently, has been outstanding. Planning by the central government and by each state no doubt has played an important role in this impressive record. But planning has worked (not fully but with increased competence) because Malaysia had a consensus on goals: increasing the participation of Malays in the economy, protecting the economic status of the Chinese and other minorities while helping them to participate in politics, and eradicating poverty among all groups. Malaysia's success in achieving growth, moderating ethnic rivalries, closing the economic and political gaps among its peoples (at least somewhat), and reducing poverty (at least somewhat) have some well-known causes: abundant natural resources, the British legacy, and Chinese entrepreneurial skills. What should not be overlooked is the perhaps too obvious fact that Malays have been in charge since independence. And further, since Malays are Muslims, the widespread belief that equates Islam with traditionalism cannot be sustained. Islamic Malays have been progressive and pragmatic from the beginning and there is evidence since the ascension to power of Datuk Seri Mahathir Mohammad in 1981 that Islamic moral values are now being wedded to the requirements of the work ethic.[19]

The economic slowdown of the mid-1980s (part of a worldwide slowdown) is associated with some ominous developments in Malaysia's political and ethnic relations. Serious infighting developed in the dominant Malay political party and the traditional "Malay way," emphasizing conciliation and courtesy, has been a victim. The prime minister has resorted to authoritarian measures against the press, public assemblies, and the judiciary. Disputes have broken out over Chinese education and the public has seriously questioned mismanagement and corruption in state operations. Regardless of whether it is characterized by dependency, Marxist, or

---

[18]For a valuable history of class formation and contention from precolonial Malaysia to the present, which adopts a nondogmatic Marxist explanation as against mainstream dependency theory, see K. S. Jomo (Jomo Kwame Sundaran), *A Question of Class: Capital, the State, and Uneven Development in Malaysia* (New York: Oxford University Press, 1986).

[19]For this thesis, see Diane K. Mauzy and R. S. Milne, "The Mahathir Administration in Malaysia: Discipline Through Islam," *Pacific Affairs* 56 (Winter, 1983–84): 617–48.

liberal theory, Malaysia's political troubles stem from its economic troubles (and the latter are much affected by the world market).

SRI LANKA (CEYLON)[20]

Land and People

Sri Lanka is an island off the Southwestern tip of India about 270 miles long and 150 wide. Its climate is hot and humid and its topography is quite varied. The center of the island is mountainous and rivers flow down all sides of its raised interior to the coastal plains. Sri Lanka is not well endowed with natural resources apart from some agricultural staples. Its basic crops are coconut, rubber, tea, and sugar cane. Its population in 1985 numbered approximately 16 million and its growth rate was an easily supportable 1.8 percent.

Ethnic Composition

Sri Lanka is a segmented (multiethnic, multicommunal) society.[21] Seventy-four percent of the population is Sinhalese (mostly Buddhists but also some Roman Catholics), 18 percent is Tamil (mostly Hindu but some Roman Catholic), 7.4 percent Muslim, plus

0.4 others. The Tamils are divided further between Sri Lankan Tamils (12.6 of the population) or early settlers (third century B.C.) and Indian Tamils (5.6 percent of the population), or those brought in from India during the colonial period to labor on the plantations.

The tension between Sinhalese and Tamils is a product of colonialism, modernization, and nation building. The violence and political instability that has marked the relations between these two original settlers has occurred largely since independence in 1948. Their hostility focuses not so much on religion as it does on language, but language differences (as we saw in the case of Canada) reflect a deeper problem: the access that language gives to scarce economic goods. The differences between these groups is aggravated by the fact that each has a historical memory in which *it* is the aggrieved minority—the Sinhalese have experienced domination by invaders from India (a country that erased Buddhism from its boundaries) while the Tamils feel threatened by the political dominance of the Sinhalese since independence. Ethnic relations are exacerbated because the Tamils did well in education and government service under British rule and now find themselves being displaced by Sinhalese. Ethnic rivalry can occur more easily because the Tamils, while a significant minority throughout Sri Lanka, dominate the Northern part of the island.

Historical Background

Sri Lanka's historical experience was shaped by two things: water and outsiders. The Sinhalese population of Sri Lanka came from North India in about 500 B.C. and the Tamils came in 300 B.C. from South India. The original peoples date back to paleolithic times but little trace of them exists. Outsiders were important in the next two thousand years in a variety of forms. South Indians invaded the island on a number of occasions and even ruled it for a time. The Portuguese arrived early in the sixteenth century and the

---

[20]The Republic of Sri Lanka (Ceylon) and Sri Lanka (Ceylon) are the official and short terms for this country. Ceylonese is the official adjective and term of reference for the people. However the term *Sri Lankan* seems to have caught on better than the term *Ceylonese*. *Sri Lanka: A Country Study* (Washington, DC: U. S. Government Printing Office, 1970), Foreign Area Studies, The American University is badly out of date.

[21]For basic data and discussions, see Virginia A. Leary, *Ethnic Conflict and Violence in Sri Lanka*, (Geneva: International Commission of Jurists, 1981); James Manor, *Sri Lanka in Change and Crisis* (New York: St. Martin's Press, 1984); S. J. Tambiah, *Sri Lanka: Ethnic Fratricide and the Dismantling of Democracy* (Chicago: University of Chicago Press, 1986); and K. M. de Silva, *Managing Ethnic Tensions In Multi-Ethnic Societies: Sri Lanka 1880–1985* (Lanham, Md: University Press of America, 1986). All volumes tend to stress ethnic, historical, and political variables and to neglect economic factors.

Dutch in the seventeenth century. Both were ousted by the British who turned it into a colony starting in 1795 and ending in 1948. The impact of the Western colonial powers was considerable, essentially transforming Sri Lanka's economy away from subsistence to export and, on the whole, predisposing it to dependency on the vagaries of the outer world.[22]

The other great influence on Sri Lanka's social structure is water or, perhaps better stated, geography. Sri Lanka developed its agriculture through irrigation, creating a food surplus which, as in other societies, led to a flourishing complex civilization. However, geography prevented Sri Lanka from becoming a centralized state such as the other great hydraulic civilizations. Both internally and because it is an island, Sri Lanka did not face chronic military problems and, consequently, the military has not played a big role in its domestic political life. And Sri Lanka had no one river system to harness but a number of smaller ones. As a result it developed as a series of small feudal kingdoms.

Economy[23]

Sri Lanka is primarily an agricultural country and relies on a small number of crops for export earnings: tea, rubber, and coconut products. Manufacturing accounts for about 15 percent of its total product. It has no other important natural resources and while the Ceylonese (as they prefer to be called) people have a standard of living that is relatively good by Asian/Third-World standards, they nonetheless live in a poor country. In 1987 Sri Lanka's GNP was $6.5 billion yielding a per capita income of $400.[24]

As a commodity exporter Sri Lanka is vulnerable to volatile price shifts in the world markets, price shifts that are mostly downward because of world overproduction. This, in addition to crop failures because of weather and the jump in oil prices from 1974 on, has meant a tough economic existence for Sri Lanka during its period of independence. Given the export-skewed economy, Sri Lanka cannot feed itself and unemployment is extremely high. It has relied on foreign assistance, mostly by Western countries but also from China, to see it through.

Sri Lanka has devoted significant resources to helping its poor, improving living conditions, and raising educational standards. It has also embarked on some development projects, especially the giant Makaweli Dam, and has encouraged export manufacturing, in various ways, including the establishment of a free-trade zone. In 1977, a new government committed the country to free enterprise. Economic regulations and controls were reduced, more emphasis was placed on capital investment and less on subsidies for consumption, and state enterprises were slated for private ownership. The new incentives invigorated the economy but predictable negative results also occurred: continued balance of payments problems, inflation, and high unemployment (25 percent).

Polity

Sri Lanka has had representative government since its independence in 1948. Its parliamentary government became a mixed presidential-parliamentary system in 1978. The president is now elected directly and has considerable power as chief executive and as a political leader. The president appoints the cabinet and while he can dissolve parliament for new elections, the government does not fall if it does not have

---

[22]For a full-scale study, which finds Sri Lanka to be a classic case of underdevelopment through colonial modernization, see Asoka Bandarage, *Colonialism in Sri Lanka: The Political Economy of the Kandyan Highlands, 1833–1886* (New York: Mouton, 1983).

[23]B. L. C. Johnson and M. Le M. Scrivenor, *Sri Lanka: Land, People, and Economy* (London: Heinemann, 1981) and Peter Richards and Wilbert Gooneratue, *Basic Needs, Poverty, and Government Policies in Sri Lanka* (Geneva: International Labor Office, 1980).

[24]The World Bank, *The World Bank Atlas 1988* (Washington, D.C.: The World Bank, 1988), p. 9.

the confidence of the legislature. Voting is by proportional representation and voters cast ballots for parties not candidates—this gives the political parties enormous control over its members.

Sri Lanka's voters have turned out six governments since independence. Their political system gives them a choice between two general political orientations: welfare state (moderately socialist) and free enterprise governments. In 1977, they decisively turned out a welfare state oriented government and have opted for free enterprise since.

Despite its success at maintaining representative government, Sri Lankan politics have not been altogether stable or peaceful. A serious insurrection by an ultra-left group occurred in 1971 in response to bad economic conditions. But the most important form of instability has been intercommunal strife. Tension between Sinhalese and Tamils has been apparent since independence but has broken into open violence since 1983.

Sri Lanka's Tamils did well under the British and felt threatened when the large Sinhalese majority took over the government in 1948. Sinhalese was made the official language, which meant that the Tamils who had done well in education and had been able to do well in government positions and the professions, would be unable to compete fairly in the new Sri Lanka (Tamil was eventually declared a national language[25]). The Northern part of the island where the Tamils predominate is not well endowed economically. The government was not only giving preference to Sinhalese for government positions but its settlement policies in new lands were also considered threatening by the Tamils.

Domestic Inequality

Sri Lanka is a very unequal society, though inequality declined somewhat between 1953

and 1973. Still, in 1973 the richest 10th received 30 percent of the total income while the poorest 10th received 1.8 percent. The welfare programs of successive governments have curbed absolute poverty and Sri Lanka is one of the societies in which slow growth has combined with less inequality and poverty. But the recent governments have also instituted free-market policies which will make further reductions in poverty difficult.

Foreign Policy, Dependency, and Adaptive Capacity

Sri Lanka pursues a policy of not getting entangled with other nations. By and large, it enjoys good relations with all countries. It is an active member of the nonaligned movement. Before 1977 it was anti-Western and since then it has been pro-Western. It has made some limited overtures toward Communist China as part of its effort to diversify its trading partners but is primarily oriented to the capitalist West. In 1982 its application to join ASEAN (the Association of Southeast Asian nations) was turned down largely because it is outside ASEAN's geographical area. Relations with the United States are good but so far only a small amount of trade with the United States has developed. In addition, American corporations have not invested much in Sri Lanka.

Sri Lanka tends to vote with the developing nations at the United Nations, and more with the Soviet Union than the United States (which is not surprising given the deep isolation of the United States in the UN).[26]

Forty years after independence Sri Lanka is still a viable country. In a world where regime failure, rebellion, and dictatorship are common, this is no mean achievement. When analysis shifts and asks, however, how well has Sri Lanka done? the mood changes. Economic growth has been slow and faltering. Government economic policies have lacked coherence, and implemen-

---

[25]English fell into disuse but the government has made an effort to revive it largely because of its international importance.

[26]H.S.S. Nissanka, *Sri Lanka's Foreign Policy: A Study in Non-Alignment* (New Delhi, India: Vikas, 1984).

tation has been indecisive. Sri Lanka has all the signs of an underdeveloped society. Above all, the dominant Sinhalese have failed to forge bonds of intercommunal harmony.

The welfare state erected prior to 1977 is not the cause of low economic growth,[27] but failure to act decisively to either nationalize the British estates or not, led to a lack of investment in Sri Lanka's basic export products. There were failures to develop new crops for export, to use irrigation water carefully, and to increase productivity through small-scale projects. The socialist-leaning government up until 1977, coupled with widespread labor and ethnic unrest, also made foreign investment unattractive.

Since 1977 the economy has revived under free enterprise but the society as a whole cannot be said to be better off. Inflation, unemployment, and a widespread perception that economic rewards are inequitably distributed have also followed the government's free-market philosophy. Inflation has hit the poor and the urban working class hard. Savings have not increased. Little has been done to spur exports and import substitution manufacturing continues as before. A large part of the investment budget has come from foreign assistance and foreign investment.

The dislocations and worsening conditions for the lower classes that have attended the market-oriented policies of the government since 1977, have exacerbated ethnic tensions. Both Tamils and Sinhalese have suffered because the competitive economy has created new anxieties, frustrations, and insecurities. The unemployed see prosperity all around, but they feel it is unattainable for them. A new class of Sinhalese small business people have assumed considerable political power at all levels and have used it to further their interests even when the rules of representative government have to be bent. They have also stirred ethnic tension by using the Tam-

ils (and Muslims and Indians), who are visible in commerce, administration, and the professions as scapegoats for the frustrations of the population (a similar fate has befallen "middlemen," broker populations such as Greeks, Armenians, Jews, Asian Indians and Chinese in many societies in various historical periods).

Since the Sinhalese ruling coalitions are multiclass, they have found it difficult to forge and implement coherent and decisive programs. Intercommunal strife has also worsened the economic situation. But in the last analysis, Sri Lanka's failures are social and historical rather than due to specific policies or party programs.[28] How different the period since independence would have been had the British invested the profits from rubber, tea, coconut, and other exports in building Sri Lankan society prior to independence. How different independence would have been had the British fostered an associational rather than a segmented society.

Beyond all this, Sri Lanka would still be a society too small and too little endowed with the resources for industrialization to be more than a dependent and precarious undertaking. Much of Sri Lanka's future lies in how well it can resolve communal strife. Unlike Malaysia, where a bare majority of Malays faced a powerful Chinese (and Indian) minority, the Sinhalese were tempted into thinking that they could turn their 75 percent majority into an across-the-board dominance. In 1983 a civil war erupted that has devastated Sri Lankan society. Sri Lanka is fortunate that India is not only not officially supporting the Tamil minority but is lending its good offices toward achieving a settlement (partisan interference by outside powers has aggravated ethnic relations in Northern Ireland and Cyprus since their independence). In 1987 an accord was signed between India and the Sri

[27]Peter Richards and Wilbert Gooneratne, *Basic Needs, Poverty, and Government Policies in Sri Lanka* (Geneva: International Labor Office, 1980).

[28]For a comprehensive analysis linking Sri Lanka's troubles to its colonial past and its dependence on the contemporary world market, see Satchi Ponnambalam, *Dependent Capitalism In Crisis: The Sri Lankan Economy 1948–1980* (London: Zed Press, 1981).

Lankan government. This accord has not been maintained and Sri Lankan civil strife has continued. A Sinhalese insurrectionist group has emerged to prevent concessions to the Tamils. A further casualty of the war has been the erosion of democratic practices. In 1989 the Sinhalese government bypassed India and its own extremist wing and invited the most radical wing of the Tamils to the negotiating table. The Tamil acceptance was promising but a rapid healing, even if begun, cannot be expected.

CHAPTER
17

SAUDI ARABIA, ISRAEL, ZIMBABWE, THE REPUBLIC OF SOUTH AFRICA, AND PEACEFUL SOCIETIES
Smaller Exceptional Societies

SAUDI ARABIA

Land and People[1]

Saudi Arabia, an arid land of approximately 10,800,000 people (including 2 million foreigners) sits atop one-quarter of the world's known reseves of oil. It holds interest for other reasons. It has succeeded so far in modernizing as a hereditary monarchy; it has done so from a herding, tribal social base; and it is part of the Arab coalition against Israel. The United States is on friendly terms with Saudi Arabia, since both have a vital stake in checking Soviet and Iranian expansion in the Middle East and protecting oil supplies to the West.

The Saudi are a homogenous people of Sunni Muslims with only a small minority (10 percent) of Shia.[2] It has imported a substantial foreign labor force but so far has kept itself insulated from it.

Family and the Position of Women

The Arab family is patrilineal on an extended basis: the couple, children, married sons and their wives, and their sons' children. This extended structure acts as a single economic unit and all assets are vested in the male head. An elder son may set up a separate household (sponsored by the family including a share of the family assets). Marriages are carefully arranged to benefit the family and it is common to marry relatives, the latter leading to a further diversity of kinship relations.

---

[1]*Saudi Ariabia: A Country Study*, Foreign Area Studies, The American University, 4th ed. (Washington, D.C.: U. S. Government Printing Office, 1984) provides a comprehensive introduction to Saudi society.

[2]With the exception of Egypt, Arab society is exceptional in that it derives from trade rather than agriculture; see the section, Preindustrial Hybrids: The Unique Arab World in Chapter 3. This section also discusses the cleavage between Sunni and Shia Arabs.

So far the Saudi family, derived from its nomadic, tribal past, has not undergone much change with urbanization. One reason is that economic statuses are deeply embedded in the family. Another is the example of the royal family, which has successfully handled the assets of the nation. And another is the sharp sexual segregation between men and women.

Arab belief and the Muslim religion combine to produce an explicit normative system that declares that men are strong, rational, and unemotional and that women are weak, emotional, and irrational. The purity of the inferior woman is a matter of family honor (and all men are expected to honor all women) and has led to a strict segregation between the sexes. Women are kept at home and even live separately at home (men, of course, can enter public spaces for work and other activities). Reverence for women is high and women are not without power. They have important knowledge about other families and are valuable to their husbands and sons when they negotiate marriages and engage in other activities outside the home.

In recent years the Saudi government has provided extensive educational opportunities for women, largely so that they can become teachers and do medical work. All this has been done under the assumption that sexual segregation will continue even as women enter the economy and government service.

Economy

Oil provides Saudi Arabia with much of its GNP of $83 billion (1986) and a per capita income of $12,000, among the highest in the world.[3] To decrease its dependence on crude oil exports, Saudi Arabia has undertaken an ambitious program of industrialization, largely to process its hydrocarbon resources. Education, including technical training abroad, has high priority. The Saudi have also stressed relative food self-sufficiency and have invested heavily in obtaining adequate supplies of water.

Once the oil began to flow in the 1960s the Saudi had to choose between slow and fast development. Arab society does not separate religion and society, and important Saudi voices felt that economic development would adversely affect the religious society that the Saudi royal family had so carefully built, but other voices, including the royal family, prevailed and Saudi Arabia embarked on a rapid program of economic development.

The economic development of Saudi Arabia from 1970 on is impressive. Stressing high-quality capital-intensive productive facilities, the Saudi hope to decrease their dependence on imported goods and labor. To service this new economy the Saudi embarked on the construction of roads, ports, airports, and other infrastructure and by the mid-1980s had eliminated earlier bottlenecks. All in all, they are poised for continued growth using their oil wealth to buy what they need.[4]

The commitment to economic development did not lead to poverty, unemployment, and political instability as it has in some other countries (the contrast with Muslim Iran is especially revealing). The Saudi monarchy struck a bargain with the Saudi people based on Saudi Arabia's Muslim religion and its tribal heritage—it shared the wealth and shared it openly and generously. Schooling at all levels is free. All health care is free. All are entitled to a plot of land and an interest-free home loan of $80,000. There are state subsidies for a wide variety of goods and services, for example, water, electricity, and gasoline. And there are no personal income taxes.

The government took the ownership of its oil away from foreigners but relied on foreign technicians and administrators to run both its production wells and its petrochemical industries, but trained Saudi have gradually taken over and by the late 1980s, the Saudi were running the upper levels of their entire economy.

---

[3]The World Bank, *The World Bank Atlas 1988* (Washington, D.C.: The World Bank, 1988), p. 9.

[4]Ali D. Johany, Michel Berne, and J. Wilson Mixon, Jr., *The Saudi Arabian Economy* (Baltimore: The Johns Hopkins University Press, 1986).

The government has stressed private initiatives in the economy but has had to take the lead since Saudi business people do not feel comfortable making long-term investments in manufacturing. Accordingly, the Saudi economy has a very large public sector. Despite having one of the world's highest per capita incomes and despite the large range of free public services such as health and education, Saudi society is still very unequal in both income and wealth.

Polity

Saudi Arabia has no constitution, legislature, or political parties. It is an absolute, hereditary monarchy that so far has succeeded in building a diversified, relatively "modern" society. Political power resides in the king and the large royal family. Decisions are arrived at collectively in secret and members of the royal family are in charge of the various branches of government.

The achievement of the Saudi royal family in building an integrated nation state out of a collection of warring nomadic tribes dates from its alliance in the eighteenth century with Wahhabism, a puritanical version of Sunni Islam. Led by Ibu Saudi, who reigned from 1902 to 1953, Saudi Arabia developed a central government, emphasized permanent settlements, and food self-sufficiency. In 1927 the British, followed by others, recognized the Saudi as an independent state. Thanks to their central authority, infused and legitimated by Wahhabism, the Saudi were ready to utilize the oil wealth that began to flow in 1938. With the adoption of modern bookkeeping and other administrative reforms, the working, adaptive royal family, energized by a vital religious ethic, has succeeded in bringing about an extensive modernization of Saudi society.

Saudi Arabia remains a highly stable society despite its rapid prosperity and despite the abrupt decline in its oil revenues during the 1980s. Internally, there is no political dissent because there are no political parties, no labor unions, no independent press, and no autonomous private groups. Effective politi-

cal authority in Saudi Arabia does not require much direct coercion. A vital religion provides much of the authority and legitimacy of the monarchy. The competence of the royal family is widely acknowledged. And of course, some of the stability can be explained by the extensive range of free public services and by the fact that foreigners make up a large part of the labor force and do the kind of work that the Saudi look down on.

To govern, the king relies on a large range of professionals, which include many members of the royal family, and on religious leaders. The strong Arab custom of charity and holding open house hearings so that individuals with problems can voice their wishes and complaints serves as a functional equivalent for Western-style politics.

Foreign Policy

Saudi foreign policy has a number of objectives: one, to keep oil flowing at the best price, two, to oppose the spread of communism, three, to oppose the state of Israel, and four, to oppose the spread of Shia Islamic fundamentalism from Iran (the latter is seen as a threat to its neighbors, as well as to itself, and to its international status among Muslims as the custodian of the Great Mosque in Mecca, Islam's most sacred shrine).

Saudi Arabia pays a great deal of attention to the rest of the Arab world, keeping its lines of communication open with all, especially Egypt, Syria, and Iraq. Despite its wealth, it is not a military power (as yet), it does not lead the Arab world intellectually, and it is politically and religiously more conservative than the rest. Accordingly, it pursues a policy of balancing all Arab countries to prevent any from becoming dominant. It also cultivates relations with the United States since both have many mutual interests.[5]

The Saudi founded the Organization of the Islamic Conference in 1970, an organization

---

[5]For background, see William B. Quandt, *Saudi Arabia in the 1980s: Foreign Policy, Security and Oil* (Washington, D.C.: The Brookings Institution, 1981), especially Chapters 1, 2, and 9.

that allows Arab and non-Arab Muslim nations to express themselves on the international scene. It is an influential member of the oil cartel, the Organization of Oil Exporting Countries (OPEC), made up of a wide variety of developing countries. The Saudi use their oil power and wealth as a political weapon, including the funding of the Palestinians in the latter's fight with Israel. Despite all of the above, they rely on the United States for arms and overall political support, though they also purchase arms from Great Britain, China, and elsewhere since the U.S. Congress, under pressure from Jewish Americans, continually balks on the issue of supplying it with the arms it wants. In 1988, meeting more resistence from Congress and Jewish-Americans on a request to purchase advanced weapons, the Saudi negotiated a huge $25 billion arms deal with Great Britain. Today the United States is no longer its biggest supplier of arms and since Great Britain has put no restrictions on the arms it is selling, both the United States and Jewish Americans have lost what measure of control they had over Saudi actions.

Despite its wealth Saudi Arabia feels vulnerable. It is small in population, surrounded by volatile, often hostile, societies and is dependent on selling a highly specialized product, oil, in the world market. In the late 1980s its revenues were drastically cut by the oil glut. For much of that time it also had to fear an Iranian military victory over Iraq and was no doubt relieved when that war ended in 1988 in a stalemate (thanks to some extent to its support of Iraq).[6]

How Stable Is Saudi Arabia?

All indications are that the radical transformation of Saudi society under sacral-monarchical authoritarianism has not yet created internal cleavage or conflict, but it is difficult to insulate an economy from other institutions and Saudi society already shows an erosion of traditional values. The quasicapitalist, anything goes, atmosphere has led to huge often unearned fortunes and considerable corruption. The easy wealth has made it somewhat difficult to interest Saudi youth in the arduous education needed for a modern economy and society. Crime, including alcohol and drug offenses, has risen and there is considerable hypocrisy about consumption and sexual morality. Saudi youth, including women, are exposed to foreign teachers and mass media, and they travel abroad in large numbers.[7]

Nonetheless, Saudi society appears internally stable. But the powers that be have unleashed expectations that will require adroit handling for the foreseeable future.

Oil, Modernization, and the World Economy[8]

The possession, purchase, or control of oil (or other energy sources such as coal) was an important reason for successful economic growth in the United States, Canada, the capitalist countries of Europe, and the Soviet Union. Since World War II oil has increased its importance in the world economy as new discoveries were made around the globe. One pattern that has emerged is that oil is much like any other resource: it does not automatically translate into economic or social success. The United States, Canada, Europe, Japan,

---

[6]For a detailed historical picture of Saudi foreign policy, see Nadav Safran, *Saudi Arabia: The Ceaseless Quest for Security* (Cambridge, Mass.: Harvard University Press, 1985). Safran correctly points to Saudi Arabia's vulnerabilities but exaggerates the weakness (immobility) of its political system, neglects its success in building a more balanced economy, and overlooks its determination to build its military strength. Safran ends his analysis by advising the United States (unbelievable as it may sound) that its short- and long-term vital interests should be disengaged from the policy and fate of Saudi Arabia.

[7]For an analysis, see Saad Eddin Ibrahim, *The New Arab Social Order: A Study of the Impact of Oil Wealth* (Boulder, Colo.: Westview, 1982), Chapter 5. The remainder of this book provides valuable coverage of a variety of Arab countries.

[8]For a succinct overview of the international oil industry, see *Saudi Arabia: A Country Study*, 4th ed. (Washington, D.C.: U. S. Government Printing Office, 1984), appendix B.

the Soviet Union continue to benefit from its use. Great Britain and Norway have used their new North Sea oil wealth to great advantage (it has perhaps given Great Britain a respite from its economic decline). But among developing countries, oil wealth has not been an unmixed blessing. Of these only the Arab countries of the Arabian peninsula and Iraq have managed to use their oil for stable development. Venezuela and Algeria have had only moderate success in translating their oil wealth into stable social development. Some smaller countries have benefitted from their oil but have not necessarily grown in a stable manner, for example, Libya, Ecuador, and Gabon. Three large countries, Indonesia, Nigeria, and Mexico, have failed to turn their enormous oil wealth into steady economic growth. And Iran under the Shah failed to share its oil wealth or develop public services and gave way in 1979 to an unstable revolutionary regime based on a charismatic religious leader.

The OPEC countries (Algeria, Ecuador, Gabon, Indonesia, Iran, Iraq, Kuwait, Libya, Nigeria, Qatar, Saudi Arabia, United Arab Emirates, and Venezuela) are quite varied in ethnic, religious, and "racial" composition. They also vary considerably in their politics and mode of development. Some are socialist, others capitalist, some absolute monarchies—all are authoritarian except Venezuela, which has the rudiments of representative government. Some are aligned with the United States, for example, Saudi Arabia, and some tend to lean toward the U.S.S.R., for example, Algeria and Libya. The OPEC nations have cartelized their oil production and pricing and have power vis a vis the First World largely because of the latter's dependence on imported oil. The huge price increase that OPEC obtained in 1973 had a profoundly adverse impact on the economies of the world, especially developing nations.

The power of the cartel receded during the early 1980s because of the worldwide recession, energy conservation, new oil discoveries outside of OPEC, and conversion to other energy sources. The relative surplus of oil will last (at least by current estimates, which are far from reliable) into the mid-90s. But the dramatic enhancement in world standing and the increase in power of the countries of OPEC (plus other oil-rich countries) are real and likely to increase at century's end.

The possession of oil has given some developing countries a means to change their relative standing in the hierarchy of nations. China is more likely than India to become an economic power for a number of reasons but one is that it has important oil reserves (for the contrast between these two countries, see Chapter 18). Mexico also has possibilities for improving its relative world position because of its large oil reserves, but so far has not succeeded. Over and beyond all this is the fact that the world's oil supplies will not last much beyond 2025. Given the so far intractable problems associated with nuclear energy (safety, disposal of radioactive waste) and the polluting effects of coal, the world faces a precarious future. In all this, one thing is certain: Saudi Arabia's control of much of the world's oil reserves will make it an important player on the world scene over the next quarter century.

ISRAEL[9]

Exceptional Features

Israel is exceptional because it is a complete society established by Westerners (who were also Jewish) in a nondeveloped part of the world. It is not merely a settler society but a full complement of people intent on establishing a homogeneous homeland. It is exceptional because the establishment of Israel

[9]For a discussion of ancient Israel's contribution to Western civilization, see Chapter 3. See also *Israel: A Country Study*, Foreign Area Studies, The American University, 2nd ed. (Washington D.C.: U. S. Government Printing Office, 1979) is dated but provides useful background material. The most recent book on Israeli society, S. N. Eisenstadt, *The Transformation of Israeli Society* (Boulder, Colo.: Westview, 1985) is for insiders and too wordy and too self-absorbed in the mystique of Jewish civilization to be more than a reference work.

was not amidst peoples who lived in horticultural tribes (like the white settler societies
set up by England in North America, Australia,
Kenya, and Zimbabwa) but amidst Arabs, and
Palestinians at that, the most Westernized
people of the Arab world. It is exceptional
because its legitimacy is denied by its neighbors and it exists by force of arms.

Israel is also exceptional because it is a
unitary associational society deeply divided
by multiple ethnicities. The first cleavage is
between Jews themselves, the Ashkenazi more-
Westernized Jews, and the Sephardim Jews,
who came to Israel from throughout the Middle East. From 1948 to the mid-70s the Westernized Jews under the socialist Labor Party
developed Israel as a typical Western class
society. The upper classes were Westerners
and their children enjoyed advantages in the
Western-style educational and occupational
system. Recently the Sephardim Jews have
used their political power and, under the
Likud Party, have begun to close the gap
somewhat between themselves and the Ashkenazi Jews.[10]

The next cleavage is between Israeli Jews
(3.5 million, 1985) and Israeli Arabs (750 thousand). The latter represent a sizeable minority
and though they are ostensibly full citizens,
they are essentially a subjugated people.[11]

The third cleavage is between Israel's Jews
and the Palestinian majority in the occupied
West Bank (813 thousand) and the Gaza Strip
(526 thousand). The total Arab population
equals 2 million or 37 percent of the population. Given their higher birth rate, Arabs in
Israel and the occupied territories will number somewhere between 42 and 46 percent of
the population by the year 2000. In December
of 1987 the Palestinians in the occupied territories began an uprising (using stones) that
was endorsed by Israeli Arabs. The Israelis
have tried to suppress the uprising by force,
expulsions, jailings, curfews, and killings ever
since but with only partial success (this remarkable popular uprising by an unarmed
population was well into its second year by
the end of 1989).

The establishment of Israel came after World
War II prompted by the Holocaust, the murder of six million Jews (and millions of other
minorities) by Nazi (Fascist) Germany. The
Jews of ancient Israel were dispersed by Rome
in the first century A.D. For almost two thousand years Jews lived in various parts of the
world diversified by language, ethnicity, and
cultural level. A political movement (Zionism) to create a Jewish state in the biblical
land of their ancestors originated in the nineteenth century in Eastern Europe, largely because of the continued persecution of Jews.
World War I produced a British mandate over
Palestine and Jewish demands for some form
of homeland increased. The Nazi's attempt to
wipe out Jews (and other minorities) made a
Jewish homeland more imperative for Jews
and gave the idea legitimacy in the minds of
non-Jews in the West. In 1948 the United
Nations (at that time dominated by the developed countries of the West) adopted a recom-
mendation for a partitioned Palestine, which
Jews accepted and the Palestinian Arabs
rejected. In the ensuing armed conflict, the
better-organized and well-supported Jews prevailed and the state of Israel began.

Economy

The influx of Westernized Jews and large
amounts of outside capital made Israel different from its Arab neighbors. Its agriculture is
highly advanced and productive (but forms
only a small percent of its GNP). Israel has a
fairly advanced manufacturing economy, especially diamonds, airplanes, electronics, and

---

[10]For analyses of this earlier period, see S. N. Eisenstadt,
Israeli Society (New York: Basic Books, 1967); Michael
Curtis and Mordecai S. Chertoff, eds., *Israel: Social Struc-
ture and Change* (Brunswick, N.J.: Transaction Books,
1973); and Leonard Weller, *Sociology In Israel* (Westport,
Conn.: Greenwood Press, 1974). For the Palestinian per-
spective, see Ibrahim Abu-Lughod, ed., *The Transforma-
tion of Palestine* (Evanston, Il.: Northwestern University
Press, 1971); Elia T. Zureik, *The Palestinians in Israel: A
Study in Internal Colonialism* (Boston: Routledge and Kegan
Paul, 1979); and Edward W. Said, *The Question of Palestine*
(New York: Times Books, 1979).

[11]For an analysis of how Israeli policies have kept
Arab Israelis in a subordinate position, see Ian Lustick,
*Arabs In The Jewish State: Israel's Control of a National
Minority* (Austin, Tx.: University of Texas Press, 1980).

computers. In 1988 it became the eighth country in the world to launch its own communications satellite.

Israel's gross national product in 1987 was $29.8 billion. Its per capita income of $6810[12] is considerably higher than its neighbors but there are drawbacks. Much of its income must be spent on defense; its national debt is one of the highest in the world (on a per capita basis); it is massively dependent on outside aid, especially from the United States; and it very much depends on a cheap and exploited labor force composed of Israeli Jews, and disproportionately of Israeli Arabs and Arabs in the occupied territories.

Israel faces severe military and political problems that are well known. Less known are the economic difficulties that have beset it since the 1970s. Israel's economy is essentially state-run and state-directed. The government owns oil refinery, chemical, arms manufacturing, rail, airline, television-radio, water, electricity, and telephone monopolies. The government controls and allocates credit, subsidizes exports, and taxes imports. The government also endorses agricultural monopolies. The trade union that represents almost all Israeli workers also owns over 20 percent of the economy and provides the economic strength of the Labor party. Israel's highly politicized economy has become inefficient and rigid, and is probably the most important reason why Israeli economic growth has gone from a robust 5 to 6 percent in the 1960s to less than 1 percent since the early 1970s. The reasons for the state-centered economy are many: a strong socialist tradition brought to Israel by Jews from Europe, the need to act as a refuge for world Jewry, and the need to keep the economy on a semiwar footing.

A large military budget is a second reason for Israel's economic woes. The already battered economy was dealt a heavy blow starting in December of 1987 and continuing through 1989 by the Palestinian uprising.

---

[12]The World Bank, *The World Bank Atlas 1988* (Washington, D.C.: The World Bank, 1988), p. 7.

Polity

Israel is also unusual in the Middle East because it has a genuine multiparty parliamentary system, that is, a Western-style system of representative government. It has had one from the beginning which means that here, as well as in its economy, science, the professions, and military skills, Israel is essentially a transplanted Western society.

The new development in its polity is the relative decline in political power of Westernized-European Jews and the rise to power of "Oriental" Jews (the Likud party). The latter originated from the Middle East and North Africa and occupy the lower reaches of the economy and class structure. Their rise to political power has meant a stalemate between the relatively equal Likud and Labor parties (the latter represents the Westernized upper classes).

The struggle between these parties is twofold: the Likud party stands for military vigilance and permanent possession of occupied land while the Labor party wants a political settlement swapping land for peace; a socioeconomic struggle exists between the lower and upper classes, represented respectively by the Likud and Labor parties.

In the 1948 fight over setting up a partitioned Palestine, up to one million Palestinian refugees fled Israel. In 1967 another Israeli military victory produced more refugees and the occupation of the West Bank and the Gaza Strip, the home of 1.3 million Palestinians. In 1973, another war, less easily won and with great cost, sobered Israel. In 1979 thanks to an initiative by the Egyptian leader Sadat, and the good offices of the United States, it entered into the Camp David accords in which it returned Egyptian territory and agreed to Palestinian self-rule in the occupied territories in return for normal relations with Egypt. Unable to face the prospect of a political settlement with the determined Palestinians (in effect reneging on the Camp David accords), Israel attempted a military solution to its problems by mounting a full-scale invasion of Lebanon in 1982. Its goal of destroying the military strength of the Palestinian Liberation Organization (PLO) and giving Christians control of Lebanon, thus securing its Northern border, failed.[13]

The invasion of Lebanon marked a turning point in Israel's short history. For the first time Israel had waged a war that was not in defense of Israeli land. The war caused many Israeli deaths and even larger number of Palestinian and Lebanese (largely civilian) deaths. The war also revealed to the Israeli that they were a divided nation torn between two unpalatable alternatives: continued reliance on military strength that brings neither victory nor peace and a political settlement that would trade land for peace and weaken Israel militarily.

Israel is isolated on the world scene, receiving strong, open support only from the United States (the United States gives Israel and Egypt $3 billion per year, the bulk of all its foreign aid[14]), lukewarm support from the rest of the First World, and is opposed by the rest of the world. So far American support has remained strong and the Israeli have worked hard to maintain that support.[15] However, the United States could not ignore the Palestinians' uprising in the occupied territories and it could not ignore a proclamation by the PLO of a Palestinian state along with a statement that it recognized Israel's right to exist. The United States could also not ignore the fact that it was isolated on the world scene in its support of Israel.

Early in 1989 it announced that it was willing to talk to the PLO, in effect, giving it legitimacy as the representative of the Palestinian people. In a May, 1989 speech, Secretary of State Baker pointedly announced a more neutral posture in the Israel-Palestinian conflict, in effect, edging away from America's traditional unilateral support of Israel.

What the future will bring cannot be said. The Palestinians are a determined people with support from Arab countries whose wealth and power are increasing.[16] Israel's victories bring no peace; one loss in war could bring the peace of extinction. The United States' willingness to talk to the PLO has increased pressure on Israel to come to a political settlement.

Another reason that Israel's future is uncertain is that its population now numbers 3.5 million Jews and 2 million Arabs, and the latter have a higher birth rate. Israel's dream of a Jewish state is already a matter of contention between Jews who think in terms of a secular society and a militant minority who want a strict Orthodox religious society. And with the occupation of the West Bank and the Gaza Strip, Israel has to monitor the activities of a huge population of half citizens (Arab residents of Israel) and half noncitizens (Palestinian residents of the occupied territories). At stake are not only the idea of a Jewish society but of a liberal democratic society.

The election of late 1988 revealed Israel's dilemma. While a 58 percent majority voted for parties favoring giving up territory for peace, the need for a coalition or union government between the two major parties gave control of foreign policy to the Likud party, which wants to keep the occupied territories and increase Jewish settlement. In return the Labor party took over control of government economic agencies, thus guaranteeing a continuation of the policies that have led to Israel's bloated and stagnant economy.

---

[13]The deeper reasons for attacking PLO bases in Lebanon were the growing political strength of the PLO and its growing legitimacy among other nations. Since its setback in 1982 the PLO has gathered increased political strength thanks to the Palestinian uprising and to the fact that the overwhelming bulk of the world's countries supports the idea of a separate Palestinian state.

[14]For a discussion of the Palestinian problem in United States foreign policy, see *The Palestinian Problem and United States Policy: A Guide to Issues and Reference*, text by Bruce R. Kuniholm and bibliographic essay by Michael Rubner (Claremont, Calif.: Regina Books, 1986).

[15]Ostensibly to further American interests but also because of its deep isolation, Israel had developed relations with South Africa and the right-wing cause in Nicaragua—see Jane Hunter, *Israeli Foreign Policy: South Africa and Central America* (Boston, Mass.: South End Press, 1987).

[16]Kemal Kirisci, *The PLO and World Politics: A Study of the Mobilization of Support for the Palestinian Cause* (New York: St. Martin's Press, 1986).

ZIMBABWE

Zimbabwe (formerly Rhodesia) is a landlocked country of about 9 million people (8.8 million blacks, 100 thousand whites, 20 thousand mixed, 10,000 Asians) located in Southeastern Africa. It is a poor country dependent on exporting commodities (per capita income of $590 and a GNP of $5.2 billion in 1987).[17] Like many Third-World countries it has a population growth rate that is unsupportable.

The territory now known as Zimbabwe was penetrated and ruled by the British South Africa Company incorporated under royal charter in 1889. As a chartered company, it was the effective government and provided a framework for a white-settler society. From 1890, settlers arrived dispossessing the black population, which lived as horticultural tribes. The seizure of land was not easy and the settlers met continued resistence by the native tribes. The settlers had another problem, South Africa, which assumed from the beginning that this valuable territory would be incorporated into itself. A referendum in 1922 rejected incorporation and Rhodesia was established as a self-governing (white only) British Crown Colony in 1923.

Black resistance never ceased and became more insistent with post-World War II world developments. The white minority refused to share political power and declared Rhodesia an independent nation in 1965. After having protested peacefully for decades, blacks resorted to armed struggle in 1966 and after years of guerrilla war, the independent black nation of Zimbabwe emerged in 1979.[18]

Economy

Zimbabwe has one of black Africa's most industrialized economies (29 percent of GNP

in 1983) and a productive agricultural sector of large commercial farms. But it is deeply dependent on the world market—indeed, its economic development in the first place came from abroad in the form of skilled settlers and foreign investment.[19] Even UN-sponsored sanctions from abroad against the attempt by whites to assert control helped Zimbabwe's economy because it forced the whites to diversify the economy in the direction of manufacturing and self-sufficiency. Zimbabwe is also deeply dependent economically on South Africa. And, overall, it is deeply dependent on world trade in commodities, another example of its dependence on the outside world.

Polity

Zimbabwe has a multiparty parliamentary system of representative government. The Zimbabwe African National Union party led by Robert Mugabe has ruled since independence. A sizable minority party led by Joshua Nkomo has led a dissident movement. In 1988 Nkomo joined the government and a reconciliation appeared to be in the making.

Exceptional Features

Zimbabwe is a classic case of white-settler imperialism. Starting in 1890, a small core of Westernized whites seized the best land and reduced the large black majority to noncitizen laborers. Variations on this pattern occurred throughout the world and Zimbabwe is not so much exceptional in this regard as a good example. White settlers or ethnically different settlers are part of the history of the Carribean and Latin American societies, Vietnam, the Pacific Island societies, Ireland, Algeria, the Republic of South Africa, Angola, and Mozambique (not to mention the spread of English settlers to Australia and New Zealand, and along with the French to North America). The state of Israel is yet another variation on this pattern.

---

[17]The World Bank, *The World Bank Atlas 1988* (Washington, D.C.: The World Bank, 1988), p. 9.

[18]For histories of Zimbabwe, see Martin Meredith, *The Past Is Another Country: Rhodesia (1890–1979);* Miles Hudson, *Triumph or Tragedy? Rhodesia to Zimbabwe* (London: Hamish Hamilton, 1981); and David Martin and Phyllis Johnson, *The Struggle For Zimbabwe* (New York: Monthly Review Press, 1981).

---

[19]It cannot be repeated too often that economic growth does not necessarily benefit the mass of the people.

Zimbabwe is exceptional on a number of other grounds. A black guerrilla movement won an armed struggle against whites. The victorious blacks, recognizing that they needed the whites for economic reasons, have worked hard to build a multiparty, parliamentary system that would ensure a place for whites. For a while, the tiny group of whites, Asians, and people of mixed blood, who make up 1 percent of the population were given 20 percent of the seats in parliament. The fact that the former exploitative minority has stayed on is in sharp contrast to the French in Algeria and Vietnam and to the Portuguese in Angola and Mozambique.

Zimbabwe has a socialist party running a government that is presiding over a capitalist economy. In its brief history Zimbabwe has raised the living standards and self-esteem of the black population. It has championed the cause of black national liberation movements throughout Africa and is active in the Non-Aligned Movement. Zimbabwe has important economic ties with its neighbor South Africa but nonetheless has assisted black movements wherever possible (South Africa in turn assists dissident movements in countries governed by blacks and is particularly unhappy with Zimbabwe, a concrete example of a successful black society brought into being by armed struggle). And Zimbabwe had its aid from the United States cut between 1986 and 1988 because it actively opposed American policies at the United Nations.

The decline of the world economy in the 1980s hit Zimbabwe hard. Its dominant black group (tribe) has been able to overcome its serious differences with a dissident black group (tribe) and its fortunes may pick up. Foreign investment, however, has been slow in coming. Hardpressed, Zimbabwe is being pulled in one direction by leaders who want it to participate in a free-market capitalist world (using its government to supervise multinationals) and those who want it to move toward socialism and self-sufficiency. Regardless of which course it follows, it will be imposed from above.[20]

THE REPUBLIC OF SOUTH AFRICA[21]

The Southern tip of Africa was first settled by the Dutch (Boers) in 1652. The British took control in 1815 and fought the Boers in 1899–1902 to maintain control. A self-governing union of whites emerged in 1910 and the English settlers were the effective governors until 1948. In 1948 the descendants of the Boers, the Afrikaners, came to power with an explicit platform of *apartheid*. Euphemisms aside, apartheid is an explicit policy of building and maintaining a racist society. Despite the trappings of representative government, South Africa is an authoritarian society increasingly given to totalitarian methods in which approximately 2.5 million white descendants of the original Dutch settlers rule 3 million English-origin whites, 2 million "coloreds" (mixed ancestry), 800 thousand Asians, and 24 million blacks.

Economy

South Africa has one of the world's larger developed economies with a GNP of $62.9 billion (1987) and a per capita income of $1,890[22] (the latter is meaningless since the bulk of the GNP supports the high standard of living of nonblacks, especially whites, and the repressive state machine).

South Africa lacks oil, but is endowed with all the other natural resources needed for a developed industrial economy. These resources, which include gold and diamonds, earn large sums of foreign exchange in addition to providing South Africa with its own needs. In addition, South Africa enjoys leverage in world economic and political markets because it contains huge amounts of scarce minerals (especially, chrome ores, vanadium, and manganese). These minerals are indispensable to modern industry and warfare and the only

---

[20]Michael G. Schatzberg, ed., *The Political Economy of Zimbabwe* (New York: Praeger, 1984).

[21]*South Africa: A Country Study*, Foreign Area Studies, The American University, 2nd ed., (Washington, D.C.: U. S. Government Printing Office, 1981), though dated, provides valuable background material.

[22]The World Bank, *The World Bank Atlas 1988* (Washington, D.C.: The World Bank, 1988), p. 9.

other country to have large deposits of them is the Soviet Union.

South Africa is a pariah nation subject to economic and arms sanctions and has been expelled from the United Nations. Its experience with sanctions has forced it to develop a more self-sufficient economy and defense industry, and it has made a major effort to overcome its deficiency in oil by using coal and synthetic energy. Over and beyond this, world economic sanctions, including stock divestment by American companies, universities, and governments has had little real practical effect. The United States, West Germany, Japan, and the United Kingdom are major suppliers of capital goods and funds, and in turn receive agricultural products and vital minerals. Israel is a major buyer of diamonds and the International Monetary Fund continues to lend it money.[23]

Over the years, blacks have been brought into the economy. Blue collar, including skilled jobs, are no longer reserved for whites. Trade unions are legal and black workers have mounted hundreds of strikes (while black unions want political reform including majority rule, most strikes have been for modest economic gains). There is little doubt that the prosperity of the whites is structurally dependent on the large reservoir of cheap black labor.[24]

Polity

South Africa has an elaborate political system to create a facade of representative government. But it is a de facto dictatorship in that half of the whites rule the rest of the population in an authoritarian and arbitrary manner. During the 1980s the black population became increasingly restive and the government has had to use considerable force against an essentially unarmed populace.

Exceptional Features

What makes South Africa exceptional is not so much racism, which is a universal disease, but its attempt to use a racially defined labor force (usually associated with plantation agriculture) to help develop an urban-industrial society.[25] With the aid of modern technology and organizational techniques, its willingness to use force both internally and externally,[26] and its mineral wealth (which buys the hypocritical support of most of the world's advanced capitalist societies, including Israel), the Afrikaners have so far withstood considerable pressure to change.[27]

PEACEFUL SOCIETIES

Chapter 17 has cited a variety of societies with exceptional features. The purpose of the chapter is to reinforce the text's theme that generalizations about society and human behavior are difficult to justify. In keeping with this theme, it is important to note that generalizations about human aggressiveness and war are also suspect. Despite the prevalence of war in human history, there are numerous exceptions in the form of peaceful societies.[28] The present expenditures and

[23]The Investor Responsibility Research Center, Washington, D.C. provides continuous information on foreign investment and divestment in South Africa.

[24]Barbara Rogers, *White Wealth and Black Poverty: American Investments in Southern Africa* (Westport, Conn.: Greenwood Press, 1976) underscores this point.

[25]For an earlier reference to this point, see Box 4-3, South Africa: A Class-Caste Hybrid.

[26]One change of significance, however, occurred in 1988 because South Africa faced the prospect of white casualties against Cuban forces defending Angola—South Africa agreed to pull out of its (illegal) occupation of Namibia in return for Cuba's withdrawal of its troops.

[27]For recent developments, see Robert M. Price and Carl G. Rosberg, eds., *The Apartheid Regime: Political Power and Racial Domination* (Berkeley, Calif.: Institute for International Studies, University of California, 1980); Ernest Harsch, *South Africa: White Rule, Black Revolt* (New York: Monad, 1980); Elizabeth Schmidt, *Decoding Corporate Camouflage: U.S. Business Support For Apartheid* (Washington, D.C.: Institute for Policy Studies, 1980); Richard Leonard, *South Africa at War: White Power and the Crisis in Southern Africa* (Westport, Conn.: Lawrence Hill, 1983); and Steven Anzovin, ed., *South Africa: Apartheid and Divestiture* (New York: H. W. Wilson, 1987).

[28]For a valuable compilation of 52 societies that have enjoyed peace for a century or more, see Matthew Melko, *Fifty-two Peaceful Societies* (Oakville, Ontario: Canadian Peace Research Institute, 1973). Also see Ashley Mon-

BOX 17-1. Aggression: cultural or genetic?

Richard E. Leakey and Roger Lewin[1] have flatly denied the argument by Konrad Lorenz, Desmond Morris, and Robert Ardrey that humans are innately aggressive. Leakey and Lewin argue that even much of the alleged violence in nature is ritual. Humans are culturally programmed not biopsychologically programmed. Those who point to killer instincts to explain violence are diverting attention from the real causes of violence and war. The seeds of war, for example, argue Leakey and Lewin, were planted 10 thousand years ago when our farmer ancestors began to assert possession over nature, and elites could expand their possessions through conquest and plunder.

Following this line of thought, one should look for peaceful societies and seek the causes of violence in culture. Violence in the home is associated with poverty and an unsatisfactory employment record. What role do sports play in fostering aggression? Far from being innate, aggressive sports must be learned. Anthropologists have found a clear association between cooperative sports and cooperative societies, and competitive sports and competitive societies. Among the cooperative Tangu of New Guinea, for example, a game is played which ends when both sides have scored equally.[2] Mock combat through sports is a ritualized way to settle grievances among the Gahuko tribes of New Guinea.[3] Sports in the United States is at the other end of the pole—winning is the whole point of play. Tie games (which were common in hockey and golf) were an incongruous element in American culture and were abolished—now tied teams play until "sudden death," that is, until one scores to win (the terms we use in sports are indicative of their violent nature). Far from being in our genes, both aggressive and peaceful-cooperative behavior must be learned. Ruth Benedict's[4] classic contrast between the peaceful Zuni and the fiercely competitive Dobu and Kwakiutl is another reminder of the power of culture.

[1]"Is It Our Culture, Not Our Genes, That Makes Us Killers?," *Smithsonian* 8 (November 1977): 56–64.

[2]Kenelm O. L. Burridge, "Disputing in Tangu," *American Anthropologist* 59 (1957): 763–80.

[3]Kenneth Read, *The High Valley* (New York: Scribner's, 1965), pp. 150–51.

[4]Ruth Benedict, *Patterns of Culture* (Boston: Houghton Mifflin, 1959), orig. published 1934.

world trade in military goods is so large and the threat of global destruction so present that it is important to be reminded that war and aggression are social products, not derivatives of human nature.[29] Peaceful societies may be exceptional but they are not alien to human nature (See Box 17-1, Aggression: Cultural or Genetic?).

[29]For an annual accounting of world military expenditures and the cost of war contrasted with expenditures for social goods such as education, health care, and so on, see Ruth Leger Sivard, *World Military and Social Expenditures* (Washington, D.C.: World Priorities, Annual). For a fuller discussion of the social causes of war, see below, Chapter 19.

tagu, ed., *Learning Non-Aggression* (New York: Oxford University Press, 1978).

18

OLD, NEW, AND EMERGING WORLD POWERS

The West, Japan, the People's Republic of China, India, and Brazil

THE RELATIVE DECLINE OF THE WEST AND THE CONTINUED PRIMACY OF THE CAPITALIST WORLD MARKET

Societies have risen and fallen throughout history and none can claim to have found the secret of eternal vigor: Sumer, Babylonia, Egypt, ancient Greece, Rome, China, India, Holland, France, Spain, Portugal, England, Sweden, Austro-Hungary, the Ottoman Empire. Some decline absolutely and others decline in a relative sense.[1] England, France, and Germany, the giant powers of the nineteenth century saw their relative positions vis-a-vis each other change and then in the twentieth century all three saw themselves overshadowed by the United States and the Soviet Union.

Since then, a rising power, Japan, though defeated in World War II, has risen to become a giant economic power (third in the world). By the twenty-first century China will be a world industrial power and so might India and Brazil.

The United States has had a relative decline in economic power since the 1960s and may well find itself merely one among many world powers by the twenty-first century. The same fate has befallen the Soviet Union. Effective economic and political union could well propel Europe back into primacy among the societies of the world, less as an imperial force and as a pathleader in economic development than as a leader in politics and social welfare.[2]

---

[1]For a study stressing relative decline, largely because of excessive reliance on military might, see Paul Kennedy, *The Rise and Fall of the Great Powers: Economic Change and Military Conflict 1500 to 2000* (New York: Random House, 1987).

[2]The European Community (EC) represents a series of political agreements among Western European countries to cooperate on a number of economic fronts: coal and steel, atomic energy, expediting trade, and finally full economic integration. Begun in 1951, the European Community now has 12 members: France, Germany,

349

Regardless of what happens, the future of the world's societies will depend greatly on their location in and ability to cope with the world-market economy. An important trend in the latter half of the twentieth century was the phenomenal increase in world trade and the inability of any country to stay out of the world market.

The future may also hold an absolute decline in the fortunes of all societies as economic growth falters through overpopulation, pollution, scarce resources, military expenditures, and other social overhead costs.[3] Declining productivity and a stagnant, even declining, standard of living have appeared throughout the world, perhaps most noticeably in the United States and the Soviet Union.

THE UNITED STATES AS A DECLINING WORLD POWER

Relative Decline

The United States acted vigorously in the post-World War II period to shore up and defend the capitalist world order. In this it scored notable successes, especially the Marshall Plan and the Truman doctrine, which helped save Europe from Soviet-style communism. It also scored an underappreciated victory in the Pacific Rim by restoring capitalist Japan and helping South Korea, Taiwan, Hong Kong, and Singapore become dynamic industrializing capitalist societies.

By the late 1980s the basic world economy and the overwhelming number of the world's nation states were capitalist but neither the United States nor the world's societies were healthy. The United States' relative decline was unmistakeable, much of it unavoidable:

other countries had simply grown rapidly and the unique period between 1945–60 when the United States, emerging unscathed from World War II, had dominated the world economy, was over. But some of the relative decline *was* avoidable. American foreign policies were too often wrongheaded and out of touch with reality. There was avoidable failure in the Middle East, Latin America, and Southeast Asia (Vietnam and the Philippines).

American domestic policies were also shortsighted, irrelevant, and self-damaging. As an extremely diversified society it was difficult for American elites to enunciate public policies on how best to direct American society without raising protests from powerful groups threatened by those policies. The result was a consensus to stress individualism and impersonal market forces and to denounce state intervention. By the late 1980s, the United States was the only society in the world that had no positive sense of its central government. By the late 1980s, its political system was badly stalemated and largely an exercise in manipulating an electorate that was anxious, unsophisticated, and apathetic (largely as a result of a mismanaged society). With no effective control over the use of private money in politics, with a gerrymandered and alienated electorate, the two American (capitalist) parties, especially the Republican party, stressed patriotism, morality, and equal opportunity for individuals to compete in a market society, all in abstract terms.

The Reagan administration of the 1980s hastened the United States' relative decline by not targeting tax cuts to productive activities, by excessive spending on military weapons, by cutbacks in public services (which increased social problems producing heavy costs), by failure to invest in infrastructure (magnifying costs), by failure to protect worker safety (magnifying costs), by failure to protect the environment (magnifying costs), by failure to direct the nation's educational efforts toward a more up-to-date labor force (professionals and workers), by a failure to develop new public services to meet new problems (for example, comprehensive health insurance, child care), and by abandoning

---

Belgium, Italy, Luxembourg, the Netherlands, Denmark, Ireland, the United Kingdom, Greece, Spain, and Portugal. Significantly, these countries have agreed on economic integration (to be completed in 1992) and to consider political union. With 320 million people and a gross national product of $4.6 trillion, the EC will be a potent world actor.

[3]For a discussion of these problems, see Chapter 19.

enforcement of the antitrust laws, which allowed not only new levels of economic concentration to emerge but which encouraged huge amounts of unproductive "paper entrepreneurialism."

All these activities and policies were legitimized by basic American beliefs and values (largely derived from the eighteenth and nineteenth centuries). These beliefs and values made it difficult for the American electorate to evaluate or oppose government policies. Further, the policies led to enormous economic disruptions producing high insecurity and anxiety among the electorate. With a zero-sum economy, all were desperate to hang on to what they had. The result was that the electorate was further "massified" and more easily manipulated. The 1988 presidential election was a high point in issueless and negative campaigning.

Absolute Decline

Far more serious is the real possibility that the United States is in absolute decline. The first and most important indicator of absolute decline is the decline in productivity that has characterized the American economy since the 1960s. This decline has also appeared as a decline in real wages and a decline in standard of living. The United States is far behind other developed capitalist societies in infant mortality rates and lags in other health areas. It has by far the largest teenage pregnancy rates in the world and by far the highest blue collar crime rates in the world. There are no comparative data on crime in the industrial world by the upper classes but the evidence suggest that the United States is the world's leader here too.

The United States has a deeply entrenched academic world that continues to stress academic knowledge, which has no proven positive nature, and that lags badly in training scientifically oriented professionals and competent citizens, while continuing to educate scientists for our First- and Third-World competitors.

The United States has a huge backlog of replacements for decaying bridges, highways, sewers, and other facilities. The nation's colleges and universities have decaying and outmoded facilities of all kinds, including scientific equipment and laboratories. The haste to develop nuclear energy (much of it propelled by government lies) has led to a large number of unsafe, expensive to operate, and terribly expensive to decommission nuclear power plants (both civilian and military).

The United States' leadership role in the early post-World War II period shows signs of being an illegitimate dominance. It has been unable to live within its means. Instead of providing political leadership that engages in useful debate and along the way educates the electorate, American elites, especially working through the Republican party, have opened the United States to cheap foreign imports and encouraged capital to search for profits anywhere. The result is low inflation (due to cheap imports and a soggy work force forced to accept lower wages and unemployment) which is politically popular. But the result is also a loss of industrial competitiveness because American industry must compete with low-wage countries that have few labor standards, welfare costs, and environmental protection expenses. The result is huge public, corporate, and individual debt. And it means borrowing from foreigners at levels that will further reduce the nation's standard of living as interest on that debt continues to mount.

The United States' descent into a chronic borrower means that domestic elites are bought off with high interest rates (to keep them from sending even more money abroad). It means that the United States' inability to manage its affairs (basically its inability to tax itself to curb consumption unwarranted by its low productivity) means that it must keep interest rates high to attract domestic and foreign lenders. This has also worsened the debt problem of Third-World countries, who then cannot buy American products, further hurting the American economy.

The American economy is also hurt by the United States' attempt to mount economic embargoes against countries it dislikes. Though countries like Vietnam, Cuba, and

Nicaragua have been hurt by this policy, they have managed slowly (at least the former two) to develop economic relations with a wide variety of other countries in the capitalist world. As late as the end of 1988, the United States was still thinking in terms of avoiding open trade with the Soviet Union when it was clear that all the major European capitalist societies and Japan were eagerly extending credit to the Soviet Union so that it could modernize its consumer industries. Here again the United States, its mind-set still in the pre-Gorbachev era, is losing economic ground because of failure to adapt to a changing world.

The one winner in all of the above are America's multinational corporations, which, despite all the problems besetting the nation, have kept their share of the world's trade. In the final analysis the laissez-faire philosophy and military buildup begun by the Democratic administration in the late 1970s and continued with a vengeance by the Republican administrations of the 1980s has benefited propertied and professional interests almost exclusively, but especially geocentric corporations.

American hegemony has continued (deserved or not) because it continues to have an economy twice as large as its nearest competitors (the U.S.S.R. and Japan) and it has a gigantic military establishment.[4] But in any long-term frame, the deficiencies in the United States' basic social institutions point only to continued relative and absolute decline.

JAPAN

Land and People[5]

Japan is an archipelago that has few resources, and its population of approximately 120 million makes it the seventh largest in the

world and fifth highest in population density. Qualitatively, the Japanese are a homogeneous people (racial and ethnic differences, except for a few enclaves, are nonexistent). Japan also has a highly disciplined population given to conforming and obeying and thus easily channelled into directions decreed by Japan's ruling elites, whether landed, military, or industrial.

Historically, Japan's population increased steadily (until recently) to supply its economy and military with plentiful supplies of cheap, disciplined labor. Family, neighborhood, school, workplace, and general public life combine to produce a highly homogeneous, obedient, skilled, and energetic people.[6] The future of Japan's labor force population is not as rosy. The declining birth rate (now at replacement level) has led to an aging population and a significant decrease in the number of workers in relation to those (especially the elderly) out of the work force.

Becoming Modern

The transition to modern society has been marked by severe social strains and violence in almost all countries regardless of their cultural and social background. Societies do not ordinarily change from one system of society to another without considerable friction and violence. People take the constitutive structure of their society very seriously and as a rule react violently to perceived threats to its security. Before institutionalized methods for reforming society emerged, it was extremely difficult for disputants to settle grievances through peaceful negotia-

---

[4]For an important argument claiming that the United States is still dominant in security, production, finance, and knowledge, see Susan Strange, "The Persistent Myth of Lost Hegemony", *International Organization* 41 (Autumn, 1987): 551–74.

[5]*Japan: A Country Study*, Foreign Area Studies, The American University (Washington, D.C.: U. S. Govern-

ment Printing Office, 1974) is useful but dated. An informative, if uncritical, general account of all aspects of life in Japan may be found in Edwin O. Reischauer, *The Japanese* (Cambridge, Mass.: Harvard University Press, 1977). An extremely readable general account, with a sure touch for the differences between the Japanese and Americans (and other Westerners), is Robert C. Christopher, *The Japanese Mind: The Goliath Explained* (New York: Simon and Schuster, 1983).

[6]For a good introduction to Japan's powerful and uniform system of socialization, see Joy Hendry, *Becoming Japanese: The World of the Pre-School Child* (Honolulu: University of Hawaii Press, 1986).

tion and compromise. What usually occurred was a metaphysical confrontation between groups prepared to resort to violence. Ancient Greece witnessed perhaps the most savage "class" struggles of all time as oligarch and democrat contended for supremacy in one city-state after another.

A transition from one system of society to another, therefore, is not very frequent. One should not confuse systemic change with, for example, church-state disputes, palace revolutions, coup d' etats, collective bargaining, election results, the rise of the welfare state, or the existence of labor governments. India and China, for example, have undergone constant internal turmoil but did not experience challenges to their respective systems of society until the twentieth century: that is, their institutional systems remained intact for over two thousand years. Feudal Europe's transition to modern society was also no abrupt event: it lasted approximately from the eleventh to the nineteenth century. This long and torturous transition to a capitalist society was characterized neither by foresight nor by peaceful adjustment.

Violent Social System Change: France, the Typical Pattern

The transition from feudal to modern society was marked by blind drift and incredible violence, neither of which is anywhere more dramatically evident than in the development of French society.[7] After centuries of slow economic expansion, France in the eighteenth century harbored in its bosom two contradictory principles: the principle of ascription and the principle of achievement.[8] While most of the French accepted the supremacy of the nobility and the noble way of life, a contradictory element had emerged in French society: a sizeable bourgeoisie representing the principle of personal achievement in a nonvalued

activity (business). Nothing better illustrates the nonrevolutionary nature of the French middle class than its anxiety to shed the stigma of lowly birth and lowly experience (the making of money). To accommodate this anxiety and to afford the nobility ways to compensate for its relative economic decline, French society developed a number of avenues of social mobility that enabled the bourgeoisie to translate its wealth into enhanced social status. The main method of achieving upward mobility was the purchase of hereditary offices and titles. Marriages to impoverished noblemen were an option for those who could afford large dowries. Status could also be enhanced by the purchase of a military commission. Finally, and importantly, one could enhance one's status by adopting the noble way of life, i.e., country house, elaborate dress, idleness, conspicuous consumption.

As long as these avenues of mobility remained open, the bourgeoisie wanted nothing more than to escape the stigma of business and join the dominant stratum. They cared little for politics, though there was some grumbling about financial matters. The two principles of ascription and achievement were basically antagonistic, however, and the aristocratic reaction that set in during the eighteenth century brought this contradiction to a head. The aristocracy's growing exclusiveness about noble rank, growing legal monopolization of high political, military, and ecclesiastical offices, and refusal to pay taxes blocked upward mobility. This in turn stimulated revolutionary feelings among a middle class that until the eve of the Revolution had rarely questioned the legitimacy of the feudal way of life. The two principles that France had accommodated for centuries at last collided, causing a revolution in 1789 whose consequences left French society unstable for over a century and a half.

France in the eighteenth century is an example of a deeply *anomic society*,[9] a social system with a relatively large middle class but no symbolic or institutional mechanisms

---

[7]For an earlier discussion of violent bourgeois revolution, see the section, The Unique Bourgeois Revolutions in Chapter 5.

[8]Much of the following is neatly summarized in Elinor G. Barber, *The Bourgeoisie in Eighteenth Century France* (Princeton: Princeton University Press, 1955).

[9]See the glossary to jog your memory about this important concept.

to legitimate or ingest such a group. The result was the typical pattern of blind drift and violence: first, the development of social fictions to disguise the problems created by change, followed by a growing self-consciousness on the part of threatened groups, and finally the descent into the abyss of confrontation and civil war. So deep were the wounds inflicted by the Revolution, the Terror, and the Restoration that France still suffered from estate-class conflicts long after it began to experience the problems of industrialization and the conflicts emerging from *within* its class system.

Peaceful Social System Change: Japan, an Exception

Japan is a major exception to the generalization that societies undergoing systemic change always experience struggle and violence (Prussia is another major example of peaceful modernization under feudal-authoritarian auspices[10]). Before 1600 Japan was a relatively static estate society, characterized by a hierarchy of warrior, peasant, artisan, and merchant estates.[11] Each estate was theoretically closed and restricted as to permissible occupations, residence, food, and dress. Despite the growth of a merchant class, there was no middle class to threaten the supremacy of the warrior estate. Japan had all the earmarks of a static hierarchical society. But something happened in the period between 1600 and 1868 that allowed a peaceful revolution to sweep away the estate structure and inaugurate a society based on individual (male) achievement (class).

The two and one half centuries of peace (the Tokugawa Period) after 1600 obviously made difficulties for the warrior estate. A few thousand warrior families were set apart by lineage and income, but the bulk of such families ("several hundred thousand") were quite poor. Changes in the warrior estate itself were of great importance to the transformation of Japanese society. Unthreatened from below, the warrior estate was transformed internally in directions leading away from feudalism. Basic to this change was the appropriation from most warriors of direct control of land and direct personal responsibility for social functions (such as justice). Instead, the lord restricted his warrior vassals' power over their fiefs, forbade them to administer local justice, relocated them in the towns that grew up around his castle, decreed the taxes they could collect, and eventually collected taxes himself, paying his warrior vassals stipends in money or in kind. Japan could be governed in this nonfeudal manner only by means of extensive bureaucratization. The advent of bureaucratic government was accompanied, significantly, by a decline in the personal bonds between the dominant warrior lords and their subordinate warriors and by the rise of impersonality and functional ability in office.

In 1868 there emerged a central government that swept away the local empires of the dominant warrior families. The new government abolished estate restrictions and gave extensive civic—though not political—rights to all. Especially important was the establishment of free public schools and the principle of qualification for office and occupation. The bulk of the warrior estate, having been separated from the land and having had centuries of experience in office holding, did not view this phenomenon as a threat to its estate privileges—especially in contrast to, for example, the French nobility. On the contrary, it saw in these reforms new and fresh opportunities for achievement. After 1868 there occurred an explosion of individual energies as the lesser warriors took the lead in developing careers in business, industry, and the professions. Thus a peaceful revolution *within* its warrior aristocracy allowed Japan to transform itself from above and to make the transition to a modern social system without experiencing the bitter social cleavages that marked such transitions in the West.

---

[10]For an earlier discussion of revolution from above, see the section, Revolution From Above in Chapter 5.

[11]The following section is based on Thomas C. Smith, "Japan's Aristocratic Revolution," *Yale Review* 50 (March, 1961): 370–83; and Barrington Moore, Jr., *Social Origins of Dictatorship and Democracy* (Boston: Beacon Press, 1966), Chapter 5.

Unbalanced Modernization: Japanese Militarism

The feudal elite that congealed into a dynamic central government in 1868 did so largely to protect its society from threats from abroad.[12] It did not modernize to protect itself from below or to develop a society of self-governing citizens (here the parallel to Prussia continues). It was clear to Japan's rulers, especially by the end of the nineteenth century, that it and all of Asia were under threat from the imperial expansion of the United States and the European powers.

Japan's prospects for modernizing on its own terms depended on staying out of the orbit of the imperial world economy and in this it succeeded. Rather than being penetrated by the economically superior Western powers, Japan used the international economy to import technology and science, while keeping out other elements of Western culture. It also embarked on a successful outward expansion defeating Czarist Russia in 1905 and conquering Korea in 1910. By the 1930s it was Asia's only modern industrial society though it was still heavily agricultural and still a society marked by small enterprises.

Japan's successful industrialization was largely a result of state action. A feudal elite, used to the idea of governance, simply governed to build an industrial nation and a military. Its strategy did not include individualism, competition, or the free market. Basically, it took the idea of the family, along with Confucianism (and the state-oriented, nationalistic religion of Shintoism), to create the idea of the nation as a family under a divine Emperor. Thus modern Japan was built fully and explicitly out of feudal elements mixed with a fear of foreign domination and an acute sense of its economic and thus political vulnerability. All in all, Japan successfully blended particularism, hierarchy, and ethnocentrism with the capitalist values of science, futurism, and efficiency.

By the 1930s, Japan was a militarized nation state of considerable industrial power.[13] It was also clear that Asia had a vacuum (a weak China) and that it represented an opportunity for colonial adventure, actually a way to acquire cheaply the raw materials that Japan needed. And it was clear to Japan's rulers that unless it acted, outside powers, especially the United States, would fill that vacuum and make Japan a secondary power in its own region. It is also clear that Japan was not being modernized for internal social development: Japan's warrior modernizers had nowhere to go but outward. Thus the invasion of China in the mid-30s and the attack on the United States in 1941.

Unbalanced Modernization: Japan, the Topheavy Economic Superpower[14]

World War II was an industrial war and Japan was beaten by the United States, a much larger industrial power. The American occupation after the war furthered Japan's modernization by eliminating the power of landlords (and thus weakening the important agricultural sector), by supplying Japan with an imported system of representative government, and by helping Japan to put aside a large military establishment. The outcome was a miracle of industrial expansion as the same combination of practices and values that had modernized Japan between 1868 and the 1930s were given full reign. But now instead of "nation and army," Japan concentrated on "nation," by which it meant economic growth. From an impoverished nation in 1945, Japan grew at an astounding rate over the next decades surpassing the

---

[12]For a sociological picture of the society of pre-World War II Japan, see Tadashi Fukutake, *The Japanese Social Structure* (Tokyo: University of Tokyo Press, 1982), Part I.

[13]For valuable background on Japan's industrialization both before and after 1930, see Jon Halliday, *A Political History of Japanese Capitalism* (New York: Pantheon Books, 1975) and Bruce Cumings, "The Origin and Development of the Northeast Asian Political Economy: Industrial Sectors, Product Cycles, and Political Consequences", *International Organization* 38 (Winter, 1984): 1–40.

[14]For a sociological picture of Japan, see Tadashi Fukutake, *Japanese Society Today*, 2nd ed. (Tokyo: University of Tokyo Press, 1981).

major capitalist countries of Europe in GNP by the 1970s. Today Japan has the third largest economy in the world surpassed only by the United States and the Soviet Union. Its gross domestic product of $1925 billion in 1987 was over 40 percent of the United States', yielding a per capita income of $15,770 (the Federal Republic of Germany had a GDP of $879 billion in 1987, the world's fourth largest).[15]

The strategy pursued by Japan was fairly simple. Japan's rulers and population know that Japan must export or die. The population was easily convinced that production came first and consumption last. The political system was unlikely to produce much deviation from this outlook but it actually produced a government run by the same capitalist party for the entire postwar period. This government, along with Japan's large, monopolistic corporations, targeted one manufacturing area after the other: textiles, machine tools, automobiles, shipbuilding, electronics, computers. Given access to the American market (and other markets around the world), Japan quickly came to dominate one field after the other because of high quality and low prices.[16] Government ministries, especially MITI (Ministry of International Trade and Industry) gave manufacturers direction (not always wise or efficient) and created a maze of import barriers that hampered foreign competitors. Government subsidies and a system of national savings through giant banks gave Japanese industry all the low-cost capital it needed. Japan has a hardworking population that saves because of the government's deliberate policy of preventing private and public consumption (little is spent on defense, public works, social welfare, or public pensions). Of special importance is the role of Japan's giant banks. As keepers of the nation's savings, banks accumulate giant pools of money that they use to not only extend credit but to become investors in Japan's economy. With huge pools of steadily supplied savings, banks can not only take a long-term view but can easily switch from declining economic sectors to those that are rising. The government's deliberate policy of high domestic prices and low public services[17] also forced an inflow of women into the labor force thus further insuring adequate supplies of cheap labor.

American authors have singled out various aspects of Japanese life to explain its success and to draw lessons for America. Some have admired Japan's managerial style but have not made realistic comparisons.[18] Chalmers Johnson provides a valuable historical picture of Japan's Ministry of International Trade and Industry and Japan's struggle to develop an industrial policy (a state-guided, private, development-oriented economy) between 1925 and 1975.[19] Johnson's recommendations for the United States (develop a civil service trained in economics and give it independence from political pressures) betrays his technocratic liberalism. Robert B. Reich also refers to Japan's industrial policy (along

---

[15]The World Bank, *The World Bank Atlas 1988* (Washington, D.C.: The World Bank, 1988), p. 7.

[16]The United States' policy of opening its markets to Japan, Taiwan, Korea, Hong Kong, and Singapore, even at considerable cost to its own people, must be seen as a way to bolster capitalism on the Pacific Rim against the Soviet Union, China, and Vietnam.

[17]Japan has a smaller public sector than the European capitalist societies, even smaller than the United States, relying more on private employers and families to care for the elderly, the sick, and funding for education and pensions; see Naomi Maruo, "The Development of the Welfare Mix in Japan" in Richard Rose and Rei Shiratori, eds., *The Welfare State East and West* (New York: Oxford University Press, 1986), Chapter 5.

[18]Ezra F. Vogel, in his free-wheeling, insightful essay, *Japan As Number One: Lessons for America* (Cambridge, Mass.: Harvard University Press, 1979) was one of the first to find many lessons for the United States in Japanese institutions. Vogel is careful to qualify his comparisons and lessons to take sociocultural distinctiveness into account but his essay format leads him into trouble. For example, Chapter 6 on Japan's industrial organization and managerial style is not a full and accurate picture. Since Vogel's book, others have either mistated or overstressed the importance of Japan's managerial style—for example, William G. Ouchi, *Theory Z: How American Business Can Meet The Japanese Challenge* (New York: Avon, 1981).

[19]Chalmers Johnson, *MITI and the Japanese Miracle: The Growth of Industrial Policy, 1925–1975* (Stanford, Calif.: Stanford University Press, 1982).

with similar practices in capitalist Europe) as a reason for its success and as something the United States could benefit from. Reich also stresses the value of Japan's flexible manufacturing (the ability of companies to move quickly into new products and to compete on the basis of quality and design as well as price (as opposed to mass production manufacturing).[20] Reich's analysis is a fully developed left liberal proposal—his recommendations for reinvigorating American manufacturing are supported by a comprehensive set of proposals to solve America's social problems.[21]

Japan's modernization both before and after World War II clearly shows similarities in capital accumulation (the core meaning of modernization) with other societies, capitalist or socialist: essentially, capital formation came from the exploitation of farmers and workers with the state working hand in hand with commercial and industrial property owners.[22] Japan's process of capital formation is closer to that of the United States as compared to the European capitalist societies in that it is largely private (the Japanese state supports capital formation in a variety of important ways but not by developing a public economic sector). Japan, however, is similar to all other capitalist societies in that wealth is highly concentrated, for example, in 1980 1 percent of all shareholders in Japan's corporate economy owned 75 percent of the total number of shares.[23]

Capital formation is also fostered by the widespread overlapping of banking and corporate business. Banks in Japan, overflowing with savings, are allowed to become owners of businesses and thus become identified with the corporate economy on a long-term basis. As owners they reap profits and not merely interest on loans. The result is that Japanese corporations are assured cheap capital on a long-term basis.

Capital formation also results from the exploitation of the work force. To understand labor exploitation in Japan one must look beyond the myth of "lifetime permanent employment." Some companies do provide permanent employment for some of their labor but only until age 55. And only approximately 55 percent of the labor force is covered by even this limited security. Japan has a huge labor force of temporary, parttime labor, mostly women, which is underpaid and which receives few benefits. But to really appreciate labor exploitation one must savor the account by Kamata of the almost inhuman automobile factory, which, like much of Japan's modern economic sector, is run like a prison camp.[24] This overall political economy, rather than unique Japanese management practices, or commitment to work, is what has produced the Japanese miracle. Actually, it is not at all clear that Japanese industrial organization is so different from other capitalist societies.[25]

Japan's uneven development means that it may be third in GNP but its standard of living lags behind most of the First World. Internally, its political power structure, based on a coalition of monopoly corporations, pampered farmers, and a network of inefficient small retailers and distributors, has kept taxes low (the lowest in the industrial world), social welfare expenditures low (the lowest in

---

[20]For an interesting comparative analysis of flexible manufacturing contrasted with mass production, see Michael J. Piore and Charles F. Sabel, *The Second Industrial Divide* (New York: Basic Books, 1984). For a case study of Japan's commitment to flexible manufacturing (which overstates its importance in Japan's economic success), see David Friedman, *The Misunderstood Miracle: Industrial Development and Political Change in Japan* (Ithaca, N.Y.: Cornell University Press, 1988).

[21]Robert B. Reich, *The Next American Frontier* (New York: Times Books, 1983).

[22]The process of capital formation is a prominent feature of Rob Steven's sophisticated Marxian analysis, *Classes In Contemporary Japan* (New York: Cambridge University Press, 1983).

[23]Rob Steven, *Classes In Contemporary Japan* (New York: Cambridge University Press, 1983), Table 1-1, p. 15.

[24]Satoshi Kamata, *Japan In The Passing Lane: An Insider's Account of Life In a Japanese Auto Factory*, tr. and ed. Tatsurn Akimoto with an intro. Ronald Dore (New York: Pantheon, 1982).

[25]James R. Lincoln and Kerry McBride, "Japanese Industrial Organizations In Comparative Perspective" *Annual Review of Sociology* 13 (Palo Alto, Calif.: *Annual Reviews*, 1987): 289–312.

the industrial world), and consumption low (by keeping prices high through tariffs and by favoring inefficient farmers and retailers).

By the mid-80s Japan was aware that its singleminded emphasis on exports had alienated foreign countries and it altered its policies somewhat. It has also expanded its foreign aid (by 1989 it surpassed the United States in foreign aid), and it began to assert itself more in world councils as befits its economic status.

By the 1980s, it was also clear that Japan had begun to resemble other advanced industrial systems. Its aging population now resembles those in the other developed capitalist societies. Actually, Japan faces a serious problem because of its aging population because, unlike say the United States, it has not taxed itself to pay what is owed under its public pension (social security) system. In the next two decades, the need to increase taxes just to pay what has been promised to its elderly will divert significant sums from the nation's savings.[26] For this and other reasons, Japan's social overhead and thus public sector will grow significantly in coming years. Its welfare and health care costs are bound to become more burdensome than in the past.[27] Marriage, family, and the status of women are changing (slowly) in ways familiar to Westerners.[28] The group-oriented world, in which each generation is molded to conform and which found its focus in the workplace, appears to be in decline. Consumer demands are on the rise. Economic practices such as guaranteed employment and full employment are threatened as Japan faces competition by low-wage competitors. Here Japan has also done what the other capitalist societies have done: faced by a shortage of industrial sites, pollution problems, and high domestic labor costs, it has exported capital to take advantage of cheap labor elsewhere. This has produced a decline in good jobs for Japan's own population and may increase domestic political pressures.

Japan has also realized that its favorable post-war position of being able to buy raw materials cheaply in the open market has changed. Consequently, it has gone abroad to develop favorable agreements with developing countries in order to ensure the supplies it needs for the future (here is the deeper meaning of its new interest in foreign aid). All types of industries and services have gone abroad with most being immature and not necessarily the most advanced technologically. But in the developing world its firms will act polycentrically (dealing with individual countries on a case-by-case basis for presumed mutual advantage) while in the United States and Europe, Japanese firms will benefit from their advanced technology and will act ethnocentrically (for their own advantage on an alleged impersonal, global basis, that is, as geocentric firms).[29]

The exploitation of women in the labor force (women make up a large majority of the deeply underpaid labor force of temporary, parttime workers) has also made some less satisfied with their lot. Crime, though still low by Western standards, is rising. And Japan has gradually increased its military over the past decade and the government has disavowed the traditional ceiling for military expenditures of 1 percent of GNP. This

---

[26]For a discussion, see Yukio Noguchi, "Overcommitment in Pensions: The Japanese Experience" in Richard Rose and Rei Shiratori, eds., *The Welfare State East and West* (New York: Oxford University Press, 1986), Chapter 8.

[27]For background on the Japanese health care system, which consumes about the same percent of GNP as the European capitalist societies but much less than the United States (for equal or better results), see Edward Norbeck and Margaret Lock, eds., *Health, Illness, and Medical Care in Japan* (Honolulu: University of Hawaii Press, 1987). This otherwise excellent study fails to provide information on social class and health.

[28]Joy Hendry, *Marriage in a Changing Japan: Community and Society* (New York: St. Martin's Press, 1981; Charles Tuttle edition, 1986); Sumiko Furuya Iwao, "The Feminine Perspective In Japan Today" in Kenneth A. Grossberg, ed., *Japan Today* (Philadelphia: Institute for the Study of Human Issues, 1981), pp. 16–27.

[29]Terutomo Ozawa, *Multinationalism, Japanese Style: The Political Economy of Outward Dependency* (Princeton, N.J.: Princeton University Press, 1979).

increased interest in an expanded military is no doubt a result of Japan's far-flung investments and economic interests (as well as of pressure by the United States).

The real challenge of the future is whether Japan's rulers are willing and able to develop Japanese society internally. To spend money on housing, social facilities (Japan lags, for example, in percent of homes connected to sewer systems), and to support the elderly in the coming era of labor shortages and increased competition from abroad means that the power of Japan's capitalist class and its ally, the state, will diminish. Whether Japan is capable of making such a significant change peacefully a second time remains to be seen.

Social Class, Adaptive Capacity, and the Future

In a broad sense Japan demonstrated a remarkable capacity to adjust to defeat in World War II. In another sense, the problems it faced were clear to all as were the solutions. Japan had no choice but to stress economic development and an export economy. To this purpose, it mobilized its population using the full powers of its feudal-authoritarian tradition. The pervasive, near total control over the lives of ordinary people that Japan's rulers exercise may not bode well for democracy but it does give Japan an enormous ability to adjust to problems.[30]

Japan, however, is no monolith. The idea of Japan, Inc. is a myth. Japan is a highly differentiated society with a large number of conflicting interest groups.[31] In addition, policy decisions are made by a wide variety of power groups and there is a significant pattern of mistakes and failure to act on pressing problems.[32] In many ways Japanese politics has begun to exhibit the same immobility that is characteristic of other First-World political systems.

Based on the record, however, there can be no doubt that Japan's governing class has succeeded in inducing both growth (in the economy and general welfare) and stability. Building on its solid support by big business, it has reached out to support and protect farmers, small business (both manufacturers and retailers), white collar workers, the sick, and the retired. Kent Calder has confirmed this history of political dominance by the ruling Liberal Democratic party in the post-World War II period. Puzzled by the contradiction in Japan's public policy between support for highly efficient big industries and support for inefficient farmers and small businesses, redistributive welfare policies, unneeded public works, and inequitable land use, Calder has found a "crisis and compensation" dynamic in Japan's political economy. Faced with the novel threat of pluralist democracy in the immediate postwar years, Japan's conservatives (authoritarian-minded) worked hard to forge a dominant coalition. The conservatives of Japan's governing class have also been helped in building a coalition beyond big business because the individual members of the Liberal Democratic party are politically insecure. The result has been that they have reached out to undercut political opposition on the left, in keeping with felt pressures (crisis) from below. Calder argues that the Liberal Democratic party and government become passive when the crisis passes, and have shown a capacity to cut back somewhat on its promises. He also argues that demands by Americans and others to remove barriers to trade will not succeed easily, if at all, because to remove them would

---

[30]For this pattern ranging from the precise registration of households and neighborhood police supervision through schools and the military-like work environment, see Yoshio Sugimoto, "The Manipulative Bases of 'Consensus' in Japan" in Gavan McCormack and Yoshio Sugimoto, eds., *Democracy In Contemporary Japan* (Armonk, N.Y.: M.E. Sharpe, 1986), pp. 65–75.

[31]For a valuable collection of essays that dispels the false image of a harmonious Japan, and which is also a contribution to the sociology of conflict, see Ellis S. Krauss, Thomas P. Rohlen, and Patricia G. Steinhoff, eds., *Conflict in Japan* (Honolulu: University of Hawaii Press, 1984).

[32]T. J. Pempel, ed., *Policymaking In Contemporary Japan* (Ithaca, N.Y.: Cornell University Press, 1977).

threaten the party's dominance and are, in any case, fiercely resisted by Japan's farmers and small businesses.[33]

Japan is a highly unequal society not much different from other capitalist societies. It has considerable poverty and a highly organized structure of exploitation that bears down hard on male workers at all levels, on day laborers and "gypsy workers" (those who do dirty dangerous work in nuclear power plants), on small farmers, and on female workers.[34] In a general comparison of income distribution, Japan is somewhat more equal than the United States (its income distribution resembles Sweden's), but it is very much like the United States in its opposition to redistribution through government intervention or taxation.[35] All this should be noted, despite the fact that, when asked, 90 percent of Japanese regard themselves as middle class (a prime example of false consciousness, or belief that deviates from reality).

The image of Japan as middle class has some basis in fact. There is enormous homogeneity of dress, consumption, and behavior. There is a widespread belief that Japan is a meritocracy fostered to a large extent by its unusual educational system. Education is no doubt a source of strength and adaptiveness for Japan. Long an explicit tool for developing nationhood under state direction, education in the post-World War II period responded fairly quickly to the demands made of it by industry. Education appears meritocratic because all of it is aimed at university entrance examinations and anything that might differentiate students by class is suppressed both by wearing common uniforms and by strict conformity to group norms. But all this is misleading. Japan's crucially important high schools are differentiated by social class. In recent years, the public system has lost ground to private high schools, clearly a trend toward open class education (in 1982, half of the freshmen at the University of Tokyo, Japan's most prestigious, came from private schools). While Japan provides the appearance of equal education and equal opportunity up to the age of 18 (an appearance fostered by the high completion rate of high school), the university entrance examination clearly reveals the class (and sexual) basis of Japanese education. Those who succeed come from the established classes. The examination sorts the population by class into those who go to the better universities and thus get the better jobs.

The Japanese educational system helps create an obedient, well-behaved population whose *average* cognitive skills are very high, especially in mathematics and natural science (the high school graduate in Japan is roughly equivalent to a college graduate in the United States). This is one of the reasons that the level of public discourse in Japan is higher than in the United States. Perhaps most importantly, the educational system helps create a thoroughly house-broken population, something not unimportant in keeping down social overhead.[36]

Japan's educational system also promotes legitimacy for the overall system and helps create its growing political mainstream. The system's stress on passive learning to pass examinations can no more be related to work performance or good citizenship than the United States' system which puts more emphasis on versatility and critical, innovative self-expression. Japan's overall system is a unique combination of American egalitarianism and European elitism. But regardless of stated purpose or surface appearances, Japan's

[33]Kent E. Calder, *Crisis and Compensation: Public Policy and Political Stability In Japan, 1949–1986* (Princeton, N.J.: Princeton University Press, 1988).

[34]In addition to many of the works cited above, see *The Other Japan* edited with an introduction by E. Patricia Tsurumi for the *Bulletin of Concerned Asian Scholars* (Armonk, N.Y.: M.E. Sharpe, 1988).

[35]Sidney Verba et al., *Elites and the Idea of Equality* (Cambridge, Mass.: Harvard University Press, 1987), Chapter 1.

[36]For a running comparison of Japanese and American education, see Thomas P. Rohlen, *Japan's High Schools* (Berkeley, Calif.: University of California Press, 1983).

egalitarian educational system has the latent function of providing support and legitimacy for a highly unequal, bureaucratic, class society. In this, it is similar to education in the United States and Europe. Education in the socialist system, it should be noted, also has latent functions: while openly stressing equality of opportunity, nation building, and the development of a rational division of labor through socialism, it too protects an unexamined society and maintains it over time by favoring the offspring of powerholders and the upper classes.

Japan's maturing industrial economy faces a host of new problems and no one can predict what the future holds. Japan could commit itself to internal development and become a force for cooperative intersocietal relations. But this would threaten the power of Japan's rulers. Democratic political forms may not be strong enough to direct Japan's economic surplus into an enhanced standard of living, and the realities of the competitive world economy may not permit it to be generous on the international scene. The prospects lean toward more of the Japan that we know.[37] The Liberal Democratic Party, dominant since World War II, has broadened its base to include the young, blue collar workers, and urban residents. It is now clearly identified with the successful merger of Japanese ways with modernization and is clearly seen by the electorate as the main force to maintain Japan's gains in an era of slower economic growth and an unstable foreign environment. But whether the LDP prevails or not, Japan in the 1990s will remain the Japan we know.[38]

THE PEOPLE'S REPUBLIC OF CHINA

Land and People[39]

China is the third largest country in the world and by far the most populous (1 billion people or 20 percent of the world's population). It is situated largely in the temperate zone and has a rich natural environment: good soil and abundant energy and mineral resources. Though the various parts of China speak different versions of Chinese and though there are 55 non-Chinese nationalities numbering 56 million, China is essentially a homogeneous and distinct cultural entity.

The Historical Background

China as a distinct cultural entity dates back 4,000 years and descends from one of the great agrarian (hydralic) civilizations of the past. Its achievements in the few centuries between 600 and 200 BC rival the achievements taking place at the same time elsewhere in the world, including ancient Greece. By the time of the period Westerners call medieval (1000 to 1350 AD) China matched any other society in the arts, technology, and governance. But its centralized feudal system was anchored in a traditionalized humanities and in magic (normative formalism) and failed to support innovation in science, technology, the arts, or economic enterprise. Combined with population growth and internal dissension, China could not experience the economic breakthrough that occurred in the West. By the nineteenth century China was easy prey for the Western imperialist powers: Britain, France, Japan, and the United States. The Manchu dynasty that had ruled since the

---

[37]For a wideranging analysis that assumes that democratic political forms in Japan are only skin-deep and that the future will be more of the same, if not openly fascistic, see Gavan McCormack and Yoshio Sugimoto, eds., *Democracy In Contemporary Japan* (Armonk, N.Y.: M.E. Sharpe, 1986).

[38]For an approving, optimistic view of Japanese politics, which stresses the above, see Gerald L. Curtis, *The Japanese Way of Politics* (New York: Columbia University Press, 1988).

[39]For an indispensable reference work, see *China, A Country Study*, Foreign Area Studies, The American University (Washington: D.C.: U. S. Government Printing Office, 1981). For a superb collection of essays by European scholars on all aspects of contemporary Chinese society reflecting the new stream of data that has become available in recent years, see Stephan Feuchtwang, Athar Hussain, and Thierry Pairault, eds., *Transforming China's Economy in the Eighties*, 2 vols. (Boulder, Colo.: Westview Press, 1988).

seventeenth century underwent a rapid decline between the Opium War (lost to Britain
in 1839–42) and the Revolution of 1911 inspired by Sun-Yat-Sen (which set up the Republic of China, an attempt at a middle-class
system of representative government in a country without a middle class).

The 1920s were a period of ferment as
China pondered its future. Representative government failed to take root and in 1937, a
weak and divided China was invaded by
Japan (which had embarked on an imperial
expansion through military conquest). The
most effective resistance to the Japanese was
provided by a communist army under Mao
Tse-Tung. Despite massive American aid, the
nationalists did not actively engage the Japanese invader. Led by Chiang Kai-shek, the
nationalists were a corrupt and inept aggregate of warlords, landlords, and urban
merchants and were easily defeated by the
Communists when World War II ended. The
communist army's success was due to more
than its military strength—its ideological mes-
sage of land reform struck a responsive chord
in a population overwhelmingly rural. In 1949
it took effective control of mainland China
(the nationalists fled to the island of Formosa,
to form the Republic of China, now known
as Taiwan).

Why Did China Fail to Develop?

China showed no signs before 1949 that it
could modernize. Lippit has asked, what
caused nondevelopment in China? Lippit
frames his analysis of China in terms of the
"development of underdevelopment" but our
use of the term *underdevelopment* is quite different. China was never shaped to be a supplier of raw materials for outside powers
(the basic meaning of underdevelopment).
However Lippit's argument that China's inability to develop was due to internal forces
rather than pressure from imperial powers is
sound. China's traditional agrarian social
structure, dominated by a landed gentry,
succeeded in establishing a system that channelled economic surplus into the pockets of

a consumption class rather than into productive enterprises.[40] China did not develop for
the same reason that the agrarian civilizations of Babylonia, Egypt, India, and so on
did not develop: its landed, consumption-
oriented power groups were content and development ran counter to their interests and
values.

Modernization Under Chinese Communism

The basic strategy of modernization under
Chinese (Mao's) communism was to base it
on a broad platform of egalitarianism and
balanced growth. By socializing all property
the Communist party abolished concentrated
wealth, luxury consumption, and made it
clear that all would start from the same position. The party also stressed decision making at the local level and in effect this meant
the vast majority of the population, the poor.
At the same time broad provisions were made
to provide all with basic necessities including health and education. For the first time in
China's history, the direct producers of wealth
could see a correspondence between their
efforts and their rewards.

China's success in modernizing also depended on building on China's strengths.
The pronounced familism of China and the
Confucian philosophy stressing harmony and
hierarchy based on family roles were modified to eliminate aspects that ran counter to
dynamic economic performance. The traditional subservience of women was flatly
and radically denounced. At the same time
China stressed collective efforts and asserted
the primacy of progressive groups, especially
the party over the life of the individual.

China's balanced modernization avoided
a top-heavy commitment to heavy industry
(as the Soviets did under Stalin). It also did
not seek an export-led growth. Unlike many
developing nations, it sought self-sufficiency

---

[40]Victor D. Lippit, *The Economic Development of China*
(Armonk, N.Y.: M.E. Sharpe, 1987), Part II; originally
published in 1978.

and this meant above all that China must feed itself. In an outstanding performance, China succeeded in feeding 1 billion people, the first time in 4,000 years that hunger did not stalk the land. Despite considerable emphasis on heavy industry, China also stressed light industry and simple consumer goods. While many services were deliberately not developed, the Communist party placed heavy emphasis on health and education clearly indicating that it knew the importance of each to economic growth. In a remarkable achievement, life expectancy doubled putting low-income China in the company of middle-income countries.

China's strategy was to use its abundant labor as fully as possible. The Chinese people were already well-disciplined, hardworking, pragmatic, and earthy. The early period of modernization from 1949 to the late 1970s stressed full employment for all, collective decision making, and collective group effort and reward. There was a deliberate policy against allowing private property in skills and knowledge—instead an effort was made to distribute economic and professional skills as widely as possible.

China already had local orientations in business, industry, and farming, and economic decentralization was stressed to avoid long transport costs, to use labor already in place, and to avoid extremes in development among the countryside, cities, and the various regions. By the 1970s China had had notable successes in enlisting the labor of women, in health, education, and science, in population control, and in urban planning.[41] But there were difficulties as well: despite efforts, the disparity between rural and urban incomes had grown. The one-child per family policy could not be maintained indefinitely, and the enormous problem of moving rural labor into urban industrial centers was daunting in the extreme, especially given the backlog in infrastructure, especially housing.

Adaptation to a Changing World

Mao's philosophy of egalitarianism served China well and was probably quite appropriate for China's initial stage of development (certainly under socialism). But Mao could not adjust to the new needs of a developing China and his attempt to reassert egalitarianism (the Great Leap Forward and the Cultural Revolution) ran counter to the inherent needs of a developing society. After Mao's death in 1976, China's leadership took stock and quickly enacted practices to overcome the weaknesses that had emerged because of Mao's failure to adapt.[42]

Essentially, Chinese communism has acknowledged the inability of a central planning body to allocate resources and to make the basic decisions regarding all matters big and small. Though the overall growth record by the late 1970s had been outstanding (despite the disastrous experience with the Cultural Revolution), food production was lagging, there were widespread inefficiencies in industry, services were backward and hampering other economic activities, and China was not keeping up with world technology.

Since the late 1970s China has introduced material incentives by abolishing collective farms and allowing farmers to grow food for the state and for profit (with a consequent huge spurt in production) and has begun to decentralize economic decision making to allow managers more discretion in running their plants (which also means using labor more efficiently). It has emphasized the importance of mental work and has entered the world market in an effort to remain competitive. It not only exports but has vigorously sought foreign enterprises, some joint, and some

---

[41]Neville Maxwell, ed., *China's Road To Development* (New York: Pergamon Press, 1979).

[42]The period since 1978 is the focus of the essays in Stephan Feuchtwang *et al.*, *Transforming China's Economy In the Eighties*, 2 vols. (Boulder, Colo.: Westview Press, 1988). These essays supply technical discussions of all aspects of China's economy, with comparisons to other countries, framed in political terms. The collection stresses the options faced by China as well as the uniqueness of its socialism and the difficulty of knowing what the future will bring.

completely foreign owned. As a result, industrial production has also spurted.

China is also allowing private ownership of enterprises by its own citizens (serviced by a bond and stock exchange) and this too has become a dynamic sector. All in all, there is a movement to establish a price system for everything as the basis of economic planning and resource allocation. The Communist party is also withdrawing from the day-to-day management of public life in favor of a merit civil service. But on the whole there has been no opening up of public debate and no increase in political freedom, dissent, or pluralism.

China's commitment to economic liberalization without political liberalization resulted in a large student-led protest movement in the late spring of 1989, which culminated in bloodshed (hundreds, perhaps over a thousand unarmed students and civilians were killed by government troops). The students had occupied the public plaza (Tiananmen Square) associated with the seat of power in China (formerly the site of the emperor's palace, now Communist party and central government headquarters) demanding free speech and the end of corruption. For some reason the government did not respond for almost two months and the movement swelled as hundreds of thousands of students came to Beijing, other cities had rallies, and various groups (journalists, civilians) joined in the massive but peaceful protests. The students also asked for the resignation of 84-year-old Deng Xiaoping, China's leader. It soon became clear that hard-line opponents of liberalization were in command of the government, martial law was declared, and a stalemate developed. Some students began to go home but others continued to occupy Tiananmen Square; they erected a crude facsimile of the Statue of Liberty, and began to organize on a China-wide basis to continue their movement. Suddenly the government acted and the People's Army spilt the people's blood. Shortly thereafter, and despite condemnation from around the capitalist world, the government began a mass crackdown on the so-called democracy movement. China's reputation had suffered, its ability to maintain economic re-

lations with the developed capitalist countries was damaged, and the relation of the Communist party and government to the Chinese people had been altered.

All this has been recounted because it helps us in making an analysis of a society different from our own (no account of the above event either by American journalists, political figures, or government-intelligence figures in the United States did anything more than provide ahistorical, acultural support for the student movement—or express understandable outrage at the killing of unarmed protestors).

How did the party and government see the student movement and what do the events tell us about China's future? We can assume from the long delay in responding that serious discord exists at the top of the party about all matters pertaining to economic and political liberalization. We also know what Deng said after the crackdown, "A very small group of people created turmoil and this eventually developed into a counterrevolutionary rebellion trying to overthrow the Communist party, topple the socialist system and subvert the People's Republic of China so as to establish a capitalist republic."[43]

Beyond that we can only speculate about the reasoning behind the government's actions. The economic liberalization since 1978 had spurred growth but also serious discontent about inflation, unemployment, and visible disparities between city and farm, coast and interior, rich and poor. Deng, who favored opening up the economy through markets and foreign investment, had announced a slowdown of economic liberalization shortly before the students, themselves largely the offspring of party members, and in any case led by students in programs designed to prepare party leaders, faced a future with fewer opportunities (it is important to know too that students in China live under conditions that prison inmates in most countries would consider intolerable). Their cry against corruption was aimed at the way in which China's

---

[43]*The New York Times*, June 10, 1989, p. 1.

too-few vacancies in top positions were being allocated: through nepotism and bribery.

The party and government had no ideological quarrel with the demand for the end of corruption. This could be interpreted as a demand for continued economic growth through liberalization (even free speech might have been seen in this light). The student movement took on a revolutionary character when it demanded the resignation of China's leader. And it became a revolutionary movement when students began to organize on a China-wide basis (the Statue of Liberty facsimile in Tiananmen Square was salt in the wound, tantamount to raising the hammer and sickle on the Washington Mall).

Perhaps party leaders were unable to face a future in which they had less power or in which they could not guarantee the future of their own children. Perhaps they were unable to sense that China's success in satisfying basic needs would lead to rising and difficult-to-control expectations. Perhaps they felt that the party was the only legitimate source of power and that the party's record in bringing China from a helpless giant to an emerging world power in 40 years could excuse mistakes and even the taking of blood. Perhaps they felt that China was not the U.S.S.R. and could only be hampered by political liberalization (and thus become like other developing countries that had been retarded by premature attempts at representative government). Perhaps China's leaders did not realize that economic liberalization, forced by the need to keep pace with the world system, also places these leaders under both domestic and world system pressure to liberalize politically (it is no accident that students used signs printed in English and a facsimile of the Statue of Liberty as they appealed to world opinion). In any case, the ruling Communist party has allowed a split to develop between it and the Chinese people and it must now not only work to solve China's complex and changing problems but to restore whatever legitimacy it lost by killing unarmed protestors.

The June, 1989, massacre of protestors will no doubt make it difficult for the party and government to govern. The Communist party will no doubt try to restore public confidence by taking measures to stem the rise of inflation, by continuing to open up the economy (but more slowly than in the past), by continuing to woo foreign investors (who will resume their activities after a brief halt because none dares to be left out of the giant Chinese market), and by at least creating the appearance that moderates (political liberalizers) are again welcome in the party and government. What the party needs to realize is that its own actions have produced reactions that it appears unwilling to accept. Uneven development, no less than uneven power, creates its own dynamic. Ideas, values, and practices are relative to history and social context. Just as the Communist party in the Soviet Union has had to contend with its own success (creating an educated citizenry) and go beyond its once useful but now outmoded practices (the command economy), the Chinese Communist party will have to face up to its own success.

China: A Superpower of the Twenty-first Century?

China in the 1990s faces novel problems, most appearing because of the very success of its previous policies. What might have been is always intriguing but Mao's path from 1949 to the 1970s suited China. Essentially, this was a policy of centralized control (a socialist command economy) emphasizing broad-based development and the satisfaction of basic needs. Growth rates averaged an impressive 4 percent and China avoided the traditional problems created by the trickle-down philosophy of capitalist development: high economic concentration, luxury living amidst widespread poverty, a sharp separation between elite and led, and a political system in the service of property groups (with perhaps political instability).

China's new problems are to continue the impressive economic growth of over 6 percent between 1979–86 produced by its new "capitalist" practices (the leanings toward a socialist market economy) as it faces novel decisions about the proper mix of industry, investment in agriculture, and a wide variety of services (transport, law, insurance, restaurants, etc.).[44] China faces new health problems because its success in doubling life expectancy now means that the diseases of old age will strike China far sooner than most developing countries.[45]

China will no doubt be a superpower in the twenty-first century. Its leadership has proven itself to be pragmatic, willing to abandon ideas and practices that do not work, determined, even ruthless, and it has acquired considerable skill in the management and development of society. China is a large country with abundant resources and a huge but economically valuable population. Even if its GNP or per capita income is not among the highest, its size and dynamism will put it among the powers of the globe.[46]

Why Is Modernization in China Succeeding?

China's success in modernizing is part of the general success of East Asia. China's pattern is later and different from Japan, South Korea, Taiwan, Hong Kong, and Singapore.

Observers have made invidious comparisons among these countries. Some are superficial (for example, Milton Friedman points to laissez-faire economic policies as the reason for the success of capitalist East Asia). Some make comparisons between apples and screw drivers to show the superiority of capitalism (for example, Alvin Rabushka, *The New China: Comparative Economic Development In Mainland China, Taiwan, and Hong Kong*, Boulder, Colo.: Westview, 1987), and many think of China as lagging behind its fellow Asian societies and in need of considerable doses of capitalism if it is to catch up.

Dwight Perkins has argued that the East Asian societies of Japan, Korea, Taiwan, Hong Kong, and Singapore have left their rural societies far behind and are now urban-industrial systems comparable to those in the West (while China has not). These East Asian societies succeeded, says Perkins, because they were rich in human resources (disciplined, literate populations experienced in urban life and in the management of large organizations) and because they had long-term stable and supportive governments.[47]

Perkins' explanation would take on added life if he had stressed the feudal-authoritarian background common to all the Chinese-based societies. The various peoples derived from Chinese culture are secular, achievement oriented with a Confucian philosophy that stresses obedience to authority. That authority can focus on agrarian values as it did in the past or it can focus on economic development as it has done from the nineteenth century on (outside China proper).

China did not develop because it was a giant country whose central government was always a reflection of landlords (and merchants). It did not develop because political instability, internal civil war, and foreign pressures kept it divided and off-balance. But in 1949, it succeeded in establishing a strong central authority (which happened to be socialist). Like the other East Asian societies, it

---

[44]For an appreciation of China's economic achievement and a careful analysis of what the needs of the future are, all with an empathetic understanding of the socialist context, see Edwin Lim et al., *China: Long-Term Development Issues and Options* (Baltimore: The Johns Hopkins University Press, 1985), a World Bank report. For a briefer analysis, also citing impressive growth in the 1980s, and which itemizes in a comparative table the greater distance travelled by China toward market practices than the Soviet Union, see Central Intelligence Agency, *China: Economic Performance In 1987 and Outlook for 1988* (Springfield, Va.: National Technical Information Services, 1988).

[45]For an appreciation of China's health care system, see Victor and Ruth Sidel, *A Healthy State: An International Perspective on the Crisis in United States Health Care* (New York: Pantheon, 1977). For background on the evolution of China's health care, see David M. Lampton, *The Politics of Medicine in China: The Policy Process, 1949–1977* (Boulder, Colo.: Westview Press, 1977); and Marilynn M. Rosenthal, *Health Care In The People's Republic of China* (Boulder, Colo.: Westview Press, 1987).

[46]In 1987 China's GNP was $319.7 billion and its per capita income was $300. The World Bank, *The World Bank Atlas, 1988* Washington, D.C., 1988), p. 6.

[47]Dwight H. Perkins, *China: Asia's Next Economic Giant?* (Seattle, WA: University of Washington Press, 1986), Part I.

overcame the power of landlords. And it began a process which like the other East Asian countries built on its feudal-authoritarian past (the U.S.S.R. after 1917 is a similar example).

The truth of the matter is that China's economic (and social) achievement is second to none! Judgments here are of course tricky and subjective. But a quick look at Japan reveals a simple job of modernizing (a resource-scarce, island kingdom that must export or die) with ready access to world markets, especially one provided by the United States for political reasons, and no defense or welfare burdens. Taiwan's story is much the same, and one can also say the same for Hong Kong and Singapore.

China, of course, has not yet made a breakthrough to sustained industrialization and Western-level living standards. But one can confidently assume it will (the same cannot be said of any of the other large developing societies such as India, Brazil, Indonesia, Pakistan, Nigeria, or Mexico). China's path has been authoritarianism in the service of the working population (whereas Japan's has been authoritarianism in the service of property groups, the military, and the state). Whether it can keep to this path and not shift to state capitalism remains to be seen.[48]

INDIA

Land and People[49]

India is the seventh largest country in the world but its population of 800 million places it second in population. Its geographical features are quite varied and contain a considerable depth and diversity of natural resources.

Historical Background: The Caste System

The most explicit, thoroughgoing, and inflexible structure of social stratification is the caste system. In general, a caste system declares that a differential in some ascriptive condition is supremely important and forms an unalterable and inviolate basis for the unequal distribution of all social benefits. While a number of societies (for example, Ceylon, parts of Africa, Japan, and the United States) have developed approximations of caste stratification, probably the only true example is India.[50]

Disregarding origins and historical irregularities, what appears to have happened on the Indian subcontinent is that the Hindu religion cystallized in such a way as to transcend class and power, and came not only to express economic and political forces but to dominate them. This is not to minimize the importance of economic and political factors. Reading the following description of the underlying religious rationale for caste, it should be kept in mind that India was an agrarian society, the vast bulk of whose population worked in a labor intensive, low technology agricultural economy. Given a static village economy, it is not surprising that a complex, sophisticated religion such as Hinduism could provide the simple productive system with a religious sanction and eventually envelop it altogether. And the same thing is true of family, governmental, and military relations: together with economic functions, these realms eventually were also absorbed into a hierarchic mosaic of religiously defined castes and subcastes. With behavior in all areas of life subject to a religiously determined division of social labor, the individual castes were self-sufficient in terms of marriage and reproduction, the socialization of the young, eating patterns, kin obligations and mutual help, the settlement of disputes, and the practice of

[48]For an interpretation of Chinese history in terms of class dynamics, with a discussion of whether or not China can avoid the Soviet pattern (in which the state bureaucracy served itself and its children first), see Victor D. Lippit, *The Economic Development of China* (Armonk, N.Y.: M.E. Sharpe, 1987).

[49]For a valuable reference work, see *India: A Country Study*, Fourth Edition, Foreign Area Studies, The American University (Washington, D.C.: U. S. Government Printing Office, 1985).

[50]For a wideranging historical and comparative analysis of various stratification systems, which sees class forces behind caste divisions including racial slavery in the American South, see Oliver Cromwell Cox, *Caste, Class and Race* (Garden City, N.Y.: Doubleday, 1958).

religion per se, while at the same time they were committed to occupations and caste relations that incorporated them into village-wide, regional, and all-India divisions of social labor.

In all societies always, there is a basic thrust toward consistency of class, prestige, and power (especially at the upper levels), and India was no exception. Modern empirical research has revealed considerable inconsistency—even conflict and mobility—in twentieth-century India, but evidence suggests a high degree of consistency in the classic period among the statuses of each caste and subcaste in each dimension of stratification. The system of caste and subcaste cannot be described exactly. At a high level of abstraction, Indian society was a hierarchy composed of four varnas (broad all-Indian castes) and the untouchables (the outcaste). This scheme was derived from a religious literary tradition three thousand years old. However, the reality of Indian stratification lay in its thousands of subcastes.[51]

The classic caste system of India was based on the all-pervasive importance of religious status at birth (Hinduism). Both the Hindu religion and the social system it eventually brought under its sway are vastly different from the religions and societies Westerners are accustomed to. They lacked the theology, explicit organizational structures, functional staff (clergy, civil servants), and degree of legalization and formal political authority that Westerners associate with religion and society. Despite the apparent formlessness of the Indian caste system, however, it effectively controlled Indian society for well over two thousand years. This is all the more remarkable in light of the fact that the caste and subcastes could never be precisely identi-

fied, described, ranked, or even numbered. Each of the four main castes—the Brahmans (priests and scholars), the Kshatriyas or Rajputs (princes and warriors), the Vaishyas (merchants), and the Sudras (peasants, artisans, laborers)—contained many subcastes, and the total numbered in the thousands. Below these, the outcastes (untouchables) made up approximately 20 percent of the population.

It is impossible to understand the absolute inequality that prevailed under the Indian caste system without understanding the main tenets of Hinduism:

1. *Samsara*, or reincarnation, is life after death—in this world not another.
2. *Dharma*, or correct ritual behavior, specifies the behavior appropriate to one's caste.
3. *Karma*, or causality, is dependent on how well one adheres to correct ritual behavior (dharma) independently of social conditions.

In Hinduism, there is no supreme creator: life, or the soul, has always existed and manifests itself in caste. One can improve one's caste in the next (social) life, and failure to adhere to the dharma of one's caste can cause one to be downgraded either in this social life or the next one, but no one can climb the social hierarchy during any given lifetime.

There is little that is obligatory for all Hindus. All must respect the Brahmans, believe in the sacredness of the cow, and accept the castes into which they are born. The main thrust of Hinduism (and thus of Indian culture) is toward prescribing different modes of behavior and different benefits for each caste. There is no universal standard of right and wrong, and no improvement is possible in this life; all deprivations and hardships are ordained and explained by religion, and the only recourse against worldly suffering and the only avenue to social mobility is the possibility of a better life in some future reincarnation. Unlike Christianity, which has universal moral rules (the Ten Commandments), universal ethical ideals (love and brotherhood), and declares all individual souls equal before God, Hinduism sets a radically different course for each caste and sub-

---

[51]For an excellent formal description of the Indian caste system, see Egon E. Bergel, *Social Stratification* (New York: McGraw Hill, 1962), pp. 35–67. For a theoretical discussion of caste, see Anthony de Reuck and Julie Knight, eds. *Caste and Race: Comparative Approaches* (London: J. and A. Churchill, 1967), especially Chapters 1, 5 and 7. Probably the best introduction for the beginning reader is Taya Zinkin, *Caste Today* (London: Oxford University Press, 1972).

caste, in effect saying that different castes are worth different amounts in the divine scheme of things.

The enormous power and stability of the Indian caste system resulted from the extension of religion into every aspect of behavior: occupation, marriage, eating and drinking, friendship, and many other pursuits were explicitly regulated by caste status. The radical particularism of religion thus resulted in a social and cultural particularism so deep that it precluded even a minimal degree of equality. The Indian subcaste was a prestige group without parallel in the history of stratification. It constituted the consciousness of its members and controlled their economic and political relationships down to the smallest particular. Westerners' deeply implanted sense of the public, ingrained universalism, and easy use of abstractions in dealing with themselves, others, and nature make the cultural diversity (particularism) represented by India's thousands of subcastes almost incomprehensible. Nevertheless, the caste system was not random or unpatterned. Relations between the subcastes were strictly prescribed according to a logic provided by the Hindu concept of ritual purity—a concept blurred obviously by such phenomena as conquest, migration, British imperial control, urbanization, and industrialization.

Given this strict and narrow definition of identity, there was no formal consistency between the hierarchies of class, prestige, and power. Formally, each of the top three castes monopolized the top of one hierarchy and each was formally positioned hierarchically in relation to the others: Brahmans (prestige), Kshatriyas or Rajputs (power), and Vaishyas (class). But beneath the forms of the Indian caste system there is a general consistency of status in the major dimensions of stratification: all three of the top castes, for example, enjoyed high or substantial economic status and were roughly equivalent in their other statuses. Only a minority of Brahmans for example, followed a priestly calling; while Brahmans could not pursue certain occupations, such as medicine and moneylending, without jeopardizing their caste positions,

they were landlords and practiced all the learned professions. Of course, there was a considerable amount of both rivalry between castes and subcastes and upward and downward mobility (of subcastes, not individuals) due to military conquest, the settlement of new lands, the emergence of new occupations, and British rule. But all this notwithstanding, the classic Indian caste system was a uniquely rigid system of virtually total inequality.

Historical Background: India as a Colony

India (or rather the many subsocieties of India) was subject to Arab and European traders and imperialists from the earliest times. In modern times Portugal, France, and England were the main competitors for India's riches. India was effectively taken over by force of arms by the English East India Company in 1757. In the next hundred years the East India Company plundered India (with the help of Indians) greatly helping England's economic development. In 1859 the English Crown took over the direct administration of India (after a serious uprising) and proceeded to forge a nation state out of India using the railroad, a common legal system, and a civil service to both unify and expand India's boundaries. During the period from 1857 until India's independence in 1947, India served England well, both as a market for its goods and as a political and military counter to Czarist Russia.

Independence and Development Under Representative Government

World War II was a turning point in the colonial era—both winners and losers had to give up their colonial empires soon after. Some colonies were freed only after prolonged wars of liberation (the French, for example, had to be forcefully evicted from Algeria and Vietnam). Some colonies became free without war—India was one of these, becoming an independent country in 1947 largely through peaceful means (and the exhaustion of Great Britain).

India approached the future with a system of representative government and a commitment to self-reliant development under planning, socialism (a large public sector), and capitalism (a large and varied private sector). India inherited an advanced civil service and had experienced no protracted war of national liberation (which were so costly say to Vietnam and Algeria). Its pluralist strategy for development seemed ideal and India's growth rate compared to the period under British rule was up significantly.[52] Investment per annum was high and India's industrial sector could boast of important achievements. But despite high rates of growth through the 60s the Indian economy could not maintain its pace and a relative stagnation set in. Thus by the 1980s India's economic growth, along with its type of growth, had not been enough to raise living standards or bring the majority of its population out of absolute poverty. The contrast with China is especially illuminating—both countries had the same per capita income in the 1950s and in 1987 still had the same per capita income.[53] China by the 1980s had not only eliminated absolute poverty, doubled life expectancy, brought its population under some control, but was poised for significant breakthroughs into industrialization and a middle-income standard of living. India, on the contrary, was treading water.

Why Has Indian Modernization Failed?

Economic development in England and the United States occurred prior to their gradually evolving system of representative government. Both countries evolved into full-fledged representative government (full-fledged means no property qualification and the elimination of ascriptive barriers to political rights) only after they achieved breakthroughs to industrialization.

Most other economic modernization has occurred or is occurring under authoritarian auspices: Prussia, Russia, Japan, Union of South Africa, South Korea, Taiwan, and Singapore are examples of successes while Latin America and Africa are examples of failure. India is a unique example of a Third-World country attempting modernization under a full-fledged system of representative government committed to planning and a mixed economy. What this has meant in reality, however, is the emergence of a wide variety of economic (and other) classes and interest groups and a general intertwining of these groups with the state. Over the decades, industrialists large and small, rich and middle-rich farmers, small-service businesses, and professionals (private and public) all emerged to voice and get their demands. Such a polity has been too much for even the developed societies, which have had a surplus to give them elbow room. In India the net result of this pluralistic system (among the upper and middle property classes) has been to retard growth.[54]

The explanation for India's relative failure to modernize goes deeper. While India was a full agrarian civilization with cultural achievements as notable as any, it never developed into a full system of feudal-authoritarism. Alone of the agrarian civilizations, India remained a deeply particularistic system. While it had a central government, India's caste system effectively blocked the emergence of a single hierarchical system with a discernible apex. This particularism was combined with the political pluralism of the postindependence era to yield a full-fledged collection of preindustrial and industrial elements in a state of noisy stalemate.

India's colonial experience also hampered its efforts to modernize—while India was too large to be turned into an underdeveloped society, the British exploited it and effectively

---

[52]For a comprehensive history and analysis of the Indian economy, see V.N. Balasubramanyam, *The Economy of India* (Boulder, CO: Westview, 1984).

[53]India's GNP in 1987 was $241.3 billion. The World Bank, *The World Bank Atlas 1988* (Washington, D.C.: The World Bank, 1988), p. 7.

[54]For two similar analyses, see Prem Shankar Jha, *India: A Political Economy of Stagnation* (Bombay: Oxford University Press, 1980) and Pranab Bardhan, *The Political Economy of Development In India* (Oxford, UK: Basil Blackwell, 1984).

stagnated its economic development (the decades before World War II were a period of almost no growth). And while the British left a modern civil service in place, there was no powerful political force that could use it to bring about modernization.

Another way of looking at India's failure is to note that successful modernizers have all overcome "the problem of landowners." The Soviet Union gave first priority to eliminating the power of landowners (and gave agricultural development low priority). Japan undermined the power of feudal landlords in 1868 and land reform under the American occupation effectively reduced the power of landlords. Land reform in South Korea during the American occupation also eliminated any threat from big landowners. And of course, China effectively rid itself of the plague of landlords by collectivizing agriculture as soon as the Communist party took control. India joins those societies that have had their development retarded by the presence of powerful private rural interests. Here it is closer to Latin America, the Philippines, and Africa than to the successful modernizers.[55]

BRAZIL

Land and People[56]

The Federative Republic of Brazil is the fifth largest country in the world and its population of 137 million (1986) makes it the world's sixth most populous country. Brazil

has enormous resources (except oil), enough to make it an economic superpower. By the 1980s, Brazil had the tenth largest economy in the world, having experienced spectacular growth during the post-World War II period. Its GNP of $314.6 billion (1987) yielded a per capita income of $2020.[57]

Brazil's population is racially and ethnically diverse. Brazil had (black) slavery until 1888 and, like the United States, has a society divided on racial grounds. Brazil's "races" are somewhat different from the United States in that extensive intermarriage has produced a large mulatto group and has prevented Brazilians from thinking, as Americans do, in biracial terms. Nonetheless, Caucasians (roughly 55 percent of the population) consider themselves better than darker-skinned Brazilians (38 percent mulatto, 6 percent black).[58] More importantly, Caucasians dominate in all fields and there has been little upward mobility for darker-skinned Brazilians.

Family and Religion

Brazil's patriarchical family is extreme even by Latin American standards. This can be seen most clearly in the decidedly inferior position of women.[59] Among the upper classes the extended family serves as an important economic and political interest group. The lower classes do not have the resources for maintaining extended families and must often improvise just to keep primary families intact.

Brazilians are overwhelmingly Roman Catholic, making Brazil the largest Roman Catholic country in the world. For the first half of the twentieth century, the church served

---

[55]The case of Argentina is instructive—a rich and prosperous country when the twentieth century opened, Argentina's development was effectively blocked by its powerful rural interests. Incidentally, the same fate may befall Australia.

[56]For a valuable though somewhat dated reference work, see *Brazil: A Country Study*, Fourth Edition, Foreign Area Studies, The American University (Washington, D.C.: U. S. Government Printing Office, 1983). If one were to read one book on Brazil it would have to be Charles H. Wood and Jose Alberto Magno De Carvalho, *The Demography of Inequality In Brazil* (New York: Cambridge University Press, 1988). Using a sophisticated sociological context for population dynamics, the authors construct a highly insightful picture of Brazil's macrosocial development.

[57]The World Bank, *The World Bank Atlas, 1988* (Washington, D.C.: The World Bank, 1988), p. 6.

[58]All data on Brazil's racial groups are highly ambiguous and subjective.

[59]For a sophisticated Marxian analysis of the position of women in Brazil, which is also a valuable historical-class analysis of Brazilian history to 1960, see Heleieth I. B. Saffioti, *Women in Class Society* (New York: Monthly Review Press, 1978), Part II. Saffioti's analysis would have been improved had she noted that women in the upper classes are in many ways better off than both men and women in the lower classes.

the middle and lower middle classes. In the post World War II period, important elements in the church (including the upper as well as the lower clergy) have decried the human costs of Brazil's economic development. Liberation Theology (Christian values and beliefs infused with Marxian analysis to support secular redemption for the poor against capitalism and imperialism) has brought the clergy into conflict with the state and property groups. Though muted somewhat in the 1980s, Liberation Theology and church-sponsored local organizations continue to seek the protection of Brazil's poor.[60] So far no great success can be reported.

Health and Education

Brazilians have benefited in terms of health care from Brazil's economic growth. Life expectancy has reached 62 years and infant mortality rates have improved. But health care is largely an urban and class phenomenon—it has not received public attention and support (as is true, say, of the People's Republic of China). And the same is true of education—literacy has lagged and university education is the monopoly of the upper classes.

Historical Background

Brazil was a colony of Portugal from 1500 to 1822. It had a partial system of representative government from 1894 to 1930, a corporatist dictatorship from 1930 to 1945, a partial system of representative government from 1945 to 1964, a military dictatorship from 1964 to 1985, and is currently commit-

---

[60]For two essays, one on the church's national effort to establish local Christian communities for political action and the second, a case study of a religiously organized neighborhood reform movement, see Thomas C. Bruneau, "Brazil: The Catholic Church and Basic Christian Communities" and Scott Mainwaring, "Brazil: The Catholic Church and the Popular Movement in Nova Iguacu, 1974–1985" in Daniel H. Levine, ed., *Religion and Political Conflict In Latin America* (Chapel Hill: University of North Carolina Press, 1986), Chapters 6, 7.

ted to a full system of representative government.

Portugal did not attempt to transform its colonies into outposts of its values as Spain had tried. It was somewhat more accepting of what it found. Nonetheless, it, like Spain, was a nondynamic agrarian monarchy and its imprint on Brazil is a major reason for Brazil's failure to develop in a balanced manner.

Dependent Development

Brazil has long been a major exporter of coffee, sugar, cocoa, tobacco, and cotton, a pattern that became noticeable during the first Republic (from the 1890s to 1930). While production of these staples remained in the hands of Brazilian landowners, along with considerable profits, the infrastructure of export was in the hands of foreigners. For its part, the Brazilian government was an active facilitator of this early export economy, by and large, an ally of the export landowners under a philosophy of laissez-faire liberalism.

The basic investors in Brazil during the First Republic were Great Britain, the United States, and European countries. Much of Brazil's dependence on others took the form of portfolio investment (state guaranteed loans). While the state was active in promoting an export economy during the First Republic, it became more active during the Vargas dictatorship and the post-World War II period, branching out to develop both internal industry and manufacturing exports. Here the state and local capital entered into agreements with multinationals, especially from the United States.

Brazil's economic growth, especially after World War II, prevented underdevelopment, but only to bring it to a state of dependent development. Despite an impressive overall rate of economic growth, Brazil has not found the secret to sustained and steady growth, and has failed to raise the living standards of large portions of its population. The state has grown largely to manage and run the economy, to placate interests groups, and to be an employer of last resort, all with negative effects on the economy.[61]

Class, Politics, and Adaptive Capacity

Brazil has inherited a small number of powerful large landowners from its past. It has a large number of insecure small landowners. It has a large, landless rural labor force. At the same time, it has urbanized quickly and received large inflows of immigrants from Europe and Japan. Its cities are huge and unmanageable. It has an urban middle class, working class, and a diverse poverty class. With only partial success at representative government in the past, Brazil in the late 1980s returned to civilian government, but the debate on the nature of its constitution was not encouraging. All indications point to stalemate and instability caused by its deeply divided power groups.

The Brazilian state is economically extremely active, but corruption is widespread and deeply planted. Huge sums are wasted or pocketed by the middle and upper classes. All in all, Brazil's dependent development is aggravated by an extremely uneven social development. By the 1980s Brazil had an economy that could not be directed and it was a huge debtor nation, essentially unable to pay its debts. A few years of recession, a few years of high growth, followed by a few years of recession made it clear that Brazil was not in charge of its economy. Its external debt and high inflation made it difficult for Brazil to borrow abroad or to receive foreign investment. But to further increase its difficulties, it now has a civilian government pressured by a wide variety of interest groups.

Historically, Brazil's growth has been the work of governments that were nonrespon-

sive to the broad public. It was this that allowed Brazil to invest large amounts of capital in productive enterprises. Brazil's growth transformed it into an urban society overnight, led to a large increase in secondary and tertiary occupations, and perhaps the most spectacular rates of social mobility in human history. But it also led to one of the most unequal income distributions in the world and a neglect of basic needs among large portions of the population.[62] The return to civilian government has created new problems for Brazil. It can no longer assume a steady supply of capital from abroad or a steady supply of savings from the exploitation of labor at home. The state has begun to increase its economic activity but much of this new activity is to placate interest groups and does not represent investment in productive enterprises and there is little prospect that Brazil will be able to make the investments needed in health, education, and other public services to maintain economic growth with political stability.

Brazil's size and its dynamism have given it a position among the powers of world. Whether it can reach superpower status or even maintain its present relative position will require important changes in its domestic power structure.[63]

---

[61]For these developments, see Steven Topik, *The Political Economy of the Brazilian State, 1889–1930* (Austin, Tx.: University of Texas Press, 1987) and Peter Evans, *Dependent Development: The Alliance of Multinational, State, and Local Capital In Brazil* (Princeton, N.J.: Princeton University Press, 1979).

[62]For basic data on these aspects of Brazil's political economy, see Carlos A. Hasenbalg and Nelson do Valle Silva, "Industrialization, Employment, and Stratification In Brazil" in John D. Wirth, Edson de Oliveira Nunes, and Thomas E. Bogenschild, eds., *State and Society in Brazil* (Boulder, Colo.: Westview Press, 1987), Chapter 3. The most recent data on income and land inequality may be found in Charles H. Wood and Jose Alberto Magno De Carvalho, *The Demography of Inequality In Brazil* (New York: Cambridge University Press, 1988), pp. 75–85.

[63]For a collection of essays by a wide variety of social scientists and public figures, including many Brazilians, which is optimistic about Brazil's future, see Julian M. Chacel, Pamela S. Falk, and David V. Fleischer, eds., *Brazil's Economic and Political Future* (Boulder, Colo.: Westview Press, 1988).

CHAPTER
19
MAJOR WORLD PROBLEMS

Chapter 19 covers three broad areas: the international economy (including population and environmental issues), the problem of war (including arms control and reduction), and the problem of the United States' diminished ability to manage itself and its lackluster performance in world affairs.[1]

THE ALL-IMPORTANT DOMESTIC AND WORLD ECONOMY

The economy is the main determinant of how people behave. Today, the peoples of the world all share the same economic expectations—they desire and look forward to a better standard of living. The peoples of the world are also all implicated in the world economy—what happens to them domestically is affected by their economic relations to other nations. The countries of the world are all aware of this but find it difficult to manage their affairs. The United States is no exception; indeed, it is uniquely handicapped by a metaphysical outlook that bears little correspondence to reality. American elites, including mainstream social scientists, continue to believe that America's economic and political institutions are something other than historical creations. From the mid-eighteenth century to the Great Depression of the 1930s, Western social scientists created a fictitious social world allegedly governed by natural laws. Economic theory was the stronghold of this fiction, though history, political science, and sociology were eager participants in it.

The Great Depression of the 1930s made clear what should have been apparent from

---

[1] Three annual publications provide supplementary materials for all these areas: Suzanne Ogden, ed., *Global Politics*, Robert M. Jackson, ed., *Global Issues*, and John Allen, ed., *Environment*, all from Dushkin Publishing, Guilford, CT.

the actual behavior of people—the social world is a created thing and the economy, far from being natural, results from the selfish, often uninformed, often clashing actions of corporations, professions, consumers, workers, governments, citizens, churches, schools, research institutes, criminals, and cultural groups.

Today, the fiction of a natural economy continues under the names of free enterprise, market economics, free trade, and comparative advantage. Nonetheless, all societies openly accept the role of government in guiding the economy ("We are all Keynesians"). Even the United States under the Reagan administration of the 1980s was Keynesian (state management of the economy favoring producers), a variant of Keynesianism that has been proven wrong (favoring producers through tax cuts led to reduced, not increased, capital investment during the 1980s and the resulting budget-trade deficits became a large drag on the American economy). Today, societies negotiate among themselves on a variety of economic matters and have set up a variety of international organizations to help coordinate their domestic economic systems. Even the Reagan administration, whose outlook on the world economy adhered to nineteenth century laissez-faire economic and social theory, was eventually forced (from 1985 on) to act politically on the international scene in an effort to revive the sluggish American and world economy.

CHANGES IN THE ECONOMIES OF THE DEVELOPED NATIONS

The developed capitalist and communist countries enjoyed a stage of economic development that appears to be historically unique, perhaps a one-time thing. Far from being a law of nature, the economic growth of the past few centuries and the rise in the standard of living in the West between the 1850s and the 1960s (and in the Soviet Union from 1917 to the 1960s) may be over.

Speaking broadly, economic growth occurred because inexpensive resources, tech-nology, and cheap and eager labor could be united in easy and obvious ways.[2] People worked hard because they needed the essentials of life. Economic growth occurred because governments, religion, schools, and social scientists provided a congenial and supportive social context. Gradually, a general consensus developed that economic growth was not only good but a law of nature and that the same law would see to it that the fruits of growth would be distributed fairly. The emergence of trade unions (in the capitalist countries) and the welfare state in all countries was part of this consensus.

The 1970s ushered in a new era—slower economic growth, a decline in productivity, a stagnating standard of living. The economic boom of the 1950s and 1960s in the West had rested to some extent on the huge backlog of demand for housing, appliances, and automobiles created by World War II and the Great Depression of the 1930s. By the 1970s this demand, though still strong, had slackened. Resources had become scarcer and more expensive. Labor had become expensive. Large-scale enterprise developed inefficiencies largely because management styles were inappropriate for emerging new problems[3] and social overhead increased both in amount and in complexity. The general public wanted a large variety of services, including government initiatives to promote egalitarian values. The welfare state now included massive new interferences with market mechanisms: help to business, farmers, and professionals through a bewildering array of grants, subsidies, price supports, and tax preferences. And the state took on complex new services such as regulating medical services, safeguarding the environment, keep-

---

[2]For a deeper discussion of why economic growth started in the first place, see the section in Chapter 4 on the rise of capitalism and the section in Chapter 5 on the many routes to the modern world.

[3]For a devastating indictment of complacency, greed, and incompetence in the oligarchic American automobile industry, see Richard Halberstam, *The Reckoning* (New York: William Morrow, 1986).

ing advertisers honest, promoting research, and protecting the consumer.

The result was to narrow the options of government and to produce rigidity and stalemate. To make things worse, the domestic economies of the entire world were being increasingly affected by new developments in the international economy.

THE NEW INTERNATIONAL ECONOMY

The contemporary world of 165 nation states began with Europe's outward expansion in the fifteenth century.[4] The great age of exploration also ushered in the great age of colonialism. There is no doubt that there was an international economy after 1450. The impact of the European colonial powers on most of the world was profound, as we saw abundantly in previous chapters. By and large, colonialism transformed the horticultural and agrarian systems of the non-European world into cash-crop dependencies. At the same time international trade had an impact on the internal development of the European nations, and later the United States and Canada. Profits from overseas provided additional investment funds for the emerging capitalist nations while their ability to import cheap food and other resources enabled them to shift their economy and labor force toward manufacturing and services.

Two things stand out about international trade from the nineteenth century to 1950:

1. The amount of economic activity among nations was small in relation to domestic activity and most of it was in terms of commodities.
2. The international economy was hegemonic, that is, England was the accepted pacesetter and standard setter especially in the period up to World War I.

---

[4]Two books are especially useful as overviews of the present world economy: Lars Anell and Birgitta Nygren, *The Developing Countries and the World Economic Order* (New York: Methuen, 1980) and Lars Anell, *Recession, The Western Economies and the Changing World Order* (London: Frances Pinter, 1981).

After World War II (climaxing trends that had occurred as early as World War I), the United States became the hegemonic power in the world economy. From the end of World War II to approximately 1970, the United States dominated the world economy, and this, combined with its military strength, also made it the dominant political actor on the world scene. However, its hegemony was short-lived. During the 1970s and 1980s, a new international order rose to the surface:

1. International economic activity had grown so as to dwarf the pre-World War II period.
2. The United States was no longer the dominant economic or political-military actor. The Soviet Union's rapid economic and military growth had transformed it into a world power. And Germany and Japan, thanks in measure to American support (much of it in the form of a free ride on defense), became significant industrial rivals to the United States. In addition, industrializing Third-World countries, such as South Korea, Taiwan, Hong Kong, Singapore, China, and Brazil, were providing significant inputs into the world economy. By the 1970s the world economy had no hegemonic leader, no center of gravity. By the 1980s, the United States' share of world production had slipped from 50 percent of the world's total to 20 percent.[5]

The Capitalist World Economy

The basic world economy is essentially a capitalist system. The vast bulk of trade takes place among the developed capitalist countries and the same countries dominate trade with the Third World. The various groups that make up this economy are private corporations, governments, and international organizations (World Bank, IMF, GATT, OPEC, commodity cartels). Lesser players are professional associations, labor unions, churches, and universities. It is clear that the Soviet Union, the Eastern European countries, and the People's Republic of China are also firmly in the world economy with both feet.

---

[5]For an earlier discussion of the relative and perhaps absolute decline of the United States, see Chapter 18.

Not only is there a world economy (actually a world political economy) but economies have become increasingly intertwined. No longer does one have only a multinational company that is clearly a visible owner of a foreign plant. The new phenomenon is the multinational that uses the entire globe to perform its operations: manufacturing in different countries, assembling in still other countries, and selling everywhere. Also new is the practice of multinationals operating jointly and using each other's developed country as part of their own.

The world economy is massively affected by domestic politics, and states around the world openly intervene to pursue economic, political, and military goals. For example, the United States' basic policies give carte blanche to multinationals even as the United States practices selective protectionism, Taiwan and Korea manage their currencies and curb consumption so that their prices and imports remain low, thus helping them to build trade surpluses.

As countries experience difficulties all find it easy to blame foreigners rather than themselves or domestic groups and this has led to increased protectionism and nationalism. Given the dense intertwining of many of the world's economies and our lack of knowledge about how the world economy works, most nations pursue policies in the blind.

The North-South Split

The nations of the world are deeply divided by economic status, especially the split between the industrial countries (capitalist and communist), which have diversified economies and the Third-World countries (most of which are located in the Southern Hemisphere), which are still exporters of staples and only partially industrialized.[6]

The two most important new aspects of the stratification between the First and Third World are (1) the Third World is not only getting poorer in relation to the First but much of it is mired in absolute poverty, and (2) there is no longer an acceptance of low living conditions anywhere in the world.

Declining Productivity: The Global Economic Slowdown

In recent decades some countries have risen relatively and on an absolute economic scale (Japan, China, South Korea, Taiwan, Singapore, Hong Kong, Malaysia, and the oil-rich nations). Some have experienced continued growth but have suffered a relative decline (United States, U.S.S.R., Great Britain, France). Others have floundered or are in what appears to be chronic trouble, unable to make either relative or absolute gains (examples are Argentina, Mexico, Nigeria, and the Philippines, but much the same is true of most of Latin America and Africa).

Beyond all these ups and downs by individual countries, however, lies the ominous slowdown in productivity of *all* the world's economies.[7] With no understanding of how the world economy works, with no established procedures for settling disputes or fostering cooperation, the world's societies are drifting.

Population Pressures

The inability of the world economy to provide for a large majority of the world's peoples or to hold out the promise of a better future is partly due to population pressures.[8] The population problems facing the countries of the world come in various forms. There are:

[6]Independent Commission on International Development Issues, *North-South: A Program For Survival* (Cambridge, Mass. MIT Press, 1980)—the Brandt Report. For the history of negotiations between Europe and its former colonies in Africa and other places, see John Ravenhill, *Collective Clientelism: The Lome Conventions and North-South Relations* (New York: Columbia University Press, 1985).

[7]John Kendrick, ed., *International Comparisons of Productivity and Causes of the Slowdown* (Cambridge, Mass.: Ballinger, 1984).

[8]D. Gale Johnson and Ronald D. Lee, eds., *Population Growth and Economic Development: Issues and Evidence* (Madison, Wisc.: University of Wisconsin Press, 1987).

1. too many people.
2. compositional problems: too many young, too many old, population segments with too many different cultural values.
3. political problems posed by conflict over values (abortion in the United States for example) or by conflict between ethnic-racial groups (for example, many African countries, Sri Lanka, Israel, South Africa).
4. high consumption practices and expectations. The developing countries now have populations that have tasted and expect a better life. The high consumption of the developed countries is a heavy burden on the planet (both on themselves and the developing countries) even as the peoples of developed countries expect more.

Population pressures and conflicts over population policy represent a drag on economic production and a threat to the environment. Significant steps have been taken by many developing countries to curb excessive population growth. The developed countries have provided a great deal of aid in helping countries adopt family planning programs. The United States government and private groups have been generous (though controversy over abortion has cut government funding), but the developed countries must do their part to ease population pressure on the environment. Their task is to curb excessive consumption.

Environmental Pressures

Of special concern is the widespread and diverse impact of economic development on the natural environment. Here one need only list some of the problems to see the enormity of the pressure being exerted on the planet: deforestation as trees are cut for firewood and settlement; the spread of deserts (mostly because of inappropriate use of land); the pollution of air, water, and soil in all countries; the depletion of the ozone layer; the heating up of the planet; and the dumping of dangerous, longlasting toxic wastes.

Strong support exists for environmental protection in many countries and the United States has some tough, well-funded laws on the books that may yield significant gains if they are enforced. Some international cooperation has emerged in both population and environmental protection. By the 1980s the long decline toward an irreversible pollution of the Mediterranean Sea had been (perhaps) reversed thanks to international cooperation. In 1986 the Reagan administration announced it would seek international cooperation to cut back on the production of fluorocarbons, the chemical that depletes the ozone layer protecting the earth from harmful solar radiation, and by 1988 an important international agreement to phase out the use of flurocarbons was in place.

Nonetheless, it is clear that industrialization has put the planet's survival at risk. The United States is far from enforcing its environmental laws and there has been on balance no halt to the degradation of the environment. The developing countries are not responsive to environmental concerns seeing themselves as scapegoats for the excesses of the developed countries. With little scientific consensus on the extent of damage and no established procedures for the nations of the world to discuss environmental issues, the future does not look good.[9]

The basic outlook of environmentalists runs counter to the power structure and the nationalism that characterizes modern societies. Environmentalists think in terms of ecology and social ecology. *Ecology* is a branch of biology (and botany) that analyzes the interaction of microorganisms, plants, animals, and the general natural environment of water, soil, and air. Its concern ranges from the survival and adaptation of single organisms to that of the entire planet. *Social ecology* brings human beings into the equation: it focuses on various aspects of the natural environment (plants, animals, water, soil, terrain, energy, chemicals, microorganisms) and studies their

---

[9]For discussion of environmental problems, see William Ophuls, *Ecology and the Politics of Scarcity* (San Francisco: W. H. Freeman, 1977), Charles Pearson and Anthony Pryor, *Environment North and South* (New York: Wiley, 1978), Kenneth A. Dahlberg *et al.*, *Environment and the Global Arena: Actors, Values, Policies, and Futures* (Durham, N.C.: Duke University Press, 1985).

impact on human life. Just as important, perhaps more so, it analyzes the impact of social life on the natural environment.

Fundamental to the ecological perspective is the image of interdependence and exchange. Life forms exchange substances. We humans breathe air to get the oxygen that our blood needs and we exhale carbon dioxide as waste. Plants and trees do the opposite. The total "breathing" by plants, trees, and animals helps to keep the planet's atmosphere at livable levels. Invisible microorganisms help transform dead things into reusable ingredients. Worm tunnels help distribute needed air to the soil, bees pollinate both wild plants and farmers' crops. In short, nature and human nature are implicated in a far-reaching, complex, and largely invisible division of labor.

Social ecology focuses on how nature shapes social life and vice versa. Plentiful supplies of water are the basis of all the great agrarian civilizations. Cities develop in terms of geography: as ports, inland crossroads, or military bases. In turn, social structures have an impact on nature, especially in the industrial era. Industry deposits wastes in air, water, and soil. Pesticides kill off birds and other organisms and contaminate the water supply. Paving over the earth to build homes, streets, shopping centers, and so forth causes flooding because the earth cannot absorb rain. The human impact on the environment can disrupt a part of the interdependent ecosystem: cutting down trees and emitting waste into the air changes the composition of the atmosphere—when it rains contaminated air falls as acid rain and destroys lakes, rivers, plants, and trees. Recreational vehicles can destroy the thin soil of semiarid or mountainous areas thus killing off plants and causing flooding. Snowmobiles compact the snow on a lake and block the sun from reaching plant life in the water; plants cannot give off the oxygen fish need; eventually the plants die thus consuming more oxygen; finally the fish die. Run-off of pesticides, acid rainfall, and ocean dumping of garbage have caused serious damage to the coastal waters of the eastern United States, threatening, for one thing, the supply of fish and thus endangering a vital source of human protein.

Today, environmentalism stresses the interdependence of each and every thing on the planet. It sees human well-being implicated in the rhythm of marshlands and the integrity of rain forests. It sees connections between industry and pollution, between pollution and disease, and between what goes on in the bedroom and pressure on resources. Environmentalism is especially concerned about technology. All technology poses a risk to humans and the natural environment. Animals are an important technology but the pig was banned in the Middle East because it is ecologically destructive in that environment. The use of the hoe and plow to turn up the soil makes farmers much more productive; but clearing the land for farming can lead to soil erosion and the depletion of nutrients in the soil.

Modern industry has expanded our ability to produce by a millionfold because it allows us to process nature, conquer its spaces, transform it, and create new materials, including new life forms. But the technology of the modern economy is also a warehouse of evils. In a brilliant sociological analysis, Charles Perrow has made an assessment of various forms of technology and ranked them in order of safety.[10] No amount of care, safety devices, training, or organizational restructuring, says Perrow, will make nuclear power safe. The reason is that the generation of nuclear power is "a system of high complexity and tight coupling," so high and so tight that a catastrophic accident is inherent in it (or normal). Because making nuclear power (and weapons) safe is hopeless, we should abandon it. Research into and production of DNA are also extremely dangerous but here a large increase in safety procedures may do the job and allow us to reap the technology's considerable promise. Other technologies are dangerous, says Perrow, but do not pose the risk of catastrophe, for example, marine transport. Chemical plants, airline and automobile travel, dams, mining, power plants, and industry in gen-

---

[10]Charles Perrow, *Normal Accidents: Living With High-Risk Technologies* (New York: Basic Books, 1984).

eral are also risky but lend themselves to improvement.

Perrow's assessment focuses on "systems" and not individuals, ideologies, or components. He also focuses on how we go about assessing risk. Power groups, he argues, impose technologies on us, and power groups have able defenders in the new science of risk assessment. The professionals who do risk assessment (risk-benefit analysis, cost-benefit analysis) tend to justify existing technology just as their predecessors (shamans, priests, court advisors, astrologers, lawyers) did for kings and landlords in the past. The pretense that precise quantitative figures about the relation of costs to benefits can be arrived at, says Perrow, should be abandoned because the attempt ignores a great deal that cannot be quantified. Risk assessment, with its stress on market principles and its focus on less government regulation (to provide elites, but not ordinary people, with more freedom), is essentially a defense of the existing structure of power. Instead of the formalism of expert risk assessment, says Perrow, we should focus on the concrete systems of technology and make political assessments of their role in the overall social system (how do they enhance or threaten personal and community values?).

The environmental movement is a broad coalition of specific interest groups. Some environmental groups are concerned with the survival of particular kinds of plants or organisms: the whale, the tiger, marsh grass, rare birds. Others are concerned with the erosion of beaches or soil. Others worry about the shrinkage of farm acreage or the overuse of fertilizer and pesticides and the effect on the soil and water. Others are concerned about chemicals spewed into the air by smokestacks and automobiles. Others want wilderness areas protected against industrial, farm-ranch, extraction, and tourist businesses. Some focus on acid rain and the damage this is doing to forests, lakes, and rivers. Some worry about the chemicals that are being manufactured for consumption by humans and also by the chemicals that go into the animals that feed us. Still others are concerned over the thousands of dumps holding chemical wastes or by the discharge of dangerous toxins into our streams and drinking water. Some environmentalists are especially concerned about the dangers inherent in nuclear energy.

On a broader scale many people worry about the so-called greenhouse effect, the warming of the earth by an atmospheric dome formed by industrial waste. (In 1988 climate experts testifying at congressional hearings stated that the greenhouse effect is inevitable and has probably already started). The ozone layer that protects us against the sun's radiation has already been breached by human-made chemicals. Some environmentalists are concerned about what will happen to the planet's climate if forests are destroyed. Still others are worried by population pressures, both the smaller but high-consumption populations of the developed world and the huge but still low-consumption populations of the developing world. Finally some environmentalists argue that we have already exceeded the planet's carrying capacity (see Box 19-1, America Still Has Slaves: The Reality of Ghost Slaves).

Scholars do not agree on how much stress has been placed on the planet or how soon resources will be depleted. Most agree, however, that the planet is under threat. Perhaps our most reliable monitor is the Worldwatch Institute's annual report.[11] That we have exceeded sustainable levels is widely accepted. But how soon we will reach irreversible levels is not known. What to do is clear in general but breaks down when it comes to specific actions. Building a sustainable society means reevaluating the main thrust of American culture and this will be difficult. But the United States also has a rich tradition of opposition to materialist modes of life that might prove helpful.[12]

---

[11]Lester Russell Brown, *et al., State of the World: A Worldwatch Institute Report on Progress Toward a Sustainable Society* (Washington, D.C.: Worldwatch Institute, Annual).

[12]David E. Shi, *The Simple Life: Plain Living and High Thinking in American Culture* (New York: Oxford University Press, 1985).

BOX 19-1. America still has slaves: the reality of ghost slaves

William Catton, along with other environmental theorists, has warned that industrial society is committed to a scale of living that exceeds the sustainable carrying capacity of our finite planet.[1] The industrial countries import food, raw materials, and energy but no one worries about total supplies for the planet's population over time. These are "ghost" supplies says Catton based on ghost acreage. The industrial countries rely not only on "elsewhere" but on "elsewhen." The energy base of industrial civilization rests on fossil fuels that took hundreds of millions of years to develop. Converted to slave labor, this process equals the work of an incredibly large work force (tens of thousands of slaves stacking 2,3000,000 blocks of stones each weighing 5000 lbs. for 20 years would equal the energy spent in a few minutes by a 3-stage Saturn V rocket!). The cost of using coal, oil, and gas has been cheap because no labor had to be paid to produce them. The cost of producing energy from our own sustainable resources (for example, from corn oil) would be 13 times higher—high enough to prevent us from committing ourselves to a scale of living based on ghost slaves and exhaustible energy. Today, both the United States economy and society are based on 80 ghost slaves for each American (there are 10 ghost slaves for each member of the world's population). The United States' standard of living is 4 parts phantom acreage and 1 part real carrying capacity. The world as a whole is based on 90 percent phantom carrying capacity. We are drawing 10 times more from the earth, concludes Catton, than the earth is replacing (or we need 10 planet earths to match present consumption).[2]

[1] William R. Catton, Jr., *Overshoot: The Ecological Basis of Revolutionary Change* (Urbana, Ill.: University of Illinois Press, 1980).
[2] For a careful empirical survey that finds food production holding up for the foreseeable future but declines in fish and forestry products and the disappearance of oil and the end of cheap energy, see F. Landis MacKellar and Daniel R. Vining, Jr. "Natural Resource Scarcity: A Global Survey" in D. Gale Johnson and Ronald D. Lee, eds., *Population Growth and Economic Development* (Madison: University of Wisconsin Press, 1987), Chapter 8.

The environmental movement has succeeded in arousing public concern about the environment. It has succeeded in making people aware that the despoilation and exhaustion of nature's resources pose a threat to human health and survival. It has succeeded in getting laws passed whose intent is to protect endangered species, clean the air and water, ensure workplace safety, and clean up toxic waste dumps. But enforcement lagged from the beginning. With the Reagan administration, the pretense that government would protect the environment was dropped. From 1981 on, the enforcement of environmental laws at the federal level was relaxed and efforts were even made to weaken the laws.

Evaluating where we stand in the struggle to protect the environment is not easy. It is safe to say, however, that no overall progress can be reported in making the air or water cleaner, protecting nature in general, or in guarding human beings from various chemicals and harmful products. If anything, the situation has gotten worse and we have come closer to the threshold of irreversible decline.

The reason why so little progress has been made is that environmentalism is fundamentally out of step with the logic of industrialism (whether capitalist or socialist). Powerful industries and agribusinesses, with the help of government, have blocked the environmental movement. Environmentalism is also out of step with the logic of development in the Third World. There, extensive damage to the environment has already occurred—soil erosion, the spread of deserts, deforestation, the decline of food production, and the pollution of air and water through uncontrolled industrialization and urbanization. The interdependence of the world economy is seen in the following irony: as Western nations raise pollution safeguards, capital flows to Third-World countries that lack pollution standards. The Third World is also a dumping ground for products that have been banned in the industrial world.

The environmental movement in the United States has stalled, or rather, has been depoliticized. Even most environmentalist groups have taken it for granted that they are dealing with solvable problems within the structure of capitalism. They have been only too ready to assume that laws will do the job and that technical solutions will be found. Few have seen the need for framing the problem of the environment in terms of an overall theory of society. But that, it appears, is what is needed.[13]

MANAGING THE WORLD ECONOMY: THE INTERRELATIONS BETWEEN THE INNER AND OUTER WORLDS OF THE NATION STATE

The most important idea for understanding the contemporary world is that domestic power structures are under enormous internal pressures and constraints (that they may be losing control of) even as constraints from the outside (that they have even less control of) have increased. This applies to giants like the

United States and the Soviet Union as well as smaller countries.

The major capitalist societies have carefully stayed away from the United Nations as the forum for discussing the world's economy. Instead, they rely on the capitalist world banking system (private banks as well as the World Bank, IMF, and so on), negotiations among themselves (annual economic summits), or negotiations among developed and developing countries in selected formats such as GATT (the General Agreement on Tariffs and Trade), which is a working consensus among approximately 125 countries on the rules of the economic game (which undergo periodic updating). Moreover, GATT is also an organization and efforts are afoot to strengthen it so that parties to the agreement will have a mechanism to resolve their disputes.

GATT has worked fairly well in the past few decades. It has committed the majority of the world's nation states to free trade, which is also an acknowledgment that their economies are interdependent (in 1986 the Soviet Union further acknowledged its dependence on the world market by asking to join GATT as an observer, and in 1988 it applied for membership). Further, GATT has worked to prevent harmful protectionism by periodic meetings in which multilateral negotiations have succeeded in lowering trade barriers. A new round of negotiations began in 1986 in an effort to do something about the glut in farm products and to see if free trade in services could be established. With its advanced service economy, the United States was pushing hard to open up world markets for its banking, insurance, engineering, construction, telecommunications, legal, mass media, and publishing companies.

The United States is still the most powerful country in the world with a GNP twice the size of its nearest competitor. It still has enormous power in world councils. But its experience and its beliefs and values are out of kilter with the world it faces. For one thing it relies heavily on GATT not realizing that GATT and the actual world economy are two very

---

[13]For three overall views based on the assumption that overdevelopment is upon us, see Andre Gorz, *Ecology as Politics*, tr. Patsy Vigderman and Jonathan Cloud (Boston: South End Press, 1980); originally published 1975; Kirkpatrick Sale, *Human Scale* (New York: Coward, McCann, and Geoghegan, 1980); and William R. Catton, Jr., *Overshoot: The Ecological Basis of Revolutionary Change* (Urbana, Ill.: University of Illinois Press, 1980).

different things.[14] The United States' ritual enunciation of universalistic norms and values (formalism) also makes it difficult for the United States to understand the world's diversity. Its belief in natural economic laws and its equation of political-legal rights with democracy are not shared by most of the peoples of the world. The United States' belief in its exceptional status, while a source of strength, is also a blinding pride. The world faces a future in which its most powerful member wants stability when most of the world wants change.[15] For most of the post-World War II period the United States believed that the private economy of the nineteenth century, which consisted of an increased input of private resources and labor, referred by a neutral state, was the path to economic growth and prosperity. By the 1980s it learned that governments in Japan, Germany, France, Italy, and some of the industrializing Third World countries such as South Korea and Brazil were developing policies and making capital available on a long-term basis so that their respective economies could be leaders in strategically important sectors of manufacturing. Now that the United States is aware of the uncompetitiveness of its economy (an awareness found in numerous reports), it seems unable to change from its commitment to nineteenth-century ideas and practices.

Whether the United States can learn to negotiate with other powerful countries, both capitalist and socialist, to understand the varieties of society in its outer environment, to channel liberation movements into viable pluralistic systems (rather than relying on right-wing dictatorships), to share the planet's resources, and to accept its position as first among equals is not an assumption that can be taken for granted.

---

[14]Raymond Vernon, *Exploring the Global Economy* (Lanham, MD: University Press of America, 1985).

[15]For a careful empirical study showing the deep isolation of the United States at the United Nations, see Miguel Marin-Bosch, "How Nations Vote In the General Assembly of The United Nations" *International Organization* 41:4 (Autumn, 1987): 705–24.

THE PROBLEM OF WAR

War as a Sociohistorical Phenomenon

War is a social phenomenon and has little to do with human nature[16] and little to do with the empty words spoken on its behalf by belligerents. Until recently, it was widely believed that war would gradually disappear with economic growth and the spread of democracy. We now know that these are false assumptions. Essentially, war is a way in which power groups solve their problems.

War is found throughout history, varying in goals, form, and intensity depending on the type of society. The fact that it varies in intensity and type (and is absent in some societies and periods) is very encouraging. This fact means that we are dealing with a sociohistorical rather than a fixed, natural phenomenon. For example, war is extremely uncommon among hunting-gathering peoples and when it occurs its purpose is to alleviate some other problem by setting things right in the cosmos, to restore the problem-free status quo. War among simple societies is heavily ritualized (often it is enough to kill one enemy). It is not conducted to seize territory or large stores of booty.

Rather than stemming from our alleged innate aggressive nature, war arises from the way we humans have organized our various societies. The anthropologist Marvin Harris places the cause of war among primitive peoples in their economic system, or more specifically, in the lack of a natural equilibrium between human population growth and material provisions for sustaining life.[17] Population control occurs in various ways: abortion, abandoning the old, infanticide. Killing female babies is an effective way to control population, says Harris, and he adds that there is a basic connection between female

---

[16]See Box 17-1, Aggression: Genetic or Cultural? and the section Peaceful Societies in Chapter 17.

[17]Marvin Harris "The Origin of War" in his book *Cannibals and Kings: The Origins of Cultures* (New York: Vintage, 1978), Chapter 4.

infanticide and the male monopoly over hunting and war. Hunting and "war" are central to the life and survival of hunting-gathering societies and by making them male monoplies, males become more important than females. This clears the way, says Harris, for female infanticide and for the general subordination of women.

Max Weber's analysis of why Rome was imperialistic and warlike is also instructive.[18] The Roman economy rested on male slavery. Rome could not generate its own slave labor force and was under chronic pressure to conquer other peoples to replenish its supply of male slaves. An economy based on slavery (and in general, on a servile population) cannot motivate people for economic growth and again war is the way to increase wealth and pay for the overhead of war itself. As long as there is a plentiful supply of cheap labor, there is no incentive to improve technology and economic practices, and as long as economic and political institutions based on servile, cheap labor exist, war is inevitable.

These who study war are now agreed that the great turning point in the development of war was the emergence of horticultural and herding societies. Horticulture produced enough surplus to enable a monarch and his retainers (eventually a noble class) to live without working. Warfare becomes much more frequent than in hunting-gathering societies, perhaps offering a substitute for the excitement of the hunt. Herding societies from the ancient Jews to the Mongols and Arabs were also warlike. Herding peoples have religions based on monotheism (God is a shepherd) which is also associated with a centralized political and military command structure (a Messiah among the Jews meant a deliverer king, often conceived as a military leader, who would deliver them from their enemies). The herding economy easily leads to the encroachment on other people's territory and thus disputes that lead to war.

War appears to emerge when societies turn nature into "private" property. People who are used to taking what they want from nature cannot adjust easily to a world of boundaries. War is also not easy to distinguish from economic behavior in general—one lived by taking from nature or from others, one lived by violence either against animals or human animals (ethnocentric cultures prevented people from seeing themselves in terms of a common humanity).

Technological developments are important to war. Herding peoples learned to ride horses and camels, and when this skill was turned to warfare it gave them an important edge. Bronze, an alloy, is far more durable than iron or copper, and bronze weapons gave those who had them an edge. Another innovation was the shift from militias to professional standing armies. The rise of capitalism meant new productive technology but it also led to a continuous series of new and deadly weapons. It has also seen new organizational systems designed to make armies more efficient.

A qualitative and quantitative jump in militarization came with the far more productive agrarian society. There economic surplus is used to augment state power and to develop professional armies. The basic power structure yields a surplus that is then used to take what the masses produce away from them. Though force is everpresent, agrarian society develops symbolic justifications, especially religion, to legitimate the upward flow of economic surplus. But the overall thrust of the system retards productivity. There is little incentive on the part of the masses to work hard or to innovate when the rewards go to others. Thus, while the first two thousand years of the agrarian age (which began about 7,000 years ago) were extremely inventive and productive, there is a marked slow-down between 5,000 and 2,500 years ago as agrarian elites perfected the institutions that milked the masses. Once specialized to be parasitic and predatory, the feudal elite could not reverse itself or adapt to new conditions. A feudal nobility cannot engage in vulgar pursuits like working or even managing. The only way to increase its revenues was from

---

[18]Max Weber, *The Agrarian Sociology of Ancient Civilization,* tr. R. I. Frank (London: Verson, 1976), Chapter 1.

war booty (and a further squeeze on its servile labor force).

War has persisted into the industrial age and here too we must look to social institutions as the cause. Early liberals were wrong to think that economic growth, science, education, and political democracy would end war. War is a product of power relations inside society. Is there a relation between the capitalist economy and war? Is there something about the industrial economy common to both the capitalist and communist countries that causes inner tension which is then projected outward? Have we so deeply institutionalized the military and weapon development that they now have a life of their own?

Today, during the post-World War II period, war has become a many-sided phenomenon. Most wars are undeclared and nonlegal, often illegal. Though much of the thought about war centers on ways to avoid a nuclear confrontation, the world is filled with "dirty little" wars and has been for 40 years and more. It is no longer easy to distinguish between war between nations and civil war. And wars do not end in peace treaties but more often in stalemate and exhaustion, peace being a mere interlude of rest before the next round of hostilities.[19]

Social Change, Insecurity, Anxiety

The past 600 years have seen unprecedented change as the capitalist West emerged and spread across the planet. First capitalist and now any and all of the world's societies routinely subject members to change, insecurity, and anxiety. The engines of development yank serfs, farmers, and peasants from their timeless routines. The village and town dweller meet the city dweller. Craft skills emerge only to become obsolete before the march of the machine. The machine owner finds his machinery obsolete. Prosperous farmers using the latest tools go bankrupt, undone by their success at producing more food than can be bought. Loyal workers are laid off as profit-oriented, faceless corporations move to another city or country.

The modern system of society must be seen as a breeder of anxiety. Or perhaps better, as a society with members who hunger for certainty and security and are thus a prey for power groups with simplistic answers. Here lie the reasons for the revival of religion, the spread of nationalism, and rival secular truths.

Hatreds from the Past

The confrontation between the superpowers stems partly from their histories: each has a long history of violence. But the many dirty little wars across the planet and many of the festering local conflicts also derive from the past. Here again we see the scars of imperialism, here again we have a developing planet living in the past: Arab-Israeli, Greek-Turk, Nicaragua-United States, Vietnam-Cambodia-China-Thailand, Muslim versus Hindu, Muslim versus Christian, and a long list of stateless peoples, some very old, some new.

Arms Control and Reduction

Arms control and reduction are not new—the rival societies of Europe, the United States, and Japan held conferences and came to agreements beginning with The Hague Conference of 1899 down to the naval agreements of the 1930s. The atomic bomb that exploded on Hiroshima in 1945 gave new urgency to arms control. Since the end of World War II, a large number of agreements have been negotiated, not only by small countries but also by the two superpowers (see Table 19-1).

Arms control and arms reduction are complex and difficult matters. Neither the United States nor the Soviet Union trusts the other. Each has its unique defense capabilities and problems. The U.S.S.R. is a land power with large conventional forces and a heavy emphasis on long-range, land-based missiles. The United States places less reliance on conventional forces and has a three-part nuclear offensive force: nuclear missiles on subma-

---

[19]For valuable reviews of the causes and nature of war and for various views about war, see Martin Shaw, ed., *War, State, and Society* (New York: St. Martin's Press, 1984) and Seyom Brown, *The Causes and Prevention of War* (New York: St. Martin's Press, 1987).

TABLE 19-1. Arms Control Agreements and Partial Agreements Since 1959.

1959: Antarctic Treaty demilitarizes the Antarctic. 23 nations.

1963: Limited Test Ban Treaty bans nuclear weapons tests in the atmosphere, in outer space and under water. 109 nations.

1963: U.S.-Soviet Hot Line Agreement establishes a direct emergency communications link between the superpowers.

1967: Outer Space Treaty bans placing of nuclear or any other weapons of mass destruction in outer space and the establishment of military bases, installations or fortifications on the moon or other celestial bodies. 80 nations.

1967: Latin American Nuclear-Free Zone Treaty prohibits the testing, use, manufacture, production or acquisition of nuclear weapons in Latin America. Under Protocol II the nuclear-weapons states agree to respect the military denuclearization of Latin America. 22 nations, including all Latin American states except Argentina, Brazil, Chile and Cuba.

1968: Non-Proliferation Treaty (NPT) prohibits the transfer of nuclear weapons by states that have them and the acquisition of such weapons by those that do not and requires nuclear-weapons states to seek nuclear disarmament. 117 nations.

1971: Seabed Treaty bans placement of weapons of mass destruction on the seabed beyond a 12-mile zone outside a nation's territory. 68 nations.

1971: U.S.-Soviet "Accidents Measures" Agreement pledges each party to guard against accidental or unauthorized use of nuclear weapons and provides, *inter alia*, for immediate notification of any accidental, unauthorized incident involving a possible detonation of a nuclear weapon.

1972: Biological Weapons Convention prohibits the development, production, stockpiling or acquisition of biological agents and any weapons designed to use such agents. 90 nations.

1972: ABM Treaty and 1974 protocol limit U.S. and Soviet deployment of antiballistic missile defenses to a single site.

1972: Interim Offensive Weapons Agreement (technically expired October 3, 1977 but is still observed) froze the number of U.S. and Soviet strategic ballistic missile launchers for five years. (This agreement and the ABM Treaty are known as SALT I.)

1973: Agreement on the Prevention of Nuclear War provides that the United States and USSR will make the removal of the danger of war and the use of nuclear weapons an objective of their policies, practice restraint in their relations toward each other and all countries, and pursue policies dedicated to peace and stability.

1974: Threshold Test Ban Treaty limits U.S. and Soviet underground tests of nuclear weapons to 150 kilotons. Signed by both U.S. and USSR but not ratified by U.S.

1976: Peaceful Nuclear Explosions Treaty (PNE) limits U.S. and Soviet underground nuclear explosions for *peaceful* purposes to 150 kilotons. Signed by both U.S. and USSR but not ratified by U.S.

1977: Environmental Modification Convention prohibits the hostile use of techniques that could produce substantial environmental modifications. 32 nations.

1979: SALT II sets equal aggregate ceilings on a number of strategic nuclear systems, including the maximum number of strategic nuclear delivery vehicles (ICBMs, SLBMs and intercontinental bombers), the maximum number of launchers of ballistic missiles with multiple warheads (MIRVs) and the maximum number of luanchers of MIRVed ICBMs. The treaty also bans construction of additional, fixed ICBM launchers and a number of other improvements to existing weapons. Signed by both U.S. and USSR but not ratified by the U.S.

Source: Alice Hughey, "The Quest for Arms Control: Why and How" (Washington, D.C.: League of Women Voters, 1983), p. 2. In 1987 the United States and the Soviet Union signed the INF Treaty eliminating all intermediate nuclear missiles from their arsenals.

rines, nuclear bombs and missiles on airplanes, and land-based missiles. An obvious example of the difficulty of achieving arms reduction in the proposal for an across-the-board reduction in all nuclear weapons is that that would give the Soviet Union's conventional forces a military edge. The United States relies heavily on maintaining a technological superiority to make up for its deficiency in conventional forces—thus it has consistently refused to sign a treaty banning nuclear testing. Ironically, one way to reduce the chance of nuclear war is for the United States to increase its conventional forces.

The march of technology has already produced military capabilities that may be uncontrollable. Seen from each side, each advance is thought to provide superiority and invulnerability. By the 1990s, for example, the United States will have submarines that are undetectable and which for the first time will be equipped with accurate first-strike missiles. Beyond that the United States is pursuing a far-reaching defense system (SDI or Strategic

Defense Initiative also known as "Star Wars") which when put in conjunction with offensive weapons becomes an offensive system. Because few believe that SDS can ever provide an effective defense, SDI is a way for the United States to continue what it does best, rely on technological fetishism to avoid making political agreements with the Soviet Union.

Similarly, the argument that agreements are not worth pursuing because the Soviet Union violates them is a politically inspired falsehood. All thinking analysts including the Joint Chiefs of Staff and the CIA agree that the Soviet Union has abided by all the major provisions of all existing treaties and that alleged violations are minor and stem from ambiguities in the treaty. Incidentally, the treaties include a mechanism for resolving such differences but the United States has refused to evoke them or participate in them.

Arms Control-Reduction as a Secondary Issue

The prevention of war through arms control (or through an arms buildup) is to turn war into a social problem on the order of crime, divorce, or poverty. Tackling a social problem directly assumes that it is solvable within the existing social order (much as Sherlock Holmes can solve a mystery because he lives in a predictable, supportive society). But social problems are now so interconnected and result so directly from a society's power structure that they cannot be solved on a piecemeal basis. The social problem approach is probably obsolete, and social problems are now quite secondary to the problem of society itself. If there is any lesson to be learned from the comparative study of societies, it is that society itself is always the problem.

Another way to look on arms agreements is that they simply allow societies to modernize their arms not reduce them. In addition, arms control lends legitimacy to the idea that national interests can be defended and promoted by force. It is the rival claims that societies make against each that must be examined and evaluated. Thinking of peace as the result of equitable arms agreements be-

tween the United States and the Soviet Union, therefore, may be a dead end. One must be prepared to assume that neither country can make the concessions needed for peace through arms negotiations. What then is needed? Or put another way: What initiatives should the United States take that will promote peace (and other social goods)?

CHANGING THE UNITED STATES TO ACHIEVE PEACE AND OTHER SOCIAL GOODS

Rethinking Mindless Economic Growth

The economic expansion of the West has had a large component of mindlessness. Economic growth has been given unqualified approval even though it means producing a large range of harmful products and services, harmful both to humans and the environment. The pursuit of economic growth means that property owners and professionals must ceaselessly develop new products and services often with no regard for other social goods. It means that capital flows to the best sources of profit even if it means upsetting meaningful social routines both at home and abroad. And the spread of capital around the globe in the form of multinational corporations makes it difficult to hold these corporations accountable even as they ask for military protection and other political supports. Certainly the alliance of property groups across national boundaries far exceeds any counterpressure from labor, consumers, or governments.

Living Within Our Means

The United States has been running a large internal budget deficit and a large trade deficit since 1977.[20] These deficits appear to be

---

[20]For a fine overview of where the United States stands (but which lacks concrete policy proposals for positive changes), see Sven W. Arndt and Lawrence Bouton, *Competitiveness: The United States in World Trade* (Washington, D.C.: American Enterprise Institute for Public Policy Research, 1987).

structural, that is, they emerge from the fundamental American power structure. They appeared because public policy decisions allocated American resources toward rearmament and away from enhancing productivity. They appeared because public policy allowed American capital to go overseas. To govern, American governments have cut taxes and kept interest rates high to attract the loans needed (from its citizens and from foreigners) to finance its deficits. High interest rates made the dollar strong, which made imports cheap. Americans enjoyed low-priced imports, which helped to keep inflation low. But while this made for political peace in some respects it also created unrest—low-priced imports, for example, hurt many American industries and communities.

Allowing easy access to the American market also promoted American foreign policy objectives—by opening its markets the United States produced strong, friendly capitalist societies in the Pacific Basin and elsewhere. But its need to borrow to finance its deficits produced high interest rates, which also produced a debt crisis in Latin America and Africa.

The United States must make painful decisions in the coming years if it is to arrest the absolute decline in its standard of living that has already occurred and which will grow more noticeable with each passing year. Consumption must be curbed; problem-preventing public services expanded; corporations better managed; research and development (including environmental research) enhanced; and every effort must be made to cut the social overhead represented by idle people, crime, superfluous armaments, unnecessary illness and disability stemming from unsafe factories, and so on. None of this is likely, however, unless the United States is further democratized.

Promoting Democracy at Home

A major unfinished business for the United States is the establishment of full popular government. American elites talk largely to each other and hold periodic elections, mostly devoid of meaning, to give themselves legitimacy. The uncontrolled use of private money in conjunction with gerrymandered electoral districts and the new technology of television and computers have made it possible to hold elections in which few issues are discussed and no mandate for governance received. All this has led to a politics of stalemate and drift (for a fuller discussion and for suggestions about reforms, see Chapters 7 and 10). In its broadest context, democracy means politicizing issues, including the core values, beliefs, and institutions of society. This means that the American electorate must be given carefully reasoned alternatives to how the economy is now run. The United States must also reverse the general process found in schools, religion, civil ceremonies, popular culture, and social science (thinking of society in natural terms), which depoliticizes social problems.

Loosening the Grip of the Iron Triangle

The United States has developed a potent military-industrial-political complex that has a stake in the conditions that usually lead to war. Keeping one's eye on the possibility that the United States may itself be a military-industrial-political complex, all that can be done to bring the iron triangle (Congress, the Pentagon, giant defense contractors) to heel should be done (for an earlier discussion, see Chapter 7).

Rethinking Foreign Policy

The United States relies far too heavily on anticommunism and military strength in its foreign policy. Its formalistic foreign policy has developed under the thought-numbing ideal of bipartisanship (the foreign policy counterpart to nonpartisan domestic politics). All thinking analysts from the CIA to private scholars would probably agree with a recent study that the Soviet Union does not have much world power, that it has little ability to control events beyond its borders, and the high point of what little power it has was reached in 1958.[21]

Domestic power structures that do not provide for the equitable distribution of the fruits of social life are the major cause of world troubles. World problems, including the threat of war, result from the imperialist actions of feudal, capitalist, and communist societies over the past centuries as power groups struggled to make their inequitable societies work.

The United States can protect itself and promote world peace by abandoning the fiction of a natural economy linking domestic and international economic transactions. America can promote world stability by focusing on viable economic development and popular government throughout the world, including at home. It was apparent during both the Carter and Reagan administrations that each was badly divided by contradictory forces. These came from the contradictory voices of a divided American power structure. To operate more effectively the United States must drastically improve its ability to understand other countries. The first barrier to be overcome is American ethnocentrism: seeing the world through American assumptions. The federal executive (State Department, Department of Defense, other civilian departments that deal with the outside world, and all intelligence agencies) is woefully deficient in its ability to read the outside world. Congress, not so directly involved in day-to-day operations, tends to see the world more clearly through its expert staffs and committees, but its voting record (subject to our oligarchic system of politics) is not consistent with its knowledge.

The United States has a dismal record in the Third World. One administration after the other has suffered defeats there (Vietnam, Lebanon, Central America, Iran, the Middle East) and there is little evidence that the United States has learned much from its experiences.[22] Americans must learn to understand the Third World and the first step is to understand itself, especially the fact that it is not necessarily a relevant model for the rest of the world. It must also rethink its goals in the world arena, its "global commitment" outlook that says that interests are to be defended and our global credibility strengthened by making firm commitments to Third-World allies. Far from failing to live up to our commitments, says Jentleson, our problems stem from the fact that we have lived up to them only too well with the result that our decision making became inflexible, the tail wagged the dog, and we have been forced into a misuse of military means (all these factors further undermining policy because they led to domestic opposition).[23]

Foreign policy is largely a matter of economic interests and here the United States must reexamine its commitment to unmanaged economic growth, its furtherance of the conditions that allow free rein to multinational corporations, and its failure to address the domestic problems that keep the general public agitated and off-balance. American trade policy (the political management of its economic policies toward other countries) must take into account the many "invisible" costs of so-called free trade. Far from leading only to efficiency and comparative advantage benefits, free trade means that the Third World will have large and growing numbers of poor, large amounts of unemployment and labor repression, unmanageable cities, and no protection of the environment. To compete with such societies means that much the same takes place in the United States. On top of all these costs is the added expense of military expenditures to keep political peace.

---

[21]For an earlier discussion, see Chapter 10.

[22]For a classic case study of the United States' faulty policy making structures and its failure to learn from experience, see Lloyd S. Etheredge, *Can Governments Learn? American Foreign Policy and Central American Revolutions* (New York: Pergamon Press, 1985).

[23]Bruce W. Jentleson, "American Commitments In The Third World: Theory vs. Practice, *International Organization* 41:4 (Autumn, 1987): 667–704.

The United States need not wait for prior agreements before undertaking tension-reducing acts. This does not mean that the concrete steps to be taken are easy—but certainly the philosophy that links all of the world's tension to communism must be abandoned. It also requires abandoning the assumption that the Soviets are absolutely untrustworthy (which simply breeds distrust) and building on the already effective inspection procedures that both sides agreed to in the INF Treaty of 1988. The logic behind breeding trust and progressive levels of tension reduction is TIT for TAT[24] (or responding in kind).

Finally, perhaps the most difficult assumptions to rid ourselves of are the ideology of rational self-interest and the psychology of interest maximizing, both of which have failed in our domestic life, yet are still thought to be somehow useful in international affairs. The rational pursuit of self-interest has been associated strongly with war from the nineteenth century on. The usual support for rational action is the parallel fallacy that wars come out of stress, mistaken views of opponents, and political-bureaucratic constraints on rational decisionmaking.[25] The involvement of churches in foreign policy matters in recent years is encouraging (some fundamentalist Christian sects, ignorant of the social causes of war, are essentially covers for right-wing political extremists, and a better managed economy and society will make it difficult for these sects and groups to find followers). And certainly the great cry for internationalizing the school curriculum at all levels is encouraging.

---

[24]William F. Allman, "Nice Guys Finish First", *Science 84*:5 (October, 1984): 25–32.

[25]For a creative look beyond this two-sided assumption, see Bruce Bueno de Mesquita, *The War Trap* (New Haven: Yale University Press, 1981).

20
THINKING ABOUT SOCIAL TYPES AND THEIR INTERRELATIONS

SOCIAL THEORY AS A REFLECTION OF SOCIAL EXPERIENCE

Social theory invariably reflects social experience; distinctive forms of social experience lead to distinctive ways of thinking about social existence. Even the origins of social theory itself (secular, systematic rational thought about society) reflected social experience. Social theory emerged when the ancient Greeks experienced social conflict and cultural diversity. Unable to fall back on supernatural and other traditional explanations, they turned "society" (the city-state) into a scientific-moral-political problem. Thought about society also lags behind social developments. Here too the Greek example is instructive. By the time the Greeks, especially Plato and Aristotle, undertook systematic social thought, social existence as the Greeks had known it was beyond repair. Their failure to understand their experience was many sided. They could not escape naturalistic thinking,

see beyond the traditional labor force of their day (slavery), or bring women into the human race. And despite the overwhelming influence of foreign affairs in their lives and the obvious obsolescence of the city-state system, they continued to think of society as a small, intimate group in which the privileged male citizens could interact personally to decide the collective fate of the many (women, slaves, resident foreigners). Instead of rethinking their world, they vainly looked for certainty and solace in a world of objective reason.

The interplay of thought and social experience can also be seen in ancient Rome. Rome expanded into an empire of enormous ethnic diversity, and Roman social theory looked for ideas that could transcend and make sense of this unique social world. Not by accident, they chose Stoicism and the cyclical theories of Polybius because these best suited the needs of a static, multicommunal, agrarian-military empire: Stoicism talked

391

about individual human beings and their common humanity and cyclical explanations made sense of their fluctuating but unchanging world. Here again there was recourse to a world of ideas lying beyond history.

Medieval social theory in the West saw yet another image of society as Europe settled into a localized, simple feudal system. Social existence and theory became one. How people lived derived from God and human nature. Social forms were considered part of a natural hierarchy extending from the natural through the human natural to the supernatural. This image is even clearer if we focus on agrarian societies without the legacy of Greek rationalism. From ancient Babylonia through medieval China and on to modernizing Japan, there is a characteristic inability to think of society as a human creation, as a problem subject to human solutions, or as an inclusive polity that puts ordinary people on a par in at least some respects with elites. In short, there is an inability in agrarian societies to think of the societal entity as one composed of individuals and to search for commonalities among them.

The concept *modern society*, which appears in the West in the seventeenth century, reflected the radically new social experience created by the dynamic capitalist economy and polity that emerged from the fifteenth century on. Our current concept of society emerged almost full-blown with Hobbes and Locke and reached maturity during the French Enlightenment as the French middle class struggled to redefine feudalism out of existence. Building on Locke, the *philosophes* postulated a natural civil society that needed a proper government. The French middle class, freed from local reality but faced with feudal particularism, created the concept of a civil society to provide a place for property groups other than a landed aristocracy. By defining society as a functional collection of self-propelled individuals, it effectively eliminated the nobility as a special ascriptive group. And since self-propulsion was something only people with property could exhibit, it also excluded dependent rural and factory workers from effective influence in society.

The liberal concept of society emerged differently in England, France, and the United States but was similar in content. Rethinking this concept is the major problem of our time, but first we must be sure of what the liberal concept of society is.

THE LIBERAL IMAGE OF SOCIETY

The concept of *modern society* in liberal thought has always had a pronounced formalism, one needed if middle-class interests were to prevail. Our comparative study of social types clearly indicates that the concept, modern society, is hopelessly vague and a distortion of reality.[1] The liberal image of society is one of homogeneous atoms acting out internal urges to improve themselves, especially by acting against nature. These atoms do not remain homogeneous but become differentiated and unequal according to natural strengths, weaknesses, and propensities. The relations among humans are essentially harmonious and there is no need for special integrative mechanisms, except to deal with transitory disturbances.

Liberal social theory in the modern period is just as reliant on naturalistic thinking as social theory in earlier periods—liberals think that society has laws similar to those in nature (plants, animals, the solar system). And, as in nature, they assume an underlying unity to the diverse types of society; in effect, they believe in a true and valid society (either at the beginning or end of history). Liberal social theory from the French Enlightenment on saw unity in an alleged linear development of social existence ending in modern (capitalist) society. From Condorcet on (actually from Vico on) social typologies were fairly similar—human history, we were told, had a linear pattern in which sacred-traditional society would be followed by secular-dynamic society. Humanity, argued theorists, was evolving toward higher social forms through the

---

[1]Readers will recall that the Soviet image of society is remarkably similar to that of mainstream capitalist thinkers.

march of science and technology, normative growth, and a more rational division of social labor.

Sociologists developed variations on this theme in keeping with their nationality and the politics of the day. English and American theorists equated the march of humanity with private property, biopsychologically based individualism, competition, achievement values, and representative government. French and German sociologists tended to think more in terms of groups, institutions, and social classes. But they too took an essentially liberal view—modern society meant capitalism. Looking back, it is clear that the bulk of social typologies (Karl Marx being a conspicuous exception) were apologies for the emerging capitalist society. Almost all typologies took private property for granted and assumed that science, technology, and the liberal division of labor would serve the public good. Almost all took capitalist society as the terminal of human history (considered as an evolutionary pattern of progress) and assumed that progress would continue after the triumph of capitalism because of it and within it (see Table 1-2).

Given the different historical development of capitalism in England and the United States (long-term gradual growth of small-scale economic units marked by individualism), English and American sociologists lost sight of society and spent much of the twentieth century struggling to understand what Aristotle, Rousseau, Burke, Marx, Durkheim, and Weber already knew—that humans are social animals and that society is problematic. The pecularities of American history made it particularly difficult for Americans to see themselves as social actors or the United States as a problem. Uninhibited by rival world views, American sociology equated American capitalism with an individualized human nature, reason, and processes in the universe at large. American sociology thought whatever problems existed were vestiges from the past representing merely transitional difficulties. After Sumner, Ward, and Cooley, sociologists rarely thought much about the economy or polity—their focus was on the rest of society.

They worried about the problems of cities, conformity, racism, poverty, the family, and so on, all within the assumption that society (the essential political economy) was sound and could reform these problems away. Complacency about society led to a virtual absence of comparative research.[2]

Talcott Parsons and a host of social scientists were still formulating new typologies and new variations of modernization theory within the tradition of evolutionary liberalism as late as the 1960s and early 1970s. The whole world was thought to be moving in the direction of the first modern society, the United States. Over the past two decades, however, making such typologies has fallen out of favor (though the tradition has been carried on by Gerhard Lenski). Social typologies no longer roll off our tongues or pens as easily as they once did. By the 1960s there was evidence that rationality was not necessarily the basis of Western culture. Given World Wars I and II, the Great Depression, and Hitler and Stalin, Westerners were no longer so sure that they were part of a progressive evolutionary scheme. Certainly the United States found it difficult to think of itself as a dynamic functional society led by scientifically based elites. But perhaps the most important inhibition to the making of evolutionary typologies was the emergence of dozens and then scores of new societies from the 1950s on. Dependency theory helped to shatter our complacency about modernization, especially its argument that developing societies were extremely diverse and that most of them were unable to develop

---

[2]For an indictment of sociology's continuing lack of interest in comparative research, see Paul Hollander, "Comparative Sociology in the United States and Why There Is So Little Of It" in Scott G. McNall and Gary N. How, eds., *Current Perspectives in Social Theory*, Vol. 2 (Greenwich, Conn.: JAI Press, 1981), pp. 21–9. For an analysis of a parochial American social science concerned only with American society and ignoring the social science of other countries, see Frederick H. Gareau, "The United States as a Center of Social Science" *Social Science Quarterly* 65 (September, 1984): 840–47. In an article following Gareau's, Norval Glenn argues that American sectarianism also stems from narrow specialization within social science and within each of the social sciences; *ibid*, pp. 848–53.

because of the negative effects of imperialist exploitation. By the 1970s, linear typologies had become obsolete because they had been contradicted by the empirical record. Nonetheless, it is the rare introductory text in sociology that does not assume, indeed often state openly, that modern society (epitomized of course by the United States) is the culmination of human progress having transcended various inferior social types.

The old typologies are false guides because they were based on arbitrary, time-bound, culture-bound assumptions. What questions should be asked to help build future typologies? Should we also question the assumption that abstract typologies are possible? Is it possible that each country is unique and that grouping countries makes sense only for purposes of policy. Perhaps the major orientation of social science should be toward politics rather than truth. It may be that human societies are inherently empirical (that is, unique historical phenomena) and that therefore our science must be applied rather than pure, empirical rather than rational, political and subjective rather than academic or objective.

In any case, our analysis of a representative set of societies and our examination of societies with exceptional features has had two weighty consequences: (1) liberal (and Marxian) social science, especially mainstream American social science, has failed to understand both the United States and the rest of the world, and (2) Americans in general do not understand their society or the world of other societies.

RETHINKING THE NATURE OF MODERN SOCIETY

Clearly, modern society has not corresponded much to our ideas about it. Liberal theorists in the seventeenth and eighteenth centuries may have talked about individuals and their rights but white male suffrage emerged only in the 1850s in the United States (the property qualification lasted even longer in Great Britain). The standard of living improved only after 1850 and while science and education grew, one cannot say that modern populations are under the sway of science or of knowledge acquired through education. One can also not say that ordinary people are in charge of society either as consumers or voters.

The liberal picture of society in mainstream social science was altered somewhat roughly between the last third of the nineteenth century and the middle of the twentieth. With the emergence of corporate capitalism, a professionalized sociology, political science, and economics now saw society as composed of groups under the guidance of educated, professional elites. Society was not so much changing as it was ripening, a moving equilibrium of interest groups. In recent decades these individual interest groups were seen as needing some coordination. On the intersocietal scene there was a corresponding development: societies also needed coordination in their relations and thus came about the liberal emphasis on internationalism and global understanding.

The liberal image of society was marked by an ideology of objectivity as was, for example, social theory in ancient Greece and Rome, and as all social images have been, whether secular or religiously inspired. Objectivity is merely consensus among elites and its emergence across the liberal disciplines marks the complacency of American elites and the effectiveness of liberal institutions in coopting even its educated classes. As empiricism, the value-neutral objectivity of social science tends to fragment the educated classes, puts them to work solving specialized, small problems, and thus acts to depoliticize them.

Liberal social theory talks of democracy but reality speaks differently. The emergence of capitalism, starting with England and including the successful growth systems in Japan, Korea, and so on, is strongly associated with strong, nondemocratic states. Democratic forms were *added* to deeply established capitalist systems to provide accurate barometers of problems and to give propertied-professional elites legitimacy, and it is debatable if modern liberal societies are really democracies (meaning a society that is run by and for ordinary and poor people). Though the liberal image of society is still dominant, a significant number of theorists have been able to see that it bears little relation to reality. Even as liberals in the 1950s and 1960s were falsifying the process of modernization with linear images of progress under liberal institutions, a strong current of historical-comparative work was shaking the foundations of liberalism. Much of this criticism of liberal metaphysics, however, was itself based on metaphysics, that of Karl Marx.[3]

The real problem of society appears if we assume that all images of society are reflections of historical experience and if we assume that there is no objective society and therefore no objective social science. The many words we use to characterize and classify social systems are largely worthless. Referring to modern society as *democracy* is a case in point. References to the "people" as the fount of power are found in the legitimating ideology of all societies, agrarian and industrial. Aristotle wisely distinguished between monarchy (rule by the rich), constitutionalism (rule by middle-level economic units), and democracy (rule by the lower classes and the poor). It is essential to note that there are no polities in the world that are democratic, to repeat, polities controlled by and in the service of ordinary people and the poor.

The social typologies of sociology have not been very sophisticated on this score. Most sociologists in the nineteenth century simply assumed that the wider popular base of the emerging capitalist society had made it a democracy. The same distinction carried into the twentieth century as social theorists compared multiparty capitalist societies and one-party state socialist societies. But one-party states can be very diverse—developed, one-party Marxist Yugoslavia stresses decentralization and mass participation in decision making while developing Mexico has a "one-party" system that favors a small propertied elite. The need to break out of the formalisms that mar social-type analysis is dramatically illustrated by the fact that the one party that controls the U.S.S.R. and the one party that controls Mexico both have deeper roots in and better representation from its respective population than the two American political parties put together. In addition, while there is much cynicism about Marxism among the Soviet people, the Communist party enjoys solid public support and cannot be said to have less legitimacy or vitality than the political parties and leadership of the United States (if anything the reverse is true).

The term *pluralism*, like the term democracy, also expresses an ideal not a fact and should be avoided in characterizing contemporary societies, including the United States. There is also no such thing as a *postindustrial* society or a *high-information* society. Contemporary society still subjects its members to exacting work performed in bureaucratized stores, offices, schools, hospitals, and factories. Information or knowledge has emerged as merely another form of property. If anything we are losing ground in the effort to base society on choices informed by knowledge, as witness, for example, the issueless presidential campaigns that emerged prominently in the 1980s.

The word *totalitarian* should also be dropped from our vocabulary of basic social types. The term is quite serviceable when used to refer to societies with power structures that seek to control their populations totally and brook no diversity. Examples in the past were Germany (1933–45) and the U.S.S.R. (1917–60s). More recently, efforts to close off a society and bring it under the total sway of a particular vision have appeared frequently in Albania, Argentina, Burma, Cuba, Iran, North Korea, El Salvador, Cambodia, Indonesia, and so on, but the outstanding feature of all these

---

[3]Marxist elites in developed and developing socialist societies, most notably the U.S.S.R. and China, have also recognized that their images of society do not square with reality. By and large, American elites, whether in policy or social science positions, are far from understanding the formalism with which they see their society.

attempts is that they are short-lived.[4] A totally controlled society is possible only with advanced technology and the use of terror (deliberately induced unpredictability). But conformity induced by fear and unpredictability is also incompatible with a society having such technology. Thus, while totalitarianism represents an important variation on social organization, it cannot be considered a basic type of society or political system.[5]

Our escape from the false image of a modern society also requires a redefinition of the following terms:

Authoritarianism: A polity with a clear source of power. Here the contrast should be drawn, not between nonexistent democracy or pluralism, but with semipluralism or diversified oligarchy. Authoritarian systems come in various subforms reflecting the history of a society, its geopolitical status, and its complexity (these will be discussed shortly).

Capitalism: A society in which an economy based on private property, science, and self-interest generates a polity which, either through a command or market economy, promotes a capitalist way of life. Capitalist societies are extremely varied and the term capitalism should be used with extreme caution.[6]

Socialism: A society in which an economy based on public property, science, and qualified self-interest has a polity, which, either through a command or market economy, promotes socialism. Extreme caution should also be used when referring to socialism (see the introduction to Chapter 14).

The idea of an *autonomous* society must also be redefined if not discarded. Our study

---

[4]North Korea has had a long run but under the special circumstances of being part of a divided nation. By the late 1980s it had become increasingly isolated and was giving signals that it wanted to change course at least somewhat.

[5]For background, see Michael Curtis, *Totalitarianism* (New Brunswick, N.J.: Transaction Books, 1979).

[6]Peter L. Berger, *The Capitalist Revolution: Fifty Propositions about Prosperity, Equality, and Liberty* (New York: Free Press, 1986) fails to provide a useful set of generalizations since of his 50 propositions some are truisms, many dubious, and 17 struck me as wrong.

has stressed that no society of any complexity can live in self-sufficient isolation. Complex societies, whether agrarian or industrial, rely on other societies for military purposes, resources, and markets. Even large and relatively self-sufficient societies such as the United States and the Soviet Union depend on other societies for many of their needs. Modern social science developed simultaneously with the nation state and it is not surprising that social scientists and social typologists came to regard the single society as a valid, ultimate unit of study. For many reasons this is a mistake. Nation states (and such things as the rise of capitalism, the development of the middle class, industrialization, class structures and processes, and social revolution) cannot be explained without referring to the interaction of societies themselves, the world-market economy, and links between various systems of social stratification (to form systems of societies and the various kinds of imperialism). At the same time, the relations among societies cannot be understood unless they are seen as a reflection of domestic power relations. Thus it is important not to conjure up an all-explanatory demiurge called a "world system."

The origins of the contemporary world of unequal nation states lie deep in the past. To understand today's rivalries, hatreds, and inequalities one must place them in at least a 600-year context. The contemporary world reflects the emergence of a market economy and the nation state in the West. By the fifteenth century the unique 600-year-old process in which a market economy emerges and shapes society to its values is clearly in evidence. The rise of capitalism is accompanied by the development of a strong central government soon defined as sovereign vis-a-vis local governments and sovereign vis-a-vis foreign governments. As the age of exploration, the fifteenth century is also the beginning of the large-scale impact of the West on the rest of the globe. The contemporary world of 165 unequal nation states caught up in a world-market economy mediated by sovereign governments (and other actors such as churches) is a direct result of this 600-year-old process. Social-type analysis and our understanding of modern society are profoundly altered once this perspective is developed. The vocabulary of social theory must now include the concepts *world market* and *system of societies*.

CRITERIA FOR ANALYZING SOCIAL SYSTEMS

Analyzing society scientifically is both an empirical (factual) and a value analysis. Investigators, be they laypeople or professionals, need to know how society works as a causal system (a cluster of structured variables). They need to know how causal structures generate and block values. Investigators must be aware of the assumptions they are using to identify issues, facts, and values. Above all, they must be aware of the many and varied ways that causes and values have expressed themselves in human history.

Our analysis of representative societies, our look at societies with exceptional features, and our picture of the changing power relations among the world's societies contained many insights into the nature of macrosocial systems. Let's put these in the form of a series of questions. As always, the first step in evaluating a society is to know its economy.

What Types of Economies Are There?

Economies can be classified and evaluated on the level of day-to-day, year-to-year policy making by asking the following questions:

1. How does an economy rank in the use of energy? How does it rank in research and development?
2. What is its GNP and what is its trend in economic growth? What is its inflation rate and its record in regard to controlling inflation? Who owns the economy? What is its per capita income and what are its trends in regard to income and wealth? What is the state of its labor force, unemployment rate, and labor policies?
3. What are its living standards as measured by infant mortality, life expectancy, available doctors, food consumption, housing, and education?

4. What are its people's economic expectations? Are they anxious about the future? Do they believe that their government and political institutions are benefitting the people at large?
5. What is the debt ratio to GNP? Is there a pattern of capital flight?
6. What is its pattern of imports and exports?
7. What is its policy toward the natural environment?

On a more theoretical level, one can classify economies by distinguishing between *use* and *exchange* economies. The former are also termed *consumption, subsistence, precommercial* economies. Use economies are found in hunting and gathering, horticultural, and agricultural societies while exchange economies are found in commercial and industrial capitalist societies. In precapitalist societies, work and production are directed at uses; in capitalist society work is for wages paid by owners who produce whatever will sell for profit.

Among industrial societies one must now distinguish between state capitalist and state socialist economies. The former are those where private property interests predominate (with the help of the state) and are characterized by high living standards, considerable income inequality, a tiny group of very rich and a large group of very poor, highly concentrated private ownership of productive property, a wide variety of quality consumer products, unemployment, inflation, and economic ups and downs. State socialist societies, which claim they will ultimately develop use economies, are characterized by a concentration of publicly-owned productive property, central planning, slightly less income inequality than capitalist economies, a large group of very poor, "full employment and price stability," living standards that are growing very slowly, low quality, scarce, and often nonexistent consumer goods. One socialist society, Yugoslavia, has a distinct socialist market economy, while another, Hungary, has combined central planning with an extensive use of market mechanisms (both the U.S.S.R. and China are moving in the latter direction).

Our knowledge about the workings of the exchange economy is extensive but there are no generally accepted economic principles (that is, agreed-on beliefs) on how the economy works, and economists have a dismal record of forecasting how the economy will behave. The failure of liberal economics is a serious indictment of liberalism's belief that modern society can generate the knowledge it needs to work properly; this failure is now being acknowledged by significant numbers of liberal economists. The record among Marxist economists and among Soviet thinkers and policy makers is no better. Overall, neither liberal nor socialist societies correspond to their legitimating ideology. In the 1980s the Thatcher government in Britain and the Reagan administration in the United States pushed hard for a return to a market economy. State socialism in Hungary relies considerably on market mechanisms. State socialism in China has made some well-publicized moves toward providing "capitalist" incentives and market mechanisms, but deep down it is clear that a market economy is a cultural fiction. There are capitalist societies with variations on market and command economies but none has a market economy, that is, an economy governed by pure economic interests and values. And there are socialist societies with variations on market and command economies. Economics has floundered because of its inability to understand this.

A move toward market mechanisms means that economic values (growth and efficiency) are being stressed. The use of prices means greater predictability for economic actors. Market mechanisms give all a greater ability to pinpoint responsibility for success and failure. A move toward market mechanisms means that economic incentives are being used to motivate elites and workers. But it also means less attention to protecting the environment. It means enhancing the power of propertied and professional groups. It means the victimization of some small businesses and farmers, and significant portions of the labor force and it means formalism and hypocrisy in how society is depicted. Market-oriented capitalism is when dominant groups are too diversified to be openly directed from a central source and they agree to compete in

a society which assumes (falsely) that a class system and unequal property groups can ensure a fair contest. Socialist societies are not much different. They too permit competition and resort to market mechanisms all within the assumption that the "propertied and nonpropertied" can compete (the propertied in socialism are those who have class-derived educational credentials and politically derived positions in the economy and polity).

The similarities between capitalist and socialist economies are obvious. However, the similarities are even wider than most are aware. The American and Soviet economies are both highly unequal, highly concentrated, and directed from above (that is, basic investment decisions are not subject to democratic discussion and control). In both societies the economy receives massive support and direction through political mechanisms. In both societies heavy military expenditures are a drag on productivity and living standards. And both appear to suffer from formalism, the ritualized enunciation of abstract principles (liberalism and Marxism), despite their evident irrelevance to today's world.

Our confusion about social types also derives from false ideas about economic growth (modernization and productivity). There is no consensus on this matter but there are many false operative assumptions. Is there a pattern to economic growth that can be associated with a specific set of variables? Liberalism and sociology assume that economic growth results from freedom, individualism, competition, private property, representative government, conducive religions, and science (or some variation of these such as abstract notions of the market, incentives, professionalism, or technology). However, keeping in mind that variations in economic growth rates and in living standards are due largely to different starting times, historical experiences, and natural environments, there appears to be no one mix of variables that leads to economic growth. Economic growth rates, as far as they are comparable, seem to be very similar in capitalist societies across a wide range of developed and developing countries and regardless of whether they have representative or authoritarian governments. And to complicate matters, the various socialist dictatorships (both developed and developing) have also experienced high economic growth rates.

Our view of modernization must be drastically altered. There are no economic laws at work and thus one must focus on concrete historical, sociocultural systems in interaction with the world system. The absence of economic laws is apparent in analyses of income, poverty, and growth. The famous Kuznets curve of development economics, that income inequality increases in the early stages of economic growth and decreases in later stages, has received little empirical confirmation. Rather, income inequality or equality occurs depending on type of country and the policies pursued by governments.[7]

Earlier studies had to rely on cross-national data; in recent years longitudinal data have become available and reveal a wide variation among income inequality, poverty, and growth. Rapid economic growth tends to reduce poverty, although this was not the case in Brazil and the Philippines. Slow growth, however, can also lead to a reduction of poverty, for example, Sri Lanka. As for the relation between rapid growth and income inequality, one pattern leads to an increase in income inequality (Brazil, the Philippines), another to a decrease (Taiwan, Costa Rica). Slow-growing Sri Lanka also experienced a reduction in income inequality. As Fields, concludes, the type of growth is what counts, not growth per se.

Brian and Rachel Griffith have also pointed to many of the examples used by Fields to show wide diversity in the relation among economic growth, poverty, and income inequality. They also point to political factors as important in reducing poverty and iden-

tify effective nationhood and a supportive normative/value system as factors in growth. They err in employing a false dichotomy between market economies and those that have governments active in the economy to explain economic growth (market systems grow). Almost all growth in history and in the contemporary developing world has had a large input from government, which is not to deny that governments can also stifle growth. The Griffiths also fail to discuss socialist countries, which would have further qualified their celebration of so-called market economies), and they too fail to place countries in the world market.[8]

Economic growth derives from a number of factors and can take a number of forms. It depends far more on state action than Americans are aware. False notions about economic growth are damaging in another sense—they do not allow us to adapt to new conditions. All societies have experienced significant and perhaps chronic declines in productivity[9] and a lag in living standards. Thus not only are the variables responsible for economic growth not what we assumed, but it turns out that whatever variables are responsible for growth may also be short-lived. The assumption that some form of modern society (either liberal or socialist) is capable of unending material progress may be problematic.

The slowdown in productivity in the developed countries suggests that social differentiation beyond a certain point does not necessarily add up to a more rational division of labor. It suggests that it is difficult to maintain capital investment when consumption incentives must be used to motivate a population. Concentrated control from above over investment in both material and human resources leads to rigidities, mistakes, and antisocial consequences. The increased com-

---

[7]This, with the examples that follow, is the general thrust of Gary S. Fields, "Income Distribution and Economic Growth" in Gustav Ranis and T. Paul Schultz, eds., *The State of Development Economics* (New York: Basil Blackwell, 1988), Chapter 15. Fields' fine summary is marred by a failure to stress that policies flow from power structures, to include an analysis of socialist societies, and by his failure to place countries in the world market.

[8]Brian and Rachel J. Griffiths, "Variables of Success and Failure in Third World Development" in Peter L. Berger, ed., *Capitalism and Equality in the Third World* (Lanhan, Md.: Hamilton Press, 1987), pp. 301–41.

[9]John Kendrick, ed., *International Comparisons of Productivity and Causes of the Slowdown* (Cambridge, Mass.: Ballinger, 1984).

plexity in the division of labor means that an ever larger number of interest groups has to be placated making it difficult to keep society's budget under control.

In recent decades we have also begun to realize that much of the spectacular economic growth of the capitalist and socialist economies was due to cheap natural resources. The end of the era of cheap resources is no doubt a part of the explanation for productivity declines. Economic growth was also due more than we realize to cheap labor—exploited male workers but also slaves, immigrants, children, and women. Looking back, it is easy to see that much of our social theory was a way to legitimate the exploitation of nature and labor. Looking back it is easy to see that much of the rivalry among nations was really a scramble for cheap resources and cheap labor.

In an important analysis Zolotas has found that economic growth as measured by GNP is not a good guide to economic vitality. Rising expenditures for social overhead (social security, welfare for the poor, crime control, military defense, environmental costs) prevent rises in the GNP from being turned into rises in the standard of living.[10] If there are limits to economic growth, then our entire understanding of modern society must change.[11] All in all, the image of modern society which assumes that it will progress indefinitely because of science, technology, and a rational division of labor must be seriously qualified if not abandoned. A shift from a positive-sum game (a society with a growing pie to share among competitors) to a zero-sum game (a society in which one actor's gain is at the expense of others) will drastically alter the world we have known. In Chapter 1 we asked,

is industrialization sustainable, is an industrial society really possible? and the answer is, perhaps not.

WHAT TYPES OF POLITIES ARE THERE?

A society's polity (politics, government, and law) reflects its economy and history. In complex society, a state emerges to coordinate efforts and interests and to suppress the interests of those that run counter to the most powerful interests. A strong state is associated with an advanced economy (centralized horticultural and agrarian states) and with economic growth out of agrarianism into industrialism. The rise of European capitalism is everywhere associated with royal centralization. The success of societies outside the West in developing is clearly associated with strong, non-"democratic" polities (U.S.S.R., Japan, South Korea, Taiwan, Hong Kong, Singapore, and the People's Republic of China).

This pattern holds for the United States as well. The United States inherited England's advanced (liberal) political forms. It used these forms to help it gain its independence. And it developed taking nationhood, government, law, taxation, and so on for granted. It too developed with the aid of a strong central government (canals, railroads, highways, tariffs, land grant colleges, farm subsidies, federal calvary, and so on). It too developed behind a facade of democracy just like some of the developing countries in the twentieth century: the United States was a growth machine *before* the introduction of universal (white) male suffrage and mass education in the 1850s and had a mature industrial economy *before* the extension in the twentieth century of high school education to the masses, the grant of the vote to women, or effective civil rights for minorities.

It is also clear that societies without a clearly developed and effective polity are having difficulty in developing. Certainly the horticultural and simple "feudal" societies of Africa and Latin America have been deeply handicapped by their inability to develop

---

[10]Xenophon Zolotas, *Economic Growth and Declining Social Welfare* (New York: New York University Press, 1981). For an earlier Marxist perspective that broadens the concept of social overhead to include government tax and spending policy in general, see James O'Connor, *The Fiscal Crisis of the State* (New York: St. Martin's Press, 1973).

[11]For a discussion of limits to economic growth from an environmental perspective and for references to books that have sought to interpret what this means, see the section, Environmental Pressures in Chapter 19.

strong effective governments and a sense of nationhood. Often these governments are consumers rather than producers or facilitators of economic growth. Central American governments (such as in El Salvador, Guatemala, Honduras), black African governments (such as in Tanzania, Zaire, Nigeria) are either parasitical or ineffective facilitators of growth. These autocratic governments contrast sharply with the strong, effective autocratic governments in the People's Republic of China, Korea, and Singapore, which direct government energies at facilitating economic growth (state investment, health, education, and so on).

Horticultural and simple feudal systems do not engender a sense that the elites and mass are part of the same universe. Nobles and landlords are separate and different in a static world. The greater complexity and relative dynamism of feudal-authoritarian systems require nobles and political figures to think in more universal terms, to see their own well-being in the management and relative well-being of the masses, and to coopt intermediate powers into state and "national" purposes. As such, the problems of economic growth and the challenges of external competition presented by the modern world merely continue the world of feudal-authoritarian elites in new forms.

This pattern can be seen in another way. The emergence of "democratic" forms in a non-industrialized society may also be a handicap in modernizing. The classic cases of "premature democracy" are Argentina, Chile, India, and perhaps Australia.[12] Here the state, while autonomous, is also stalemated by society's various classes and interest groups. It is clear that the state can become autonomous and either benefit or oppress society. It is also the case that a state cannot long remain autonomous—even when its actions help a society

develop (India, Brazil, Taiwan, Korea) or aims to restore society or portions thereof to its normal structure (the welfare state in the United States since the 1930s), the state stimulates opposition, new forces to contend with, and eventually loses its former autonomy.[13]

Recent developments in the U.S.S.R. and the People's Republic of China confirm the essential historicity of social development. A strong and creative government in the U.S.S.R. created a society that needed new ways to remain strong and creative. In the People's Republic of China a strong and creative government satisfied most basic needs but unleashed expectations going beyond authoritarianism. And both societies, like all others, found themselves coping with an outer world they neither understood nor could insulate themselves from. The Marxist elites of the U.S.S.R. and China should have had an edge on the ahistorical elites of the capitalist world in understanding history but did not. Ironically, they, like their capitalist counterparts, are reactors to history's ironies rather than the anticipators and shapers of history.

The role of the state in developing or directing society has also led to a heightened interest in analyzing public policy and welfare states on a comparative basis. The knowledge garnered by comparative welfare state analysis promises to improve the adaptive capacities of all countries. The capitalist democracies of Europe have developed their welfare states in different ways but are now fairly similar. The United States lags in providing public services and Japan's welfare state is even less developed than the United States' (in the United States inadequate public services hamper growth and productivity; in Japan low public consumption spurs them). It is also clear that the smaller, less complex societies with socialist governments (Sweden, Australia, New Zealand) have managed to reduce the high inequality of capitalist society to a significant extent (still leaving

---

[12]For Australia's relative decline, see Jocelynne A. Scutt, ed., *Poor Nation of the Pacific? Australia's Future* (Boston: Allen & Unwin, 1985). For a more positive appraisal, see Rodney Maddock and Ian W. McLean, eds., *The Australian Economy In The Long Run* (New York: Cambridge University Press, 1987).

[13]For useful comparative insights into the behavior of states, see Peter Evans, Dietrich Rueschemeyer, and Theda Skocpol, eds., *Bringing The State Back In* (New York: Cambridge University Press, 1985).

them quite unequal). It is also clear that having a fully developed welfare state is compatible with economic growth, and more importantly, with productivity growth (West Germany, for example). In point of fact, the contrast with the United States is so sharp that one must also conclude that the welfare state and a commitment to full employment are the reasons for West Germany's success.[14]

The difficulties that developing countries have had with representative government provide an insight into the fuller meaning of representative government in the West. Economic growth cannot be attributed to representative government since the West grew before and without most of the trappings of what we call representative government. Great Britain in the post-World War II period had the world's most developed system of representative government with the most secure civil liberties, but its pluralist democracy, especially its socialist governments, coincided with a period of economic stagnation. The more authoritarian (large, secure majority) of the Thatcher government gave Britain the legitimated victims (labor and all those hurt in the cutbacks in housing, health care, education, and so on) it needed to spur economic growth. In the same way the greater "democracy" introduced into the United States in the 1960s coincides with political stalemate and sluggish economic growth. All this places the current focus on classifying and judging societies according to whether they have free elections, civil rights, and a free press in context. The real issue is problem solving, not "democracy."

Nonetheless, it is important to classify societies by their polities. The developed capitalist societies all have representative governments. The polities of the developing societies are varied. India, Sri Lanka, and Malaysia are examples of societies with a substantial history of representative government (despite difficulties and lapses). Some of the other developing capitalist societies (with good growth records) have shifted from authoritarian government to representative government; Greece, Spain, Portugal, and South Korea are major examples.[15] Taiwan, also a country with a good growth record, is taking some steps toward political democracy. Indeed, one of the new developments of the late 1980s (perhaps a function of the world system or rather the inability of governments to block out the world-wide dissemination of knowledge of representative government and liberal institutions through world-straddling communication networks) was the movement toward elections in authoritarian countries as varied as South Korea, Pakistan, Paraguay, Poland, Jordan, and, of course, the Soviet Union.

In Latin America, the attempt to establish representative government has met with failure. Costa Rica is the only example of success (because of unique historical reasons). Mexico, despite the trappings of representative government, was a one-party state for most of the twentieth century (until 1988 when economic failure resulted in a near defeat for the ruling party and the emergence of what appears to be a more pluralistic political system). Venezuela, Chile, Argentina, Brazil, Colombia, Peru all have had successes and failures with representative government. The Philippines can be included in this category.

Authoritarian government is the prevailing system of political power in about 130 of the 165 nation states in the world. The developing capitalist world in black Africa is also

---

[14]For good guides in comparative public policy (all deficient, however, in not putting their subject matter in the context of the world economy), see Arnold J. Heidenheimer, Hugh Heclo, and Carolyn Teich Adams, *Comparative Public Policy: The Politics of Social Choice in Europe and America*, 2nd ed. (New York: St. Martin's Press, 1983); Meinolf Dierkes, Hans N. Weiler, and Ariane Berthoin Antal, eds., *Comparative Policy Research: Learning From Experience* (New York: St. Martin's Press, 1987); and Peter Flora, ed., *Growth To Limits: The Western European Welfare States Since World War II* (New York: Walter de Gruyter, 1988), 2 vols.

[15]Small countries, especially the former colonies of Great Britain such as Cyprus and Jamaica, also have functioning systems of representative government.

authoritarian though a few black African nation states have had some success with representative government. The newly industrializing countries (NICS) are authoritarian although South Korea has moved toward representative government and Taiwan is leaning in this direction (Singapore and Hong Kong remain authoritarian). The Arab world and the non-Arab Muslim world are largely "authoritarian" systems. In the Arab world these range from secular one-party government (espousing vague socialist goals) to religiously oriented monarchies. Non-Arab Muslim Bangladesh and Indonesia have straightforward authoritarian (military-backed) governments (as did Pakistan until 1989 when an elected civilian government was installed). A mostly Muslim non-Arab Malaysia, on the other hand, has had a success with representative government).

The socialist world (developed and developing) is also authoritarian, but here too we must distinguish between forms of authoritarianism. In East Germany a strong tradition of nationhood and government has led to an economic success that compares well with the West. Poland, lacking a viable authoritarian tradition, has floundered economically. The Soviet Union, Vietnam, and Cuba are centrally planned systems with stagnant economies (the former two are trying to decentralize their economies in the direction that one-party Hungary has already taken). Yugoslavia is a uniquely one-party state that stresses worker management, decentralized market economics, and mass participation (largely to make a deeply divided multicommunal society work).

Authoritarianism is a large abstraction covering many variations to match the particular strengths and weaknesses of a country's historical, geopolitical experience. Midlarsky and Roberts distinguish three types of (authoritarian) states in Latin America (which we can expand to include the rest of the world):

1. The instrumentalist [authoritarian] state: in El Salvador and Guatemala, the state is openly a direct instrument of class domination (places like this rely on naked force to keep power and can be thought of as nonsocieties. Algeria and Vietnam as colonies are other examples of nonsocieties).

2. The autonomous [authoritarian] personalist state: here the state is led by a caudillo-type ruler, which while serving the class interests of the propertied class, is not directly its agent—allied with factions of the dominant class, the personalist state openly exploits for its own interests. This has also been called "neo-patrimonialism" (Eisenstadt). Examples are Cuba's Batista, Venezuela's Jimenez, the Dominican Republic's Trujillo, Paraguay's Stroessner, and the Somozas of Nicaragua. (One can add the Marcos of the Philippines, some black African societies, some Arab societies, and Iran under the Shah).

3. The autonomous [authoritarian] institutional state: here the state serves a wider variety of property-class interests and can achieve a structured existence apart from them to pursue policies of national development (Mexico and Brazil).[16] This is also known as bureaucratic authoritarianism (G. O'Donnell). In a wider sense, its successful forms range from Prussia and modernizing Japan and Korea to failure in Peru and elsewhere. Given a certain level of complexity, societies of this type evolve means of receiving feedback from below and to legitimate themselves, and often evolve into representative government as the means of insuring the interests of property groups.

The autonomous institutional state has been successful in societies coming out of feudal-authoritarianism with a strong sense of ethnic identity (Prussia, Japan, Korea). When rid of its landlord class, China and Chinese-led Taiwan, also became dynamic under authoritarianism (one left-wing and the other right-wing authoritarianism). To fully understand this dynamism, which runs counter to American assumptions, one must employ an insight by Lucian Pye—referring to what he calls Asian paternalistic authoritarianism, Pye sees Confucian societies fostering group conformity as the source of

---

[16]Manus I. Midlarsky and Kenneth Roberts, "Class, State, and Revolution In Central America" *Journal of Conflict Resolution* 29 (June, 1985): 181–83. Of the three, argue Midlarsky and Roberts, the autonomous personalist state is most vulnerable to multiclass-led revolution.

personal identity, a dependency he shrewdly notes, which is also psychologically liberating since it frees individuals from responsibilities outside their immediate work-family roles.[17]

Authoritarianism must also include the Union of South Africa which is a racially split society in which a diversified white capitalist society has seriously crimped its system of representative government so that the dominant faction can keep control of subordinated whites and the large majority of exploited blacks.

The autonomous institutional state can have a participatory facade for purposes of legitimacy. Examples are the U.S.S.R., Mexico, Thailand, Indonesia. Often this form of state will shift to representative government as, for example, postwar Japan, contemporary Brazil and Korea, and, from appearances, the Soviet Union.

Social-type theorizing has also been deficient because of its failure to fully understand that most societies are multiethnic and that premodern values and beliefs are still powerful throughout the developed as well as developing worlds. Polities, therefore, must also be judged and classified in terms of their ability to cope with multiple ethnic groups. At one end are societies that will not tolerate autonomous ethnic groups—Turkey, Iraq, and Iran, for example, strongly oppose their Kurd minorities. Some black African societies (Nigeria, Zimbabwe, and others), Lebanon, Northern Ireland, Indonesia, Malaysia, Sri Lanka, and Cyprus have all had internal troubles centered on ethnic (or tribal) rivalries. Belgium, Canada, Yugoslavia, the Soviet Union, and Switzerland have all had varying degrees of success in accommodating their ethnic groups. Here again social analysts must be aware that modern populations have again and again shown that they cannot live by the impersonal ethic of either liberalism or Marxism (at least not up to now).

What Types of Political Economies Are There?

Ultimately one must combine questions about a society's economy and polity, and ask, what is the nature of a society's *political economy* and how well is it solving problems? Which are stable, legitimate? Essentially, the successful developed societies are those that can muster coalitions or governments strong enough to tackle problems. This applies to the elitist capitalist coalitions that engendered economic growth in the United States and that saw it through problems including the Great Depression, as well as the elitist systems of Japan and Korea that modernized successfully and the elitist system of Sweden in which socialist governments instituted successful policies of economic growth, urban planning, and social welfare.[18]

The old typologies of society judged adaptive capacity by the growth of science, education, and individualism. Today, we must reverse all these because they are largely consequences of state-led economic growth. The problem of evaluating adaptive capacity has taken another turn. The traditional typologies assumed that social development was marked by a growth in adaptive capability with modern (Western) society at the apex of this process. Today it is hard to think of modern society and its polity as being a functioning, problem-solving entity. Here another peculiarity appears. All polities appear to be having trouble coping with problems, but among developed societies, the United States may be in the worst shape of all in this regard. Alone of all developed societies, the United States has no positive or even realistic image of government or the political process. True, for much of its history, representative government in the United States provided a way for

---

[17]Lucian W. Pye with Mary W. Pye, *Asian Power and Politics: The Cultural Dimensions of Authority* (Cambridge, Mass.: Harvard University Press, 1985).

[18]Marick F. Masters and John D. Robertson in their article, "Class Compromises In Industrial Democracies," *American Political Science Review* 82 (December, 1988): 1183–99, cite evidence that the state in 20 developed capitalist societies (the First World) was able to mute conflicts between capital and labor (between 1965 and 1983) by providing resources (public employment) conducive to class consent and social stability.

elites to interact and reach an accommodation on problems (and to a lesser extent for elites and masses to interact). In recent decades, however, ominous developments have occurred in the American political system: the collapse of political parties, gerrymandered, nonrepresentative electoral districts, issueless campaigns, widespread electoral apathy, wide cleavages in how elites and masses define problems, and the inability of government to act. Not surprisingly, the legitimacy of its political institution is threatened. The relative decline of the United States from the 1960s on was partly unavoidable as other countries grew in power. But a good deal of this decline was due to faulty and outmoded policies, most of them caused by the United States' underdeveloped and stalemated polity.

The liberal social sciences with their narrow specialization and artificial distinctions among institutional areas obscure reality. This is especially pronounced in the United States. Economics and political science are limited and irrelevant to the extent that they do not merge to focus on political economies.[19] No society makes sense unless it is put into its complete historical-institutional setting. Capitalist political economies run a spectrum between those in which the state promotes the semblance of competition through markets (but is really promoting a wide variety of class interests that cannot be synthesized, for example, the United States), and those where the state, still supporting property interests, openly directs a "less complex" economy with policies more easily derived because the solutions are more apparent (for example, West Germany, Japan, Korea). Capitalist political economies, therefore, run the gamut from capitalist market societies to capitalist command societies.

Socialist political economies also run the gamut between socialist market and socialist command societies. Socialist market political economies are found in Yugoslavia, Hungary, and increasingly in China. Socialist Command political economies are still the norm in the U.S.S.R. (with stirrings of liberalization), throughout the Eastern European Soviet bloc (except for Hungary and Poland), Cuba, and Vietnam (the latter is also beginning to liberalize its economy).[20]

Skill at characterizing political economies is important to policy makers. Achieving stability in the Third World, for example, will fail if American policy makers employ vague notions about the benign effects of economic growth. With shades of meaning, American policy makers and social scientists have simply assumed that capitalist dictatorships will evolve into representative government. Thus American policy has stressed political forms, though occasionally there is talk of land reform. What is needed, of course, is an attack on economic concentration in general and an insistence that the fruits of growth be shared. What is needed is an attack not on economic inequality but on types of inequality (those that stem from a failure to develop economic opportunities, free labor markets, education, health care, and the satisfaction of basic needs).[21] What is needed in other words is understanding that economic power is linked to political power and that to talk of changing something without changing the fundamental structure of social power is an

---

[19]Charles E. Lindblom's attempt to do this (*Politics and Markets: The World's Political-Economic Systems*, (New York: Basic Books, 1977) fell flat because Lindblom based his analysis on two false assumptions: that the developed capitalist societies are based on popular rule leading to political pluralism, and on consumer-driven market economies.

[20]The Soviet Union's complexity has led to failure by its centralized planning system because its huge diversity of interests cannot easily be synthesized. Thus, like the United States, it it moving toward a more competitive system in which responsibility for failure can be pinpointed while the ideologically defined system gets the credit for success.

[21]For a variety of approaches, which all fail to understand the dynamics of social system change, see Jeane J. Kirkpatrick, *Dictatorships and Double Standards: Rationalism and Reason in Politics* (New York: Simon and Schuster, 1982) and Hans Binnendijk, ed., with Peggy Nalle and Diane Bendahmane, *Authoritarian Regimes In Transition* (Arlington, Va.: Center for the Study of Foreign Affairs, Foreign Service Institute, U. S. Department of State, 1987).

exercise in formalism and futility. What is needed in understanding the relation between polity and economy (and society) is a fuller sense of the political—which means a fuller sense of human action as contingent, ironic, and historical. For example, a state may work to develop an economy favorable to producers but also create a working class that opposes producers and the state (or the producers may become autonomous).

What is also needed is to place countries and their problems in the world economy or rather world political economy. Nations may be dependent in various ways depending on their particular institutions. They can work to change their position in the international order. Powerful nations can act to further geopolitical causes (which are usually but not always consonant with their economic interests), and powerful nations can also change their position in the relative scheme of things.[22]

To understand social systems, in other words, it is necessary to put them in their distinctive historical and international contexts. It is necessary to know their distinctive internal systems of power. The transition from authoritarianism to representative government will be quite different in Southern Europe and Asia than in Latin America and Africa. American policy makers are badly handicapped by their ahistorical outlook and by their outmoded ideas about how economies and polities work.[23]

_____

[22]For a full-scale analysis displacing the arid concept of *international relations* with the concept, *international political economy,* see Robert Gilpin, with the assistance of Jean M. Gilpin, *The Political Economy of International Relations* (Princeton, N.J.: Princeton University Press, 1987). Gilpin also leaves this world floating insubstantially, however, by separating it (explicitly) from the mainspring of human action, domestic power structures.

[23]For some useful guides to how various societies in Southern Europe and Latin America have handled the transition from less to more developed, and from authoritarianism to representative government, see David Collier, ed., *The New Authoritarianism In Latin America* (Princeton, N.J.: Princeton University Press, 1979), and Guillermo O'Donnell, Philippe C. Schmitter, and Laurence Whitehead, eds., *Transitions From Authoritarian Rule: Prospects for Democracy* (Baltimore, Md.: Johns Hopkins University Press, 1986).

What Types of Modal (Prevalent) Social Relations Are There?

Traditional typologies classified societies by how differentiated they were, or rather by their movement away from primary-personal-ascriptive-particularistic relations toward secondary-impersonal-achievement-universalistic relations. This approach was parochial and biased, bounded by the experience of Westerners. It assumed all societies were headed toward liberal (modern) society. It assumed that vestiges of the past would eventually be erased by the march of modernity. It assumed that social differentiation enhanced efficiency and achievement and assured progress in mastering nature and social problems.

Today we know that socialist societies are also deeply differentiated. We know that there are associational and segmented (multicommunial) societies. We know that the associational societies (whether capitalist or socialist) often are marked by deep ethnic and racial divisions (and are making no progress toward ideal associationalism, that is, a society characterized by self-directed, mobile, achieving individuals).

We also know that modern, developed societies are deeply marked by the past. Modern societies are far from being run or even guided by science, knowledge, professionalism, or education (see the next section). We know that the developed societies have considerable deviance (crime, mental illness, family instability, alcoholism, managerial and professional incompetence, and so on). They are also characterized by collective behavior representing disaffection and instability. Do their social movements yield adaptation or stalemate? How much do contemporary societies rely on deviance for their identity and regeneration? We also know that mass behavior leading to a mass society (associated by some theorists with decay, decline, and breakdown) is not out of the question.

Our Western way of looking at institutions is narrow and unreal in other ways. The political relations known as authoritarianism and the positive functions served by government are a major blindspot in American life, both within its politics and social science. The role of religion in facilitating social cohesion and adaptation is also real and does not fit our traditional social typologies. The family is also misperceived. The family stabilizes society but the United States, thanks to its erratic economy, underdeveloped welfare state, and idealization of individualism, has put it under great pressure and has no family policies. The family can also be dynamic (or static). In Japan the strong family tradition divides up labor so that the absorption of the female with family matters allows the male complete freedom to put in a long, intense work day. In Taiwan, the strong Chinese family system had grafted on it a dynamic family-based entrepreneurialism.

What Types of Normative/Value Systems Are There?

Traditional typologies and social science assumed a polar opposition and a transition between tradition and modernity—in short, the world was heading in the direction of science and secular humanism. This ideology dominates both developed capitalist and socialist societies. We now know that there is no unitary, static, antimodern tradition and there is no easily identified modernity. Some traditional systems resist new ideas and values (African magic, peasant customs, Islam in Iran), some combine with them (Islam in Saudi Arabia or Malaysia), and some can actively both support the status quo and facilitate extensive modernization (for example, Confucianism can serve landlords and emperors as well as capitalists and prime ministers). We also know that modernity can mean many things: for example, science and technology in the service of better living standards or the imperialism of Nazi Germany or Imperial Japan.

The sociology of science is crucial for understanding modern society. For one thing, science cannot easily substitute for deeply held emotions. We now know that religion, ethnicity, and nationalism are important forces in the world (no matter that these

are often ways of expressing economic and political frustrations and aspirations). It is important to remember that Protestantism in the West emerged *after* the rise of capitalism and is best thought of as a religious revival offering certainty and comfort in a surging world of change. We know that fundamentalist Protestantism in the American South is a response to industrialization after 1945 and the intrusion of foreign ideas and gods. And we can be sure that concern for ethnic identity, whether in the United States, the Middle East, inside the Soviet Union, and so on, emerges from the unsettling pace of economic and social change.

There are other things we must know about science. Over time, many took it on faith that modern science would generate the knowledge that modern society needs. Is this true? There is now considerable skepticism about the ability of natural and social science, the educational world, the political process, the news media, or the voluntary sector to generate the kinds of knowledge we need, or to see to it that knowledge is located in the proper persons and social statuses. Here again we need to raise questions about attempts to characterize modern society by its professions, its universalistic symbol system, or its knowledge-technology base.

With the exception of Max Weber (and the social philosopher Pitirim Sorokin), social typologists have also taken the value system of capitalism for granted. But was Max Weber right about the destructive power of formal rationality? Has the precontractual solidarity of capitalism (derived from the Judaic-Christian tradition, feudal traditions, and the secular humanism of early liberalism) been eroded by the ceaseless calculations and reciprocal debunkings of its competing individuals, elites, and bureaucracies? Is even the strong precontractual solidarity of ethnocentric Japan eroding under the diversifying pressures of advanced capitalism?

Mainstream sociology assumed that modern society had a dominant value system (Soviet elites also characterize their society in the same terms). Is this true? Is there a dominant American belief system or are there rival sources of truth and morality? Are American norms integrated, clear, and operational, or are they marked by contradiction, vagueness, and unreality? How much consensus does the United States have in the sense of agreement or homogeneity of beliefs and values, especially about the ultimate nature of reality, the social division of labor, and the basic goals of human life? Above all, does it have norms and values that effectively address problems and result in functional, problem-solving behavior?

In recent decades we have come to question the alleged effectiveness and rationality of science and the professions. Many theorists have begun to notice that objectivity is only that which elites agree on. Others have noticed that elites are beginning to agree on less. Still others have noticed that the generation of knowledge is done selectively in keeping with elite interests, and that the general realm of science, scholarship, and information has gradually been transformed into private property (a process that the Reagan administration of the 1980s accelerated).[24] Depictions of modern society as under the guidance of science are wide of the mark in other ways. Illiteracy and functional illiteracy rates are high. Education in general (from college graduates to high school dropouts) may not have improved if judged by whether people know what they need to know in order to function in their various social statuses. Astrology is alive and flourishing. Even the most transparent confidence racket finds its market. Eighteen state legislatures have equated the biblical version of creation with that of biology. The Reagan administration of the 1980s had one foot in a science fiction future and the other in the Old Testament. Organized, civil, and popular religion join popular culture in creating a mythological world view

that depoliticizes socially created problems. Looked at in this light, the United States is far different than the way our social typologies and textbooks depict it.

We now know that the normative-value world is derived from social experience and reflects the structure of social power. By and large, knowledge is what power groups say it is. In the United States, knowledge is essentially private property masked by the ideology of education, IQ, free press, and research (professionalism).

Any inquiry into a society's normative-value system should ask, what method (or methods) does a society use to obtain truth: magic, intuition, revelation, deduction, induction, "free" science, "use" science, and so on? What are the sanctions for its normative-institutional systems (supernatural versus natural; moral versus nonmoral; custom versus positive law; history; evolution; psychology, biology, race, sex)? How much consensus does it have in the sense of agreement or homogeneity of beliefs and values, especially about the ultimate nature of reality, the social division of labor, and the basic goals of human life? Another way of asking these questions is to analyze societies by the extent of conflict (either recognized or unrecognized, overt or covert, violent or peaceful)—conflict that reflects disagreement among classes, castes, estates, ethnic and racial groups, and contradictions among institutions, statuses, norms, and values. And above all, one must ask, exactly how do norms and values work in given sociocultural (power) contexts; exactly what norms and values animate policy makers and citizens?

What Types of Modal Personalities Are There?

Different societies and different stages of social development produce different types of personality. What are these? Some of the familiar terms in this mode of inquiry are: Apollonian versus Dionysian; traditional versus dynamic; and achievement, Protestant-bourgeois, inner-directed, authoritarian, modern man, bureaucratic, and socialist personality

---

[24]Anito R. Schiller and Herbert I. Schiller, "The Privatizing of Information; Who Can Own What America Knows?" *The Nation* (April 17, 1982): 461–63; Diane Smith, "The Commercialization and Privatization of Government Information" *Government Publications Review* (January–February, 1985): 45–63; and David Dickson, *The New Politics of Science* (New York: Pantheon Books, 1984).

types.[25] How much do we know about comparative personalities? Here one must include recent quality-of-life studies in which scholars have been probing the world of subjectivity in new ways.[26] Despite its large number of psychologists, perhaps because of them, the United States does not really understand personality. Here it should be assumed that personality derives from social experience and that a personality should be judged by how well it performs social roles. To understand societies we must avoid psychological explanations (innate drives or needs, whether emotional or cognitive) and focus on how the psychology is shaped by various power structures. We must be aware of the many mixtures of beliefs and values that can be lodged in the human personality (see the previous section on normative-value systems). We must ask, how is a society socializing its members, and is it producing adaptive citizens appropriate for that society? And in doing comparative personality studies, we must not neglect the United States. There is considerable evidence that Americans have settled on a narrow definition of individualism, one in which earlier versions emphasizing civic responsibility and participation are giving way to self-centeredness.[27] There is evidence that American society is not socializing its members to acquire a competent personality, that is, the ability to perform social roles. Certainly, Americans, both ordinary citizens and policy makers, are ignorant, indeed mistaken, about the nature of other societies.

Beyond our borders lies a world of diverse personality types. What do we know of them at their core: what do we know of them in terms of their nuances? Do we know foreigners well enough to interpret what they mean when they speak or act? Do we understand the diverse negotiating styles that emerge from different sociocultural backgrounds?[28] We must come to understand the personalistic personality of Latin America (and the Philippines) and distinguish it from the personalism of Confucian, Muslim, and Hindu societies. We need more studies like Lucien Pyle's *Asian Power and Politics: The Cultural Dimensions of Authority.*[29] Pyle's effort to explain the success of Asian societies is not successful because he does not use a multi-causal approach stressing economic and political variables. Nonetheless, he provides some valuable clues to personality by making subtle distinctions among various kinds of Confucianism and by exploring personality in Muslim and Hindu Asia.

WHAT TYPES OF SOCIETIES ARE THERE?

Even Development: The Ideal Developed Society

Our standard for classifying contemporary societies will be the *ideal* of a society that satisfies basic material needs, socializes its

---

[25]Comparative studies have been greatly enhanced by the superb *Handbook of Cross-Cultural Psychology,* ed. Harry C. Triandis and William Wilson Lambert (Boston: Allyn and Bacon, 1980), 6 vols. Also extremely useful is Ruth H. Munroe, Robert L. Munroe, and Beatrice B. Whiting, eds., *Handbook of Cross-Cultural Human Development* (New York: Garland, 1981).

[26]Alexander Szalai and Frank M. Andrews, ed., *The Quality of Life: Comparative Studies* (Beverly Hills, Calif.: Sage, 1981).

[27]Robert N. Bellah, Richard Madsen, William M. Sullivan, Ann Swidler, and Steven M. Tipton, *Habits of the Heart: Individualism and Commitment in American Life* (Berkeley, Calif.: University of California, 1985). Bellah and his associates based their thesis on selected interviews with white middle-class Americans of both sexes. Norval D.

Glenn has treated their thesis as a hypothesis and has found it confirmed by attitude studies conducted between the 1950s and 1980s; see his "Social Trends In the United States: Evidence From Sample Surveys," *Public Opinion Quarterly* 51 (Winter, 1987), 4, Pt. 2: 109–26. By and large, Americans have withdrawn allegiance from political parties, religion, and family, and opted for a self-centered individualism.

[28]Two extremely useful publications, emphasizing the different ways in which the peoples of the world perceive the negotiation process, are Allen R. Janger and Ronald E. Berembeim, *External Challenges to Management Decisions: A Growing International Business Problem* (New York: Conference Board, 1981) and Hans Binnendijk, ed., *National Negotiating Styles* (Arlington, Va.: Foreign Service Institute, U.S. Department of State, 1987).

[29]Cambridge, Mass.: Harvard University Press, 1985.

members for positive social roles, keeps its members motivated and in meaningful structured relations, resolves disputes, solves problems by providing its elites and citizens with informed choices, and has a foreign policy that helps other societies do the same. The ideal society is secular-scientific (though not unmindful of the social value of tradition, ritual, ethnicity, religion, and the need for meaningful group life at all levels). It is historical in outlook and pluralistic in its power structure. Its economy is distinctly subordinated to social purposes, said purposes determined politically by an organized public.

The concept of *developed society* is a commonplace of contemporary thinking but represents a confused merger of ideal and practice. Present-day, so-called developed societies only approximate the ideals that they allegedly embody. To be a developed society in the literature of social science means to have made the transition from agriculture to industry and to be committed to economic growth. In the ideal society, the choice of stopping or slowing economic growth must also be a choice. In the literature of social science, the developed societies have representative government and elites are recruited through achievement processes. Those who know that representative government is not the same thing as democracy (or pluralism) and that we are far from having learned how to develop competent elites will understand why the concept *developed society* has no examples. The so-called developed societies are uneven versions of full development—thus *uneven development* constitutes our first type of society in the contemporary empirical world.

Uneven Development: The Historical Developed Society

All the societies now called developed, including Great Britain, France, the United States, Germany, the Soviet Union, and Japan are really in a state of uneven development. This concept refers to societies that have modernized (become industrial) but have done so by continuing many feudal ideas and values.[30] Uneven development means that the economy is not geared to use values. It means that the economy is ecologically destructive, investment in basic infrastructure and in social facilities is neglected, society is not under the direction of elites guided by knowledge or by feedback from below, and science and education are not geared to promoting awareness and political sophistication on the part of elites or masses. Uneven development means that our most advanced societies have not yet figured out how to solve social problems on a routine basis, or rather, it means that industrial elites routinely use or rely on unemployment, poverty, bankruptcy, crime, and depoliticized polities to solve their own problems. When these don't work they are not adverse to blaming victims and foreigners, resorting to violence against their own people, exploiting weaker countries, or going to war.

Uneven development and an incapacity to solve problems are undoubtedly attributable to the concentrated and at the same time highly diversified economies that are characteristic of these advanced systems. Elites have succeeded in industrializing either through middle-class revolutions, authoritarian-military revolutions, or authoritarian revolutions in the name of the masses. They run either private or public economies, but all advanced industrial systems have elites that sit astride concentrated economies. A successful attack on social and intersocietal problems, therefore, is difficult (if not impossible) because existing power groups must generate solutions that would undermine their power.

The advanced unevenly developed societies think of themselves and their outer world in metaphysical terms (that is, as an unchanging world based on simple truths). None understands that human societies are caught in history's web, a history whose truths are profoundly antimetaphysical, which deceives by being both static and dynamic, both easy to understand and mysterious, both filled with surface phenomena and deep latent currents that whiplash those mired in metaphysics.

---

[30]See the section, Agrarian Feudalism and the Modern World, in Chapter 2.

Dependent Development

Many societies have industrialized but are not self-sustaining entities. Here we must think in terms of a spectrum. All advanced industrial systems are dependent to some important degree on the world economy. Japan and Germany are more dependent on exports than the United States and the Soviet Union, but no society is self-sufficient.

Beyond these advanced, unevenly developed societies are societies that have industrialized but are both unevenly developed and deeply dependent on the outer world, for example, Brazil, Mexico, the Republic of Korea, Yugoslavia, Taiwan, Hong Kong, and Singapore (the latter three are deeply dependent on their export economies, indeed their essential nature is a function of the open American and European markets, and in the case of Hong Kong, because of China's need for foreign trade even before the post-1978 reforms).

Beyond these lie various societies that are unevenly developed, cannot industrialize, and are dependent on the outer world to various extents. Peru and Nigeria fit this pattern as do the Philippines, Argentina and the other societies (except Brazil) on the South American continent.[31] The same is true of black Africa, most of the Arab world, and most of the non-Arab Muslim world (Iran, Pakistan, and Indonesia).

A number of countries are not yet industrialized but show some balance in their development, for example, India, Malaysia, Tanzania, Cuba, China, Greece, and Australia. Of these only China gives evidence that it will achieve a breakthrough to sustained industrialization.

Mature Dependency

There may be a need for a category called *mature dependency* to single out societies that have developed but have had their growth retarded by dependency. Canada is one example but there may be more, for example, Finland, Australia, or the Soviet bloc countries.[32]

Underdevelopment

An *underdeveloped society* is one that has been developed as a supplier of raw materials and cheap labor, thereby acquiring a structure that prevents it from developing toward industrialization. A classic instance is El Salvador (see Chapter 5) but this term probably fits many of the countries of Latin America, Africa, and Asia. In some ways, this category can include the countries that cannot develop an effective national government or nationhood such as Peru (see Chapter 13).

ARE SOCIETIES CONVERGING?

Sociology and the other social sciences had a theory of convergence that was part of the modernization theory of the 1950s and 1960s. Convergence theory was central to the limited (noncomparative, apolitical) outlook of American liberalism. Today the main thinking about the relation of the world's societies to each other and trends in their relations is being done by dependency and world system theorists. World system and dependency theorists have predicted a general convergence among core (capitalist) countries and a divergence between them and the rest of the world with perhaps growing homogeneity among all the countries in the semiperiphery (dependent development) and the periphery (underdevelopment). Peacock, Hoover, and Killian have attempted to test world system theory by analyzing the relation of selected countries over a 31-year period (1950–80). The authors found only limited support for world system theory: the core countries are becoming more equal but semiperipheral and peripheral countries are not converging internally and total world inequality is not increasing.[33]

---

[31]Even oil-rich Venezuela and Mexico have found crossing the threshold of industrialization difficult.

[32]For a discussion of Canada in this context, see Chapter 15.

[33]Walter Gillis Peacock, Greg A. Hoover, and Charles D. Killian, "Divergence and Convergence In Interna-

The study by Peacock, Hoover, and Killian is seriously deficient in a number of respects. By focusing on world system theory, they encounter the issue of whether socialist societies are in the world system, and solve it by excluding them, thus their analysis is not about the world's societies but only the capitalist ones. Second, their choice of countries to represent the core, semiperiphery, and periphery is questionable to say the least. Included in their list of 28 semiperipheral countries are Austria, Denmark, Finland, Norway, Sweden, Switzerland, Australia, and New Zealand! Third, the periphery category is weighted against the truly poor countries (least-developed countries and low-income countries as defined by the United Nations and the World Bank). Fourth, controlling for population should not really matter since population, like radios, available doctors, literacy, calories, and so on, is a function of what kind of society one is analyzing. Finally, while their data end in 1980, the authors could easily have noted that global inequality increased dramatically in the 1980s largely through a deterioration in the position of the Third World, whether peripheral or semiperipheral.

Convergence and Divergence Among Industrial Systems

The developed capitalist societies have many similarities despite their varying ideologies. Putting some differences aside, they are similar in their income distribution, economic concentration, urbanization, population dynamics, standard of living, economic growth, and welfare states.[34] Their differences are important, however, because all have experienced another similarity, a slowdown in economic growth, productivity, and standard

---

tional Development: A Decomposition Analysis of Inequality in the World System" *American Sociological Review* 53 (December, 1988): 838–52.

[34]The United States is a deviant among the developed capitalist societies in that it contains a variety of social pathologies that are the worst in that comparison group. It probably compares poorly in many areas with developed socialist societies.

of living, and perhaps they can learn from each other. For example, national health insurance in capitalist Europe and in Canada provides health care at least as good as in the United States at considerably lower cost. Worker retraining programs seem to aid productivity. And so on.

The capitalist and socialist industrial systems are also not as different as many think. Exploring the similarities here might lead to better relations. For example, the United States and the Soviet Union are the only two societies that have industrialized on a continent-wide basis, both have mass production economies, and both have experienced difficulties in adapting to the new world economy.

The Third World: Convergence Toward Disaster?

The Third World is huge and generalizations about it are difficult to come by. Except for a few dynamic Asian societies, and a few (not most) oil-rich countries, the economic and social conditions of the Third World have deteriorated over the past decade or two. Determining how much of this change is due to the countries themselves and how much due to the inability of the developed capitalist societies to manage their affairs better has first-order priority. The growing gap between rich and poor nations, and the growing poverty and debt of the Third World makes the liberal concept of trickle-down economics as false internationally as it is domestically.

Prospects for a World Culture

The industrial West (along with Japan and even the developed socialist bloc) have sent elements of their cultures to the far corners of the earth. All countries now have cars, radios, television, powdered milk, soft drinks, and blue jeans. But many countries resist cultural elements that do not harmonize with their mores. Even Japan, an advanced industrial country, resisted individualism and does not yet have much of a feminist movement. But the greatest resistance is to industrialization itself. Of the non-Western countries only those with a background in Chinese culture have really committed themselves to industry: Japan, South Korea, Taiwan, Hong Kong, Singapore, and now China. This is not to minimize the achievement of India, Brazil, and other countries, only to say that these latter countries have not yet made the transition to a viable industrialization.

We must not forget, therefore, that there has always been deep resistance to Western imperialism and to its cultural penetration and standardization. Today religion is the foremost barrier to modernization (either toward capitalism or socialism). Certain forms of Islamic religion are especially hostile to the secular values of the West and industrial development. Religion is still a powerful force in all parts of the world and is far from having made its peace with modernity. As Hinduism, it resists change in India. In Hispanic societies, Roman Catholicism is still a conservative force although some elements of the Roman Catholic clergy have tried to promote reform. Even in the United States, powerful religious currents run counter to secularism, science, and humanism.

The various regions and blocs of the world are quite diverse. The Third World is filled with military and communist dictatorships. The Arab world is very diverse. Black African countries are having extreme difficulty in feeding themselves, let alone entering the modern world. And the superpowers have shown only a glimmer of understanding that they have much in common and many mutual interests.

Thus it is a mistake to think that a world culture is emerging that will integrate the societies of the world. True, the United Nations provides a common forum for discussion. Many dissimilar societies work in and derive mutual benefit from its many specialized agencies. The United Nations has had some success in its peacekeeping missions, especially in recent years. A body of international law has developed and the World Court's authority has been enlarged. All of the world's societies are dependent on the world-market economy and maintain a wide network of economic and other relations. But when all this is said the fact remains that the planet is now inhabited by 165 sovereign nation states most of which have very little in common and few accepted ways of interacting. The countries of the world have made little progress in establishing problem-solving mechanisms and they have a long history of resorting to violence to solve problems. In short, the present intersocietal system has many of the earmarks of anomie.

But intersocietal anomie has its roots in the domestic power structures of the various societies. A world culture is in its infancy but the prospects for cooperation and peace are not promising as long as the world's domestic power structures are not geared to democratically derived policies that ensure food, shelter, work, a protected environment, and meaningful social roles for all.

Prospects for a World Government

There is little likelihood of a world government in the foreseeable future. Government arises from social complexity and there will no doubt be world pressures for world government as the complexity of world affairs continues to grow and affects people within their societies. The United Nations and its specialized agencies may well form the core of an effective future world polity. There are numerous private, public, and quasipublic institutions at the intersocietal level that can be built on, but the major world powers must find world government in their interests and at present they fear any popular world government because they would be outvoted by the Third World. However, incremental steps may occur—for example, in 1987 the U.S.S.R. proposed an increase in the mandatory jurisdiction of the World Court and in 1989 agreed to accept its jurisdiction over a number of areas that it had formerly said were matters of sovereign right.

THE ANOMIC WORLD SOCIETY

The planet is inhabited by 165 dissimilar societies, most of them problem societies. It is no longer easy for social analysts or elites to distinguish (or understand) internal from external relations. Societies, now more interdependent than ever, have few ways of interacting that can be relied on to solve disputes and satisfy mutual needs. Even the two superpowers cannot impose their will and have had great difficulty in coping with the external environment of other countries. In addition, the powerful thrust of technology has created many novel conditions for international relations. The destructiveness of contemporary military technology has produced an unprecedented situation: the possibility that war could end life on the planet. Even a limited nuclear war could usher in a nuclear winter. The basic processes of economic development spill out beyond national boundaries. Acid rain produced in Ohio contaminates Canada; acid rain generated in one European country affects ten other countries. The clearing of the Amazon forest could adversely affect the climate of North America. Industrial waste could gradually accumulate in the atmosphere, destroy the ozone that protects us from harmful rays from the sun, or block the escape of heat from the earth, in effect warming it, beginning a meltdown of polar ice, and creating catastrophic flooding.

With the emergence of the 165 new nation states from the middle ages on (most of them since 1945), hundreds of territorial disputes have also emerged. Ethnic minorities and stateless people clamor for new arrangements. Internal struggles and regional disputes are more important to many countries than arguments between the United States and the U.S.S.R., although some regional disputes such as Vietnam and its neighbors and the Arab-Israel confrontation are also linked to superpower rivalry.

The bipolar confrontation between the superpowers is softened somewhat by the fact that the United States and the Soviet Union have a number of important common interests. Both see the developing nations as suppliers of raw and semiprocessed materials. As naval powers both have a stake in keeping the world's waterways open to international traffic. There is no better example of the strange bedfellow world of intersocietal pol-

itics than the fact that the United States, which banned the sale of wheat to the U.S.S.R. and organized a boycott of the Moscow Olympics after the Soviet invasion of Afghanistan in 1979, continued to supply it with advanced oil drilling and production equipment for fear that Soviet oil production would decline and thus create excessive demand pressures on world oil supplies.

Neither the United States nor the Soviet Union is acting to create international institutions that can solve problems. As the leader of the powerful bloc of capitalist societies, the United States bears a special responsibility in this regard. Like other societies, it pursues interests in terms of its internal power structure. Far from developing a framework for resolving world conflicts, which would require acknowledging its dependence on others and its fallibility, it has proclaimed itself the world's judge and declared its resolve not to share the planet's land and oceanbeds or space with anyone that is not its ally or client.

In the unique multiple-system world, all actors are involved in a global system but in different ways. Some societies are interested mostly in local or regional interests. Some are involved in more than one region. Others are involved locally and in their own regions but are also interested in broadly defined world problems. Some are active at all levels and in all world problems. Nonetheless, the world's many dissimilar societies and blocs have few accepted ways of behaving toward each other. Worse still, all think of themselves as essentially sound and seek the causes of their problems in the malevolent actions of outsiders. This holds for the United States as much as any other society. The American foreign policy establishment has no idea that the world's major problem society is the United States. The American people and government have a long and settled faith that the United States is an exception to the corruptions that have always beset societies whereas the reality is otherwise.

In recent decades the American government and national legislature have reflected the growing complexities of American society. What coherence and unity there is in

American foreign policy consists of simplistic slogans and well-intentioned blunders. In an important sense there is no American foreign policy. In another sense the reality of American foreign and domestic policy furthers the interests of American corporate and professional elites.

The incoherence in American foreign policy, reflecting the incoherence of American society, is also reflected in the organization of the federal executive and in the policy-making organs of the general polity. A large and diverse set of agencies formulate incoherent and ineffective policies under the assumption that order and stability are the natural condition of humankind. They accept no responsibility for being part of the cause of world disorders. Assuming order as a natural condition, American elites are constantly surprised by the frequency and seriousness of the outbursts against their country: Pearl Harbor, Korea, Cuba, Vietnam, Iran, Central America, Lebanon.

Private organizations have also failed to disabuse Americans of their conceit that their society is an exception to run-of-the-mill humanity. Private organizations are also powerful promoters of poor policies. The theory of intersocietal relations from 1500 to 1945 focused narrowly on internation state relations. Even today it is not sufficiently recognized that the state-centric model of world affairs is much too narrow and that many other actors such as intergovernmental bodies, churches, ethnic lobbies, criminal groups, individuals, labor unions, militant liberation groups, professional associations, law firms, foundations, and a wide variety of powerful, geocentric corporations play a significant role in the fortunes of the world's peoples. Needless to say, such quasipublic and private groups add to the contradictions and confusions in the relations among societies.

American social science has not been much help in clarifying the anomic nature of intersocietal relations. Mainstream economics has simply extended the idea of laissez-faire to the world economy, completely unaware that free trade is simply a cover to legitimate the selfish interests of powerful countries (like England in the nineteenth century and the United States in the twentieth) and multinational corporations. Mainstream political science and its subspecialty, international relations, along with sociology, have only limited conceptions of the real forces at work in the world. Introductory sociology texts continue to ignore foreign relations in their depiction of American society and their concluding chapters on social change are an embarrassment to the profession. By and large, American social science takes the United States at face value and assumes that it is or can be a force for good.

A realistic assessment of intersocietal relations sees them as a dumping ground for internal frustrations and a way to divert attention from internal failure. Another cause of anomie in worlds affairs is that the elites of the world are facing different problems and cannot easily negotiate or cooperate. The United States' go-it-alone policy at the United Nations has isolated it in that forum. Despite some promising changes, it continues the Cold War practice of linking all troubles to world communism. The United States has acted under the assumption that the Soviet economy, being socialist, is fundamentally flawed and can thus be pressured and outspent into a fatal decline. The Soviets in turn have many false assumptions about the capitalist economy. Despite their many similarities and common problems, there is much pluralistic ignorance between the United States and Soviet Union. Neither senses that all developed societies are problematic. Nor can modern society remain a taken-for-granted backdrop for sociology. Sociology's research, textbooks, teaching, social-type theorizing, and politics will all change once sociology begins to ask, is an industrial society really possible, and if so, how?

GLOSSARY

Adaptive capacity The ability of a society to perform social functions (provide itself with economic necessities and new members, socialize its members to perform social roles, and settle internal and external disputes). *Also see* **Anomie, Elite, Institutions, Rationalization, Technology,** and **Uneven development.**

Advanced horticultural society A horticultural society using more advanced tools and techniques of production. As a result inequality increases, hereditary statuses emerge, symbolic forms justifying the new society are elaborated, and elites become warlike and expansionist.

Agrarian era Emerged slowly from 10,000 to 5,000 years ago and lasted until the rise of capitalism in the West (1200–1800), the spread of the capitalist world economy (1450–1945), and the demise of most feudal elites (1650–1950).

Agrarian society (*also see* **Feudal-authoritarian**) A highly unequal ascriptive society with a central state based on the cultivation of large plots using advanced technology (for example, plow, irrigation, fertilizer, crop rotation, human and animal energy) and legitimated by abstract beliefs and norms (universal religion).

Agriculture A form of farming as distinguished from horticulture (in which families cultivate gardens using simple tools) in which large plots of land (fields) are cultivated with the use of plows, irrigation, fertilizer, terracing, and human and animal energy.

Anomic society A society whose institutions (and thus norms and values) are profoundly contradictory, whose power groups are in conflict, and which characteristically generates large amounts of deviance, including revolutionary movements. Characterizes England in the seventeenth century, France in the eighteenth century, and many Third World societies in the post-World War II period, for example, Vietnam. *Also see* **Anomie, Conflict perspective,** and **Functional analysis.**

Anomie A social condition induced by change under which social control becomes ineffective. Instead of being in a congruent set of statuses (and thus norms and values), individuals find themselves in statuses whose norms and values are vague, contradictory, or lacking. As a result individuals experience personality upsets and deviate from expected behavior. Anomie can be present in various social situations at the microlevel or can be characteristic of an entire society or of the relation among societies (the nation states of the West from 1450 to 1945; the world system today).

The term *anomie* is associated with Emile Durkheim but the idea is a staple of Western conflict social theory (which generally focuses not on individuals but on groups and social classes).

In an important use of the concept, Robert K. Merton has argued that Americans experience emotional problems and commit deviant behaviors because all are subject to classless norms and values (the universalistic Protestant-bourgeois success ethic) while at the same time many are held back by the very real, *de facto* class system.

The deviance that results from anomie can exist without disturbing the stability of society—indeed, it can contribute to it as appears to be the case in the United States. But anomie can also undermine a social system, be it a family, craft, a whole society, or an intersocietal structure.

Authoritarianism A large abstraction covering many variations and serving many ideologies. Most forms, from feudal through industrial societies, serve property groups but authoritarianism has also served socialist societies. See Autonomous institutional state, Autonomous personalist state, Bureaucratic authoritarianism, Instrumentalist state, Neo-patrimonial state.

Autonomous institutional state An authoritarian polity in which the state serves a variety of property-class interests and can achieve a structured existence apart from them to pursue policies of national development (Mexico and Brazil). This is also known as Bureaucratic Authoritarianism (G. O'Donnell). In a wider sense, its successful forms range from Prussia and modernizing Japan and Korea to failure in Peru and elsewhere.

Autonomous personalist state An authoritarian polity in which the state led by a caudillo-type (strongman) ruler, serves the class interests of the propertied class but is not directly its agent. Allied with factions of the dominant class, the personalist state openly exploits its members for its own interests. This has also been called "neo-patrimonialism" (Eisenstadt).

Examples are Cuba's Batista, Venezuela's Jimenez, the Dominican Republic's Trujillo, Paraguay's Stroessner, the Somozas of Nicaragua, the Marcos of the Philippines, some black societies, some Arab societies, and Iran under the Shah.

Bourgeoisie *See* Liberalism, Middle class, Revolution from the middle.

Bureaucracy A hierarchy of statuses organized to implement or administer the policies of power groups efficiently and responsibly. Those who own or control the bureaucracy (nobility, business people, religious leaders, elected leaders, and so on) can hold employees responsible for carrying out orders and policies by supplying them with equipment, recruiting them according to qualifications, making their work a career, and requiring written records in an explicit chain of command. *Also see* **Patrimonial administration.**

Bureaucratic authoritarianism *See* **Autonomous institutional state.**

Capitalism An economy and society in which the means of producing goods and services are privately owned and used for income (profit). In such a society basic investment decisions are made by private elites (with the support of government). Such a society requires legally free labor (that is, labor that can be hired and fired) and extensive political supports such as the protection of property, currency, credit, roads, education, health, and government tax, spending, or credit policies to keep the economy on an even keel. Capitalist societies vary in how much they rely on markets and in how open their markets are. Markets help provide business people, governments, and consumers with predictability and yield relative efficiency but they are also unpredictable and generate insecurity and assorted problems; in fact, pure or free markets are extremely rare and short lived because power groups, for example, consumer organizations, churches, environmental groups, labor unions, and especially government, business, and professional groups, continuously seek to control and even to monopolize them. *Also see* **State capitalism.**

Colonialism See Imperialism.

Command economy A type of socialist economy based on the public ownership of productive facilities in which decisions about production and distribution are made by political elites using multiyear plans. The goals of socialism (in contrast to market capitalism) stress full employment and food, shelter, education, and health care for all before efficiency, new products and services, and consumption for leisure, comfort, and luxury.

Communism A future state of society hypothesized by Marx in which the distribution of goods and services would be based on need; a society in which there is no undeserved inequality and all are free to fulfill their potential.

Comparative-historical method The awareness that comparison is the essence of rational-scientific thought and the systematic search for the variables that cause human behavior. To be genuinely comparative one must go beyond one's own society because the variables that constitute it have invariably been frozen into a taken-for-granted world that misleads even elites, including social scientists.

Scholars in comparative studies fall into schools, for example, liberals and socialists, with some emphasizing a functionalism that sees society veering toward harmony and progress through the growth of knowledge and morality, and with others seeing the essence of society centered in conflict (in values and beliefs and/or economic institutions). Some comparative scholars focus on variables that can be quantified while other tend to stress qualitative variables. Some scholars focus on variables such as per capita income, literacy, and energy consumption, assuming that facts and values can be separated, while others focus on institutions and national power structures, assuming that facts and values cannot be separated (the latter is the focus of this text). *Also see* **Conflict perspective, Cultural relativism, Ethnocentrism, False consciousness, Functional analysis,** and **Sociology of knowledge.**

Conflict perspective A viewpoint that stresses the conflicts in society as the cause of behavior. Liberals tend to assume that the conflicts of capitalism can be solved through reform; radicals, especially Marxists, assume that the conflicts of capitalism are so pronounced that only a new society can resolve them.

Convergence theory An argument by liberal theorists that all societies, especially the developed capitalist and even socialist societies, are becoming similar in their basic structures. The argument goes further to specify that the driving force of these similarities is knowledge and technology and that all advanced societies are entering a postindustrial phase of declining ascriptive inequality and increasing mobility and adherence to achievement criteria (meri-

tocracy). Socialists and increasingly, perhaps most, liberal thinkers have rejected or seriously qualified this view.

Cultural relativism The belief that behavior, material objects, and values and norms make sense and can be evaluated only in terms of the cultural context in which they occur. For example, a low-level of public services helps productivity in Japan but harms it in the United States; a low birth rate helps Greece but hurts Israel; individualism may have been more useful to the United States in the eighteenth and nineteenth centuries than it is in the twentieth century. *Also see* **Ethnocentrism, False consciousness, Functional analysis, Sociology of knowledge.**

Culture The complete set of values and norms that order (and disorder) the lives of society's members. The values and norms of a people considered as a complete range of symbols includes definitions of people, statuses, groups, history, nature, artifacts (technology and the like), space, time, the hereafter, and so on. Definitions of culture vary but most analysts stress that culture has a powerful influence on behavior and is socially learned and not the direct result of biopsychic forces.

Democracy A society based on and for the benefit of ordinary people and the poor, that is, the majority who do not have much economic power. Strictly speaking, democracy is an ideal—there are no examples though both capitalist and socialist societies call themselves democracies.

Dependent development A society that escapes or moves beyond underdevelopment (*see* **Underdeveloped society**) to include a significant manufacturing and service sector but which finds it difficult to cross the threshold to self-sustaining industrialization and escape vulnerability to world markets.

Developing-countries *See* **Third World, Less developed world, Modernization.**

Development A change from one type of society to another, for example, hunting-gathering to horticulture, agrarian to industrial (*also see* **Dependent development, Mature dependency, Underdeveloped society, Uneven development**).

Elite Used interchangeably with the term "power group" to mean historically and institutionally created individuals and power groups who emanate from distinctive economies or historically unique situations and who can make decisions, especially about the use of economic resources, affecting the life of both their own and other societies. Some use the term differently to refer to individuals who allegedly have innate qualities that propel them to leadership. *Also see* **Adaptive capacity.**

Ethnocentrism Literally, to make one's ethnic group or society the center of the universe. Sociologically, it refers to the tendency of all societies (their power groups) to make their own values and norms absolute and to use them to judge (and misjudge) their own and other societies. *Also see* **Cultural relativism.**

False consciousness When dominant classes or societies, using ideas and values divorced from observable reality, nonetheless succeed in persuading themselves and those subordinate to them that existing power relations are in everybody's best interest and, in any case, are natural and unalterable.

Feudal-authoritarian An agrarian society with a landed nobility, a large mass of unarmed, dependent farm laborers, and a central power that can prevail against both nobility and mass.

Feudalism (simple) A social form in which land is in effect owned by a landlord class, inherited in family lines, and which gives landlords economic and political-legal power over both serf-tenants and against a central authority.

Functional analysis A viewpoint that stresses the interdependence of social phenomena and also stresses that given elements in society can be understood in terms of their usefulness in fulfilling personal and social functions. This viewpoint can assume a harmony among social phenomena (characteristic of laissez-faire liberals) or conflict, even contradiction (characteristic of reform liberals, radicals, Marxists, dependency theorists). *Also see* **Anomic society, Anomie, Conflict perspective, Comparative-historical method, Functional equivalent,** and **Latent function.**

Functional equivalent A social practice or cultural element in one society that serves the same purpose as a different practice or cultural element in another society. For example, the dowry serves to protect women and serves some of the purposes of an economic market; a low-level of public services helps productivity in Japan while a large welfare state in the Federal Republic of Germany has the same outcome. *Also see* **Cultural relativism, Latent function.**

Governing class The social class or classes from which the political leaders of a society are recruited.

Gross domestic product (GDP) The monetary value of the goods and services produced in one year by an economy not counting foreign trade.

Gross national product (GNP) The monetary value of all the goods and services produced by a nation during a year.

Group A social group forms when there is recurring interaction between the occupants of statuses who have expectations of each other. This can refer to small groups (friendship or family) or to large groups (a corporation or a government).

Hegemony The theory that a governing class or a dominant society can impose itself successfully on subordinate classes or societies. *Also see* **False consciousness** and **Sociology of knowledge.**

Horticultural era The period when horticulture was the most productive society (approx. 10,000 to 5,000 years ago).

Horticulture A simple form of farming in which small plots of land (gardens) are cultivated by families using hand tools.

Hunting and gathering era The tens of thousands of years up to about 10,000 years ago when gathering wild food and hunting animals were the most advanced form of society.

Hunting and gathering society One whose members make a living through the collection of wild vegetables, nuts, and fruits and hunting wild animals.

Imperialism The outward expansion characteristic that is apparently inherent in all complex societies, including contemporary capitalist and socialist societies.

Before World War II the basic pattern of capitalist imperialism was for a developed country to take over another country militarily and shape its economy (with or without colonial settlers) to export raw materials. The colonial power would also lend the colony's government money (portfolio investment) to build the facilities needed for an export economy, putting a lien on its tax revenues so that the loan's interest and principle could be repaid. After World War II the basic pattern of capitalist imperialism became direct foreign investment (ownership or control of corporations in other countries) and foreign economic and military aid (which ties a country to the imperial power). The functions formerly performed by portfolio imperialism are now performed by the World Bank, the International Monetary Fund, and various regional banks, ostensibly public agencies but essentially capitalist bodies which do the bidding of the First World and pressure debtor countries to adopt capitalist practices complementary to the economies of the advanced capitalist societies. *Also see* **Imperialism of the capitalist world market, Imperialism of empire, Multinational corporation,** and **Internationalization of capital.**

Imperialism of the capitalist world market The exploitation by advanced (and even semi-advanced) capitalist (and even socialist) societies of weaker countries (whether intended or not) through the use primarily of economic but also political and other means. The imperialism of the capitalist world market is justified by an ideology of free trade, comparative advantage, and economic growth as a panacea (imperialist socialist societies talk of liberation from capitalism and an eventual classless society of freedom but tend to engage in many of the same practices as capitalist societies). *Also see* **Internationalization of capital, Multinational corporation.**

Imperialism of empire The acquisition of territory (mostly through force) by an advanced horticultural, agrarian, or early capitalist society in order to resolve internal problems and augment its economy and power. The building of empires has been justified by religion, philosophy, and racial ideologies.

Individualism Liberals define individualism as behavior that emerges from preexisting forces in human beings. As such, individuals own themselves and should have the right to use their labor and skills as they see fit (possessive individualism). Understood this way, individualism leads to economic and political progress. Anglo-American reform liberals see the need for helping individuals express and develop their innate abilities. Continental (European) liberals, such as Emile Durkheim and Max Weber, and socialists, including Marxists, see individualism as a social product. Some liberals and all socialists believe that capitalist individualism may once have been necessary to spur economic growth but is now a destructive social force and must be transformed by cooperation and a greater sense of collective responsibility.

Industrialization The process by which a society comes to be characterized by an economic system and a mode of social existence based on the rationalization of life. An important spur to such a society (which gave it its name) is industry: the introduction of machine manufacturing and the use of inanimate energy. But services and agriculture, both highly mechanized, are also part of the rationalized economy. In addition, an industrial society needs support from a rational-legal state, education, the nuclear family, and other sources. *Also see* **Capitalism, State capitalism, Industrial society,** and **Rationalization.**

Industrial society A socioeconomic system mobilized to create wealth through the rationalization of all institutional sectors. Presently industrial society exist in two basic forms, capitalism and socialism. After centuries of development as commercial capitalism, this social form was propelled massively into its present form by the use of machines powered by inanimate energy (coal, oil, gas, hydroelectricity, nuclear power). The use of machines in manufacturing also occurred in services and agriculture. Despite reserving some of the new output for investment and despite the need to use a good part for social overhead, the capitalist societies of the industrial West improved the standard of living of ordinary people (at least between 1850 and 1950). The capitalist industrial societies of the Pacific Rim (Japan, the Republic of Korea, Taiwan, Hong Kong, and Singapore) are also improving their standard of living while remaining productive.

The developed socialist societies have different priorities and are not easily compared with the capitalist West. After a spectacular growth the Soviet Union's productivity and standard of living stagnated from the 1970s on. The German Democratic Republic compares favorably with its capitalist counterpart, the Federal Republic of Germany.

It should be noted that all industrial societies have experienced economic slowdowns, have what appear to be sizable and chronic amounts of poverty, assorted, seemingly intractable, social problems, and are having trouble living within their means.

It should also be noted that industrial society relies on social technology as well as physical technology, such things as writing and mass literacy, organizational forms such as free interchangeable labor, bureaucracy, the factory system, law, banking, consumer persuasion, Keynesianism, and so on. Thus the management of industrial society requires policies derived from a full sociopolitical analysis rather than ideology or technical economic analysis.

Institutions A cluster of values, norms, statuses, and groups that emerges to provide one or more basic social needs (functions): obtaining food and shelter, having and raising children, defending one's territory, and settling disputes. Institutions tend to specialize: thus the family is a cluster of statuses organized around reproduction and socialization, the economy specializes in producing goods and services, religion in elaborating goals and arranging them in an order of priority, and the state in achieving social integration and defending against outside enemies. But institutions do more than one thing and are found in many combinations. *Also see* **Adaptive capacity, Cultural relativism, Elite,** and **Functional analysis.**

Instrumentalist state An authoritarian polity in which the state is openly a direct instrument of class domination (places like this rely on naked force to keep power and can be thought of as nonsocieties because they are chronically unstable and lack legitimacy). Present-day examples are El Salvador and Guatemala, and from the past, revolutionary Algeria and Vietnam.

Keynesianism The use of the state's tax, credit, or spending power to stimulate or curb demand or otherwise keep an economy on an even keel in keeping with capitalist values. *Also see* **State capitalism.**

Latent function A social practice or cultural element that in addition to or in spite of its intended or manifest function serves other functions that actors are not aware of. For example, the dowry facilitates marriage but also has the latent function of making property mobile and thus serves as an equivalent of a free economic market. *Also see* **Functional equivalent.**

Legitimacy A felt sense that power relations are valid and the ideas and values they embody are true and moral because all derive from the nature of human beings, from a divine source, from the natural order, or from revered lawgivers. *Also see* **Cultural relativism** and **False consciousness.**

Legitimation The process of convincing ordinary people that those in power belong there and are exercising power for the common good. *Also see* **Legitimacy.**

Less-developed societies A euphemism for the 40 or so nations, largely in black Africa but also in Latin America and Asia, which live in poverty and whose prospects for the future are bleak unless they receive outside aid.

Liberalism The basic thoughtways of capitalism from Thomas Hobbes (1650) and John Locke (1690) to the present. In the Anglo-American world a belief that individuals exist prior to society and that the latter should take its form from the actions of these self-oriented individuals. As they behave, individuals transform themselves and nature into private property and the resulting economy exhibits growth. It also exhibits conflict, which requires a political mechanism to resolve disputes. The state has support functions to perform but is primarily a neutral referee mediating and arbitrating among competitive groups (laissez-faire economics). In the United States Republicans (right-wing liberals) are more likely to advocate a value-neutral state while Democrats (left-wing liberals) tend to advocate a more active state. Continental (European) liberalism defines individualism and private property as social phenomena (for example, Emile Durkheim and Max Weber). The state is seen as an active shaper of society but, unlike socialists, continental liberals believe that a private property economy and private voluntary groups are more likely to produce a choice-oriented and thus moral society.

Liberation theology The indictment by some Roman Catholic clergy of oppressive societies (in Latin America) as antithetical to basic Christian values and their support of actions that would oppose both capitalism and imperialism.

Macrosociology The analysis of large-scale forms of social organization, especially entire societies and the world system of societies. Macrosociology relies heavily on comparison across time (history) and space (among various societies). *Also see* **Comparative-historical method.**

Mass society Used to characterize industrial societies as having a uniform consumption of goods and values and, thus, lifestyles. Some celebrate mass society as the march of democracy, equalitarianism, and achievement. Others see it as a threat to elite values, while still others see it as the result of elite dominance.

Mature dependency A theory arguing that a core society (for example, Canada) can also be dependent. Such a society, while enjoying economic growth, would have been even more prosperous had it controlled its own capital formation.

Meritocracy The belief that society should be ruled by a natural elite. Found, for example, in Plato and in modern, technocratic liberalism. *Also see* **Technocracy.**

Microsociology The analysis of small groups and face-to-face social relationships.

Middle class A term referring to the new commercial and manufacturing property class that emerged inbetween the nobility and the peasant masses from the Middle Ages on in the West. Today the historic middle class has diversified so much that it is best to refer to an upper class (of very rich), an upper-middle class (of well-to-do business people and professionals), and lower-middle class (of small business people, local professionals, semiprofessionals). *Also see* **Capitalism, Liberalism, Revolution from the middle.**

Modernization All the long-term changes associated with the rationalization of life starting in the late Middle Ages in the West and continuing to the present, both in the West and throughout the globe. Attempts to explain and understand this process are the heart of contemporary politics and social science. *Also see* **Capitalism, Convergence theory, Industrialization, Rationalization,** and **State capitalism.**

Multinational corporation (MNC) The common term for corporations that operate in a number of countries (polycentric corporations) or throughout the globe (geocentric corporations). The term for such corporations preferred by the United Nations and others is *transnational corporation* (TNC) because it clearly refers to a corporation in a particular nation that operates beyond its borders.

Liberals argue that MNCs promote economic growth on the part of all countries because they are the most efficient way to allocate human and material resources. MNCs see to it that capital in the form of money and technology flows to where it is needed and will do the most good. Further, MNCs help to undermine traditionalism by uniting progressive elites around the world and are especially valuable in overcoming the nonmarket irrationalities erected by misguided governments. Thus seen MNCs are the progressive vanguard of an emerging rational division of international labor.

Socialists and left liberals argue that MNCs represent the institutional or group form inherent in the dynamics of capitalism (*see* the **Internationalization of capital**). MNCs are merely the continuation of the contradiction in capitalism whereby a social process of production is subject to the self-serving power of those who own material capital and scarce skills. As a result, MNCs promote economic concentration, poverty, dependency, and environmental degradation both in their home countries and throughout the First and Third Worlds, escaping control, regulation, and taxation in all countries. *Also see* **Imperialism, Imperialism of the capitalist world market,** and **Internationalization of capital.**

Neolithic Revolution The major technological and social transformation, beginning about 10,000 years ago, associated with the beginnings of advanced horticulture and agrarian society. The shift to food production through the cultivation of plants (thus harnessing the power of the sun) soon led to feudalism, urban life, more technological innovations, and the creation of elaborate often universalistic, normative and religious systems to cope with the diversity and conflict now characteristic of society. Also referred to as the *agricultural revolution.*

Norms The rules that ideally govern the behavior of an occupant of a status, especially in relation to someone in a related status. Whereas values provide general orientations, specific situations require specific directives, hence norms, or the rules of conduct appropriate to concrete situations. For example, the United States values human life but specific norms in law and medicine govern the way citizens and doctors must behave in order to realize the general value placed on human life. Murder is legally prohibited, killing someone in self-defense is legally permissible. Doctors must do all they can to keep people alive: they are not legally allowed to put patients with incurable diseases to death, and so on.

Oligarchy Literally, control by the few. Sociologically, the tendency of group leaders from families to corporations to governments to rule in their own interest and not to live up to the legitimating ideology of their statuses (which always includes a claim that power serves the common good).

Patrimonial administration Under simple feudalism the central authority is weak and must give over administrative duties (taxes, justice, military) to local landlords. These offices become the private property of landlords and thus part of the estate which passes to heirs. *Also see* **Bureaucracy.**

Peasant A farmer, who is in an economically and politically subordinate relationship either as a serf or tenant to those who own or control land (can also refer to farmers who own their land as in modern France).

Periphery In world-system and dependency theory those parts of the world that are exploited by core and semiperipheral societies because they are weak and are weak because they are exploited.

Pluralism The belief that power in contemporary capitalist societies is dispersed among a wide range of contending groups so that no group (or small set of groups) consistently dominates the rest. Further, that society benefits by the competition among groups. Probably, this is no longer accepted as a realistic picture of society by most sociologists.

Polity The political-governmental-legal institution (the state) whereby a society maintains internal law, supports the performance or functions of other institutions, and carries out relationships with other societies.

Positive-sum game A competitive relationship in which the gains of one individual or group are not necessarily at the expense of others (compare with **Zero-sum game**).

Postindustrial society A popular misconception (both in and out of social science) that claims or believes that industrial society has come under the sway of knowledge elites and that it no longer need worry about the harmful effects of having self-interested property owners and others running society (also referred to as a high information society).

Power elite Those at the apex of the concentrated economy and the central state who allegedly are powerful enough to make the key decisions affecting the life of society. A view held by what is probably a small minority of sociologists.

Rationalization The attempted transformation of social relationships into an explicit search for the most efficient ways to achieve goals. Thought to involve confrontation with particularistic, ascriptive, sacred worlds; also known as the disenchantment of the world, in short, modern society, capitalist and socialist. Associated with the work of Max Weber. Traditional values, for example, nationalism, ethnicity, racism, sexism, have not always succumbed, however, to rationalization.

Revolution A movement, peaceful or violent from one social order to another, for example, hunting-gathering to advanced horticulture or agrarian society, from the latter to capitalism, from developing capitalist to developing socialist.

Revolution from above An attempt, not necessarily successful, by a property-based elite, or its military, to transform or modernize a social system, largely by developing a more up-to-date polity.

Revolution from below An attempt, not necessarily successful, by an elite representing the masses (usually rural) to overturn an existing society and produce a new one in the interests of the masses.

Revolution from the middle (bourgeois revolution) An attempt, not always successful, by a new property class (commercial and manufacturing capitalist class) who seek the transformation of society from one based on land and ascription to one based on economic achievement by individuals in any line of work. In effect, a bourgeois revolution, usually accompanied by declarations of freedom, equality, and democracy, establishes property in general as the animating and differentiating principle of society. *Also see* **Capitalism, Liberalism.**

Semiperiphery Societies that have enough strength to modify or withstand exploitation by dominant powers and to be exploiters on their own of peripheral societies.

Serf Those who work the land as members of families under advanced horticulture or agrarian society. In return for their labor they receive protection and are provided with a symbolic world that justifies and makes meaningful the prevailing power relations.

Simple horticultural society One whose members earn a living through gardening using simple tools.

Simple society One that has a relatively simple level of either hunting-gathering, pastoral, or gardening technology and is organized according to patterns of kinship.

Slavery A form of human property used for labor in some advanced horticultural, agrarian, and premodern hybrid societies. Slavery tends to arise where there is undesirable work to be performed (labor in the fields, especially in remote areas, quarries, rowing ships, and so on) but slaves also do domestic work.

Social class Households sharing a similar social and political position by virtue of their economic position (wealth, income, and occupation). In Marxian sociology, social classes are essentially two fold, those who own the means of production (and who thereby also have power over the rest of society) and those who are propertyless.

Social institution Any part of a sociocultural system that involves established and regularized patterns of social behavior and consciousness in order to provide specific functions such as material sustenance, reproduction, socialization of new members, social control and integration, e.g., the economy, the polity, family, religion, education.

Socialism An ideal society in which social problems, usually associated with the private ownership or control of the economy, are largely done away with. The main tradition of socialism is associated with Karl Marx, who pictured a future classless society without private property in which all would fulfill their potential working in a cooperative world. Socialism can also be inspired by religion (especially Christianity and Muslim) or can take the form of an incremental reform-welfare state (Great Britain, Sweden). When found in the Third World it is heavily committed to national liberation from imperialism and to nation building.

Socialist society Actual socialist societies take a variety of forms though all stress a commitment to subordinating the economy to moral and social purposes. Under planned (or state) socialism (the U.S.S.R.) the government owns the economy and directs it in terms of a central plan. Under market socialism (Yugoslavia) workers own businesses and make investment decisions (subject to some central guidance) based on an assessment of the market. Most planned forms of socialism have begun to introduce market mechanisms.

Socialization The process whereby the members of a society transmit the content of their culture to new generations through various forms of child training and education. Socialization also occurs through public ceremonies, elections, church attendance, popular and elite culture, and so on.

Social mobility The upward or downward movement of individuals, groups, or categories of people among positions in the class hierarchy of a society.

Social stratification A society with a hierarchy of households that enjoy different levels of economic existence, prestige, and political-legal power. Also a world of societies arranged in a hierarchy of power that yields different benefits.

Social structure Regularized patterns of social behavior (both conformist and deviant) common to the members of a sociocultural system.

Sociology of knowledge The argument that beliefs, values, and aesthetics derive from social experience, especially in the economy. Some who hold this view feel it is compatible with the idea of objectivity or truth, for example, Karl Marx, while others do not, for example, Max Weber.

State *See* **Polity.**

State capitalism All advanced capitalist societies are state capitalist though some acknowledge the role of the state openly (Great Britain, France, Japan, the Republic of Korea) and some do not (the United States). State capitalist societies rely heavily on the state to manage their economies and to deal with other countries. By and large, the state serves large corporate interests through various means: by managing the business cycle through its tax, credit, and spending policies, through subsidies and by making unprofitable capital outlays, by nationalizing unprofitable businesses, by controlling labor costs, by promoting a welfare state to pacify workers and ward off socialist movements, and by entering agreements with other countries, either directly or through international organizations, to prevent harmful capitalist rivalry, to ward off the threat of socialism, and to stabilize the Third World.

State socialism A socialist society (for example the U.S.S.R. or Cuba) in which the government owns the economy and directs it from a central point using a multiyear plan (also called a command economy).

Status A social position that directs behavior, especially toward the occupant of related statuses, according to rights and duties that are generally known and accepted.

Technocracy The singleminded stress by some liberals and socialists on giving knowledge elites control of society.

Technology The sociocultural elements and personality structures that make up the adaptive capacity of society. Too often the concept technology is restricted to tools and machines (digging stick, plow, draft animals, steam engine, railroad, computer, and so on). The concept also includes such cultural elements as writing, arithmetic, work norms and values, and so on, and social relations such as lord-serf, master-slave, owner-worker, patrimonial and bureaucratic administration, and so on, along with types of human beings (serfs, lords, slaves, laborers for hire) and cognitive and emotional forces in the human personality (shame, guilt, literacy, skills, ambition, past-or-future orientation, tolerance for risk and ambiguity, self-reliance, and so on).

Third World The large majority of the world's societies. They are characterized by low technology levels, reliance on human energy, and the export of food, raw materials, and labor, and find it difficult to raise enough capital to achieve a breakthrough to sustained industrialization; extremely diverse by material level, size, and prospects.

Totalitarianism The attempt by a power group to exercise total control over the life of society. Includes political control over social institutions, positive incentives, persuasion, and physical and psychic coercion.

Underdeveloped society A society developed by outside powers to be a dependent supplier of food, raw materials, or labor to more developed societies.

Uneven development A movement toward economic differentiation and growth accompanied by a failure to update political, governmental, legal, educational, and other institutions. Characteristic of all modern societies, including developed capitalist and socialist systems. This shortfall in adaptive capacity has led to a collection of social problems (unemployment, poverty, slums, assorted family pathologies, environmental degradation, crime, racism, sexism, and so on) which appear to be chronic and perhaps an unsolvable tangle (unsolvable within the institutions of presentday societies since these institutions are the cause of the problems).

Values The things, behaviors, states of personality, and states of existence in general that social actors (individuals and groups) deem good-bad, right-wrong, acceptable-unacceptable, desirable-undesirable. Values are usually stated in broad abstract terms, placed in a hierarchy of importance, and are effective in a general way in coordinating behavior. In complex societies values are both compatible (for example, individualism, civil rights, privacy) and contradictory (for example, competition versus brotherhood, individualism versus equality).

World economy The capitalist economy that emerged in the late middle ages that first consisted of European-Mediterranean trade routes and than spread through exploration and imperialism to encompass the world.

World system The interaction of power groups, including governments, across nation state boundaries to form a structure and to influence domestic behavior. Generally used to refer to the widening set of relationships that started in Western Europe in the late middle ages and now encompasses all the nation states of the world. The world system lacks a polity to integrate it and is subject to severe competitive strains, including war. Some integration occurs through hegemonic powers, core dominance, regional alliances, the United Nations, and international organizations.

Zero-sum game A competitive relation in which the gains of one actor are at the expense of other actors (compare positive-sum game). A society with no or little economic growth can become a zero-sum game (and thus characterized by suffering, conflict, and instability) while those undergoing growth can enjoy a positive-sum game experience (provided elites do not take all the economic growth for themselves).

A MAP OF THE NATION STATES OF THE WORLD

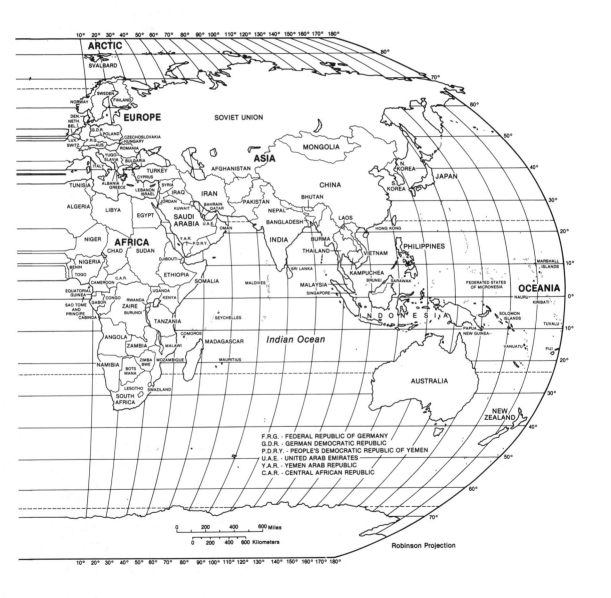

F.R.G. - FEDERAL REPUBLIC OF GERMANY
G.D.R. - GERMAN DEMOCRATIC REPUBLIC
P.D.R.Y. - PEOPLE'S DEMOCRATIC REPUBLIC OF YEMEN
U.A.E. - UNITED ARAB EMIRATES
Y.A.R. - YEMEN ARAB REPUBLIC
C.A.R. - CENTRAL AFRICAN REPUBLIC

Robinson Projection

B

RESEARCHING THE UNDERGRADUATE PAPER IN COMPARATIVE STUDIES

PICKING THE TOPIC

Instructors assign term papers for two main reasons: to help reinforce aspects of their course and to give students experience with research and writing. The first question you must ask yourself, therefore, when tackling a research paper is, how does the topic I'm thinking of writing about relate to the course I'm taking? To answer this question, look at the course outline, the text, and any other assigned or recommended reading. If the instructor has passed out a list of suggested topics, scrutinize it carefully. It, together with the course outline, provides clues to what the instructor hopes to achieve and what is on the instructor's mind.

Once you are relatively sure that your topic is relevant (remember you can refocus a topic as you go along), by all means see how well it relates to your other courses. A comparative paper on crime, for example, can fit into a political science course that deals with law enforcement or the constitu-

tional rights of criminal defendants. Comparative child care or health care might overlap with another sociology course. And so on.

FORMULATING YOUR THESIS

All interesting writing has a thesis: a point or an argument. If it interests you, it could also interest others. What do you want to say? More than that, what do you want to argue for or against? Sociology is the scientific search for what is going on. Often its findings contradict some widely held belief. The conflict perspective can help set the mood of your paper and perhaps supply some ideas. Once you have a general idea of what you want to say (your thesis), keep it in mind as you attend lectures, watch television, or talk to your friends. New ideas about your topic can appear from anywhere and it helps if you are on the alert. More than likely, though, your topic will come to a clear focus only after you have consulted sources in the library.

USING THE LIBRARY

For your research paper you will more than likely do library research, that is, you will use the research already done by others. The library is like the human brain only it is more orderly and fixed and less creative. There is a logic to it and you will enjoy getting in tune with it once you know how it is organized. But getting to know the library is like meeting a stranger on a train—there is always a little awkwardness at first. By the way, knowing how to use a library will hold you in good stead in quite a number of occupations long after you finish school.

There is no first step in using the library, only the step required by your particular need. Let's suppose you are intrigued with the role of sports in various societies but you have no specific topic. The first step calls for rummaging or browsing. The card catalog contains books by author and subject. Look under the subject, Sociology of Sports, and you will find authors. You can also start with an author referred to in your text. Be sure to use your text and other course readings for ideas and information because that will help keep you in touch with the main thrust of your course. Jot down titles and library call numbers on 3 × 5 cards. As you read and browse put some ideas on 4 × 6 cards. Using cards is useful because it keeps your information flexible—you can rearrange cards to suit your developing project.

Libraries have a section containing indexes to published work of all kinds. The *Social Sciences Index,* including the latest unbound volumes, could well give you some juicy leads to your topic as well as providing a general orientation. *The Reader's Guide To Periodical Literature* is also useful. Indexes such as these put you in touch with a wide variety of magazines and scholarly journals. Don't hesitate to consult the *Encyclopaedia of the Social Sciences* (1930–1934) or its sequel, the *International Encyclopaedia of the Social Sciences*

(completed in 1968). Two major sources of information are the U.S. Bureau of the Census, *Statistical Abstract of the United States* (published annually) and the United Nations, *Statistical Yearbook* (published annually).

Along the way you will encounter the titles of journals and reference works. These are valuable sources but you should not rely on chance encounters. Libraries have a directory of the journals they carry—get to know the journals your library carries by browsing through the directory. You will undoubtedly find comparative journals that deal with the world-at-large, with geographical regions, and with specialized topics (urban, Soviet studies, etc). As for reference works, you may want to start with a reference to reference books such as Eugene P. Sheehy, ed., *Guide To Reference Books*, 10th ed. (Chicago, Il: American Library Association, 1986). Here you can look up reference works in sociology, political science, or area studies and then tighten your focus depending on your interests. Once you have an author and title you can then look it up in the general card catalog.

To locate material about specific events and people, consult the index to the *New York Times* and then put the microfilm of the issue you want on a display machine. The latest machines also allow you to make a copy for your records and convenience. Incidentally, most libraries now have copying machines—don't hesitate to make copies of important articles or book segments.

For a lengthier introduction to the library, as well as discussions of a wide variety of research materials, students should also look at (or buy, especially if they plan to take more sociology courses) Pauline Bart and Linda Frankel, *The Student Sociologist's Handbook*, 4th ed. (New York: Random House, 1986). The social sciences also stress quantitative data and for this and other reasons, it may be a good idea to browse through a book such as Richard J. Light and David B. Pollemer, *Summing Up: The Science of Reviewing Research* (Cambridge, Mass.: Harvard University Press, 1985).

One last tip—do ask the librarians for assistance. They are trained to know how the library's brain is arranged and they are eager to help you.

WRITING

As early as possible attempt a short statement about your topic. Don't show it to anybody because it will embarrass you. You will soon find, however, that it improves as you interact with it. Also as soon as possible, make an outline of how you think you will develop your topic. The outline will also change as you uncover new materials and gain new insights. Remember that no topic has a natural or obvious boundary like a tennis court or this page. You are in charge and you must construct the fences that will set off your topic. If possible use your paper as an opportunity to get acquainted with the word processor. You must know how to type and it is never too late to start learning how. A word processor allows you to store your writing for easy recall on a screen where it can easily be corrected or revised. When you are finished, a printer attached to it will give you a copy(s). The word processor is widely used in business, government, and the professions, and skill in using it and knowledge about its capabilities will hold you in good stead in almost any line of work. It will also be useful in your remaining years of school.

Write simply and avoid long rambling sentences. Think of your paper as a half-hour of 90-second commercials linked together to tell a coherent story. Use active verbs and focus on causation—who did what, when, and to whom? Remember the interactionist perspective—human behavior is acted out by goal seeking, willful, decision-making individuals and groups. In writing a paper you should think of yourself as an actor trying to influence another actor by telling a good story about social action. You will make your essay interesting by constructing a narrative or story. Make it convincing by citing sources and by showing you are aware of positions different from yours. When you are through no one will know how many times you recast your argument or rearranged your outline. No one will know how you struggled to find a better word or a later source. All they will see is an interesting argument and perhaps wonder why they never thought of things that way.

APPENDIX
C
GUIDES TO STUDY, WORK, AND TRAVEL OPPORTUNITIES ABROAD

The world economy and events around the world affect our lives in many ways. Much can be learned about the outside world by staying at home but there is a special quality to studying abroad (the main benefit in all likelihood is to get to know your own country better). The place to start is your school's Career Services Office (or equivalent name) and with the foreign study official usually located in the academic dean's office.

"Studying abroad" is a big term referring to studying away for a whole year, a semester, or for the summer, and it is often combined with work and travel. Here are some basic references to help you decide if and where you want to go:

Work, Study, Travel Abroad: The Whole World Handbook by Marjorie Adoff Cohen. 9th ed. (New York: St. Martin's Press, 1988).

Invest in Yourself: The Catalogue of Volunteer Opportunities by Susan G. Angus, ed. (New York: Commission on Voluntary Service and Action, 1986).

Careers For People Who Love To Travel by Joy Mullett and Lois Darley (New York: Arco, 1986).

Living Overseas by Ted Ward (New York: The Free Press, 1984).

Funding For Research, Study and Travel: Latin America and the Cariibbean by Karen Cantrell and Denise Wallen, eds., (Phoenix: Oryx Press, 1987).

Volunteer! The Comprehensive Guide To Voluntary Service in the U.S. and Abroad, 1985–86 (New York: Council on International Educational Exchange, 1984).

Study Abroad by UNESCO (Paris: United Nations Educational, Scientific, and Cultural Organization, 1987).

Vacation Study Abroad 1988 by Edrice Marguerite Howard, ed. (New York: Institute of International Education, 1988).

1989 Directory of Overseas Summer Jobs by David Woodworth, ed., (Oxford, U.K.: Vacation-Work, n.d.; dist. by Writer's Digest Books, Cincinnati, Ohio).

APPENDIX
D
GUIDES TO CAREER OPPORTUNITIES FOR STUDENTS IN COMPARATIVE STUDIES

Comparative studies will hold you in good stead for all occupations, both those located in the United States and those located abroad. Actually most of the valuable jobs requiring cross-societal understanding and knowledge about foreign countries are located in the United States proper.

Careers in comparative studies encompass all fields: certainly teaching and comparative research and certainly the large variety of federal civilian, military, and intelligence occupations. You will think naturally of business careers when thinking of multinational corporations, but here one must branch out: multinational corporations want computer experts, engineers, lawyers, environmental scientists, and even educators. The field of journalism beckons as do organizations dealing with refugees, disaster relief, intersocietal credit arrangements, and so on. In other words, stay loose and start by browsing in your college or university's Career Services and, of course, by discussing your career choice and

major-minor fields with your adviser and teachers.

Your Career Services office should have most of the following basic sources:

Careers in International Affairs. School of Foreign Service, Georgetown University (Washington, D.C., 1985).

Directory of American Firms Operating in Foreign Countries. 3 vols. (World Trade Academy Press, 50 E. 42nd St., New York, NY).

101 Ways To Find an Overseas Job by Will Cantrell and Terry Marshall (Merrifield, VA: Cantrell Corporation, 1987).

International Affairs Career Bulletin by Francis M. Jeffries (Poolesville, Md.: Jeffries and Associates, February 1989, Bimonthly).

Making It Abroad: The International Job Hunting Guide by Howard Schuman (New York: Wiley, 1988).

The Total Guide To Careers In International Affairs by Francis M. Jeffries (Poolesville, Md.: Jeffries and Associates, 1987).

Overseas Development Network Opportunities Catalog: A Guide to Internships, Research, and Employ-

ment with Development Organizations (Overseas Development Network, P.O. Box 1430, Cambridge, Mass., n.d.).

Employment Abroad: Facts and Fallacies (Publications Fulfillment, Chamber of Commerce of the United States, 1615 H Street, NE, Washington, D.C.).

How To Get a Job Overseas by Curtis W. Casewit, 2nd ed. (New York: Arco, 1984).

International Jobs: Where They Are, How to Get Them, by Eric Kocher, ed (Reading, Mass.: Addison-Wesley, 1986).

Looking for Employment in Foreign Countries (World Trade Academy Press Inc., 50 East 42nd Street, New York, N.Y.).

Your career choice may be enhanced by an internship. By all means use your summers to find out about various lines of work. And since many high-level jobs require graduate training, be sure to consult Peterson's guides to graduate study. The following list of books should help you with your career choice:

Occupational Outlook Handbook (Washington, DC: U.S. Department of Labor, 1988–89), revised every two years.)

National Employment Listing Service (Huntsville, Tx.: Sam Houston State University, 1979). A monthly bulletin with specific job descriptions many of which call for a B.A. in sociology.

1982–1983 National Directory For Summer Internships For Undergraduates (Haverford, Penn.: Career Planning Offices of Bryn Mawr and Haverford Colleges, 1981).

The Student Guide to Mass Media Internships, by Ronald H. Claxton and B.A. Powell (Boulder, Colo.: School of Journalism, University of Colorado, 1980).

Directory of Washington Internships, 1983–1984 (Washington, D.C: National Society For Internships and Experimental Education, 1983).

First Suplement to Directory of Career Training and Development Programs (Santa Monica, Calif.: Ready Reference Press, 1981); a guide to training programs in corporations, government agencies and professional associations.

Peterson's Annual Guides To Graduate Study, 5 vols. (Princeton, N.J.: Peterson's Guides). Peterson's guides contain a wealth of information about graduate and professional programs, admission requirements, admission tests and minimum scores required, costs, financial aid, combined degree programs, and directories of education in specialized areas. Volumes (books) 1 and 2 (Graduate and Professional Programs: An Overview, and Humanities and Social Sciences) are of special interest to sociology majors and minors.

NAME INDEX

Abu-Lughod, Ibrahim, 342n
Adams, Carolyn Teich, 16n, 402n
Adams, Gordon, 136
Adams, Robert M., 32n
Aganbegyan, Abel, 242n
Agnew, John, 117n
Akimoto, Tatsurn, 357n
Albright, David E., 21n
Alexander, Stella, 319n
Allen, John, 374n
Allende, Salvador, 198n
Allman, William F., 390n
Almond, Gabriel A., 16
Altbach, Philip G., 200n
Alter, Jonathan, 144n
Aluko, Olajide, 326n
Amin, Samir 51n, 76, 276n, 296n
Anatol, Ariane Berthoin, 16n
Anderson, Barbara A., 246n
Andrews, Frank M., 409n
Anell, Lars, 376n
Angell, Norman, 75n
Antal, Ariane Berthoin, 402n
Anthony, Dick 160n
Antonio, Robert, 50n

Anzovin, Steven, 347n
Apeldoorn, G. Jan van, 324n
Ardalan, Cyprus, 315n
Arensberg, Conrad, 26n
Aristotle, 4, 48, 124f., 393
Armstrong, Hugh, 304n
Armstrong, Pat, 304n
Armstrong, Robert, 83n
Arndt, Sven W., 387n
Arner, Michael, 4n
Arnstein, Walter L., 40n
Asad, Talal, 201n
Aston, T. H., 60n
Atkinson, M. M., 314n
Atkinston, Dorothy, 233n
Azreal, Jeremy, 216, 217

Bachrach, Peter, 207n
Bahagwate, Jagdish, 120n
Baker, James, 344
Balasubramanyam, V. N., 370n
Balayra, E. A., 83n
Baldwin, Frank, 270n
Bandarage, Asoka, 333n
Baratz, Morton S., 207n

435

SUBJECT INDEX